The Handbook of Humanitarian Law in Armed Conflicts

The Handbook of Humanitarian Law in Armed Conflicts

EDITED BY

DIETER FLECK

IN COLLABORATION WITH

Michael Bothe, Horst Fischer, Hans-Peter Gasser, Christopher Greenwood,
Wolff Heintschel von Heinegg, Knut Ipsen, Stefan Oeter,
Karl Josef Partsch†, Walter Rabus, Rüdiger Wolfrum

OXFORD
UNIVERSITY PRESS

OXFORD
UNIVERSITY PRESS

Great Clarendon Street, Oxford OX2 6DP

Oxford University Press is a department of the University of Oxford.
It furthers the University's objective of excellence in research, scholarship,
and education by publishing worldwide in

Oxford New York

Auckland Bangkok Buenos Aires Cape Town Chennai
Dar es Salaam Delhi Hong Kong Istanbul Karachi Kolkata
Kuala Lumpur Madrid Melbourne Mexico City Mumbai Nairobi
São Paulo Shanghai Taipei Tokyo Toronto

Oxford is a registered trade mark of Oxford University Press
in the UK and in certain other countries

Published in the United States
by Oxford University Press Inc., New York

First published 1995
First published new as paperback 1999
Reprinted 2003

British Library Cataloguing in Publication Data

Data available

Library of Congress Cataloging in Publication Data

Handbook of humanitarian law in armed conflicts/
edited by Dieter Fleck . . . [et al.].
p. cm.
Includes bibliographical references and index.
1. War victims—Legal status, laws, etc. 2. War (International law)
I. Dieter, Fleck.
JX5136.H34 1995 341.697—dc20 95-30486

ISBN 0–19–825835–6
ISBN 0–19–829867–6 (Pbk)

Printed in Great Britain
on acid-free paper by
Biddles Ltd, *www.biddles.co.uk*

PREFACE

The *Handbook*, first published in 1994[1] and 1995,[2] responded to a need felt by academic experts and practitioners and was well received in the growing community of international humanitarian law. Numerous reviews of the book in many countries, its use in academic activities to support dissemination and research, and the frequent references made to it by legal advisers in military headquarters, were encouraging for both the authors and the editor. It is therefore hoped that this paperback edition will be a welcome addition to continuing efforts undertaken to support the application of international humanitarian law and its further development.

Since the first edition, numerous people of different origin, tasks, and expectations were challenged with new forms of armed conflict. Declared wars or other armed conflicts between two or more states, in which the 1977 Protocol I Additional to the Geneva Conventions (AP I) applies, remained very exceptional, but the standard setting role of this important international instrument has gained considerable weight over time. To a very large extent the provisions of AP I constitute customary law today. They are influencing also other forms of military operations including peace-keeping missions and non-international armed conflicts, as explained in Sections 208 and 211.

It was agreed to reprint the unchanged text of the handbook here, as its contents are still valid and the preparation of a revised edition would have posed problems that could have prevented publication for a considerable time. Nevertheless, some new developments of the last five years shall be recalled here:

— Efforts to strengthen international criminal jurisdiction gained considerable weight with the establishment, under Security Council Resolutions 827 (1993) and 995 (1994), of the *Ad Hoc* Tribunals in the Hague for the former Yugoslavia and Rwanda. The Rome statute of 17 July 1998 on the International Criminal Court—ICC—provides the first multilateral comprehensive definition of war crimes and crimes against humanity which includes crimes committed during non-international armed conflicts.

— A Fourth Protocol to the 1980 Inhumane Weapons Convention was adopted on 13 October 1995, prohibiting the employment of laser weapons specifically designed, as their sole combat functions, to cause permanent blindness to unenhanced vision, that is to the naked eye or to the eye with corrective eyesight devices.

— The Second Protocol (mines, booby-traps and other devices) to the 1980 Inhumane Weapons Convention was revised on 3 May 1996.

---

[1] Fleck (ed.), *Handbuch des humanitären Völkerrechts in bewaffneten Konflikten*, München (C. H. Beck) 1994.
[2] Id. *The Handbook of Humanitarian Law in Armed Conflicts*, Oxford University Press, 1995.

— The Convention on the prohibition of the use, stockpiling, production, and transfer of anti-personnel mines and on their destruction, adopted at Oslo on 18 September 1997, was signed in Ottawa on 3 December 1997 and soon supported by more than forty states.
— A Second Protocol to the 1954 Hague Convention on Cultural Property was adopted on 26 May 1999.
— Multinational military operations in which not only Parties to AP I participated have facilitated the acceptance of standards set by AP I as customary law.
— Customary law in non-international conflicts is clearly expanding today, even if it may still be disputed to what extent specific rules are applicable in such situations.

These developments have not changed but supplemented substantial rules explained in this handbook, stressing at the same time their importance.

With our co-author Professor *Karl Josef Partsch*, who died on 30 December 1996, we have lost a dear friend and most highly esteemed colleague, whose contributions in many areas of international law remain unforgotten. His creativity, diligence, and unfailing good nature had met with an exceptional range of experience. I am personally grateful for the intellectual benefit and happy memories that were derived from his participation in our endeavours.

States and international organizations, members of armed forces and civilians, practising lawyers, and academics alike remain challenged with the complex task of expanding knowledge of existing rules of humanitarian law, ensuring its application under ever difficult circumstances and cooperating in its further development.

Bonn, July 1999   *Dieter Fleck*

CONTENTS

INTRODUCTION

During the past few decades the international humanitarian law applicable in armed conflicts has been subject to a progressive development which culminated in the four 1949 Geneva Conventions, the 1977 Protocols Additional to these Conventions, the 1954 Hague Convention for the Protection of Cultural Property, and the 1980 Weapons Convention. These treaties put in concrete form three general legal restrictions which are described in Section 130 of the present handbook as follows: even in war the use of force is permissible only if it is directed against military objectives, if it is not likely to cause unnecessary suffering, and if it is not perfidious.

Extensive international co-operation, which had been encouraged above all by the Additional Protocols and is today practised by extensive contacts between official, academic, and private institutions and individuals, has contributed decisively to the worldwide dissemination of international humanitarian law. This co-operation has paved the way for the far-reaching and continuously progressing establishment of the rules of international humanitarian law in the customary law of all cultures.[1] It has also underlined its political significance for security and co-operation in Europe and throughout the world. These co-operative efforts, however, have also shown that fundamental work in both national and international implementation remains to be done,[2] which poses a challenge to political decision makers and to their legal and military advisers many of whom must assume this task in addition to their other duties and in spite of the pressure of other priorities.

There have been gross violations of international law which have brought home to the general public time after time the importance of humanitarian protection. The International Committee of the Red Cross has repeatedly, and with complete justification, launched appeals for humanitarian mobilization, addressed to all states, in accordance with common Article 1 of the Geneva Conventions, not only to respect but also to ensure respect for international humanitarian law in all circumstances.[3] After a long period of restraint, the Security Council of the United Nations has recently been more explicit in its condemnation of gross violations of international humanitarian law.[4] In Resolution 827 the Security Council went so far as to enact the Statute of the *ad hoc* International Tribunal on the prosecution of war crimes and other crimes against international law in the former Yugoslavia, thus creating the germ of a permanent International Criminal Court, the legal basis of which still requires considerable negotiating efforts within the International Law Commission, the UN General Assembly, and between states. The International

---

[1] Meron, 246 ff.   [2] Bothe, in Bothe/Macalister/Smith/Kurzidem (Eds.), 261 ff.
[3] Sommaruga, *IRRC* 286 (1992), 74–93.
[4] S/RES/688 (5 Apr. 1991), S/RES/771 (13 Aug. 1992), S/RES/780 (5 Oct. 1992), S/RES/794 (3 Dec. 1992), S/RES/808 (22 Feb. 1993), S/RES/819 (16 Apr. 1993), S/RES/824 (6 May 1993), S/RES/827 (25 May 1993), S/RES/836 (4 June 1993).

Conference for the Protection of War Victims, in its Final Declaration of 1 September 1993, has called for practical measures of implementation which are to be submitted to the next session of the International Conference of the Red Cross and Red Crescent, and above all to nation states.

There is an urgent and continuing need for investigatory and punitive measures as well as for measures to prevent future violations of the law. Such measures would be in line with the extended concept of international humanitarian law as part of the law of human rights,[5] which includes an obligation owed by states to individual persons and establishes for each of those parties international humanitarian rights and obligations of their own. As early as 1975, the Conference on Co-operation and Security in Europe Final Act signed in Helsinki emphasized in Principle VII the right of the individual to know and act upon his rights and duties in the field of human rights. At the same time, it stressed the duty of participating states constantly to respect these rights and freedoms in their mutual relations and to endeavour jointly and separately (including co-operation with the United Nations) to promote universal and effective respect for these rights and freedoms.

Article 82 AP I which obligates the Contracting Parties to ensure that legal advisers are available to the armed forces constitutes a provision of prime importance for the endeavour to ensure the respect of international humanitarian law. Ever since its inception in 1956, the German *Bundeswehr* has had a legal advisory organization whose task is to advise military commanders and to instruct the armed forces also in aspects of international law. Germany has always been highly interested in the implementation of the international humanitarian law, not least because for several decades its territory contained the line of confrontation between two opposing military alliances. Accordingly, and in view of the differences in the status of national ratifications of the Additional Protocols within the North Atlantic Alliance, German initiatives aim to settle problems regarding the conduct of combined operations by reaching agreement on common standards for the application of the law, and to support legal co-operation in this area extending far beyond the members of the Alliance.

The present handbook is the result of close co-operation between scientific research and practice. It is designed to support not only further academic studies but also the legal instruction of the armed forces. Its key statements, which are **printed in bold type**, were promulgated for the *Bundeswehr* in August 1992 as Joint Services Regulations (ZDv) 15/2. The importance of this now complex branch of law for both the conduct of military operations and international co-operation is shown here in context. The publication of this service regulation follows intensive co-operation between practitioners and scholars and an international conference of government experts.[6] The results of this co-operation have benefited not only the wording of the Joint Services Regulations but also the commentary presented here.

In **Chapter 1** the handbook explains the historical evolution and the existing legal foundations of the international humanitarian law. It brings into relief the ethical and political prerequisites for legal development, the origins of which are not exclu-

---

[5] Patrnogic/Jakovlevic, 26.   [6] See Fleck, *HuV–I* (4/1991), 213–15.

sively European or Christian. At a time which is characterized by rapid societal changes and diminishing distances, the establishment of a multicultural basis for humanitarian rules is of the utmost importance. **Chapters 2 to 10** describe the law of the conduct of military operations in all theatres and at all levels. Here, the distinctions between Geneva Law and Hague Law, developed at different points in history, have lost their importance, as have those between the law of treaties and customary law. The Protocols Additional to the Geneva Conventions and the ongoing process of their adoption as customary law have now made obsolete such distinctions, which military commanders have always considered to be artificial. **Chapter 11** contains rules of the law of neutrality concerning the protection of the victims of armed conflicts, and which must be considered as part of international humanitarian law. These rules as well as questions of law pertaining to the conduct of military operations at sea are the subject of a continuing international discussion between experts. While for this reason in Chapters 10 and 11 of Joint Services Regulations 15/2 a certain restraint is exercised, the commentary presented here lays more stress on the details of innovative proposals and possibilities for development. **Chapter 12**, which deals with the most important part of Joint Services Regulations 15/2, describes and evaluates measures to ensure respect for international humanitarian law which contribute to, and encourage compliance with, its rules. The **Annex** contains a survey of the international instruments, the international distinctive emblems, and the various military and Red Cross manuals which are particularly relevant as *opinio iuris*. The list of references is not meant to replace more comprehensive bibliographies[7] but only to provide additional information on the sources mentioned in the footnotes.

Like Joint Services Regulations 15/2, the present handbook is a collaborative work and could not have been compiled without the preparatory involvement of many members of the growing community of experts. This dialogue on humanitarian law must be continued. The attempt to make this area of international law, which has become difficult to survey and has often been neglected, the subject of a restatement has sometimes inevitably resulted in the presentation here of less detail than would perhaps have been desirable, and a number of worthwhile proposals have had to be left out of account. My thanks are due to all who took part in this process by giving critical advice. It is in keeping with the character of the Joint Services Regulations that all proposals for its improvement remain anonymous, while the editor assumes sole responsibility for its contents including any shortcomings. This applies equally to the present commentary. I should, however, like to express my particular gratitude to M. Henri Meyrowitz, *Docteur en droit, Avocat honoraire à la Cour d'Appel*, Paris. He has read and reviewed the draft Joint Services Regulations 15/2 with passionate interest. With his criticism he has set an example both of the necessary co-operation between academia and practice and of the great value of the exchange of experience in international law between the generations. The present commentary has also benefited from his opinions.

---

[7] International Committee of the Red Cross & Henry Dunant Institute, *Bibliography of International Humanitarian Law Applicable in Armed Conflicts*, 2nd edn., Geneva (1987), xxix, 605 pages.

A heavy burden has fallen on our co-author Christopher Greenwood who agreed to read the manuscripts of the entire book and patiently removed linguistic mistakes. I express my sincere gratitude for this important support.

I am grateful to Oxford University Press and in particular to Richard Hart and John Whelan for their professional co-operation.

A German edition has been published by C.H. Beck Verlag, Munich.[8]

Bonn, December 1994

Dieter Fleck

---

[8] Fleck (Ed.), *Handbuch des humanitären Völkerrechts in bewaffneten Konflikten*, München (1994).

LIST OF CONTRIBUTORS

Prof. Dr. Michael Bothe, Institut für Öffentliches Recht, Johann-Wolfgang-Goethe-Universität, Frankfurt/Main

Dr. Horst Fischer, Director, Institut für Friedenssicherungsrecht und Humanitäres Völkerrecht, Ruhr-Universität Bochum

Dr. Dieter Fleck, Director, International Agreements and Policy, Federal Ministry of Defence, Bonn; Member of the Council, International Institute of Humanitarian Law, San Remo

Dr. Hans-Peter Gasser, LL.M., Senior Legal Adviser, International Committee of the Red Cross, Geneva

Christopher J. Greenwood, M.A., LL.B., Director of Studies in Law, Magdalene College, Cambridge

Ass. Prof. Dr. Wolff Heintschel von Heinegg, Ruhr-Universität Bochum

Prof. Dr. h.c. Knut Ipsen, LL.D. h.c., Ruhr-Universität Bochum, President of the German Red Cross

Dr. Stefan Oeter, Research Fellow, Max-Planck-Institut für ausländisches öffentliches Recht und Völkerrecht, Heidelberg

Prof. (em.) Dr. Karl Josef Partsch, Universität Bonn

Dr. Walter Rabus, Reader, Seminarium voor Volkenrecht en Internationale Betrekkingen, Universiteit van Amsterdam

Prof. Dr. Rüdiger Wolfrum, Director, Max-Planck-Institut für ausländisches öffentliches Recht und Völkerrecht, Heidelberg

TABLE OF ABBREVIATIONS

HC IV	Hague Convention (IV) of 18 October 1907 concerning the Laws and Customs of War on Land
HC V	Hague Convention (V) of 18 October 1907 concerning the Rights and Duties of Neutral Powers and Persons in Case of War on Land
HC VI	Hague Convention (VI) of 18 October 1907 concerning the Status of Merchant Ships at the Outbreak of Hostilities
HC VII	Hague Convention (VII) of 18 October 1907 concerning the Conversion of Merchant Ships into War Ships
HC VIII	Hague Convention (VIII) of 18 October 1907 concerning the Laying of Automatic Submarine Contact Mines
HC IX	Hague Convention (IX) of 18 October 1907 concerning Bombardment by Naval Forces in Time of War
HC XI	Hague Convention (XI) of 18 October 1907 concerning Certain Restrictions with regard to the Exercise of the Right of Capture in Naval War
HC XIII	Hague Convention (XIII) of 18 October 1907 concerning the Rights and Duties of Neutral Powers in Naval War
HRAW 1923	Hague Rules of Air Warfare, drafted 19 February 1923
HUV-I	*Humanitäres Völkerrecht—Informationsschriften*
ICAO	International Civil Aviation Organization
ICLQ	*International and Comparative Law Quarterly*
ICRC	International Committee of the Red Cross
ILM	*International Legal Materials*
IRRC	*International Review of the Red Cross*
ItalYIL	*Italian Yearbook of International Law*
IYHR	*Israel Yearbook of Human Rights*
LondonDecl 1909	London Declaration of 26 February 1909 concerning the Laws of Naval War
LondonProt 1936	London *Procès-Verbal* of 6 November 1936 concerning the Rules of Submarine Warfare
MercenaryConv	Mercenary Convention of 4 December 1989
NATO	North Atlantic Treaty Organization
NethYIL	*Netherlands Yearbook of International Law*
NWP9	US Navy Department, NWP9 A/FMFM 1–10, *The Commander's Handbook on the Law of Naval Operations*, 1989 and *Annotated Supplement to the Commander's Handbook* (Rev. A)/FMFM 1–10, 1989
NZWehrr	*Neue Zeitschrift für Wehrrecht*
para.	paragraph
ParisDecl 1856	Paris Declaration of 16 April 1856 concerning Maritime Law
PetersburgDecl 1868	St Petersburg Declaration of 29 November/11 December 1868 Renouncing the Use, in Time of War, of Explosive Projectiles under 400 Grammes Weight

Prot.	Protocol
RDMilG	*Revue de Droit Militaire et de Droit de la Guerre*
Reg.	Regulation
RegEx	Regulations for the execution of the Convention for the Protection of Cultural Property in the Event of Armed Conflicts of 14 May 1954
Res.	Resolution
RIC	*Revue Internationale de la Croix-Rouge*
UN	United Nations
USNIP	US Naval Institute Proceedings
VaJIntL	*Virginia Journal of International Law*
WeaponsConv	Inhumane Weapons Convention of 10 October 1980
WEU	Western European Union
WVR	*Wörterbuch des Völkerrechts*
ZaöRV	*Zeitschrift für ausländisches öffentliches Recht und Völkerrecht*

LIST OF INTERNATIONAL INSTRUMENTS

18 October 1907	**Hague Declaration (XIV)** Prohibiting the Discharge of Projectiles and Explosives from Balloons (not yet in force)
26 February 1909	Declaration Concerning the Laws of Naval War (**London Declaration—LondonDecl 1909**)
19 February 1923	**Hague Rules of Air Warfare,** drafted by a Commission of Jurists (**HRAW 1923**)
17 June 1925	Protocol for the Prohibition of the Use of Asphyxiating, Poisonous or Other Gases, and of Bacteriological Methods of Warfare (**Geneva Gas Protocol—GasProt**)
27 July 1929	Convention for the Amelioration of the Condition of the Wounded and Sick in Armies in the Field (replaced by the Ist Geneva Convention of 1949)
27 July 1929	Convention concerning the Treatment of Prisoners of War (replaced by the IIIrd Geneva Convention of 1949)
15 April 1935	Treaty on the Protection of Artistic and Scientific Institutions and Historic Monuments (**Roerich Pact**)
6 November 1936	*Procès-Verbal* relating to the Rules of Submarine Warfare set forth in Part IV of the Treaty of London of 22 April 1930 (**London Protocol— LondonProt 1936**)
9 December 1948	Convention on the Prevention and Punishment of the Crime of Genocide (**Genocide Convention—GenocidConv**)
12 August 1949	**Geneva Convention (I)** for the Amelioration of the Condition of Wounded and Sick in Armed Forces in the Field (**GC I**)
12 August 1949	**Geneva Convention (II)** for the Amelioration of the Wounded, Sick and Shipwrecked Members of Armed Forces at Sea (**GC II**)
12 August 1949	**Geneva Convention (III)** concerning the Treatment of Prisoners of War (**GC III**)
12 August 1949	**Geneva Convention (IV)** concerning the Protection of Civilian Persons in Time of War (**GC IV**)
14 May 1954	Convention for the Protection of Cultural Property in the Event of Armed Conflict (**Cultural Property Convention—CultPropConv**)
10 April 1972	Convention on the Prohibition of the Development, Production and Stockpiling of Bacteriological (Biological) and Toxin Weapons and on their Destruction (**Biological Weapons Convention—BWC**)
18 May 1977	Convention on the Prohibition of Military or any Other Hostile Use of Environmental Modification Techniques (**ENMOD**)
8 June 1977	Protocol Additional to the Geneva Conventions of 12 August 1949, and concerning the Protection of Victims of International Armed Conflicts (**Protocol I—AP I**)
8 June 1977	Protocol Additional to the Geneva Conventions of 12 August 1949, and concerning the Protection of Victims of Non-International Armed Conflicts (**Protocol II—AP II**)
10 October 1980	Convention on Prohibitions or Restrictions on the Use of Certain Conventional Weapons Which May be Deemed to be Excessively

1

Historical Development and Legal Basis

$(43 - 8 \ UNC)$

I. DEFINITION OF THE TERM 'HUMANITARIAN LAW'

The use of force is prohibited under Art. 2(4) of the UN Charter. States may resort   101
to force only in the exercise of their inherent right of individual or collective self-defence (Art. 51 UN Charter) or as part of military sanctions authorized by the Security Council (Arts. 43–8 UN Charter). International humanitarian law applies with equal force to all the parties in an armed conflict irrespective of which party was responsible for starting that conflict. It comprises the whole of established law serving the protection of man in armed conflict.

1. *Introduction.* Although the subject of this Manual is the law applicable to the conduct of hostilities once a State has resorted to the use of force (the *ius in bello*), that law cannot be properly understood without some examination of the separate body of rules which determines when resort to force is permissible (the *ius ad bellum*). The modern *ius ad bellum* is of relatively recent origin and is based upon Art. 2(4) and Chap. VII of the UN Charter.

2. *The Charter Prohibition on the Use of Force.* Art. 2(4) of the UN Charter states that: 'All Members shall refrain in their international relations from the threat or use of force against the territorial integrity or political independence of any State, or in any other manner inconsistent with the purposes of the United Nations.' By prohibiting the use of *force*, rather than *war*, this provision avoids debate about whether a particular conflict constitutes war. Although some writers have endeavoured to read Art. 2(4) narrowly, arguing that there are instances in which the use of force may occur without it being directed 'against the territorial integrity or political independence of any State' or being 'in any other manner inconsistent with the purposes of the United Nations',[1] the prevailing view is that any use of force by one state against the forces of another, or on the territory of another, will contravene Art. 2(4) unless it can be justified by reference to one of the specific exceptions to that provision.

3. *The Right of Self-Defence.* Art. 51 of the Charter provides that: 'Nothing in the present Charter shall impair the inherent right of individual or collective

---

[1] See the discussion of this question by various writers in Cassese (Ed.).

self-defence if an armed attack occurs against a Member of the United Nations, until the Security Council has taken measures necessary to maintain international peace and security. Measures taken by Members in the exercise of this right of self-defence shall be immediately reported to the Security Council and shall not in any way affect the authority and responsibility of the Security Council under the present Charter to take at any time such action as it deems necessary in order to maintain or restore international peace and security.' The term 'armed attack' is not defined. In its decision in *Nicaragua* v. *United States* the International Court of Justice held that armed attacks included 'not merely action by regular armed forces across an international border', but also 'the sending by or on behalf of a State of armed bands, groups, irregulars or mercenaries, which carry out acts of armed force against another State of such gravity as to amount to [*inter alia*] . . . an actual armed attack conducted by regular forces ·. . . or its substantial involvement therein'.[2] On this basis, systematic terrorist attacks organized, or perhaps sponsored, by a State could constitute an armed attack to which the victim State could respond in self-defence. However, the Court went on to set a threshold by ruling that terrorist or irregular operations would constitute an armed attack only if the scale and effects of such an operation were such that it 'would have been classified as an armed attack rather than as a mere frontier incident had it been carried out by regular armed forces'.

a) In addition to an attack upon the territory of a state, it appears to be accepted that an attack against a state's warships, military aircraft, or troops overseas will amount to an attack upon the state itself. It has sometimes been argued that an attack upon a merchant ship should not be treated as an armed attack upon the state whose flag it flies and will not, therefore, trigger the right of self-defence.[3] This view is not, however, accepted by the majority of naval states. During the Iran–Iraq War, for example, most of the states which deployed naval forces to the Gulf made clear that those forces would defend merchant ships flying the same flag from attack. There have also been a number of cases (of which the best known is the Entebbe incident) in which one state has used force to protect its citizens from attack in the territory of another state. The legality of such actions has been questioned. Nevertheless, a state consists of people as well as territory and it would be a strange law of self-defence which allowed a state to use force in response to the military occupation of an uninhabited island but not in response to an attack which threatened the lives of its citizens. Where a state deliberately attacks foreign nationals on its territory, it seems a reasonable exercise of the right of self-defence for the state of those nationals to use force to rescue them.[4]

b) A particularly difficult question left open by the International Court in the *Nicaragua* case is whether a state must wait until it is attacked before it can respond in self-defence or whether it is entitled to pre-empt an attack by taking measures of

---

[2] ICJ Reports1986, p. 14, at para.. 195. The Court was quoting from Art. 3 of the Definition of Aggression, annexed to UN GA Res. 3314.

[3] Bothe in Dekker/Post, 209.

[4] See Ronzitti, *Rescuing Nationals Abroad.*

'anticipatory self-defence'.⁵ Although the text of Art. 51 appears to rule out any concept of anticipatory self-defence, it does not *create* the right of self-defence but preserves a right described as 'inherent'. Before 1945 it was generally assumed that the right of self-defence included a right of anticipatory self-defence provided that an armed attack was imminent.⁶ Since 1945 there have been numerous instances of states asserting a right of anticipatory self-defence. Apart from Israel's invocation of this right in 1967, for which it was not condemned by the Security Council or the General Assembly, the United States has repeatedly asserted a right of anticipatory self-defence and this was reflected in the rules of engagement issued to United States naval forces in the Persian Gulf during the Iran–Iraq War (The United Kingdom, France, the USSR, and on one occasion during the Congo conflict the UN itself have also claimed a right of anticipatory self-defence.⁷ It is noticeable that when Israel relied upon this argument in attempting to justify its destruction of Iraq's nuclear reactor in 1981, debate in the UN Security Council centred not upon whether there was a right of anticipatory self-defence but upon whether any threat to Israel was sufficiently close in time to bring that right into operation. The Security Council concluded that any threat posed by Iraq to Israel in 1981 was too remote to meet the requirement that an armed attack must be 'imminent'.⁸

c) The notion of collective self-defence is that one state may come to the assistance of another which has been the victim of an armed attack. In the *Nicaragua* case, the International Court of Justice held that for a state to be able to justify going to the assistance of another state by way of collective self-defence, two requirements must be satisfied: the second state must have been the victim of an armed attack (or such an attack must be imminent), so that that state is itself entitled to take action by way of individual self-defence, and it must request military assistance from the first state. In the absence of a request for assistance from the state attacked, the Court considered that the right of collective self-defence could not be invoked.⁹

d) The right of self-defence is preserved only 'until the Security Council has taken measures necessary to restore international peace and security'. It is not clear what action on the part of the Council will put an end to the right of self-defence. Purely verbal condemnation of an aggressor by the Council cannot be sufficient for, as the UK Representative at the UN stated during the Falklands conflict, Art. 51 'can only be taken to refer to measures which are actually effective to bring about the stated objective'.¹⁰ When Iraq invaded Kuwait, however, the Security Council reinforced its immediate demand for Iraqi withdrawal by imposing economic sanctions upon Iraq.¹¹ A number of commentators argued that the imposition of sanctions

---

⁵ Compare Bowett, *Self-Defence in International Law* with Brownlie, *International Law and the Use of Force by States.*

⁶ The *Caroline* dispute between Britain and the United States in 1837; see *Jennings, AJIL* 32 (1938) 82.

⁷ Not all of these claims were well founded. The USSR's claim of anticipatory self-defence as a justification for its intervention in Czechoslovakia in 1968 was fanciful. The point, however, is that so many states expressly recognized that such a right exists.

⁸ Debate of 12 June 1981, S/PV 2280.   ⁹ *Nicaragua case*, supra fn. 2.

¹⁰ UN Doc. S/15016.   ¹¹ Res. 661 (1990).

removed the scope for military action against Iraq under Art. 51 unless the Security Council adopted a further resolution specifically authorizing military action. Yet to argue that as soon as the Security Council adopts any kind of sanctions, the right of self-defence is suspended strains the meaning of Art. 51, since it ignores the requirement that the measures must be 'necessary' to maintain peace and security. If any action by the Council required the victim of an armed attack to suspend action in self-defence, that would scarcely induce states to refer situations of this kind to the Security Council. The better view is that only when the Security Council takes measures which are effective in terminating an armed attack, or expressly calls upon a state to cease action in self-defence, are Art. 51 rights suspended.[12]

e) Not all the conditions for a valid exercise of the right of self-defence are stated in Art. 51 of the Charter. It was accepted by both parties in the *Nicaragua* case, and confirmed by the International Court, that measures taken in self-defence must not exceed what is necessary and proportionate. These requirements have been described as being 'innate in any genuine concept of self-defence',[13] and it is these requirements which distinguish the modern law of self-defence from the traditional concept of the 'just war'. In just war theory, once a state had a valid reason for resorting to force, there was no limit on the extent of force which could be employed (other than those which stemmed from the humanitarian requirements of the law of armed conflict). Self-defence, by contrast, permits only the use of force to put an end to an armed attack and to any occupation of territory or other forcible violation of rights which may have been committed. That does not mean that the state which uses force in self-defence must use no more force than has been used against it. Such a rule would be practical nonsense. The United Kingdom, for example, could not have retaken the Falkland Islands after the Argentine invasion of 1982 using only the degree of force which had been used by Argentina, for Argentina had placed a far larger force on the Islands than the small British garrison overcome in the initial invasion. The correct test is that stated by Sir Humphrey Waldock when he said that the use of force in self-defence must be '. . . strictly confined to the object of stopping or preventing the infringement [of the defending state's rights] and reasonably proportionate to what is required for achieving this objective'.[14] In the case of the Falklands, the United Kingdom was entitled to use such force as was reasonably necessary to retake the Islands and to guarantee their security against further attack. The limitations which the principles of necessity and proportionality impose upon the degree of force which may be used have implications for the conduct of hostilities which are examined in the commentary to Section 130 of this Chapter, below.

4. *Other Possible Justifications for the Use of Force.* Self-defence is much the most important and the most frequently invoked justification for the use of force by a state. On occasions, however, a number of other possible justifications have been advanced. Reprisals, the protection of nationals abroad, humanitarian interven-

---

[12] Greig, *ICLQ* 40 (1991), 366; Greenwood, in *The World Today*, Vol. 47 (1991).
[13] Brownlie, 434.   [14] Waldock, *Recueil des Cours* 81 (1952), 451.

tion, intervention to promote self-determination, and intervention in an internal conflict at the request of the government of the state concerned have all been cited. Of these, intervention to protect nationals can plausibly be regarded as an aspect of the right of self-defence, for the reasons given above. Armed reprisals, though once lawful, have been condemned by both the Security Council and the General Assembly and their legal basis must now be regarded as highly doubtful.[15] Humanitarian intervention has also been controversial, although the interventions by western states in northern Iraq in 1991 and southern Iraq in 1992 to protect the civilian population of those areas from large-scale attacks by the Iraqi armed forces suggest that a principle of intervention in cases of extreme humanitarian necessity is now accepted as lawful. Those cases were, however, unusual both in the extent of the humanitarian emergency and in the fact that the Security Council had condemned the Iraqi Government's attacks on the civilian population as a threat to international peace and security in Resolution 688 (1991). Intervention to promote self-determination is also of doubtful legality. Even if it might be said to exist in the classic case of a colonial people fighting a war of independence, it is unclear that it could be extended to more modern cases of pro-democratic intervention. Finally, intervention in a state with the consent of the government of that state has generally been taken as involving no use of force *against* that state, unless the state concerned was already in a condition of civil war.

5. *Military Sanctions authorized by the Security Council.* The extensive limitation placed by the Charter upon unilateral resort to force by states is linked to, but not dependent upon, the system of collective security in Chap. VII of the UN Charter. Under Art. 39 of the Charter, the Council is empowered to 'determine the existence of any threat to the peace, breach of the peace, or act of aggression'. Once it has taken this step, Arts. 41 and 42 give the Council power to take measures to restore international peace and security.

a) Under Art. 41, the Council may call upon member states to apply economic sanctions, a power which it has recently used in relation to Iraq's invasion of Kuwait,[16] Libya's refusal to co-operate with investigations into terrorist attacks on aircraft,[17] and the situation in the former Yugoslavia.[18] Where the Council has imposed sanctions under Art. 41, it may authorize States to use limited force to prevent ships or aircraft from violating those sanctions.[19]

b) Art. 42 then provides: 'should the Security Council consider that measures provided for in Art. 41 would be inadequate or have proved to be inadequate, it may take such action by air, sea or land forces as may be necessary to maintain or restore international peace and security. Such action may include demonstrations, blockade, and other operations by air, sea or land forces of Members of the United Nations.'

---

[15] See, however, Bowett, *AJIL* 66 (1972), 1.   [16] Res. 661 (1990).
[17] Res. 748 (1992). See also the decision of the International Court of Justice in *Libya* v. *United Kingdom* (*Provisional Measures*) ICJ Reports 3 [1992].
[18] Res. 757 (1992).   [19] e.g. Res. 665 (1990).

c) To give effect to this provision, Art. 43 envisaged that member states would conclude with the UN a series of bilateral agreements under which they would make forces and other facilities available to the Council on call. Arts. 46–7 provided that plans for the use of armed force were to be made by the Council with the assistance of a Military Staff Committee which was charged by Art. 47 with responsibility, under the Council, for 'the strategic direction of any armed forces placed at the disposal of the Security Council'. Due to Cold War rivalries and different perceptions of the UN's military role, no Art. 43 agreements were concluded and the Military Staff Committee has never functioned as intended.[20] Nevertheless, the Security Council has authorized a number of operations which have involved the deployment of military forces.

d) Most of these operations were peace-keeping operations, in which UN forces, made up of units contributed on a voluntary basis by various member states, were deployed with the consent of the states in whose territory they operated. The sole purpose of these forces was to police a cease-fire line or to monitor compliance with a truce or deliver relief supplies. The UN forces in Cyprus, Cambodia, Croatia, Lebanon, and on the Iran–Iraq border are all examples of this kind of peace-keeping by consent. Although peacekeeping forces are not intended to engage in combat operations, they have sometimes become involved in fighting when attacked.[21]

e) On occasions, however, the Council has come closer to taking enforcement action of the kind envisaged in Art. 42. In the Korean conflict in 1950 the Council (which was able to act because the USSR was boycotting its meetings) condemned North Korea's invasion of South Korea, and called upon all member states to go to the assistance of South Korea.[22] Following Iraq's invasion of Kuwait in 1990 the Council adopted Resolution 678, which authorized those States co-operating with the Government of Kuwait to use 'all necessary means' to ensure that Iraq withdrew from Kuwait and complied with the various Security Council resolutions on the subject and to 'restore international peace and security in the area'. It was this resolution which provided legal authority for the use of force by the coalition of states against Iraq in 1991. In the absence of Art. 43 agreements, the Council was not able to require states to take part in these operations. Instead, it relied upon voluntary contributions of forces from a wide range of states.[23] Nor did the Council and the Military Staff Committee direct the two operations. In Korea, the Council established a unified command under the United States and expressly left to the United States Government the choice of a commander, although the contingents operating in Korea were regarded as a UN force and were authorized to fly the UN flag.[24] In the Kuwait conflict, the Council authorized the use of force, but command and control arrangements were made by the states concerned and the coalition forces fought as national contingents, not as a UN force.

---

[20] Bowett, *UN Forces*, 12.   [21] e.g. in the Congo.   [22] Bowett, *UN Forces*, 29.
[23] In Korea, sixteen states contributed forces. The coalition forces in the Kuwait conflict were drawn from twenty-eight states.
[24] Res. 84 (7 July 1950).

Greenwood

f) It has been argued that neither the Korean nor the Kuwaiti operation constituted enforcement actions of the kind provided for in Art. 42 of the Charter, because neither operation was controlled by the Council and neither was based upon the use of forces earmarked for UN operations under Art. 43 agreements. Yet there is nothing in Art. 42 which stipulates that military enforcement action can only be carried out using Art. 43 contingents, nor does Chapter VII preclude the Security Council from improvising to meet a situation in which military operations can effectively be conducted only by large national contingents contributed by states which wish to retain control in their own hands. Moreover, the Charter expressly envisages that the Council might authorize an *ad hoc* coalition of States to carry out its decisions, for Art. 48 provides that: 'The action required to carry out the decisions of the Security Council for the maintenance of international peace and security shall be taken by all the members of the United Nations or by some of them, as the Security Council may determine.' While the wording of the key resolutions in both Korea and Kuwait leaves room for argument on this point, both operations should be seen as instances of enforcement action authorized by the Council.[25]

g) If the legal basis for an operation is to be found in the enforcement powers of the Security Council, then the objectives for which force is used may go beyond the limits of what is permissible in self-defence. In the Kuwait case, a military action which was based on the right of collective self-defence could not lawfully have gone beyond liberating Kuwait and ensuring Kuwait's future security, whereas enforcement action against Iraq would have justified more extensive measures to re-establish peace in the region. The fact that Res. 678 authorized the coalition to ensure that Iraq complied with all relevant Security Council resolutions and 'to restore international peace and security in the area'[26] indicates that the operation was seen by the Council as enforcement action.

h) Only the Security Council has the authority to authorize enforcement action but it may choose to make use of other organizations (or, as in Kuwait and Korea, *ad hoc* coalitions) to carry out such action. Arts. 52 and 53 of the Charter provide that regional organizations may undertake enforcement action with the authorization of the Security Council. The recent decision of the Organization on Security and Co-operation in Europe (OSCE) to constitute itself as a regional organization under Art. 53 makes it possible for the CSCE, with the consent of the Security Council, to undertake action of this kind in Europe. In such a case, there seems to be no legal obstacle to the OSCE using NATO or the WEU as the military vehicle for conducting such operations.

6. *The Equal Application of International Humanitarian Law.* Once hostilities have begun, the rules of international humanitarian law apply with equal force to both sides in the conflict, irrespective of who is the aggressor. On the face of it, this seems completely illogical. To place the aggressor and the victim of that aggression

---

[25] Bowett Greenwood, *Modern Law Review* 55 (1992); compare 153; Schachter, *AJIL* 85 (1991), 452; Rostow, *AJIL* 85 (1991), 506.

[26] Res. 678, para. 2.

on an equal footing as regards the application of humanitarian law appears to con-travene the general principle of law that no one should obtain a legal benefit from his own illegal action: *ex injuria non oritur ius*. Yet the principle that humanitarian law does not distinguish between the aggressor and the victim is well established. In the Diplomatic Conference which adopted the two 1977 Protocols Additional to the Geneva Conventions,[27] the Democratic Republic of Vietnam argued that states which committed acts of aggression should not be allowed to benefit from the pro-visions of humanitarian law. This argument was roundly rejected and the Preamble to Additional Protocol I reaffirms that: 'the provisions of the Geneva Conventions of 12 August 1949 and of this Protocol must be fully applied in all circumstances to all persons who are protected by those instruments, without any adverse distinction based on the nature or origin of the armed conflict or on the causes espoused by or attributed to the Parties to the conflict.'

7. A number of war crimes trials held at the end of the Second World War make clear that the provisions of the earlier Hague Conventions on the laws of war[28] are also equally applicable to all parties in a conflict.[29] The reason for this apparently illogical rule is that humanitarian law is primarily intended to protect individuals, rather than states, and those individuals are, in general, not responsible for any act of aggression committed by the state of which they are citizens. Moreover, since in most armed conflicts there is no authoritative determination by the Security Council of which party is the aggressor, both parties usually claim to be acting in self-defence, as Iran and Iraq did throughout the 1980–88 Iran–Iraq War. Any attempt to make the rules of humanitarian law distinguish between the standards of treatment to be accorded to prisoners of war or civilians belonging to the aggres-sor and those belonging to the state which was the victim of aggression would thus almost certainly lead to a total disregard for humanitarian law. As Sir Hersch Lauterpacht said, '. . . it is impossible to visualize the conduct of hostilities in which one side would be bound by rules of warfare without benefiting from them and the other side would benefit from them without being bound by them'.[30] After initial hesitation,[31] similar reasoning has led to general acceptance that a UN force, or a force acting under the authority of the Security Council, is also bound to observe the rules of international humanitarian law.

102   **International humanitarian law constitutes a reaffirmation and development of the traditional international laws of war (*ius in bello*). In this context, most rules of the law of war now extend even to those international armed conflicts which the parties do not regard as wars. The term 'international humanitarian law' takes this development into account.**

---

[27] See Section 127 below.   [28] See Section 126 below.

[29] See e.g. *United States* v. *List* Annual Digest 15 (1948), 632 and the *Singapore Oil Stocks* case ILR 23 (1956), 810.

[30] Lauterpacht, *BYIL* 30 (1953), 206, 212; see also Greenwood, in *Review of International Studies* 9 (1983), 221, 225.

[31] Bowett, UN Forces 484; see Section 208 below.

Greenwood

1. *The Scope of 'International Humanitarian Law'.* The term 'international humanitarian law' is of relatively recent origin and does not appear in the Geneva Conventions of 1949.[32] International humanitarian law comprises all those rules of international law which are designed to regulate the treatment of the individual— civilian or military, wounded or active—in international armed conflicts. While the term is generally used in connection with the Geneva Conventions and the Additional Protocols of 1977, it also applies to the rules governing methods and means of warfare and the government of occupied territory, for example, which are contained in earlier agreements such as the Hague Conventions of 1907 and in treaties such as the Inhumane Weapons Convention of 1980. (For a full list of these treaties, see Sections 125–8.) It also includes a number of rules of customary international law. International humanitarian law thus includes most of what used to be known as the laws of war, although strictly speaking some parts of those laws, such as the law of neutrality, are not included since their primary purpose is not humanitarian. This Manual, however, deals with all of the rules of international law which apply in an armed conflict, whether or not they are considered to be part of international humanitarian law.

2. *Humanitarian Law and the Law of Human Rights.* International humanitarian law obviously has much in common with the law of human rights, since both bodies of rules are concerned with the protection of the individual.[33] Nevertheless, there are important differences between them. Human rights law is designed to operate primarily in normal peacetime conditions, and within the framework of the legal relationship between a state and its citizens. International humanitarian law, by contrast, is chiefly concerned with the abnormal conditions of armed conflict and the relationship between a state and the citizens of its adversary, a relationship otherwise based upon power rather than law. Nevertheless, the law of human rights and the powers of human rights tribunals have become increasingly important in armed conflicts, particularly in relation to the government of occupied territory.[34]

a) Another difference between humanitarian law and human rights law is that a state which becomes a party to a human rights treaty assumes an obligation to treat all persons within its jurisdiction in accordance with the treaty's requirements, even if they are citizens of a state not party to that treaty. Humanitarian treaties, by contrast, are binding only between states which are parties to those treaties. In the Kuwait conflict, several of the coalition states (such as Italy, Canada and Saudi Arabia) were parties to AP I but they were not obliged to apply its provisions in the conflict because Iraq was not a party to the Protocol.[35] However, once it is established that a humanitarian law treaty is binding upon states on both sides in a conflict, the application of the treaty is not dependent upon reciprocity. As the ICRC Commentary to the Geneva Conventions puts it, a humanitarian law treaty does not constitute '. . . an engagement concluded on the basis of reciprocity, binding

---

[32] Partsch, *EPIL* 3, 215.   [33] Robertson, in Swinarski (Ed.), 793; Eide, *op. cit.* 675.
[34] *Cyprus* v. *Turkey, ILR* 62, 4 (European Commission of Human Rights).
[35] Many provisions of AP I were, however, declaratory of customary law and as such were applicable to all the states in the Kuwait conflict (see commentary to Section 127).

each party to the contract only in so far as the other party observes its obligations. It is rather a series of unilateral engagements solemnly contracted before the world as represented by the other Contracting Parties'.[36]

b) Thus, the fact that one side in a conflict violates humanitarian law does not justify its adversary in disregarding that law.[37] Moreover, it is not necessary today that all the states involved in a conflict must be parties to a particular humanitarian treaty for that treaty to apply in the conflict. If there are states on both sides of the conflict which have become parties to a particular humanitarian treaty, the treaty is applicable between them, even though it does not bind them in their relations with those states which have not become parties. In this respect, humanitarian law has changed since the beginning of the twentieth century, for the older humanitarian law treaties contained what was known as a 'general participation clause', under which a treaty would apply in a war only if all the belligerents were parties to that treaty.

3. *Application of Humanitarian Law to Armed Conflicts.* Another significant development in the law is that, whereas the older humanitarian treaties applied only in a 'war', today humanitarian law is applicable in any international armed conflict, even if the parties to that conflict have not declared war and do not recognize that they are in a formal state of war. This matter is discussed further in the commentary to Chapter 2.

103 **International humanitarian law sets certain bounds to the use of force against an adversary. It determines both the relationship of the parties to a conflict with one another and their relationship with neutral states. Certain provisions of international humanitarian law are also applicable in the relationship between the state and its own citizens.**

1. International humanitarian law is not concerned with the legality of a state's recourse to force. That is a matter for the *ius ad bellum*, discussed in the commentary to Section 101. Humanitarian law sets limits to the way in which force may be used by prohibiting certain weapons (such as poison gas) and methods of warfare (such as indiscriminate attacks), by insisting that attacks be directed only at military objectives, and even then that they should not cause disproportionate civilian casualties. It also regulates the treatment of persons who are *hors de combat*: the wounded, sick, shipwrecked, persons parachuting from a disabled aircraft, prisoners of war, and civilian internees, as well as the enemy's civilian population. Although primarily concerned with the relationship between the parties to a conflict, a distinct branch of the laws of armed conflict, the law of neutrality, regulates the relationship between the belligerents and states not involved in the conflict. Unlike the rules dealing with the relationship between the parties to a conflict, the law of neutrality has not been the subject of much codification and still consists

---

[36] Pictet, *Commentary*, Vol. IV, 15.
[37] For the special case of reprisals, see Sections 476–9 and 1206.

largely of customary international law. It is considered in Chapter 11 of this Manual.

2. Most rules of humanitarian law concern the way in which a party to a conflict treats the nationals of its adversary and nationals of third states who may be serving in the forces of the adversary or resident in its territory. For the most part, humanitarian law does not attempt to regulate a state's treatment of its own citizens. Thus, it has been held, for example, that a national of one party to a conflict who serves in the armed forces of an adversary against his own state is not entitled to be treated as a prisoner of war if captured,[38] although this decision has been criticized[39] and is probably untenable in a case where nationality has been forced upon the person concerned (e.g. as a result of the annexation of the territory in which he resides) and perhaps where large numbers of people have taken up arms against the state of their nationality.[40] There are, however, some provisions of humanitarian law which are expressly intended to apply to the relationship between a state and its own citizens. Art. 3 of the four Geneva Conventions and AP II each lay down a legal regime for civil wars and internal armed conflicts. In addition, some provisions of the Geneva Conventions and AP I require a state to take positive steps in relation to its own citizens by, for example, ensuring that members of its armed forces receive instruction in international humanitarian law, or encouraging the dissemination of the principles of that law amongst the civilian population.[41] A state is also required to take steps to prevent its citizens from violating provisions of humanitarian law and must, for example, take action to prevent or prosecute grave breaches of that law by its nationals.[42]

Apart from the general rules which apply to all types of warfare, special rules   104
apply to the law of land warfare, the law of aerial warfare, the law of naval warfare,
and the law of neutrality.

The general rules of humanitarian law and their application in land and aerial warfare are considered in Chapters 2 to 9 and Chapter 12 of this Manual. The law of naval warfare is the subject of Chapter 10. Although many of the rules of humanitarian law (for example, those related to the treatment of prisoners of war) are common to all forms of warfare, naval warfare is in other respects subject to a distinct legal regime. The environment in which naval warfare takes place is very different from that of land warfare, its scope for affecting the rights of neutrals is far greater and the rules which govern naval warfare have not, for the most part, been the subject of as much attention in recent years as the rules applicable to land warfare. Apart from the Second Geneva Convention, which deals with the wounded, sick, and shipwrecked at sea, none of the post-1945 treaties have been specifically concerned with naval warfare and some of the most important provisions of AP I are not applicable to warfare at sea, except in so far as it may affect the civilian

---

[38] See the decision of the Privy Council in *Public Prosecutor* v. *Oie Hee Koi* ILR 42, 441.
[39] Levie, *Prisoners of War*, 74–6; Baxter, *AJIL* 63 (1969), 290.
[40] Oppenheim/Lauterpacht, Vol. II, 252–3.   [41] See Section 136.   [42] See Sections 1207–1213.

population on land or is directed against targets on land.[43] The result is that much of the law of naval warfare still consists of rules of customary international law. At the time of writing, the International Institute of Humanitarian Law is conducting a study of the law of naval warfare aimed at producing a statement of the laws applicable to naval warfare today.[44] The law of neutrality is also largely a matter of customary law. The entire institution of neutrality has been questioned in recent times, on the ground that the UN Charter has effectively rendered it obsolete.[45] Nevertheless, the events of the Iran–Iraq War show that the law of neutrality remains important, even if there are doubts about its exact content.

II. HISTORICAL DEVELOPMENT

105 **The following historical references may promote appreciation of the development and value of international humanitarian law.**

106 **Throughout its history, the development of international humanitarian law has been influenced by religious concepts and philosophical ideas. Customary rules of warfare are part of the very first rules of international law. The development from the first rules of customary law to the first written humanitarian principles for the conduct of war, however, encountered some setbacks.**

The laws of war have a long history,[46] as the following paragraphs show, although it has been suggested that military practice in early times fell far short of existing theory, and that such rules of warfare as can be identified in early times have little similarity to modern international humanitarian law.[47] From the Middle Ages until well into the seventeenth century discussion of the rules of war in Europe was dominated by theological considerations, although some elements of classical philosophy remained influential.[48] The codification and written development of the law did not begin until the nineteenth century.

107 **Some rules which imposed restrictions on the conduct of war, the means of warfare, and their application can be traced back to ancient times.**

– **The Sumerians regarded war as a state governed by the law, which was started by a declaration of war and terminated by a peace treaty. War was subject to specific rules which, *inter alia* guaranteed immunity to enemy negotiators.**

– **Hammurabi King of Babylon, (1728–1686 BC), wrote the 'Code of Hammurabi' for the protection of the weak against oppression by the strong and ordered that hostages be released on payment of a ransom.**

---

[43] See Art. 49 para. 3 AP I.

[44] The results of the first two meetings are published in *Heintschel von Heinegg* (Ed.), *Military Objective and Methods and Means.*

[45] See Lauterpacht, *Proceedings of the American Society of International Law* 62 (1968), 58; Norton, *AJIL* 17 (1976), 249.

[46] Verzijl, vols IX and X; Friedman, L. (Ed.).   [47] Münch, *EPIL* 4, 326.   [48] Holland, 40.

- The law of the Hittites also provided for a declaration of war and for peace to be concluded by treaty, as well as for respect for the inhabitants of an enemy city which has capitulated. The war between Egypt and the Hittites in 1269 BC, for instance, was terminated by a peace treaty.

- In the 7th century BC, Cyrus I, King of the Persians, ordered the wounded Chaldeans to be treated like his own wounded soldiers.

- The Indian epic Mahabharata (c. 400 BC) and the Laws of Manu (after the turn to a new era) already contained provisions which prohibited the killing of a surrendering adversary who was no longer capable of fighting; forbade the use of certain means of combat, such as poisoned or burning arrows; and provided for the protection of enemy property and prisoners of war.

- The Greeks, in the wars between the Greek city-states, considered each other as having equal rights and in the war led by Alexander the Great against the Persians, respected the life and personal dignity of war victims as a prime principle. They spared the temples, embassies, priests, and envoys of the opposite side and exchanged prisoners of war. For example, the poisoning of wells was proscribed in warfare. The Romans also accorded the right to life to their prisoners of war. However, the Greeks and Romans both distinguished between those peoples whom they regarded as their cultural equals and those whom they considered to be barbarians.

1. These examples show that the laws regulating the conduct of hostilities were recognized in many early cultures. The theory that humanitarian law is essentially 'Eurocentric' is in reality more a criticism of most literature on the subject than a reflection of historical fact. Thus, several of the principles of modern humanitarian law have precursors in ancient India.[49] In recent years much has also been written about the humanitarian principles which can be identified in African customary traditions.[50] As may be expected, the wide range of cultural traditions to which this paragraph refers displays a diversity of practice. Nevertheless, certain common themes can be identified, several of which continue to enjoy a prominent place in modern international humanitarian law.

a) In many cultural traditions there was an emphasis upon the formalities for opening and closing hostilities. The Sumerian and Hittite traditions are in this respect similar to the later Roman *ius fetiale* which required a formal declaration of war at the commencement of hostilities. In part, this tradition reflects the perception of war as a formal legal condition, as opposed to a factual condition, a perception which has only declined in importance in the twentieth century.[51] The attachment to formalities was also important, however, in serving to distinguish between hostilities entered into by a state and violence which had no official sanction.

---

[49] Singh, in Swinarski (Ed.), 531.   [50] Bello.   [51] See Sections 203 and 245–9.

b) The protection accorded to ambassadors and the respect for truces and for negotiations held during a war were the precursors of modern principles regarding ceasefires and parlementaires.[52]

c) The prohibition on certain types of weapon, particularly poison, is found in many different traditions and is now embodied in a number of important modern agreements.[53]

2. However, while some cultures respected the lives of prisoners and the wounded, the majority of prisoners faced death or enslavement. A similar fate usually befell the civilian population of a city which resisted attack, although in some traditions the population was spared if there was a timely surrender and the city did not have to be taken by storm.

108   **Islam also acknowledged the essential requirements of humanity. In his orders to his commanders, the first caliph, Abu Bakr (c. 632), stipulated for instance the following: 'The blood of women, children and old people shall not stain your victory. Do not destroy a palm tree, nor burn houses and cornfields with fire, and do not cut any fruitful tree. You must not slay any flock or herds, save for your subsistence.' However, in many cases Islamic warfare was no less cruel than warfare by Christians. Under the reign of leaders like Sultan Saladin in the twelfth century, however, the laws of war were observed in an exemplary manner. Saladin ordered the wounded of both sides to be treated outside Jerusalem and allowed the members of the Order of St. John to discharge their hospital duties.**

Several studies have now shown that many of the central principles of humanitarian law were deeply rooted in Islamic tradition.[54] Although Saladin was unusual amongst both Muslims and Christians during the Crusades in his humane treatment of prisoners and the wounded, he was by no means alone in regarding warfare as subject to principles of law. Three centuries after Saladin, the Turkish Sultan Mehmet extended to the population of Constantinople a greater degree of mercy than might have been expected given that the city had been taken by storm.[55]

109   **In the Middle Ages feud and war were governed by strict principles. The principle of protecting women, children and the aged from hostilities was espoused by the Latin father St Augustine. The enforcement of respect for holy places (Truce of God) created a right of refuge, or asylum, in churches, the observance of which was carefully monitored by the Church. The knights fought according to certain (unwritten) rules. The rules of arms were enforced by the arbiters of tribunals of knights. Those rules applied only to knights, not to the ordinary people. The enemy was frequently regarded as an equal combatant who had to be defeated in an honourable fight. It was forbidden to start a war without prior notification.**

---

[52] See Chapter 2.   [53] Art. 23 lit. a HagueReg and GasProt.   [54] Khadduri.
[55] Runciman, 152.

St Augustine's influence on the laws of war during the Middle Ages derived in part from his development of the theory of the 'just war'. Whereas the earliest Christian writers had generally been pacifists, St Augustine reasoned that a Christian committed no wrong by participating in a just war.[56] Augustine's views were later adopted by influential writers such as St Thomas Aquinas, who maintained that a just war required lawful authority, just cause, and rightful intention. The first requirement was important in distinguishing between hostilities entered into on the authority of a prince, on the one hand, from the lawless activities of brigands and war lords on the other. Once the idea that warfare might have a legal and theological basis was accepted, it followed naturally (at least in conflicts between Christian princes) that considerations of law and humanity should also influence the conduct of war. The rules which developed for the regulation of warfare between knights reflected these considerations as well as a general code of chivalry.[57] These rules undoubtedly had a civilizing effect and were a valuable humanitarian development. It should, however, be borne in mind that this code was largely devised for the benefit of the knights and that the purpose of some of the rules was not so much humanitarian as an attempt to prevent the development of weapons and methods of warfare which would threaten their position. Thus, the attempt by the Lateran Council in 1137 to ban the crossbow was motivated as much by a desire to get rid of a weapon which allowed a foot soldier to threaten an armoured knight as by humanitarian concern at the injuries which crossbow bolts could cause. Moreover, the code was intended to apply only to hostilities between Christian princes and was seldom applied outside that context, for example, in the Crusades.

The 'Bushi-Do', the medieval code of honour of the warrior caste of Japan,   110
included the rule that humanity must be exercised even in battle and towards
prisoners of war. In the seventeenth century the military tactician Sorai wrote that
whoever kills a prisoner of war shall be guilty of manslaughter, whether that pris-
oner had surrendered or fought 'to the last arrow'.

As a result of the decline of the chivalric orders, the invention of firearms, and   111
above all the creation of armies consisting of mercenaries, the morals of war
regressed towards the end of the Middle Ages. Considerations of chivalry were
unknown to these armies. Equally, they made no distinction between combatants
and the civilian population. Mercenaries regarded war as a trade which they fol-
lowed for the purpose of private gain.

For the modern law regarding mercenaries, see Art. 47(1) of AP I and Section 303 below.[58]

At the beginning of modern times the wars of religion, and particularly the Thirty   112
Years War, once again employed the most inhuman methods of warfare. The cru-
elties of this war particularly led to the jurisprudential consideration of the *ius in*

---

[56] Russell.   [57] Keen; Draper, *IRRC* 7 (1965), 3.   [58] Hampson, *NYIL* 32 (1991), 3.

bello and established a number of dictates to be observed by combatants. In his work '*De iure belli ac pacis*', published in 1625, Hugo Grotius, the father of modern international law, signalled the existing bounds to the conduct of war.

The savagery of warfare in the late sixteenth and early seventeenth centuries is summed up by Grotius in a passage in which he explained why he wrote about the laws of war: 'I saw prevailing throughout the Christian world a licence in making war of which even barbarous nations should be ashamed; men resorting to arms for trivial or for no reasons at all, and when arms were once taken up no reverence left for divine or human law, exactly as if a single edict had released a madness driving men to all kinds of crime.'[59] In effect, what Grotius described was the breakdown of both the *ius ad bellum* of the Middle Ages (the 'just war' doctrine) and the *ius in bello*. His '*De iure belli ac pacis*' was to have considerable influence on the rebuilding of the latter body of law, although it was not until the twentieth century that any real progress was made in developing a new *ius ad bellum*. Nevertheless, Grotius was not the only writer of this period to focus on the laws of war. Gentilis, who like Grotius was an exile from his own country, published his seminal work '*De iure belli*' in England in 1598,[60] while the Spanish writer Vitoria was also influential in reviving interest in this area of the law, particularly by suggesting that rules of international law might apply to warfare between Christian states and the Indians of the New World.

113　A fundamental change in the attitude of states to the conduct of war came only with the advent of the Age of Enlightenment in the eighteenth century. In 1772 Jean Jacques Rousseau made the following statement in his work '*Le Contrat Social*': 'War then is a relation, not between man and man, but between State and State, and individuals are enemies only accidentally, not as men, nor even as citizens, but as soldiers; not as members of their country, but as its defenders . . . The object of the war being the destruction of the hostile State, the other side has a right to kill its defenders while they are bearing arms; but as soon as they lay them down and surrender they become once more merely men, whose life no one has any right to take.' From this doctrine, which was soon generally acknowledged, it follows that acts of hostility may only be directed against the armed forces of the adversary, not against the civilian population which takes no part in the hostilities. These ideas also found expression in several international treaties concluded at that time.

The acceptance during the late eighteenth century of the ideas to which Rousseau gave voice in the passage quoted was a landmark in the development of humanitarian law; it was the first recognition of the principle that the purpose of using force is to overcome an enemy state, and that to do this it is sufficient to disable enemy combatants. The distinction between combatants and civilians, the requirement that wounded and captured enemy combatants must be treated

[59] *Prolegomena* 28.　　[60] Holland, 40.

humanely, and that quarter must be given, some of the pillars of modern humanitarian law, all follow from this principle. While the French revolutionary wars were in many respects cruel by modern standards, they are important for the development of humanitarian law in that they demonstrated in military practice many of the ideas enunciated by Rousseau and other writers of the Enlightenment.[61] The treaty of friendship and commerce between Prussia and the United States in 1785, whose most important authors are deemed to be King Frederick the Great and Benjamin Franklin, contained some exemplary and pioneering provisions for the treatment of prisoners of war. It was also one of the first attempts to record new principles of humanitarian law in written form, although it was to be another seventy years before the conclusion of the first multilateral treaty on the subject.

In the nineteenth century, after a few interim setbacks, humanitarian ideas continued to gain ground. They led to remarkable initiatives by individuals as well as to numerous international treaties. These treaties imposed restrictions on both the instruments of warfare and the methods of their use.   114

The nineteenth century saw the ideas which had gained acceptance in the late eighteenth century given practical effect. A number of major international treaties, some of which are still in force, were adopted, codifying several of the customary rules of warfare and developing those rules in various ways. In addition, the initiative of a number of private individuals led to the creation of what became the International Committee of the Red Cross, which has played a central role in the development and implementation of the rules of humanitarian law.[62]

Florence Nightingale soothed the sufferings of the sick and wounded through her efforts as an English nurse in the Crimean War (1853–56). She later made an essential contribution towards the renovation of both the civil and military nursing systems of her country.   115

Although she cannot be said to have had a direct effect upon the development of humanitarian law, her work in developing a military medical and nursing service to care for the wounded and sick on the battlefield (which was also a feature of the American Civil War) was an essential prerequisite to the development of that body of humanitarian law which deals with the wounded and sick and which was the subject of the first Geneva Convention.[63]

In 1861 Francis Lieber (1800–72), a German-American professor of political science and jurisprudence at Columbia University, NY, prepared on the behalf of President Lincoln a manual based on international law (the Lieber Code) which was put into effect for the first time in 1863 and governed the Union Army of the United States in the Civil War (1861–65).   116

---

[61] Best, 31–127.   [62] See Section 1220.   [63] See Sections 117 and 118.

The Lieber Code[64] is the origin of what has come to be known as 'Hague Law', so called because the principal treaties which dealt with the subject were concluded at The Hague. Hague Law is the law of armed conflict written from the standpoint of the soldier, in the sense that it takes the form of a statement of the rights and duties of the military in a conflict. Lieber's Code was the first attempt to set down, in a single set of instructions for forces in the field, the laws and customs of war. Its 157 Articles are based on the philosophy of the Enlightenment described in the preceding paragraph, stressing e.g. that only armed enemies should be attacked,[65] that unarmed civilians and their property should be respected,[66] and that prisoners and the wounded should be humanely treated.[67] The Code is, however, far more than a statement of broad general principles. The treatment of prisoners of war, for example, is the subject of detailed regulation,[68] as are the arrangements for exchange of prisoners, truce, and armistice.[69] The Code is the more remarkable for having been issued during a civil war when the Union Government had been at pains to insist that no state should recognize the Confederacy. In that sense it was many years ahead of its time; even today the rules of humanitarian law applicable in internal armed conflicts are more limited in their scope than the provisions of the Lieber Code.

117   **The Genevese merchant Henri Dunant who, in the Italian War of Unification, had witnessed the plight of 40,000 Austrian, French, and Italian soldiers wounded on the battlefield of Solferino (1859), published his impressions in his book 'A Memory of Solferino' which became known all over the world. In 1863 the International Committee of the Red Cross (ICRC) was founded in Geneva on his initiative.**

What shocked Dunant after the Battle of Solferino was the lack of any systematic effort by the armies concerned to care for the wounded, who were left to die on the battlefield, and often robbed and murdered by local inhabitants. In so far as medical services were available, their providers appeared unprotected from attack or capture. Dunant organized teams of volunteers to collect and care for the wounded at Solferino. The ICRC, for whose foundation he was responsible, was and remains an exclusively Swiss organization which has promoted the creation of better medical services in wartime, and the adoption of international agreements dealing first with the wounded and subsequently with the whole field of humanitarian law.[70]

118   **The 1864 Geneva Convention for the Amelioration of the Condition of the Wounded in Armies in the Field defined the legal status of medical personnel. It stipulated that wounded enemy soldiers were to be collected and cared for in the same way as members of friendly armed forces. These rules were extended and improved by the Geneva Convention of 1906.**

The 1864 Geneva Convention marks the beginning of the development of what has become known as 'Geneva Law'. In contrast to Hague Law (see commentary to

---

[64] Schindler/Toman, 3.   [65] Art. 15.   [66] Arts. 22–3 and 34–8.   [67] Art. 49.
[68] Arts. 49–59.   [69] Arts. 105–47.   [70] See Willemin/Heacock; Boissier; Durand.

Greenwood

Section 116), Geneva Law is written from the standpoint of the 'victims' of armed conflict: the wounded, sick, shipwrecked, prisoners of war, and civilians. It does not purport to define the rights and duties of the military but rather to lay down certain basic obligations designed to protect those victims, while leaving to customary law and Hague Law questions which do not fall within its provisions. The borderline between Hague and Geneva Law has now largely been eroded and AP I contains elements of both these legal traditions. The 1864 and 1906 Conventions have been superseded by the more detailed provisions of GC I and GC II, 1949.[71] Certain principles are, however, common to all these treaties. All provide that the parties to a conflict must not only abstain from attacking the wounded and medical personnel caring for them, but must also collect and provide care for them. The use of the Red Cross emblem (and later the Red Crescent) as a protected sign also stems from these conventions.

The 1868 Declaration of St Petersburg was the first to introduce limitations on the   119
use of weapons of war. It codified the customary principle, still valid today, pro-
hibiting the use of weapons to cause unnecessary suffering.

1. The Declaration of St Petersburg was the result of an initiative by the Russian Government to obtain the agreement of the major powers to outlaw the use in war between themselves of 'rifle shells', small projectiles which exploded or caught fire on impact.[72] These exploding or inflammable bullets caused far worse injuries than the ordinary bullets of the time (the effects of which were almost invariably disabling and frequently fatal). The Preamble to the Declaration states that: 'the only legitimate object which States should endeavour to accomplish during war is to weaken the military forces of the enemy; for this purpose it is sufficient to disable the greatest possible number of men; this object would be exceeded by the employment of arms which uselessly aggravate the sufferings of disabled men or render their death inevitable.' It concludes that 'the employment of such arms would, therefore, be contrary to the laws of humanity'. The parties therefore agreed to renounce the use, in conflicts between themselves, of 'any projectile of a weight below 400 grammes, which is either explosive or charged with fulminating or inflammable substances'. This provision remains in force and has now acquired the status of customary international law, although the evolution of aerial warfare led to it being interpreted as permitting the use of such projectiles against aircraft.[73]

2. The importance of the 1868 Declaration lies not so much in the specific ban which it introduced as in its statement of the principles on which that ban was based. The Preamble to the Declaration reflects the theories developed by Rousseau nearly a century earlier[74] and is the classic statement of the principle that it is prohibited to employ weapons or methods of warfare which are likely to cause unnecessary suffering.[75] Humanitarian law accepts that one of the legitimate

---

[71] See Chapter 6.   [72] Kalshoven, *Arms, Armaments* 205.
[73] See e.g. Art. 18, para. 1 *HRAW* 1923.   [74] See Section 113.
[75] See now Art. 35, para. 1 AP I and Art. 23 lit. e HagueReg. See also Section 130.

objects of warfare is to disable enemy combatants (and in many cases this necessarily involves killing) but it rejects the use of weapons which cause additional suffering for no military gain.[76] That principle remains important today. It is one of the general principles of humanitarian law, by which the legality of all weapons and means of warfare fall to be measured. It also inspired a number of other international agreements banning specific weapons, such as poison gas and soft-headed or 'dum-dum' bullets.[77]

120 **The 1874 Brussels Declaration provided the first comprehensive code of the laws and customs of war. That Declaration was further developed at the Hague Peace Conferences of 1899 and 1907. The most important result was the Hague Regulations Concerning the Laws and Customs of War on Land (HagueReg).**

The conference which drew up the Brussels Declaration was also the result of a Russian initiative, although some of the inspiration for the project lay in the earlier Lieber Code. The Declaration[78] itself was never ratified but many of its provisions were incorporated into the Manual of the Laws and Customs of War adopted by the *Institut de droit international* at its Oxford session in 1880 ('the Oxford Manual').[79] The Brussels Declaration and the Oxford Manual, although not legally binding, were highly influential and many of the provisions of the HagueReg can be traced back to them. Although parts of the Regulations have been superseded by the Geneva Conventions and AP I, many remain in force and are now regarded as declaratory of customary international law.[80] Thus, the section of the Regulations dealing with the government of occupied territory is still of considerable importance and is generally regarded as applicable to Israel's occupation of territories in the Middle East.[81]

121 **World War I, with its new munitions and unprecedented extension of combat actions, demonstrated the limits of the existing law.**

The most important development of World War I, in so far as it affected humanitarian law, was the evolution of aerial warfare and other forms of long range bombardment. These took place in spite of the requirement of Art. 25 HagueReg, that attacks on undefended towns and villages were prohibited. An undefended town was defined as one which could be captured without the use of force (a legacy of early customary rules which distinguished between the treatment of a city taken by storm and one which surrendered). Aerial warfare opened up the possibility of bombarding towns hundreds of miles behind enemy lines. These towns might be undefended in the sense that no forces were stationed near them, but they did not fall within the terms of Art. 25 because they could not be captured without force. Aerial warfare thus posed an unprecedented threat to civilians for which the existing laws made no provision. World War I also revealed deficiencies in the legal protection of the wounded

---

[76] See Chapter 4.   [77] See Section 128.   [78] Schindler/Toman, 25.
[79] Schindler/Toman, 35.   [80] Decision of the International Military Tribunal in Nuremberg.
[81] Bar-Yaacov, *Israel Law Review* 24 (1990), 485.

and prisoners of war, which led to the adoption of new Geneva Conventions in 1929 (see Section 123). The widespread use of poison gas during World War I also resulted in the adoption in 1925 of the Geneva Gas Protocol.[82]

**In 1923 the Hague Rules of Aerial Warfare (HRAW 1923) were formulated,   122
together with rules concerning the control of radio communications in times of
war. Although they were never legally adopted, they were influential in the development of legal opinion.**

1. World War I had highlighted the danger to the civilian population from aerial warfare, and in the aftermath of that War numerous proposals were made to subject aerial warfare to new legal constraints. The obvious military advantages of aerial warfare, however, prevented agreement on a new legal regime at the Washington Conference on the Limitation of Armaments, 1921–22. Nevertheless, some of the states represented at that Conference appointed a Commission of Jurists, chaired by the United States lawyer John Bassett Moore, with representatives from France, Italy, Japan, The Netherlands, and the United Kingdom, to investigate the subject and to make proposals. That Commission, which reported in 1923, drew up the Hague Rules on Aerial Warfare in an attempt to achieve a balance between military interests and the protection of the civilian population. The rules[83] prohibited attacks on civilians and aerial bombardment 'for the purpose of terrorizing the civilian population'.[84] Attacks had to be confined to military objectives, and in Art. 24 the Commission attempted to draw up a list of these. Certain objectives were given special protection and the Rules also included a duty to minimize incidental civilian casualties.

2. The Hague Rules on Aerial Warfare were never legally adopted and their principles were widely disregarded during World War II.[85] The attempt to devise a list of military objectives was probably doomed to failure, since objectives which have military value will vary over time and from one conflict to another. Nevertheless, although they never entered into force, the Rules were widely regarded at the time as an important statement of the legal principles which should govern aerial warfare. The basic principles which they laid down, though not the list of targets, were embodied in a resolution of the Assembly of the League of Nations in 1938. That resolution (modelled on a statement by the Prime Minister of the United Kingdom to the House of Commons) recognized the urgent need for the adoption of regulations dealing with aerial warfare and stipulated that the Assembly: 'Recognizes the following principles as a necessary basis for any subsequent regulations: (1) The intentional bombing of civilian populations is illegal; (2) Objectives aimed at from the air must be legitimate military objectives and must be identifiable; (3) Any attack on legitimate military objectives must be carried out in such a way that civilian populations in the neighbourhood are not bombed through negligence.'[86]

---

[82] See Section 128.   [83] For more detailed consideration, see Sections 325–9 and 448–9.
[84] Art. 22.   [85] See Spaight.   [86] Schindler/Toman, 221.

Greenwood

3. After World War II the ICRC drew up in 1956 the Delhi Draft Rules for the Limitation of the Dangers Incurred by the Civilian Population in Time of War.[87] These Draft Rules and the ICRC Commentary upon them show the influence of the HRAW. More importantly, many of the principles laid down in the 1923 Rules have been adopted, albeit in a modified form, in AP I of 1977, and have thus become binding treaty law.

123   In 1929 the Convention for the Amelioration of the Condition of the Wounded and Sick in Armies in the Field and the Convention relative to the Treatment of Prisoners of War were signed in Geneva. They developed the terms of the Geneva Convention of 1906 and part of the Hague Regulations of 1907.

The 1929 Geneva Conventions[88] were influenced by the experience of World War I and contained more detailed regulations for the treatment of the wounded and prisoners of war than their predecessors. Although the Conventions were in force during World War II, some of the major protagonists, including the USSR and Japan, were not parties to them. Nevertheless, at the end of the War, tribunals in a number of war crimes ruled that the main provisions of the Prisoners of War Convention had become part of customary international law and were thus binding on all states by 1939.[89] The 1929 Conventions have now been superseded[90] by the 1949 Geneva Conventions.

124   The first regulations on naval warfare were already developed by the Middle Ages. These regulations, which primarily embodied the right to search vessels and their cargo and the right of seizure, were subsequently changed several times. The treatment of ships belonging to neutral states lacked uniform regulation and was disputed. In the north, the Hanseatic League used its almost unrestricted naval supremacy to enforce embargoes in times of war, which were not only detrimental to its adversary, but also made it impossible for neutral states to trade with that adversary. The ability of neutral states to pursue their maritime trade activities in times of war could only override the attempts by belligerents to cut their adversaries off from ship-to-shore supplies if the position of these powerful neutral states was secured. In the eighteenth century, this led to the formation of alliances between neutral states, and to the deployment of their naval forces to protect their right to free maritime trade. The 1856 Paris Declaration Concerning Maritime Law (ParisDecl 1856) was the first agreement to address the protection of neutral maritime trade.

1. Although the law of naval warfare has never been subjected to such detailed regulation by treaty as the law of land warfare, the customary law on the subject developed at an earlier date. This development was largely due to the fact that naval

---

[87] Schindler/Toman, 251.   [88] Schindler/Toman, 325 and 339.

[89] *United States* v. *Von Leeb*, 15, *Annual Digest* 376; Baxter, *BYIL* 41 (1965–66), 286.

[90] Except in the case of states party to the 1929 Conventions which have not become parties to the 1949 Conventions.

warfare involved a far greater degree of contact between combatants and neutrals and so brought into conflict the right of a combatant to conduct war effectively and the right of a neutral state's shipping to enjoy the freedom of the seas. Moreover, the law of naval warfare was unusual in that each warring nation established a tribunal (or series of tribunals) to rule on the legality of interference with neutral shipping. The British Prize Court played a particularly important part in the development of the laws of naval warfare, since throughout the eighteenth and nineteenth centuries Great Britain was the dominant maritime power. Nevertheless, belligerent treatment of neutral shipping remained a source of controversy and the United States, which remained neutral throughout the French Revolutionary and Napoleonic wars, engaged in hostilities with France (1797–1801) and Britain (1812–15) partly on account of what it regarded as the infringement of neutral rights.

2. The influence of neutral states generally declined after the late eighteenth century and the balance tipped in favour of belligerent rights, although the Paris Declaration went some way to arrest this process. The United States, which had been a champion of neutral rights in the period 1789–1815, took a broad view of the rights of a belligerent during the Civil War (1861–65), greatly extending for example the doctrine of continuous voyage. This process was taken even further during the World Wars of the twentieth century.

3. The Paris Declaration of 1856 was important not only for its provisions on neutrality but also for its abolition of privateering, in which a belligerent authorized private shipping to prey upon the enemy's merchant ships.

III. LEGAL BASIS

The four Geneva Conventions have come to be internationally binding upon all   125
states:

- ✓ **Geneva Convention I for the Amelioration of the Condition of the Wounded and Sick in Armed Forces in the Field (GC I);**
- ✓ **Geneva Convention II for the Amelioration of the Condition of the Wounded, Sick and Shipwrecked Members of Armed Forces at Sea (GC II);**
- ✓ **Geneva Convention III Concerning the Treatment of Prisoners of War (GC III);**
- ✓ **Geneva Convention IV Concerning the Protection of Civilian Persons in Time of War (GC IV).**

1. The Geneva Conventions of 1949 have now achieved almost universal participation. At the time of writing virtually all states are parties to the four conventions.

2. Since the Conventions will therefore apply as treaties in almost any international armed conflict, the question of whether their provisions have achieved the status of customary international law might be thought irrelevant. It may, however, still be significant in two respects. First, the decision of the International Court of Justice in *Nicaragua* v. *USA*[91] shows that an international tribunal may sometimes be able to apply rules of customary international law even though it lacks the competence to apply the provisions of a multilateral treaty. Secondly, in some states (noticeably the United Kingdom and many Commonwealth countries as well as Israel) treaties do not form part of national legislation and cannot be applied by national courts, whereas national courts can and do apply rules of customary international law.[92] It seems likely that most, if not all, of the provisions of the Conventions would now be regarded as declaratory of customary international law.[93]

126   The 1907 Hague Conventions were binding not only upon the contracting parties, but have been largely recognized as customary law. The documents relevant to international humanitarian law are:

– **Hague Convention III Concerning the Opening of Hostilities (HC III);**

– **Hague Convention IV Concerning the Laws and Customs of War on Land (HC IV), and Annex to the Convention: Regulations Concerning the Laws and Customs of War on Land (HagueReg);**

– **Hague Convention V Concerning the Rights and Duties of Neutral Powers and Persons in Case of War on Land (HC V);**

– **Hague Convention VI Concerning the Status of Enemy Merchant Ships at the Outbreak of Hostilities (HC VI);**

– **Hague Convention VII Concerning the Conversion of Merchant Ships into Warships (HC VII);**

– **Hague Convention VIII Concerning the Laying of Automatic Submarine Contact Mines (HC VIII);**

– **Hague Convention IX Concerning Bombardment by Naval Forces in Times of War (HC IX);**

– **Hague Convention XI Concerning Certain Restrictions with Regard to the Exercise of the Right of Capture in Naval War (HC XI);**

– **Hague Convention XIII Concerning the Rights and Duties of Neutral Powers in Naval War (HC XIII).**

1. The current importance of some Hague Conventions is greater than others. HC IV and the annexed Regulations remain of the utmost importance. Arts. 42–56

---

[91] [1986] ICJ Reports 14; Abi-Saab, *IRRC* (1987), 367.

[92] See Jacobs/Roberts; Meron, 3–78; Bothe (Ed.), *National Implementation*, 1–71.

[93] Meron, 61–2. See also the decision of the Kammergericht, Berlin, of 13 July 1967, 60 ILR 208; *Fontes Iuris Gentium, Series A, Section II, I Tomus 6* 234. The Israel Supreme Court, however, has taken a contrary view; Bar-Yaacov, fn. 81, at 495. See also Section 134.

HagueReg still constitute the principal text on the government of occupied territory and the treatment of property in occupied territory.[94] In addition the provisions on methods and means of warfare,[95] on spies,[96] on flags of truce, and on armistices[97] retain importance even though for parties to Additional Protocol I the sections on spies and methods and means of warfare have now been largely superseded. The International Military Tribunal at Nuremberg held that the provisions of the Regulations had become part of customary international law by 1939 and accordingly they are binding on all states.

2. By contrast, the provisions of HC III, which require that hostilities should not 'commence without prior and explicit warning, in the form either of a declaration of war, giving reasons, or of an ultimatum with conditional declaration of war' has been completely disregarded. Since 1945 declarations of war have become virtually unknown[98] and it is difficult to regard HC III as a rule of contemporary customary international law.

3. In some respects, the most important of the Hague Conventions are those dealing with the law of naval warfare. Their provisions and current legal status are considered in Chapters 10 and 11.

The two 1977 Protocols Additional to the Geneva Conventions are designed to   127
reaffirm and develop the rules embodied in the laws of Geneva of 1949 and part of
the laws of The Hague of 1907:

- **Protocol of 8 June 1977 Additional to the Geneva Conventions of 12 August 1949, and Concerning the Protection of Victims of International Armed Conflicts—Protocol I—(AP I); and**

- **Protocol of 8 June 1977 Additional to the Geneva Conventions of 12 August 1949, and Concerning the Protection of Victims of Non-International Armed Conflicts Protocol II—(AP II).**

1. The Additional Protocols of 1977 have not yet achieved the near-universal acceptance achieved by the 1949 Geneva Conventions. As at July 1995 there were 138 parties to AP I and 126 to AP II. Both the United States and France, however, have so far decided not to become parties to AP I.[99]

2. *The Legal Effects of AP I.* The fact that AP I has proved unacceptable to some states and has not yet been formally applicable in any major international armed conflict does not, however, mean that it is without legal significance. The Protocol is binding upon a clear majority of states, including the Federal Republic of Germany and many other members of NATO. In addition, many of its provisions are declaratory of customary international law and are thus applicable in all

---

[94] See Sections 525–81.   [95] Arts. 22–8.   [96] Arts. 29–31.
[97] Arts. 32–41.   [98] See Section 203.
[99] For the debate on US participation see Sofaer, *AJIL* 82 (1988), 784 and the Aldrich, *AJIL* 85 (1991), 1–20.

international armed conflicts.[100] The influence of the declaratory provisions of AP I is illustrated by the 1990–91 Kuwait conflict. Although the Protocol was not applicable to that conflict, since several of the main protagonists including Iraq were not parties, the targeting policy announced by the coalition states reflected Arts. 48–57 most of which are widely regarded as declaratory of custom, or as representing developments of customary law which are generally acceptable to the international community.[101] Thus, the coalition made clear that it would attack only military objectives and its announcement of this policy was in terms very similar to those of Art. 52 AP I. Coalition announcements that every effort would be made to avoid excessive collateral damage and civilian casualties were also couched in language very similar to that of Arts. 51(5)(b) and 57.[102] The ICRC's appeals to the parties during the conflict also reflected the language of the Protocol.[103]

a) Even those provisions of AP I which have not yet achieved the status of rules of customary international law (e.g. the rules on protection of the natural environment in Arts. 35(3) and 55) have influenced public opinion and the perceptions of states as to what is permissible in conflict. Thus, reference was made to the environmental provisions of Additional Protocol I in a number of governmental and ICRC pronouncements during the Kuwait conflict.[104]

b) The fact that some states are bound by AP I while others are not might be thought to raise a serious problem of interoperation, especially for an alliance with an integrated command structure such as NATO.[105] Different national assessments of what might lawfully be targeted, or what weapons or methods of attack were permissible, could cause chaos in such an alliance. In practice, however, these problems seem to have been exaggerated. Most provisions of AP I which are likely to heave a bearing on the conduct of multinational military operations are either declaratory of customary law or represent developments of the law which are generally acceptable. The areas in which there are real differences, such as the provisions on reprisals in Arts. 50–6[106] and the complicated provisions of Art. 56 on dams, dykes, and nuclear electrical generating stations,[107] are unlikely to present insuperable obstacles for NATO.

3. *Additional Protocol II.* AP II lays down rules on internal conflicts which develop the more general provisions of common Art. 3 of the Geneva Conventions. To date the only conflict in which it has been treated as applicable is the civil war in El Salvador.[108]

---

[100] Greenwood, in Delissen/Tanja (Eds.), 93; Meron, 62; Fleck, *RDMilG* 29 (1990), 497; Cassese, *UCLA Pacific Basin Law Journal* 3 (1984), 55.

[101] Greenwood, in Rowe (Ed.), ch. 4.

[102] See the US Department of Defense, Interim Report to Congress (1991); Greenwood, *loc. cit.* n. 101.

[103] *IRRC* 1991, 22; Michel (Ed.).

[104] See Interim Report, *loc. cit.* n. 102; ICRC statement at *IRRC* (1991), 25 and 27; but cf. the US Department of Defense *Final Report to Congress: Conduct of the Persian Gulf War* Appendix O, 0–26.

[105] Meyrowitz, *Etudes Internationales* 17 (1986), 549.

[106] See Sections 476–9 and 1206.   [107] See Sections 464–70.   [108] See Sections 210–11.

Other agreements refer to specific issues of warfare and the protection of certain
legal assets. The most important documents are:

- St Petersburg Declaration of 11 December 1868 Renouncing the Use, in Times of War, of Explosive Projectiles under 400 grammes Weight (PetersburgDecl 1868);

- Hague Declaration of 29 July 1899 Concerning Expanding Bullets, so-called 'dum-dum bullets' (HagueDecl. 1899);

- Geneva Protocol of 17 June 1925 for the Prohibition of the Use in War of Asphyxiating, Poisonous or Other Gases and of Bacteriological Methods of Warfare—Geneva Protocol on Gas Warfare (GasProt);

- London *Procès-Verbal* on 6 November 1936 Concerning the Rules of Submarine Warfare (LondonProt 1936);

- Hague Convention of 14 May 1954 for the Protection of Cultural Property in the Event of Armed Conflict—Cultural Property Convention (CultPropConv);

- Convention of 10 April 1972 on the Prohibition of the Development, Production and Stockpiling of Bacteriological (Biological) and Toxin Weapons and on their Destruction—Biological Weapons Convention (BWC);

- Convention of 18 May 1977 on the Prohibition of Military or any Other Hostile Use of Environmental Modification Techniques—ENMOD Convention (ENMOD);

- Convention of 10 October 1980 on Prohibitions or Restrictions on the Use of Certain Conventional Weapons which May be Deemed to be Excessively Injurious or to Have Indiscriminate Effects (WeaponsConv).

1. Most of the agreements listed in this section concern weapons and means of warfare and are dealt with in greater detail in Chapter 4. The PetersburgDecl 1868 and the HagueDecl 1899 have already been the subject of comment.[109] Both remain in force and are widely regarded as declaratory of customary law.

2. The GasProt 1925 is also still in force and now has over 100 signatories. The ban on chemical and biological weapons which it imposed has generally been observed, although Iraq employed poisonous gas in breach of the Protocol on several occasions during the Iran–Iraq War[110] and threatened to do so during the Kuwait conflict. Following the use of gas in the Iran–Iraq War, the ban on chemical and biological weapons was expressly reaffirmed in a resolution adopted by the Paris Conference on the Prohibition of Chemical Weapons in 1989.[111] Although GasProt has attracted a large number of parties, many states have made their acceptance of the Protocol subject to a reservation to the effect that they retain the right to use chemical weapons in the event that such weapons are first used against them or their allies.[112] These reservations are based on reciprocity, i.e. a state engaged in a

[109] See commentary to Section 119.   [110] See UN Docs. S/20060 and 20063 (1988).
[111] *ILM* 28 (1989), 1020. *Europa-Archiv* (1989), 111.
[112] See e.g. the reservations by France and the United States, in *Roberts/Guelff*, 144–6.

Greenwood

conflict against one of the reserving states would also be entitled to rely upon the reservation to justify a retaliatory use of chemical weapons. The Protocol is therefore at present effective only as a ban on the first use of the weapons to which it applies. The Protocol bans only the use, not the possession of these weapons. Both the possession and use (including retaliatory use) of chemical weapons will, however, be unlawful under the Convention on the Prohibition of the Development, Production, Stockpiling and Use of Chemical Weapons and on their Destruction, 1993.[113]

3. The possession of biological weapons was outlawed by the Biological Weapons Convention of 10 April 1972.

4. The Inhumane Weapons Convention of 1980 is an umbrella agreement and provisions banning or restricting the use of specific weapons or means of warfare are contained in a series of protocols annexed to it. As of 1992 there were three Protocols, dealing with weapons which injure with fragments which cannot be detected by x-rays (Protocol I), mines, booby-traps, and other devices (Protocol II), and certain uses of incendiary weapons (Protocol III). A state must accept at least two of the Protocols if it becomes party to the Convention. There is provision in the Convention for the adoption of additional protocols.[114]

5. The ENMOD Convention is designed to prevent the deliberate manipulation of the environment for military purposes (and is thus distinct from the provisions of AP I which concern incidental damage to the environment).

6. The Cultural Property Convention was adopted in 1954 in order to prevent attacks on the looting of buildings and works of cultural, historical, and religious significance which had been a feature of World War II. The Convention and the Protocol attached to it have not been ratified by a number of major military powers. The principles underlying the Convention are incorporated in Art. 53 AP I. The protection of cultural property is dealt with in Chapter 9.

7. The London *Procès-Verbal* of 1936 is discussed in Chapter 10. Its requirement that submarines should conform to the rules applicable to surface vessels in their dealings with merchant ships was widely disregarded in World War II, and the status of the Procès-Verbal today has therefore been the subject of some controversy. Nevertheless, it seems that the agreement remains valid, although some of the assumptions on which it was based may have changed.[115]

129   **If an act of war is not expressly prohibited by international agreements or customary law, this does not necessarily mean that it is actually permissible. The so-called Martens Clause, developed by the Livonian professor Friedrich von Martens (1845–1909), delegate of Tsar Nicholas II at the Hague Peace Conferences, which has been included in the Preamble to the 1907 Hague**

---

[113] See Sections 434–40.   [114] Art. 8.   [115] Tucker, 67; Nwogogu, *Commentary*, 359–60.

Convention IV and reaffirmed in the 1977 Additional Protocol I as stated below, will always be applicable:

> In cases not covered by this Protocol or by other international agreements, civilians and combatants remain under the protection and authority of the principles of international law derived from established custom, from the principles of humanity and from the dictates of public conscience. (Art. 1, para. 2 AP I; see also Preamble para. 4 AP II).

1. The Martens Clause[116] was originally devised to cope with a disagreement between the parties to the Hague Peace Conferences regarding the status of resistance movements in occupied territory.[117] Those states which had argued that inhabitants of occupied territory who took up arms against the occupying forces should be treated as lawful combatants had been unable to obtain a majority for their proposal and the provisions on combatant status in Arts. 1 and 2 HagueReg did not include resistance fighters in the list of those entitled to combatant status. The Martens Clause was seen by many states as a reminder that Arts. 1 and 2 should not be seen as the last word on the subject of combatant status and that the question of whether resistance fighters were entitled to that status should not be decided simply by pointing to their omission from Arts. 1 and 2 but should be resolved by reference to *'des principes du droit des gens, tels qu'ils resultent des usages établis entre nations civilisées, des lois d'humanité et des exigences de la conscience publique.'*[118] Today, however, the Martens Clause is applicable to the whole of humanitarian law and it appears, in one form or another, in most of the modern treaties on humanitarian law.[119]

2. The exact significance of the Clause is more difficult to assess. It certainly means that the mere omission of a matter in a treaty does not mean that international law should necessarily be regarded as silent on that subject, and serves as a reminder that the adoption of the treaty in question does not preclude protection by customary international law. What is not clear is whether the Martens Clause goes further and introduces into humanitarian law a rule that all weapons and means of warfare are to be judged against the standard of 'the public conscience' even if their use does not contravene the specific rules of customary international law such as the unnecessary suffering principle.[120] Although this suggestion has been made from time to time,[121] it is impracticable since 'the public conscience' is too vague a concept to be used as the basis for a separate rule of law and has attracted little support. The Martens Clause should be treated as a reminder that customary international law continues to apply even after the adoption of a treaty on humanitarian law and as a statement of the factors which are likely to lead states to adopt a ban on a particular weapon or means of warfare.

---

[116] Strebel, *EPIL* 3, 252.   [117] See Sections 304–12 and commentary thereon.
[118] The original form of the clause.
[119] Art. 63, para. 4 GC I; Art. 62, para. 4 GC II; Art. 142, para. 4 GC III; Art. 158, para. 4 GC IV and Preamble, para. 5 WeaponsConv.   [120] See commentary to Section 119.
[121] See e.g. *ICRC, Conference of Government Experts on the Use of Certain Conventional Weapons* (Lucerne, 24 Sept.–18 Oct.), Report, 35–6; *ICRC, Second Working Group of Experts on Battlefield Laser Weapons* (Geneva 5–7 Nov. 1990), Report, 35–6; reproduced in ICRC, *Blinding Weapons* (1994).

Greenwood

IV. HUMANITARIAN REQUIREMENTS AND MILITARY NECESSITY

130 **In war, a belligerent may apply only that amount and kind of force necessary to defeat the enemy. Acts of war are only permissible if they are directed against military objectives, if they are not likely to cause unnecessary suffering, and if they are not perfidious.**

1. *Necessity and Proportionality in Humanitarian Law.* The principle that a belligerent may apply only that amount and kind of force necessary to defeat the enemy prohibits unnecessary or wanton application of force and is a long established principle of humanitarian law. Thus, Arts. 14–16 of the Lieber Code[122] make clear that only the necessary use of force against persons and property is permissible. Similarly, the United States Naval Commanders' Handbook states, as general principles of law, that: '(1) Only that degree and kind of force, not otherwise prohibited by the law of armed conflict, required for the partial or complete submission of the enemy with a minimum expenditure of time, life and physical resources may be applied. (2) The employment of any kind or degree of force not required for the partial or complete submission of the enemy with a minimum expenditure of time, life and physical resources is prohibited.'[123] These general principles are the basis for numerous specific rules of humanitarian law, such as the prohibition of the use of weapons and means of warfare likely to cause *unnecessary* suffering (Art. 23 lit. e HagueReg), the prohibition of the unnecessary destruction of property (Art. 23 lit. g HagueReg), and the principle that even military objectives should not be attacked if this would cause excessive civilian casualties or damage to civilian objects (Art. 51, para. 5 lit. b AP I).

2. *The Effects of the* Ius ad Bellum. The changes in the *ius ad bellum* brought about by the UN Charter[124] have added a new dimension to this principle of military necessity.[125] Prior to 1945, once a state was justified in going to war it was invariably entitled to seek the complete submission of its adversary and to employ all force, subject only to the constraints of humanitarian law, to achieve that goal.[126] That is no longer permissible. Under the UN Charter, a state which is entitled to exercise the right of self-defence is justified only in seeking to achieve the goals of defending itself and guaranteeing its future security. It may therefore use whatever force is necessary (within the limits of humanitarian law) to recover any part of its territory which has been occupied as the result of its adversary's attack, to put an end to that attack, and to remove the threat which the attack poses. In an extreme case the achievement of these defensive goals might be possible only by securing the complete submission of the adversary, but that will not generally be the case. Thus, the

---

[122] Schindler/Toman, 3.

[123] *NWP 9* 5.2; see also the decision in *United States* v. *List*, 15, *Annual Digest* 632 at 646.

[124] See commentary to Section 101.   [125] Greenwood, in Dinstein/Tabory (Eds.), 273.

[126] See *United States* v. *List*, *loc. cit.* n. 123.

Greenwood

right of the United Kingdom to use force in response to Argentina's invasion of the Falkland Islands could not have justified the UK seeking the complete submission of Argentina. The only legitimate goal permitted by the inherent right of self-defence was the recovery of the Islands and their protection from further attack.

3. Although some writers have taken a different view,[127] it seems that these limitations apply irrespective of whether there is a state of war between the countries concerned. The prohibition on the use of force contained in Art. 2(4) of the Charter is the cornerstone of modern international law and has the status of *ius cogens*, i.e. a peremptory rule from which states may not derogate.[128] The creation of a state of war—if that is still possible[129]—is an act of the state or states concerned and cannot, therefore, alter the obligations of those states under the Charter. Nothing in the Charter suggests that the limitations in Arts. 2(4) and 51 were intended to apply only until an armed conflict had become a war and the Charter has not been applied in that way. Thus, in 1951 the Security Council rejected Egypt's argument that a continuing formal state of war between Egypt and Israel justified Egypt in exercising belligerent rights with regard to shipping passing through the Suez Canal. In considering the legality of Egypt's action, the Council asked whether the measures taken were necessary for Egypt's self-defence and concluded that they were not.[130] Although in this case active hostilities between the parties had ceased two years earlier, the debate in the Council suggests that even if hostilities had been continuing, Egypt would still have had to demonstrate that its exercise of belligerent rights was necessary for its own self-defence.[131] Similarly, during the Falklands conflict, the United Kingdom never denied that its use of force had to meet the criteria of proportionality and necessity and went to some lengths to show that, in view of the size of the Argentine forces, the British action met those criteria.[132]

4. The humanitarian law principle of necessity and the limitations which form part of the right of self-defence, taken together, produce the following result: (a) the humanitarian law principle of necessity forbids a state to employ force in an armed conflict beyond what is necessary for the achievement of the goals of that state; and (b) the modern *ius ad bellum* contained in the UN Charter limits those lawful goals to the defence of the state (including its territory, citizens, and shipping).

   a) In other words, a state may use only such force (not otherwise prohibited by humanitarian law) as is necessary to achieve the goals permitted by the right of self-defence.[133] In that sense, the *ius ad bellum* has an effect upon the conduct of hostilities as well as upon the initial right to resort to force.[134] That does not mean that

---

[127] Dinstein, *War, Aggression and Self-Defence*, 231–2.
[128] *Nicaragua v. USA*, [1986] ICJ Reports 14, 100–1.   [129] See Section 202.
[130] SC Res. of 1 Sep. 1951 S/2322.   [131] Higgins, 213–14.
[132] See statements at *BYIL* 43 (1982), 542, 545, 553, and 554.

   [133] Other justifications for the unilateral use of force by states, in so far as they are well founded, also permit the use of force only in order to achieve limited objectives.

   [134] Greenwood, *loc. cit.* n. 125, Lagoni, in Heintschel von Heinegg, *Military Objective*, 56; Langdon, ibid. 86; O'Connell, in Howard (ed.) *Restraints on War* (1979) 123; Ronzitti, in Ronzitti (Ed.), 2–10. For a contrary view, see Fenrick, in Delissen/Tanja, 439 and van Hegelsom, in Dekker/Post, 127.

a state which is the victim of an armed attack and exercises its right of self-defence must always fight on its adversary's terms. A state acting in self-defence may take the fighting to its adversary's territory if that is necessary to recover territory of its own or to ensure its defence. What it does mean is that such action will be lawful only if, in the circumstances, it is necessary for the defence of that state.

  b) It follows that, even if the legal basis for the coalition's use of force against Iraq in 1991 had been the right of collective self-defence with Kuwait,[135] that would not have prevented the coalition states from sending forces into Iraq itself rather than launching a frontal attack upon the Iraqi forces in Kuwait, since outflanking the Iraqi forces offered the possibility of achieving the liberation of Kuwait with far fewer coalition and civilian casualties than would otherwise have been sustained. In fact, however, the legal basis for the coalition operations against Iraq was the mandate granted to the coalition states by the Security Council in Res. 678. The permitted goals of the coalition states were laid down by the Council in that resolution: the expulsion of Iraqi forces from Kuwait, ensuring Iraqi compliance with all relevant Security Council resolutions, and the restoration of peace and security in the region. Where a state uses force under a mandate from the Security Council, it may use only such force (not otherwise prohibited by humanitarian law) as is necessary to achieve the objectives set out (expressly or impliedly) in that mandate.

5. *Distinction and Perfidy.* Section 130 also refers to two other general principles of great importance. The principle of distinction requires states to distinguish between combatants and military objectives on one hand, and non-combatants and civilian objects on the other, and to direct their attacks only against the former.[136] The principle of perfidy forbids the use of treacherous methods and means of warfare.[137]

131 **International humanitarian law in armed conflicts is a compromise between military and humanitarian requirements. Its rules comply with both military necessity and the dictates of humanity. Considerations of military necessity cannot, therefore, justify departing from the rules of humanitarian law in armed conflicts to seek a military advantage using forbidden means.**

132 **Any exception to the prescribed behaviour for reasons of military necessity shall be permissible only if a rule of international humanitarian law expressly provides for such a possibility. The Hague Regulations Concerning the Laws and Customs of War on Land, for instance, prohibit the destruction or seizure of enemy property, 'unless such destruction or seizure be imperatively demanded by the necessities of war' (Art. 23 lit. g HagueReg).**

1. Although it was at one time contended by some writers that the necessities of war prevailed over legal considerations,[138] this argument has now been decisively

---

[135] See commentary to Section 101 for the view that this was enforcement action.
[136] Arts. 51–2 API; see Sections 304–12 and 441–63.   [137] See Sections 471–3.
[138] For discussion see Oppenheim, vol. II 231.

rejected.[139] Thus, the United States Military Tribunal in *United States* v. *List* ruled that 'military necessity or expediency do not justify a violation of positive rules'[140] and a similar approach was adopted in many other war crime trials after World War II.[141] AP I also makes clear that military necessity can never justify the killing of prisoners of war, even when these prisoners have been captured by special forces units who cannot evacuate them in the manner required by GC III. Art. 41, para. 3 AP I provides that in such circumstances the prisoners must be released and 'all feasible precautions shall be taken to ensure their safety'. The reference to 'all feasible precautions' illustrates that many of the rules of humanitarian law already make allowance for considerations of military necessity. In such cases military necessity does not override the law, it is an integral part of it. The existence of these rules shows that considerations of military necessity have already been taken into account in framing the rules of humanitarian law, which are intended to achieve a balance between military necessity and the requirements of humanity. A state cannot, therefore, be allowed to invoke military necessity as a justification for upsetting that balance by departing from those rules.

2. Indeed, as Section 130 makes clear, far from justifying a state in acting contrary to humanitarian law, the principle of necessity operates as an additional level of restraint by prohibiting acts which are not otherwise illegal, as long as they are not necessary for the achievement of legitimate goals. Similarly, considerations derived from the Charter cannot justify a departure from the rules of humanitarian law.

3. It should not be assumed, however, that humanitarian law and military requirements will necessarily be opposed to one another. On the contrary, most rules of humanitarian law reflect good military practice, and adherence by armed forces to those rules is likely to reinforce discipline and good order within the forces concerned.

V. BINDING EFFECT OF INTERNATIONAL LAW FOR THE SOLDIER

The obligations of the Federal Republic of Germany under international human-   133
itarian law are binding not only upon its government and its supreme military
command but also upon every individual.

One of the unusual features of humanitarian law is that, unlike most rules of international law, it binds not only the state and its organs of government but also the individual. Thus, the individual soldier or civilian who performs acts contrary to

---

[139] Dinstein, *EPIL* 3, 274.   [140] *Annual Digest* 15, 632 at 647.
[141] E.g. Manstein, in:16 *Annual Digest* 509 at 511–13; Thiele/Steinert, in: *Law Reports Trials of War Criminals* 3 (1948), 56; *The Peleus*, ibid. vol. 1, p. 1 (1946).

Greenwood

humanitarian law is criminally responsible for those acts and liable to trial for a war crime.[142] This criminal responsibility for violations of humanitarian law applies to members of the armed forces of all ranks. By contrast, the trials held after World War II established that only those individuals at the highest levels of government and the supreme military command could be convicted of crimes against the peace, i.e. the deliberate violation of the *ius ad bellum*.[143]

134   **According to Article 25 of the Basic Law of the Federal Republic of Germany, the general rules of international law form part of and take precedence over the federal law. They entail rights and duties for all the inhabitants of the Federal territory. These general rules also include those provisions of international humanitarian law demanding behaviour consistent with the principles of humanity and the dictates of public conscience (Art. 1, para. 2 AP I; Preamble, para. 4 AP II).**

1. Article 25 of the German Basic Law gives rules of international law greater effect within the law of the Federal Republic of Germany than they enjoy in the legal systems of many other states.[144] It applies, however, only to general rules of international law. Treaty provisions thus enjoy this status only in so far as they embody general rules of customary law. In relation to the status of the Geneva Conventions 1949, a 1988 study by the German National Section of the International Society for Military Law and the Laws of War concluded: 'Article 25 of the Basic Law provides that the general rules of public international law shall be directly applicable internally and take precedence over all Acts. Consequently, as far as the provisions of the four Geneva Conventions constitute rules which are "general rules of public international law" within the meaning of this constitutional provision, i.e. as far as they are part of the universally applicable customary international law, under national law in the Federal Republic of Germany they take priority over all ordinary Acts. Today a considerable part of the provisions of the four Geneva Conventions and the Additional protocols thereto must be considered part of customary international law. This does not apply, however, to each single provision.'[145]

2. In some countries, e.g. the United States, treaties possess a status equal but not superior to federal legislation, while rules of general international law are subordinate to domestic legislation.[146] In the United Kingdom and some Commonwealth countries, a treaty cannot alter rights and obligations under national law unless it is first given effect by Act of Parliament, while rules of customary international law form part of national law but are subordinate to domestic legislation.[147]

---

[142] See Sections 1207–13.

[143] von Leeb, loc. cit. n. 89; Greenwood, *Review of International Studies* 9 (1983), 221.

[144] Oppenheim/Lauterpacht, vol. I, 52–86.

[145] *Report to the XIth Congress of the Society for Military Law and the Laws of War* (1988), RDMilG (1989), 153, 154.

[146] Restatement of Foreign Relations Law (Third) 40–69.

[147] Oppenheim/Lauterpacht, vol. I, 56–63. On the incorporation of humanitarian law into the laws of states, see the national reports in *RDMilG* 28 (1989), 37–308 and Bothe (Ed.) *Implementation*.

Greenwood

Apart from these general rules, the members of the Federal Armed Forces are   135
obliged to comply and ensure compliance with all treaties of international
humanitarian law binding upon the Federal Republic of Germany.

The duty not merely to comply but to ensure compliance by others is stated in
common Art. 1 of the Geneva Conventions and Art. 1 of Additional Protocol I.

The four Geneva Conventions and the Protocols Additional to them oblige all con-   136
tracting parties to disseminate the text of the Conventions as widely as possible
(Art. 47 GC I; Art. 48 GC II; Art. 127 GC III: Art. 144 GC IV; Art. 83, para. 1 AP I; Art.
19 AP II). This shall particularly be accomplished through programmes of instruction for the armed forces and by encouraging the civilian population to study
these Conventions (Art. 83, para. 1 AP I). Considering their responsibility in times
of armed conflict, military and civilian authorities shall be fully acquainted with
the text of the Conventions and the Protocols Additional to them (Art. 83, para. 2
AP I). Regarding the Federal Armed Forces, s. 33, para. 2, of the Legal Status of
Military Personnel Act (*Soldatengesetz*) stipulates that soldiers of the Federal
Armed Forces shall be instructed in their rights and duties under international
law in peace and war.

All soldiers of the Federal Armed Forces receive instruction in international law.   137
It is conducted in the military units by senior officers and legal advisers and at the
armed forces schools by teachers of law. The emphasis is on teaching which is
related to practice. The soldier is instructed, using examples, in how to deal with
the problems of and the issues involved in international law. This instruction is
intended not only to disseminate knowledge, but also and primarily to develop an
awareness of what is right and what is wrong. The soldier is taught to bring his
conduct into line with this awareness in every situation.

The commanding officer must ensure that his subordinates are aware of their   138
duties and rights under international law. He is obliged to prevent, and where
necessary to suppress or to report to competent authorities, breaches of international law (Art. 87 AP I). He is supported in these tasks by a legal adviser (Art. 82
AP I).

A commanding officer has a duty to ensure that the forces under his command
conduct themselves in accordance with the rules of international humanitarian
law. In the case of *Yamashita*[148] the United States Supreme Court held that General
Yamashita was guilty of a war crime for failing to control the troops under his command and to prevent the atrocities which they committed in areas occupied by the
Japanese army.

It shall be the duty of a member of the Federal Armed Forces to follow the rules of   139
international humanitarian law. With whatever means wars are being conducted,

---

[148] 327 US 1; 13 *Annual Digest* 269. See also Green, *Essays*, 215.

the soldier will always be obliged to respect and observe the rules of international law and to base his actions upon them. If, in a particular situation, he should be in doubt as to what international law prescribes, he shall refer the issue to his superior officer to decide. If this is not possible, the soldier will always be right to let himself be guided by the principles of humanity and to follow his conscience.

The statement that the rules of humanitarian law must be obeyed 'whatever means' are used to prosecute a war is of the utmost importance. The fact that a conflict is labelled 'total war' or 'guerrilla warfare' does not alter the duty to comply with the rules of humanitarian law. The use of nuclear weapons is also subject to the rules of humanitarian law, although some of the provisions of AP I do not apply to nuclear weapons.[149]

140 **The soldier shall avoid inhumanity even in combat and refrain from using force against defenceless persons and persons needing protection, and from committing any acts of perfidy and brutality. The soldier shall look upon his wounded opponent as a fellow man in need. He shall respect the prisoner of war as an opponent fighting for his native country. He shall treat the civilian population as he would wish civilians, civilian property, and cultural property of his own people to be treated by the adversary; the same applies to foreign property and cultural assets.**

This Section states some of the basic principles of humanitarian law, the details of which are elaborated in later Chapters. The duty to avoid inhumanity even in combat is particularly significant. Although many of the provisions of the Geneva Conventions deal with events outside the immediate combat zone, even in the heat of combat humanitarian law requires that certain standards be observed, for example that quarter be given to anyone who clearly evinces an intention to surrender (Art. 40 AP I) and that enemy combatants who are incapacitated by wounds should not be made the object of attack (Art. 12, para. 1 GC I; Art. 12, para. 1 GC II). The final sentence of the Section should not be read as implying a principle of reciprocity: the soldier is required to treat enemy civilians as he would want his own people to be treated by the enemy, not as the enemy actually treats them. Apart from the law of reprisals,[150] failure by the forces of a state to comply with humanitarian law does not release their adversaries from their obligations.

141 **Superiors shall only issue orders which are in conformity with international law (s. 10, para. 4 of the Legal Status of Military Personnel Act [*Soldatengesetz*]). A superior officer who issues an order contrary to international law exposes not only himself but also the subordinate obeying to the risk of being prosecuted (Art. 86 AP I).**

An officer, of whatever rank, who orders the commission of an unlawful act is himself guilty of a war crime, as is the soldier who carries out that order. The 'grave

---

[149] Sections 427–33.   [150] Sections 476–9 and 1206.

breaches' provisions of the Geneva Conventions and AP I stipulate that ordering the commission of an act amounting to a grave breach is itself a grave breach.[151]

According to German law an order is not binding if: 142
- **it violates the human dignity of the third party concerned or the recipient of the order;**
- **it is not of any use for service; or**
- **in the particular situation, the soldier cannot reasonably be expected to execute it.**

Orders which are not binding need not be executed by the soldier (s. 11, para. 1 of the Legal Status of Military Personnel Act).

Moreover, it is expressly prohibited to obey orders whose execution would be a   143 **crime (s. 11, para. 2 of the Legal Status of Military Personnel Act). Grave breaches of international humanitarian law (Art. 50 GC I; Art. 51 GC II; Art. 130 GC III; Art. 147 GC IV; Art. 85 AP I) are penal offences under German national law.**

A plea of superior orders shall not be a good defence if the subordinate realized or,   144 **according to the circumstances known to him, should have realized that the action ordered was a crime (s. 5 of the Military Penal Code [*Wehrstrafgesetz*]).**

Punishment for disobedience or refusal to obey is proscribed if the order is not   145 **binding (s. 22 of the Military Penal Code).**

These Sections state two principles of particular importance:

a) A soldier who commits an unlawful act is not relieved of criminal responsibility merely because he was carrying out an order. Superior orders do not provide a general defence to liability for war crimes, a point established in the Nuremberg and Tokyo trials and applied in numerous other war crimes trials after World War II.[152] A soldier who carries out an order by action which is illegal under international humanitarian law is guilty of a war crime, provided that he was aware of the circumstances which made that order criminal or could reasonably have been expected to be aware of them. Superior orders may, however, amount to a factor mitigating the level of punishment.

b) A soldier has no legal obligation under the law of the Federal Republic of Germany to obey an order which would result in a grave breach of international humanitarian law. On the contrary, he is legally obliged not to carry out such an order.

---

[151] Arts. 49–50 GC I; Arts. 51–1 GC II; Arts. 129–30 GC III; Arts. 146–7 GC IV, and Arts. 85–6 AP I. On war crimes see Sections 1207–13.
[152] Dinstein, *Superior Orders* and Green, *Superior Orders*.

VI. TASKS OF THE LEGAL ADVISER

146   A lawyer who is qualified to exercise the functions of a judge is assigned to every military commander at the division level and above to perform the following tasks:

 – to advise the commander (and his subordinate disciplinary superiors) in all matters pertinent to the military law and the international law;

 – to examine military orders and instructions on the basis of legal criteria;

 – to participate in military exercises (in his wartime assignment) as a legal officer whose duties include giving advice on matters pertinent to international law; and

 – to give legal instruction to soldiers of all ranks, particularly including the further education of officers.

147   The legal adviser has direct access to the commander to whom he is assigned. The commander may give directives to the legal adviser only if they are pertinent to general aspects of duty.

148   The legal adviser receives directives and instructions pertinent to legal matters only from his supervising legal adviser, via the legal specialist chain of command.

149   The legal adviser additionally exercises the functions of a Disciplinary Attorney for the Armed Forces. In the case of a severe disciplinary offence the legal adviser conducts the investigation and brings the charge before the military disciplinary court. Such a disciplinary offence may include a grave breach of international law which in addition to its criminal quality also has a disciplinary significance.

   Art. 82 AP I requires the parties to the Protocol to ensure that legal advisers are available at all necessary times 'to advise military commanders at the appropriate level on the application of the Conventions and this Protocol and on the appropriate instruction to be given to the armed forces on this subject'.[153]

---

[153] Draper, IRRC (1978) 6–17; Denny, in: *Army Lawyer* 1980, 14. On the role of legal adviser during the Kuwait conflict, see Keeva, *American Bar Association Journal*, (December 1991), 52.

2

Scope of Application of Humanitarian Law

I. ARMED CONFLICT

International humanitarian law is applicable in international armed conflicts. The international law of peace existing between the states concerned will thus largely be superseded by the rules of international humanitarian law. The international law of peace, however, will continue to be of great importance, particularly for the relationship between the parties to a conflict and neutral states.

201

1. Traditional international law was based upon a rigid distinction between the state of peace and the state of war. Countries were either in a state of peace or a state of war: there was no intermediate state, although there were cases in which it was difficult to tell whether the transition to a state of war had been made.[1] So long as two countries were at peace, the law of peace—the normal rules of international law—governed relations between them. Once they entered a state of war, the law of peace ceased to apply between them and their relations with one another became subject to the law of war, while their relations with other states not party to the conflict became governed by the law of neutrality. While the matter was not free from doubt, it was generally thought that a state of war came into existence between two countries if, and only if, one of these countries made it clear that it regarded itself as being in a state of war.[2]

2. No such clear picture can be discerned today.[3] Since 1945 countries have rarely regarded themselves as being in a formal state of war and international humanitarian law now becomes applicable as soon as there is an international armed conflict.[4] Nevertheless, there is no sharp dichotomy between peace and armed conflict in international law such as used to exist between peace and war. A state of war usually presumed a complete rupture of normal relations between the parties. Today, the outbreak of an armed conflict between two countries will not necessarily mean that all non-hostile relations between them cease. Thus, diplomatic relations between the parties will not necessarily be terminated or suspended. Although the

---

[1] Such as the 1798–1801 hostilities between France and the United States or the 1903 blockade of Venezuela, Brownlie 28–37; Grob 37–63.

[2] Brownlie 38; McNair, in *Transactions of the Grotius Society* 11 (1925), 45; Meng, *EPIL* 4, 282.

[3] Greenwood, *ICLQ* 36 (1987), 283.   [4] See Sections 202–3.

United Kingdom broke off diplomatic relations with Argentina at the start of the Falklands conflict, and most of the states which took part in the conflict with Iraq in 1991 withdrew their diplomatic missions and required Iraq to do likewise, there have been cases in which diplomatic relations were not severed. China and India did not sever diplomatic relations during their 1962 border conflict, nor did India and Pakistan in 1965, and Iran and Iraq continued to have diplomatic representatives in each other's capitals long after the outbreak of the Iran–Iraq War. Similarly, the parties may continue with arbitration proceedings, as India and Pakistan did in the *Rann of Kutch* arbitration in 1965,[5] or with proceedings in the International Court of Justice, as in the *Burkina Faso/Mali* boundary dispute.[6]

3. Moreover, whereas it was at one time widely assumed that the creation of a state of war between countries automatically terminated, or at least suspended, all treaty relations between them (except, of course, for treaties which were specifically intended to apply during wartime),[7] today neither an armed conflict nor a formal state of war has such an effect. A recent resolution of the *Institut de droit international* suggests that the effects of an outbreak of war or armed conflict on treaty relations between the parties will depend upon whether it may be inferred from the treaties concerned that it was intended that they should cease to be effective in such circumstances.[8] It has been held that human rights treaties, which may have a considerable effect upon the way in which one state treats the nationals of another, do not cease to be applicable in time of war or armed conflict.[9]

4. The outbreak of an armed conflict between two states will lead to many of the rules of the ordinary law of peace being superseded, as between the parties to the conflict, by the rules of humanitarian law. For example, if one state detains nationals of the other, it must do so in accordance with either the Third or Fourth Geneva Convention, depending on the status of the persons concerned; the rights of the states to seize one another's property and to use force against each other will become materially different. Nevertheless, the law of peace does not cease to be applicable. In matters not regulated by humanitarian law, it will continue to apply. Thus, the treaty relations between the parties, their diplomatic relations (if any), and certain aspects of their treatment of each other's citizens will continue to be regulated by the law of peace, even if that law makes allowance for abnormal conditions between the states concerned. The greater the extent to which the parties maintain non-hostile relations (a feature of a surprising number of armed conflicts), the more important the law of peace will be.

202 **An international armed conflict exists if one party uses force of arms against another party. This shall also apply to all cases of total or partial military occupa-**

---

[5] 50 ILR 1.   [6] [1986] ICJ Reports 3 and 554.
[7] McNair, *The Effect of War upon Treaties* (1943).
[8] *Annuaire de l'Institut*, 61 (1985) vol. II, 278. See also Delbrück, *EPIL* 4, 310.
[9] See the decision of the European Commission of Human Rights in *Cyprus* v. *Turkey* 62 ILR 4.

tion, even if this occupation meets with no armed resistance (Art. 2, para. 2 common to the Geneva Conventions). The use of military force by individual persons or groups of persons will not suffice. It is irrelevant whether the parties to the conflict consider themselves to be at war with each other and how they describe this conflict.

1. It is now well established that the application of international humanitarian law[10] is not dependent upon the existence of a formal state of war, or indeed upon the existence of what has sometimes been called 'war in the factual sense'[11] (in so far as that may be different from the concept of an armed conflict). In the case of the Geneva Conventions, the conditions of their applicability are governed by common Art. 2, para. 1 which provides that the Conventions apply: 'to all cases of declared war or of any other armed conflict which may arise between two or more of the High Contracting Parties, even if the state of war is not recognized by one of them.' Although the final phrase does not deal expressly with the situation in which *neither* party to an armed conflict admits that it is in a state of war, it is generally believed that the Conventions were intended to apply in such a case, so that the last phrase of Art. 2, para. 1 should be read as if it said 'even if the state of war is not recognized by one *or both* of them'.[12] That is certainly the way in which it has been interpreted in practice: in most conflicts since 1949, neither side has admitted that it was in a state of war,[13] yet they have treated the Geneva Conventions as applicable. The Conventions are also applicable in a case where a state declares war but does not engage in actual hostilities (as happened with some Latin American states during World War II), so that if such a state interns 'enemy' nationals, those internees will be entitled to the protection of the Fourth Convention.[14] Art. 2, para. 2 provides that the Conventions also apply where the forces of one state occupy all or part of the territory of another, even if that occupation meets with no resistance. This provision is not, however, intended to affect the situation in which a state occupies territory after the outbreak of actual hostilities; such a case is governed by Art. 2, para. 1.[15]

2. The Hague Conventions of 1907 and a number of the other earlier treaties on humanitarian law are stated to apply only in time of war; in practice, however, the rules which they contain are treated as applicable in an international armed conflict, whether or not that conflict is regarded by the parties as a war.[16] Art. 1, para. 3 of AP I provides that the Protocol will apply in the same circumstances as the Conventions.

---

[10] For the position regarding the law of neutrality, see Section 209.

[11] Kotzsch; Dinstein, *War, Aggression and Self-Defence*, 8.

[12] Pictet, *Commentary* Vol. IV, 21; Oppenheim, Vol. II, 369. But compare Pictet, *Humanitarian Law and the Protection of War Victims*, 49–51, which takes a different view.

[13] For the exceptions, see commentary to Section 203.

[14] Schindler, *Recueil des Cours* 163 (1979–II), 117 at 132.

[15] Pictet, *Commentary* Vol. IV, 21. See, however, the discussion of Israel's position by Bar-Yaacov, *Israel Law Review* 24 (1990), 485.

[16] See e.g. *British Manual*, para. 7, *US Field Manual* para. 9; Bar-Yaacov, *supra*.

Greenwood

3. The Geneva Conventions do not define 'armed conflict',[17] an omission which was apparently deliberate, since it was hoped that this term would continue to be purely factual and not become laden with legal technicalities as did the definition of war.[18] The ICRC Commentary on the Geneva Conventions takes a very broad view of what constitutes an armed conflict: 'Any difference arising between two States and leading to the intervention of members of the armed forces is an armed conflict within the meaning of Article 2, even if one of the parties denies the existence of a state of war. It makes no difference how long the conflict lasts, or how much slaughter takes place.'[19] When a US pilot was shot down and captured by Syrian forces over Lebanon in the 1980s the United States maintained that this incident amounted to an armed conflict and that the pilot was thus entitled to be treated as a prisoner of war under the Third Convention.[20] It is not clear, however, that countries always take such a broad view of what constitutes an armed conflict; many isolated incidents, such as border clashes and naval incidents, are not treated as armed conflicts. It may well be, therefore, that only when fighting reaches a level of intensity which exceeds that of such isolated clashes will it be treated as an armed conflict to which the rules of international humanitarian law apply. In any event, only the use of force by the organs of a state, rather than by private persons, will constitute an armed conflict.

4. In the normal course of events the term 'international armed conflict' refers to a conflict between two or more states. Art. 1, para. 4 AP I, however, provides that the term includes: '. . . armed conflicts in which peoples fight against colonial domination and alien occupation and against racist regimes in the exercise of their right to self-determination, as enshrined in the Charter of the United Nations and the Declaration on Principles of International Law concerning Friendly Relations and Co-operation among States in accordance with the Charter of the United Nations.'[21] This provision has proved highly controversial and is one of the reasons for the United States' decision not to ratify AP I.[22] However, its field of application was intended to be quite restricted.[23] Wars against colonial domination are largely a thing of the past, and the reference to alien occupation adds little to Art. 2 of the Geneva Conventions, except perhaps where the territory occupied was not part of the territory of a state at the time of the occupation, and the ICRC Commentary regards the reference to racist regimes as applying only to 'regimes founded on racist criteria'.[24] Art. 1, para. 4 AP I was not intended to apply to any conflict in which an ethnic group or the inhabitants of a territory attempted to secede from a parent state, although recent developments which have suggested an extension of the concept of self-determination outside the colonial and neo-colonial

---

[17] See Partsch, *EPIL* 3, 28.

[18] See Pictet, *Humanitarian Law and the Protection of War Victims*, at 49.

[19] Pictet, *Commentary* Vol. IV, 20.

[20] Proceedings of the American Society of International Law 82 (1988), 602–3 and 609–11.

[21] See Abi-Saab, *Recueil des Cours* 165 (1979–IV), 353.

[22] Sofaer, *AJIL* 82 (1988), 784; see also Greenwood, *IYHR* 19 (1989), 187.

[23] Wilson, 168. See also the declarations made by the UK on signing the Protocol, Roberts/Guelff, 467–8.

[24] Pilloud, ICRC *Commentary*, para. 112.

Greenwood

context[25] may involve also a wider application for Art. 1, para. 4. Where Art. 1, para. 4 does apply, Art. 96, para. 3 AP I provides that an authority representing the people engaged in such a conflict may make a declaration addressed to the depositary of the Protocol (the Government of Switzerland), undertaking to apply the Conventions and the Protocol, in which case the Conventions and the Protocol shall become binding on both parties to the conflict. Art. 7, para. 4 of the Weapons Convention 1981 contains a similar provision. Opinions differ as to whether Art. 1, para. 4 AP I can be regarded as stating a rule of customary international law.[26] The controversy which Art. 1, para. 4 has aroused ever since it was first proposed suggests that states do not regard it as declaratory of customary international law, although there is some evidence that it has had an influence on practice.[27]

The application of international humanitarian law is not dependent on a formal   203
declaration of war. Formal declarations of war (Art. 1 HC III) nowadays occur
only occasionally.

1. It has already been noted that international humanitarian law now becomes applicable in any international armed conflict, whether or not a state of war exists between the parties. It follows that a declaration of war is not necessary for the application of humanitarian law. In fact, declarations of war have become almost unknown since 1945. There are no cases of a formal declaration of war having been delivered by one state to another through diplomatic channels (as was done in World War I and II). In most cases the parties to a conflict have denied that they were in a state of war. There have, however, been cases in which states have expressed the view, by means other than a formal declaration, that they regarded themselves as being at war. Thus, in both 1948 and 1967 a number of Arab states made explicit statements to the effect that they were at war with Israel, and similar statements were made by Iran and Iraq during the 1980–88 Iran–Iraq War, as well as by Pakistan during its 1965 conflict with India.[28]

2. It has sometimes been suggested that an attempt, by whatever means, to create a state of war today would be ineffective because the legal concept of war is incompatible with the UN Charter.[29] Many nations still seem, however, to regard it as open to them to declare war and there is considerable support for this view in the literature[30] and elsewhere.[31] However, there is probably a presumption that nations do not intend to create a state of war and a leading work cautions that: 'So serious a matter as the existence of a state of war is not lightly to be implied.

[25] e.g. the EC's application of the principle of self-determination to the republics of the former Yugoslavia.

[26] Compare Abi-Saab, *Recueil des Cours* 165 (1979–IV), 353, 371–2 and Cassese, *UCLA Pacific Basin Law Journal* 3 (1984) 55, 68–71, with Aldrich, *VaJInt* 26 (1986), 703; Draper, Howard (Ed.), *Restraints in War* (1979); Greenwood, in Delissen/Tanja (Eds.), 111–12.

[27] See Murray, *ICLQ* 33 (1984), 462.   [28] Greenwood, *ICLQ* 36 (1987), 290–4.

[29] Lauterpacht, *Proceedings of the American Society of International Law* 62 (1968), 58.

[30] See e.g. McNair/Watts, 2; Dinstein, *War, Aggression and Self-Defence*, 8.

[31] See e.g. the arbitral award of Professor Lalive in: *Dalmia Cement Ltd* v. *National Bank of Pakistan* 67 ILR 611, and the practice of the Security Council discussed in Greenwood, *ICLQ* 36 (1987), 283, 292.

Greenwood

Furthermore, where leading political figures of a country engaged in hostilities refer to their country being "at war", caution must be exercised before concluding therefrom that a state of war exists in any legal sense, since such references may prove to be more of emotional and political significance than legal.'[32]

3. Only if a statement that a country is at war was clearly intended to create a state of war, in the full legal sense, will it be taken to have that effect. On that basis, it has been said that a radio broadcast by the President of Pakistan in 1965 in which he stated that Pakistan was at war with India was not sufficiently unequivocal to create a state of war in the legal sense.[33] The announcement in December 1989 by General Noriega, the *de facto* Head of State of Panama, that Panama was in a state of war with the United States should probably be considered in the same light.

204   **Nor are formal declarations of war required for exercising the right of individual or collective self-defence. Art. 51 UN Charter prescribes that measures taken in the exercise of this right of self-defence shall be immediately reported to the UN Security Council.**

The exercise of the right of self-defence preserved by Art. 51 of the UN Charter is not connected to a declaration of war or to the existence of a state of war. Thus, in the Falklands conflict, the British Foreign Secretary told the House of Commons that the United Kingdom was not at war with Argentina but was exercising the right of self-defence recognized by Art. 51 of the Charter. It has already been suggested (in the commentary to Section 130) that a country which does declare war does not thereby increase its right to use force. If it was entitled to use force by way of self-defence, the right of self-defence remains the legal basis for its actions and the country continues to be subject to the limitations which stem from the right of self-defence, in particular the requirements that measures taken be necessary and proportionate,[34] irrespective of whether it declares war.[35] Nor will a declaration of war by the aggressor in an armed conflict alter the fact that the legal basis for the use of force by the victim of that aggression is the right of self-defence. A declaration of war by the aggressor does, however, imply that the aggressor is committed to the destruction of his adversary and this will obviously be a relevant factor in determining what is a proportionate response.[36]

205   **Formal declarations of a state of armed conflict can be envisaged in alliance documents or national constitutional acts.**

In the Federal Republic of Germany the President may issue a declaration of a state of defence under Art. 115a, paras. 1 and 5 of the Basic Law. Similar provisions exist in the constitutions of other nations. In the United States, for example, the

---

[32] McNair/Watts, 8.   [33] *Dalmia Cement, supra* n. 31, at 618.
[34] See commentary to Section 101.
[35] For a contrary view see Dinstein, *War, Aggression and Self-Defence*, 232–3.
[36] Brownlie, 368; Greenwood, *ICLQ* 36 (1987), 283, 301–3.

right to declare war is vested in Congress by Article I, Section 8 of the Constitution, although the President has a limited authority to commit US forces to battle in situations falling short of war.[37] There are various ways in which the question whether a particular situation amounts to war can arise before national courts. The answer to that question, however, will generally turn on rules of national law regarding the interpretation of documents[38] or the power of the executive.[39] Only occasionally is the question of whether there is war answered by a national court by reference to the criteria of international law.

It is irrelevant to the validity of international humanitarian law whether the States   206 and Governments involved in the conflict recognize each other as States (Art. 13, para. 3 GC I; Art. 13, para. 3 GC II; Art. 4 A, para. 3 GC III; Art. 43, para. 1 AP I).

The applicability of the rules of international humanitarian law is not dependent upon whether the parties to a conflict recognize one another. Throughout the Arab–Israel conflict, the Arab states have not recognized Israel as a state,[40] yet both sides in that conflict have accepted the applicability of international humanitarian law. The question of whether the parties to an armed conflict are states is objective and not a matter to be determined by the subjective recognition policies of each party. Where, however, there is real doubt about whether one side in a conflict is a state, rather than a secessionist movement within the rival party, recognition by other states may have an important evidential effect.

The application of humanitarian law in international armed conflicts does not   207 depend on whether an armed conflict has been started in violation of a provision of international law, e.g. the prohibition against aggressive war. The victims of military aggression contrary to international law are also bound by the rules of international humanitarian law.

The principle that the rules of international humanitarian law apply equally to all the parties to an armed conflict, irrespective of which state was responsible for starting the conflict and of whether that State was guilty of an act of aggression, was discussed in the commentary to Section 101 above.

The rules of international humanitarian law shall also be observed in peace-   208 keeping operations and other military operations of the United Nations.

1. Although there was originally some doubt about the applicability of international humanitarian law to UN forces,[41] it is now generally accepted that such

---

[37] See the *War Powers Resolution*, 1973; PL 93 148; Rovine (Ed.), 560.

[38] *Kawasaki Kabushiki Kisen Kaisha of Kobe* v. *Bantham SS Co* [1939] 2 KB 544 (Court of Appeal, England) and *Navios Corp.* v. *SS Ulysses* 161 F Supp 932 (United States District Court).

[39] *R.* v. *Bottrill, ex parte Küchenmeister* [1947] 1 KB 41 (Divisional Court, England).

[40] Egypt, however, recognized Israel in 1979 when the two states concluded a peace treaty, as did Jordan in 1994. See Sections 246–8.

[41] Bowett, *UN Forces* 484.

Greenwood

forces are subject to humanitarian law,[42] whether they were established as peace-keeping forces or for the purpose of engaging in enforcement action.[43] Thus, the *Institut de droit international* has confirmed that 'the humanitarian rules of the law of armed conflict apply to the United Nations as of right and they must be complied with in every circumstance by United Nations forces which are engaged in hostilities.'[44] A second *Institut* resolution maintains that this obligation also extends to those rules of the law of armed conflict which are not of a specifically humanitarian character.[45] Given that this is the case when the UN establishes a force of its own, it is clear that the rules of humanitarian law are applicable to a force under national control which operates with the authority of the Security Council, as in the Gulf conflict.

2. The application of humanitarian law to UN forces is not only a practical necessity, it may also be said to follow from the obligation of states 'to respect and ensure respect' for the Geneva Conventions and AP I 'in all circumstances',[46] which can be said to oblige a state to ensure that its forces comply with the rules of humanitarian law even when they are serving under UN command.[47] In the 1990–91 Kuwait conflict it was accepted by all parties that the coalition forces were required to comply with international humanitarian law, irrespective of their UN mandate.[48]

3. The one qualification which must be made is that the application of the law of neutrality may be affected in a conflict in which the United Nations is involved. Almost all states are members of the United Nations and, as such, are under a legal obligation to carry out Security Council decisions relating to the maintenance of international peace and security.[49] In addition, Art. 2, para. 5 of the UN Charter provides that: 'All Members shall give the United Nations every assistance in any action it takes in accordance with the present Charter, and shall refrain from giving assistance to any State against which the United Nations is taking preventive or enforcement action.' This obligation will prevail over the laws of neutrality. A member state may not, therefore, rely upon the law of neutrality in order to evade the obligation to carry out binding Security Council resolutions. In addition, any state, whether or not a member of the United Nations, may assist a UN force or a force acting under the authorization of the Security Council even if such assistance would normally be a violation of the law of neutrality.[50]

---

[42] Schindler, in Swinarski (Ed.), 521; Seyersted; Dinstein, *War, Aggression and Self-Defence*, 161–2.
[43] See commentary to Section 101.
[44] *Annuaire de l'Institut*, 54 vol. II (1971), 466; Schindler/Toman, 903.
[45] *Annuaire de l'Institut*, 56 vol. II (1975), 541; Schindler/Toman, 907.
[46] Common Art. 1; Condorelli/Boisson de Chazournes, in Swinarski (Ed.), 17.
[47] Sandoz, *IRRC* 20 (1978), 274.
[48] See e.g. US Department of Defense, *Final Report to Congress: Conduct of the Persian Gulf War* Appendix O, and the appeal by the ICRC, *IRRC* 1991, 21.
[49] Art. 25, UN Charter.
[50] See the 1975 Wiesbaden resolution of the *Institut de droit international*, *Annuaire de l'Institut*, 56 Vol. II (1975), 541, Schindler/Toman, 907 and Dinstein, 154–5.

While a state of war exists, the law of neutrality shall be applied to the relations   **209**
between the belligerent parties and countries not participating in the conflict (Art.
2 HC III).

1. The law of neutrality is the one part of the law of armed conflict in which it may
make a real difference whether or not an armed conflict is characterized as war.
There remains considerable support for the view that the law of neutrality applies
only if there is a formal state of war. Thus, one leading commentator has suggested
that: 'Unlike the law governing the mutual behaviour of combatants, a large part of
which may be considered operative in any international armed conflict, the rules
regulating the behaviour of neutrals and belligerents remain strictly dependent for
their operation upon the existence of a state of war.'[51]

2. There is also evidence that a number of states take the same view.[52] On the other
hand, the United States *Naval Commander's Handbook* states that the law of neutrality is applicable in any international armed conflict, irrespective of whether or
not that conflict is regarded as war.[53] The first approach raises difficult questions
about the criteria to be applied in deciding whether a conflict is or is not war, and
about who is to make that decision. The second approach, therefore, probably represents the present trend in international law. Nevertheless, the matter has yet to be
authoritatively settled. This question is examined in more detail in Chapter 11.

3. During the Iran–Iraq War, the United Kingdom maintained that: '. . . under Art.
51 of the United Nations Charter a State such as Iran, engaged in an armed conflict,
is entitled in exercise of its inherent right of self-defence, to stop and search a foreign merchant ship on the high seas if there is reasonable ground for suspecting
that the ship is taking arms to the other side for use in the conflict.'[54] This statement
suggests that, while the law of neutrality may be applicable in an armed conflict
falling short of war, a state may rely upon it to justify interference with neutral shipping only if that is necessary for its own self-defence.

A non-international armed conflict is a confrontation between the existing gov-   **210**
ernmental authority and groups of persons subordinate to this authority, which is
carried out by force of arms within national territory and reaches the magnitude
of an armed riot or a civil war.

In ⸱ non-international armed conflict each party shall be bound to apply, as a   **211**
minimum, the fundamental humanitarian provisions of international law

---

[51] Tucker, 199–200. See also Schindler in Cassese (Ed.), 3, 5; Castren, 34–5; Oppenheim, Vol. II, 655 and
Bindschedler *EPIL* 4, 9.

[52] Greenwood, *ICLQ* 36 (1987), 283, 297–301; statements by India quoted in: Sharma 87 and by Canada
CYIL 21 (1983), 326.

[53] *NWP 9*, para. 7.1. See also Bothe, in Delissen/Tanja (Eds.), 387.

[54] Statement by Minister of State, Foreign and Commonwealth Office, to the House of Commons, following the interception by an Iranian warship of the British merchant ship *Barber Perseus*; *BYIL* 47 (1986),
583.

Greenwood

embodied in the four 1949 Geneva Conventions (common Art. 3), the 1954 Cultural Property Convention (Art. 19) and the 1977 Additional Protocol II. German soldiers like their Allies are required to comply with the rules of international humanitarian law in the conduct of military operations in all armed conflicts however such conflicts are characterized.

1. The application of international humanitarian law to non-international armed conflicts was only embodied in treaty form for the first time in the 1949 Geneva Conventions.[55] Today, there are two instruments which expressly apply to internal armed conflicts. Common Art. 3 of the Geneva Conventions contains a series of rudimentary provisions dealing with minimum rights and duties, such as the requirements that those *hors de combat* be treated humanely and that the wounded and sick be collected and cared for, and the prohibition against murder, torture, hostage taking, humiliating and degrading treatment, and the passing of sentences and carrying out of executions without a fair trial. AP II is a far more detailed code for application in internal armed conflicts.[56]

2. In two respects, however, AP II does not go as far as common Art. 3. First, whereas Art. 3 applies to any 'armed conflict not of an international character occurring in the territory of one of the High Contracting Parties', AP II applies only to armed conflicts '. . . which take place in the territory of a High Contracting Party between its armed forces and dissident armed forces or other organized armed groups which, under responsible command, exercise such control over a part of its territory as to enable them to carry out sustained and concerted military operations and to implement this Protocol' (Art. 1, para. 1 AP II). In addition, Art. 1, para. 2 provides that: 'This Protocol shall not apply to situations of internal disturbances and tensions, such as riots, isolated and sporadic acts of violence and other acts of a similar nature, as not being armed conflicts.' AP II will, it seems, be applicable only in a full-scale civil war. Secondly, whereas AP II applies only to a conflict between the government of a State and a rebel movement, Art. 3 is broad enough to cover a conflict between different rebel movements competing for power within a state where the government is not involved as such or has ceased to exist. The conflicts in Lebanon during the 1980s and in Somalia after 1991 are examples of this kind of internal conflict.

3. AP II was applied for the first time in the civil war in El Salvador during the 1980s.[57] The Government of El Salvador did not concede the *de iure* applicability of the Protocol but accepted that it should be applied because its provisions developed and completed the minimum provisions of Art. 3 of the Geneva Conventions.[58] Both common Art. 3 and the Protocol apply with equal force to all parties to an armed conflict, government and rebels alike.

---

[55] R. Abi-Saab, *Droit International et Conflits Internes*.

[56] Forsythe, *AJIL* 72 (1978), 272; Abi-Saab, *loc. cit. supra*; Pilloud, ICRC *Commentary*, 1305–509.

[57] See e.g. ICRC *Annual Report* 39 (1989).   [58] Greenwood, in Delissen/Tanja (Eds.), 113.

4. Although internal conflict is, in principle, subject to a different and more limited legal regime than that which applies in an international armed conflict, it is possible that some or all of the law of international armed conflicts may become applicable in a conflict which was originally classified as internal. Common Art. 3 encourages the parties to an internal conflict to conclude special agreements to bring other provisions of the Geneva Conventions into force between them. In addition, foreign intervention may have the effect of giving that conflict an international character, at least in some of its aspects. Thus, the Commission of Experts established by the Security Council to investigate allegations of war crimes in the conflicts in the former Yugoslavia stated in its Report to the UN Secretary-General that, although the classification of the various conflicts was a difficult matter: 'The Commission is of the opinion . . . that the character and complexity of the armed conflicts concerned, combined with the web of agreements on humanitarian issues the parties have concluded among themselves, justify an approach whereby it applies the law applicable in international armed conflicts to the entirety of the armed conflicts in the territory of the former Yugoslavia.'[59]

5. The final sentence of Section 211 adds an important policy rule, namely that German armed forces will comply with all rules of international humanitarian law in the conduct of any armed conflict, irrespective of whether that conflict is characterized as internal or international. Compliance with the full body of rules of international humanitarian law in non-international conflicts undoubtedly presents practical problems, but it serves not only humanitarian interests but also operational requirements. This policy has received support from a number of other sources.[60]

II. ACTS OF WAR

Acts of war are all measures of force which one party, using military instruments of power, implements against another party in an international armed conflict. These comprise combat actions designed to eliminate opposing armed forces and other military objectives.   212

The term 'acts of war' does not have the same precision or legal significance which it possessed in the days when states more commonly declared themselves to be in a formal state of war. Today it is used to describe all military operations,

---

[59] *Interim Report* of the Commission of Experts established pursuant to Security Council Resolution 780 (1992), UN Doc. S/25274 (26 Jan. 1993), para. 45. Note, however, the more cautious approach taken in the Report of the Secretary-General pursuant to Paragraph 2 of Security Council Resolution 808 (1993), UN Doc. S/25704 (3 May 1993), containing a draft statute for an International War Crimes Tribunal.

[60] International Institute for Humanitarian Law, *Declaration on the Rules of International Humanitarian Law governing the Conduct of Hostilities in Non-International Armed Conflicts*, IRRC, Sep.–Oct. 1990, 404–8; see also the discussion in *NWP 9*/FMFM 1–10, 5–3 and DoD Directive 5100.77, DoD Law of War Program, 10 Jul. 1979, para. E-1.

Greenwood

including those (such as the announcement of a blockade) which involve the threat of force, once the parties are in armed conflict. However, actions involving the threat but not the use of force before an armed conflict has begun will not necessarily constitute acts of war, in that they will not in themselves give rise to a condition of armed conflict. Thus, the measures taken by coalition shipping, pursuant to Security Council Resolution 665 (1990), to intercept shipping suspected of breaking the economic sanctions imposed upon Iraq by Resolution 661 clearly involved a threat of force; on a number of occasions shots were fired across the bows of vessels.[61] These measures were not, however, regarded as sufficient to make the states enforcing them parties to an armed conflict with Iraq before the main coalition military operations began in January 1991. Similarly, the 'quarantine' imposed by the United States around the island of Cuba in 1962[62] did not make the United States party to an armed conflict with the USSR. Nor will the commission of such an act by one state necessarily entitle the other to resort to force. A state confronted by a threat of force, as in the Cuban Quarantine, will be entitled to resort to force only if the conditions for the exercise of the right of self-defence exist, i.e. if there is an armed attack upon that state or an armed attack is reasonably considered to be imminent.[63]

213   **The term 'act of war' is not evidence of the lawfulness of such an act. The admissibility of an act of war under international law shall be subject to examination in every single case.**

The description of an act as an 'act of war' does not indicate whether or not that act is lawful. The legality of each such act must be examined to see whether, in all the circumstances, the resort to force is lawful within the terms of the *ius ad bellum*,[64] while the manner in which force is used must be scrutinized for compatibility with international humanitarian law.

214   **Support for a third party's acts of war shall generally be rated as an act of war of the supporting state if it is directly related, i.e. closely related in space and time, to measures harmful to the adversary. Co-operation in arms production or other activities to support the armed forces will not suffice.**

A state not originally party to an armed conflict will only commit an act of war, and thus risk making itself a party to the conflict, by giving direct support to the military operations of one of the belligerents. Financial, political, and intelligence support will not have such an effect. Where one of the parties to the conflict is the United Nations, or is authorized by it, a state is entitled to give support to that party without forfeiting its status as a neutral.[65] The line between participation in an armed conflict and neutrality is no longer as clear as it once was. Between the two

---

[61] Greenwood, *Modern Law Review*, 55 (1992), 161–2; US Department of the Navy, *The United States Navy in Desert Shield and Desert Storm* (1991).

[62] See Chayes.

[64] See commentary to Section 101.

[63] See commentary to Section 101.

[65] See commentary to Section 208.

there is now a grey area in which a state engages in non-neutral service without overtly becoming a party to the conflict. This is discussed in greater detail in Chapter 11.

III. AREA OF WAR

**Military operations of the parties to a conflict shall only be carried out in the area   215
of war. The area of war comprises:**

- **the territories of the parties to the conflict as defined by the national boundaries;**
- **the high seas (including the airspace above and the sea floor); and**
- **exclusive economic zones.**

Military operations may not be carried out beyond the area of war.[66] That area is, however, extensive since it includes all the territory of the parties to the conflict,[67] and the high seas, and exclusive economic zones, including the exclusive economic zones (EEZs) of neutral states[68] (although military operations in the EEZ of a neutral state must show due regard for the rights and interests of that state[69]). The territory (including internal and territorial waters) of neutral states and the airspace above them may not be made part of the area of war, unless the neutral state has allowed one of the belligerents to conduct military operations on its territory, in which case the rival belligerent has a right to take measures in that territory to terminate those operations.[70]

The national territory includes: 216
- **land territory;**
- **rivers and landlocked lakes;**
- **national maritime waters and territorial waters; and**
- **the airspace above these territories.**

**The dividing line between the airspace of the national territory of a state and outer   217
space shall be drawn where, due to existing physical conditions, the density of the
air is small enough to permit the employment of satellites. According to the present state of the art, the minimum flight altitude of satellites ranges between 80
and 110 km above ground level.**

**Although they belong to the national territories of the parties to the conflict,   218
demilitarized zones (Art. 60 AP I), in particular hospital and safety zones (Art. 23**

---

[66] Oppenheim/Lauterpacht, Vol. II, 236–44.
[67] Unless somehow excluded, e.g. by neutralization; see Sections 218–19.
[68] See Chapter 10.   [69] Art. 58, Law of the Sea Convention 1982.   [70] See Chapter 11.

Greenwood

GC I; Art. 14 GC IV) and neutralized zones (Art. 15 GC IV), are excluded from the area of war. Non-defended localities (Art. 25 HagueReg; Art. 59 AP I), however, are part of the area of war but enjoy special protection (see Section 458 below).

1. Zones within the territory of the parties to a conflict may be removed from the area of war by agreement between the parties. Thus Art. 23 GC I and Art. 14 GC IV provide for the establishment of hospital zones for the treatment of the wounded and sick. Art. 15 GC IV provides for the establishment of safety zones intended to shelter the wounded, sick, and civilians 'who take no part in hostilities'. Such zones are to be established by agreement between the parties and a Draft Agreement is attached to the Geneva Conventions as a precedent. Instances of such agreement are very rare. In the closing stages of the Falklands conflict, the United Kingdom and Argentina agreed upon the establishment of a safety zone around the Cathedral in Port Stanley but hostilities came to an end before the zone was due to come into operation. The parties can also, if they wish, establish zones on the high seas in which no hostile operations are to take place. This was done during the Falklands conflict, when a 'Red Cross box' was established in part of the South Atlantic for the protection of both states' hospital ships.[71] The provision in Art. 60 AP I for the creation, again by agreement between the parties, of demilitarized zones builds upon the concept of the safety zones in the Fourth Convention. It should be noted that the establishment of all these zones requires agreement between the parties; a unilateral announcement by one party to the conflict is not sufficient.

2. Undefended localities are those which can be occupied at will by a belligerent. They are therefore confined to 'places in or near a zone where armed forces are in contact' (Art. 59 AP I) and do not extend to places far behind a state's 'lines' since such a place, although it may have no forces anywhere near it, is not open for occupation. Undefended localities may be established without agreement between the parties. Undefended localities declared by a state remain part of the area of war but the adverse party may not bombard or otherwise attack them, although it may send forces to occupy them.

219   **Military operations shall not be carried out in the national territories of neutral or other states not parties to the conflict and in neutralized zones. These are areas in which, according to contractual agreements, no military operations shall take place, even if the state to whose area of jurisdiction they belong is a party to the conflict. There are, for instance, binding agreements not to execute any military operations in Spitsbergen, in the area of the Åland Islands, in the Suez Canal, the Panama Canal, and in the Antarctic regions.**

The duty of the belligerents not to conduct military operations in the territory of neutral states and states not parties to the conflict applies to all such states and not just to those states, such as Switzerland, with a permanent regime of neutrality. In addition, a number of treaties provide for the neutralization of areas of territory,

[71] See Junod.

even if those areas form part of the territory of a belligerent.[72] The Spitsbergen Treaty, 1920,[73] by which eleven states recognized the 'full and absolute sovereignty of Norway over the Archipelago of Spitsbergen', required Norway not to construct any naval base or fortification on the archipelago, 'which may never be used for warlike purposes'. Spitsbergen was, however, used for military operations during World War II. When Norway placed Spitsbergen under NATO command after World War II, the USSR protested. Norway replied that no bases or fortifications were to be built upon the archipelago.[74] The Åland Islands were made a 'neutral zone' by a multilateral agreement of 1921[75], following the recommendation of the Council of the League of Nations. This status was reaffirmed in Art. 5 of the Peace Treaty with Finland, 1947. Art. 1 of the Antarctic Treaty 1959[76] reserves the Antarctic for peaceful purposes and forbids the establishment of military bases and fortifications within Antarctica.[77] The Suez Canal is subject to a detailed regime regarding its use and protection in time of war, contained in the Constantinople Convention 1888.[78] However, the measures taken to close the Canal to German shipping during World Wars I and II and to Israeli shipping during the Egypt–Israel War called into question aspects of this regime. The Hay-Pauncefote Treaty 1901[79] between the United Kingdom and the United States prohibits acts of hostility within the Panama Canal Zone.[80] The Treaty Concerning the Permanent Neutrality and Operation of the Panama Canal Zone 1977[81] between the United States and Panama, and the annexed Protocol on neutrality, open to accession by all states, provides for the permanent neutrality of the Panama Canal.[82]

The zones in which military operations actually take place shall be designated as the area of operations.   220

Military operations will not normally be conducted throughout the area of war. The area in which operations are actually taking place at any given time is known as the 'area of operations' or 'theatre of war'.[83] The extent to which a belligerent today is justified in expanding the area of operations will depend upon whether it is necessary for him to do so in order to exercise his right of self-defence. While a state cannot be expected always to defend itself solely on ground of the aggressor's choosing, any expansion of the area of operations may not go beyond what constitutes a necessary and proportionate measure of self-defence. In particular, it cannot be assumed—as in the past—that a state engaged in armed conflict is free to attack its adversary anywhere in the area of war.[84]

---

[72] Oppenheim/Lauterpacht, Vol. II, 244–7 and Verosta, *EPIL* 4, 31.
[73] *LNTS* 2, 7; Hofmann, 'Spitsbergen/Svalbard', *EPIL* 12, 352.   [74] Verosta, *loc. cit.* n. 70 at 32.
[75] *LNTS* 9, 212; Modeen, 'Aaland Islands', *EPIL* 12, 1.
[76] *UNTS* 402, 71;*BGBl* 78 II 1517; Wolfrum/Klemm, 'Antarctica', *EPIL* 12, 10.
[77] Oppenheim/Lauterpacht, Vol. I, 694.
[78] Oppenheim/Lauterpacht, Vol. I, 592; Broms, 'Suez Canal', *EPIL* 12, 360.   [79] 190 *CTS* 215.
[80] Oppenheim/Lauterpacht, Vol. I, 595; Hartwig, 'Panama Canal', *EPIL* 12, 282.
[81] *ILM* 16, (1977) 1021–98; Oppenheim, Vol. I, 597–8.
[82] A number of other cases in which territory is said to have been neutralized are discussed in Oppenheim/Lauterpacht, Vol. II, 244–7 and Verosta, *loc. cit.* n. 70.   [83] Oppenheim, Vol. II, 237.
[84] This question is discussed further by Greenwood, in Dinstein (Ed.), 273, 276–8.

Greenwood

IV. TERMINATION OF HOSTILITIES

221   **Hostilities may be terminated temporarily or permanently. Even a definite cessation of hostilities does not alter the fact that there is a state of war. This state of war will be ended only by a conclusion of peace unless it has already been expressly terminated.**

Where a state of war has come into being, the fact that active hostilities have ceased is not in itself sufficient to terminate the state of war. It has generally been accepted that a peace treaty or some other clear indication on the part of the belligerents that they regard the state of war as ended is required.[85] Although active hostilities during World War II ceased in Europe in May 1945, it was not until 31 December 1946 that the United States formally announced that hostilities had terminated.[86] Even then, the state of war was regarded as continuing, pending the adoption of a peace treaty between Germany and her former adversaries. In the end, no peace treaty was concluded.[87] The state of war was, however, formally declared terminated by France (9 July 1951), the United Kingdom (9 July 1951), the United States (24 October 1951), and the USSR (25 January 1955). Similar declarations were made by Germany's other former adversaries.[88] Until those declarations were made, national courts continued to hold that the state of war obtained for most purposes.[89] The question of whether a formal instrument is needed for the termination of an armed conflict not amounting to war is considered in Sections 245–9.

1. *Parlementaires and Protecting Powers*

222   **A cessation of hostilities is regularly preceded by negotiations with the adversary. In the area of operations the parties to the conflict frequently use parlementaires for this purpose.**

Parlementaires[90] are used not only for negotiations about a cessation or temporary suspension of hostilities but also for negotiations on such matters as the recovery of wounded persons or exchange of prisoners and for communicating messages to an adversary's forces. Today, negotiations for a general cessation of hostilities are more likely to be conducted at the political level, frequently through an intermediary such as the United Nations. The use of parlementaires as the means of communication between opposing forces nevertheless remains important, especially when forces are deployed in remote areas, as in the Falklands conflict. The parlementaire must be authorized by the commander of the forces which sent him.

---

[85] Oppenheim/Lauterpacht, Vol. II, 597–9.   [86] Whiteman, Vol. X, 89.

[87] See, however, the Treaty on the Final Settlement with respect to Germany, 1990, *ILM* 29 (1990), 1186.

[88] Whiteman, Vol. X, 89–95; Kunz, *AJIL* 46 (1952), 114.

[89] See the cases discussed at Whiteman, Vol. X, 93–4.

[90] *British Manual of Military Law* (hereinafter: *British Manual*), Part III, 121–5; Dinstein, *EPIL* 3, 173; Greenspan, 380–5.

Traditionally, this authorization should be in writing and signed by the commander concerned, although there is no express provision in the Hague Regulations to that effect.[91]

Parlementaires are persons authorized by one party to the conflict to enter into   223
negotiations with the adversary. Parlementaires and persons accompanying
them, e.g. drivers and interpreters, have a right to inviolability (Art. 32
HagueReg). They make themselves known by a white flag.

1. A parlementaire has a duty to make himself and the purpose of his mission known to the adversary; his own protection may depend upon this. For that reason, the law has traditionally required that a parlementaire display a white flag (Art. 32 HagueReg). A white flag is, however, no more than a signal that an armed force wishes to open negotiations. By hoisting a white flag a force is asking its adversary whether it is willing to receive a communication. It does not necessarily indicate an intention to surrender, although it has come to indicate such an intention when raised by an individual soldier or a small group of soldiers during an exchange of fire. Although it is unlawful for a force displaying a white flag to carry on firing, great caution is necessary, for the flag may have been hoisted by some members of a unit without the knowledge or consent of the commander.[92] During the Battle for Goose Green in the Falklands conflict, some Argentine soldiers displayed a white flag without authorization from their commander and unknown to the rest of the Argentine forces engaged in the battle. A British party who went into the open to investigate were fired on and killed by other Argentine soldiers who were apparently unaware of the white flag raised by their colleagues.

2. Traditionally, a parlementaire may approach the enemy alone, carrying the white flag himself. It is, however, more usual for him to be accompanied. According to Art. 32 HagueReg, he may be accompanied by a trumpeter, bugler or drummer, a flag-bearer, and an interpreter. In modern warfare, however, the parlementaire is more likely to be accompanied by a driver, wireless or loudhailer operator, and an interpreter.[93] The interpreter need not be a member of the armed forces to which the parlementaire belongs.

When entering the territory of the adversary, parlementaires and the persons   224
accompanying them shall not be taken prisoner or detained. The principle of invi-
olability shall apply until they have returned safely to friendly territory. The
adverse party is not required to cease firing in the entire sector in which a par-
lementaire arrives.

The parlementaire and those accompanying him are accorded inviolability. This means that they may not be fired upon or otherwise attacked. Except by prior agreement, however, the approach of a parlementaire does not require opposing forces to cease firing throughout a whole sector of the battlefield.

[91] *British Manual*, para. 393.   [92] *British Manual*, para. 394.   [93] *British Manual*, para. 400.

225   The parlementaire is usually, but not necessarily, an officer. He may be of any nationality. Defectors or members of friendly forces taken prisoner by the adversary cannot have the status of parlementaires nor of persons accompanying parlementaires, and hence have no right of inviolability. They can be detained if the tactical situation so requires.

226   The commander to whom a parlementaire is sent is not in all cases obliged to receive him (Art. 33, para. 1 HagueReg).

It is legitimate for a commander to refuse to receive a parlementaire, e.g. because his forces are engaged in a manœuvre which they do not wish a member of the opposing forces to see. However, contrary to the practice before 1899, it is no longer considered lawful for a commander to announce in advance that he will not receive any parlementaires.[94]

227   It is permissible to take all necessary precautions (e.g. blindfolding) to prevent the parlementaire from taking advantage of his mission to obtain information (Art. 33, para. 2 HagueReg).

The commander who receives a parlementaire is entitled to direct the time and route by which he and his party should approach and the point at which they should enter the area controlled by his forces. Once the parlementaire is in territory controlled by the opposing forces, those forces are entitled to direct his movements in whatever way is necessary, commensurate with the safety of the parlementaire, to protect their security.

228   A parlementaire may temporarily be detained if he has accidentally acquired information the disclosure of which to the adversary would jeopardize the success of a current or impending operation of the friendly armed forces. In this case, the parlementaire may be detained until the operation has been completed. In the meantime, he shall be treated with the respect appropriate to his position and at least like a prisoner of war.

229   The parlementaire loses his right of inviolability if it is proved in an incontestable manner that he has taken advantage of his privileged position to provoke or commit an act of treason (Art. 34 HagueReg). Such a case of misuse, which implies the right to detain the parlementaire (Art. 33, para. 3 HagueReg), exists if the latter has committed acts contrary to international law and to the detriment of the adversary during his mission. This includes particularly the following activities:

   – gathering intelligence beyond the observations he inevitably makes when accomplishing his mission;

---

[94] Oppenheim/Lauterpacht, Vol. II, 539; Greenspan, 382, though compare Dinstein, *loc. cit.* n. 90, who maintains that such an announcement would be legitimate so long as it applied only for a definite period of time.

- acts of sabotage;
- inducing soldiers of the adverse party to collaborate in collecting intelligence;
- instigating soldiers of the adverse party to refuse to do their duty;
- encouraging soldiers of the adverse party to desert; and
- organizing espionage in the territory of the adverse party.

A parlementaire is entitled to observe and report on anything he sees which the adversary has not hidden. If he sees something which might endanger the enemy's forces, those forces are entitled to detain him as a preventive measure, even though he has done nothing wrong.[95] It is an abuse of the parlementaire's position, however, for the parlementaire or those accompanying him to take photographs, make sketch maps of defensive positions, engage in secret intelligence gathering, or to behave in any of the ways listed in Section 229. Should they do so, they may be detained temporarily (Art. 33,para. 3 HagueReg) and, if it is proved 'in a clear and incontestable manner' that any of them have abused their position to provoke or commit an act of treason, he forfeits his inviolability and may be tried. Any measures taken against a parlementaire or members of his party should be communicated to the enemy at once.[96]

Misusing the flag of truce constitutes perfidy and is thus a violation of international law (Art. 23 lit. f HagueReg; Art. 37, para. 1 lit. a, Art. 38, para. 1 AP I). The flag of truce is misused, for instance, if soldiers approach an enemy position under the protection of the flag of truce in order to attack.   230

Misuse of the flag of truce has long been a war crime under customary international law. Under Arts. 37 and 38 of AP I, such acts are treated as perfidy.

Apart from dispatching parlementaires, the parties to a conflict may also communicate with each other through the intermediary of Protecting Powers. Protecting Powers are neutral or other states not parties to the conflict which safeguard the rights and interests of a party to the conflict and those of its nationals *vis-à-vis* an adverse party to the conflict (Art. 2 lit. c AP I). Particularly, the International Committee of the Red Cross may act as a so-called 'substitute' (Art. 5, para. 4 AP I) if the parties to the conflict cannot agree upon the designation of a Protecting Power.   231

For discussion of the now little-used institution of the Protecting Power, see Sections 1215–17 below. The ICRC is now used more frequently as an intermediary. For example, the establishment of the Red Cross box in the South Atlantic and the safety zone in Port Stanley during the Falklands conflict was arranged between the United Kingdom and Argentina through the good offices of the ICRC.[97]

---

[95] *British Manual,* para. 412.   [96] *British Manual,* para. 414.   [97] See commentary to Section 218.

2. *Ceasefire and Armistice*

232   An armistice agreement is characterized by the intention to provide an opportunity for making preparations for the termination of an armed conflict. Its aim is to terminate hostilities permanently. That is what distinguishes an armistice from a ceasefire. An armistice may be local (Art. 37 HagueReg). As a matter of principle, however, an armistice agreement shall be designed to suspend military operations between the parties to the conflict and to pave the way for peace negotiations.

1. The distinction between a general armistice and a ceasefire has traditionally been that the armistice was considered a step on the road to a permanent end to hostilities and the conclusion of a treaty of peace. Thus the armistice of Rethondes in 1918 was a prerequisite for the commencement of negotiations which led in 1919 to the Treaty of Versailles and the termination of World War I. Since World War II, however, there have been a number of cases in which hostilities were brought to a close by the conclusion of an armistice agreement and no peace treaty was subsequently agreed. The hostilities in Korea were brought to an end by the conclusion of the Panmunjom Armistice Agreement in 1953, and the first Arab–Israeli hostilities ceased with the conclusion of the 1949 armistice agreements between Israel, Egypt, Jordan, Lebanon, and Syria.

2. Historically, it has always been considered that the conclusion of a ceasefire or an armistice did not terminate the state of war.[98] It has been questioned whether this principle is still part of the law, especially where, as in the case of the 1949 armistice agreements between Israel and four Arab states, an armistice is concluded under United Nations auspices.[99] The correct view is probably that stated by Judge Baxter, namely that such an instrument *can* terminate the state of war, if the parties intend that it should have that effect,[100] for just as the creation of a state of war is brought about by a clear expression of the intentions of a country, that state of war can also be terminated by an indication of the intention to do so.

3. On the question of whether an armistice agreement or ceasefire can terminate an armed conflict, which has not amounted to war in the legal sense, see Section 249.

233   A ceasefire is defined as a temporary interruption of military operations which is limited to a specific area and will normally be agreed upon between the local commanders. It shall generally serve humanitarian purposes, in particular searching for and collecting the wounded and the shipwrecked, rendering first aid to these persons, and removing civilians (Art. 15 GC I; Art. 18 GC II; Art. 17 GC IV). The

---

[98] Levie, *AJIL* 50 (1956), 880.

[99] See e.g. the statement by the representative of Israel, SCOR 549th Meeting, 26 Jul. 1951, paras. 40–1; Rosenne, *Israel's Armistice Agreements with the Arab States* (1951) 45.

[100] Baxter, *Recueil des Cours* RC 149 (1976), 353.

regulations governing armistices (Art. 36–41 HagueReg) shall be applied analogously.

Now that so few conflicts are treated, either by the parties or by other nations, as giving rise to a formal state of war, the dividing line between ceasefires, armistices, and other forms of suspension of hostilities has become increasingly blurred.[101] In many cases a ceasefire is of indefinite duration. That was the case with the ceasefire concluded in the Iran–Iraq War in 1988, although that was concluded under UN auspices and followed the adoption of a binding resolution of the Security Council.[102]

If the parties to the conflict have not defined the duration of an armistice, it shall, as a matter of principle, be considered a valid assumption that the armistice is designed to be the transition to a definite cessation of hostilities. The ban on the use of force embodied in the Charter of the United Nations shall also be observed during this period of transition. In contrast to the provisions of the Hague Regulations Concerning the Laws and Customs of War on Land (Art. 36 HagueReg), the parties to a conflict may not, at any time, resume operations after the conclusion of an armistice unless the exercise of the right to self-defence makes it absolutely necessary. 234

1. The changes in the law regarding resort to force brought about by the adoption of the UN Charter have had a particular effect on the right of the parties to resume hostilities after the conclusion of an armistice or ceasefire of indefinite duration. Whereas the law once admitted there was a general right to resume hostilities (Art. 36 HagueReg), today it would be a violation of Art. 2(4) for a state to resume hostilities unless the behaviour of the other party to the armistice or ceasefire amounted to an armed attack or the threat of an armed attack. Similarly, although under the traditional law the conclusion of an armistice did not prejudice the right of a party to exercise belligerent rights against shipping, such action would now be lawful only if it constituted a necessary and proportionate measure of self-defence.

2. That the law relating to the resumption of hostilities and the exercise of belligerent rights has changed in this way since the Hague Regulations were adopted was made clear by the Security Council in 1951, when it ruled that Egypt's continued exercise of belligerent rights against shipping was incompatible with the Egypt–Israel Armistice Agreement 1949. The Council ruled that: '. . . since the armistice regime, which has been in existence for nearly two and a half years, is of a permanent character, neither party can reasonably assert that it is actively a belligerent or requires to exercise the right of visit, search and seizure for any legitimate purpose of self-defence . . .'[103] It seems that there is no difference between a general, indefinite cease-fire and an armistice in this respect. Whether a

---

[101] Fleck, *EPIL* 4, 239.   [102] Res. 598 (1987); see Weller in Dekker/Post, 77–90.
[103] Resolution 95 of 1 Sep. 1951, UN Doc. S/2322.

resumption of hostilities is justified must be assessed by reference to the criteria in the Charter in each case.[104]

235   Any serious violation of a cease-fire or an armistice may give the other party a cause to recommence hostilities immediately. A denunciation of the armistice treaty (Art. 40 HagueReg) will be necessary only if the military situation so permits.

236   A violation of the terms of the armistice by individuals acting on their own initiative does not entitle the injured party to denounce the agreement but only to demand the punishment of the offenders and compensation for the losses sustained (Art. 41 HagueReg).

A serious violation of an armistice or cease-fire will give rise to a right to resume hostilities. Again, however this right exists as an aspect of the right of self-defence, rather than as a right to punish the state responsible for the violation. Hostilities may be resumed if, and to the extent that, to do so is a necessary and proportionate measure of self-defence. Violations of armistice and cease-fire conditions committed by individuals acting without the authorization of their state will not normally give rise to such a right, although the true facts may be very difficult to ascertain in a particular case. Partly for that reason, many cease-fires are now monitored by UN peace-keeping forces to deter violations and to provide an authoritative machinery for determining the truth where violations have been alleged.

237   The terms of the armistice treaty shall be strictly observed by the parties to a conflict. It is not permissible to carry out any military operations giving an advantage over the adversary. To what extent this shall also apply to other actions taken during the armistice depends on the terms of the agreements made. In the absence of any provision to the contrary (Art. 39 HagueReg), activities such as entrenching, ammunition resupply, and prepositioning of reinforcements shall be permissible. During an armistice it is, however, definitely forbidden to move forward forces who are close to the enemy, or to employ reconnaissance patrols.

Where an armistice regime becomes permanent, in the sense that all hostilities cease but normal relations are not resumed between the parties, the extent to which a party to the armistice agreement is prevented from moving its forces within the territory which it holds will depend upon the specific terms of the armistice, rather than upon any general rule.

238   The area of application of a limited armistice shall be defined as precisely as possible. If, for instance, wounded persons are to be recovered it must be clear if and up to what line bombardments further to the rear remain permissible. Sometimes it will also be necessary to co-ordinate the utilization of the airspace and the passage of ships.

[104] Bailey, *AJIL* 71 (1977), 461.

Greenwood

An armistice must be notified in an unmistakeable form and in good time.   239
Hostilities are to be suspended immediately after the notification, or on the date
fixed (Art. 38 HagueReg).

The terms of an armistice shall not deviate from the provisions of the Geneva   240
Conventions to the detriment of protected persons (Art. 6 common to GC I–III;
Art. 7 GC IV).

   International humanitarian law exists primarily to protect individuals rather
than to establish rights for states.[105] The states party to a conflict may not, therefore,
waive by agreement between them any of the rights conferred upon individuals by
international humanitarian law. However, they may of course agree to accord
greater protection than is required by international humanitarian law.

3. *Capitulation*

A capitulation is the unilateral or mutually agreed termination of hostilities. It   241
must take into account the rules of military honour (Art. 35, para. 1 HagueReg).

It may be a total capitulation applying to all armed forces of a state, or a partial   242
capitulation limited to specific units.

Every commander may declare or accept a capitulation only for his particular   243
area of command. The capitulation and its acceptance are binding upon the states
involved in the conflict. Every state may, however, call a capitulating commander
to account if he has violated his duties, e.g. offended against orders.

A capitulation must be faithfully observed by the parties to the conflict (Art. 35,   244
para. 2 HagueReg). Persons who infringe the terms of the capitulation may be
called to account by the adversary.

   While the capitulation of the forces in a particular part of the area of operations
will not affect the existence of the state of armed conflict elsewhere, when the surrender effectively applies to all the forces of one party in the area of operations and
when there is every indication that the state on which those forces depend will not
resume operations elsewhere, then the surrender may mean that active hostilities
between the parties have ceased, with consequences for such matters as the duty to
repatriate prisoners of war.[106] The surrender of Argentine forces in the Falkland
Islands in June 1982 led to the end of active hostilities and the repatriation of prisoners of war within a very short period once the British forces had taken the surrender of outlying Argentine garrisons not covered by the principal instrument of
surrender and once it became clear that Argentina had no intention of carrying on
hostilities from the mainland.[107]

[105] See commentary to Section 102.   [106] Art. 118 GC III.
[107] For the text of the instrument of surrender, see *BYIL* 53 (1982), 526–7; see also the statements at 537–8
op. cit.

4. Conclusion of Peace

245 While a cease-fire, an armistice, or a capitulation only lead to a suspension or temporary cessation of hostilities, a conclusion of peace results in the termination of the state of armed conflict.

The conclusion of a cease-fire, armistice, or capitulation will not necessarily terminate a state of war or armed conflict. See, however, the commentary to Sections 232 and 249 for the suggestion that any of these acts may have the effect of terminating a state of armed conflict and possibly a state of war if the parties so intend.

246 A conclusion of peace is generally brought about by a peace treaty. The application of humanitarian law between the parties to a conflict (save for a few provisions which, for instance, relate to prisoners of war not yet repatriated) will thereupon terminate.

247 A peace treaty may only be concluded by Heads of States or explicitly authorized representatives of the government of a state.

248 A peace treaty regularly includes provisions on the following specific areas:
- termination of all hostilities;
- re-establishment of peaceful relations between the adversaries;
- settlement of disputes which led to the outbreak of the armed conflict;
- resolution of territorial issues;
- arms restrictions or disarmament duties;
- repatriation of prisoners of war; and
- compensation for war damages.

1. Apart from the treaties arising out of World War II, peace treaties have since 1945 been rare. Nevertheless, in 1979 Egypt and Israel concluded a Treaty of Peace, Art. 1, para. 1 of which stated that: 'The state of war between the parties will be terminated and peace will be established between them upon the exchange of instruments of ratification of this treaty.'[108]

2. The unratified peace treaty between Israel and Lebanon, drawn up in 1982, was more equivocal: 'The Parties confirm that the state of war between Israel and Lebanon has been terminated and no longer exists.'[109] It is not clear, however, whether this was effected by the treaty or whether the treaty was intended merely to confirm something which the parties considered had already happened. If the latter was the intention of the parties, then the consequences of the failure to ratify the treaty are difficult to assess.

[108] *ILM* 18 (1979), 362.   [109] Art. 1 (2), *ILM* 22 (1982), 708.

3. Most of the other conflicts since 1945 in which a state of war was said to have existed have been terminated by agreements which do not deal expressly with the existence of a state of war.[110] Where an armed conflict has not been regarded as war in the formal sense, it has been even less common for there to have been anything resembling a classical peace treaty.[111]

Nowadays, armed conflicts are often terminated merely by a cease-fire without   249
any peace treaty, or by mere cessation of hostilities.

It is not clear whether a formal instrument is needed to terminate an armed conflict which does not amount to war in the formal sense. Since armed conflict is not a technical, legal concept[112] but a recognition of the fact of hostilities, the cessation of active hostilities should be enough to terminate the armed conflict. Following the surrender of Argentine forces in the Falkland Islands, the United Kingdom Government drew a distinction between 'the surrender of forces in the field and the cessation of hostilities generally'[113] and sought a formal confirmation from Argentina that the conflict was at an end. That confirmation was not given and the United Kingdom and Argentina only agreed to restore normal relations in 1989.[114] Nevertheless, in practice the United Kingdom treated the armed conflict as having come to an end in June 1982, although it maintained certain defensive measures around the Islands for some years afterwards. It seems that while a state may seek confirmation of an end of hostilities as a guarantee against their resumption and as a prelude to the restoration of normal relations, the fact that active hostilities have ceased probably puts an end to the armed conflict, irrespective of whether that confirmation is given. In any event, certain obligations, such as the duty to repatriate prisoners of war,[115] come into operation as soon as active hostilities have ended, whether or not the state of war or armed conflict continues.[116]

---

[110] See e.g. the Tashkent Declaration, 1966, settling the dispute between India and Pakistan, *UNTS* 39, 560, and the exchange of letters between Iran and Iraq in 1990, Lauterpacht (Ed.), *The Kuwait Crisis*, Vol. I, 61–70.

[111] See, however, the Agreement on Ending the War and Restoring Peace in Vietnam, Falk, *The Vietnam War and International Law*, Vol. IV, 821.

[112] See commentary to Sections 201–3.

[113] *BYIL* 53 (1982), 537.

[114] Joint Statement on Relations, 1989, ILM 29 (1990), 1291.

[115] Art. 118 GC III; Sections 730–3.

[116] This rule was introduced in 1949 in an attempt to prevent a recurrence of the delays in repatriation which occurred at the end of World War II, where the last prisoners of war were not returned until 1958.

3

Combatants and Non-Combatants

Introductory Remarks

International law regarding persons taking part in or affected by an international armed conflict makes a fundamental distinction between combatants and civilians. This distinction determines the international legal status of these two categories. They indicate the *primary status* of persons in the event of an international armed conflict. The acquisition of a new, *secondary status* is linked to this primary status when there is an actual change in circumstances (the combatant who falls into the power of the enemy becomes a prisoner of war). The primary status determines the protection afforded to a person by international law (e.g. the general protection of civilians against dangers arising from military operations). Finally, an individual's primary status determines the *legal consequences* of his or her conduct (e.g. the consequences of a violation of international law by a combatant, or of the direct participation in hostilities by a civilian).

International law applicable in international armed conflicts determines which persons are entitled to the status of combatant or of civilian. Regardless of this basic classification, persons can be in closer proximity to one or the other primary status—either due to national law or administrative measures, or because of actual circumstances. As a rule, for example, members of the armed forces of a state (or another party to the conflict which is a recognized subject of international law) are combatants; thus they are authorized, within the limits imposed by international law applicable in international armed conflicts, to participate directly in hostilities. Members of the medical and religious personnel are exceptions to this rule. In addition, other members of the armed forces may, in accordance with decisions made at national level, be excluded from a direct participation in hostilities, thus 'non-combatants' in the literal sense. Finally, persons can be attached to the armed forces without actually being members. They are generally known as 'persons who accompany the armed forces', which is an indication that their primary status is that of civilians. The authorization to fight as a combatant is denied, on one hand to 'non-combatants' *despite* their membership of the armed forces, and on the other hand to 'persons who accompany the armed forces' *because* of their primary status. However, persons who do *not* belong to the armed forces can, under exceptional circumstances, attain combatant status by virtue of an act of their state or through their own decision, as is illustrated by the inclusion of police forces in the 'armed forces' or the armed resistance of the civilian population against an invasion (the '*levée en masse*').

It follows from the above that the heading of this chapter should not be taken to indicate that combatants and non-combatants are categories on the same level of meaning. The primary status under international law of persons in an international armed conflict will be one of two categories of persons: '*combatants and civilians*'. Combatants may fight within the limits imposed by international law applicable in international armed conflict, i.e. they may (participate directly in hostilities) which members of medical or religious personnel and 'non-combatants' may not do because they are excluded—the former by international law and the latter by a legal act of their party to the conflict—from the authorization to take a direct part in hostilities.

301 **The armed forces of a party to a conflict consist of combatants and non-combatants. Combatants are persons who may take a direct part in the hostilities (Art. 3 HagueReg; Art. 43, para. 2 AP I), i.e. participate in the use of a weapon or a weapon-system in an indispensable function. The other members of the armed forces are regarded as non-combatants. The status of the various groups of service personnel will be determined by national decision in accordance with the aforementioned international legal principles.**

To the extent that the armed forces are described as consisting of 'combatants', this corresponds to the fundamental tenet of international law that one party to a conflict, being a subject of international law, exercises the force of arms against another party to the conflict through the organ of its 'armed forces' and that, in accordance with the armed forces' capacity and its tasks, its members as a rule have combatant status. This means that only a party to a conflict which is a subject of international law can have armed forces whose members are combatants. This reflects the basic relation in international law between the state (as a subject of international law), its armed forces (as its organ), and the members of the armed forces (as combatants). The armed forces are described as consisting also of 'non-combatants'; this refers to the exception that, in addition to the medical and religious personnel, other members of the armed forces are not authorized to participate directly in hostilities. The description of the armed forces as comprising combatants and non-combatants should not, however, detract from the fact that for members of the armed forces combatant status is the rule, while the classification as non-combatant is an exception. This follows both from the ordinary meaning and additionally from the historical origin of the relevant norms of international law. Art. 3 HagueReg provides that the armed forces of the parties to a conflict 'may' consist of combatants and non-combatants. This reflects the basic fact, already generally recognized at the time when the HagueReg came into being, that according to a national decision, armed forces may consist of persons both with and without combat tasks.[1] Both the ordinary meaning and the drafting history of Art. 3

---

[1] K. Ipsen, *Kombattanten und Kriegsgefangene*, 139 ff.

Ipsen

HagueReg prove that it was intended to afford to all captured members of the armed forces the status of prisoner of war, regardless of whether or not they were directly involved in the hostilities. That the combatant status of members of armed forces is the deciding factor is made particularly clear by the wording of Art. 43, para. 2 AP I, which in brackets expressly identifies medical personnel and chaplains as an exceptional group not possessing combatant status. In the light of this state of international law it would have been advisable, both in the heading of this Chapter and in the introductory Section 301, to make clear that members of armed forces as a rule are combatants and that the non-combatant status of members of the armed forces only applies in exceptional cases.

In the definition of combatants as 'all persons who may take a direct part in hostilities', the legal definition of combatants contained in Art. 43, para. 2 AP I is repeated almost word for word. The additional explanation that combatants 'participate in the use of a weapon or a weapon-system in an indispensable function' in no way restricts the ambit of the definition: naturally members of the armed forces whose function in the use of a weapon or a weapon-system is not 'indispensable' do not, for this reason, lose their combatant status. The formula of the 'indispensable function' can only serve to differentiate between combatant and non-combatant members of the armed forces in national organizational decisions. Persons who participate in the use of a weapon or a weapon-system in an indispensable function may not under any circumstances be designated as non-combatants by national decision.

Hence on the basis of the ordinary meaning, a combatant is a person who fights. As an international legal term, the combatant is a person who is authorized by international law to fight in accordance with international law applicable in international armed conflict. This authorization is not an individual right afforded to the combatant by international law, but results from the affiliation of the combatant to an organ of a party to the conflict, which is itself a subject of international law.[2]

The statement that '[t]he other members of the armed forces are regarded as non-combatants' must be taken to mean that the combatant is defined narrowly as a specific member of the armed forces and that all other members of the armed forces are non-combatants. Such a false conclusion would be diametrically opposed to the principle of international law: that members of the armed forces are as a rule combatants, and are only non-combatants in exceptional cases.

Finally, the observation that the 'status of the various groups of service personnel will be determined by national decision in accordance with the aforementioned international legal principles' does not mean that, regardless of the definition of a combatant in Art. 43, para. 2 AP I, a state or other party to the conflict which is recognized as a subject of international law has a broad discretion in classifying the members of its armed forces as combatants or as non-combatants. In fact, the opposite is true. If a state, or a party to a conflict bound in accordance with Art. 1 para. 4, Art. 96 para. 3 AP I, maintains armed forces, then the members of these

---

[2] As Kussbach states correctly in *RDMilG* XXII (1983), 381.

armed forces (with the exception of medical and religious personnel) *are* combatants by international legal definition, i.e. they are entitled to participate directly in hostilities without any further legal act beyond the act of establishing armed forces. If, however, the subject of international law maintaining the armed forces wishes to exclude members of the armed forces beyond the medical and religious personnel from direct participation in hostilities, then for *this reason alone* an internal legal act is required. Reduced to a concise formula: a member of the armed forces is a combatant by nature; the status of non-combatant can only be granted to a member of the armed forces by an internal constitutive legal act.

302 **Whereas combatants may not be punished for the mere fact of fighting, persons who take a direct part in the hostilities without being entitled to do so (unlawful combatants) face penal consequences. They do not have the right to prisoner of war status. Unlawful combatants do, however, have a legitimate claim to certain fundamental guarantees (Art. 75 AP I) including the right to humane treatment and a proper judicial procedure.**

The 'mere fact of fighting', for which combatants are not punishable, means participating directly in hostilities within the limits imposed by international law applicable in international armed conflict, provided that all of the relevant norms of this body of law with respect to military activities are observed. Thus the combatant must particularly abide by the rules on weapons and means of combat (Chapter 4 below) as well as by the regulations concerning persons receiving special protection (Chapters 5–7 below). If combatants breach rules of international law applicable in international armed conflict and relevant for their military acts, they shall be called to account in accordance with the military or military penal law of their party to the conflict. If, following the violation of international law, they come into the power of the adversary, then the punishment under criminal law is determined by Arts. 99 *et seq.* GC III (see Chapter 7 III below).

If, on the other hand, persons who do not have combatant status participate directly in hostilities then they are treated as unlawful combatants if they fall into the hands of the enemy. Such fighters cannot be classified as belonging to a state or a party to the conflict recognized as a subject of international law, and are therefore not authorized to undertake armed acts against the adversary. Such irregular fighters, i.e. fighters not belonging to a subject of international law involved in the conflict, if taken by the adversary, are prosecuted as criminals and sentenced for their direct participation in hostilities, in compliance with Art. 45 AP I. If it becomes clear that neither the assumption of prisoner of war status (Art. 45, para. 1 AP I) can be invoked for the captured person, nor that the preliminary judicial decision about prisoner of war status (Art. 45, para. 2 AP I) has been successful, then the person shall at least be treated in accordance with the fundamental guarantees of Art. 75 AP I, provided that GC IV—to the extent that it is applicable—does not grant a more favourable treatment.

**In particular, mercenaries shall be regarded as unlawful combatants. A merce-   303
nary is any person who is motivated to take a direct part in the hostilities by the
desire for private gain without being a national or a member of the armed forces
of a party to the conflict (Art. 47 AP I). The provisions of the 1989 Mercenary
Convention then also apply.**

Under Art. 47, para. 1 AP I, mercenaries are not entitled to the status either of
combatant or of prisoner of war. To regard them as 'unlawful combatants' or 'irregular fighters' does not accord with the meaning of these terms, as mercenaries can
certainly take part in hostilities on the side of a recognized subject of international
law which is a party to the conflict. The denial of the status of combatant and prisoner of war to mercenaries can be explained by the crucial and fatal role which mercenaries—especially of European and North American origin—have played in
armed conflicts on the African continent. In 1967 the UN Security Council had
already called upon states to prohibit the recruitment of mercenaries on their territory for the purpose of removing foreign governments; the Security Council
repeated this request specifically in the final phase of the negotiations in Geneva on
AP I.[3] Art. 47, para. 2 AP I defines a mercenary as fulfilling six criteria: recruitment
(locally or abroad) in order to fight in an armed conflict; actual and direct participation in hostilities; participation motivated by desire for private gain with payment which substantially exceeds that of normal combatants; lack of legal ties to
the party to the conflict based on nationality or residency in a territory controlled
by that party; lack of membership in the armed forces of the party to the conflict;
and not being on official duty in the armed forces of a state not party to the conflict.[4]
The African Mercenary Convention of 1985 and the Mercenary Convention of 1989
have adopted this definition, which is so narrow that even members of armed
forces who are not nationals of the party to the conflict are not considered to be
'mercenaries' if they serve in special units consisting only of foreigners (e.g. the
French Foreign Legion).

This particular point illustrates that the exclusion of mercenaries from combatant and prisoner of war status does not by any means constitute an example of the
renaissance of the *bellum-justum* idea[5]. First and foremost it is the person belonging to the armed forces of a party to the conflict who has the primary status of combatant. This assignment to an organ constitutes authorization to carry out armed
acts causing harm. A simple contract between an individual and a party to the conflict—fighting in exchange for payment—is not sufficient. Thus the rule regarding
mercenaries does not amount to an exception but represents a logical consequence
of the law: a person who is not a member of the armed forces is not (with the exception of participants in a *levée en masse*) a combatant either.

---

[3] UN SC Res. 239 of 10 July 1967; UN SC Res. 405 of 16 April 1977.
[4] For a detailed account see Maaß.   [5] In contrast see Maaß, 212.

Ipsen

I. COMBATANTS

The key rule for determining a person's status as combatant is contained in Art. 43 AP I, which defines armed forces and provides that members of the armed forces (not including the medical and religious personnel) are combatants.

1. *The armed forces of a party to a conflict.* The wording of Art. 43 AP I is clear and therefore requires no further interpretation; it provides that all armed forces of a party to the conflict have the legal status of an organ of that party. According to the broad legal definition of armed forces, these 'consist of all organized armed forces, groups, and units which are under a command responsible to that Party for the conduct of its subordinates'. This definition of armed forces has also been incorporated into the following formulations.

304   **The armed forces of a party to a conflict consist of all its organized armed forces, groups, and units. They also include militias and voluntary corps integrated in the armed forces. The armed forces shall be:**

  – **under a command responsible to that party for the conduct of its subordinates, and**

  – **subject to an internal disciplinary system which, *inter alia*, shall enforce compliance with the rules of international law applicable in armed conflict (Art. 43, para. 1 AP I).**

The definition of armed forces contained in the first sentence of this section is identical with the definition laid down by Art. 43 AP I. The definition is comprehensive: it refers expressly to 'all' organized armed forces of a party to a conflict. This comprehensivity puts an end to the long-standing controversy regarding the definition of 'armed forces' in international legal instruments pertaining to Geneva and Hague Law. The second sentence of this Section should not be misconstrued to mean that only those militias and voluntary corps forming a component of the armed forces according to the relevant national law are part of the armed forces. Such an interpretation could lead to a false conclusion that the differentiation made in Art. 1 HagueReg is being stressed. In this Art. 43, the distinction is made between states in which militias or voluntary corps constitute the army or a part of it, and those states which have militias or voluntary corps in addition to their army. This division is also reflected in Art. 4A Nos. 1 and 2 GC III. Section 304 is—in this respect falsely—based only on the category of No. 1 (integrated militias and voluntary corps). However, both organizational forms of militias and voluntary corps now fall within the term 'armed forces' of Art. 43, para. 1, 1st sentence AP I.

The construction of this key regulation is based on the following indispensable legal elements. Only states or other parties which are recognized as subjects of international law can be parties to an international armed conflict. However, a subject of international law can act only through its own organs. If it uses armed force, the subject can thus act only through the instruments organized for this purpose, i.e. through the armed forces. Militias or voluntary corps of which a party to an international armed conflict makes use are therefore part of its armed forces within the meaning of Art. 43, para. 1, 1st sentence AP I, regardless of whether they are incorporated into the regular armed forces, e.g. the army, or are separate. The two express requirements—of a responsible command and an internal disciplinary system—contained in Art. 43, para. 1 follow from the aforesaid construction of the term 'armed forces' contained in AP I. Each party to a conflict must in all circumstances observe the international law applicable in international armed conflict, as is stipulated for example with respect to AP I in its Art. 1, para. 1. A party to an international armed conflict acts through its armed forces as its organs. Given its fundamental duty to comply with the law, such a party is also bound to ensure that its organs' behaviour is lawful. Art. 3, 2nd sentence HC IV expressly lays down this duty with the same words as Art. 91, 2nd sentence AP I. To guarantee that this duty is performed, a command of the armed forces which is responsible to the party to the conflict for the conduct of its subordinates is required. However, a breach of international law leads to responsibility in international law of the party to the conflict recognized as a subject of international law. It is in the general interest of the party to the conflict to prevent contraventions of international law, in order to avoid responsibility. Hence it is necessary to implement a system of sanctions, together with the internal disciplinary system, both of which are required by Art. 43, para. 1, 2nd sentence AP I.

2. *Combatant status.* According to Art. 43, para. 2 AP I, only members of the armed forces as defined above (with the exception of the medical and religious personnel specially protected by Art. 33 GC III) are combatants, 'that is to say, they have the right to participate directly in hostilities'. Thus membership of the armed forces is an indispensable prerequisite to combatant status; 'armed forces' in the meaning of international law, however, have the legal status of an organ of a party to the conflict. If persons participating directly in hostilities lack either of these two prerequisite elements of combatant status, then they cannot have combatant status. Thus, if they fall into the hands of the enemy, they cannot acquire the secondary status of prisoner of war.

   To sum up, it has to be established that Art. 43, para. 1 AP I has created a standard international legal term of 'armed forces' covering all combatant forces (except participants in a *levée en masse*) which are listed in addition to the regular 'armed forces' in the older relevant conventions (HagueReg, GC); they are now included within the term 'armed forces'. It was the natural and legally logical consequence of this broad definition of armed forces to define the combatant as a member of the armed forces who is entitled to participate directly in hostilities. The fundamental structure of the term 'combatant' in international law which was established prior to AP I, however, has not been changed: it describes a person who is a member of the armed forces, being an organ of a party to a conflict which is a subject of international law. The party to the conflict determines the type and size of its armed forces in accordance with its national laws. On the level of international law, the

Ipsen

members of these armed forces are entitled to take part directly in hostilities. This point deserves emphasis. With regard to the direct participation in hostilities, combatants are privileged solely by that entitlement, the lack of which makes them criminals liable to prosecution. On the other hand, the duties of the combatant impose limits on that entitlement (see Sections 308, 309, 311 below).

3. *Women and children as combatants.* Since the primary status of combatant is derived from membership in the armed forces of a party to the conflict, women and children also have this status if they are members of the armed forces. A party to the conflict may, however, be bound by international conventions prohibiting the recruitment of children below a certain age into their armed forces or may, by national law, exclude women from direct participation in hostilities or from military service altogether.

305 **It shall be left to the discretion of the individual states to choose whether to admit women to their armed forces. Their combatant or non-combatant status is determined by the same principles as that of male members of armed forces.**

In so far as women are members of the armed forces they have the same authorization under Art. 43, para. 2 AP I as male members. They are entitled—as long as they do not belong to medical or religious personnel—to participate directly in hostilities. It is left to the discretion of the states or other parties to a conflict recognized as subjects of international law whether or not to admit women to the armed forces. The decision of the Federal Republic of Germany on this matter is recorded in its constitution: Art. 12a, para. 4, 2nd sentence of the German Basic Law excludes women from any military service (even voluntary) which involves the use of weapons. In this connection, the term 'weapon' includes any weapon-system, the operation of which constitutes a direct participation in hostilities.[6] Apart from this, women are permitted to serve in the German armed forces as volunteers.

The conscription of women into the armed forces in the state of defence is problematic. According to s. 2 No. 1 of the German Emergency Labour Control Act (*Arbeitssicherstellungsgesetz*, or ASG) of 9 July 1968, the right to terminate the employment of women between the ages of eighteen and fifty-five may be restricted. It clearly follows from s. 4, para. 1 No. 1 ASG that this restriction (ruling out termination) is also permitted in order to secure their work in the Federal Armed Forces. Remaining in an existing employment according to one's duty and the imposition of a duty to enter into a new employment are dealt with in the same way by s. 4 ASG. In so far as the imposition of new duties is concerned, however, Art. 12a, para. 4 of the German Basic Law restricts the conscription of women in the aforesaid age group to civilian duties in the civilian medical service and in the organization of permanent military hospitals. Since the legal duty to continue an existing employment has a similar effect on women as the legal imposition of a new employment, it is at least questionable whether the authorization to oblige women

---

[6] See K. Ipsen/J. Ipsen, BK, Art. 12a, n. 294.

to continue their employment in the armed forces, granted by ss. 2 No. 1, 4 para. 1 No. 1 ASG, is consistent with Art. 12a of the German Basic Law. A correct interpretation of paras. 4 and 6 of Art. 12a of the German Basic Law according to their common object and purpose leads to constitutional conformity with the legal duty to continue an existing employment with the armed forces: Art. 12a para. 6 of the German Basic Law creates the constitutional basis to ensure that the actual assignment of manpower to defence tasks is preserved. Compared to the imposition of a new employment envisaged by Art. 12a paras. 1–5 German Basic Law, the duty to continue an existing employment is a less severe infringement of the constitutional right to freedom of occupation. Furthermore, Art. 12a German Basic Law is not limited to men, and also subjects women to the possibility of a mandatory direction to remain in their current employment.[7] The consequences of the characterization of women in the armed forces as non-combatants will be discussed in connection with the relevant Section (313).

The parties to the conflict shall take all feasible measures to ensure that children   306
who have not attained the age of fifteen years do not take direct part in hostilities
and, in particular, they shall refrain from recruiting them into their armed forces
(Art. 77, para. 2 AP I; see also Art. 38 of the 1989 Convention on the Rights of the
Child).

This provision reproduces exactly the same duties as imposed upon the parties to AP I by Art. 77, para. 2 and by Art. 38, paras. 2 and 3, 1st sentence of the Convention on the Rights of the Child. The two provisions of AP I and of the Convention on the Rights of the Child cited above have identical contents. In addition, Art. 38, para. 1 of the Convention on the Rights of the Child commits the states which are parties to respect and to ensure respect for the rules of international humanitarian law applicable in armed conflicts which are relevant to children. At the same time, this is a reference to the fundamental rule of Art. 77, para. 1 AP I, according to which children in international armed conflicts have to be treated with special care.

Art. 77, para. 3 AP I takes into account the circumstances arising from a breach of the duties laid down in para. 2. If a child who has not reached the age of fifteen and has participated directly in hostilities falls into the hands of the adversary, that child is nevertheless entitled to the special protection provided under Art. 77 regardless of whether or not he or she is a prisoner of war. However, children protected under Art. 77 can only be prisoners of war if they had previously attained the primary status of combatant by being unlawfully recruited into the armed forces of one of the parties to the conflict. This is particularly significant because the combatant status protects the child against being prosecuted upon capture for its direct participation in hostilities. In conclusion: every party to a conflict bound by AP I and/or the Convention on the Rights of the Child is subject to the clear duty to keep children out of the armed forces and away from direct participation in hostilities. If a party to a conflict fails to carry out this duty then it breaches international law, but the

---

[7] Cf. in particular K. Ipsen, J. Ipsen, BK, Art. 12a GG, notes 279–300.

Ipsen

children affected are nonetheless entitled to the maximum protection provided by Art. 77 AP I and Art. 38 of the Convention on the Rights of the Child.

4. *Paramilitary or armed law enforcement agencies as part of the armed forces.* The task of armed law enforcement agencies of a state (for instance the police), even if they are of a paramilitary nature, is as a rule only to protect and maintain the internal order of the state. The legal status of such armed, possibly paramilitary, law enforcement agencies in relation to the armed forces is regulated differently by different states[8]: some states incorporate their police, or police units, into their armed forces in the event of an international armed conflict. Some states have police units permanently incorporated into their armed forces, even in peacetime. In other states there is a strict division between the armed forces and the police. The purpose of the following regulation is to establish a common denominator in international law for these different categories of national organization.

307 **Whenever a party to a conflict incorporates a paramilitary or armed law enforcement agency into its armed forces it shall notify the other parties to the conflict (Art. 43, para. 3 AP I). In the Federal Republic of Germany the Federal Border Guard Commands (including their Border Guard formations and units as well as the Federal Border Guard School) shall become part of the armed forces upon the outbreak of an armed conflict. They shall, however, remain subordinate to the Federal Minister of the Interior and shall only be employed for their police functions and for their own defence (s. 64 of the Federal Border Guard Act).**

This rule corresponds word for word to Art. 43, para. 3 AP I. It also confirms the finding described in connection with the definition of armed forces (Section 304 above) that the state or party to the conflict which is a subject of international law determines the type and size of its own armed forces through a national legal act. This also holds true in principle for the decision of whether or not to incorporate paramilitary or armed law enforcement agencies into the armed forces. The first half of the first sentence of Art. 43, para. 3 AP I is based on the assumption that the question of whether or not paramilitary or armed law enforcement agencies will be incorporated into the armed forces and thus employed as fighting forces in the armed conflict is to be determined by the sovereign decision of each state or other party to the conflict. From the point of view of international law, this decision—just like any similar internal act with international legal relevance—only becomes effective through the international legal act of notification, i.e. a either an *ad hoc* notification *vis-à-vis* the opposing party in a conflict, or *vis-à-vis* the depositary of the AP I. If such notification has been given (e.g. notification pursuant to s. 64 of the Federal Border Guard Act) then the combatant status under international law of the affected paramilitary or armed law enforcement agencies in the event of a conflict is clearly secured. The effectiveness of combatant status in international law is established—and this is crucial—solely by the fact of notification. Furthermore,

---

[8] Cf. K. Ipsen, BK, Art. 87a, notes 54–60.

international law does not take national constitutions into consideration. Any doubts regarding the conformity with the constitution or other laws of the national act are therefore irrelevant. This situation in international law is both clear and practical: it simply cannot be expected that the recipient of the notification regarding the combatant status of paramilitary or armed law enforcement agencies should become involved in a jurisprudential dispute about a foreign legal order. Along with the combatant status attained through the incorporation into the armed forces, these (police) forces also become a military target (as defined by Art. 52, para. 2 AP I) and are therefore subject to armed attacks by the opposing party to the conflict just like any other unit of the armed forces. This is also the inevitable consequence of notifying s. 64 of the Federal Border Guard Act to the Swiss depositary: after this notification has been made with respect to the Federal Border Guard Commands and the Federal Border Guard School, the latter become part of the armed forces and thus also military objectives, regardless of whether or not they are restricted by a national order only to carry out police functions and defend themselves against a combatant enemy.

Armed law enforcement agencies, especially police forces without the aforementioned notified combatant status, are protected by international law as civilians—in particular by Part IV AP I and by GC IV. International law applicable in international armed conflict does not provide for a special primary status of the police. The fact that the police receive the primary status of protected civilians creates a large number of practical and legal problems both in the theatre of operations of an armed conflict and in occupied territories (e.g. intervention against persons whose primary status either as combatants or as civilians is not recognizable; intervention against commandos who conceal their combatant status; intervention against other armed units whose primary status is doubtful).

5. *The duty of combatants to distinguish themselves from civilians.* While membership of the armed forces of a party to a conflict is the factor which determines the primary status as combatant, the distinction from civilians represents a duty deriving from the combatant status, the breach of which at worst leads to the forfeiture of the secondary status of prisoner of war. The following applies with respect to the duty of distinction.

Combatants are obliged to distinguish themselves from the civilian population   308
while they are engaged in an attack or in a military operation preparatory to an
attack (Art. 44, para. 3 AP I). In accordance with the generally agreed practice of
states, members of regular armed forces shall wear their uniform (Art. 44, para. 7
AP I). Combatants who are not members of uniformed armed forces shall wear a
permanent distinctive sign visible from a distance and carry their arms openly.

The first sentence of this regulation has the same content as Art. 44, para. 3, 1st sentence AP I. In addition this norm, which lays down the fundamental obligation of combatants to distinguish themselves from the civilian population during attacks or military activities in preparation for an attack, is expressly intended to promote the protection of the civilian population against the effects of hostilities. Interpreting this provision in the systematic context of AP I leads to the following observations. Part IV AP I, which is dedicated to the protection of the civilian population, begins with the basic rule of Art. 48 which obligates the parties to a conflict 'at all times [to] distinguish between the civilian population and combatants . . . [i]n order to ensure respect for and protection of the civilian population'. Since the explicit reason, according to Art. 44, para. 3, 1st sentence AP I, for the fundamental obligation of the combatants to distinguish themselves from the civilian population is to increase the protection of the civilian population against the effects of hostilities, the compelling result is that this duty of the combatants to distinguish themselves is the basic rule.

Following this basic rule it would be systematically appropriate subsequently to stress next the generally agreed practice by states of the wearing of uniforms by regular armed forces, as is correctly done in Section 308. Art. 44 dedicates a later paragraph, para. 7, to this principle. This is acceptable because it expressly applies to the entire article and makes clear that none of the regulations of this article are intended 'to change the generally accepted practice of States with respect to the wearing of the uniform by combatants assigned to the regular, uniformed armed units of a Party to the conflict'. Art. 44 para. 7 AP I refers to a rule of international customary law according to which regular armed forces shall wear the uniform of their party to the conflict when directly involved in hostilities. This rule of international customary law had by the nineteenth century already become so well established that it was held to be generally accepted at the Conference in Brussels in 1874.[9] The armed forces listed in Art. 4 No. 1 GC III are undoubtedly regarded as 'regular' armed forces within the meaning of this rule. This is the meaning of 'armed forces' upon which the identical Articles 1 of the Hague Regulations of 1899 and 1907 were based. Both these conventions retained Art. IX of the Brussels Declaration of 1874 without alteration. Hence Art. 4 A No. 1 GA III is based on this historically evolved meaning of regular armed forces, which No. 3 of the said provision also relies on: it specifically mentions 'regular armed forces', which unequivocally means those described in No. 1; on the other hand, the obligation to wear a uniform does not apply to the armed units listed in Art. 4 A No. 2 GC III. These do fall under the broad category of 'armed forces' covered by Art. 43, para. 1 AP I, but they are not obliged to wear a uniform, although they must wear a permanent and distinctive sign which is visible from a distance, and carry their arms openly. It confirms, though, that the basic rules regarding the distinction of forces from the civilian population apply to them as well.

This category is dealt with in Section 308, which refers to '[c]ombatants who are not members of uniformed armed forces'. Thus, members of 'militias and . . . other volunteer corps, including those of organized resistance movements, belonging to a Party to the conflict' (not incorporated into the armed forces) are mentioned. From Art. 4 A No. 2 lit. b and c, it follows that these armed groups must wear 'a fixed distinctive sign recognizable at a distance' and carry 'arms openly'. It should be

---

[9] Buß, 156.

Ipsen

noted that this category is also included in the definition of armed forces contained in Art. 43, para. 1 AP I. The category is exempted from the obligation to wear a uniform, but the fundamental duty to distinguish themselves in the manner described still applies.

The basic rule providing that combatants must distinguish themselves from the civilian population is supplemented by Art. 44, para. 3, 2nd sentence AP I which is formulated as an unambiguous exception.

Recognizing that there are situations in occupied territories and in wars of **309** **national liberation where, owing to the nature of the hostilities, a combatant (especially a guerilla) cannot so distinguish himself from the civilian population, he shall retain his status as a combatant, provided that, in such situations, he carries his arms openly:**

– during each military engagement, and

– during such time as he is visible to the adversary while he is engaged in a military deployment preceding the launching of an attack in which he is to participate (Art. 44, para. 3, sentence 2 AP I).

The term 'military deployment' refers to any movement towards the point from which an attack is to be launched.

Art. 44, para. 3, 2nd sentence AP I which is identical to this provision was one of the most controversial regulations at the 1977 Geneva Conference on the Reaffirmation and Development of International Humanitarian Law Applicable in Armed Conflicts. States which acquired their independence by successful guerilla warfare or which supported guerilla liberation movements strongly advocated the elimination of criteria distinguishing such combatants from civilians. Other states were resolutely opposed to an exception for guerillas to the rule requiring distinction from the civilian population. Art. 44, para. 3, 2nd sentence AP I represents the compromise achieved after a long argument. The delegation of the Federal Republic of Germany played an important role in the establishment of this compromise and even formulated some of the drafts. For this reason the Federal Republic of Germany's interpretation, as contained in a declaration of interpretation submitted with the document of ratification, carries significant weight. According to this declaration, the criteria used to distinguish between combatants and civilians contained in the exceptional rule apply only in occupied territories and in armed conflicts of the kind described in Art. 1, para. 4 of AP I. This is an interpretation which, in the light of the general rule of interpretation of Art. 31 of the Vienna Convention on the Law of Treaties, is undoubtedly correct. According to the wording of Art. 44, para. 3, 2nd sentence, the reason for the exceptional rule lies in the fact that 'there are situations in armed conflicts where, owing to the nature of the hostilities, an armed combatant cannot so distinguish himself' from the civilian population. However, such situations can in fact only arise if a people within the meaning of Art. 1, para. 4 AP I is engaged in a 'war of liberation' as described therein, for this is one of two typical situations of guerilla warfare. The other is the

Ipsen

situation in occupied territories which is repeatedly marked by guerilla fighting through organized resistance movements. This interpretation based on the object and purpose of the provision is supported by the historical development which has led to this exception.[10] The protagonists of guerilla warfare were mainly concerned to include all wars of liberation as defined by Art. 1, para. 4, whereas some western states in particular sought to restrict such exceptional circumstances to occupied territories. By its restrictive interpretation, which has been realized *lege artis*, the Federal Republic of Germany has taken into account both of these positions.

In addition, according to the declaration of interpretation submitted upon ratification, the Federal Republic of Germany understands 'military deployment [as] any movement towards the point from which an attack is to be launched'. This interpretation is also contained in a number of declarations submitted by other member states of AP I, but it carries a special weight as the term 'military deployment/ *militärischer Aufmarsch*' has been introduced into AP I by the Federal Republic of Germany. The German delegation had already given this explanation of the term at the Geneva Conference which had met with general approval. To date no reasons have emerged for abandoning this object- and purpose-oriented interpretation aimed at a minimal distinction.

Thus, the exceptional rule consists of a narrowing of the scope of application and of a reduction of the distinctive criteria. It only applies in occupied territories and when a people fight for national liberation according to Art. 1, para. 4 AP I; the requirement of distinction from the civilian population is already fulfilled if the combatants carry their arms openly from the time of the initial deployment to the place of attack (at the latest), and of course during every military engagement.

Paragraph 7 expressly indicates that Art. 44 is not intended to change the generally accepted practice of states concerning the wearing of uniforms by combatants who are members of the regular armed forces. This might lead to the conclusion that the exceptional rule of para. 3, 2nd sentence does not apply to members of the regular armed forces. This would, however, directly contradict the reciprocity principle which governs international humanitarian law and which is expressed for example in the Preamble to AP I.[11] Despite this legal equality the exceptional rule will in practice only be applied to guerilla fighters.

If combatants within the scope of the exceptional rule do not meet the minimal requirements of the rule, then, according to Art. 44, para. 4, 1st sentence, they forfeit their secondary status as prisoners of war in the event of capture by the enemy. Nevertheless they shall be afforded protection equivalent to that of GC III and AP I, which includes protection in the case of criminal prosecution. This is expressly mentioned in the second sentence of Art. 44, para. 4; the first sentence only takes into account the equivalence of protective provisions, not of criminal provisions (in particular Arts. 82–8 GC III). Those combatants who have forfeited their prisoner of war status under Art. 44, para. 3, 2nd sentence in conjunction with para. 4 are thus prosecuted and punished under the national criminal law of the detaining power. However, treatment equivalent to that of Arts. 99–108 GC III shall be ensured.

[10] See Bothe/Ipsen/Partsch, *ZaöRV* 38 (1978), 34 ff.

[11] Likewise, although based on different reasoning, de Preux ICRC *Commentary*, Art. 44, n. 1723.

Ipsen

If a combatant who is a member of the regular armed forces and is captured while participating directly in hostilities is not wearing the appropriate uniform, or if such a captured combatant who is a member of a militia, voluntary corps, or an organized resistance movement does not wear a permanent distinctive sign visible from a distance, then generally a breach of the duty of distinction and additionally a charge of perfidy according to Art. 37, para. 1 AP I must be considered, unless an exception under Art. 44 para. 3, 2nd sentence AP I is applicable.

6. *The levée en masse.* The combatant status generally depends—as has been clearly shown in the comments to Section 304 above—upon the authorization by the state or party to the conflict recognized as a subject in international law, because the armed forces are, within the meaning of Art. 43, para. 1 AP I, assigned to these entities as organs of the parties. Only in one situation does international law applicable in international armed conflict permit persons to participate directly in hostilities solely on the basis of their autonomous decision: this is the *levée en masse* defined by Art. 2 HagueReg and Art. 4A No. 6 GC III.

The inhabitants of a territory which has not yet been occupied who, on the   310
approach of the enemy, spontaneously take up arms to resist the invading troops
without having had time to form themselves into armed units (so-called *levée en*
***masse*) shall be combatants. They shall carry arms openly and respect the laws**
and customs of war in their military operations (Art. 2 HagueReg; Art. 4A No. 6 GC
III).

Such spontaneous resistance must therefore meet four requirements in order for the persons taking part to obtain the primary status of combatants:

(1) Spontaneous armed resistance is permitted by international law only in 'territory which is not occupied'. A territory is considered to be 'not occupied' if it is not (yet) under the factual control of the enemy as arises by *argumentum e contrario* from Art. 42 HagueReg. It follows that resistance movements which are organized autonomously by the population of an already occupied territory do not fall into the category of *levée en masse.*

(2) The population of this unoccupied territory must take up arms 'spontaneously' on the approach of the enemy. This requires two conditions to be met: first, only a resistance initiated by the population itself, not one directed or organized in advance by organs of the state, fulfils this condition. Secondly, armed resistance is only permitted against 'invading troops' and therefore not in territory which is already occupied. These two conditions are obviously not met by organized resistance movements.

(3) Furthermore, the civilians involved in armed resistance may not have had the time to organize themselves (within the meaning of Art. 1 HagueReg) as militia or volunteer corps. This requirement clearly emphasizes the principle of authorization: only a state or another party to the conflict recognized as a subject of international law has the authority to decide on the use of armed force within the framework of international law. In every developed legal order, self-help is the

Ipsen

exception. International law, as a legal order, also in principle prohibits private individuals from deciding on the use of armed force, even if their motivation in a concrete case can be recognized as stemming from patriotism or other ethical reasons. The rule in Art. 2 HagueReg is unambiguous: persons wanting to resist an attack must secure the authorization of their state by joining the armed forces, a militia, or a volunteer corps. Only if it is in fact impossible to join these armed units, and provided that the conditions of Art. 2 are met, are civilians exceptionally permitted to take up arms by their own decision.

(4) Finally, the participants in such a *levée en masse* must respect 'the laws and customs of war' and are thus bound by the basic duty which applies to all combatants.

If spontaneous resistance fighters fulfil these four conditions then they have the primary status of combatants. In the event of capture by the adverse party to the conflict they are granted the secondary status of prisoners of war. It should be noted, however, that in modern-day armed conflicts the *levée en masse* has become less significant because, as a rule, the regular armed forces of an attacking party are armed to a degree that simply cannot be countered with the weapons available to a spontaneous resistance (such as hunting weapons).

7. *The obligation to comply with international law applicable in armed conflicts.* In addition to the important duty to distinguish themselves from the civilian population (Section 308 above), combatants are also bound by the duty to abide by the applicable international law.

311   **While all combatants are obliged to comply with the rules of international law applicable in armed conflict, violations of these rules shall not deprive a combatant of his right to be a combatant (Art. 44, para. 2 AP I).**

Although the duty of all combatants to comply with the international law applicable in armed conflicts is only mentioned briefly in Art. 44, para. 2 AP I, this constitutes a codification of a general principle of international humanitarian law which applies as customary law in addition to the respective international conventions. Art. 1 HagueReg already binds the armed forces as well as (independent) militias and volunteer corps to '[t]he laws, rights, and duties of war', thereby reiterating the wording of Art. IX of the Brussels Declaration of 1874. It is a basic rule already considered to be a principle of international law at that time. Thus, the first half of the sentence in Art. 44, para. 2 AP I is a reaffirmation of a legal principle which has long been codified (and which was effective even before that). In addition, the combatant's duty to comply with the law is the expression of another fundamental principle of international law: the principle of reciprocity. General practice can only arise through reciprocity; sanctions such as reprisals are a negative aspect of reciprocity. Consequently, privileges granted under international law, such as that of combatant status which, after all, privileges those persons who use force, can only be realized on the basis of reciprocity. This means, however, that combatants are also compelled by the principle of reciprocity to act within the restrictions and limitations imposed on them by international law applicable in international armed conflict. Sporadic attempts have been made amongst legal scholars to develop a concept of international law of war which discriminates against the aggressor and whose restrictions apply only to the combatants of the aggressor, thus ruling out legal equality of treatment. This concept, however, has not found its way either into treaty law or into customary law. Therefore the duty of combatants to abide by the rules of international law applicable in armed conflicts is all-encompassing and incumbent equally upon the combatants of all parties to the conflict.

If combatants breach the rules of international law applicable in armed conflicts then it is the responsibility of the party to the conflict to which they belong to punish this behaviour through disciplinary measures or prosecution. This is an obligation attached to the party to the conflict concerned under Arts. 85, 86 AP I. If combatants fall into the hands of the adverse party after having breached international law then, according to Arts. 82–88 GC III, they shall be called to account under the applicable legal regulations of the detaining power. In principle the breach of rules of international law applicable in armed conflicts does not result in the offenders forfeiting their primary status as combatants. Thus, if they fall into the hands of the adverse party to the conflict they do not forfeit the secondary status of prisoners of war. A breach of the obligation of minimal distinction according to Art. 44, para. 3, 2nd sentence AP I (see Section 309 above) is an exception. Art. 44, para. 4 AP I lays down that a breach of this duty results in forfeiture of prisoner of war status.

8. *The secondary status of prisoner of war.* Attached to the primary status of combatant—as explained above, before Section 301—is the secondary status of prisoner of war.

**Combatants who fall into the hands of the adversary shall be prisoners of war (Art.   312
3, sentence 2, HagueReg; Art. 44, para. 1 AP I). They shall not be called to account
for their participation in lawful military operations. Violations of international
law committed by them may be prosecuted under the laws of the detaining power
and international law (Arts. 82 ff. GC III).**

Art. 44, para. 1 AP I simply confirms existing international law when it lays down that a combatant (as defined by Art. 43, para. 2 AP I) 'who falls into the power of an adverse party shall be a prisoner of war'. This basic rule was already established in Art. 3 HagueReg and Art. 4 A Nos. 1–3 and 6 GC III. It has not been altered by the new law (regarding the status of prisoners of war, see the detailed Sections 701–33).

II. NON-COMBATANTS

1. *The historical development of the division of members of the armed forces into combatants and non-combatants.* The autonomy to organize the internal structure

of their armed forces is granted to states by Art. 3 HagueReg, according to which the 'armed forces . . . may' consist of combatants and non-combatants. It has its origin in a factual situation which had already been taken into account by the Brussels Declaration of 1874. In 1874, the Brussels Conference based the negotiations on a draft presented by the Russian delegation, of which s. 10, 1st sentence reads: 'The armed forces of the belligerents may be composed of combatants and non-combatants.'[12] In a further provision (s. 38) the Russian draft provided for the 'neutralization' of medical personnel, just as Articles I–III of the Geneva Red Cross Convention of 22 August 1864 had already stated. Consequently, s. 10 of the Russian draft included all persons who—being members of the armed forces—belonged to various branches of the military administration. They were categorized as 'non-combatants'. Apart from military and religious personnel they included quartermasters, members of the legal services and other non-fighting personnel. Obviously, the actual composition of the armed forces at that time had been taken into account, with the explicit purpose of granting to all members of the armed forces the secondary status of prisoners of war in the event of capture. From this general category of 'non-combatants' the members of the medical and religious personnel were singled out again—in accordance with the Geneva Red Cross Convention signed ten years earlier—in order to grant them the 'right of neutrality' guaranteed by that Convention. Section 23 of the draft expressly repeated that combatants and non-combatants, with the exception of the neutralized medical and religious personnel, acquired prisoner of war status in the event of their capture.

As prisoner of war status was guaranteed twice, namely in ss. 10 and 23 of the Russian draft, there was inevitably some criticism in the negotiations.[13] It was suggested that s. 10 (the division into combatants and non-combatants) be entirely omitted as this rule did not establish a new principle and could lead to misunderstandings in practice. It was argued that medical and religious personnel were already protected by the Geneva Convention of 1864. Combatants and non-combatants received prisoner of war status anyway upon being captured; yet this was also guaranteed by s. 23 which said that all combatants and non-combatants are entitled to prisoner of war status. To the extent that it was desired to maintain s. 10 (laying down that the armed forces may be composed of combatants and non-combatants), it was said that a clause should be inserted stipulating that non-combatants are exposed to the misfortunes and dangers of war in the same way as the units to which they belong. The conference, however, was of the opinion that such a provision was already tacitly included in the rule.[14]

The documents cited lead to the following observation. It was obviously not the intention of the Brussels Conference to create a non-combatant status in international law determined by the fact that persons with this status are not entitled under international law to participate directly in hostilities. Nor was it intended to treat non-combatants belonging to the armed forces in the same way as civilians.

---

[12] See in this connection and to the following, *Projet d'une déclaration internationale conçernant les lois et coutumes de la guerre adoptés par la Conférence de Bruxelles, Actes de la Conférence, Bruxelles* 1874 (*juillet–aout* 1874)—translated by the author.
[13] See *Actes de la Conférence de Bruxelles*, Prot. XIII, session of 17 Aug. 1874, 183 ff.   [14] Ibid. 184.

Ipsen

Instead, the point of departure was the actual and widespread awareness that armed forces are composed both of persons who fight and of persons who (because of their function) do not take a direct part in the fighting.

The approach of the Brussels Conference was based on this finding, as illustrated by its discussion of the duty of non-combatants to wear uniform. The delegate of the German Reich raised the question of whether it would not be appropriate to require that the non-combatants mentioned in the draft should wear uniform during wartime. Without such a duty it would be difficult to distinguish between non-combatant members of the armed forces and civilians accompanying the armed forces (mentioned in s. 24 of the Russian draft). Other delegates objected to this proposal, saying that the wearing of a uniform was anyway common practice for non-combatants. It would therefore be superfluous to lay down a special duty for them to wear uniforms.[15] Immediately after this discussion, s. 10 was put into the version which was then adopted as s. 11 of the Brussels Declaration, and several decades later without further controversy as Art. 3 of the Hague Regulations of 1899 and 1907: 'The armed forces of the belligerent parties may consist of combatants and non-combatants. In the case of capture by the enemy, both have a right to be treated as prisoners of war'.

Since then the non-combatant, within the meaning of Art. 3 HagueReg, has not acquired a special status in international law entailing special rights or duties on this level. This explains why the comprehensive definition of armed forces given in Art. 43, para. 1 AP I, and the related definition of members of the armed forces as combatants in para. 2, no longer refer to non-combatants. During the negotiations on the definition of armed forces at the Geneva Conference, only one delegation pointed out that the members of armed forces could comprise both combatants and non-combatants. This comment was incorporated into the report of the Third Commission: 'It should, however, be noted that the term "members of armed forces" is all-inclusive and includes both combatants and non-combatants'.[16] In view of the wording and the historic origin of Art. 43 AP I, one should agree with the opinions of legal scholars that international law does not afford the non-combatant any better protection than the combatant.[17] Thus the non-combatant, as a member of the armed forces, is not protected from being the object of an attack. Furthermore, as non-combatants are not mentioned in Art. 43 AP I, it is argued that the differentiation in Art. 3 HagueReg between combatants and non-combatants in the armed forces is no longer useful.[18]

2. *No greater protection under international law for non-combatants than for combatants.* Even though the view stated above goes beyond that which can clearly be derived from the historical origin of the norm, one thing remains certain: the non-combatant has never enjoyed a special status under international law, either before

---

[15] Ibid. 185.

[16] Official records of the Diplomatic Conference on the Reaffirmation and Development of International Humanitarian Law Applicable in Armed Conflicts, Geneva (1974–77), Vol. XV, 390.

[17] As stated correctly by Solf in Bothe/Partsch/Solf, 240.

[18] See de Preux ICRC *Commentary*, n. 1676.

Ipsen

or after the entry into force of AP I. Before AP I, non-combatants belonged to the armed forces (according to Art. 3 HagueReg or Art. 4 A No. 1 GC III) without this membership being linked to special protection under international law. Even the classification as an enemy *hors de combat* under Art. 23 lit. c HagueReg did not provide any other protection than that afforded to combatants in the same situation. Since AP I entered into force, non-combatants are no longer even included in the members of the armed forces, although the historic origin of Art. 43, para. 1 AP I would justify their inclusion in that provision's definition of armed forces. In any event, on the level of international law the only consequence of classifying members of the armed forces as non-combatants is that they acquire prisoner of war status if they fall into the hands of the adverse party.

313   **Persons who are members of the armed forces but who, by virtue of national regulations, have no combat mission, such as judges, government officials, and blue-collar workers, are non-combatants. If they fall into the power of the adversary, they will be prisoners of war as will combatants (Art. 4A No. 1 GC III).**

As a rule, persons who are members of the armed forces are combatants—as laid down in Art. 43, para. 2 AP I—and are entitled, as such, to participate directly in hostilities. It remains in the discretion of the states and other parties to the conflict recognized as subjects of international law to restrict this entitlement of international law with respect to certain categories of the members of their armed forces and to prohibit them by legal act from direct participation in hostilities. Any such national legal act has no effect whatsoever in international law, since prisoner of war status is already attained by virtue of the fact that the non-combatant is a member of the armed forces and thus falls under Art. 4A No. 1 GC III.

It follows from this that non-combatants are not nor could they under any circumstances be protected as civilians, for Art. 50, para. 1, 1st sentence AP I determines with a negative legal definition: 'A civilian is any person who does not belong to one of the categories of persons referred to in Article 4A (1), (2), (3) and (6) of the Third Convention and in Article 43 of this Protocol.' However, non-combatant members of the armed forces clearly belong to the armed forces within the meaning of Art. 4A No. 1 GC III or Art. 43, para. 1 AP I, if these provisions are interpreted in the light of their object and purpose. This interpretation will have to take into account the stipulation's all-encompassing scope as well as its drafting history. From the negative legal definition of civilians it also follows that members of the armed forces do *not* enjoy the 'general protection against dangers arising from military operations' which Art. 51, para. 1, 1st sentence affords to the civilian population and to individual civilians. The non-combatant members of the armed forces are not protected by the prohibition of attacks according to Art. 51, para. 2, 1st sentence AP I, since they do not enjoy the protection of Art. 51. Therefore the non-combatant members of the armed forces are not merely subjected to the risk of collateral damage in the sense of Art. 51, para. 5, lit. b. Art. 51 AP I concerns exclusively the 'protection of the civilian population', to which the non-combatant members of the armed forces do not belong. AP I and international humanitarian law protect the civilian population but not the armed forces against dangers arising from military operations.

According to Art. 52, para. 2, 1st sentence AP I, 'attacks shall be limited strictly to military objectives'. The armed forces of the enemy are a military objective. This is a general principle of customary international law. The Russian draft convention negotiated at the Brussels Conference of 1874 had already taken this legal finding as a starting point. Furthermore it is clarified by the regulations of the Brussels Declaration and by the prohibition of bombardment of undefended places included in the Hague Regulations.[19] Art. 2 HC IX likewise makes clear that facilities of the armed forces also represent military objectives. Art. 24, para. 1 of the HRAW 1923 (which did not enter into force as a treaty) contains a definition of military objectives as targets 'of which the destruction or injury would constitute a distinct military advantage to the belligerent'. Finally Art. 52, para. 2, 2nd sentence AP I defines military objectives, in so far as they are objects, as 'those objects which by their nature, location, purpose or use make an effective contribution to military action and whose total or partial destruction, capture or neutralization, in the circumstances ruling at the time, offers a definite military advantage'. With the exception of the term of 'definite military advantage', this legal definition essentially contains those characteristics which are required by customary law for the determination of a military objective. Members of the armed forces (with the exception of the specially protected medical and religious personnel) are, however, military objectives as they clearly have these features of military objectives under customary law. As the organization of armed forces—including and especially with regard to their non-combatant members—is concentrated on efficiency, it must be assumed that the main purpose of armed forces is effective participation in hostilities. This participation includes their non-combatant members which, therefore, effectively contribute to military operations.

The presence of non-combatant members of the armed forces in a mobile or immobile facility representing a military objective, therefore, does not even require the attacking forces of the adversary to take special precautionary measures. They do not have to differentiate during their attack between combatant and non-combatant members of the adverse armed forces, provided that no medical or religious personnel are present. As an object of such attack, the—possibly unarmed—non combatant member of the armed forces can at best be entitled to protection as an enemy *hors de combat* within the meaning of Art. 41 AP I. Of the variations of the legal definition provided in Art. 41, para. 2, only lit. b or c come into consideration. In this respect, too, the position of the non-combatant member of the armed forces is not better than that of the combatant, to whom Art. 41 AP I applies equally.

As members of the regular armed forces, which non-combatants undoubtedly are, they are required to wear a uniform by Art. 44, para. 7 AP I. As mentioned above, this rule had already been accepted at the Brussels Conference of 1874 as also applying to non-combatants in customary law; it has not subsequently been changed through any contrary, generally recognized practice.

---

[19] See K. Ipsen, *Die 'offene Stadt'*, 153 ff.

Ipsen

3. *Competence for categorizing combatant and non-combatant members of the armed forces.* International law does not determine which state organ must decide upon the classification of persons as combatant or non-combatant members of the armed forces. International law accepts the national decision as a factual precondition, just as it accepts an organizational decision by state organs as to which of its armed agencies are to be qualified as 'armed forces' within the meaning of Art. 4A No. 1 GC III or Art. 43, para. 1 AP I in the event of an international armed conflict. The definition of armed forces in international law, therefore, follows the definition of, respectively, national armed forces as laid down by acts of state and the definition of armed forces of non-state parties to a conflict being recognized as subjects of international law.

4. *The constitutional and legal situation in the Federal Republic of Germany.* In the Federal Republic of Germany, the required organizational decision is recorded in the constitution: in Art. 87a, para. 1 of the German Basic Law. According to this, the term 'armed forces' includes the military instrument of the Federal Republic of Germany organized in the *Bundeswehr* (Federal Armed Forces), which is divided into the army, the air force, and the navy as well as the territorial forces and the central military institutions of the *Bundeswehr*.[20] The administration of the *Bundeswehr*, including the associated but organizationally and substantially independent administration of justice, does *not* belong to the 'armed forces' as defined by the constitution. According to the constitution (Art. 87b German Basic Law), it is a federal administration with own institutions and fields of activity, and with a sphere of activities limited by the constitution.[21] This constitutional regulation corresponds to the political will of the legislator who amended the constitution, according to which the future military organization should make absolutely clear that the administration of the *Bundeswehr* must be a federal non-military administration.[22] As the preliminary parliamentary work which led to this solution reveals, the main political goal was the 'demilitarization' of the military administration. The consequences of this in international law were secondary considerations or were ignored completely. There have been attempts to include members of the *Bundeswehr* administration in an international legal definition of armed forces.[23] These attempts were bound to fail, because the organizational decision provided by the constitution clearly separates the *Bundeswehr* and its administration and defines as 'armed forces' in the international legal sense only the *Bundeswehr* itself.

The organizational decision as to which persons belong to the armed forces (i.e. to the *Bundeswehr*) has been made by federal legislation in accordance with the constitution. Accordingly—as laid down by a law determining their status (*Soldatengesetz*)—members of the armed forces of the Federal Republic of Germany are the soldiers of the *Bundeswehr*. With the exception of medical personnel, they have combatant status. Apart from the soldiers of the *Bundeswehr*— and except for s. 64 Federal Border Guard Act, which remains in force despite

[20] See K. Ipsen, BK, Art. 87a, note 13.
[21] Confirming this, see *BVerfGE* 48, 177 ff.
[22] BT-Drucks. II/275.
[23] See Moritz, 49 ff.; Juschka, 145 ff., 173 ff.

attempts on the part of the police union to revise it—no organizational decision in connection with the granting of combatant status has been made.

For constitutional reasons, it is not possible to confer non-combatant status on members of the *Bundeswehr* administration simply by incorporating them into the armed forces. The division between Arts. 87a, para. 1 and 87b para. 1 German Basic Law bars the federal legislator from altering the organizational decision made on the constitutional level by passing a simple federal law which incorporates either all or some categories of members of the *Bundeswehr* administration into the armed forces.

It follows from all the above that under the present state of the constitution of the Federal Republic of Germany, there are no persons who are—as provided for by Section 313—at the same time 'judges, government officials and blue-collar workers' and also non-combatant members of the armed forces. Members of the aforementioned categories of the civil service are public servants either under public law or as employees of the Federal Republic of Germany—even if they carry out their assigned activities with or in the armed forces. They are not members of the armed forces. Judges, government officials, and blue-collar workers can only obtain the status of non-combatants, if they are first made members of the armed forces, because 'non-combatants' only exist within, not outside of, the armed forces. Therefore, it would be desirable to introduce a regulation which—similar to s. 64, para. 1 Federal Border Guard Act—determines that persons of those groups occupying positions within the armed forces are to be deemed members of the armed forces of the Federal Republic of Germany in the event of an international armed conflict. This regulation would have to be introduced by statute. According to the precedents of the Federal Constitutional Court, the legislator must make all essential decisions himself.[24] Whether a decision is essential or not is determined in particular in the light of its effect upon the basic rights of the individual. It is obvious that a measure which would make civilians such as judges, government officials, and blue-collar workers members of the armed forces would have no less effect upon those basic rights than, for example, conscription for military service. If the barrier between Arts. 87a, para. 1 and 87b, para. 1 of the German Basic Law is to be overcome, then simultaneous membership of the armed forces and retention of the status of judge, government official, or blue-collar worker can only be achieved by means of a law which expressly regulates this double status. Such a solution, however, may be regarded as unconstitutional because of the barrier referred to above.

Hence the easiest solution, realizable already under the present state of the legislation, would be to create military positions for those judges, government officials, and blue-collar workers who will definitely be required as members of the armed forces in the event of a conflict, and to fill these (civilian) positions in peacetime with persons who will become members of the armed forces through mobilization order in the event of a conflict. The mobilization order could, on the national legal level, explicitly determine the non-combatant status of these persons. If this legally acceptable method is not adopted, membership in the armed forces is ruled out by

---

[24] *BVerfGE* 49, 89 (126).

Ipsen

the present state of German law which, concerning the civilian personnel working in the armed forces, can only be altered by statute, and which is laid down by the constitution with regard to the *Bundeswehr* administration. To this extent Section 313 does not accomplish the result it intends.

5. *Medical and religious personnel.* The evolution over the last 130 years of the special position of medical and religious personnel in international law precludes their simply being listed in the category of 'non-combatants'. It is true that the Russian draft convention, which formed the basis of the Brussels Conference of 1874, classified members of the religious and medical service (in addition to quartermasters, the military judiciary, and other branches of the military administration) as non-combatants. However, persons employed in hospitals and ambulances and chaplains were immediately differentiated in that they were acknowledged to be neutral when they fell into the hands of the adversary. The draft expressly reiterated in another context that chaplains and members of the medical service could not be made prisoners of war but instead would, in accordance with Articles I–III of the Geneva Red Cross Convention of 22 August 1864, enjoy the right of neutrality. As negotiations progressed, references to combatants and non-combatants were directed solely at the fact that both have prisoner of war status in the event of capture. Thus the wording of the later Art. 3 HagueReg was laid down. It was, therefore, recognized by 1874 at the latest that the legal status of medical and religious personnel was determined by Geneva Law, i.e. by the Geneva Red Cross Convention of 1864. These regulations became more concrete through subsequent Red Cross Conventions. However, at the Brussels Conference, medical and religious personnel had already been excluded from the category of non-combatants defined by the later Art. 3 HagueReg.

314 **Members of the medical service and religious personnel (chaplains) attached to the armed forces are also non-combatants. Medical personnel and chaplains who have fallen into the hands of the adversary shall be detained only in so far as it is necessary for assisting prisoners of war. Although they shall not be deemed prisoners of war, they shall be granted the same legal protection (Arts. 28 and 30 GC I; Arts. 36 and 37 GC II; Art. 33 GC III).**

The first sentence of this Section attempts, despite the historical development of medical and religious personnel in international law as described above, to classify these persons simply as one of several categories of non-combatants. Furthermore, the intended connection with Section 313 ('. . . are *also* non-combatants') might give the erroneous impression that medical and religious personnel are a secondary group of non-combatants. The fact, however, that medical and religious personnel have been expressly removed from the scope of regulation of Hague Law and left within the scope of Geneva law since 1874 or earlier should actually have led to the inclusion in this Chapter of a Part III—Religious and Medical Personnel—of equal importance to part II—Non-Combatants. In its present form this Manual makes a distinction which had already been abandoned in Brussels by 1874.

Ipsen

The chain of provisions protecting medical and religious personnel laid down within the Red Cross Conventions since 1864 shows how inappropriate it is to include these personnel in the category of non-combatants. Art. II of the Red Cross Convention of 1864 granted medical personnel and chaplains 'the benefit of . . . neutrality'. Art. IX of the subsequent Convention of 1906 determines that medical personnel and religious personnel assigned to the armed forces 'shall be respected and protected under all circumstances'; they were not to be considered as prisoners of war. Art. IX of the Convention of 1929 included a similar regulation. Finally, the currently applicable Articles 24 and 28 GC I, 36 GC II, and 33 GC III all contain regulations with identical contents. From this it can be concluded that medical personnel belonging to the armed forces enjoy an international legal status under Geneva Law which has been developed with rare consistency and continuity. This status has not been fundamentally altered since 1864. It has, decisively, never constituted a subcategory of 'non-combatants'. Religious personnel are normally not even members of the armed forces, which is an indispensable requirement for non-combatants. All of the aforementioned Geneva Conventions assume that protected religious personnel are 'attached' to the armed forces, but not necessarily members thereof. The inconsistency of the Manual is evident: the first sentence of Section 313 classifies those persons who are members of the armed forces but do not have a combat task as non-combatants. However, in the first sentence of Section 314 there is already a divergence from this basic definition, as religious personnel are not included in the category of non-combatants, even though, as laid down correctly, these personnel are not members of but are merely *attached to* the armed forces. Consequently, it should be emphasized that medical and religious personnel have a special primary status under Geneva Law which has been developed since 1864 through all of the Geneva Conventions to the status which is now set out in GC I–III.

The second sentence of Section 314, according to which medical personnel and chaplains who have fallen into the hands of the adversary may only be detained to assist prisoners of war of their own party to the conflict, is a rule of international law which was already contained in the Red Cross Convention of 1864. This Convention ensured that the medical and religious personnel who had fallen into the hands of the adversary could either continue their duties or return to the units to which they belonged (Art. III). According to the Convention of 1906 these personnel were permitted to continue carrying out their functions under the direction of the detaining power, but were to be returned to their own country or army when their assistance was no longer required (Art. XII). The convention of 1929 contained a regulation to the same effect (Art. XII). Thus the regulations applicable today (Art. 28–30 GC I; Art. 37 GC II; Art. 33 GC III) are an uninterrupted continuation of the protection of the Geneva Law, although according to Art. 33 GC III, the return of the protected persons to their state or army of origin does not require an agreement between the parties to the conflict, an agreement which the parties are obliged to negotiate. The legal finding that members of the medical and religious personnel are not prisoners of war can also be found in all the Red Cross Conventions since 1864. As shown above (Section 313), this has led to the exclusion of medical and religious personnel from the provisions of Hague Law, which is logically correct. It is consistent that Art.

Ipsen

21 HagueReg in connection with this protection refers to the Geneva Law. This state of the law has remained unchanged. With regard to the protection of medical and religious personnel who have fallen into the hands of the adversary, the antecedents of the four Geneva Conventions of 1949 maintained the obligation upon the detaining power under all circumstances to respect and protect those personnel, even those who fell into their power. Art. 33 GC III specifies this obligation to protect by guaranteeing to the members of medical and religious personnel all the benefits and protections of this Convention as well as 'all facilities necessary' to provide for the medical care of, and religious ministration to, prisoners of war. In this respect the legal position of medical and religious personnel exceeds the best possible treatment available under GC III.

6. *The right of self-defence of the non-combatant and of medical and religious personnel.* Members of these three categories are in different situations, from the point of view of international law, when they themselves are the object of an attack by combatants of the adverse party. In general the following has been laid down.

315 **Non-combatants, too, have the right to defend themselves or others against attacks contrary to international law. Medical personnel and chaplains are allowed to bear and use small arms (pistols, rifles, or sub-machine-guns) for this purpose (Art. 22 No. 1 GC I; Art. 35 No. 1 GC II; Art. 13 para. 2 lit. a AP I). This presupposes a national authorization for the handling of fire arms and ammunition, which has been granted generally to the medical personnel of the Federal Armed Forces (see s. 2 of the General Administration Directive of FMOD Relating to the Law on the Purchase, Possession, and Carrying of Fire Arms [*Allgemeine Verwaltungsvorschrift des BMVg zum Waffengesetz*, VMB 1 1989, s. 174]).**

a) The first sentence of this Section requires correction as its present form could lead to the erroneous conclusion that non-combatants are as widely protected by international law against attacks by combatants of the adverse party as medical and religious personnel; that such attacks are therefore contrary to international law; and that non-combatants must therefore only protect themselves against attacks contravening international law. However, as non-combatants are members of the armed forces, which represent a military objective against which international law permits armed acts, they can certainly be the object of attacks consistent with international law applicable in international armed conflict. In such a case non-combatants, as members of the armed forces, are naturally authorized to defend themselves. Thus the non-combatants' right of self-defence is not restricted to those attacks which involve prohibited methods and means of warfare, such as a violation of the prohibition of perfidy (Art. 37 AP I) or of the obligation to protect an enemy *hors de combat* (Art. 41). In contrast to the applicable rules of Geneva Law regarding self-defence of medical personnel, Hague Law contains no express regulation about the right of self-defence of non-combatants. However, since membership in the armed forces according to Art. 43, para. 2 AP I generally leads to the authorization of combatants to take part in hostilities, the denial of this authorization to participate, which in any event is mere domestic law, should be regarded as obsolete if non-combatants created by a national legal act (and not by international law) themselves become the object of an attack. If they defend themselves against such an attack, they take a direct part in hostilities, which, by virtue of Art. 43, para. 2 AP I, they are permitted to do as members of the armed forces. In summary, this means: an attack against a member of the armed forces who is classified by a national legal act as a non-combatant activates the entitlement of every member of the armed forces (except medical and religious personnel) to take a direct part in hostilities. The attack activates their latent combatant status. The first sentence of Section 315 must therefore be understood to mean that non-combatants are authorized to defend themselves and others against any attack.

b) The situation regarding medical personnel is different. They are protected by the absolute rule—continuously repeated by the Geneva Conventions—of respect and protection 'under all circumstances' against *every* attack. An attack against medical personnel is, therefore, always contrary to international law. Beginning with the Red Cross Convention of 1906 (in Art. VIII No. 1), it is expressly laid down that medical personnel may be armed and may use their weapons for their own defence or for the defence of the wounded and sick entrusted to them. Art. 13, para. 2 lit. a AP I, therefore, merely confirms the law which has already long been in force when it stipulates that medical personnel 'are to be equipped with small-arms for their own defence or for that of the wounded and sick in their charge'. The firearms listed in Section 315 (pistols, rifles, or sub-machine-guns) are clearly small-arms. As is correctly noted in Section 315, on the national level an Administrative Directive of FMOD Relating to the Law on the Purchase, Possession, and Carrying of Fire Arms, which puts the law into concrete terms, is sufficient to implement this authorization in international law.

c) The legal situation concerning religious personnel is more complex. As far as their protection is concerned, the position is the same as for medical personnel; both must be respected and protected under all circumstances, which also means that every attack against religious personnel is contrary to international law. The reference in Section 315 to both medical and religious personnel and to the rules of Geneva Law applicable to the arming and authorization of self-defence for *medical* personnel should not be taken to mean that the regulations also authorize the arming and self-defence of *religious* personnel. Since the Red Cross Convention of 1906 provisions for arming and for self-defence apply exclusively to medical personnel, not to religious personnel. This is systematically confirmed by all relevant Conventions since 1906, all of which regulate the arming and the right of self-defence of medical personnel under the rubric of 'Medical Units and Establishments' and the protection of religious personnel under the rubric 'Personnel'. Finally it must be noted that these Conventions generally classify medical personnel as *members* of the armed forces, but religious personnel as chaplains '*attached to* the armed forces'. According to the legal definition in Art. 8 lit. d AP I, religious personnel may include military and civilian persons. They must, however, be exclusively engaged in the work of their ministry and at least attached to the armed

Ipsen

forces. Thus the regulations about arming and the right of self-defence applicable for medical personnel do not apply to religious personnel.

In addition, the national authorization to use firearms and ammunition (at least in the Federal Republic of Germany) presently applies only to medical units, and not to (civilian) religious personnel—leaving aside the question of whether the task of clergymen and their own perception of their role would be compatible with the carrying of a sub-machine-gun or rifle on their shoulder. Disregarding the fact that a possible authorization of religious personnel to carry weapons has not yet been regulated by national law, in international law it can be stated that, according to the principle of reciprocity, members of religious personnel are permitted to defend themselves against attacks which contravene international law if they are willing and able to do so.

7. *Doubts about the status of persons who have been captured.* The uncertainty of the primary status of a person who has participated directly in hostilities and has fallen into the hands of the adverse party usually involves the problem of whether that person is a combatant or a civilian. This problem of differentiation is determined as follows.

316   **Should any doubt arise as to whether a person who has taken part in hostilities and fallen into the hands of the adversary shall be deemed a combatant or non-combatant*), that person shall continue to be treated as a prisoner of war until such time as his status has been determined by a competent tribunal (Art. 5, para. 2 GC III; Art. 45, para. 1 AP I).**

This Section should not be taken to mean that all groups of persons listed in Sections 313 and 314 fall under the term of non-combatants. Instead, as shown above at Section 313, the correct distinction is between non-combatants on one hand and members of medical and religious personnel on the other. Here the following applies.

a) If there are doubts as to whether persons who have participated directly in hostilities are combatants or members of medical or religious personnel, then the interim treatment of these persons as prisoners of war until a tribunal has decided the matter (according to Art. 5, para. 2 GC III and Art. 45, para. 1, 2nd sentence AP I) has no effect on the treatment which GC III eventually prescribes in either case. If the persons are combatants, they are prisoners of war according to Art. 4A No. 1, 2, 3, or 6 GC III; if they are members of medical or religious personnel, then Art. 33, para. 1, 2nd sentence GC III affords them all the benefits and protection of that Convention. Depending on the type and extent of their direct participation in hostilities, the members of medical or religious personnel concerned would have to expect proceedings in accordance with Art. 85 GC III, to determine whether they

---

* *The term 'non-combatant' should be read here as 'civilian', and Section 316 should be moved from the present sub-chapter II (Non-Combatants) to the end of sub-chapter I (Combatants). This correction will also be made in future editions of the German military manual.*

Ipsen

were merely defending themselves as permitted, or whether they had committed armed acts beyond self-defence, which are not permitted.

b) However, if persons who participated directly in hostilities fall into the hands of the adversary in circumstances where there is doubt as to whether they, as members of the armed forces, are combatants or members of the armed forces who, by virtue of a legal act of their party to the conflict, are *not* authorized to take a direct part in hostilities, then this has no effect at all on their status as prisoners of war. It is abundantly clear in Art. 3 HagueReg that in the event of capture, combatants and non-combatants alike are entitled to prisoner of war status. This legal situation was not altered either by Art. 4A No. 1 GC III or by Arts. 43, 44, para. 1 AP I. Hence from the point of view of a party to the conflict who has captured a member of the enemy's armed forces having participated directly in hostilities, it is of no legal relevance whether the captive is a combatant or a non-combatant. In either case prisoner of war status unambiguously applies. Non-combatant members of the armed forces will not even be subject to proceedings in accordance with Art. 85 GC III on account of perfidy, since they are not classified as civilians uninvolved in the fighting within the meaning of Art. 37, para. 1 lit. c AP I, nor as having any other protected status within the meaning of lit. d. As mentioned above, international law does not provide any special protection for non-combatant members of the armed forces. Therefore, it does not matter whether members of the armed forces are combatants or non-combatants: in both cases they acquire prisoner of war status if they fall into the hands of the adverse party.

c) Art. 5, para. 2 GC III and Art. 45, para. 1 AP I are intended to apply when persons directly involved in the hostilities are captured and there are doubts as to whether they are combatants or *civilians*. In particular, the aforementioned cases of minimal distinction (cf. Section 309) could raise such doubts.

8. *Criminal punishment for direct participation in hostilities.* If during direct participation in hostilities, members of the armed forces (combatant or non-combatant) abide by the international law applicable in international armed conflicts then they cannot be punished, either by their own party to the conflict or by the competent tribunals of the adversary, in the event of their capture. This is the essential message of the first half of the sentence of the following Section.

A captive shall not be prosecuted for his participation in hostilities unless he has   317
been positively identified as an unlawful combatant.

a) The context of the first phrase shows that this Section refers solely to those prisoners of war who are either members of the armed forces (whether combatant or non-combatant) under Art. 4A No. 1 or combatants under Art. 4A Nos. 2, 3, or 6 GC III, thereby falling under the new comprehensive notion of armed forces of Art. 43, para. 1 AP I. The other two categories mentioned in Art. 4A as being entitled to prisoner of war status in the hands of the adversary (civilians accompanying the armed forces without actually being members thereof, and members of crews of the

Ipsen

merchant navy and of civil aircraft) are *not* entitled to take a direct part in hostilities. In the event of such participation as unlawful combatants (Section 302 above) they must expect to be prosecuted in the same manner as all other civilians who are prohibited from taking a direct part in hostilities.

b) Persons whose prisoner of war status is unquestionable because they belong to the categories listed in Art. 4A Nos. 1, 2, 3, or 6 GC III and who have engaged in any activity contrary to international law must also expect to be prosecuted while in the hands of the adversary. This follows from Art. 85 GC III. That provision guarantees convicted prisoners of war the benefits listed in GC III, i.e. the right of appeal, notification of the judgment to the Protecting Power in accordance with Art. 107, a (humane) enforcement procedure in accordance with Art. 108, and—in the event of a death penalty—suspension of the execution for a period of six months following notification of the Protecting Power according to Art. 101. If, however, it is clearly established by the courts that the person in question is not entitled to prisoner of war status according to Art. 4A Nos. 1, 2, 3, or 6 or Art. 43 in conjunction with Art. 44, para. 1 AP I, then his or her direct participation in the hostilities was also unauthorized. He or she is thus an unlawful combatant and responsible under criminal law for all acts committed against the adversary. The detaining power is obliged under international law to afford to every prosecuted person of the adverse party to a conflict the treatment which is more favourable either under GC III or under Art. 75 AP I.

9. *Sentencing and punishments based on a judgment.* The punishment of criminal acts within the meaning of substantive criminal law is subject to special conditions imposed by international law (as for the punishment of disciplinary offences, see Section 726 below).

318   **No sentence may be passed and no penalty may be executed except pursuant to a conviction pronounced by an impartial and regularly constituted court respecting the generally recognized principles of regular judicial procedure (Art. 84 GC III; Art. 75, para. 4 AP I).**

This section repeats word for word the main contents of Art. 75, para. 4, 1st sentence AP I, which in turn corresponds to the special regulation for prisoners of war contained in Art. 84 GC III. Thus the principle of more favourable treatment laid down in Art. 75, para. 1 AP I applies here as well. Art. 75, para. 4 only applies—to fill in the gaps, as it were—in so far as it provides for more favourable treatment of prisoners of war than the applicable provisions of Chapter III GC III in respect of the sentencing and execution of punishments. In particular, in Articles 86 and 99 to 108, Chapter III sets down a standard of treatment not less favourable than that in Art. 75, para. 4. Thus, according to the general rule of interpretation of Art. 31, para. 3 lit. c Vienna Convention on the Law of Treaties, this regulation, which to a large extent was modelled on the judicial guarantees in Articles 14 and 15 of the International Covenant on Civil and Political Rights, must be referred to in interpreting Chapter III GC III. Therefore the principle '*nulla poena sine lege*' contained in Art. 99 GC III is specified by Art. 75, para. 4 lit. c, just as the procedural guarantees of Art. 105 GC III are put into concrete terms through lit. d (presumption of innocence until proven guilty according to the law), lit. e (the right of persons charged to be present at trial), and lit. f (no compulsion to confess guilt). With regard to the execution of a punishment, Art. 108 GC III contains detailed rules which are not found in Art. 75 AP I.

III. PERSONS ACCOMPANYING THE ARMED FORCES

Persons accompanying the armed forces have, by definition, the primary status of civilians. The following is therefore correct.

Persons who accompany the armed forces without being members thereof, such   319
as war correspondents, members of labour units, or of services responsible for the
welfare of the soldiers, shall not be deemed combatants. If they fall into the power
of the adversary, they shall become prisoners of war (Art. 4A No. 4 GC III).

    Civilians accompanying the armed forces are formally protected by the obligation of the armed forces which they accompany to provide them with identity cards, an example of which is contained in Annex IV A of GC III. Substantially, the members of this category are protected as civilians. The function for which they (as civilians) accompany the armed forces must be recorded on the identity card. Their function should be stated in such a manner that they cannot be suspected of having taken a direct part in the hostilities. Art. 50, para. 1, 2nd sentence AP I states clearly that 'in any case of doubt as to whether a person is a civilian, that person shall be considered to be a civilian'. However, if a person accompanying the armed forces is suspected of combatant behaviour, and if this suspicion is confirmed, then this regulation, which was intended as a protective provision, has adverse repercussions on the person in question. If persons accompanying the armed forces conduct themselves according to their status as civilians then they run the risk of collateral injury. Conversely, the responsible military leader who attacks a military objective containing civilians accompanying armed forces must carry out the precautionary measures stipulated by Art. 57 (especially in para. 2 lit. a) in order to keep collateral injuries to the civilians accompanying the armed forces to a minimum. If civilians accompanying the armed forces fall into the hands of the adversary then they attain prisoner of war status in accordance with Art. 4A No. 4 GC III. Apart from merchant navy or civil aircraft crews, civilians accompanying the armed forces are therefore the only category of civilians without combatant status who attain the status of prisoner of war.

Ipsen

IV. SPECIAL FORCES

In past international armed conflicts, long-distance reconnaissance patrols (with or without combat tasks) and task forces on remote missions against military objectives located to the rear of the adversary have repeatedly raised the problem of whether members of armed forces involved in such actions could permissibly be camouflaged in plain clothes or in the uniform of the enemy, at least during the phase preceding military engagement. The following clear position is adopted in this regard.

320 **It shall be lawful for combatants recognizable as such (by their uniform, insignia, etc.) to participate in raids, acts of sabotage, and other attacks carried out by special forces in the enemy's hinterland or in forward areas. Combatants who commit such acts wearing plain clothes or the uniform of the adversary are liable to be punished. They shall nevertheless have the right to a regular judicial procedure (Arts. 82 ff. GC III; Art. 75, para. 4 AP I).**

This regulation adopts a clear position towards a question which remains controversial even today. During the Second World War, the camouflaging of long-distance reconnaissance patrols or of task forces wearing plain clothes or the uniform of the adversary was regarded as perfidious and was universally accepted as being prohibited (the prohibition against the misuse of the adversary's uniform was already expressly contained in Art. 23 lit. f HagueReg).[25] After the Second World War, the acquittal in the *Skorzeny* case led to some legislation adopting a partial rather than a total prohibition against using the adversary's uniform as camouflage. The case concerned the deployment of commando forces to the German *Wehrmacht* in connection with the Ardennes offensive in December 1944 against military objectives to the rear of western Allied forces, during which the advance was carried out in the enemy's uniform, the actual fighting being carried out in the uniform of the *Wehrmacht*. The conclusion drawn from the case that such camouflaging is permitted under international law was, appropriately, countered with the argument that such generalization is incompatible with both the ordinary meaning and the historical origins of Art. 23 lit. f HagueReg.[26] However, the same controversy arose again during the Geneva Conference on the Reaffirmation and Development of International Humanitarian Law Applicable in Armed Conflicts. Several states supported a clear and universal prohibition, allowing no exceptions, while other states were of the opinion that only the use of the enemy's uniform or other insignia for camouflage and to make operations easier should be prohibited. The compromise now contained in Art. 39(2) is—as can be seen—closer to this second position.

If Section 320 is interpreted correctly, i.e. in connection with Section 308, 2nd sentence, then the meaning of this regulation is unequivocal: participation in

[25] In this connection see the detailed remarks in Fleck, *Beiträge*, 118 ff.
[26] As Fleck states correctly in *Beiträge*, 119 ff.

Ipsen

armed acts causing harm by special forces in the forward area or to the rear of the adversary is a permitted act provided that the members of the armed forces involved can be identified by their uniform (in so far as they are members of the regular armed forces) or by other clearly recognizable distinctive emblems. If this requirement, which derives from the basic rule of distinction contained in Art. 44, para. 3, 1st sentence AP I, is not fulfilled, then the following alternative legal consequences apply, depending on the type of camouflage used. If the members of special command units wear plain clothes and if the other conditions are fulfilled, then there is a violation of the prohibition of perfidy under Art. 37, para. 1, lit. c AP I, unless all the conditions of the special situation envisaged in Art. 44, para. 3, 2nd sentence AP I, i.e. the ordered minimum degree of distinction (see the comments to Section 309 above), are met. It is, therefore, possible that the legal result will be the forfeiture of the combatant status provided by Art. 44, para. 4, 1st sentence AP I. If, on the other hand, members of armed forces involved in special units wear the uniform of the adverse party to the conflict, then they violate the prohibition under Art. 39, para. 2 AP I. The alternative contained in this norm (as a result of the compromise described above) will normally be present cumulatively: members of commando forces wear the uniform of the enemy above all in order to 'shield, favour, [and] protect . . . military operations'. If they fall into the hands of the adversary prior to their attack against the chosen military objective, then as a rule the wearing of the enemy's uniform provides the intended prohibited purpose. This result is supported by a further consideration: Art. 44, para. 3, 2nd sentence lit. b AP I describes the special situation wherein arms are required to be carried openly during 'a military deployment preceding the launching of an attack' and thus clearly equates this phase with an act of military operations. As described above (at Section 109), the Federal Republic of Germany interprets such activity as including any movement towards a location from which an attack is to be launched. This legal position clearly falls within the scope of interpretation of the applicable provision of the Protocol. Consequently a military deployment preceding an attack or an advance of commando forces *as a whole* is deemed to be an act of military operations within the meaning of Art. 39, para. 2 AP I, and thus invariably the wearing of the enemy's uniform will be deemed to be for the prohibited purpose of shielding, favouring, or protecting that military operation. If members of the armed forces involved in special units are caught wearing the uniform of the adverse party to the conflict 'while engaging in attacks', then the violation of the prohibition contained in Art. 39, para. 2 AP I is evident.

Undoubtedly, therefore, the Federal Republic of Germany is acting legitimately in classifying camouflage in plain clothes or the enemy's uniform by members of special units of armed forces as a violation of the applicable norms of international law, for which legally permissible sanctions may be imposed. The framework set out in international law for such sanctions has been dealt with in detail above (see Section 318).

V. SPIES

In the light of the sophistication of modern-day reconnaissance with electronic instruments, especially satellite-supported reconnaissance, it may come as a surprise that 'spies' are dealt with in the Manual under a rubric comparable to that dedicated to combatants. Apart from the fact that most states do not (as yet) have at their disposal the highest standard of reconnaissance technology, international law applicable in international armed conflict must take a position on the issues of who is a spy, and how spies may be treated.

321   **Spies are persons who clandestinely, or under false pretences, i.e. not wearing the uniform of their armed forces, gather information in the territory controlled by the adversary. Even if they are members of armed forces, they do not have the right to prisoner of war status. Persons who fall into the hands of the adversary while engaged in espionage shall be liable to punishment (Arts. 29–31 HagueReg).**

The definition of spies in the first sentence of this regulation stems from Art. 29, para. 1 HagueReg and Art. 46, para. 2 AP I. For this reason the individual elements of this definition must be determined according to the HagueReg or AP I. In so far as the definition speaks of 'persons', these can have the primary status of either civilians or combatants. Art. 46 AP I, contained in the section 'Combatant and Prisoner-of-War Status', only applies to persons who are members of the armed forces, and says nothing about spies whose primary status is that of civilians. In contrast the definition contained in Art. 29, para. 1 HagueReg applies to both civilians and members of the armed forces who do not wear the uniform of their party to the conflict. The first sentence of Section 321 seems to make use of the definition of the HagueReg; however, it is ambiguous in that it explains 'false pretences' as the lack of a uniform 'of their armed forces'. This suggests that only members of armed forces can be meant here, since only they are permitted to wear a uniform. It would be an unacceptably narrow interpretation of the first sentence of Section 321 to define spies simply as members of the armed forces who clandestinely or under false pretences gather information in the territory controlled by the adversary. For one thing, spies can—as stated above—also have the primary status of civilians, which means that, as a rule, they are in any event not entitled to prisoner of war status if they fall into the hands of the adversary. On the other hand, persons within the meaning of this regulation could have the primary status of civilians and, at the same time, of persons accompanying the armed forces (see Section 319 above). As such they are certainly entitled to prisoner of war status. Properly understood, therefore, three groups of persons are involved: persons who have the primary status of civilians and who do not become prisoners of war even if they fall into the hands of the adversary; civilians who have the primary status of civilians but who, in the event of their capture by the enemy, attain prisoner of war status in accordance with Art. 4A GC III; and

Ipsen

finally persons who are members of armed forces but who engage in activities described in Art. 29, para. 1 HagueReg, Art. 46, para. 2 AP I without wearing the uniform of their party to the conflict.

As for the requirement regarding location, the Section's phrase 'in the territory controlled by the adversary' makes use of the further requirement of Art. 46, para. 2 AP I (Art. 29, para. 1 HagueReg: zone of operations of a belligerent). This location requirement, therefore, refers to the entire territory held by the party being spied upon, either under sovereign power as state territory or under occupational force as occupied territory.

As for espionage activity, this relates to information gathering which occurs 'clandestinely or under false pretences'. This is the literal formulation used in Art. 29, para. 1 HagueReg, which incidentally is also contained in the Lieber Code (Art. 88) and in the Brussels Declaration of 1874 (Art. 19). The fact that Art. 46, para. 2 AP I does not specify the gathering of information in the same way should not obscure the fact that AP I has left the old law unaltered in this respect. Instead, it follows from the connection between para. 2 (definition) and para. 3 (information gathering on territory occupied by the adversary), where espionage is understood to be an activity carried out under false pretences or deliberately in a clandestine manner, that in this respect the Hague Law has not been altered.

Following these comments it can be stated that espionage activity, i.e. the gathering of information clandestinely or under false pretences, has been construed in the same way from the time of the Lieber Code until the date of AP I.

Spies are not entitled to prisoner of war status even if they are members of the armed forces, persons accompanying the armed forces, or members of merchant navy or civil aircraft crews, and notwithstanding that these categories of persons do without exception acquire prisoner of war status in the hands of the enemy (according to Art. 43, para. 1 AP I in conjunction with Art. 4A Nos. 1–5 GC III) when they are not involved in espionage. As far as members of the armed forces are concerned, this follows explicitly from Art. 46, para. 1 AP I. With regard to the aforementioned civilians who are entitled to prisoner of war status this derives from Art. 29, para. 1 in connection with the *argumentum e contrario* drawn from Art. 31 HagueReg. The fundamental permissibility of punishing spies who have fallen into the hands of the adversary arises from Art. 46, para. 1 AP I and Art. 29, para. 1 HagueReg in conjunction with Art. 30 HagueReg.

Even if captured while engaged in espionage, a spy shall not be punished without   322
prior conviction pursuant to regular judicial proceedings (Art. 30 HagueReg; Art.
75, para. 4 AP I).

The Brussels Declaration of 1874 already contained the rule that a spy who is caught in the act of spying is treated and prosecuted in accordance with the detaining power's applicable laws (Art. 20). The HagueReg has put this into more concrete terms by prohibiting the punishment of spies caught in the act of spying without prior conviction (Art. 30). This judicial guarantee is again made concrete by Art. 75, para. 4 AP I as set out above (at Section 318).

Ipsen

A spy who, after rejoining his own or allied armed forces upon completion of his mission, is subsequently captured by the adversary, shall be treated as a prisoner of war and incur no responsibility for his previous acts of espionage (Art. 31 HagueReg; Art. 46, para. 4 AP I).

This regulation represents a rule already contained in the Brussels Declaration of 1874 (Art. 21) which was adopted almost literally by the two Hague Regulations (HagueReg 1907: Art. 31). This traditional rule has been specified in relation to members of the armed forces who have been engaged in espionage on the territory of the adversary, although not residing there, and who have then returned to a unit or a formation of their own armed forces. This could be the case, for example, if a member of the armed forces who has been active as a spy in an occupied territory joins a long-distance reconnaissance patrol or a commando unit of his own party to the conflict. If he is captured, he shall be deemed to have returned to his armed forces and is entitled to prisoner of war status.

324   **Combatants, such as reconnaissance patrols, who, marked as such, reconnoitre the adversary's area of operations shall not be deemed engaged in espionage (Art. 29, para. 2 HagueReg; Art. 46, para. 2 AP I).**

The substance of this regulation corresponds to Art. 29, para. 2 HagueReg and, furthermore, is a logical legal consequence of the rule contained in the first sentence of Section 321. This Section repeats the broad territorial criteria of AP I (territory controlled by an adverse party) while Section 324 uses the narrower formulation of the HagueReg (zone of operations of the hostile army). This does not mean that long-distance reconnaissance is only permitted within the zone of operation of the hostile army. Rather, Section 324 must be understood as also permitting members of the armed forces (within the meaning of Art. 43, para. 1 AP I) who can be identified as such (as members of the regular armed forces: by their uniform), to gather information in the entire territory controlled by an adverse party to the extent that this is efficient and feasible from a military and tactical point of view. This is expressly confirmed by Art. 46, para. 2 AP I.

A special rule worth noting in this context results from Art. 46, para. 3 AP I, which recognizes the loyalty of a member of armed forces to his own party to the conflict. If a member of armed forces who is a resident of territory occupied by an adverse party gathers information of military value in that territory, then this is not regarded as espionage, unless he gathers information clandestinely or through an act of false pretences. If those characteristics of espionage are met by a member of armed forces who is caught in the act, he may be treated as a spy, as has been the case since the Brussels Declaration.

VI. SPECIAL ASPECTS OF AERIAL AND NAVAL WARFARE

Since the Second Geneva Convention of 1949 there have been no universal international treaties on the law of naval warfare. The same is true of air warfare. However, as shown by the Hague Convention for the Protection of Cultural Property in the Event of Armed Conflict of 1954, and by Art. 49, para. 3 AP I—which makes Section I, Part IV of AP I applicable to any land, air or sea warfare—these dimensions of armed conflicts have not been disregarded. Sections 325 ff. deal only with a limited aspect of air and sea warfare, namely that which concerns combatant and prisoner of war status.

Unlike military ground vehicles, manned military aircraft and ships are required   325
to bear external marks indicating their nationality and military character. Non-
uniformed members of armed forces who take part in hostilities using correctly
marked military aircraft or ships shall remain combatants. When captured by the
adversary they shall prove their military status by an identity card.

A warship is a ship belonging to the naval forces of a state and bearing external marks which distinguish the warship and its nationality (Section 1002 below). Likewise, a military aircraft is defined as an aircraft belonging to the air forces of a state and bearing external military marks distinguishing its nationality. Apart from the controversial issue of warships displaying false flags and emblems during their approach and the obligation to display their own flag before opening fire (Section 1018 below),[27] warships and military aircraft shall be clearly and unambiguously recognizable as military objectives by their external marks. This accords with the requirement of distinction which in the case of ground forces is met by the obligation of the individual combatant to wear uniform or other distinguishing emblems in order to protect the civilian population. Consequently, members of armed forces not wearing uniforms on board a properly marked warship or military aircraft and taking part in hostilities are and remain combatants regardless of this circumstance. Naturally, the same applies to armed forces members on board such warships or military aircraft who, according to national decision, although members of the armed forces are non-combatants. To this extent a cardinal error is included in Section 1017 below, stating (third point): 'The parties to the conflict shall at all times distinguish between combatants and non-combatants'. As proved and explained in detail above (in Sections 301 and 313), both combatants and non-combatants are members of armed forces. If combatants and non-combatants find themselves on board a military aircraft or warship, then the aircraft or ship in question becomes a military objective which the adversary is allowed to attack with the permitted weapons and means of warfare. The adversary cannot—and is not required to—take into consideration the fact that there are non-combatants on board in addition to the combatant crew

---

[27] Cf. Fleck, *Beiträge*, 134 ff.; W. Fenrick, *Military Objectives*, 38; Hegelsom, 16 ff.

(with the exception, of course, of the specially protected medical and religious personnel). Combatants and non-combatants (excluding medical and religious personnel) as armed forces members are military objectives who according to international law may be attacked. In contrast to the false assumption contained in Section 1017, there is clearly *no* duty to distinguish between combatants and non-combatants, for instance during a use of arms against a military aircraft or warship.

If crew members of a military aircraft or warship not in uniform fall into the hands of the adversary, they must prove their membership of the armed forces by displaying an identity card (if necessary with an identification tag).

326   **No aircraft other than military aircraft of the parties to an international armed conflict shall engage in any form of hostilities (Art. 16, para. 1 HRAW 1923).**

The prohibition contained in Art. 16, para. 1 HRAW 1923, that no aircraft other than belligerent military aircraft shall engage in hostilities in any form, never entered into force as a provision of international treaty law, but is regarded as a rule of customary international law (see Section 1016 below). This principle corresponds with Art. 44, para. 3, 1st sentence AP I: 'In order to promote the protection of the civilian population from the effects of hostilities, combatants are obliged to distinguish themselves from the civilian population while they are engaged in an attack or in a military operation preparatory to an attack.' The civilian aircraft is a civilian object which is fully protected in international law by Art. 52, para. 1 AP I. The military aircraft, on the other hand, is a military objective according to Art. 52, para. 2 AP I, must be identifiable, and is permitted to take part directly in military operations, but may also be the object of armed attacks by the adversary.

327   **A military aircraft shall be under the command of a duly commissioned soldier. The crew must be subject to military discipline (Art. 14 HRAW 1923).**

This provision reiterates the contents of Art. 14 HRAW 1923. This requirement of international law, which must be met by the internal organization of the party to the conflict, has been applied to ground forces in various respects (Art. 1 No. 1 HagueReg, Art. 13 No. 2 lit. a GC II, Art. 4A No. 2 lit. a GC III, Art. 43, para. 1 AP I). This principle of customary law takes into account the principle of authorization, which is an essential prerequisite for classification as a combatant (see Section 304 above). If a party to a conflict acts in accordance with international law applicable in international armed conflict through its armed forces as the organ provided for this purpose, then the connection between the armed forces and the state party to the conflict must be guaranteed. This requirement is fulfilled by the chain of command and by a system of military discipline.

328   **No private aircraft, when outside the jurisdiction of its own country, shall be armed in international armed conflict (Art. 16, para. 3 HRAW 1923).**

Ipsen

The term 'private aircraft' obviously refers to 'civilian aircraft' as defined below in Section 1009 (the expression 'private aircraft' is an inaccurate translation of Art. 16, para. 3 HRAW 1923). It is, however, questionable whether this prohibition against arming civilian aircraft, which has not entered into force as treaty law, has become customary law. The correct definition of civilian aircraft as an object which is neither a military nor a public aircraft and 'exclusively' serves the civilian transport of passengers or cargo (see Section 1009 below) conflicts with the permissibility of arming civilian aircraft during an international armed conflict even within the jurisdiction of its own state. In order to establish this limited prohibition as a rule of customary law, proving general state practice and acceptance as law will be extremely difficult. Besides, such a limited prohibition would be of little practical relevance. The arming of a civilian aircraft for the purpose of direct participation in hostilities over the state territory would in any event be incompatible with the principle of distinction which has become customary international law. The purpose of the principle of distinction between combatants and civilians is the protection of the latter. The arming of a civilian aircraft for the purpose of direct participation in military operations (for purposes of attack) can therefore be ruled out from the outset. If one wishes to arm a civilian aircraft within the jurisdiction of its own country in the case of a conflict for the purpose of countering an attack (i.e. in self-defence) then under the present state of technological development this purpose would be better served by equipping the aircraft with electronic defence systems against radar target detection, missile attacks, etc., than by arming it. Thus it is incorrect or at least highly questionable to classify Section 328 as permission in customary international law to arm a civilian aircraft within the jurisdiction of its own country; also, it is of very little practical relevance.

Public non-military aircraft shall be treated as private aircraft (Arts. 5 and 6   329 HRAW 1923). Public aircraft employed for jurisdictional purposes (customs, police) shall also carry papers and bear marks evidencing their non-military character (Art. 4 HRAW 1923). Public aircraft shall be subject to confiscation. Private aircraft shall be made the subject of prize proceedings (Art. 32 HRAW 1923).

This provision deals with the same problem in international law as has occurred in connection with paramilitary or armed law enforcement agencies of a party to a conflict; a problem which has been regulated by Art. 43, para. 3 AP I (see Section 307 above). It follows particularly from Art. 43, para. 3 AP I that members of armed law enforcement agencies of a party to a conflict always have the primary status of civilians unless the party incorporates them into its armed forces and properly notifies the adversary thereof. The inevitable legal result is that the aircraft of armed law enforcement agencies which are not incorporated into the armed forces are civilian objects, just as their members are civilians. Furthermore, it follows that a public non-military aircraft must be marked in order to distinguish it from military aircraft belonging to armed forces.

The statement contained in Section 329 that public aircraft are subject to confiscation whereas private aircraft shall be made the subject of prize proceedings is not consistent either with Art. 32 HRAW 1923 or with customary international law. HRAW 1923, which is not treaty law, lays down in Art. 32 that public non-military aircraft are subject to confiscation 'without prize proceedings'. It is incorrect to conclude *a contrario*, as the authors of Section 329 have obviously done, that prize proceedings are required in the case of civilian aircraft, since HRAW 1923, Chapter VII, clearly differentiates between enemy and neutral private aircraft. Enemy private aircraft 'are liable to capture in all circumstances' (the exact wording of Art. 52). A neutral private aircraft, by contrast, is only liable to capture under certain preconditions (Art. 53). The capture of an aircraft or of the goods on board shall only be brought before a prize court in so far as neutral claims must be heard and determined (Art. 55). If a private aircraft is proven to belong to the adverse party to the conflict, it may even be destroyed after any persons on board have been placed in safety. However, the rules of HRAW 1923 (as expounded so far) may be put aside, for the seven decades following its formulation have not evolved a corresponding state practice and *opinio iuris*. For the most part in international armed conflicts, in particular during the Second World War, public non-military aircraft and private aircraft that had fallen into the power of the adversary have been treated by the adversary power as booty and have been confiscated, without prize proceedings regularly being carried out for civilian aircraft.

With regard to the law of AP I, public non-military aircraft are usually, and civilian aircraft always, civilian objects in the sense of Art. 52, para. 1, 1st sentence AP I and therefore they may neither be attacked nor made the object of reprisals. It could prove difficult to differentiate in cases where public non-military aircraft are used as airborne headquarters of the state leaders; in such a case it would be difficult to exclude such an aircraft from the definition of military objectives in Art. 52, para. 2 AP I.

330 **Special provisions relating to warships are contained in Chapter 10 (Sections 1001 ff.).**

Note that special provisions concerning military, public non-military, and civilian aircraft are contained in the 'Definitions' in Chapter 10.

4

Methods and Means of Combat

Introductory Remarks

1. *Historical Development of the Rules on Warfare and Weapons.* The concern to protect the civilian population, as well as combatants, against excessive and exceptionally cruel violence might have been the beginning of all moral and philosophical attempts to mitigate the horrors of war (Sections 107–22). The ancient civilizations experienced—as did the cultures of the Far East, India, and Islam[1]—religiously motivated efforts to set bounds to the spread of belligerent violence (*supra* Section 107). These attempts to control war, however, succeeded only to a limited degree.

Like all 'modern international law' the contemporary law of war has its roots primarily in European history since the Middle Ages.[2] Christian moral theology and the natural law theories of early modern times made intense efforts to alleviate the sufferings of war but they failed to find real resonance in the belligerent practice of medieval feuds or the religious wars of the sixteenth and seventeenth centuries.[3] The code of honour of European chivalry had imposed certain ritual limits on the permitted forms of combat towards 'equal' enemies, but did little to protect the hostile 'civilian population'.[4] Combat to the prejudice of the peasant and urban population reached a sad climax in the Thirty Years War of 1618–48, when a third of Central Europe's population fell victim to the excesses of unlimited warfare.

This background must be kept in mind when dealing with the desperate endeavours of the classical authors of international law to achieve a legal limitation of belligerent practice. The famous work of Hugo Grotius, *De Jure Belli ac Pacis Libri Tres*, was primarily a treatise on laws of war founded on natural law theory. '*Necessaria ad finem belli*' for Grotius was the ultimate limit of admissible use of force in war.[5] The rise of disciplined professional armies, the monopolization of the means of force in the hands of the developing state bureaucracy, and the `nationalization of war' by the absolutist regimes of Europe were the basic conditions of the ongoing process of 'delimitation' of permissible means of use of force, as well as of the

---

[1] Concerning Japanese and Islamic traditions cf. Adachi, 31–6, and Sultan, 47–60.
[2] See Kunz, 'Kriegsrecht im Allgemeinen', *WVR* II, 354, as well as Kimminich, *Schutz der Menschen in bewaffneten Konflikten*, 16.
[3] See Verzijl, Vol.IX, 131–5.   [4] See Grewe, 141–3.
[5] Cf. Kunz, *loc. cit.*, 354; Draper, *Le développement*, 90.

connected concept that war constitutes a struggle between states but does not create a relation of enmity between its citizens.[6]

The fundamental idea underlying all humanitarian rules on methods and means of warfare has since that time always been the concept of **military necessity**. According to the traditional approach, only the use of those weapons and means of combat which is necessary to attain the military purposes of war, purposes based on the ultimate goal of overpowering the enemy armed forces,[7] are permitted. Accordingly, the civilian population and civilian objects do not constitute legitimate military targets, as was recognized by the Lieber Code of 1863;[8] equally prohibited is the deliberately cruel killing of enemy combatants by weapons which uselessly aggravate suffering, a principle codified at around the same time in the St. Petersburg Declaration of 1868.[9] Because these principles of 'limited warfare' which were formed during the nineteenth century became the nucleus of the (originally customary) laws of war, *opinio juris* and the practice of the nineteenth century have had a decisive impact on the shaping of modern humanitarian law.[10]

Nevertheless, the attempt at codification of these humanitarian rules by the two Hague Peace Conferences of 1899 and 1907,[11] proved unsuccessful. The Hague Regulations were scarcely ever applicable as treaty law, due to the extreme form of the general participation clause.[12] Moreover, the substantive provisions of the Hague Regulations proved to be too cautious, and in a sense also fragmentary, since to a large degree they were oriented towards the problems of the past. Art. 22 Hague Regulations had of course explicitly settled the basic principle that 'The right of belligerents to adopt means of injuring the enemy is not unlimited' , and in Art. 23 the Hague Regulations had prohibited the use of poison and poisoned weapons as a means of warfare, as well as the employment of 'arms, projectiles, or material calculated to cause unnecessary suffering'. The same article also stated that it was prohibited 'to destroy or seize the enemy's property, unless such destruction or seizure be imperatively demanded by the necessities of war'. The proper prohibition of indiscriminate warfare, however, had only found a rather imperfect echo in the treaty provisions on the laws of war; Art. 25 Hague Regulations merely prohibited the 'attack or bombardment, by whatever means, of towns, villages, dwellings, or buildings which are undefended'. The most important achievement of the Hague Conferences was probably the so-called 'Martens clause' which was included in the Preamble of the Fourth Hague Convention, a dynamic reference to customary law not affected by the Conventions and to the 'principles of the law of nations, as they result from the usages established among civilized peoples, from the laws of humanity, and the dictates of public conscience'.[13]

---

[6] Cf. Grewe, 247–54, 428–9 and Best, 53–9.   [7] Kunz, *loc. cit.*, 355.

[8] Cf. Pilloud/Pictet, ICRC *Commentary*, 585 (paras. 1823–4) and Parks, *Air Force Law Review* 32 (1990), 7–8.

[9] See Kunz, *Kriegsrecht im Allgemeinen*, 354; Sandoz, *Des armes interdites*, 16–22; Schindler, *RDMilG* 21 (1982), 24, and in particular detail Kalshoven, *Recueil des Cours* 191 (1985 II), 205–13.

[10] See in particular Best, 128–215.

[11] Draper, *Le développement*, 92–3; Parks, *Air Force Law Review* 32 (1990), 8–20 (esp. 19); Sassòli, 247–50.

[12] See Geck, *WVR I*, 28–9; Bothe, 'Land Warfare, *EPIL* 3, 240; Kalshoven, *Recueil des Cours* 191 (1985 II), 292–3.

[13] Strebel, 'Martens Clause', *EPIL* 3, 252–3; Münch, *ZaöRV* 36 (1976), 347–73.

The most serious problem of rapidly developing modern warfare soon proved to be the use of the air force. In less than three decades the air weapon became an important military instrument. An early attempt to regulate the ensuing problems of air warfare were the Hague Air Warfare Rules of 1923.[14] They failed, however, because the consent of the states concerned was lacking; this abortive attempt never found a successor, and the (draft) Hague Air Rules unfortunately remained without a parallel. In addition to the frustration of attempts to codify the rules of air warfare, technical developments in warfare on land (the emergence of gas warfare is an example) brought increased risks for the civilian population in its wake.

World War II finally demonstrated the immense discrepancy between the noble but lofty principles of customary law and a practice which had been barbarized by technological changes and ideological polarization.[15] The killing of civilians and widespread destruction of civilian objects (in particular at the Eastern, Russian, front and in the territories occupied by Nazi Germany) took place on a massive scale, while air warfare was taken to horrifying excesses, consigning almost to oblivion the basic principle that the civilian population should be protected as far as possible.[16] In World War I civilian casualties amounted to some 5 per cent of those killed, whereas in World War II they rose to nearly 50 per cent.[17]

The indiscriminate use of the air force, which made terrorizing the civilian population the dominant purpose of air warfare, threatened to bury all restrictions on the use of force which were derived from the guiding principle of military necessity.[18] Unleashed by the German side, the practice of total disdain for all the traditional customary principles quickly became a widespread practice of all parties.[19] At the instigation of the Allied Powers the violation of the principle of discrimination was excluded from the charges brought at the Nuremberg trials.[20]

The main question concerning the regulation of weapons and means of warfare, an adjustment of warfare to the principles of military necessity and humanity, was subsequently also excluded from the work of the Red Cross meetings which preceded the Geneva Conventions, although the Geneva Red Cross Conventions of 1949 made an effort to regulate most of the problems that had arisen in the wake of World War II (and to fill the gaps which had become obvious in earlier treaties).[21] The Fourth Geneva Convention developed a rather detailed legal regime for the problems of military occupation, but the questions of possible limits on air warfare and on arms that cause unnecessary suffering (which were at least as delicate as the

---

[14] Concerning the Hague Air Rules, cf. Spetzler, 156–7; Randelzhofer, *Flächenbombardement*, 475–7; Verzijl, Vol.IX, 328–31; Spieker, *HuV-I* 3 (1990), 134–8; Parks, *Air Force Law Review* 32 (1990), 25–36; Sassòli, 252–4; Hanke, *RIC* 75 (1993), 13–49.

[15] Concerning this problem see in detail Parks, *Air Force Law Review* 32 (1990), 50–4.

[16] See esp. Sassòli, 257–66.

[17] Schindler, *L'évolution du droit de la guerre*, 28; Randelzhofer, *Flächenbombardement*, 471.

[18] Best, *Humanity in Warfare*, 262–85.

[19] See esp. Randelzhofer, *Flächenbombardement*, 478–9; Meyrowitz, *ZaöRV* 41, (1981), 12–18, and De Zayas,'Civilian Population, Protection', *EPIL* 3, 98.

[20] Pilloud/Pictet, ICRC *Commentary*, 587 (para. 1828); cf. also Doswald-Beck, *The Value of the Geneva Protocols for the Protection of Civilians*, 145–6.

[21] For the reasons underlying that approach cf. Kunz, *AJIL* 45 (1951), 58–61; Schwarzenberger, *Yearbook of World Affairs* 28 (1974), 302; Draper, 'Indiscriminate Attack', *EPIL* 3, 220; Parks, *Air Force Law Review* 32 (1990), 55–9.

problem of occupied territories) were left to customary law with all its inherent lacunae and vagueness.

Eventually, during the decades after 1945 there appeared on the scene the third (and most recent) complex of problems of humanitarian law, namely the question of weapons and means of warfare affecting the environment. Not only did lawyers pay attention to the (rather dated) problem of collateral effects of warfare damaging the environment, but also to the possibility of deliberate destruction of the environment as a means of weakening the enemy. The large-scale deforestation carried out by the US Army in the course of the war in Vietnam[22] and then by the Soviet campaign in Afghanistan which, at least in part, deliberately destroyed the environment of peasant regions which resisted,[23] demonstrated that the question of environmental modification is not merely a question of pure theory, but now constitutes a part of military reality. The deliberate employment of burning oil-wells as an environmental weapon in the Kuwait War in 1991 thus represents only a sad climax of a practice which has developed over many decades.[24]

The concern that these hitherto neglected problems needed to be addressed on a solid basis in treaty law dominated the Diplomatic Conference on the Reaffirmation and Development of International Humanitarian Law Applicable in Armed Conflicts, held in Geneva from 1974 until 1977.[25] At the conference it soon became clear how difficult a practicable codification of the traditional principles of customary law would be, if one wanted to give the principles some concrete contours. With the provisions of Art. 51 AP I on the protection of the civilian population and of Arts. 52–6 AP I on the protection of civilian objects an attempt was nevertheless made to achieve such a concretization and specification of customary rules, although it remains open to debate to what extent these provisions constitute a pure codification of (pre-)existing customary law and to what extent they constitute further development or even creation of new rules. The provisions accordingly were heavily attacked by some military experts, and—in connection with the absolute prohibition against reprisals against the civilian population contained in AP I—they are probably the main reason why important military powers still refuse to ratify the First Additional Protocol. In particular, on the hotly disputed question of the legal status of nuclear weapons, which has repeatedly provoked doubts about the compatibility of the traditional doctrines of nuclear deterrence with the new regime of AP I, the treaty's provisions have often been perceived as constituting too radical a shift, to the detriment of the requirement of military necessity.

With regard to the prohibition against excessive damage to the environment, however, Additional Protocol I regulates only a part of the question, namely the

---

[22] Kalshoven, *Constraints*, 81.

[23] See the report of the special rapporteur appointed by the UN Human Rights Commission in order to investigate human rights violations in Afghanistan, Felix Ermacora, UN Doc. E/CN.4/1985/21 of 19 Feb. 1985, 33 (paras. 122–3).

[24] Concerning the use of environmental damage as a means of war in the Kuwait War 1991, see *York*, 269–90; Witteler, 48–58; Momtaz, 203–19; Roberts, *RIC* 72 (1990), 559–77; Leibler, *California Western International Law Journal* (1992), 126–32; Lijnzaad/Tanja, 169–71.

[25] For the course of the Conference, cf. Bothe/Ipsen/Partsch, *ZaöRV* 38 (1978), 1–85; Kimminich, *Schutz der Menschen in bewaffneten Konflikten*, 60–79; Parks, *Air Force Law Review* 32 (1990), 76–94; Sassòli, 289–93.

issue of collateral damage. The international community (at the same time as the Geneva Diplomatic Conference) concluded a special treaty, the 1977 Convention on the Prohibition of Military or Any Other Hostile Use of Environmental Modification Techniques (ENMOD) to deal with the problem of environmental damage as a deliberate means of warfare. The prohibition against arms calculated to cause excessive suffering also received only marginal attention in the course of the negotiations on the Additional Protocols and has been touched on only in a minor provision. In its Art. 35, para. 2 Additional Protocol I reaffirmed the old (and imprecise) prohibition against excessive sufferings by a formula nearly identical to Art. 23(e) of the Hague Regulations. Concrete shape was given to this prohibition by the UN Weapons Convention negotiated in the wake of the Geneva Diplomatic Conference, a treaty supplemented by specific protocols on non-detectable fragments, mines and booby traps and incendiary weapons.[26]

2. The Relationship between Treaty Law and Customary Law. Customary law might still be said to have a decisive role in the international regulation of warfare, bearing in mind that until recently the treaty provisions on weapons and means of warfare were somewhat rudimentary, and also due to the fact that the new provisions of the Additional Protocols, the ENMOD Convention, and the UN Weapons Convention were not of universal application[27]. A majority of Third World states, some of the NATO States, and the overwhelming majority of former Warsaw Pact members (including the Soviet Union/Russia) have ratified the Additional Protocols; not bound by the Protocols are, however, the three Western nuclear powers, the USA, the UK, and France, as well as most Third World states actually involved in armed conflicts. The UK announced in 1993 that it would ratify both AP I and AP II. Accordingly, the most severe international armed conflicts of the last decades, namely the First and the Second Gulf Wars, were mainly fought by armed forces of states not subject to the rules of the First Additional Protocol,[28] which renders serious comment on the practical effects of the provisions of AP I almost impossible.

To a large degree, however, the combat operations of the armed forces involved were adjusted to comply with the legal guidelines of AP I, which is probably due to the fact that the provisions of Articles 51–60 AP I are mostly considered to represent established rules of traditional customary law. Also it may be that there is a certain effect of 'radiation' of the provisions of AP I concerning the protection of the civilian population, because these relatively specific rules are much easier to apply than the vaguer principles of customary law.[29] Even more, 'Operation Desert Storm' demonstrated that the advance of modern weapons technology[30] facilitates respect for the guarantees of AP I, so far as the protection of the civilian population is

---

[26] Concerning the UN Weapons Conference and its results see Fenrick, *CYIL* 19 (1981), 229–52 (esp. 239–40); Würkner-Theis, 21–7; Kalshoven, *Recueil des Cours* 191 (1985 II), 251–65; Roach, *Military Law Review* 105 (1984), 3–72; Kalshoven, *RIC* 72 (1990), 559–63.

[27] Cf. the general studies of Penna, Swinarski (Ed.), 201–25; Cassese, *UCLA Pacific Basin Law Journal* 3 (1984), 55–118; Greenwood, in Delissen/Tanja (Eds.), 93–114.

[28] See Gasser, *HuV-I* 4 (1991), 30–1.   [29] Ibid.

[30] Cf. the observations of Parks, *Air Force Law Review* 32 (1990), 113 n. 353.

concerned, since discrimination between military and civilian objectives can be implemented much more easily with the new generations of 'precision-guided munitions'[31] than was possible with traditional weapons.

So far as conventional warfare is concerned, therefore, there is every reason to believe that customary law standards will come into line with the provisions of Arts. 51–6 AP I (even if only *de lege ferenda*), with a resulting merger of relevant conventional and customary norms. With regard to nuclear operational planning (as well as the use of chemical weapons for reprisals), however, the question of what actually constitutes the customary standard of feasible protection for the civilian population remains a matter of contention. Even if the provisions of Articles 51–6 AP I, which are intended to specify and develop customary law, have any effect upon these problems, (cf. Sections 428–30), the Western nuclear powers still remain subject to the traditional regime of discriminate warfare, which imposes in principle an obligation to distinguish between military and civilian objectives, but not to all the other specific provisions of Part III of Additional Protocol I.

Comparable questions arise as to the regulation of non-international armed conflicts, a problem which is of enormous importance in practice. It is generally recognized now that common Art. 3 of the four Geneva Conventions, which requires that the utmost care should be taken of the civilian population even in internal armed conflicts, constitutes a reflection of fundamental principles of customary law, if not an expression of the 'elementary considerations of humanity' referred to in the Martens' Clause.[32] Since these principles have been expressed in a formula of considerable vagueness—even in its reflection in common Art.3—whereas the more specific provisions of Additional Protocol II are subject to certain conditions which must be fulfilled before Protocol II becomes applicable (not to mention the absence of ratifications by the states most concerned) the question arises: to what degree does a parallel customary law exist which could fill the gaps left by treaty law?[33]

Even with respect to the provisions of the UN Weapons Convention it would be interesting to clarify how far the treaty provisions are paralleled by any analogous customary law. One could argue in that direction, since (at least in theory) the provisions of the Convention constitute only a specification and development of the general prohibition against unnecessary suffering which dates back to the St. Petersburg Declaration of 1868, later codified in the Hague Regulations in Art. 23(e). It is, however, to say the least, open to doubt how far it is really possible to deduce from the general customary prohibition of *maux superflus* the concrete prohibitions of specific weapons stated by the three Weapons Protocols to the 1980 Convention;[34] comparable problems are raised by the question of whether there exist further

---

[31] Gasser, *HuV-I* 4 (1991), 31.

[32] See the Judgment of the ICJ in the Nicaragua case, *Case Concerning Military and Paramilitary Activities in and against Nicaragua (Nicaragua v. United States of America)*, Judgment of 27 June 1986, ICJ Reports 1986, 114 (para. 218); cf. also the report of the special rapporteur W. Kälin to the UN Human Rights Commission concerning human rights violations of Iraq in occupied Kuwait, UN Doc. E/CN.4/1992/26 v. 16.1.1992, 10–11 (paras. 35–8).

[33] See Kalshoven, in Cassese (Ed.), *Current Problems of Customary International Law*, 267; ibid., *Recueil des Cours* 191 (1985 II), 295–6; Plattner, *RIC* 72 (1990), 605–19; Gardam, 164–80; Goldman, 61–2.

[34] The problem is raised by Kalshoven, *RIC* 72 (1990), 563–6.

prohibitions of weapons besides the specific prohibitions of the UN Weapons Convention, i.e. additional prohibitions deduced directly from the general principle of prohibition of unnecessary suffering codified in Art. 23(e) Hague Regulations.[35]

Concerning the prohibition of methods of warfare that cause widespread, long-term, and severe damage to the natural environment[36] one could even raise the question of whether there exists any possibility at all of a parallel customary law. The entire problem has only recently arisen in military practice so that it is difficult to conceive that one could find any substantial state practice in that respect. Thus, it will be nearly impossible to prove the formation of a specific rule of customary international law from state practice. One could point to the fact, however, that even this complex of rather novel provisions constitutes only an implementation and materialization of the old maxim of customary law that the ultimate barrier of any legally permitted warfare is to be found in the principle of military necessity (understood in the sense that the damaging action must be imperatively required by operational necessities).[37] The traditional formula, which has found expression in Art. 22 Hague Regulations and in Art. 35, para. 1 AP I, provides that: 'the right of belligerents to choose methods or means of warfare is not unlimited' ('to adopt means of injuring the enemy' in the language of the Hague Regulations). One might deduce from this principle a requirement that the weapons or means employed to achieve a military goal should be in an adequate proportion to the destruction and suffering inflicted by the operation, which accordingly would mean that one could construct under existing traditional customary law a far-reaching prohibition against excessive damage applicable also to environmental warfare.[38]

I. GENERAL RULES

The right of the parties to an armed conflict to choose means (Art. 22 Hague   401
Regulations) and methods (Art. 35, para. 1 Additional Protocol I) of warfare is not unlimited. It is particularly prohibited to employ means or methods which are intended or of a nature:

—to cause superfluous injury or unnecessary suffering (Art. 23(e) Hague Regulations; Art. 35, para. 2 Additional Protocol I);

—to cause widespread, long-term, and severe damage to the natural environment 'Arts. 35, para. 3, and 55, para. 1 Additional Protocol I; ENMOD Convention); or

—to injure military objectives, civilians, or civilian objects without distinction (Art. 51 paras. 4 and 5 Additional Protocol I).

[35] See Kalshoven, *Recueil des Cours* 191 (1985 II), 295–6.

[36] As to the established principles concerning environmental warfare see Kiss, Swinarski (Ed.), 181–92; Witteler, 48–58; Goldblat, *Bulletin of Peace Proposals* 22 (1991), 399–406; Kalshoven, *Constraints*, 81; Bothe, *GYIL* 34 (1991), 55–8; Green, *CYIL* 29 (1991), 222–36; Lijnzaad/Tanja 178–89; Bouvier, *RIC* 73 (1991), 599–611; Leibler, *California Western International Law Journal* 1992, 96–112; B. Baker, 358–76 and the collection of essays edited by Plant (esp. the contribution by Falk, 78 *et seq.*).

[37] See Falk, in Plant (Ed.), 84 *et seq.*; Leibler, *loc. cit.*, 97–9; B. Baker, 360–3; Lijnzaad/Tanja, 183–4.

[38] Falk, *op. cit.*, 84–6; Bothe, *GYIL* 34 (1991), 55–56; Leibler, *loc. cit.*, 98–9; Lijnzaad/Tanja, 183–5.

Oeter

1. The fundamental maxim of humanitarian rules on warfare which is reproduced in the first sentence constitutes the basis of any regulation of the methods and means of warfare employed.[39] The formula puts in a nutshell the customary principle that any act of warfare should be guided by the requirements of military necessity. The formula expressed in the version cited had already been adopted in Art. 22 of the Hague Regulations; now it is repeated almost verbatim in Art. 35, para.1 AP I and in the Preamble of the UN Weapons Convention. The principle forms one of the core 'principles of international law derived from established custom, from the principles of humanity, and from the dictates of public conscience' in the sense of the Martens' Clause. As Jean de Preux has written in the ICRC commentary on the Additional Protocols,[40] all of Part III of AP I is implicitly (but clearly) based on the assumption of a final rejection of the idea of 'total war'. The opposing principle, the principle of 'limited warfare', which is intimately connected to the condition of 'military necessity', thus has a key function in relation to the other provisions of Part III (and implicitly probably also Part IV) of Additional Protocol I.[41] The basic approach of 'limited warfare', which dominates the modern laws of war, requires every belligerent to strike a balance between the conflicting concerns of humanity and military necessity.[42] To curtail the objective of humanization of warfare is justified only in so far as military necessity inevitably requires a certain military operation, not to mention the further condition that the damage inflicted must be proportionate to the military advantage sought.[43] What should be perceived as an adequate equilibrium between the damage likely to result from the operation and the military advantage aspired to is a question further elaborated, and regulated in detail, by the specific provisions of humanitarian law which will be explained in the following Sections. All customary as well as conventional regulation of means and methods of warfare could be understood in one sense as a comprehensive attempt to give the principle of 'limited warfare', i.e. the limitation of belligerent use of force by the condition of military necessity, some specific and practical shape.

2. Flowing from the general principle of 'limited warfare' (limited to what is militarily absolutely necessary in order to achieve the military objectives[44]) several sub-principles have developed historically, giving the rule of military necessity its specific contours. These specific expressions of the principle of military necessity have different purposes and reflect very different historical stages of the evolution of humanitarian law.

3. The concept of the utmost protection of the civilian population constitutes the oldest stage, or layer of that evolution, a layer now reflected in the binding rules of

---

[39] See Bothe, 'Land Warfare', *EPIL* 3, 240 and Kalshoven, *RIC* 72 (1990), 556–63.

[40] de Preux, ICRC *Commentary*, 382 (para. 1367).

[41] Cf. in the same sense Solf, in Bothe/Partsch/Solf, 193–8 and Dinstein, 'Warfare', *EPIL* 4, 338; Sassòli, 344–7.

[42] Cf. Bretton, *Principes humanitaires et impératifs militaires*, 37–8; de Mulinen, *A propos de la conférence de Lucerne et Lugano*, 122–3; Dinstein, 'Military Necessity, *EPIL* 3, 274; Sassòli, 344.

[43] Cf. Bretton, *Principes humanitaires et impératifs militaires*, 47–8; Venturini, 145–50.

[44] For the dazzling relationship between the political objective pursued by war and the 'military objective' in the sense of AP I cf. Meyrowitz, *RDMilG* 22 (1983), 95 ff.

Art. 48 AP I (basic rule) and Art. 51 AP I (specific provisions on the protection of the civilian population). The humanitarian principles of Islamic legal culture and the moral theological postulates of medieval scholars already contemplated a principle of distinction between combatants and civilians and called for extensive protection of the civilian population.[45] More recently, the legal practice of the nineteenth century established the prohibition against indiscriminate warfare as a customary rule.[46] In the Hague Regulations, however, this customary rule was only incompletely reflected (see Arts. 23, para. 1 (g), and 25 Hague Regulations). The requirement of discrimination did not find expression in a general formula nor was the question of collateral damages in the course of attacks on military objectives regulated by any of the provisions. The Hague Rules on Air Warfare, which some decades later attempted to codify the prohibition of indiscriminate attacks by air, did not find acceptance. Nevertheless, the customary validity of the prohibition of indiscriminate warfare was never seriously disputed.[47] Even the excesses of World War II did not change the basic validity of the customary protection of the civilian population.[48] In Part IV of Additional Protocol I these firmly established principles of customary law were explicitly laid down in a treaty for the first time. Art. 48 AP I formulates the basic principle of discrimination: 'In order to ensure respect for and protection of the civilian population and civilian objects, the Parties to the conflict shall at all times distinguish between the civilian population and combatants and between civilian objects and military objectives and accordingly shall direct their operations only against military objectives.' The overall validity of this principle today is beyond any doubt. However, even bearing in mind that the principle of distinction, as enshrined in Art. 48 AP I, constitutes an ancient and established rule of customary law, and not a new principle created recently by conventional law,[49] one must admit that concrete shape is given to the fundamental maxim mainly by the detailed treaty provisions of Arts. 50–6 AP I (cf. Sections 441–70).

4. The prohibition against *maux superflus*, i.e. against weapons and materials causing excessive suffering, is also an old normative principle. The prohibition of poisoned weapons and of the use of poison as a means of warfare, which had been so deeply rooted in medieval custom, could be seen as a precursor. The objective of banning superfluous injury/unnecessary suffering was formulated for the first time *expressis verbis* in the St Petersburg Declaration of 1868 which outlawed explosive projectiles under 400 grammes weight.[50] This regulatory approach was

---

[45] Cf. Pictet, *Development and Principles*, 5–25; esp. concerning the Islamic concepts cf. Sultan, 56–9.

[46] Cf. Pilloud/Pictet, ICRC *Commentary*, 585–6 (paras 1823–7).

[47] See Kunz, *Kriegsrecht und Neutralitätsrecht*, 75–6 with extensive references to the contemporary literature; but cf. also Oppenheim/Lauterpacht, Vol.II, 346–7; Castrén, *The Present Law of War and Neutrality*, 174–8; Greenspan, 154–6; Schwarzenberger, *Yearbook of World Affairs* 28 (1978), 109–17; Rousseau, 67–9; Detter De Lupis, 232–44; McCoubrey, 114–15.

[48] The intense discussion about this question is reflected in detail in the articles of Randelzhofer, *Flächenbombardement*, 479–87 and Meyrowitz, *ZaöRV* 41 (1981), 24–5.

[49] See in extensive detail Sassòli, 342–59 (esp. 359). Cf. also Meyrowitz, *RDMilG* 1982, 128; Solf, *The American University Journal of International Law and Policy* 1 (1986), 129; Venturini, *Necessita*, 149; Rogers, *RDMilG* 1982, 295–6, 303.

[50] See esp. Kalshoven, *Recueil des Cours* 191 (1985 II), 205–13 and Sandoz, *Des armes interdites*, 16–22.

Oeter

continued in the Hague Declaration of 1899 concerning dum-dum bullets. As a general prohibition of arms or material 'of a nature to cause superfluous injury' (HagueReg 1899) or 'calculated to cause unnecessary suffering' (HagueReg 1907) it was included in Art. 23(e) of the Hague Regulations. The bans on the use of poisonous gases as a means of warfare provided for by the Geneva Gas Protocol of 1925 and the Biological Weapons Convention of 1972 were further steps on the way to a total ban on the use of certain particularly barbaric weapons. Additional Protocol I now contents itself with repeating the abstract prohibition of weapons causing unnecessary suffering, in Art. 35, para. 2. The UN Weapons Convention of 1980 and its three Protocols gave a much more precise content to the prohibition of specific weapons, originally intended for inclusion in Additional Protocol I.[51] Thus, the prohibition of *maux superflus* is characterized by a particularly complex mixture of very definite prohibitions of certain specific categories of arms on one hand, and a rather abstract prohibition of means of warfare which cause unnecessary sufferings on the other; the relationship between these two sets of rules is far from clear. How far the definite prohibitions are only specific expressions or materializations of the general prohibitory provision, and to what extent they are, to the contrary, constitutive developments of a merely political programme envisaged in Art. 23(e) Hague Regulations, is a question which still needs careful consideration.[52]

5. Similar questions can be asked about the most recent exposition of the principle of 'limited warfare', namely the prohibition against methods of warfare which cause widespread, long-term, and severe damage to the natural environment (cf. Section 403). This sub-principle might also be deduced logically from the requirements of military necessity, and from its supplement, the principle of proportionality of the damages inflicted in relation to the military objective.[53] However, the military practice of the last decades demonstrates considerable carelessness on the part of belligerent forces as to the preservation of the natural environment. Thus, it seemed sensible to embody provisions which explicitly include the environment as an object entitled to the protection granted by the rules of humanitarian law.[54] The Convention on the Prohibition of Military or Any Other Hostile Use of Environmental Modification Techniques (ENMOD Convention) of 1977 and Articles 35, para. 3 and 55, para. 1 AP I accordingly addressed that problem. The relationship between these treaties, however, as well as their relationship to the rules of customary law is problematic and needs further analysis (cf. Section 403).

402   **'Superfluous injury' and 'unnecessary suffering' are caused by the use of weapons and methods of combat whose foreseeable harm would be clearly excessive in relation to the lawful military advantage intended.**

[51] For the attempts to include prohibitions of specific categories of arms in Additional Protocol I see Solf, in Bothe/Partsch/Solf, 197–8; cf. Würkner-Theis, 16–20.

[52] The question is elaborated by Kalshoven, *RIC* 72 (1990), 563–6.

[53] See Falk, in Plant (Ed.), 84 *et seq.*

[54] Kalshoven, *Constraints*, 81; Antoine, *RIC* 74 (1992), 540–50; concerning the recent efforts to ameliorate the protection of the environment in times of armed conflict see Bouvier, *RIC* 74 (1992), 578–91.

1. The provision of Art. 35, para. 2 AP I, which was taken as a precedent when formulating the rule above, clarifies the principle of 'limited warfare'. It is a reaffirmation of the prohibition of *maux superflus* laid down in the St Petersburg Declaration of 1868 and later codified in the Hague Regulations.[55] The attempt to link the use of force to the requirement of 'military necessity' is thus given a much more precise shape: to inflict physical or psychological harm is justified only in so far as it is really necessary to attain the military advantage intended.[56] Necessity and proportionality of the means employed thus become conditions of the lawfulness of the use of specific weapons.[57]

2. Article 23 lit. e HagueReg and Art. 35, para. 2 AP I prohibit in a nearly identical formula the use of weapons, projectiles, and materials of war calculated to cause superfluous injury or unnecessary sufferings.[58] The category of 'superfluous injury', which was newly integrated in the provision of Art. 35, para. 2 AP I, implicitly clarifies what should properly constitute the decisive criterion of proportionality. Injuries can only be 'superfluous' either if they are not justified by any requirement of military necessity or if the injuries normally caused by the weapon or projectile are manifestly disproportionate to the military advantage reasonably expected from the use of the weapon. The first will only rarely be the case, since the intended injuring effect generally serves a military goal, namely the neutralization of enemy combatants or military material. The second condition will only be fulfilled if the weapon is at least relatively superfluous—which requires a comparative judgment as to how much suffering various weapons cause and whether alternative military means could achieve the same results with less suffering.[59]

3. Concerning the classical formula of 'unnecessary suffering' (*maux superflus*) it is much more difficult to find an adequate description of the effects of weaponry which are intended to be outlawed by the choice of that wording. The notion of 'suffering' is not quantifiable under a medical perspective, for it is defined according to psychological criteria.[60] Accordingly attempts have been made to find alternative formulae, which are more accessible to technical operationalization, and recent terminology favours the (more objective) term of 'injury'.[61] The traditional notion of 'unnecessary suffering' means essentially the same, namely a physical or emotional impairment which cannot be justified by military necessity. To this extent it is a concept which enables the effects of various methods of warfare to be

---

[55] For the historical development of the prohibition of *maux superflus* see Kalshoven, *Recueil des Cours* 191 (1985 II), 205–24 and Kalshoven, *RIC* 72 (1990), 557–63.
[56] In that sense already provided in the Preamble to the St Petersburg Declaration of 1868—see Kalshoven, *Recueil des Cours* 191 (1985 II), 206, 212.
[57] Concerning that problem see the comments on Art. 35, para. 2 AP I by de Preux, in ICRC *Commentary*, 399–410 (paras. 1410–39) and by Solf, in Bothe/Partsch/Solf, 195–8.
[58] Concerning the textual differences between the two provisions see Solf, in Bothe/Partsch/Solf, 195 and Rogers, *RIC* 72 (1990), 568–9.
[59] Solf, in Bothe/Partsch/Solf, 196.
[60] See Bretton, *Principes humanitaires et impératifs militaires*, 39.   [61] Ibid.

compared, and also opens to question the military usefulness of a weapon in relation to its adverse consequences on those affected by it.[62]

4. 'Relevant military advantage' in this sense is judged only by reference to direct attacks upon military objectives, irrespective of the fear and terror caused among enemy personnel and the civilian population. The notion of 'lawful military advantage intended', which is used in Section 402, refers to this type of direct advantage. The precise definition of a military advantage justifying the use of arms is provided elsewhere in the law on methods and means of warfare (see Sections 442 to 444).

5. The practical significance of the question is demonstrated by the continuing discussion on the legality of laser guns, a new weapon which can cause blindness. There are convincing arguments that such laser weapons could be useful in a military conflict, but they are also claimed to cause 'superfluous injury' in the sense of aggravated suffering not justified by corresponding advantages in neutralizing enemy combatants. The ICRC has accordingly proposed a new Protocol to the 1980 UN Weapons Convention prohibiting all types of laser guns.

403   **'Widespread', 'long-term', and 'severe' damage to the natural environment is a major interference with human life or natural resources which considerably exceeds the battlefield damage to be regularly expected in a war. Such damage to the natural environment by means of warfare (Arts. 35, para. 3, and 55, para.1 AP I) and severe manipulation of the environment as a weapon (ENMOD) are likewise prohibited.**

1. Against the background of US warfare in Vietnam[63] the UN Committee on Disarmament drew up a specific treaty concluded in 1977, the Convention on the Prohibition of Military or Any Other Hostile Use of Environmental Modification Techniques (the ENMOD Convention).[64] Art. I of the Convention prohibits 'to engage in military or any other hostile use of environmental modification techniques having widespread, long-lasting, or severe effects' for the purpose of destroying, damaging or injuring the enemy. The subject matter of the treaty is thus the use of so-called 'environmental modification techniques' as military instruments, i.e. the calculated abuse of the environmental damage for offensive purposes.[65]

2. Definitions of 'widespread', 'long-lasting', and 'severe' were provided by the UN Committee on Disarmament in a series of so-called 'Understandings'.[66] Damage is 'widespread' if it affects an area which encompasses several hundred square kilo-

---

[62] Solf, in Bothe/Partsch/Solf, 196; see also Kalshoven, *Recueil des Cours* 191 (1985 II), 234–6.

[63] See Witteler, 49 and the contribution of Falk in Plant (Ed.), 90.

[64] Concerning ENMOD see Witteler, 53 *et seq.*; Goldblat, 401; R. Falk, in Plant (Ed.), 90; Leibler, *California Western International Law Journal* 23 (1992), 81–3; Lijnzaad/Tanja 185–9.

[65] See Witteler, 54; Goldblat, 401.

[66] For the text of the 'Understandings' see UN Doc. CCD/520 of 1976 Sep. 3, Annex A; printed also in Delbrück, *Friedensdokumente* (Vol. 2), document number 300.

Oeter

metres; 'long-lasting' (or 'long-term') means damage lasting for a period of several months, or approximately a season, while 'severe' was defined as involving serious or significant disruption or harm to human life, natural or economic resources, or other assets. If any one of these thresholds is crossed then the ENMOD prohibition is breached. This link between the prohibition against environmental modification techniques and the crossing of a certain threshold of application was (and is) often heavily criticized.[67] It seems, however, that such a formula is sensible, because it pursues the objective of distinguishing warfare by environmental modification techniques, which is generally condemned, from the common practice of intervening in the environment on an operative level. ENMOD was not intended to affect the established practice of tactical intervention in the environment in the framework of specific combat operations, like the flooding of restricted sectors of ground or the burning of isolated woods.[68] The definition of both categories nevertheless remains a difficult undertaking, which is not altogether achieved in 'Understandings' annexed to the ENMOD Convention.

3. An even more delicate question is the delimitation of the various fields of application of the relevant provisions of the First Additional Protocol. By Art. 35, para. 3 AP I and the complementary provision of Art. 55 AP I, the Diplomatic Conference in Geneva has introduced—going beyond the traditional requirement of 'military necessity'—an absolute prohibition against severe environmental damage.[69] In the case of 'widespread, long-lasting or severe damages to the natural environment' even the claim of military necessity may not justify the use of weapons or means of warfare which are intended or likely to cause such damage; calculated imposition (and reckless disregard) of long-lasting and severe damage to the environment was accordingly banned absolutely.[70] The provisions in AP I therefore go much farther than the prohibition in ENMOD, covering not only the intentional infliction of damage to the environment in the course of warfare (as in the ENMOD Convention), but also purely unintentional and incidental damage.[71]

4. Since every method of warfare causes collateral damage to the environment, the question arises as to the exact thresholds of application of Arts. 35, para. 3 and 55 AP I. The Diplomatic Conference made use of the threshold notions (analogous to the ENMOD Convention[72]) of 'widespread', 'long-lasting' and 'severe', although it

---

[67] See e.g. Goldblat, 403; cf. also Plant, Introduction, in Plant (Ed.), 3 *et seq.* (27–8) as well as the discussion ibid., 104 *et seq.*, 117 *et seq.*

[68] See York, *South African Journal of Human Rights* (1993), 287–8.

[69] For the history of Arts. 35, para. 3 and 55 AP I see de Preux, in ICRC *Commentary*, 411–14 (paras. 1444–9); Solf, in Bothe/Partsch/Solf, 344–5; Kiss, 182–4; Lijnzaad/Tanja, 178–81.

[70] See de Preux, in ICRC *Commentary*, 410–11 (paras. 1440–3); Kiss, 184–6.

[71] Concerning the difficult relationship between Art. 35, para. 3 AP I and the ENMOD Convention see de Preux, in ICRC *Commentary*, 414–18 (paras. 1450–6) and Solf, in Bothe/Partsch/Solf, 347; see also Kiss, 187, 187; Bouvier, *La protection de l'environnement naturel*, 609; Lijnzaad/Tanja, 197–8, and Baker, 368–70.

[72] For the parallels of wording in Arts. 35, para. 3 and 55 AP I and the ENMOD Convention, negotiated simultaneously, see Witteler, 56; de Preux, in ICRC *Commentary*, 416–17 (paras. 1452–4). It has to be admitted, however, that the analogous wording does not automatically mean that the notions have to be interpreted identically in both Conventions, although textual logic seems to point in that direction.

Oeter

used them not alternatively (as in ENMOD) but cumulatively.[73] Collateral damage is covered by the prohibitions of Arts. 35, para. 3 and 55 AP I only if it affects large areas *and* lasts for a long period *and also* causes severe damage to the natural environment.[74] The usual collateral damage caused by large military operations in the course of conventional warfare (which can be quite considerable) are thus excluded from the scope of the prohibitions against environmental damage of AP I[75] and accordingly continue to fall under the basic requirement of military necessity.

5. The fundamental principles of military necessity also form the basic long-stop provision of humanitarian law when the conventional provisions of AP I and ENMOD are not applicable, as for example in the Kuwait conflict ('Operation Desert Storm') of 1991.[76] The specific prohibitions against environmental warfare in ENMOD and the prohibitions against environmental damage in AP I probably still have no customary equivalents, for they prohibit (under specific circumstances) environmentally damaging methods of combat which in principle could be justified as militarily necessary. According to customary law, however, only those impairments of the environment which are manifestly superfluous under the principle of military necessity are prohibited, since they are in no way militarily required.[77]

404   The prohibition of indiscriminate warfare means that both the civilian population as a whole and individual civilians shall be spared as far as possible from attack.

1. The prohibition of indiscriminate warfare probably constitutes the most important expression of the principle of 'limited warfare'. It is both the greatest consequence of and a modification of the fundamental orientation of warfare towards the requirements of 'military necessity'.[78]

2. The requirement to distinguish between the civilian population and the combatants, as well as between military objectives and civilian objects (Art. 48 AP I) is a classical result of the attempt to restrict warfare to acts of violence against the enemy which are strictly 'necessary' from a military perspective. Use of force is permitted only in so far as it is directed against a specific military objective, be it a military installation, an object used for military purposes, or an individual combatant or group of combatants.[79] A 'specific military objective' accordingly is the funda-

[73] Solf, in Bothe/Partsch/Solf, 347; Witteler, 57.

[74] Where the threshold of application of Arts.35, para. 3 and 55 AP I really lies, remains in dispute—see Witteler, 51–2 and Aldrich, *Virginia Journal of International Law* 26 (1986), 711; Solf, in Bothe/Partsch/ Solf, 347–8; de Preux, ICRC *Commentary*, 416–18 (paras. 1454–6); Kiss, 189–90.

[75] See Witteler, 51; de Preux, in ICRC *Commentary*, 417 (para. 1454); Lijnzaad/Tanja, 180–5.

[76] Concerning the legal problems of environmental warfare in the Gulf in the course of 'Operation Desert Storm' against Iraq see York, 269–90; Witteler, 48–58; Roberts, *RIC* 72 (1990), 559–77.

[77] See Falk, in Plant (Ed.), 84 *et seq.* and Bothe, ibid., 117–18.

[78] See Pilloud/Pictet, in ICRC *Commentary*, 585–9 (paras. 1822–37) and Sassòli, 342–50.

[79] Concerning the classical principle of distinction see Kunz, *Kriegsrecht und Neutralitätsrecht*, 75–7; Castrén, *The Present Law of War and Neutrality*, 174–83; Mirimanoff-Chilikine, 8 *Revue Belge* 101–42 (1972);

mental precondition for an act of force to be justifiable under humanitarian law.[80] The use of force must not only be directed against this specific (and separable) target, but it must also employ specific weapons and methods of warfare that are limited (or at least limitable) in their results. In its effects the military instrument may not exceed what is warranted by the military objective of the operation.[81] The following conclusion can be drawn: the use of means of force must, in its intention, be limitable to combat against purely military objectives, and in its results it must be limited to damaging only military targets (Art. 51, paras. 2 and 4 AP I).[82]

3. The prohibition against indiscriminate warfare, however, potentially exceeds even that limitation to the requirements of 'military necessity' by laying down the fundamental principle of proportionality.[83] The use of means and methods of warfare may be illegal, even if collateral damage to the civilian population and civilian goods could be justified in principle by reference to 'military necessity', on the grounds that such damage is unavoidable in mounting an effective attack on a military objective in the centre of the operation. Manifestly disproportionate collateral damage inflicted in order to achieve operational objectives will result in the action being deemed an (illicit) form of indiscriminate warfare (Art. 51, para. 5, lit. b AP I).

4. Accordingly, all methods and means of warfare which primarily damage the civilian population, such as the practice of indiscriminate area bombing[84]—a strategy used excessively by both sides during World War II[85]—are prohibited. Likewise, 'scorched earth' strategies on enemy territory, the indiscriminate dispersal of mines and booby traps on enemy territory (see Sections 410–415), and several other forms of warfare which primarily damage the civilian population, such as the use of incendiary weapons against civilian settlements (see Section 423), starving the population of besieged areas, artillery bombardment of 'enemy' settlements, or the use of snipers to terrorize the 'enemy' civilian population are also forbidden.[86]

5. One specific achievement of the Additional Protocols was the prohibition against starvation as a method of warfare, as provided by Art. 54, para. 1 AP I.

Kalshoven, *The Law of Warfare*, 27–35; Rosenblad, *International Humanitarian Law*, 53–63; Kimminich, *Schutz der Menschen in bewaffneten Konflikten*, 131–5; Randelzhofer, 'Civilian Objects', *EPIL* 3, 93; Draper, 'Indiscriminate Attack', *EPIL* 3, 219–21; Pilloud/ Pictet, in ICRC *Commentary*, 598–600 (paras. 1863–71).

[80] See Section 442; cf. v.d. Heydte, 'Military Objectives', *EPIL* 3, 276–9.

[81] See Cassese, *Prohibition of Indiscriminate Means*, 171–82; Kimminich, *Schutz der Menschen in bewaffneten Konflikten*, 139–46.

[82] See the comments of Solf on Art. 51 AP I, in Bothe/Partsch/ Solf, 299–311 and Arrassen, 260–4; Baxter, *Comportement des combattants*, 146–58; Blix, *Moyens et méthodes de combat*, 174–8.

[83] Concerning the principle of proportionality generally regarded as already embodied in customary law see Randelzhofer, *Flächenbombardement*, 484–93; Kimminich, *Schutz der Menschen in bewaffneten Konflikten*, 152–7; Cassese, *UCLA Pacific Basin Law Journal* 3 (1984), 85–6; Bretton, *Principes humanitaires et impératifs militaires*, 47–8; Venturini, *Necessita*, 145–50; Greenwood, in Delissen/Tanja (Eds.), 109.

[84] See Art. 51, para. 5(a) AP I; cf. also Bruha, 'Bombardment', *EPIL* 3, 56; Randelzhofer, *Flächenbombardement*, 488–93; Draper, 'Indiscriminate Attack', *EPIL* 3, 220–1; Blix, *BYIL* 49 (1978), 52–69; Meyrowitz, *ZaöRV* 41 (1981), 55–68; DeSaussure, *Annals of Air and Space Law* 4 (1979), 469–72, 477–81.

[85] See De Zayas, *EPIL* 3, 98 and Randelzhofer, *Flächenbombardement und Völkerrecht*, 478–9; DeSaussure, *loc. cit.*, 473–5; Parks, *Air Force Law Review* 32 (1990), 1–2.

[86] See in detail Kimminich, *Schutz der Menschen in bewaffneten Konflikten*, 139–49.

Oeter

Methods of warfare that attempt to destroy the logistical basis of the enemy were traditionally popular in military tactics.[87] Sieges of encircled settlements deliberately tried to force the enemy to lay down their weapons by starving out the civilian population; strategies of 'scorched earth' employed during a retreat from enemy territory or in the abandonment of one's own territory were an instrument frequently used by belligerents in order to prevent the enemy from achieving its strategic goals.[88] Since these ways of conducting war are primarily damaging to the civilian population, the international community has outlawed such methods and means of warfare; narrow bounds have been set by Arts. 54 AP I and 14 AP II to traditional tactics of siege, laying waste of areas, etc.[89] (For further details see Section 463).

6. The general prohibition against indiscriminate warfare applies independently of Arts. 48 and 51 AP I. The relevant provisions of the Additional Protocols merely codify pre-existing customary law, because the principle of distinction belongs to the oldest fundamental maxims of established customary rules of humanitarian law.[90] It is also virtually impossible to distinguish between international and non-international armed conflict in this respect, since common Art. 3 of the Geneva Conventions already provides for extensive protection of the civilian population even in internal armed conflicts. Although the law of 'non-international armed conflict' has no specific notion of 'the combatant', it is undisputed that attacks on the life and health of civilians, in particular intentional killing and cruel treatment such as torture and mutilation, are absolutely prohibited under the customary minimum standards set out in common Art. 3.[91] The ICJ has recently reaffirmed, in the *Nicaragua* judgment, the particular dignity of these minimum rules, qualifying them as general principles of law which flow from 'elementary considerations of humanity' (in a clear reference to the Martens' Clause).[92]

405 **In the study, development, acquisition, or adoption of new means or methods of combat it shall be determined whether these means and methods are compatible with the rules of international law (Art. 36 AP I). The agency responsible for this assessment in the Federal Armed Forces is the Federal Ministry of Defence, International Legal Affairs Directorate (VR II 3).**

In order to guarantee effective implementation of the prohibition of certain means and methods of warfare emanating from the principles described above it is neces-

---

[87] See Dinstein, *Siege Warfare*, 145–7.

[88] See Solf, in Bothe/Partsch/Solf, 337 and Dinstein, *Siege Warfare*, 146–7.

[89] Concerning Art.54, para. 1 AP I see Pilloud/Pictet, in ICRC *Commentary*, 652–3 (paras. 2083–91); Solf, in Bothe/Partsch/ Solf, 336–42; Dinstein, in Delissen/Tanja (Eds.), 148–52.

[90] See Cassese, *loc. cit.*, 82 ff.; Greenwood, in Delissen/Tanja (Eds.), 108–10; Fleck, *RDMilG* 1990, 500–1.

[91] See Kalshoven, *Recueil des Cours* 191 (1985 II), 296; Gardam, 176–80.

[92] International Court of Justice, *Case Concerning Military and Paramilitary Activities in and against Nicaragua (Nicaragua v. United States of America)*, Judgment of 27 June 1986, ICJ Reports 1986, 114 (para. 218); see also the report of special rapporteur W. Kälin to the UN Human Rights Commission concerning the human rights violations of Iraq in occupied Kuwait, UN Doc. E/CN.4/1992/26 of 16 Jan. 1992, 10–11 (paras. 35–8).

sary to provide for an efficient procedure to ensure the legality of new weapons.[93] Some states had already created such procedures prior to the elaboration of the Additional Protocols (Federal Republic of Germany, USA, Sweden),[94] but for most states such a form of preventive control will be a novel institution. Originally an internationalized procedure of control had even been considered.[95] In view of the legitimate requirements of secrecy that surround the development of new weapons, however, the concept of the internationalization of controls proved to be impracticable and refuge was taken in the already established procedures of national control of legality, although these control procedures were made obligatory.[96]

II. MEANS OF COMBAT

1. Certain Conventional Weapons

In the 1868 St Petersburg Declaration the use of explosive and incendiary projec-   406
**tiles weighing under 400 grammes was prohibited, since these projectiles were
deemed to cause disproportionately severe injury to soldiers, which is not necessary to put them out of action. This prohibition is now only of limited importance,
since it is reduced by customary law to the use of explosive and incendiary projectiles of a weight significantly lower than 400 grammes which can disable only
the individual directly concerned but not any other persons. 20 mm high-explo-
sive grenades and projectiles of a similar calibre are not prohibited.**

1. The St Petersburg Declaration of 1868 was the first instrument to outlaw specific weapons.[97] One of its most interesting parts is the Preamble, where the motivation (and dilemma) of all humanitarian prohibitions of weapons has found a convincing expression. In the Preamble the states parties declared their acceptance of an oblig-ation to restrict the use of certain projectiles considering that 'the progress of civi-lization should have the effect of alleviating as much as possible the calamities of war' and that 'the only legitimate object which States should endeavour to accom-plish during war is to weaken the military forces of the enemy'. For this purpose it is sufficient 'to disable the greatest possible number of men'; this object would be exceeded 'by the employment of arms which uselessly aggravate the sufferings of disabled men, or render their death inevitable', not to mention that 'the employ-ment of such arms would be contrary to the laws of humanity.' The only legitimate purpose of any use of weapons is the disabling of enemy combatants.[98]

---

[93] See Solf, in Bothe/Partsch/Solf, 199 and de Preux, in ICRC *Commentary*, 421–5 (paras. 1463–71).

[94] See Solf, in Bothe/Partsch/Solf, 199 n. 1 and de Preux, in ICRC *Commentary*, 423 (para. 1467), 426–7 (n. 19).

[95] Solf, in Bothe/Partsch/Solf, 200.

[96] Ibid.; for the standards of control see also de Preux, in ICRC *Commentary*, 425–8 (paras. 1472–7).

[97] For the historical background see Kalshoven, *Recueil des Cours* 191 (1985 II), 205–13.

[98] For an analysis of the Preamble to the St Petersburg Declaration 1868 see Kalshoven, in *Recueil des Cours* 191 (1985 II), 206–7, 212.

Oeter

2. According to the judgment of the International Military Commission which assembled at St Petersburg at the instigation of the Imperial Cabinet of Russia,[99] the use of explosive projectiles against infantry failed to meet this standard. The laws of war, as the principles 'at which the necessities of war ought to yield to the requirements of humanity', should not prohibit the use of explosive projectiles *per se*. The use of such projectiles as artillery munition had already been long established and was perceived to be militarily necessary. However, the use against individual combatants of explosive projectiles was seen to be avoidable in military terms, and therefore superfluous.[100] The weight limit used to distinguish between infantry and artillery munitions (400 grammes) was set rather arbitrarily; artillery projectiles of the time were considerably heavier, whereas infantry munitions were much lighter than 400 grammes. The absolute weight limit set in 1868 should therefore not be taken too strictly.[101] The basic principle of the declaration has, therefore, been transformed not into customary law as a prohibition of explosive projectiles weighing under 400 grammes, but into a prohibition against infantry munitions with explosive or inflammable effects.[102] Modern artillery munitions under the weight limit of the St Petersburg Declaration are therefore legally permissible under international customary law (as a Convention provision, the St Petersburg Declaration is scarcely ever applicable, due to its general participation clause).

407   **It is prohibited to use bullets which expand or flatten easily in the human body (e.g. dum-dum bullets) (Declaration Concerning Expanding Bullets of 1899). This applies also to the use of shotguns, since shot causes similar suffering unjustified from the military point of view. It is also prohibited to use projectiles of a nature:**

—to burst or deform while penetrating the human body;

—to tumble early in the human body; or

—to cause shock waves leading to extensive tissue damage or even lethal shock (Arts. 35, para. 2 and 51, para. 4, lit. c AP I; Art. 23 lit. e Hague Regulations).

1. The attempt to outlaw excessively cruel weapons, which was the basis of the St Petersburg Declaration of 1868, was continued in the Declaration Concerning Expanding Bullets adopted at the Hague Peace Conference in 1899.[103] The intended object of the prohibition was the projectile developed by the British Army for use against tribesmen in India, which had become known as the 'dum-dum bullet'. The declaration must be seen as an undertaking parallel to the prohibition against the use of poison or poisonous weapons included by the Hague Peace Conference in Art. 23, lit. a HagueReg and to the (admittedly rather general) prohibition of 'arms, projectiles, or material calculated to cause unnecessary suffering' in Art. 23 lit.e Hague Regulations (see *supra*, Section 402).

---

[99] Kalshoven, in *Recueil des Cours* 191 (1985 II), 205–8, 212–13.   [100] Ibid.

[101] Kalshoven, *loc. cit.*, 207.

[102] See e.g. Meyrowitz, *RIC* 50 (1968), 545 and Kalshoven, *Recueil des Cours* 191 (1985 II), 222–3; cf. Sandoz, *Des armes interdites*, 18–19.

[103] Reprinted in Schindler/Toman, 109–11; as to its historical background see Kalshoven, *Recueil des Cours* 191 (1985 II), 213–17 and Fenrick, *CYIL* 19 (1989), 239–40.

Oeter

2. What exactly is covered by the firmly established prohibition against (in the original French version) *'maux superflus'* remains however, in doubt, although the Geneva Diplomatic Conference 1974–77 reaffirmed the basic prohibition in Arts. 35, para. 2 and 51, para. 4 lit. c AP I in a formula nearly identical to Art. 23 lit.e Hague Regulations. One could reasonably argue, as the German administration for example does, that the use of shotguns has essentially to be regarded as prohibited under these provisions, since shot inflicts extremely painful wounds which cause grave difficulties in medical treatment, but is not much more efficient in its effects than normal infantry munition. Nevertheless, no real consensus has developed on this issue. The same could be said of other variants of recently developed infantry weapons and munitions which cause excessive injuries without achieving particularly impressive military advantages: projectiles which burst or deform while penetrating the human body; projectiles which tumble early in the human body (causing particularly severe internal injuries); and weapons and munitions which cause shock waves leading to extensive tissue damage or even lethal shock. The analogy with the dum-dum bullets outlawed in 1899 is obvious, and a prohibition under the general ground of 'excessive suffering' suggests itself; an explicit prohibition anchored in treaty law, however, has not yet been agreed by the international community. Also far from easy to evaluate is the question of precisely which new weapons are covered by the prohibitions in Art. 23 lit.e Hague Regulations and Art. 35, para. 2 AP I. That discussions on modern small-calibre high-velocity weapons systems over the last decades has produced no agreement is telling in that respect.[104]

**It is also prohibited to use any weapon the primary effect of which is to injure by   408
fragments which in the human body escape detection by X-rays (Protocol I to the
WeaponsConv).**

The prohibition laid down in the Protocol on Non-detectable Fragments is the only specific prohibition of a weapon in the tradition of the St Petersburg Declaration and Art. 23, lit. e HagueReg which met with unanimous approval by state representatives at the meetings of experts in Lucerne and Lugano in the 1970s, and then at the concluding UN Weapons Conference of Geneva in 1980.[105] As Protocol No. I it was annexed to the Convention of 10 October 1980 'on prohibitions or restrictions on the use of certain conventional weapons which may be deemed to be excessively injurious or to have indiscriminate effects'.[106] The Federal Republic of Germany ratified the Convention, including its Protocols, in 1992.[107]

The prohibition in Protocol I is formulated restrictively, being deemed to cover only weapons the primary effects of which lie in the spread of non-detectable

---

[104] See Kalshoven, *Recueil des Cours* 191 (1985 II), 259–61 and Fenrick, *loc. cit.*, 250–2; as a re-evaluation of the discussion on the basis of new ballistic findings see Granat, 157–68.

[105] See Kalshoven, *Recueil des Cours* 191 (1985 II), 241–4, 251–3 and Fenrick, *loc. cit.*, 242.

[106] Reprinted in Schindler/Toman, 179–96; as to the framework agreement of the UN Weapons Convention system see the detailed comments by Roach, *Military Law Review* 1984, 16–68 and Fenrick, *La Convention sur les armes classiques*, 542–55.

[107] Cf. the draft of an approving statute in BR-Drs. 117–92 of 21 Feb. 1992 and BT-Drs. 12/2460, 12/2904.

fragments ('weapons which were *designed* to injure by such fragments', according to the report of the working group),[108] and also it covers only the extreme cases of fragments not readily detectable, namely those not detectable even by X-rays. This means, in particular, fragments of plastic, wood, or glass which cause unnecessarily severe suffering because medical care is impeded and long periods of rehabilitation become unavoidable if such weapons are used.[109] However, weapons which contain plastic or other non-metallic parts for purposes other than those aimed at by Protocol No. I, such as grenades or mines with plastic detonators, are not covered.[110]

409 **The use of mines and other devices on land is, in principle, permissible (Art. 1 Protocol II to the UN Weapons Convention of 1980). According to this Understanding:**

—**'mine' means any device placed—or remotely delivered—under, on, or near the ground or other surface area and designed to be detonated or exploded by the presence, proximity, or contact of a person or vehicle (Art. 2, No. 1 to the WeaponsConv);**

—**'other devices' means manually emplaced munitions or devices designed to kill, injure, or damage and which are actuated by remote control or automatically after a lapse of time (Art. 2, No. 3, Protocol II to the WeaponsConv).**

1. The most important result of the negotiations on conventional weapons that culminated in the UN Weapons Convention of 1980 was the 'Protocol on prohibitions or restrictions on the use of mines, booby-traps, and other devices'. Contrary to Protocol I (on non-detectable fragments) it did not use the prohibition against unnecessary suffering as its starting-point, but the prohibition against indiscriminate warfare and against weapons with indiscriminate results. This does not prohibit the possession or even the use of mines and booby-traps as such; the purpose of the Protocol is only to prohibit the use of mines and booby-traps in certain situations, where the danger of indiscriminate effects is particularly grave.[111] Therefore, the Protocol in principle recognizes the legality of the use of mines in common practice. Beside this relative, situational prohibition against the use of mines the Protocol also contains absolute prohibitions against the use of certain perfidiously hidden explosive devices (booby-traps) which are often, in practice, deployed not against combatants, but for the sake of terrorizing the civilian population in order to break its will to resist (as demonstrated especially in, e.g., the war in Afghanistan).[112] A particular problem is posed by modern mines that can be remotely delivered deep into the enemy hinterland by the use of mortars, rockets,

---

[108] Roach, *loc. cit.*, 69–70.

[109] See the memorandum of the German Government annexed to the draft of an approving statute to the Weapons Convention, BR-Drs. 117/92, 25.

[110] Ibid.

[111] For technical details of the mine protocol see in particular Carnahan, *Military Law Review* 1984, 73–95 and A.P.V. Rogers, *RIC* 72 (1990), 573–83.

[112] See the Memorandum of the German Government, BR-Drs. 117/92, 25.

or air vehicles. The Protocol here has obliged states to undertake certain safeguarding measures, by which the dangers of such uncontrolled minefields shall be reduced as far as possible.[113]

2. Art. 2 of Protocol II defines exactly what constitutes mines and booby-traps. According to that definition, a 'mine' is 'any munition placed under, on, or near the ground or other surface area and designed to be detonated or exploded by the presence, proximity, or contact of a person or vehicle'. The essential point in the definition is the detonation or explosion of the device by an action of a third person or vehicle. Such third party intervention is the characteristic which distinguishes between 'mines' and 'other devices', which are detonated by remote control or delayed-action cap.

It is prohibited to direct the above-mentioned munitions—even by way of   410
reprisals—against the civilian population as such or against individual civilians
(Art. 3, para. 2, Protocol II to the WeaponsConv). Any indiscriminate use of these
weapons is prohibited (Art. 3, para. 3, Protocol II to the WeaponsConv).

1. Art. 3 of the Mine Protocol lays down the fundamental principle of the entire regulation. It is forbidden to use any of the weapons covered by the Protocol (mines, booby-traps, and other devices) against the civilian population or against individual civilians[114] in any circumstances, whether offensive, defensive, or by way of reprisal. All forms of indiscriminate use are likewise prohibited, i.e. any use which is not specifically directed against a military objective, which employs a weapon or means of delivery which cannot be limited in its effects to military objectives, or which is likely to cause disproportionate collateral damage.[115]

2. Careful analysis of the elementary safeguards of Art. 3 reveals that they merely reaffirm the principle of distinction and the prohibition against indiscriminate warfare, now codified in the provisions of Arts. 48 and 51 AP I (see Sections 441, 451, 454, and 456). Both fundamental rules are expressly repeated here with regard to mine warfare, without adding anything to the content of either principle.[116] This is made explicit, in particular, by paragraph 3 of Art. 3, Protocol II (prohibition of indiscriminate use) which adopts almost verbatim the wording of Art. 51, para. 4 AP I.[117] Thus the provisions of Art. 3 could be seen as merely affirming a truism, namely that the general provisions on weapons and means of warfare in Art. 51 AP I are applicable also to mine warfare.[118] It is therefore stressed that the specific

---

[113] For the fierce debate on remotely delivered mines that had developed at the conferences of Lucerne and Lugano and at the UN Weapons Conference in 1980 see Rauch, *GYIL* 24 (1981), 269–80; Carnahan, *loc. cit.*, 79–80; Würkner-Theis, 152–3.

[114] Cf. also Würkner-Theis, 109–20.

[115] For the parallel legal consequences resulting from Art. 51, para. 4 AP I see Würkner-Theis, 141–52, 160–71.

[116] To the contrary conclusion, see Rauch, *GYIL* 24 (1981), 270–8 (esp. 274, 278).

[117] Kalshoven, *Constraints*, 153.

[118] See Rauch, *loc. cit.*, 265–6, 279; Würkner-Theis, 98–103 (esp. 102–3); cf. however, Fenrick, *CYIL* 19 (1981), 243–4.

Oeter

regulation of Protocol II constitutes nothing more than a concretization of the basic principles of distinction and the prohibition against 'indiscriminate warfare' which were in any event applicable to mine warfare.[119] Therefore, even when parties to a conflict are not bound by the UN Weapons Convention, they will be bound by most of the specific provisions of Protocol II to the extent that these represent the general principles embodied in Art. 51 AP I for the special case of mine warfare.[120]

3. The same considerations are true for non-international armed conflicts, in which a comparable prohibition against indiscriminate use of mines also applies. It must be assumed that the utmost protection of the civilian population is required (as provided by common Art. 3 of the Geneva Conventions) as an 'elementary consideration of humanity', a rule which in principle requires every armed force to employ in non-international conflicts only weapons and means of combat which are directed against members of enemy armed forces and against military objects.[121] Assuming this (as one must do), the parties, even of purely internal armed conflicts, are not permitted to make unlimited use of mines and other explosive devices. Even in non-international armed conflicts, mining operations must be designed in such a way that the civilian population is not excessively damaged, i.e. the principles described below, which give the guiding principle of distinction more concrete shape, must be applied in principle even by parties to purely internal conflicts.[122] Admittedly, however, there exist serious difficulties concerning the implementation of the fundamental rules for the protection of the civilian population against the dangers of mines in civil wars. The problem of the millions of mines scattered today throughout areas of conflict undoubtedly constitutes one of the main scourges for the civilian population of regions plagued by civil wars.

411 **All feasible precautions shall be taken to protect civilians also from unintended effects of these munitions (Art. 3, para. 4 Protocol II to the WeaponsConv).**

Art. 3, para. 4 of Protocol II on Mines repeats once again the fundamental rule of Art. 57 AP I, although with a specific orientation towards problems of mine warfare (see Section 457), but even here in a formula nearly identical to the wording of Art. 57 AP I.[123] The general explanations given above under Section 410 as to Art. 3 Protocol II are valid also concerning this provision: the 'active' precautions required in general by Art. 57 AP I ('every precaution practically feasible') must in principle always be taken by the responsible military leaders, including cases of mining operations. The employment of mines and booby-traps is of particular importance, since the dangers for the civilian population arising from such means of combat are particularly high. Accordingly, the location of a minefield must be chosen with due regard to civilian protection; the location and pattern of the minefield should be recorded, in

---

[119] See Kalshoven, *Constraints*, 153–4; A. P. V. Rogers, *RIC* 72 (1990), 572; Aubert, *RIC* 72 (1990), 536–7.

[120] See Würkner-Theis, 283–302.

[121] See Kalshoven, in Cassese (Ed.), 267–85 (esp. 281–2); Plattner, *La Convention de 1980*, 607–10.

[122] The point is impressively elaborated by Plattner, *RIC* 72 (1990), 610–19.

[123] Concerning the parallelism of Art. 57, para. 2 AP I and Art. 3, para. 4 Weapons Protocol II see Würkner-Theis, 181–97 (esp. 191–5).

order that the mines may be removed as soon as they are no longer needed, and the mines should be guarded and marked, as far as is feasible, in order to prevent unnecessary civilian casualties.

Mines and other devices shall not be used in any built-up area, or other area pre-   412
dominantly inhabited by civilians, in which there is no actual or imminent com-
bat between ground forces (Art. 4, para. 2 Protocol II to the WeaponsConv).
Exceptions are permissible if:

—these munitions are placed on or in the close vicinity of a military objective; or

—measures are taken to protect civilians from their effects, for example, the post-
ing of warning signs, the posting of sentries, the provision of fences, or the issue
of warnings (Art. 4, paras. 2, lit. a and b Protocol II to the WeaponsConv).

1. The above rule repeats Art. 4 of the Mine Protocol. That provision contains special guidelines for the use of manually emplaced conventional mines and explosive
devices in towns, villages, or other areas with a similar population density of civilians, to the extent that such use is not a compelling military necessity arising
immediately out of situations of combat (which can only be the case when combat
between ground forces takes place or appears to be imminent directly in the zone
of a settlement).[124] Inside such zones or settlements the use of mines has in practice been shown to pose particularly serious dangers.[125] Art. 4 therefore provides for
a general prohibition on the use of mines in such areas—as long as they are not
inside the combat zone.

2. The use of mines in densely populated areas, however, is exceptionally admissible according to the provision of Art. 4 if mines are employed directly to protect a
military installation, or for combat against an enemy military objective (placement
directly 'on or in the close vicinity of a military objective'[126]), or when precautionary measures have been taken which reduce the risk for the civilian population to a
tolerable degree.[127] Art. 4, para. 2 lit. b enumerates some examples of these precautionary measures: the posting of warning signs, the posting of sentries, the issue of
warnings, and the provision of fences. The following conclusion may be drawn. The
preventive placement of minefields is permitted even in conurbations and settlements,[128] if these minefields are guarded and secured against intrusion by civilians—a modification which seems sensible, since under those conditions the
dangers for the civilian population are kept in reasonable bounds.[129]

---

[124] For a criticism of the distinction between combat zone and hinterland see Rauch, *GYIL* 24 (1981),
280–1.
[125] See the Memorandum of the German Government on the UN Weapons Convention, BR-Drs. 117/92,
26.
[126] As to that formula see Rauch, *loc. cit.*, 278–9.
[127] For the debate on that formula see Carnahan, *Military Law Review* 1984, 81–2.
[128] Of a different opinion, however, is Rauch, *loc. cit.*, 281–2.
[129] See the Memorandum of the German Government on the UN Weapons Convention, BR-Drs. 117/92,
26; moreover, see Fenrick, *CYIL* 19 (1981), 245.

Oeter

413   The use of remotely delivered mines is prohibited unless such mines are only used
       within an area which is itself a military objective or which contains military objec-
       tives (Art. 5, para. 1 Protocol II to the WeaponsConv). After emplacement, their
       location shall be accurately recorded (Art. 5, para. 1, lit. a Protocol II to the
       WeaponsConv). If a mine no longer serves its military purpose, a self-actuating
       mechanism shall ensure its destruction or neutralization within a reasonable
       lapse of time (Art. 5, para. 1, lit. b Protocol II to the WeaponsConv).

1. The particular problem of remotely delivered mines led to fierce debates during
the Weapons Conference of 1980, debates which had already arisen at the preparatory meetings of Lucerne and Lugano.[130] While many states (particularly those from
the Third World) had demanded that a total prohibition against the use of remotely
delivered mines should be included in Protocol II, most of the industrialized states
argued that a complete prohibition against such devices would be in total contra-
diction with requirements of military necessity. In particular the member states of
NATO claimed that the possibility of employing mines in enemy territory in order
to hamper the enemy's operations in its hinterland and to block deployment areas
was militarily absolutely necessary. The reasons are obvious: NATO states thought
it necessary to retain the option of disturbing and delaying the advance of the second and third attack formation of Warsaw Pact armies.[131] Finally, in a night session
at the 1980 Conference, delegations agreed to the compromise now embodied in
Art. 5 of the Mine Protocol. Art. 5 does not completely ban the use of remotely delivered mines, but it requires the parties to the treaty to take far-reaching precautionary measures and technical safeguards against the risks to the civilian population
resulting from such devices.[132]

2. Thus, remotely delivered mines may only be employed within an area which
itself constitutes a military objective (gathering areas of attack formations) or which
contains military objectives.[133] A purely preventive placement of minefields with a
view to potential future operation is thus prohibited. The location of remotely delivered mines must be recorded with the utmost possible precision,[134] and in principle remotely delivered mines must be fitted with a neutralizing mechanism which
renders them unserviceable as soon as they lose their military purpose.[135] Such a
neutralizing mechanism may be self-actuating if the duration of the military purpose which the mine is intended to serve can be foreseen; or it can be a remote control mechanism by which the mine is rendered harmless or brought to detonation
when the mine ceases to serve the military purpose for which it was emplaced.[136]

[130] See Carnahan, *loc. cit.*, 79–80; Rauch, *loc. cit.*, 269–80; Würkner-Theis, 152–9.

[131] Such is the reasoning of the German Government's Memorandum, submitted to Parliament before
ratification, see BR-Drs. 117/92, 26.

[132] For the compromise character of Art. 5 see Würkner-Theis, 172–97 (esp. 193–7) and Rogers, *RIC* 72
(1990), 576–7.

[133] As to the problem what constitutes a military objective in the use of remotely delivered mines see
Würkner-Theis, 121–40.

[134] See Würkner-Theis, 175–6 and Rogers, *loc. cit.*, 577.

[135] Whether this requirement is really mandatory has been disputed, see Rogers, *loc. cit.*, 576–7.

[136] As to technical questions of the possible neutralizing mechanisms see Würkner-Theis, 173–5.

Oeter

3. From the wording of Weapons Protocol II it could be argued that the fundamental prohibition against the use of mines in densely populated areas and settlements, provided for in Art. 4 for all other types of mines, does not apply to remotely delivered mines. Nevertheless, it must be doubted whether this is a sensible conclusion. The general prohibition against 'indiscriminate warfare' covering all uses of mines, which was reaffirmed in respect of mine warfare by Art. 3, para. 3 of Weapons Protocol II, leads to the same conclusions as were explicitly drawn by Art. 4, even without the formal applicability of that provision.[137] The employment of remotely delivered mines in densely populated areas poses extremely high risks to the civilian population (even in cases of neutralization of rear areas), because minefields deep in the enemy hinterland cannot be marked or controlled or guarded. How the use of remotely delivered mines in densely populated areas could ever be justifiable, given the prohibition against indiscriminate warfare, remains difficult to conceive, unless the civilian population has fled the combat area or been evacuated.

Effective advance warning shall be given of any delivery or dropping of remotely delivered mines which may affect the civilian population, unless circumstances do not permit this (Art. 5, para. 2 Protocol II to the WeaponsConv).   414

In order to protect the civilian population against the dangers of remotely delivered mines the party responsible for their use is obliged to give an effective advance warning if the civilian population actually risks damage by such mines.[138] This warning may only be omitted if the specific circumstances of the operation make it impossible (as to the warning prior to an attack in general, see Section 453). It is open to debate, however, in what situations circumstances do not permit a warning. Some authors argue that tactical necessities, such as ensuring surprise or the necessity to protect the delivering aeroplane, may justify a deviation from the basic rule of Art.5, para. 2 Weapons Protocol II.[139] Whether this is true, or whether Art. 5, para. 2 Protocol II should not be read more restrictively, remains in dispute.

It is prohibited in all circumstances to use: 415

a) any booby-trap in the form of an apparently harmless portable object (Arts. 2, para. 2 and 6, para. 1, lit. a Protocol II to the WeaponsConv);

b) booby-traps which are in any way attached to or associated with:

—internationally recognized protective emblems, signs, or signals;

—sick, wounded, or dead persons;

—burial or cremation sites or graves;

—medical facilities, transportation, equipment, or supplies;

—food or drink;

—objects of a religious nature;

---

[137] The point is argued impressively by Rauch, *loc. cit.*, 283.
[138] See Würkner-Theis, 200–2.   [139] Ibid. 201 and Rogers, *loc. cit.*, 576.

Oeter

—cultural objects;

—children's toys and all other objects related to children;

—animals or their carcasses (Art. 6, para. 1, lit. b); or

c) booby-traps designed to cause superfluous injury or unnecessary suffering (Art. 6, para. 2).

Art. 6 of Weapons Protocol II lays down an absolute prohibition against the use of certain types of booby-traps. The humanitarian necessity of such a prohibition was and is undisputed. The so-called 'booby-traps', i.e. devices which are constructed to kill or injure by an explosion initiated unexpectedly 'when a person disturbs or approaches an apparently harmless object or performs an apparently safe act' (the definition in Art. 2, No. 3 Protocol II),[140] have gained tragic prominence in recent practice. In Afghanistan, in particular, they were frequently used: despite the pre-existing prohibition in the UN Weapons Convention.[141] Due to their apparent harmlessness, booby-traps are extremely dangerous for the civilian population, and their primary effect is to terrorize the civilian population, a purpose strictly prohibited under humanitarian law. Art. 6, para. 1, lit. b of the Protocol enumerates some of the most repellent variants of booby-traps, the express prohibition of which is not strictly necessary.[142] The same is true for the general principle embodied in Art. 6, para. 2, which repeats the fundamental prohibition of *maux superflus* in respect of the employment of booby-traps.[143] So far the provision, and probably all of Art. 6, seems to be merely declaratory, since such means and methods of combat are already prohibited under the general rules.

416   This prohibition does not apply to fixed demolition appliances or to portable demolition devices lacking any harmless appearance.

The admissibility of the use of other explosive devices results from the basic approach of Art. 6 Weapons Protocol II by way of an *argumentum e contrario*. All fixed demolition appliances, and portable demolition devices not disguised as harmless objects, are permitted, provided that they are immediately recognizable as dangerous devices and have not been heavily camouflaged. Even these demolition devices, however, fall under the general rules of Articles 3 and 4, and are therefore covered by the prohibition against indiscriminate warfare as well as that against weapons and munitions which have indiscriminate effects, not to mention the strict limitations on the use of explosive devices in populated areas. In particular, with camouflaged demolition devices which function by an actuating mechanism such as a trip wire, the belligerent parties must take strict precautionary

---

[140] As to the definition of Art. 2, No. 3 Mine Protocol see Carnahan, *loc. cit.*, 89–90.

[141] See the findings of the special rapporteur appointed by the UN Human Rights Commission to investigate human rights violations in Afghanistan, Felix Ermacora, in his report presented in 1988, UN Doc. A/43/742 of 24 Oct. 1988, 23 (paras. 103–4).

[142] See Carnahan, *loc. cit.*, 91–2; Kalshoven, *Recueil des Cours* 191 (1985 II), 255.

[143] See Carnahan, *The Law of Land Mine Warfare*, 90 and Fenrick, *Use of Conventional Weapons*, 245.

measures, in most cases probably by guarding the appliances in order to prevent triggering of the device by civilian persons not involved in combat.

**The location of minefields, mines and booby-traps shall be recorded. The parties   417
to the conflict shall retain these records and, whenever possible, by mutual agreement, provide for their publication (Art. 7 Protocol II to the WeaponsConv). In the Federal Armed Forces the Territorial Command authorities are responsible for the documentation of mines.**

1. The Weapons Protocol II provides a rudimentary obligation to record the existence of minefields and booby-traps. In the case of pre-planned minefields and of large-scale pre-planned booby-traps, Art. 7 of the Protocol requires the parties to the conflict to record their location;[144] other minefields, mines, and booby-traps delivered *ad hoc* in the wake of combat operations, however, are covered only by a clause requiring best efforts: 'The parties shall endeavour to ensure the recording of the location of all other minefields . . .'.[145] In order to concretize the recording obligation embodied in Art. 7 the parties to the treaty have agreed on additional minimum standards of recording, laid down in a non-binding 'Technical Annex' to the Protocol; the guidelines on recording set by the Annex should facilitate the discovery and neutralization of mines.[146] These minimum standards also distinguish between pre-planned minefields and demolition appliances and other uses of mines and explosive devices. In all cases, however, the required information is limited to information on the geographic location of minefields, booby-traps, and demolition appliances.[147] This is obviously insufficient. The Federal Republic of Germany (like other western states) has accordingly stressed in its final declaration that, in order to achieve the humanitarian purposes of the Protocol, it is desirable that these rules should be interpreted generously. If feasible, parties to a conflict should also record information on the nature and quantity of the mines delivered, and also information on eventual safeguards for removal.[148]

2. The creation of records not only about location, but also nature, quantity, and patterns of delivery will normally be in the military interest of the parties to the conflict, since systematic mining documentation enables the parties to protect their own armed forces against the dangers arising from uncontrolled minefields.[149] Particularly in the case of complex and rapidly moving combat operations, the armed forces of a belligerent can only be protected against the dangers of minefields placed by allied units if the minefields and booby-traps are carefully documented and the mining documentation is systematically collected and

---

[144] Concerning the problematic notion of 'pre-planned minefields' see Carnahan, *loc. cit.*, 84; Fenrick, *loc. cit.*, 245–6, and Würkner-Theis, 203–7.

[145] As to the obligation contained in Art. 7, para. 2 see Würkner-Theis, 209–12.

[146] See Carnahan, *loc. cit.*, 84–5; Würkner-Theis, 208.

[147] See Würkner-Theis, 207–9; Carnahan, *loc. cit.*, 84.

[148] See the Memorandum of the German Government on ratification of the UN Weapons Convention, BR-Drs. 117/92, 27.

[149] See Fenrick, *loc. cit.*, 242–3.

administered. An equally strong argument can also be made for extensive documentation concerning the removal of mixed fields which combine anti-tank mines and anti-personnel mines with fragmentation mines; rapid and secure removal of such minefields by a different unit from that which planted the field becomes possible only if exact documentation is available on the location and pattern of delivery. Without solid documentation, removal of one's own minefields would endanger engineer units. Thus in the German armed forces it is required that every unit placing a minefield records the necessary information in a standardized document; these documents are continually collected and combined into all-embracing mining documents for the respective territories by territorially competent regional command authorities.[150]

3. After the end of hostilities the parties, according to Art. 7, para. 3 of the Mine Protocol, must take all feasible measures to protect the civilian population against danger from minefields and other explosive devices.[151] Weapons Protocol II distinguishes in this respect different sets of cases. If parties to the conflict are still in occupation of enemy territory, then the obligation is limited to the usual 'necessary and appropriate measures', including the use of records by the occupying authorities, to protect civilians from the effects of minefields, (Art. 7, para. 3, lit. a (i));[152] the military authorities of the occupying powers must mark the minefields, warn the civilian population, and in some cases guard minefields. By contrast, in cases where no territory remains under occupation by the adverse party, the parties shall make available to each other all information in their possession concerning the location of minefields, mines, and booby-traps in the territory of the adverse party (Art. 7, para. 3, lit. a (ii)), on the intervention of the Secretary-General of the United Nations to whom the records must also be made available. Once complete withdrawal of the forces of one party from occupation of the territory of another has taken place, the parties are also required to make available all other information on minefields and booby-traps. In the meantime, however, the obligation is limited in Art. 7, para. 3, lit. c merely to endeavour to provide 'whenever possible, by mutual agreement . . . information concerning the location of minefields . . .'.[153] The much more extensive mandatory requirement to release *all* information available immediately after the cessation of active hostilities which was sought by the Federal Republic of Germany was unfortunately not achieved at the UN Weapons Conference.[154]

4. One further point arising from the customary minimum standards on the protection of the civilian population must be mentioned when describing the guidelines on recording and on safeguards against continued endangering of civilians after the end of hostilities. If one takes seriously the concept of the best feasible pro-

---

[150] See the Memorandum of the German Government on ratification of the UN Weapons Convention, BR-Drs. 117/92, 27.

[151] See Carnahan, *loc. cit.*, 85 ff.; Würkner-Theis, 219 ff.

[152] Concerning the scope of these obligations to protect, see Würkner-Theis, 224–5.

[153] As to the compromise character of that rule see Carnahan, *loc. cit.*, 86–7 and Würkner-Theis, 220–3.

[154] See the detailed reasoning given in the Memorandum of the German Government on ratification of the UN Weapons Convention, BR-Drs. 117/92, 27; see also Fenrick, *loc. cit.*, 246.

Oeter

tection of civilians after the end of hostilities, one must wonder whether the *ad hoc* use of non-metallic anti-personnel mines outside pre-planned (and therefore unrecorded) minefields should still be regarded as permissible.[155] If the exact location of these mines is not recorded, or the records are not made available to the party concerned, it is nearly impossible to detect and systematically clear such mines; accordingly they become a permanent threat to the civilian population, which is incompatible with the standards of responsible warfare which requires respect for the prohibition against indiscriminate warfare.

When a United Nations force or mission performs peace-keeping, observation, or   418
similar functions, each party to the conflict shall, if requested:

—render harmless all mines or booby-traps;

—take such measures as may be necessary to protect the force or mission while carrying out its duties; and

—make available to the head of the force or mission all pertinent information in the party's possession (Art. 8, para. 1, lit. a to c Protocol II to the WeaponsConv).

The protection of the force or mission shall be ensured at all times (Art. 8, para. 2 Protocol II to the WeaponsConv).

Besides the general safeguards provided by the prohibitions against indiscriminate warfare, excessive suffering, and perfidious methods of warfare, Weapons Protocol II also includes provisions concerning the duty of parties to co-operate with United Nations forces and missions in respect of mines. The Protocol undoubtedly creates new obligations in requiring parties to an armed conflict to protect UN forces and missions against dangers resulting from mines and to assist and co-operate with such forces or missions.[156] Practical experience has shown that peacekeeping forces and observer missions[157] of the United Nations are particularly endangered by minefields and booby-traps, since these units and missions must often move between the lines of the adverse armed forces. Extensive safeguards and protective measures for UN forces and observer missions are thus undoubtedly necessary. Of particular relevance will be the general duty of the parties to provide to the head of the UN force or mission all available information on the location of minefields, mines, and booby-traps in the area concerned.

After the cessation of an international armed conflict, the parties to the conflict   419
shall, both among themselves and, where appropriate, with other states or inter-
national organizations, exchange information and technical assistance necessary

---

[155] Concerning the problems of non-metallic anti-personnel mines see the observations based on the experience of the Falklands War made by Rogers, *loc. cit.*, 580–1 and the technical remarks by Cauderay, *RIC* 75 (1993), 293–308.

[156] See Carnahan, *loc. cit.*, 94–5.

[157] The provision refers only to these two categories of UN personnel; fighting troops of the UN in enforcement operations under Chapter VII are probably not protected under this provision—see Carnahan, *loc. cit.*, 95.

Oeter

to remove or otherwise render ineffective minefields, mines, and booby-traps (Art. 9 Protocol II to the WeaponsConv).

Art. 9 of the Protocol on Prohibitions or Restrictions on the Use of Mines, Booby-traps, and Other Devices provides for a minimum core of international co-operation in the removal of minefields after the cessation of active hostilities.[158] The parties shall endeavour, according to Art. 9, to agree (both among themselves and, where appropriate, with other states and with international organizations) on co-operation in the neutralization and removal of minefields, mines, and booby-traps. That agreement should cover the provision of information on the location and nature of minefields and booby-traps, and provision of technical and material assistance in the clearance of minefields and the removal of mines and booby-traps, including in appropriate circumstances joint operations for removal.[159] In most cases the realization of these objectives would constitute a great step forward, particularly in view of the fact that it is normally the civilian population which suffers as a result of lack of co-operation in the neutralization and removal of mines after the cessation of hostilities. The experience of the last decades proves, however, that non-international armed conflicts in practice cause the main problem in this respect; yet the Weapons Protocols are not applicable to internal armed conflicts according to the wording of the 1980 Treaty. The legal instrument of the UN Weapons Convention with its Protocols thus fails to address the major problems that arise from military practice, except in so far as it reiterates general standards of customary law prohibiting indiscriminate warfare in the use of mines, applicable even to non-international armed conflicts (see Section 410).

420 **Incendiary weapons are weapons or munition primarily designed to set fire to materials or objects or to cause burn injury to persons through the action of flame, heat, or a combination thereof. Examples are: flame-throwers, fougasses (hand-held weapons containing liquid incendiaries), shells, rockets, grenades, mines, bombs and other containers of incendiary substances (Art. 1, para. 1, lit. a Protocol III to the WeaponsConv).**

One of the main topics of the 1980 UN Weapons Conference was the issue of incendiary weapons (the US air force use of napalm bombs in Vietnam were still fresh in the memory).[160] Some of the states participating at the conference (including Sweden, Mexico, and the majority of the non-aligned states) demanded a complete ban on incendiary weapons, for these weapons—such was the argument—always cause unnecessary suffering and generally have also indiscriminate effects;[161] but the superpowers, led by the USA and the USSR, openly declared that—due to the military importance of incendiary weapons—they would accept, at the maximum,

---

[158] See Würkner-Theis, 229–32.

[159] For examples of such agreements see Carnahan, *loc. cit.*, 82–3.

[160] Concerning the military background to the use of incendiary weapons see Fenrick, *loc. cit.*, 247.

[161] See the Memorandum of the German Government on ratification of the UN Weapons Convention, BR-Drs. 117/92, 27; see also Fenrick, *loc. cit.*, 248; Kalshoven, *Recueil des Cours* 191 (1985 II), 256–7; Parks, *RIC* 72 (1990), 588–94.

Oeter

a few (and limited) restrictions on the use of such weapons.[162] The traditional military powers thought these weapons to be militarily absolutely necessary to attack certain objectives, and particularly specific operations such as 'close air support' in the combat zone against immediately adjacent enemy positions.[163] A compromise only became possible when the delegation of the USA began to request a prohibition of all air-launched attacks by incendiary weapons (including napalm) in settlements and populated areas, thus providing an opening for the resumption of the stalled negotiations.[164] The resulting definition of the incendiary weapons covered by Protocol III of the WeaponsConv is extremely broad, since it includes not only incendiary materials based on hydrocarbon (like napalm) but also all means of combat designed to set fire to objects or to cause burn injury to persons through the action of flame, heat, or a combination thereof.[165] The only important factor in the definition is the causation of burns through chemical reaction of a substance brought on the target.

Incendiary weapons do not include: 421

—munitions which may have incidental incendiary effects (e.g. illuminants, tracers, smoke or signalling systems) (Art. 1, para. 1, lit. b (i) Protocol III to the WeaponsConv); or

—munitions designed to combine penetration, blast, or fragmentation effects with an additional incendiary effect (e.g. armour-piercing projectiles, fragmentation shells, explosive bombs). The incendiary effect shall only be used against military objectives (Art. 1, para. 1 (b) (ii) Protocol III to the WeaponsConv).

Art. 1, para. 1 of the Protocol excludes from its definition of 'incendiary weapons' all means of combat which produce burns only as a side-effect of a different primary objective (like illuminants, smoke or signalling systems).[166] It also excludes weapons which cause burns only as part of an integrated mode of action mainly involving other mechanisms, i.e. munitions not specifically designed to cause burn injury to persons (like anti-tank munitions with an armour-piercing projectile working by extremely high temperature, or fragmentation shells and explosive bombs which combine penetration, blast, or fragmentation effects with an additional incendiary effect).[167] The exclusion of such munitions makes sense in the light of the overall objective of Protocol III, since such munitions with a combined effect are normally used for operation against 'hard' military targets, and not against persons.[168]

[162] Ibid.

[163] See in particular Fenrick, *loc. cit.*, 247–8; cf. also the Memorandum of the German Government on ratification of the UN Weapons Convention, BR-Drs. 117/92, 27.

[164] See the Memorandum of the German Government on ratification of the UN Weapons Convention, BR-Drs. 117/92, 27 and Fenrick, loc.cit., 248.

[165] On the definition of Art.1, para. 1 see Kalshoven, *Recueil des Cours* 191 (1985 II), 257; Fenrick, *loc. cit.*, 248; Parks, *loc. cit.*, 594–5.

[166] Fenrick, *loc. cit.*, 248; Parks, *loc. cit.*, 596.

[167] See Fenrick, *loc. cit.*, 249; Kalshoven, Constraints, 156; Parks, *loc. cit.*, 597–8.

[168] See the Memorandum of the German Government on ratification of the UN Weapons Convention, BR-Drs. 117/92, 27.

Oeter

422 When incendiary weapons are used, all precautions shall be taken which are prac- ticable or practically possible, taking into account all the current circumstances, including humanitarian and military considerations (Art. 1, para. 5 Protocol III to the WeaponsConv).

The parties to an armed conflict are already obliged, under the general rules on weapons and means of combat, to take all precautions which are practically possi- ble in order to protect civilians or civilian objects from unnecessary damage (Art. 57 AP I; see Section 457). Art. 1, para. 5 defines exactly what are 'practically possible precautions' for the purpose of Weapons Protocol III: namely, those precautions which are 'practicable or practically possible, taking into account all circumstances ruling at the time, including humanitarian and military considerations'. Responsible military leaders must with all due diligence take such precautions before an attack, because the risks of indiscriminate effects are extremely high in the case of attack with incendiary weapons. This is particularly the case in attacks on settlements and other concentrations of civilian population; Art. 2, para. 3 of the Protocol requires explicitly that parties take 'all feasible precautions'. That formula requires particular precautions to limit the incendiary effects on the military objec- tive. However, attacks with incendiary weapons *outside* any concentration of civil- ians also requires a considerable degree of diligence, even if the Protocol on Incendiary Weapons is not intended to protect combatants.

423. The civilian population, individual civilians, and civilian objects shall be granted special protection. They shall not be made the object of attack by incen- diary weapons (Art. 2, para. 1 Protocol III to the WeaponsConv).

Art. 2, para. 1 of the Protocol repeats the prohibition of deliberate attacks on civil- ians and civilian objects (particularly, the prohibition of terrorizing attacks) and directs this general prohibition explicitly to the use of incendiary weapons. Thus the provision merely repeats the self-evident, elementary minimum standards of modern humanitarian law which can be deduced directly from Art. 51, para. 2 AP I[169] (see Section 451).

424. It is prohibited under any circumstances to make any military objective located within a concentration of civilians the object of attack by incendiary weapons (Art. 2, paras. 2 and 3 Protocol III to the WeaponsConv).

1. Strictly speaking the Protocol on Incendiary Weapons distinguishes in its sub- stantial provisions between incendiary weapons delivered by the air (e.g. the noto- rious napalm bombs) and other incendiary weapons used on land. Concerning attacks with air-delivered incendiary weapons Art. 2, para. 2 of the Protocol sets up an absolute prohibition against attacks on any objective located within a concen-

---

[169] See Kalshoven, *Constraints*, 157, who claims that the provision is 'strictly speaking,[a] redundant reaffirmation'.

Oeter

tration of civilian population.[170] Attacks with other incendiary weapons are, in principle, also prohibited inside settlements and other concentrations of civilian population; however, under certain conditions specified in Art. 2, para. 3 they remain admissible, namely insofar as the attack is directed against a military objective which is clearly separate from the concentration of civilians and provided that all feasible precautions are taken to limit the incendiary effects so that they damage only the military objective, and to avoid, or to minimize, incidental loss of life and incidental damage to civilian objects.[171]

2. These restrictions on the use of incendiary weapons undoubtedly constitute the core of Protocol III. The civilian population is protected against attacks by incendiary weapons (and in particular by incendiary bombs) within its cities, villages, and comparable settlements. At the same time military necessity is respected by delimiting the object of protection not in purely spatial terms, but in qualitative aspects. Not every area of a settlement is protected, only the concentration of civilians within that settlement. This means that attacks on important military objectives remain legally possible under certain conditions, even if they are located within inhabited areas, as long as these military objectives are not inseparably linked to real concentrations of civilian population (as would be probably: harbour facilities, airports, fuel and munition depots, anti-aircraft gun positions inside large parks, etc.)[172].

It is further prohibited to use incendiary weapons against forests or other kinds of   425
plant cover except when such natural elements are used by the adversary to cover,
conceal, or camouflage a military objective, or are themselves military objectives
(Art. 2, para. 4 Protocol III to the WeaponsConv).

In this rule Protocol III clearly exceeds its original objective of protection, i.e. the prohibitions against unnecessary suffering and indiscriminate warfare. The provision was included in the Protocol following a proposal by the USSR (supported by numerous Third World states). It extends the scope of protection to certain kinds of natural plant cover, in particular forests.[173] The provision is not problematic in military terms, since it explicitly excludes protection in all cases in which flora is used to conceal military objectives, or in which natural cover itself constitutes a military objective.[174] The provision exceeds even the scope of Arts. 35, para. 3 and 55, para. 1 AP I and the ENMOD Convention, in that it is designed to cover isolated attacks on the natural environment even if these are spatially limited, in contrast to the

---

[170] Concerning the complicated drafting history of that provision see Kalshoven, *Recueil des Cours* 191 (1985 II), 258–9; Fenrick, *loc. cit.*, 248; Parks, *loc. cit.*, 591–4, 600–1.

[171] See the Memorandum of the German Government on ratification of the UN Weapons Convention, BR-Drs. 117/92, 28; see also Parks, *loc. cit.*, 602.

[172] See Fenrick, *loc. cit.*, 249; cf. also the Memorandum of the German Government on ratification of the UN Weapons Convention, BR-Drs. 117/92, 27.

[173] See Fenrick, *loc. cit.*, 250; cf. also the Memorandum of the German Government on ratification of the UN Weapons Convention, BR-Drs. 117/92, 28.

[174] See the Memorandum of the German Government on ratification of the UN Weapons Convention, BR-Drs. 117/92, 28.

Oeter

general prohibitions of environmentally damaging warfare, which cover only 'widespread', 'long-term', and 'severe' damage to the environment.

426   **It is prohibited to employ poison and poisoned weapons (Art. 23, lit. a HagueReg).**

The prohibition against poison referred to above is probably the most ancient prohibition of a means of combat in international law.[175] Since the late Middle Ages the use of poison has always been strictly prohibited. With Art. 23 lit.a of the Hague Regulations that firmly established prohibition was codified in an international treaty.[176] Beyond any doubt, the ancient prohibition of poison is still valid today.

2. NBC Weapons

a. Nuclear Weapons

427   **Numerous multilateral and bilateral treaties already exist which are designed to prohibit the proliferation of nuclear weapons, to restrict the testing of nuclear weapons, to prohibit the stationing of nuclear weapons, to provide for nuclear weapon-free zones, to limit the scope of nuclear armament, and to prevent the outbreak of nuclear war. These include:**

—Treaty on the Non-Proliferation of Nuclear Weapons of 1 July 1968;

—Treaty Banning Nuclear Weapon Tests in the Atmosphere, in Outer Space, and under Water of 5 August 1963;

—Outer Space Treaty of 27 January 1967;

—Seabed Treaty of 11 February 1971;

—Treaty on the Prohibition of Nuclear Weapons in Latin America of 14 February 1967;

—Treaty on the Establishment of a Nuclear Weapon-Free Zone in the Southern Pacific Area of 6 August 1985;

—Treaty on the Elimination of American and Soviet Intermediate-Range and Shorter-Range Missiles of 8 December 1987.

When dealing with weapons of mass destruction, and in particular with nuclear weapons, one should bear in mind that production and possession of nuclear weapons are primarily issues of arms control, and not questions of humanitarian law. However, the possibility of the future use of nuclear weapons obviously has an important humanitarian aspect which makes it impossible to relegate the subject matter to be dealt with according to the usual political calculations of arms control treaties. Nuclear weapons are also of extreme importance for modern security policy, a policy that is embedded in a system of deterrence backed by the threat of mutual destruction. Accordingly, the question of the military–technical balance of

[175] See Sandoz, *Des armes interdites*, 11–14.

[176] Concerning Art. 23(a) Hague Regulations and the problem of defining exactly what constitutes 'poison' see Sandoz, *Des armes interdites*, 27–8.

powers is so weighty that it must be seen as legitimate for the superpowers (as well as for the international community) to evaluate, primarily as a matter of security policy, whether and to what degree production and possession of nuclear weapons should be limited.[177] The regulatory instruments of bans and limitations of nuclear armaments are therefore arms control treaties, and not primarily the humanitarian rules of the Geneva Conventions and the Additional Protocols. Over the last decades states have concluded a whole network of treaties about nuclear arms control and disarmament on the global as well as the regional level; the most important of these treaties are listed above.[178]

The international law in force, however, does not contain any explicit prohibition against the use of nuclear weapons, nor can any such prohibition be derived from current contractual and customary law.   428

1. The principle formulated above deals with what is probably the most delicate question of current humanitarian law. For decades the question of whether the use of nuclear weapons is permissible has placed state practice and international doctrine in a kind of religious war, leaving unresolved the problem of whether humanitarian law implicitly answers the question of legality of possession, and especially of use of nuclear weapons.[179] It is indisputable that customary law imposes limitations on the use of nuclear weapons in specific situations. It is not clear, however, whether one can deduce from these traditional restrictions on methods and means of warfare a comprehensive prohibition of nuclear weapons. Under merely quantitative criteria the above formulated (official) position of the Federal Republic of Germany (and of the other Western states) probably now constitutes a minority position, since the number of doctrinal studies attempting to prove an absolute prohibition on the use of nuclear weapons is overwhelming.[180] Whether the arguments of these studies are really convincing in the perspective of current state practice, however, remains open to doubt. Neither the claim that there exists a customary prohibition, founded mainly upon the principle of 'limited warfare' and the resulting prohibition of indiscriminate warfare,[181] nor the attempt to derive a general conventional prohibition from the ban on the use of poisonous gases in the Hague Regulations (Art. 23a) and the Geneva Gas Protocol of 1925[182] is really convincing.

[177] As to the eminently political character of these treaties see Graf Vitzthum, *Rechtsfragen der Rüstungskontrolle*, 110–14.
[178] As a comprehensive study on the current system of arms control treaties see Bothe, ibid. 36–79; cf. also the articles by Woodliffe, Cameron, Grief and Freestone/Davidson in Pogany (Ed.) and the relevant chapter in the US Navy's *Annotated Supplement to the Commander's Handbook on the Law of Naval Operations*, NWP 9 (Rev.A)/FMFM 1–10, 10–3 to 10–6.
[179] Concerning the course of debates in the relevant international forums see the instructive presentation by Kalshoven, *Recueil des Cours* 191 (1985 II), 271–83.
[180] See Schwarzenberger, *Legality*, 35–49; v. d. Heydte, *AVR* 9 (1961), 162–82; Brownlie, *ICLQ* 14 (1968), 441–51; Castrén, *University of Toledo Law Review* 3 (1971), 89–98; Sandoz, *Des armes interdites en droit de la guerre*, 62–74; Falk/Meyrowitz/Sanderson, *Indian Journal of International Law* 20 (1980), 561–95; David, Swinarski (Ed.), 325–42; Nahlik, *International Law and Nuclear Weapons*, 283–99.
[181] See in particular Singh/McWhinney, 313–19, for further references.
[182] See also Singh/McWhinney, 307–12, for further references.

2. The argument that a customary prohibition on the use of nuclear weapons exists has two important weaknesses. First, the principle of distinction between combatants and civilians and the corresponding prohibition of indiscriminate warfare, which were rooted solely in customary law until their codification in AP I, present rather blurred contours in practice (see Sections 441, 451, and 454 to 457). It is certainly possible to find a consensus that there exists such a principle; how far its normative effects reach, however, and to what extent it effectively prohibits belligerents from using certain weapons, is hopelessly disputed. Even the general prohibition on indiscriminate target-area bombardment, affirmed in principle by so many authors, has always remained in dispute in that a real consensus has never been reached on the extent of permissible collateral damages.[183]

3. At the same time, the argument that the use of nuclear weapons *per se* constitutes prohibited indiscriminate warfare is founded on an image of nuclear war which perhaps had some justification in the era of the doctrine of 'massive retaliation', but which fails to appreciate the current options of use, which include militarily targeted employment of precision-guided warheads with limited destruction capability. The option most likely to be adopted under the hitherto dominant 'flexible response' doctrine (and even more so under a new succeeding military doctrine of NATO), use of precision-guided tactical nuclear warheads in limited operations against purely military objectives, would result in consequences which cannot be adequately dealt with by a broad reference to principles such as the prohibition of indiscriminate warfare and the protection of the civilian population. The collateral damage likely to be caused by such attacks is not necessarily much higher than the damage to be expected from modern conventional weapons, which are now designed to create comparable explosive force.[184]

4. As a consequence only one conclusion seems possible: the claimed customary prohibition on the use of nuclear weapons is more an aspiration *de lege ferenda* founded in natural law theory and moral philosophy than a definite provision of positive customary international law derived from state practice and *opinio juris*.[185] This does not mean, however, that no legal limitations to the use of nuclear weapons follow from the prohibition of 'indiscriminate attack': on the contrary it must be stressed that legal limits *in concreto* may be deduced from the general rules

---

[183] See Spaight, 270–8, 280–1; Stone, 627–31; Greenspan, 336; Rosenblad, *Area Bombing*, 53–111; Randelzhofer, *Flächenbombardement und Völkerrecht*, 471–93; Bruha, 'Bombardment', *EPIL* 3, 53–6; Blix, *BYIL* 49 (1978), 54–61; Sassòli, 409–11.

[184] As to the compatibility of certain uses of nuclear weapons with the general humanitarian requirement to distinguish between combatants and civilians see Rauschning, 'Nuclear Warfare and Weapons', *EPIL* 4, 49; Ney, 276–81, 285, 292–8; Meyrowitz, *Etudes Internationales* 17 (1986), 560–2; Fleck, *NZWehrr* 1987, 221–9.

[185] To the same conclusion come Oppenheim/Lauterpacht, Vol.II, 351; Stone, 343–8; Tucker, 50–5; McDougal/Feliciano, 830–1; Kimminich, *Kernwaffenfrage*, 407–23; Rauschning, 'Nuclear Warfare and Weapons', 48–9; Ney, 292–3; Kalshoven, *Recueil des Cours* 191 (1985 II), 283–8 (esp. 286–8); M. N. Shaw, in Pogany (Ed.), 1–18; Pilloud/Pictet, in ICRC *Commentary*, 594 (para. 1857); Bring/Reimann, *Netherlands International Law Review* 33 (1986), 99; Green, in *Denver Journal of International Law and Policy* 17 (1986), 1–27; Pechstein, *loc. cit.* 295.

on means and methods of warfare, notwithstanding that these limits are only relevant as to the concrete fashion in which the weapons are employed, and do not constitute an absolute prohibition on any one category of weapons.[186]

5. Comparable objections should be raised against broad generalizations which assume that nuclear weapons always qualify as 'poisonous weapons' in the sense of Art. 23 lit.a Hague Regulations, or as 'poisonous gases' in the sense of the Geneva Protocol of 1925.[187] Admittedly both notions were deliberately expressed in an 'open' fashion, in order to cover future advances in weapons technology. At the same time, however, it is beyond doubt that new means of combat were intended to be covered by these 'open' provisions only to the extent that the physical effects of such weapons are subject to the same principles as the means of warfare originally covered by the ban. However, it is precisely this comparability of operating principles which may be doubted with plausible arguments concerning nuclear weapons. The physical destruction of enemy objectives by nuclear weapons relies on the same effects as the operation of conventional explosive warheads, namely the results of the explosion (i.e. the pressure wave and subsequent burn effects), whereas the release of poison is an unintended side-effect. In this respect the use of nuclear weapons is different from the use of 'poison' or 'poisonous gases' which are by definition intentionally designed to cause poisoning.[188] Only in so far as nuclear weapons are also designed intentionally to cause poisoning (or radiation) as the primary instrument to weaken the enemy, as with the so-called 'neutron bomb', can one argue plausibly for a 'progressive' and 'dynamic' interpretation which extends the scope of these provisions to cover recent weapons.[189]

International humanitarian law, however, imposes the same general limits on the   **429**
use of nuclear weapons as on the use of conventional weapons: it is prohibited to make the civilian population the object of attack. A distinction shall at all times be made between persons who take part in hostilities and members of the civilian population, who are to be granted maximum protection.

To conclude that the general rules of customary and convention law impose no absolute prohibition on the use of nuclear weapons is not to say that the use of nuclear weapons is free of all legal limitation. On the contrary: nobody has ever claimed seriously that the traditional principles concerning warfare and weapons have been derogated as regards nuclear weapons; such a claim could not be argued

[186] See esp. Bring/Reimann, 99–105 and recently also Reimann, *Das internationale Regime der ABC-Waffen* 308–9; cf. Kalshoven, *Recueil des Cours* 191 (1985 II), 286–7 and the US Navy's *Annotated Supplement to the Commander's Handbook on the Law of Naval Operations*, NWP 9 (Rev.A)/FMFM 1–10, 10–1.
[187] So argue e.g. Schwarzenberger, *Legality*, 48; Sandoz, *Des armes interdites*, 62–5; Falk/Meyrowitz/Sanderson, *Indian Journal of International Law* 20 (1980), 561 *et seq.*; Singh/McWhinney, 307–12.
[188] For the same conclusions see Kimminich, *Kernwaffenfrage*, 418–23; Rauschning, 'Nuclear Warfare and Weapons', *EPIL* 4, 47–8; Kalshoven, *Recueil des Cours* 191 (1985 II), 283–4; Ney, 186–91, 290–1.
[189] See the detailed analysis by Ney, 188–9, 291; see also US Department of the Army Pamphlet 27–161–2, *International Law*, Vol.II (1962), 43.

Oeter

plausibly.[190] This leads to the conclusion: that the above-mentioned general rules of customary law are applicable also to the use of nuclear weapons. The most important consequence of this is that the general prohibition of indiscriminate warfare must cover the use of nuclear weapons. Nuclear weapons may be employed only under strictly specified conditions and only after taking restrictive precautions to restrict their effect on civilians (except in reprisal, so far as reprisals are permissible,[191] see Sections 476 to 479). First use, or use beyond the law of reprisals, is only permissible for modern, precision-guided munitions furnished with nuclear warheads which are employed against military objects and concentrations of armed forces in uninhabited or sparsely populated areas. Care must always be taken to ensure that the pressure wave, the consequent burn effects, and the radioactive fallout cause the minimum possible damage or injury to the civilian population (as to the principle of proportionality, see Section 456).

430   **The new rules introduced by Additional Protocol I were intended to apply to conventional weapons, irrespective of other rules of international law applicable to other types of weapons. They do not influence, regulate, or prohibit the use of nuclear weapons.**

1. When the original draft of the Additional Protocols was presented, and during the later negotiations at the Diplomatic Conference in Geneva 1974–77, there was intense controversy over whether the new Convention should also cover the use of nuclear weapons. The position of the ICRC and of the most important military powers was, from the beginning, that the Additional Protocol should not affect nuclear weaponry.[192] Accordingly, at the opening of the negotiations in 1974 the mandate of the Diplomatic Conference had been restricted to conventional weapons. The German Government—like most of its NATO allies—has stressed this precondition of consent by submitting a corresponding declaration upon its ratification of AP I. The declaration says: 'It is the understanding of the Federal Republic of Germany that the rules relating to the use of weapons introduced by Additional Protocol I were intended to apply exclusively to conventional weapons without prejudice to any other rules of international law applicable to other types of weapons.'[193]

2. The German Government in this interpretative declaration implicitly refers to the declarations filed by the United States of America and the United Kingdom when signing the Additional Protocols.[194] In these 1977 declarations the nuclear powers explicitly referred to the general 'nuclear consensus' which existed at the

---

[190] See Kimminich, *Kernwaffenfrage*, 421–3; Rauschning, *loc. cit.*, 48–9; Ney, 150–64; Roberts, *VaJIntL* 26 (1985), 163–4; Meyrowitz, *Etudes Internationales* 17 (1986), 553–5.

[191] See esp. Kalshoven, *Recueil des Cours* 191 (1985 II), 286 and Kalshoven, *Belligerent Reprisals*, 353–61.

[192] For a description of the historical background see Kalshoven, *Recueil des Cours* 191 (1985 II), 278–83 and Pilloud/ Pictet, ICRC *Commentary*, 590–1 (paras. 1842–6); cf. also Fischer, *Der Einsatz von Nuklearwaffen*, 119–30.

[193] Published in BGBl 1991 II, 968.   [194] Printed in Bothe/Partsch/Solf, 190, 721–2.

outset of the negotiations,[195] a general understanding which purported to exclude discussion on nuclear weapons from the negotiations.

3. This limitation of the negotiations may be explained by the original negotiating proposal of the ICRC. In its introduction is the following formula concerning the question of nuclear weapons: 'Problems relating to atomic, bacteriological and chemical warfare are subjects of international agreements or negotiations by governments, and in submitting these draft Protocols the ICRC does not intend to broach these problems.'[196]

4. In the course of the Diplomatic Conference of 1974–77 the United States, Great Britain, and France repeatedly stressed the limitation of the negotiations, while other states openly attempted to extend the scope of Additional Protocol I to include express regulation concerning nuclear weapons. However, those attempts to take up the question of nuclear warfare finally failed. Nevertheless, no formal agreement on the scope of application could be reached until the end of the conference, which was why the USA and Great Britain annexed their declarations to the Treaty on the occasion of its ratification.[197]

5. By these declarations the so-called 'nuclear consensus' has become directly relevant to the interpretation of the Treaty, because all treaties shall be, according to Art. 31, para. 1 of the Vienna Convention on the Law of Treaties of 1969, 'interpreted in good faith in accordance with the ordinary meaning to be given to the terms of the treaty in their context'. Pursuant to Paragraph 2 of Art. 31 of that Convention the context there is included *in the list of matters* relevant to the interpretation of a treaty provision, in addition to the text (including any preamble and annexes), and 'any instrument which was made by one or more parties in connexion with the conclusion of the treaty and accepted by the other parties as an instrument related to the treaty'. The declarations which were deposited by the USA and the United Kingdom are such instruments, and are directly connected to the text of the Treaty.[198] It is undisputed that they were made on the occasion of the conclusion of the Treaty. It should also be indisputable—although this is questioned by some authors[199]—that the declarations were 'accepted by the other parties as an instrument related to the treaty'. Acceptance by the other parties, referred to in Art. 31, para. 2(b) of the Vienna Convention, requires only a consensus on the connection with the treaty, not a consensus on the substantial content of the declaration.[200] Those authors who argue to the contrary misunderstand that basic principle if they

[195] See Meyrowitz, 25 *GYIL* 219, 229–37 (1982) and Kalshoven, *Recueil des Cours* 191 (1985 II), 282–3.

[196] Printed in Bothe/Partsch/Solf, 188–9; as to the background of the exclusion of NBC weapons from the negotiations see Kalshoven, *Recueil des Cours* 191 (1985 II), 271–82.

[197] As to the history of the negotiations see Solf, in Bothe/Partsch/Solf, 188–92; Kimminich, *Kernwaffenfrage*, 419–23; Ney, 193–209; Fischer, *Der Einsatz von Nuklearwaffen*, 120–46; Pilloud/Pictet, in ICRC *Commentary*, 589–93 (paras. 1839–51).

[198] The same is is argued by Solf, in Bothe/Partsch/Solf, 191 n. 12.

[199] See Fischer, *Der Einsatz von Nuklearwaffen*, 155–60.

[200] See Kühner, *Vorbehalte zu multilateralen völkerrechtlichen Verträgen*, 37 (with further references) and Pechstein, *AVR* 30 (1992), 292.

Oeter

contend that the so-called 'nuclear consensus' is irrelevant in the light of the 'unequivocal' wording of the Additional Protocol, and that the preparatory work of the Treaty and the circumstances of its conclusion are relevant only as a supplementary means of interpretation, pursuant to Art. 32 Vienna Convention, if on the textual interpretation the meaning is ambiguous or obscure.[201] An interpretation based on these assumptions is plausible only if the declarations do not belong to the 'general means of interpretation' in the sense of Art. 31 Vienna Convention. Yet the exclusion of Art. 31, para. 2(b) can be argued only if it is mistakenly assumed that instruments according to Art. 31, para. 2(b) require a consensus on the correctness of the substance of the declaration.[202] The correct construction of the declarations of the Western nuclear powers is that they are complementary instruments in accordance with Art. 31, para. 2(b) Vienna Convention, and it therefore follows from the context of AP I that there was no consensus among the parties concerning the scope of the new rules. Accordingly, to clarify the question of whether AP I covers the use of nuclear weapons, one must rely upon the preparatory work and the circumstances of conclusion of AP I, which sources in turn prove that the (politically delicate) question of use of nuclear weapons was excluded from the scope of the Treaty.[203]

6. It follows that the rules of the Additional Protocol are not applicable as treaty law on the use of nuclear weapons. The customary rules, reaffirmed by the provisions of AP I, are, however, applicable to nuclear warfare.[204] Accordingly, the 'nuclear clause' is of importance primarily regarding Art. 51, para. 6 AP I (prohibition of reprisals towards the civilian population and civilian goods) and regarding Art. 49, para. 2 AP I (inclusion into the scope of AP I of the territory of a party which is under the control of the enemy). These two provisions undoubtedly constitute new rules introduced into humanitarian law by Additional Protocol I.[205] In addition to these two obviously new rules, the provisions of Art. 51, paras. 2–5 and Art. 52 AP I could be considered as exceeding traditional customary law. Although they intended only to give more concrete shape to the customary prohibition of indiscriminate warfare, they in fact contain a decisive element of new law. Although these provisions primarily reaffirm and develop customary law, it must also be admitted that it is extremely difficult to distinguish the expression of pre-existing rules from the more innovative elements inherent in any codification, particularly concerning convention codification of pre-existing customary rules, i.e. of rules previously not fixed

---

[201] See Ipsen, in Bothe/Ipsen/Partsch, 44–5; Fischer, *Der Einsatz von Nuklearwaffen*, 167–72; Rauch, *Revue Hellénique du droit international* 30 (1980), 53–60.

[202] Fischer, *op. cit.*, 156–8.

[203] With the same result see Meyrowitz, *Revue Générale de Droit International Public* 83 (1979), 933–8; Aldrich, *AJIL* 75 (1981), 781–2; Kimminich, *Kernwaffenfrage*, 419–23; Meyrowitz, 25 *GYIL* 238–42 (1982); Solf, in Bothe/Partsch/Solf, 188–92; Ney, 193–209: Aldrich, *Virginia Journal of International Law* 26 (1986), 718–19; Kalshoven, *Recueil des Cours* 191 (1985 II), 283; Pilloud/Pictet, in ICRC *Commentary*, 593 (para. 1852), 594 (para. 1858); Fleck, *NZWehrr* 1987, 227; Pechstein, *AVR* 30 (1992), 290–4.

[204] In that regard see Meyrowitz, 25 *GYIL* 243–51 (1982); cf. also Pilloud/Pictet, in ICRC *Commentary*, 593 (para. 1852).

[205] See Meyrowitz, *Etudes Internationales* 17 (1986), 555 and Kalshoven, *Recueil des Cours* 191 (1985 II), 283.

with sufficient precision in written form.[206] Such attempts at codification always involve both the definition of pre-existing customary law and the creation of new law by treaty, and are inevitably, as Henri Meyrowitz has expressed it: 'a mixture . . . of elements of the *lex lata* and of the *lex ferenda*'.[207] Particular difficulties are created in that regard by the basic rules of paragraphs 4 and 5 of Art. 51, in particular by the codification of the principle of proportionality in Art. 51, para. 5(b) AP I, parts of which are seen as new rules created by the Protocol, but other parts as mere reaffirmation of customary law already in existence at the time of codification.[208] That the principle of proportionality as such existed in previous customary law is beyond doubt. Its specific expression in Arts 51, para. 5(b) and 57, para. 2(a)(ii) AP I, however, should only be applied to the use of nuclear weapons with some caution.

Under Article I of Protocol No. III to the Brussels Treaty (WEU Treaty) of 23   431 October 1954 the Federal Republic of Germany undertook not to manufacture nuclear weapons on its territory. Under the Treaty on the Non-Proliferation of Nuclear Weapons of 1 July 1968 the Federal Republic of Germany further undertook: not to receive from any transferor any nuclear explosive devices or control over such devices whether direct or indirect; not to manufacture or otherwise test nuclear explosive devices; and not to grant or receive any assistance in the manufacture of nuclear explosive devices. These commitments were confirmed under Article 3 of the Treaty on the Final Settlement with respect to Germany (2+4 Treaty) of 12 September 1990. Under the German Law on Arms Control—revised on 22 November 1990—any contravention of these provisions shall incur penalty.

Concerning Germany the special regulatory framework resulting from the occupation after World War II has created specific limitations on the possession or manufacture of nuclear weapons. Under the WEU Treaty the Federal Republic of Germany was already bound to renounce the right to manufacture or possess nuclear weapons. The renunciation of any right to possess nuclear weapons later was consolidated by Germany's accession to the non-proliferation regime of the Treaty on the Non-Proliferation of Nuclear Weapons of 1 July 1968. The German renunciation was further (and finally) reaffirmed by the settlement concerning Germany which was agreed after reunification in the so-called '2+4 Treaty' of 1990, a treaty which was necessary in order to replace the Allied occupation regime.[209] The corresponding prohibition on the development and manufacture as well as on the possession of atomic weapons is incorporated into German national law mainly by the provisions of the German statute on Arms Control, which prohibits and designates as criminal offences any act of development, manufacture, or distribution of nuclear weaponry. Even providing assistance to or collaborating in foreign nuclear weapons projects is in principle prohibited to German nationals by the

---

[206] As to that problem see Meyrowitz, *Etudes Internationales* 17 (1986), 554.

[207] Ibid.

[208] See Meyrowitz, 25 *GYIL* 247–51 (1982), and, by the same author, *Etudes Internationales* 17 (1986), 556–7.

[209] As an informative description of the régime of that treaty see Marauhn, *HuV-I* 4 (1991), 62–9.

Oeter

latest reform of the statute unless the project is under the control of one of Germany's NATO allies.[210]

432   **As weapons of last resort, nuclear weapons continue to fulfil an essential role in the overall strategy of NATO to prevent war by ensuring that there are no circumstances in which the possibility of nuclear retaliation in response to military action might be discounted.**

1. It is difficult to evaluate the repercussions of customary law rules on the strategic planning of the North Atlantic Alliance. This is due partly to the current state of flux of NATO's overall strategy, but also to the fact that such repercussions can be discussed in practical terms only concerning the concrete details of operational planning. On an abstract level one can only state that a strategy of 'massive retaliation'—at least in the form of a threat of first strike or of escalation—is probably not compatible with the general principles of distinction and the prohibition of indiscriminate warfare.[211] A retaliatory operation against a population centre would only be permissible if it constituted a pre-emptive strike qualifying as a military reprisal (concerning the law of reprisals, see Sections 476 to 479).

2. Attacks with tactical nuclear weapons (and perhaps also with precision-guided strategic weapons) could be legally permissible if they are specifically aimed at military objectives and they are also proportionate, with collateral damage to civilian objects being commensurate with the military purpose intended.[212] It is, however, absolutely necessary in these cases that the requirements of distinction and of proportionality are strictly observed.[213]

3. An assessment of nuclear strategy remains essential even after the profound political changes in Central and Eastern Europe of recent years, which have radically improved the security environment. Also, under the 'New Strategic Concept' of the NATO Alliance[214] nuclear forces will continue to fulfil—as declared at the meeting of heads of state and government of NATO in London, July 1990—an essential role in the overall strategy of the Alliance: 'to prevent war by ensuring that under no circumstances can the possibility of nuclear retaliation in response to military action be discounted'.[215] As formulated in the Alliance's 'New Strategic

---

[210] Concerning the drastically aggravated provisions on crimes in the War Materials Control Act see Epping, *Recht der internationalen Wirtschaft* (1991), 463–70.

[211] As to the repercussions of the general rules on methods of war on the legality of strategies of massive retaliation see Rauschning, 'Nuclear Warfare and Weapons', *EPIL* 4, 49; Ney, 275; Meyrowitz, *Etudes Internationales* 17 (1986), 560.

[212] See Rauschning, 'Nuclear Warfare and Weapons', *EPIL* 4, 49; Ney, 277–98; Kalshoven, *Recueil des Cours* 191 (1985 II), 287.

[213] As to the problems resulting from such principles see Meyrowitz, *Etudes Internationales* 17 (1986), 560–3.

[214] New Strategic Concept, agreed by the heads of state and government participating in the meeting of the North Atlantic Council in Rome, 7–8 Nov. 1991, published in: *NATO Review* No. 6 (Dec. 1991), 25–32.

[215] London Declaration on a Transformed North Atlantic Alliance, issued by the heads of state and government participating in the meeting of the North Atlantic Council in London, 5–6 July 1990, *NATO Review* No. 4 (August 1990), 32–3.

Oeter

Concept': 'Nuclear weapons make a unique contribution in rendering the risks of any aggression incalculable and unacceptable. Thus, they remain essential to pre-serve peace'.[216] Nuclear forces are still needed to ensure uncertainty in the mind of any aggressor about the nature of the Allies' response. 'They demonstrate that aggression of any kind is no rational option.'[217] It is true that in the light of the dras-tically changed security situation the Alliance can 'significantly reduce their sub-strategic nuclear forces', in particular nuclear artillery and ground-launched short-range nuclear missiles, which are no longer required and will be eliminated. The Allies will maintain, however, 'adequate sub-strategic forces based in Europe which will provide an essential link with strategic nuclear forces, reinforcing the transatlantic link'.[218] To conclude: the threat to use nuclear weapons continues to be regarded by the NATO Allies as an essential instrument for the prevention of war, although nuclear forces now will truly become weapons of last resort.

The threat and use of nuclear weapons are subject to political control, which shall   433
observe the principles of proportionality, limiting damage on the territory of the
enemy as well as the risk of damage on friendly territory.

Decisions on whether to use nuclear weapons are not purely military. On the contrary, nuclear forces have a primarily political character. Their purpose is pri-marily to keep a balance of mutual deterrence, not intervention in combat opera-tion. Accordingly, decisions on the use of such weapons cannot be left to the military alone. Nuclear strikes have such far-reaching political implications that they must be authorized by the highest political authorities. This is true not only for all states which possess nuclear weapons, but also for states on whose territory nuclear weapons are deployed. The political decision to use such weapons should be taken with due regard to the question of legal justification of the operation, and its concrete modalities, and in strict observance of the relevant legal rules. These legal considerations are of the utmost importance since the boundary between legally permissible combat and prohibited indiscriminate attack can easily be over-stepped in nuclear warfare. The criteria of proportionality, of limiting damage on the territory of the enemy as well as limiting the risk of damage on friendly territory, are of paramount importance.

b. *Chemical Weapons*

The use in war of asphyxiating, poisonous, or other gases, and of all analogous   434
liquids, materials, or similar devices is prohibited (GasProt 1925; Art. 23 lit.a
HagueReg). This prohibition also applies to toxic contamination of water-supply
installations and foodstuffs (Art. 54, para. 2 AP I; Art. 14 AP II) and the use of irri-
tant agents for military purposes. This prohibition does not apply to uninten-
tional and insignificant poisonous secondary effects of otherwise permissible
munitions.

---

[216] 'New Strategic Concept', *op. cit.*, para. 39.   [217] Ibid. para. 55.   [218] Ibid. para. 57.

Oeter

1. There is no dispute as to the basic rule: the use of chemical weapons is prohibited. A prohibition on wartime use of potentially lethal substances which cause asphyxiation or poisoning effects had already been codified in Art. 23 lit.a of the Hague Regulations (prohibition against using poison or poisoned weapons, see *supra*, Section 426). Despite that regulatory safeguard, massive military use was made of poisonous gases in World War I. After the war it was therefore felt that the prohibition should be reaffirmed. The Geneva Protocol of 17 June 1925 for the Prohibition of the Use of Asphyxiating, Poisonous or Other Gases, and of Bacteriological Methods of Warfare thus consolidated the general prohibition of poisonous weapons in 1925 and explicitly outlawed all use of the gas weapon which had been so common during World War I.[219]

2. The general prohibition against the use of poisonous gases—which now constitutes a rule of customary law[220]—applies not only to their direct use against enemy combatants, but extends also to the toxic contamination of water-supply installations and foodstuffs. This could in theory be deduced from the pre-existing general prohibition of poison and poisoned weapons in Art. 23 lit.a HagueReg; nowadays it is expressly provided for in Arts. 54, para. 2 AP I and 14 AP II on the protection of objects and installations indispensable to the survival of the civilian population (see Section 463). As the analogous regulation in Additional Protocols I and II already indicates, the prohibition on the use of chemical weapons is applicable irrespective of whether the conflict is international or non-international. Even in internal conflicts it is prohibited to use chemical agents to place members of armed forces *hors de combat* or to terrorize the civilian population; contaminating water supplies and foodstuffs is only one example of such illicit chemical warfare the primary goal of which is to spread terror among the 'enemy population' (as demonstrated most strikingly by Iraq's 'Operation Anfal' against its Kurdish population[221]).

3. Concerning the category of 'irritant agents', which is included in the scope of the prohibition by sentence 2 of the above-cited Section 434 of the Manual, it should be noted that a serious dispute continues as to whether these substances were covered by the traditional prohibition of chemical weapons. State practice was not unequivocal in that regard; one thinks of the US operations in Vietnam.[222] Art. 1, para. 5 of the Chemical Weapons Convention of 1993 now settles the controversy by explicitly prohibiting the use of 'irritant agents' in warfare (under the notion 'riot control

---

[219] Concerning the legal regime of the two convention prohibitions see Bothe, *Das völkerrechtliche Verbot des Einsatzes chemischer und bakteriologischer Waffen*, 4–18, 21–9; Frailé, 31–6; Kassapis, 6–28.

[220] See Kassapis, 48–79 (esp. 73–9) and Bothe, *Das völkerrechtliche Verbot des Einsatzes chemischer und bakteriologischer Waffen*, 39–47.

[221] See the reports on human rights in Iraq, prepared by the Special Rapporteur of the UN Commission on Human Rights, Max van der Stoel, UN Doc.A/46/647, paras. 22, 23, 74, and 75; UN Doc.E/CN.4/1993/45 of 18 Feb. 1992, paras. 49, 50, 102; UN Doc.E/CN.4/1993/45 of 19 Feb. 1993, paras. 89–97.

[222] Concerning the problem of 'irritant agents' see Bothe, *Das völkerrechtliche Verbot des Einsatzes chemischer und bakteriologischer Waffen*, 49–61; Kassapis, 79–83; Kalshoven, *Recueil des Cours* 191 (1985 II), 268 and the US Navy's *Annotated Supplement to the Commander's Handbook on the Law of Naval Operations*, NWP 9 (Rev.A)/FMFM 1–10, 10–18 *et seq*.

Oeter

agents').[223] In addition, the Preamble of the new Convention also refers to herbicides,[224] although the reference is not as clear as the explicit prohibition of 'irritant agents'. The most important point concerning all these disputes about the definition of 'poisonous gases' (clarified to a large extent by the new Chemical Weapons Convention) is the intentional design of a weapon in order to inflict poisoning as a means of combat. Only in so far as the poisoning effect is the intended result of the use of the substances concerned does the use of such munitions qualify as a use of 'poisonous gases'. If the asphyxiating or poisoning effect is merely a side-effect of a physical mechanism intended principally to cause totally different results (as e.g. the use of nuclear weapons), then the relevant munition does not constitute a 'poisonous gas'.[225] Nuclear weapons, for example, are not prohibited as 'poisonous weapons' although they cause asphyxiation and poisoning as secondary effects.

The scope of this prohibition is restricted by the fact that, when signing the Geneva Gas Protocol, numerous states declared that this Protocol should cease to be binding in regard to any enemy state whose armed forces fail to respect the prohibition embodied in the Protocol. According to the principle of reciprocity, states which did not record such a reservation will also not be legally bound by the Protocol with respect to a follow-on use of chemical weapons against states which launch, support, or assist in planning an attack by chemical weapons contrary to international law.   435

1. Nearly all the important military powers have lodged reservations to the Geneva Gas Protocol which limit the Protocol to a prohibition only against first use and/or restrict the effects of the prohibition as between the contracting parties.[226] The results of such reservations must be judged according to the general rules on legal effects of reservations in Art. 21 of the Vienna Convention on the Law of Treaties. Accordingly, a reservation modifies the provisions of the treaty to which it relates also for the other contracting parties as far as their convention relations with the reserving state are concerned. This means in effect that in the treaty relations with the major military powers the prohibition of chemical weapons is generally reduced to a prohibition against first use.[227] Even beyond the technical effects of reservations, the general principle of reciprocity applies in that (prohibited) first use by one contracting party would entitle the adversary to make subsequent use of chemical weapons by way of military reprisal, as long as the subsequent use is not proscribed by specific prohibitions against reprisals.

---

[223] Convention on the Prohibition of the Development, Production, Stockpiling and Use of Chemical Weapons and on their Destruction, Paris, 13 Jan. 1993, 32 *ILM* 800 (1993); for a brief description of the new Convention's approach see also T. Taylor, *ICLQ* 42 (1993), 913–14.
[224] On the dispute concerning herbicides see Kassapis, 83–6.
[225] See n. 188 above.
[226] As to the reciprocity reservations see Bothe, *Das völkerrechtliche Verbot des Einsatzes chemischer und bakteriologischer Waffen*, 66–78; Kassapis, 43–5; Kalshoven, *NYIL* 21 (1990), 73–4 and the US Navy's *Annotated Supplement to the Commander's Handbook on the Law of Naval Operations*, NWP 9 (Rev.A)/FMFM 1–10, 10–15 n. 21.
[227] On the legal effects of reservations see Kalshoven, *loc. cit.*, 74.

2. Apart from the above, chemical weapons are covered by the same fundamental principles which apply to nuclear weapons. The use of chemical weapons is also subject to the general customary rules on weapons and warfare, and particularly the basic principle of military necessity and the prohibition of indiscriminate warfare.[228] Retaliatory use is justifiable only under the aspect of reprisal, and the legal limits of the law of reprisals must also be observed, in particular the requirement that reprisals be restricted to measures absolutely necessary in order to put an end to the infringement of law by the state who first violated the law (making first use of chemical weapons). The specific prohibition of reprisals in Art. 51, para. 6 AP I, however, does not in principle apply to the use of chemical weapons (as in the case of nuclear weapons), since the so-called 'nuclear consensus'—which was an agreement to leave out of consideration the whole complex of ABC weapons—leads to the non-applicability of the new rules of Additional Protocol I, *inter alia* Art. 51, para. 6 AP I.[229]

436 **The UN Convention on Chemical Weapons of 13 January 1993 includes comprehensive prohibitions of any development, production, stockpiling, transfer, and use of chemical weapons, as well as provisions on international control of compliance with these provisions.**

1. For decades the member states of the UN have negotiated within the framework of the UN Conference on Disarmament in order to reach agreement on a treaty prohibiting not only the use, but also the production and stockpiling of chemical weapons.[230] In 1992 they finally succeeded, after the decisive participation of German diplomacy, in concluding the new Chemical Weapons Convention. The Convention comprehensively bans all development, production, stockpiling, and transfer of chemical weapons and provides for a detailed regulatory framework on the destruction of stockpiled resources.[231] It thus goes far beyond what had been provided for in the old 1925 Geneva Gas Protocol which had prohibited only the *use* of chemical weapons. Since the Biological Weapons Convention of 1972 the new treaty is only the second to outlaw completely a specific category of weapons.

2. One characteristic decisively distinguishes the new Chemical Weapons Convention from the Biological Weapons Convention of 1972, however, and that is its comprehensive verification regime,[232] the preparation of which was the major impediment during decades of negotiations.[233] Under the new verification regime there will be for the first time in history a far-reaching system not only of routine inspections, but also of 'challenge inspections' at the request of a state party, to

---

[228] Bothe, 'Chemical Warfare', *EPIL* 3, 85.

[229] See Solf, in Bothe/Partsch/Solf, 188–91 and the literature cited above in n. 202.

[230] Concerning the course of negotiations see the detailed analysis by Kassapis, 124–322.

[231] On the final phase of the negotiations see Bernauer, *The Chemistry of Regime Formation*, 27–30; concerning the Convention's new legal regime see T. Taylor, *ICLQ* 42 (1993), 912–14.

[232] See Bernauer, *The Projected Chemical Weapons Convention*, 119 *et seq.*, 164 *et seq.*, 173 *et seq.*

[233] As to the course of negotiations see Bernauer, *op. cit.*, 18–59 and Kassapis, 124–202, 266–321.

investigate allegations of non-compliance. Even the private chemical industry will be included in the system of on-site inspections.[234]

3. In August 1992 the negotiating delegations approved the Treaty at the UN Conference on Disarmament. The Convention was then approved by the UN General Assembly, and at a subsequent conference of all UN member states, was laid open to signature. It will enter into force when the required number of ratifications has been obtained.

Under Article I of Protocol III to the WEU Treaty the Federal Republic of Germany undertakes not to manufacture chemical weapons on its territory. On signing the Convention on the Prohibition of the Development, Production, and Stockpiling of Bacteriological (Biological) and Toxin Weapons and their Destruction on 10 April 1972, the Federal Republic of Germany further declared that, in accordance with its attitude, it would neither develop nor acquire nor stockpile under its own control chemical weapons whose manufacture it has already abstained from. This commitment was confirmed by Article 3 of the Treaty on the Final Settlement with Respect to Germany (2+4 Treaty) of 12 September 1990. Under the Law on Arms Control, revised on 22 November 1990, any contravention of these provisions shall be liable to penalty. 437

As far as chemical weapons are concerned, the same legal regime applies concerning disarmament and unilateral commitments to abstain from possession and manufacture as was described above under Section 431 in regard to nuclear weapons. The Federal Republic of Germany has renounced in a number of legal instruments (both multilateral and unilateral) any right to develop, manufacture, or stockpile chemical weapons and has declared a comprehensive renunciation of that category of weapons in the German military arsenal. Accordingly, German nationals are subjected to strict controls also concerning any activity related with the development, manufacture, or transfer of chemical weapons; their participation in any chemical weapons project would render them liable to severe penalties.

c. *Bacteriological (Biological) and Toxin Weapons*   438

The use of bacteriological weapons is prohibited (Geneva Gas Protocol of 17 June 1925).

The prohibition of use laid down in the Geneva Gas Protocol is not limited to 'poisonous gases' in a strict sense; the wording of the Treaty covers also bacteriological weapons.[235] Even according to customary law one must assume an absolute prohibition of any use of bacteriological weapons,[236] be it in international or internal conflicts.

---

[234] See T. Taylor, *loc. cit.*, 915–16; Bernauer, *The Chemistry of Regime Formation*, 38–9.
[235] See Bothe, *Das völkerrechtliche Verbot des Einsatzes chemischer und bakteriologischer Waffen*, 25; Rauch, 'Biological Warfare', *EPIL* 3, 45.
[236] Bothe, *op. cit.*, 48–9; Rauch, *loc. cit.*, 46.

439 The development, manufacture, acquisition, and stockpiling of bacteriological (biological) and toxin weapons is prohibited (Biological Weapons Convention of 10 April 1972). These prohibitions apply both to biotechnological and synthetic procedures serving other than peaceful purposes. They also include genetic engineering procedures and the alteration of micro-organisms through genetic engineering.

The Biological Weapons Convention of 1972 was the first universal treaty to codify the prohibition of an entire category of weapons.[237] According to the Convention, the development, manufacture, acquisition, or stockpiling of bacteriological weapons, as well as their use in any military conflict, are prohibited. The Convention requires the complete destruction of all such weapons—without, however, providing for a specific regime of verification. The Convention also refrains from defining exactly what constitutes bacteriological (biological) weapons.[238] Nevertheless there seems to exist general agreement that all living organisms fall under the Treaty which could be used to cause or spread diseases, or which are intended to cause the death of humans, animals, or plants, in so far as these organisms are designed to be used for hostile purposes in armed conflicts. Such organisms may be bacteria, microbes, viruses, fungi, or rickettsiae, or other living organisms damaging to other organisms. The notion 'biological weapons' covers also so-called 'toxins', i.e. all substances extracted from living organisms designed to be used for hostile purposes.[239]

440 Under Article I of Protocol III to the WEU Treaty the Federal Republic of Germany undertakes not to manufacture biological weapons on its territory. This commitment was confirmed under Article 3 of the Treaty on the Final Settlement with Respect to Germany (2+4 Treaty) of 12 September 1990. Under the Law of Arms Control, revised on 22 November 1990, any contravention of these provisions shall be liable to penalty.

The Federal Republic of Germany has also accepted the obligation not to develop, manufacture, acquire, or possess biological weapons. A whole series of international legal instruments confirms that renunciation, beginning with Art. I of Protocol III to the WEU Treaty and ending with the '2+4 Treaty' of 1990. (See Sections 431 and 437 concerning the legal regime of these treaties and the ensuing consequences for commercial activities.)

---

[237] Concerning the substance of the Convention see the brief description by Bothe, *op. cit.*, 36–8, and the detailed analysis of the Convention's legal regime by Stein, *Recueil des Cours* 133 (1971 II), 337 *et seq.*, 358 *et seq.*

[238] See Bothe, *op. cit.*, 37.   [239] See Rauch, *loc. cit.*, 45.

III. METHODS OF COMBAT

1. *Military Objectives*

**Attacks, i.e. any acts of violence against the adversary, whether in offence or in   441
defence (Art. 49, para. 1 AP I), shall be limited exclusively to military objectives.**

1. The basic principle laid down in Section 441 is an attempt to codify the customary requirement of distinction and to transform it into a specific rule of combat. Military use of force is only permissible—such is the basic requirement of customary law—against an objective which constitutes a military objective by virtue of its being part of the military endeavours of the adversary. Only for the purpose of combat against such objectives does the regulation of customary international law recognize military necessity.[240] Whether the conflict is international in character or non-international makes no difference, because even in internal conflicts states are obliged under customary law to spare the civilian population and civilian objects.[241]

2. Art. 48 AP I, which explicitly lays down such a maxim of 'limited warfare', makes use of the rather untechnical term 'operations' ('. . . shall direct their operations only against military objectives'). Art. 49, para. 1 AP I goes on to give an express definition of what constitutes an 'attack' in the technical sense of the Protocol: 'Attacks' are all 'acts of violence against the adversary, whether in offence or in defence'. This definition raises another question, however: namely whether the term 'attacks'—which must be understood as identical with 'acts of violence against the adversary'—has a narrower meaning than the rather wide term 'military operations'. The answer must be yes, since many types of military operations are carried out without any direct violence against the adversary. Such military operations performed without the direct use of violence do not need any limitation concerning legitimate objectives of attack, i.e. 'military objectives', since they entail no risk of direct violence for the civilian population.[242]

3. The Protocol's use of the term 'attacks' to include all acts of violence against the adversary has been severely criticized by some military writers. The main point of criticism has been that such an interpretation removes the terminology of the Protocol too far from daily language (W. Hays Parks has claimed it to be 'etymologically inconsistent with its customary use' and even 'contrary to its ordinary meaning').[243] To label even a purely defensive operation an 'attack' on the basis that violence is employed—so claim the critics of AP I—is incomprehensible for the

---

[240] As to the basic set of rules see the comments of Solf on Art. 48 AP I, in Bothe/Partsch/Solf, 282–6; see also Arrassen, 260–4; Baxter, *Comportement des combattants*, 146–55; Blix, *Moyens et méthodes de combat*, 174–8.

[241] See Kalshoven, *Recueil des Cours* 191 (1985 II), 296; Gardam, 176–80.

[242] See also Solf, in Bothe/Partsch/Solf, 289 and Kalshoven, *Constraints*, 87.

[243] Parks, *Air Force Law Review* 32 (1990), 114 and 115.

Oeter

non-lawyer and places a pejorative value-judgment on any use of armed force.[244] This critique is certainly exaggerated; but it must be admitted that the all-embracing use of the term 'attack' as including all acts of violence can be quite confusing and does not always assist the understanding of the provisions of Additional Protocol I.[245] On the other hand, the definition of the notion 'attack' is primarily intended to clarify that the point of departure of the provisions of the Protocol is the individual military operation of a specific unit,[246] and not the entire network of all co-ordinated military operations of a party to the conflict (as to the problems resulting from such an approach, see Section 444). If the term 'attack' is understood as a short formula for any kind of 'combat action', the semantic combination of offensive and defensive operations in a single unitary concept has a striking advantage: it unmistakably brings home to commanders and soldiers in combat that the 'defensive character' of a specific act of violence does not exempt it from the provisions for the protection of the civilian population.[247] This applies under certain conditions even for a party's preventive operations in its own 'hinterland', as e.g. in the case of laying mines in anticipation of a future offensive by the adversary.[248]

4. The same basic lesson is also given by Paragraph 2 of Art. 49 AP I which expressly provides that the provisions of the Protocol, particularly the provisions on protection of the civilian population, apply not only to operations on the territory of the adversary but also to combat operations on the national territory of a party, even if this is occupied by the adversary.[249] Thus the pretence is excluded that the safeguard provisions of humanitarian law should be seen to protect only the enemy civilian population and not a party's own population. Even the civilian population of a state which comes under the control of the adversary in the course of the armed conflict enjoys the protection of the Protocol against actions by its national armed forces[250] (see also Section 463). Thus, a party to the conflict may not mount attacks on objects which are indispensible to the survival of the population in its own territory being occupied by the adversary, but it may destroy, in case of imperative military necessity, such objects in territory still under its own control in order to counter the invasion. Such destructive acts by a belligerent on his own territory will often not even constitute an 'attack', for they may be acts of violence which are not mounted 'against the adversary'.[251]

5. Paragraph 3 of Art. 49 regulates the scope of the Protocol's provisions on the protection of the civilian population. Included are attacks by sea or air against

---

[244] See esp. Parks, ibid. 113–16; cf. Pilloud/Pictet, in ICRC *Commentary*, 603 (para. 1879).

[245] See Pilloud/Pictet, ibid.   [246] Solf, in Bothe/Partsch/Solf, 288.

[247] Pilloud/Pictet, in ICRC *Commentary* 603 (para. 1880); Kalshoven, *Constraints*, 87.

[248] Pilloud/Pictet, in ICRC *Commentary*, 603 (para. 1881); cf. also Rauch, *GYIL* 24 (1981), 270–8; Würkner-Theis, 98–103 (esp. 103); Kalshoven, *Constraints*, 153–4.

[249] Sassòli, 337–41, proves that such an understanding corresponds to the basic approach of the relevant rules of customary law.

[250] Pilloud/Pictet, in ICRC *Commentary*, 604–5 (paras. 1883–91); Solf, in Bothe/Partsch/Solf, 289–90; Kalshoven, *Constraints*, 87.

[251] Pilloud/Pictet, in ICRC *Commentary*, 604–5 (paras. 1888, 1890).

Oeter

objectives on land, and also any air or sea warfare which may affect the civilian population or civilian objects on land. By contrast, armed conflict at sea or in the air with no consequences for the area protected under Part IV of the Protocol (which refers uniquely to land territory) is not covered by Art. 49, para. 3 AP I.[252] However, these operations are covered by the relevant general rules of customary law. As paragraph 4 of Art. 49 expressly states, the provisions of the Protocol are *additional to* the other rules concerning humanitarian protection contained in the Fourth Geneva Convention and in other international agreements as well as to the customary rules relating to the protection of civilians; those rules are not replaced by the provisions of the new Protocol.[253]

Military objectives are armed forces—with paratroops in descent (Art. 42, para. 3 442
AP I) but not crew members parachuting from an aircraft in distress (Art. 42, para.
1 AP I)—and also objects which by their nature, location, purpose, or use make an
effective contribution to military action and whose total or partial destruction,
capture, or neutralization, in the circumstances ruling at the time, offer a definite
military advantage (Art. 52, para. 2 AP I).

1. The attempt to define exactly what constitutes a military objective is an essential step in making the principle of distinction operative. For a long time belligerent practice tended to leave uncertain the precise contours of the notion. Accordingly, belligerents were often tempted to manipulate the rules by choosing—according to the situation—either a restrictive or an extensive definition of the term 'military objective'.[254]

2. Since time immemorial enemy combatants have constituted the principle 'military objective'.[255] The category of 'combatants' includes units of land armies, navies, and air forces, also under certain conditions guerilla fighters as well as the civilian population of an invaded territory taking part in hostilities in the wake of a *levée en masse*. (As to lawful combatants, see Sections 304 to 310.)

3. The specific problem of air force crews parachuting in distress merits attention. It has been disputed under what circumstances crew members of a military aircraft may be fired upon. Concerning parachute troops and airborne combat units it is beyond doubt that they constitute a lawful military objective, because in parachuting from aircraft they perform an offensive operation (an 'attack'). Thus, even while parachuting they may be perceived and attacked as legitimate military objectives (Art. 42, para. 3 AP I).[256] One exception, however, was stated by the rapporteur of

---

[252] See Sassòli, 334–7.

[253] See the observations on Art. 49 in the Memorandum of the German Government annexed to the statute transforming the Additional Protocols—BR-Drs. 64/90 of 2 February 1990, 111.

[254] See v.d. Heydte, 'Military Objectives', *EPIL* 3, 277.

[255] See the Preamble to the St Petersburg Declaration of 1868 which is worded: 'Considering . . . that the only legitimate object which States should endeavour to accomplish during war is to weaken the military forces of the enemy . . .'.

[256] See de Preux, in ICRC *Commentary*, 501 (para. 1652); cf. also the US Navy's *Annotated Supplement to the Commander's Handbook on the Law of Naval Operations, NWP 9* (Rev.A)/FMFM 1–10, 11–10.

Oeter

the Diplomatic Conference in that regard: when a plane has been shot down, i.e. in cases of emergency descent outside the target area of the intended attack, even airborne troops should not be counted as military objectives.[257] Nevertheless, this exception probably will be of no relevance in practice. The land troops of the adversary will not normally know when parachuting results from an emergency, and will have to assume that enemy parachute troops are carrying out an attack operation. Accordingly, they will treat airborne troops as a military objective unless it is obvious that they are *enemies hors de combat*, either from signs that they have no hostile intent or from surrender (which would bring them under the protection of Art. 41 AP I).

4. The contrary applies to crew members of an aircraft in distress, according to Art. 42, paras. 1 and 2 AP I. For some time it was not clear whether crew members parachuting in distress should still be treated as military objectives—as during a flight which constitutes an attack—or whether during their descent they qualify as persons *hors de combat*.[258] Art. 42, para. 1 AP I now settles the question by providing that with the descent from an aircraft in distress the 'combat action' of its crew is terminated and they may no longer be attacked.[259] Having landed, it is presumed that they constitute persons *hors de combat* who have no hostile intent. The adversary must give them an opportunity to surrender and may continue to attack them as a military objective only if it becomes obvious by their commission of a hostile action that they intend to continue combat.[260]

5. The definition of the boundary between military objectives and civilian objects remains a critical problem. By Art. 52, para. 2 AP I the international community has attempted to clarify the question of how to distinguish between these categories.[261] The general definition of 'military objectives' in Art. 52, para. 2 AP I, however, constitutes one of the most heavily debated provisions of the Additional Protocol and, in particular, military circles in Western countries have been extremely hostile to it.[262] The background to this condemnation is the restrictive nature of the definition, which purports radically to limit the category of legitimate objectives of military operations.[263] For that purpose the provision uses two basic elements which are combined with one another.[264] First, Art. 52, para. 2 AP I requires that military objectives should be objects 'which by their nature, location, purpose, or use make an effective contribution to military action'. The formula used constitutes a general

---

[257] See de Preux, in ICRC *Commentary*, 501 (para. 1652).

[258] See de Preux, in ICRC *Commentary*, 494–501 (paras. 1634–51); Penna, in Swinarski (Ed.), 212–14 and Hailbronner, *Notsituation*, 86–8.

[259] See in detail de Preux, in ICRC *Commentary*, 496–7 (paras. 1639–43).

[260] See in detail de Preux, in ICRC *Commentary*, 497–501 (paras. 1644–51); cf. also Hailbronner, *Notsituation*, 89–90 and the US Navy's *Annotated Supplement to the Commander's Handbook on the Law of Naval Operations, NWP 9* (Rev.A)/FMFM 1–10, 11–10.

[261] As to the drafting history of Art. 52, para. 2 AP I see Sassòli, 370–2.

[262] For the massive criticism from the US military see e.g. Parks, *Air Force Law Review* 32 (1990), 137–44.

[263] Parks, *Air Force Law Review* 32 (1990), 138–41.

[264] As to the systematic structure of Art. 52, para. 2 AP I see Pilloud/Pictet, in ICRC *Commentary*, 635 (para. 2018); Meyrowitz, *ZaöRV* 41 (1981), 35.

criterion the existence of which can be judged *in abstracto*. Under the category of 'military objectives' therefore are installations, buildings, or ground sectors which are directly involved in the military endeavour of the enemy, i.e. which make an effective contribution to the military operations due to their inclusion in the military dispositions of the adversary. In essence this is a return to the restrictive definitional approach of the Hague Rules of Air Warfare, with the corresponding purpose of repressing the subsequent (and extremely broad) construction of 'military objectives' favoured by the proponents of 'strategic air warfare'.[265] Almost boundless interpretations of 'military objective' have been adopted in doctrines of 'total warfare', such as that advanced by Air Marshall Trenchard in 1928, which included as military objectives 'any objectives which will contribute effectively towards the destruction of the enemy's means of resistance and the lowering of his determination to fight'.[266] These are now replaced by the more recent doctrine of 'limited warfare'. It must be admitted that such an approach considerably limits the military opportunities for a belligerent and is therefore not without problems, since successful modern warfare requires great strategic and tactical flexibility.[267] The purpose of any military action must always be to influence the political will of the adversary,[268] especially in defence where the enemy's determination to pursue its goals by violence must be broken; the destruction of the enemy's military apparatus is thus never an end in itself. The protection of civilian populations, however, requires a basic limitation of violence, a restriction on the use of force against the enemy's military organization. If the intention directly to influence the enemy population's determination to fight were recognized as a legitimate objective for military force, then no limit to warfare would remain. This is what happened in World War II. The limitation of admissible military objectives is accordingly a step of the utmost importance for the implementation of the principle of non-combatant immunity. The legitimate interest of states to preserve strategic and tactical manœuvring space can be taken into account only by interpreting and applying the inherent definition of 'military objectives', not by abandoning any limitation of lawful military objectives. (As to the precise construction of the notion 'military objectives', see Section 443).

6. Art. 52, para. 2 AP I combines this 'objective' element (concerning the capacity to contribute effectively to military operations) with a second 'subjective' criterion which refers to the military purposes of the acting state. It is not sufficient that the objective contributes to the military arrangements of the adversary; the destruction, capture, or neutralization of the objective must also offer the belligerent, in the specific circumstances obtaining at the time of the attack, a 'definite military advantage'.[269] This is both a 'situative' element, since Art. 52, para. 2 refers

[265] See Parks, *Air Force Law Review 32* (1990), 138–41.   [266] See Parks, ibid. 139 n. 412.
[267] Concerning this problem see Parks, *Air Force Law Review* 32 (1990), 139–44.
[268] Ibid., 141.
[269] On the background and problematic of the formula see Pilloud/Pictet, in ICRC *Commentary*, 635 (para. 2019) and 637 (para. 2027); Parks, *Air Force Law Review* 32 (1990), 141–4; Solf, in Bothe/Partsch/Solf, 324–6.

Oeter

expressly to the 'circumstances ruling at the time',[270] and also a 'relative' criterion since the 'military advantage' can only be realistically evaluated in the light of the tactical and strategic goals of the belligerent.[271] The attack must profit the armed forces using violence; to put it in extremely simple terms: it must be militarily necessary in order to reach a permissible operative goal. (For details, see Section 444.) Attacks launched for the purpose of terrorizing the enemy civilian population, to break its determination to fight, are accordingly prohibited, as are attacks of a purely political purpose, whether to demonstrate military strength, or to intimidate the political leadership of the adversary.[272]

7. The abstract definition laid down in Art. 52, para. 2 AP I has a distinct advantage over the lists of admissible military objectives proposed earlier, namely the flexibility of its practical implementation, preserved by the abstraction of the formula. However, the same abstraction can be a disadvantage, in that it leaves a wide margin of interpretation which allows belligerents to construe it with completely different results according to their particular interest.[273] It also means that an officer, in determining whether a specific target is a lawful military objective, requires precise information as to the exact nature, purpose, and use of the objective concerned.[274] AP I appears to presuppose 'a greater certainty in the mind of an attacker as to the connection between a segment of a target system and military operations than an attacker normally would possess'.[275] Exact reconnaissance and the procurement of precise information by military intelligence services become key factors of lawful warfare. The technologically and institutionally highly developed military organizations of the industrial states could probably manage these requirements;[276] military actors without efficient means of reconnaissance and intelligence, however, will encounter serious difficulties in meeting the requirements of Art. 52, para. 3 AP I. However, these problems seem to be unavoidable if one wants to improve the protection of the civilian population by imposing legal restrictions on permissible means and methods of combat. The problems described result from the enormous complexity of the questions which need to be regulated, and not from a misguided politico-legal approach or a malicious conspiracy against specific military powers.

443   **Military objectives include particularly:**

- **armed forces;**
- **military aircraft and war ships;**
- **buildings and objects for combat service support; and**
- **commercial objectives which make an effective contribution to military action (transport facilities, industrial plants, etc.).**

---

[270] See Meyrowitz, *ZaöRV* 41 (1981), 43; Solf, in Bothe/Partsch/Solf, 324.
[271] See Meyrowitz, *ZaöRV* 41 (1981), 39–43.   [272] Ibid., 40–1.
[273] See Meyrowitz, *ZaöRV* 41 (1981), 35–6.
[274] Ibid., 36; see also Parks, *Air Force Law Review* 32 (1990), 141 n. 416.   [275] Ibid., 140–1.
[276] As an example, the experience of the Allied armies (in particular the US armed forces) in the course of 'Operation Desert Storm'; see Keenan, *HuV-I* 4/1991, 36.

Oeter

1. As explained above, the ICRC and the Diplomatic Conference employ an abstract definition in order to limit the scope of the term 'military objective'. Such an approach has been criticized repeatedly, for it leaves a large margin of interpretation.[277] Ultimately, however, the Conference had no real choice but to take such an approach, since it would have been impossible for the delegations participating at the Conference to reach agreement on a detailed and exhaustive list of permissible military objectives.[278] There is, however, a precedent which could be used as an interpretative aid: the list of 'military objectives' drafted by the ICRC as an annex to the 'Draft Rules for the Limitation of Dangers incurred by the Civilian Population in Time of War' adopted in 1956 by the Red Cross Conference in New Delhi.[279]

2. At the heart of the category of military objectives are the armed forces of the adversary, including all military auxiliary organizations and paramilitary units fighting side by side with the regular armed forces. As well as the regular units of army, navy, and air force, and all militia and volunteer corps incorporated in the armed forces, that group also includes all other persons who, together with (or instead of) the armed forces fight against the adversary (see Section 304). This also includes any part of the population of a non-occupied territory who, on the approach of the enemy, spontaneously takes up arms to resist the invading forces (the so-called '*levée en masse*'; see Section 310), and also guerilla forces in occupied territories (see Section 309). The group of 'lawful combatants' also includes paramilitary or armed law enforcement agencies which are incorporated to the armed forces in accordance with Art. 43, para. 3 AP I (see Section 307). Most police forces, which in general serve to enforce law and order and in principle do not take part in hostilities, however, are not included in the category of legitimate 'military objectives'; normally they do not possess arms suitable for military combat, being armed at most with small-arms and light equipment.[280] The only exception is needed for regular police in the enemy hinterland in the case of commando operations; police officers pursuing an enemy detachment become an admissible military objective.[281]

3. Also valid as a military objective is equipment serving a navy or air force for combat purposes, namely military aircraft (see Sections 326–7) and warships (see Sections 1001–6, 1021).

4. The installations and objects for immediate combat service support, which are usually regarded as having a military nature, such as barracks, fortifications, staff buildings, military command and control centres, military airfields, port facilities of the navy (also ministries of a military nature, e.g. of the Army, Navy, Air Force,

---

[277] See e.g. Rosenblad, *International Humanitarian Law of Armed Conflict*, 71.
[278] See Meyrowitz, *ZaöRV* 41 (1981), 32.
[279] Reprinted in Pilloud/Pictet, in ICRC *Commentary*, 632 n. 3 and Parks, *Air Force Law Review* 32 (1990), 138–9; see also v. d. Heydte, 'Military Objectives', *EPIL* 3, 278 and Meyrowitz, *ZaöRV* 41 (1981), 45 *et seq.*
[280] See de Preux, in ICRC *Commentary*, 517–18 (paras. 1682–3); Solf, in Bothe/Partsch/Solf, 240.
[281] See Solf, ibid., 240.

Oeter

National Defence, Supply) also constitute traditional military objectives.[282] Also included in that category are logistical bases of the armed forces, namely stores of arms or military supplies, munition dumps, fuel stores, military vehicle parks, etc.

5. The term 'buildings and objects for combat service support' has an additional layer of meaning which creates many more problems of delimitation than the case of buildings with an obvious military function. What is meant here is the category which is covered by the notion (in the terminology of the Red Cross list of 1956) of 'positions, installations or constructions occupied by the forces' and of 'combat objectives'.[283] The term 'positions, installations or constructions occupied by the forces' prompts thoughts of civilian objects and ground positions temporarily used for military purposes by an armed force in the course of its operations. These might be schools, hospitals, or residential premises used to lodge troops or to serve staff purposes; but they can also be buildings or installations where troops have entrenched themselves, where observation posts have been installed, or which serve military purposes in another way. The notion 'combat objectives' (or better: 'combatted objects') indicates objects or topographically exposed ground positions which in the course of a specific military operation suddenly become important for both sides, and the possession or destruction of which accordingly becomes decisive in achieving operative goals (e.g. church or other towers, hills, steep slopes, exposed farms, etc., the control of which both sides try to achieve). The German Federal Government, on ratification of the Additional Protocols, filed an interpreting declaration, according to which the Federal Republic construes Art. 52 to mean 'that a specific area of land may also be a military objective if it meets all the requirements of Article 52, paragraph 2'.[284]

6. The most delicate distinction between permissible military objectives and civilian objects concerns the 'commercial objectives which make an effective contribution to military action'. It has long been hotly disputed as to what exactly is covered by this category. Even the different attempts to draw up specific lists of recognized 'military objectives' did not bring about a real clarification. The ICRC's 1956 list, for example, includes under this heading lines and means of communication, broadcasting and television stations, as well as telephone and telegraph installations, in so far as all these are of fundamental military importance, and also the 'industries of fundamental importance for the conduct of war'.[285] *In abstracto*, these categories seem to be capable of finding consensus. The difficulties begin when one attempts to delimit the permissible objectives of attack in detail. Certain lines of communication such as railway lines, roads, bridges, or tunnels may undoubtedly be of

[282] See no. 3 of the Red Cross list of 1956: 'installations, constructions and other works of a military nature, such as barracks, fortifications, War Ministries (. . .) and other organs for the direction and administration of military operations'; see also nos. 4 and 5 of the list.

[283] See no. 2 of the Red Cross list annexed to the New Delhi 'Draft Rules'.

[284] See BR-Drs. 64/90 of 2 Feb. 1990, 132; see also the explanations given to Art. 52 in the Memorandum of the German Government submitted with the draft of a statute transforming the Additional Protocols, BR-Drs. 64/90 of 2 Feb. 1990, 112.

[285] See nos. 6, 7, and 8 of the list—cf. ICRC *Commentary*, 632 n. 3.

Oeter

fundamental military importance, and as such would be legitimate objectives for attack. The adversary belligerent, however, will be able to compensate for the destruction of such 'strategically important' lines of communication by switching to railway lines or roads which had previously been totally unimportant.[286] But does this not lead to the conclusion that such objects or lines which for the present seem 'unimportant' may be perceived as militarily important from the beginning, and may accordingly constitute relevant military objectives *ab initio*? Comparable questions may be asked of networks of telecommunication. In the case of modern densely interlinked infrastructures of telecommunication, it may be doubted whether any 'unimportant' installation still exists (with the exception of the periphery of the network). The practice of the Kuwait 'Desert Storm' operation in 1991 demonstrated that an attacker nowadays must probably destroy a network of telecommunication *in toto* (or at least its central connection points) in order to paralyse the command and control structures of the enemy armed force, which in themselves clearly constitute a legitimate military objective.

7. Considerable problems are created also by the exact delimitation of what constitute 'industries of fundamental importance for the conduct of war'. It is indisputable that industries for the production of armaments fall within this category, as also the heavy industries delivering the metallurgical, engineering, and chemical products upon which that industry relies, as well as storage and transport installations serving the armament industries and the heavy industries assimilated to it.[287] Also generally counted as undisputed 'military objectives' are the numerous installations for the production of electric energy for mainly military purposes (here again arises the above-mentioned problems of internetting and delimitation between military power supplies and 'purely civilian' energy installations[288]), and finally the research and development facilities of the armaments sector. There remain large uncertainties, however, concerning the supply industry of armaments production and subcontractors of the defence industry. If those enterprises were also brought within the notion of 'industries of fundamental importance for the conduct of war', then nearly all areas in a highly developed industrial society with an elaborate division of labour in production would comprise lawful military objectives, thus undermining the overall attempt to limit warfare. Yet if such industries are excluded, there is created an enormous (and extremely dangerous) opportunity to 'immunize' armaments production by subcontracting, and decentralizing production into 'civilian' firms,[289] which would ultimately erode the basis of the entire system, tempting states to ignore the whole regulatory framework and to return to strategies of 'total war', aiming directly at the economic capacity of the adversary. This dilemma probably cannot be solved in the abstract. However, a careful implementation of the relevant rules by *bona fide* interpretation of the requirements of Art. 52, para. 2 AP I should be capable of producing satisfactory results in individual cases.

[286] As to that problem see Parks, *Air Force Law Review* 32 (1990), 139–40 n. 413.
[287] See nos. 8(a), (b), (c), and (d) of the ICRC list of 1956.
[288] See Parks, *Air Force Law Review* 32 (1990), 141 n. 415.   [289] Ibid., 140 n. 414.

Oeter

444   The term 'military advantage' refers to the advantage which can be expected from
an attack as a whole and not only from isolated or specific parts of the attack.

The First Additional Protocol relies on a relatively specific concept of 'attack'
(provided for in Art. 49, para. 1 AP I) as an isolated ground operation by a specific
unit. This notion is linked to that of the 'military objective', and both are relevant to
the determination of the 'definite military advantage' which is to be expected from
the attack concerned. Such a conceptual foundation seems to suggest a very narrow
idea of what constitutes a 'definite military advantage' under Art. 52, para. 2. One
could be tempted to conclude that a 'military advantage' which justifies classifying
an object as a 'military objective' must result from the specific military operation
which constitutes the 'attack'. Such a construction, however, would ignore the
problems resulting from modern strategies of warfare, which are invariably based
on an integrated series of separate actions forming one ultimate compound operation. The separate action within an operation, that could be described as a specific
'attack', is hardly ever an end in itself. Normally such an action is directed towards
a goal which lies outside the single action, as part of the complex mosaic of a bigger
integrated operation conceived in a kind of division of labour, and thus depends in
its purpose on the aggregate strategy of the party to the conflict. The aggregate military operation of the belligerent may not be divided up into too many individual
actions, otherwise the operative purpose for which the overall operation was
designed slips out of sight. It is this elementary condition of any sensible interpretation of the concept of 'military advantage' which the German Government—in
accordance with important voices in international legal literature[290]—took into
account when it annexed to its ratification an interpreting declaration concerning
the construction of what constitutes a 'definite military advantage'. The declaration
is worded: 'In applying the rule of proportionality in Article 51 and Article 57, "military advantage" is understood to refer to the advantage anticipated from the attack
as a whole and not only from isolated or particular parts of the attack'.[291] Although
the declaration expressly refers only to the rule of proportionality in Arts. 51 and 57
AP I, it seems also to apply the same interpretation to the construction of what constitutes a 'definite military advantage' in the sense of Art. 52, para. 2 AP I.

445   Civilians present in military objectives are not protected against attacks directed
at those objectives; the presence of civilian workers in an arms production plant,
for instance, will not prevent opposing armed forces from attacking this military
objective.

1. Persons who are not combatants according to Art. 4 Geneva Convention III and
Art. 43 AP I must be seen as 'civilians'. Both the civilian population and individual
civilians according to Art. 51, para. 1 AP I enjoy 'general protection against dangers
arising from military operations'; they shall not be made the object of an attack (Art.

---

[290] See particularly Solf, in Bothe/Partsch/Solf, 325, who uses the example of preparations of the invasion in Normandy in 1944.
[291] See BR-Drs. 64/90 of 2 Feb. 1990, 132.

Oeter

51, para. 2 AP I; see Section 4451 and Section 451). Even the presence within the civilian population of individual combatants does not deprive the population of its civilian character, and thus it retains the protection accorded to it under Additional Protocol I.[292]

2. Only if civilians fight side by side with the regular armed forces is the position different, and then only as long as they directly take part in hostilities (Art. 51, para. 3).[293] These civilians, by taking up arms against the enemy, become lawful military objectives (e.g. the case of police officers in a commando operation—see Section 443, para. 2). The same is true for civilians present in military objectives, i.e. civilian persons who are integrated into the military endeavours and logistics of a belligerent. The classic example of such integration is that of civilian workers in arms production plants (or, more extremely, the civilian personnel of armed forces who maintain military installations). These workers do not become combatants by working in arms factories or military installations; however, their workplace is a permissible military objective. The qualification of such an installation as a military objective is not changed by the presence of civilians who work in it, even if there are hundreds or thousands of them.[294] Even the deliberate use of parts of a civilian population as a 'human shield' does not change the status of an installation (as a military objective), as long as it delivers an effective contribution to the military activity of the belligerent. The actions of the Iraqi Government during 'Operation Desert Storm' are a relevant example. Iraq deliberately arranged the presence of civilians in military installations in order to 'immunize' those installations against air raids. Attacks against such installations remain lawful in principle; only the principle of proportionality may cause the attacker difficulties when trying to justify such an attack (see Section 456).

3. One point remains unclear in respect of the prohibition of disproportionate attacks. It must be asked whether the deliberate taking of the risk by any civilian who stays in a military installation should influence the balance which must be struck between the intended military advantage and the collateral damage to be taken into account. What has been clarified is only the basic premise that collaboration in the military endeavours of the belligerent does not make the civilian a 'quasi-combatant', the civilian is therefore not a military objective himself.[295] Direct bombardment of civilian living quarters of arms production plant workers (such as occurred in World War II) can no longer be justified by the argument that these workers are military objectives by virtue of their essential contribution to warfare.[296] Whether collateral damage to civilians working in military objectives (and thus contributing to the military endeavour of its state) is of lesser weight in striking a balance with the military advantage than potential damage to 'innocent' civil-

---

[292] See de Zayas, 'Civilian Population, Protection', *EPIL* 3, 97.

[293] See Pilloud/Pictet, in ICRC *Commentary*, 618–19 (paras. 1942–5); Solf, in Bothe/Partsch/Solf, 301–4; and Kalshoven, *Constraints*, 91.

[294] See Kalshoven, *Constraints*, 91–2, and Sassòli, 393–4; cf. (as an extremely critical voice towards AP I) Parks, *Air Force Law Review* 32 (1990), 120–35 (esp. 134–5).

[295] Doswald-Beck, in Meyer (Ed.), 154.   [296] Ibid.

ians is a question not yet answered, but which needs careful study. Although an affirmative answer might create serious ethical difficulties, reasons of military practicability (and of soldiers' common sense) might point in that direction.

446 **An objective which is normally dedicated to civil purposes shall, in case of doubt, be assumed not to be used in a way which makes an effective contribution to military action (Art. 52, para. 3 AP I), and shall therefore be treated as a civilian object.**

1. The presumption laid down in Art. 52, para. 3 AP I is complementary to the complex provision of Art. 52, para. 2 (definition of 'military objectives'). The presumption expressly refers to objects which are normally dedicated to civilian purposes, 'such as a place of worship, a house or other dwelling or a school', but which may, if used to make an effective contribution to military action, become a military objective.[297] Only with respect to those objects which originally had a purely civil purpose can there be any serious doubt as to the military nature of the objective. Means of transport and of communication (which it was proposed, at the beginning of the Diplomatic Conference, should also be covered by the presumption) fall into a different category. They were excluded from the presumption because, if they are of military utility at all, there can be no doubt as to their 'contribution to military action'.[298]

2. Ultimately, when applying Art. 52, para. 3 AP I, one should bear in mind that, according to the external circumstances and the information available to the attacker, before the presumption comes into play there must be a serious doubt as to whether the object in question contributes to military action. In most situations such doubt will not exist; in the combat zone, for example, there will normally be no question and the combatants will generally assume that an object constitutes a military objective the possession or destruction of which is essential for both sides. 'Combatants are not likely to entertain any doubt about the military use of buildings located in an area on land where the forward elements of opposing forces are in contact with each other, especially where they are exposed to direct fire from the ground'.[299] The decisive factor in that respect should be the perspective of the soldier acting on the ground, or of the military commander deciding on the attack: serious doubts must be obvious from his perspective before there is any reason to invoke the presumption contained in Art. 52, para. 3. Several NATO states filed declarations confirming such an understanding when ratifying the Additional Protocols; the German declaration says that 'the decision taken by the person responsible has to be judged on the basis of the information available to him at the relevant time, and not on the basis of hindsight'.[300]

---

[297] Critical towards this regulation are Roberts, *VaJInt* 26 (1985), 150–1 and Parks, *Air Force Law Review* 32 (1990), 136–7.

[298] Solf, in Bothe/Partsch/Solf, 326. [299] Ibid., 327.

[300] See BR-Drs. 64/90 of 2 Feb. 1990, 132 (Federal Republic of Germany), 125 (Belgium), 127 (Italy), 129 (Netherlands), 130 (Spain); see also Schindler/Toman, 707, 712, 714, and 717.

Oeter

**Attacks against military objectives shall be conducted with maximum precau- 447
tions to protect the civilian population (Art. 51, para. 1 AP I; Art. 13 AP II). Attacks
which may affect the civilian population shall be preceded by an effective warning, unless circumstances do not permit this (Art. 26 HagueReg; Art. 57, para. 2,
lit. c AP I). These rules shall also apply to attacks by missiles and remotely controlled weapons.**

1. The corollary of the principle of distinction and the subsequent limitation of
legally permissible military objectives is the fundamental maxim that the civilian
population must be spared as far as possible.[301] As a customary rule this maxim has
long been recognized;[302] indeed it is arguable that the principle of distinction and
of non-combatant immunity today constitutes one of the few peremptory norms of
humanitarian law, and accordingly also a part of '*jus cogens*'[303] which is applicable
regardless of whether the conflict is international or internal in character.[304] In Art.
51 AP I and Art. 13 AP II the maxim is now reaffirmed and codified. The rule prohibits not only attacks against the general civilian population but also attacks likely
to cause incidental loss of civilian life, injury to civilians, or damage to civilian
objects which are excessive in relation to the expected advantage. This formula covers all kinds of attacks which, under the perspective of military necessity, could
cause unnecessary violence and which accordingly would unduly endanger the
civilian population (measured according to the strict requirements of military
necessity).[305] Thus there must be inherent in the principle of utmost protection of
the civilian population a rule requiring that the military use of force be both necessary and appropriate, whenever damage to the civilian population is to be
expected.[306] Collateral injury to the civilian population must be minimized by the
operational arrangements under which the attacks are performed, either by an
exact delimitation of the targets of the attack, by the use of precisely targetable
weapons in the 'weapons mix' used for the attack, or by other precautionary measures in planning or implementing the military operations.[307] It will be difficult,
however, to deduce from such general principles a specific rule that any particular
type of weapons (in particular 'precision-guided munitions') must be used in a specific case; precision-guided munitions are still too expensive and too rare for even
military super-powers to be required to use them in all cases where civilian losses
might thereby be minimized.[308] The armed forces of belligerents therefore retain

---

[301] As to the codification of that maxim in Art. 51 AP I see Solf, in Bothe/Partsch/Solf, 299; Pilloud/Pictet,
in ICRC *Commentary*, 615–17 (paras. 1923–33, 1935); Gardam, 114–18.

[302] See Greenwood, in Delissen/Tanja (Eds.), 108–11; Venturini, 127–50; Sassòli, 344–50; Gardam,
132–62.

[303] In that sense argue e.g. Miyazaki, in Swinarski (Ed.), 436–9 and Fleck, *RDMilG* 29 (1990), 501.

[304] See e.g. Gardam, 176–9.

[305] As to the practical difficulties of implementing the general rule see Parks, *Air Force Law Review* 32
(1990), 152–63.

[306] In this sense see para. 3 of *US Army Manual* FM 27–10: 'The law of war . . . requires that belligerents
refrain from employing any kind or degree of violence which is not actually necessary for military purposes'; see Sassòli, 346.

[307] On the relevant experiences of the Kuwait War see Keenan, 36; Gasser, *HUV-I* 4/1991, 31.

[308] Quite far-reaching in that regard is Gasser, *HUV-I* 4/1991, 31.

Oeter

considerable discretion, which will be exercised primarily according to military considerations, in the framework of operational priorities, and not mainly according to humanitarian aspects.

2. The rule of utmost protection of the civilian population includes the requirement of a previous warning, if possible. This requirement was already recognized by customary law. In so far as the planned attack is likely to cause serious losses to the civilian population, the competent authorities of the adversary shall be given an effective warning prior to the attack, allowing an opportunity to evacuate the civilian population, or at least to place the population in specifically protected locations (see Section 453). Art. 26 of the Hague Regulations provided that the 'commander of an attacking force, before commencing a bombardment, except in the case of an assault, should do all he can to warn the authorities'. Only in the case of an assault attack, namely an attack primarily based on the element of surprise, is such a warning logically excluded by considerations of military necessity.[309] Art. 57, para. 2(c) AP I, which addressed the question again, in essence goes no further than the traditional rule codified as early as 1907,[310] since it requires nothing more than an effective advance warning—unless the specific circumstances of the planned operation do not permit such a warning, as especially before an assault.[311]

3. The same principles apply to attacks by missiles and remotely controlled weapons. The danger of militarily excessive collateral damage in these cases is particularly high (unless the attack uses the new generation of remotely controlled 'precision-guided munitions'), since the targeting capabilities of remotely controlled weapons are traditionally extremely bad. Accordingly, it is unlawful not only to use such weapons against the civilian population as such in order to terrorize it (as was done by the Iraqi 'Scud' attacks on Israel in the course of the Kuwait War 1991), but also to use these weapons indiscriminately against military pin-point targets in urban settlements or other concentrations of civilian population. Such supposedly 'military' use of remotely controlled weapons against military installations in urban areas makes little sense from a military perspective, since the low targeting capability of such weapons leads to minimal success in combating a specific military objective; the collateral damage from such attacks, on the other hand, is usually extremely high. Traditional remotely controlled weapons and missiles may thus be used only with extreme precaution, for example against concentrations of enemy forces in scarcely populated areas of deployment, or (if precisely targeted) against lines of communication in the enemy hinterland.

4. It is not only the attacker who is subject to specific obligations to minimize civilian casualties and collateral damage. The state responsible for a certain territory is

---

[309] Concerning the regulation of Art. 26 HagueReg see Parks, *Air Force Law Review* 32 (1990), 157.

[310] Of a different opinion is Parks, ibid., 158; to the point, however, Solf, in Bothe/Partsch/Solf, 368.

[311] See Pilloud/Pictet, in ICRC *Commentary*, 686–7 (paras. 2223–5) and Solf, in Bothe/Partsch/Solf, 367–8.

also obliged to avoid collateral damage therein.[312] Art. 58 AP I requires that parties to a conflict shall endeavour to remove the civilian population and civilian objects under their control away from the vicinity of military objectives (the traditional practice of evacuating the population of important cities),[313] and that the responsible state shall avoid locating military objectives within or near densely populated areas,[314] and obliges the belligerents to 'take other necessary precautions to protect the civilian population, individual civilians and civilian objects under their control against the dangers resulting from military operations'.[315] The last covers preparations for civil defence, such as the provision of adequate shelters, the training and build-up of civil defence organizations, and the maintenance of adequate fire-fighting brigades.

**In the aerial war zone enemy military aircraft may be attacked without warning in   448
order to make them crash or land. Downed aircraft shall become spoils of war.
The members of the crew and the passengers—save unlawful combatants and
mercenaries—shall become prisoners of war (Art. 36, para. 1 HRAW 1923).**

In aerial warfare the military aircraft of all parties to a conflict are entitled to take part in hostilities and to attack military objectives (see Section 326). At the same time, military aircraft constitute a lawful military objective, against which violence may be used. The attack against such objects is permitted at any time and requires no specific safeguards.[316] Even if there are persons on board such aircraft who are civilians according to the general rules, this does not prevent these aircraft from qualifying as military objectives, since those passengers voluntarily run the risk of being shot down. The attacking enemy has the choice of shooting down the aircraft or of forcing it to land. Any planes shot down or forced to land are legitimate booty of war pursuant to established practice, and may be used by the adversary for its own military purposes.[317] Crew members and passengers become prisoners of war, because they are deemed to be combatants due to integration in the military structure of the enemy (only *franc tireurs* and mercenaries, who are covered by particular rules of international law, are excluded; see Sections 302 and 303). Captivity begins, however, only when those persons are taken into custody by state organs of the adversary. Accordingly, those who have parachuted or made an emergency landing do not acquire prisoner of war status immediately upon leaving their aircraft; for as long as they remain uncaptured, they are still regular combatants and must conform to the general rules governing troops who have advanced behind the enemy's lines (such as patrols or commandos). They must therefore wear uniform and carry their weapons openly.

---

[312] See Pilloud/Pictet, in ICRC *Commentary*, 692 (paras. 2239–44); Solf, in Bothe/Partsch/Solf, 371–3; Sassòli, 490–3.
[313] Details can be found in the studies of Sassòli, 493–5, and in the comments by Pilloud/Pictet, *op. cit.*, 693–4 (paras. 2247–50).
[314] Concerning details see Pilloud/Pictet, *op. cit.*, 694 (paras. 2251–6); Sassòli, 496–8.
[315] See Sassòli, 498–9 and Pilloud/Pictet, *op. cit.*, 694–5 (paras. 2257–8).
[316] See v. d. Heydte, *EPIL* 3, 8.   [317] Ibid.

449   **Other enemy public aircraft shall not be attacked without warning. They may, however, by force of arms, be compelled to land (Art. 34 HRAW 1923). Such aircraft may be attacked if they:**

    – **escort enemy military aircraft;**

    – **fly through an aerial zone interdicted by the adversary; or**

    – **take part in hostilities.**

Other public aircraft, i.e. planes and helicopters which are used by state organs but which are not designed for military purposes and do not take part in the hostilities, are not a legitimate military objective. The neutralization of such aircraft will not normally be militarily necessary, because they make no contribution to the military activities of the adversary. On the contrary, they should usually be considered as civilian objects. Therefore, like aircraft that enter foreign territory without authorization in peacetime, they may be forced to land, but they may not be shot down without previous warning. The only exception applies if such aircraft escort enemy military aircraft, enter into an interdiction zone, or participate directly in hostilities. In those cases aircraft become military objectives. Even a non-military aircraft, by its integration in the operative framework of the enemy's warfare, then renders itself liable to attack.

450   **It is prohibited to order that there shall be no survivors. It is also prohibited to threaten an adversary with such an order or to conduct military operations on that basis (Art. 40 AP I; Art. 23, lit. d HagueReg).**

There is an ancient customary principle prohibiting orders 'to give no quarter' to captured enemies.[318] This well established rule has now been reaffirmed by Art. 40 AP I; it constitutes in essence a logical expression of the principle that the legal use of military violence is strictly limited to what is required by military necessity; clearly there is no necessity to kill persons *hors de combat*. Only for so long as the enemy combatant participates in hostilities is he to be considered as a legitimate military objective.[319] As soon as he lays down his arms or drops out of combat because of wounds, to kill him becomes a useless act from the perspective of strict military necessity,[320] since it contributes nothing to the military objectives of the belligerents (see also Art. 41 AP I; see Sections 601 and 705). The mere intimidation or terrorization of the adversary with no other purpose, however, is not permitted under international law.

    The principle codified in Art. 40 AP I has been seriously violated even in our century, particularly in the practice of World War II (Hitler's order to kill all Soviet commissars, liqidation of so-called 'irregulars', martial law executions of 'saboteurs' and parachute commandos),[321] but also in numerous civil wars since 1945, when

---

[318] Concerning the historic background of this customary rule see de Preux, in ICRC *Commentary*, 474 (paras. 1589–90).

[319] See Solf, in Bothe/Partsch/Solf, 219–23.   [320] Ibid., 217.

[321] See de Preux, in ICRC *Commentary*, 476 (para. 1595); Solf, in Bothe/Partsch/Solf, 217.

the minimum standard of common Art. 3 would have prohibited such an action. The Diplomatic Conference therefore thought it necessary explicitly to codify such a maxim in Additional Protocol I (Art. 40) as well as in Additional Protocol II (Art. 4, para. 1, last sentence), although there is a considerable overlap with the fundamental rules of Arts.41 and 51, para. 4. AP I, for combatants *hors de combat* do not constitute lawful military objectives. Even without the specific provision of Art.40 AP I attacks on those *hors de combat* would thus have been regarded as unlawful indiscriminate attacks.[322]

2. Protection of Civilian Objects

It is prohibited to fire at or bombard—whether to terrorize them or for any other   451
purpose—members of the civilian population not taking part in hostilities (Art.
51, para. 2 AP I), and to make civilian objects the object of attack. Such attacks in
reprisal are also prohibited (Arts. 51, para. 6, 53, lit. c, 54, para. 4, 55, para. 2, 56,
para. 4 AP I).

1. The prohibition against attacks on civilian persons and on the civilian population as such (the principle of non-combatant immunity) is the logical consequence of the fundamental principle of limited warfare and of the rule ensuing from this basic foundation, namely the principle of distinction between military objectives and the civilian population. Since only attacks on military objectives are admissible under the rule of military necessity (see Sections 441–3), it is clear that neither the civilian population nor individual civilians can ever be permissible objects of attack. As a fundamental maxim of customary international law this rule has been undisputed for decades;[323] Art. 51, para. 2 AP I is therefore a reaffirmation of established principles of customary law.[324]

2. The same is true of the prohibition against terror attacks stated in Art. 51, para. 2, 2nd sentence AP I. An attack solely designed to spread terror among the civilian population constitutes a special case of unlawful attack on the civilian population. The bombardment of the civilian population or of civilian objects in such cases is deliberately intended to intimidate the adversary and the enemy civilian population.[325] Although it constitutes a blatant violation of fundamental humanitarian law,[326] which undoubtedly falls within the category of 'grave breaches' which

---

[322] See de Preux, in ICRC *Commentary*, 476–7 (para. 1598).

[323] See Sassòli, 387–8, with further references; see also Oppenheim/Lauterpacht, Vol.II, 524–30; Castrén, *The Present Law of War and Neutrality*, 174–5; Kalshoven, *Law of Warfare*, 59–70; Detter De Lupis, 239–44; Green, *Essays on the Modern Law of War*, 143; Mirimanoff-Chilikine, *Revue belge de droit international* 8 (1972), 1057; Bruha, 'Bombardment', *EPIL* 3, 55; Rogers, *RDMilG* 1982, 296; Cassese, *Tentative Appraisal*, 477–80.

[324] That was the position argued by the ICRC and the negotiating delegations when drafting the Additional Protocols, as well as the position of subsequent state practice—cf. Sassòli, 388–9.

[325] See in particular Gasser, *Genfer Abkommen und Terrorismusverbot*, 73–4; Sassòli, 396–402; Solf, in Bothe/Partsch/Solf, 300–1.

[326] Already concerning the traditional customary law, to the same conclusion come Greenspan, 337; Castrén, *The Present Law of War and Neutrality*, 200–1; Spetzler, 191–2; Ney, 224–5; Sassòli, 398–9.

Oeter

should be sanctioned as war crimes, this particularly barbarian variant of 'total' warfare is unfortunately used regularly by military actors in practice. The 'Yugoslav', or rather Serbian army, for example, has repeatedly launched terror attacks on the civilian population and threatened attacks on purely civilian objects in the course of the wars in Croatia in 1991 and in Bosnia since 1992, in order to intimidate the 'secessionist' republics and to expel the indigenous population from the territories claimed as 'historically Serbian'.[327] Soviet warfare in Afghanistan during the 1980s[328] and the Iraqi attacks with 'Scud' missiles on Saudi and Israeli cities during the Kuwait War in 1991[329] also provide recent examples of such blatantly illegal belligerent practices, to which the international community has not yet found an adequate mode of reaction.

3. The lack of any adequate response to such barbaric excesses is connected with a dilemma besetting the international community, which has found only a rather one-sided solution (in favour of direct humanitarian concerns) in the First Additional Protocol. For a long time it was disputed whether cases of blatant violation of the rules safeguarding the civilian population justify reprisals which injure the enemy's civilian population.[330] Additional Protocol I now unequivocally states that reprisals against the civilian population and against civilian objects are absolutely prohibited. The strictly reciprocal character inherent in traditional rules of humanitarian law has thus been superseded by an 'objective regime' which marginalizes the interests of individual member states in favour of 'community interests' of a purely humanitarian nature.[331] The fundamental provisions of Part IV of AP I cannot therefore be brushed aside under the system of the Protocol even for reprisal, i.e. by a reaction in deliberate disregard of international law to a prior violation of the law by another state.[332] The prohibition of attacks on the civilian population and on purely civilian objects (Arts. 51, para. 6 and 52, para. 1 AP I), on important cultural objects(Art. 53(c) AP I), on objects indispensable to the survival of the civilian population (Art. 54, para. 4 AP I), on works and installations containing dangerous forces (Art. 56, para. 4 AP I), and on the natural environment (Art. 55, para. 2 AP I) is now absolute and may not be waived even in reprisal, according to a whole series of provisions scattered throughout Chapters II and III of Part IV AP I. The peremptory character of these fundamental safeguards for the benefit of the civilian population is thus most clearly emphasized.

452   Defended localities or buildings may be fired at or bombarded in order to:

—break down active resistance (conquering fire, bombardment);

[327] See Oeter, *HuV-I* 5/1991, 6; as to Bosnia see the detailed materials on the practices of so-called 'ethnic cleansing' contained in the reports of the Special Rapporteur on Bosnia of the UN Commission of Human Rights, Mazowiecki, esp. UN Doc.A/47/418 of 3 Sep. 1992, 4–9, and UN Doc.A/47/666 of 17 Nov. 1992, 6–12; see also the appeal to the parties of the conflict by the ICRC on 13 Aug. 1992, *RIC* 74 (1992), 511–12.

[328] See Ermacora, *Der Afghanistankonflikt*, 206.   [329] Cf. White/McCoubrey, 366.

[330] As to that debate see Kalshoven, *Belligerent Reprisals*, 353–61; cf. also Bierzanek, *Reprisals*, 237–47.

[331] As to the problems of that approach see Kalshoven, *NYIL* 21 (1990), 54–67 and Nahlik, in Delissen/Tanja (Eds.), 172–3.

[332] As to 'reprisal' see Sassòli, 428–32, and esp. Kalshoven, *Belligerent Reprisals*, 11–33.

Oeter

—eliminate military objectives located therein (destructive fire, bombardment).

In both cases, the fire or bombardment shall be locally limited to the actual resistance and the military objectives.

Unlike 'undefended localities' (see Sections 458–60), which the prohibition of attacks on the civilian population covers, 'defended localities' constitute legitimate military objectives.[333] Whole cities or villages, however, do not become military objectives merely because some combatants resisting enemy forces remain there. Contemporary humanitarian law in that regard deviates from the approach traditional before World War II, which qualified defended (and in particular besieged) localities as legitimate military objectives *in toto*, thus permitting wholesale destruction of such settlements.[334] Even against such localities, military force is permissible only if and in so far as the violence is justified by military necessity, in order to neutralize enemy resistance and to destroy specific military objects located in it. Only if bombardment of such a locality could achieve military purposes in a strict sense is the use of force justifiable under Art. 52, para. 2 AP I. Accordingly, those sections of such a locality the bombardment of which does not offer a definite military advantage must be spared the bombardment—although it must be admitted that the defence of a locality will normally lead to practically all the important objects becoming military objectives.[335]

Effective advance warning shall be given of any bombardment, unless circumstances do not permit this (Art. 57, para. 2, lit. c AP I; Art. 26 HagueReg).   453

Customary law already included an obligation, deduced from the principle of utmost minimization of collateral civilian casualties, that the opposing side should be given advance warning. The enemy authorities should be given the opportunity to evacuate the civilian population (or at least to lodge them in specifically protected localities, such as prepared shelters). Accordingly, Art. 26 HagueReg required that the commander of an attacking force should inform the competent authorities of the target location of the fact that a bombardment is planned. Only in a case of assault, i.e. when the success of an attack depends on surprise, was such a warning deemed to be superfluous (or rather: militarily counter-productive), and therefore a warning of assault is logically excluded by considerations of military necessity.[336] Art. 57, para. 2, lit. c AP I addressed again the question of warning. In essence the new provision in AP I does not go much beyond what was contained already in Art. 26 Hague Regulations,[337] since Art. 57, para. 2, lit. c does not require anything other than an effective advance warning in cases where the attack is likely to cause severe civilian casualties and collateral damage to civilian goods. The attacker may

---

[333] See Sassòli, 355–8; Doswald-Beck, in Meyer (Ed.), 158; Meyrowitz, *ZaöRV* 41 (1981), 28.

[334] See Oppenheim/Lauterpacht, Vol.II, 421; Castrén, *The Present Law of War and Neutrality*, 201; Meyrowitz, *loc. cit.*, 28; Rauch, *RDMilG* 1980, 234; Sassòli, 356–7.

[335] In that regard see the detailed reasoning of Meyrowitz, *loc. cit.*, 28–9; see also Sassòli, 357–8.

[336] As to the regulation of Art. 26 Hague Regulations see Parks, *Air Force Law Review* 32 (1990), 157, and Sassòli, 478–81.

[337] Of a different opinion seems to be Parks, *Air Force Law Review* 32 (1990), 158; to the point Solf, in Bothe/Partsch/Solf, 368 and Sassòli, 481–4.

dispense with a warning if 'circumstances do not permit', namely when the specific circumstances of the planned operation do not make it possible to inform the defender because the purpose of the operation could not then be achieved (which in essence is no more than an abstract description of the 'assault' problem).[338] The formulation of the exception in Art. 57 AP I is even more vague than the old one contained in Art. 26 Hague Regulations; but again the formula must be interpreted in the light of the overarching principle of military necessity. That means *in concreto* that the advance warning really must be excluded under a military perspective, because e.g. the element of surprise is crucial for the success of the whole operation. Two problems therefore become decisive, namely the repercussions of the warning on the chances of success of the operation on one hand, and the casualties which the attacking forces are likely to sustain if a warning is issued on the other hand.[339] A general preference for leaving the adversary in doubt about one's operations is obviously not sufficient to fulfil the criteria of the 'exception formula'; the relevant yardstick, however, must not be exaggerated, since it would undermine the plausibility of the system if too high a level were imposed on the extent of casualties which attackers should risk in order to provide an opportunity for evacuation.

454   **It is prohibited in any circumstances to fire at or bombard civilian and military objects without distinction (Art. 51, paras 4 and 5 AP I; Art. 24, para. 3 AP II).**

1. Art. 51, paras. 4 and 5 AP I states the most important consequence of the principle of limited warfare. Essentially, the prohibition against indiscriminate attacks is no more than a logical conclusion from the principle of distinction. The fundamental maxim of distinction and non-combatant immunity not only prohibits attacks on the civilian population but also requires that belligerents must always distinguish between military objectives on one hand and the civilian population and objects on the other.[340] The prohibition of indiscriminate attacks laid down in Art. 51, para. 4 AP I is thus a more or less self-evident inference from the fundamental rules of humanitarian law, if not from 'elementary considerations of humanity'. The ICRC and government delegates who were decisive in negotiating, and the Diplomatic Conference as a whole, accordingly considered it—in its abstract version—to be a fundamental rule of humanitarian law firmly established in custom.[341]

2. At the same time, however, the prohibition of indiscriminate attack as enshrined in Art. 51 AP I, in its detailed version with many specific rules on combat, is also a development of convention law which far exceeds the customary core of traditional practice.[342] For example, it is way beyond a mere logical deduction from military

---

[338] See Pilloud/Pictet, in ICRC *Commentary*, 686–7 (paras. 2223–5) and Solf, in Bothe/Partsch/Solf, 367–8.

[339] See Carnahan, *American University Law Review* 31 (1982), 866, with an illustration of the practical problems in the case of the US bombardment of Northern Vietnam in December 1972.

[340] See Kalshoven, *Law of Warfare*, 64; Blix, *BYIL* 49 (1978), 47; Falk/Meyrowitz/Sanderson, 564–5; Rauch, *loc. cit.*, 228; Sassòli, 403.

[341] See Sassòli, 405–8.   [342] Sassòli, 407.

necessity to state that losses among the civilian population, even if resulting from an attack on a military objective and being necessary in a military perspective, may not always be legally permissible. Such a proposition cannot, in pure logic, be derived from the principle of military necessity. The restrictive approach which outlaws collateral damage even if 'militarily necessary' in the traditional sense, therefore needs a further value-judgement and a second fundamental principle, namely the essential principle of proportionality.[343] Only if the concept of military necessity is combined with the principle of proportionality, can one come to the conclusion that collateral damage which is unavoidable in achieving certain military objectives may nevertheless be prohibited by law.[344] The traditional approach, according to which all collateral damage that is unavoidable in attacking a certain military objective must be accepted, is no longer valid.[345] Extreme cases demonstrate the point: the accidental presence of a civilian in a military objective does not render it immune under the rule of distinction; equally, an attack upon a military objective inside a city but which is in itself totally unimportant does not justify an attack on the city as a whole which causes enormous damage to the civilian population. The prohibition of excessive damage, inherent in the prohibition of indiscriminate attack, requires belligerents to relate the military advantage which is expected from an attack to the possible civilian losses.[346] Only if the expected military advantage is of such tactical or strategic importance as to outweigh the collateral damage is the attack justifiable under Art. 51 AP I. The criteria of such a balancing act necessarily remain indefinite, and inevitably leave considerable latitude in the assessment of probable consequences and the balancing of the various concerns.[347] However, there is no alternative. The intellectual process of balancing the various elements is so complicated, needs to take into account such a huge amount of data and so many factors, that any attempt to design a formula which is both comprehensive and precise would be ridiculous. In short: common sense is irreplaceable.

Indiscriminate firing and bombardment means attacks:　　455

—which are not directed at a specific military objective (Art. 51, para. 4, lit. a AP I);

—which cannot be directed at a specific military objective (Art. 51, para. 4, lit. b AP I); or

—whose intended effects cannot be limited to the military objective (Art. 51, para. 4, lit. c AP I).

1. Art. 51, para. 4, AP I, sub-paras. (a) to (c) undertakes to give concrete meaning to the notion of 'indiscriminate attack'. Whether such a definition is helpful, and whether it does not risk confusing soldiers involved more than it enlightens them (which was the initial purpose of the provision) was a question hotly debated in the

[343] On the rule of proportionality in the context of humanitarian law see Fenrick, *Military Law Review* 98 (1982), 91–127; Parks, *Air Force Law Review* 32 (1990), 168–85; Venturini, 127–50.
[344] Solf, in Bothe/Partsch/Solf, 304–5.
[345] See Solf, *Protection of Civilians*, 119; Pilloud/Pictet, in ICRC *Commentary*, 619 (para. 1946).
[346] See Sassòli, 404.　　　　　　　　　　　　　[347] See Fenrick, *loc. cit.*, 126.

Oeter

course of its drafting.[348] Ultimately the opinion prevailed that the laconic sentence 'indiscriminate attacks are prohibited' would be too imprecise and would fail to provide practical guidance to the field commanders and staff officers who have to plan and implement military operations.[349] The 'official' explanation of the term 'indiscriminate attack' which, despite its use of a rather abstract formula, already goes into more detail than the earlier definitions, thus tries to elaborate the definitional approach. It carves out three different types of specific attacks which must be considered as violations of the rule of distinction.[350]

2. Art. 51, para. 4 lit. a AP I prohibits attacks which are not directed at a specific military objective; in essence a self-evident consequence of the rule of distinction. The attacker must be sure that the target against which the use of force is directed constitutes a military objective in accordance with humanitarian law, and he must restrict his action as far as possible to that specific objective alone, not objects and persons around it.[351] This raises two particular concerns. The attacking force must—using all available means of intelligence—make sure of directing its operation against a genuine military objective, i.e. it must clarify whether the object or ground position against which firing or bombardment is directed actually constitutes a military objective the neutralization of which is essential.[352] Blind fire into territory controlled by the adversary is clearly forbidden, which means that firing without reliable information about the objective, and therefore without a clear idea of the nature of the objective, is now strictly outlawed.[353] Also forbidden is the practice of releasing bombs over enemy territory, particularly over settlements, after missing the original objective, which was common in World War II. Such an attack constitutes a paradigm case of indiscriminate warfare. Modern rules of engagement usually exclude this method of disposal of bomb loads; in 'Operation Desert Storm' the rules of engagement of the Allied forces expressly ordered air crews to bring home the entire bomb load when target identification had failed. In addition, the attacker must direct fire specifically at the identified military objectives. In combating a certain objective (or a compound of objectives) he may spread his fire power over a certain area, either as 'harassing fire' against the enemy's lines and deployment areas,[354] or as 'interdiction fire' against certain strategic points, bridgeheads, or ground positions the use of which is intended to be denied to the adversary.[355] Even such kinds of 'barrage fire' covering a certain area, however, must fulfil the basic condition of being directed against a specific objective. Accordingly, in these cases the ground area serving as a target must be definable as a military

---

[348] Sassòli, 405.   [349] Pilloud/Pictet, in ICRC *Commentary*, 620, para. 1950.

[350] That it is not a mere list of examples but a genuine definition 'by law', is demonstrated convincingly by Fischer, *Der Einsatz von Nuklearwaffen*, 183–90.

[351] As a general explanation of Art. 51, para. 4, lit. a AP I see Sassòli, 420–2; Pilloud/Pictet, in ICRC *Commentary*, 620–1 (paras. 1951–5) and in much detail Fischer, op. cit., 185–90.

[352] Pilloud/Pictet, in ICRC *Commentary*, 620–1 (para. 1952); Fischer, *Der Einsatz von Nuklearwaffen*, 189–90.

[353] Sassòli, 421.

[354] Cf. Solf, in Bothe/Partsch/Solf, 307 and Kimminich, *Schutz der Menschen in bewaffneten Konflikten*, 142–4.

[355] Solf, in Bothe/Partsch/Solf, 308; Pilloud/Pictet, in ICRC *Commentary*, 621 (para. 1955).

Oeter

objective in its entirety, i.e. the whole ground sector must in itself be militarily relevant. It is prohibited to combine clearly separate objectives in one single target area covered by an overall 'area bombardment', since such untargeted fire exposes the civilian population and civilian goods in the intermediate zones to risk.[356] The basic requirement of Art. 51, para. 4, lit. a AP I that the attack should be directed against a 'specific' military objective, draws a boundary which the belligerent may not overstep.[357] The same applies to the use of mines (cf. Sections 409–14). Although it is impossible to deduce a general prohibition on the laying of mines from Art. 51, para. 4 AP I, even the ground sector blocked by mines must always constitute a military objective in itself. The neutralization (or closing) of the target area of a mine attack must be militarily necessary, and the surveillance and timely removal of the minefield must ensure that the civilian population will not be injured by the mining operation.[358]

3. Art. 51, para. 4 lit. b AP I prohibits attacks which cannot be directed against a specific military objective. This also concerns methods of warfare which are obviously prohibited by customary law as indiscriminate. The drafters of the provision had primarily in mind traditional remotely controlled weapons with extremely low target accuracy, such as long range missiles with only a rudimentary guidance system. In these cases the construction of the weapon itself (in combination with the specific operative modalities under which these weapons are used) leaves no doubt as to the nature of the attack. The mode of operation of such an attack usually makes it impossible to distinguish between military objectives and civilian objects.[359] Thus, the attack is inherently unable to fulfil the requirements of distinction. The prime example of such an operation which *per definitionem* leads to an indiscriminate attack is the German use of V2 missiles against British cities in World War II.[360] More recent practice also provides examples of such indiscriminate missile attacks, such as the series of missiles lauched on Iraqi and Iranian cities during the Gulf War and the Iraqi attacks with 'Scud' missiles on Israel in the Kuwait War of 1991.[361] Aside from these self-evident cases it remains in dispute how far (beyond the core just described) the prohibition in Art. 51, para. 4, lit. b really reaches. For example, there are many arguments in favour of including in the prohibition certain kinds of conventional bombing raids, at least those where the bombardment cannot in practice be limited to specific military objectives. Night attacks without adequate targeting equipment fall into this category, or bombing raids from extremely high altitudes where the target accuracy becomes unacceptably low.[362] The prohibition seems, however, not to cover specific categories of weapons as such. Some states

[356] See Kimminich, *Schutz der Menschen in bewaffneten Konflikten*, 145–6; Sassòli, 421–2.
[357] See Sassòli, 421–2; Fischer, op. cit., 186, 188–9.
[358] See Solf, in Bothe/Partsch/Solf, 308 (he mainly refers to Art. 51, para. 4, lit. b AP I); Würkner-Theis, 102–3, 141–8; and Rauch, *GYIL* 24 (1981), 270–80.
[359] Sassòli, 422–5.
[360] See Spaight, 214–17; Castrén, *The Present Law of War and Neutrality*, 204; Greenspan, 365–7; Kimminich, *Der Schutz der Menschen in bewaffneten Konflikten*, 132–3; Fischer, *Der Einsatz von Nuklearwaffen*, 192–3.
[361] See White/McCoubrey, *International Relations* 10 (1991), 366.
[362] See Ney, 226; Sassòli, 424.

insisted on this during the drafting of the provision.[363] Certain operational uses of dangerous weapons were thought to be outlawed under Art. 51, para. 4, lit. b: operations where the distinction between military objectives and civilian objects is by definition impossible because the weapons cannot be directed specifically at individual military objectives. In principle, this sounds convincing. However, there remains an inherent tendency which extends the provision's application beyond a mere prohibition of certain operational designs; 'blind' weapons such as long-range missiles without adequate guidance systems, or traditional minefields laid without customary precautions (i.e. unrecorded, unmarked, and not designed to destroy themselves within a reasonable time) are difficult to imagine as compatible with Art. 51, para. 4, lit. b[364].

4. Art. 51, para. 4, lit. c AP I outlaws attacks whose intended effects cannot be limited to the military objective, and is the most controversial part of the definition of indiscriminate attacks. Lit. c of Art. 51, para. 4 reads as follows: 'Indiscriminate attacks are . . . (c) those which employ a method or means of combat the effects of which cannot be limited as required by this Protocol.' This refers to a whole series of limitations on the use of force: the rules on the protection of the environment (Arts. 35, para. 3 and 55, para. 1), the prohibition of attacks on works and installations containing dangerous forces (Art. 56), and the principle of proportionality.[365] Proportionality in particular has been a point of a fierce controversy. It was debated to what extent a prohibition of excessive damage really constitutes an established part of previously existing customary law, or to put it in another way, to what extent Art. 51, para. 4, lit. c AP I refers to an established principle of proportionality.[366] The starting-point is the fact that the version of the rule which was finally adopted by the Diplomatic Conference deliberately included the problem of disproportionate attacks. The formulation of this, however, was rather cryptic, since it implicitly focused on methods of warfare which necessarily cause excessive losses to the civilian population.[367] Thus, the weapons primarily concerned are those whose effects are spread over a wide area, such as phosphorous incendiary bombs or other variants of incendiary weapons, or so-called 'cluster bombs'. If these undirected weapons are used in densely populated regions their effects will necessarily be disproportionate[368] and accordingly they are prohibited under Art. 51, para. 4 lit. c AP I. Although the international community has concluded special agreements on most of the armament items inherently covered by the provision (UN Weapons Convention of 1980; see Sections 402, 409–25) it remains to be resolved under a general perspective whether the particular convention rules which refer only to specific categories of weapons (excluding e.g. cluster bombs) are really exhaustive, or whether the general rule of Art. 51, para. 4 lit. c AP I should not be seen as providing an overriding legal framework which imposes a final limit. Most considerations

---

[363] Solf, in Bothe/Partsch/Solf, 306; Sassòli, 424.

[364] Convincingly argued by Solf, in Bothe/Partsch/Solf, 305.

[365] See Kimminich, *Schutz der Menschen in bewaffneten Konflikten*, 141–2; Solf, in Bothe/Partsch/Solf, 305–6.

[366] See Fischer, *Der Einsatz von Nuklearwaffen*, 195; Sassòli, 427.

[367] Fischer, *op. cit.*, 195.   [368] See Sassòli, 426–7.

speak in favour of such a proposition, so that weapons not regulated by the 1980 Convention (cluster bombs being the most obvious example) are subject to the more general principle codified in Art. 51, para. 4 lit. c AP I.[369]

5. Particular problems arise from the definition of legally permissible uses of nuclear weapons (see Sections 428 to 430). If one assumes, as did the ICRC in its original draft, and which the nuclear powers later confirmed in their declarations, that the Additional Protocol did not intend to broach the question of legality of nuclear weapons, a further question arises immediately. Must Art. 51, para. 4 lit. c AP I be considered as an expression of established customary law, which continues to exist alongside the convention regulation in Additional Protocol I?[370] As long as Art. 51, para. 4 lit. c is seen to rely only on an established principle of proportionality, that question must be answered in the affirmative. Therefore, the use of weapons of mass destruction, which inevitably cause disproportionate collateral damage if used in densely populated areas, would in principle have to be considered as prohibited by public international law, independent of Art. 51, para. 4 lit. c AP I as a convention norm. At least first use of such nuclear munitions against urban settlements is accordingly already prohibited under customary principles. Only modern precision-guided nuclear warheads for combat against purely military objectives, and retaliatory use of nuclear weapons by way of reprisal, remain permissible, and not subject to the legal obstacles imposed by the customary standards here analysed.

Attacks and bombardments are also to be considered as indiscriminate if:

—**a number of clearly separate and distinct military objectives located in a built-up area are attacked as if they were one single military objective (Art. 51, para. 5, lit. a AP I);**   456

—**they are likely to cause loss of civilian life, injury to civilians or damage to civilian objects which would be excessive in relation to the concrete and direct military advantage anticipated (Art. 51, para. 5, lit. b AP I);**

—**they also cause excessive injury and damage to civilians or civilian objects located outside the actual target area and its immediate vicinity.**

1. The still abstract definition of what constitutes an 'indiscriminate attack' contained in Art. 51, para. 4 AP I is supplemented in paragraph 5 of Art. 51 by two examples of situations which had long been debated. Art. 51, para. 5 now states expressly that they are covered by the prohibition of indiscriminate attack.[371] The clarification concerns on one hand the practice of 'area bombardment' which had become common in World War II and which was claimed to be legal by the Allied Powers at the time.[372] It is true that discussion has continued for decades as to whether area

---

[369] So argues Sassòli, 427–8.   [370] Ibid., 426–8.

[371] On Art. 51, para. 5 AP I see Solf, in Bothe/Partsch/Solf, 309–11; Pilloud/Pictet, in ICRC *Commentary*, 623–6 (paras. 1967–81).

[372] See Spaight, 270–81; Greenspan, 336; Randelzhofer, *Flächenbombardement und Völkerrecht*, 478–80; Rousseau, *Le droit des conflits armés*, 366; DeSaussure, *Annals of Air and Space Law* 4 (1979), 481; Blix, *BYIL* 49 (1978), 36–7.

Oeter

bombardments are not already outlawed under the customary prohibition of indiscriminate attacks,[373] 'area bombardments' being defined as bombardments which combine a number of clearly separate and distinct military objectives located in a built-up area and treating them as one single military objective. State practice hitherto had not demonstrated its willingness to accept such a prohibition,[374] although it is not difficult to argue that a prohibitory rule follows from the general prohibition of indiscriminate attacks. Thus, Art. 51, para. 5, lit. a AP I constitutes an important innovation, since it makes clear that such practices of area bombardment are generally inadmissible.[375] Only where a genuine target area is attacked (i.e. a passage or ground sector the whole of which constitutes a military objective, or where several military objectives are so intermingled that they are practically inseparable and thus can only be attacked together) does bombardment of a wide area remain permissible.[376]

2. The second important point of debate clarified by Art. 51, para. 5 AP I is the validity and scope of the principle of proportionality. Admittedly it had already been widely accepted before the adoption of AP I that attacks on military objectives are subject to elementary restrictions. If collateral damage is likely to affect the civilian population and civilian goods as a consequence of the attack, the anticipated damage must not be excessive in relation to the intended military advantage.[377] Beyond that minimum requirement, Art. 51, para. 5, lit. b now ultimately settles that all damaging effects of military operations must be measured on the yardstick of proportionality.[378] The collateral damage which inevitably occurs on the occasion of nearly every attack is justifiable only in so far as losses to the 'innocent' civilian population are commensurate with the military advantage which the operation sought to achieve.[379] As a general rule this sounds reasonable. However, the principle of proportionality creates serious difficulties in practice, since it necessarily remains

[373] See Spaight, 270–3, 280–1; Stone, 627–31; Mirimanoff-Chilikine, *Revue belge de droit international* 8 (1972), 130; Bruha, *Bombardment*, 55; Rosenblad, *Area Bombing and International Law*, 94–5; Baxter, *Comportement des combattants*, 148; Blix, *loc. cit.*, 54–8.

[374] See Sassòli, 409–11, with a detailed presentation of the relevant state practice.

[375] See Aldrich, *AJIL* 75 (1981), 780; DeSaussure, *loc. cit.*, 468–9; Randelzhofer, *Flächenbombardement und Völkerrecht*, 489; Sassòli, 411; Blix, *loc. cit.*, 61–9; cf. also G. B. Roberts, 151–2; Rogers, *Conduct of Combat*, 306; Solf, *loc. cit.*, 131; Fischer, *Der Einsatz von Nuklearwaffen*, 232; Meyrowitz, 25 *GYIL* 250 (1982).

[376] See Solf, in Bothe/Partsch/Solf, 309; see also the US persistence during the negotiations on the condition of a 'significant distance' between the different military objectives; cf. Parks, *Air Force Law Review* 32 (1990), 161.

[377] On the customary rule of proportionality see Venturini, 127–32; O'Brien, 38 *et seq.*; Fenrick, in *Military Law Review* 98 (1982), 126–7; Parks, *Air Force Law Review* 32 (1990), 168–75; Solf, *Protection of Civilians*, 128; Solf, in Bothe/Partsch/Solf, 309; Delbrück, 'Proportionality', *EPIL* 7, 398; Greenspan, 335; Fleck, *Rotkreuzentwurf*, 70 *et seq.*, 114; Carnahan, *Air Force Law Review* 17 (1975), 56–7; Rosenblad, *International Humanitarian Law of Armed Conflict*, 140–1; Randelzhofer, *Flächenbombardement und Völkerrecht*, 484–5; Kimminich, *Schutz der Menschen in bewaffneten Konflikten*, 154–5; Rauch, *RDMilG* 1980, 213–14; Aldrich, *AJIL* 75 (1981), 778; Meyrowitz, 25 *GYIL* 250 (1982); Rogers, *RDMilG* 1982, 297–8; Cassese, *Geneva Protocols and Customary International Law*, 85–6; G.B. Roberts, *Virginia Law Review* 26 (1985), 151; Bring/Reimann, *Netherlands International Law Review* 33 (1986), 103–4; Doswald-Beck, in Meyer (Ed.), 156; Sassòli, 412–15.

[378] Concerning the rather controversial debate on including criteria of proportionality in AP I see Fenrick, *Military Law Review* 98 (1982), 91–112; Pilloud/Pictet, in ICRC *Commentary*, 683–5 (paras. 2204–18); Solf, in Bothe/Partsch/Solf, 309–10, 361; Sassòli, 415–18.

[379] See Solf, in Bothe/Partsch/Solf, 310.

loosely defined and is subject to subjective assessment and balancing. In the framework of the required evaluation, the actors enjoy a considerable margin of appreciation.[380] This is particularly true in view of the strongly prognostical character of any such assessment, which must always be an assessment of the future effects of the operation. Objective standards for the appraisal of expected collateral damage and intended military advantage are virtually non-existent. In the final result, therefore, it is for the competent military commander and the staff planning the operation—who should know best the possible results and repercussions—to assess the consequences of the operation and to ensure its proportionality.[381] Final responsibility is thus laid in the hands of the military, which can act only on the basis of the information available at the time of the decision. Germany, like most other NATO members ratifying AP I, therefore filed a declaration that 'the decision taken by the person responsible has to be judged on the basis of all information available to him at the relevant time, and not on the basis of hindsight'.[382] In a second interpretative declaration Germany stated that by 'definite military advantage' in Art. 51, para. 5, lit. b AP I it understands 'the advantage anticipated from the attack considered as a whole and not only from isolated or particular parts of the attack'.[383] This means that the point of reference of the required balancing is not the gain of territory or other advantage expected from the isolated action of a single unit, but the wider military campaign of which that action forms part. Only in the framework of the more complex overall campaign plan of a belligerent can one assess the relative military value of the specific purpose of an individual attack.[384] In essence this should be self-evident: actions of individual units are not ends in themselves in modern integrated warfare. To the contrary, they must be placed in their operational context.

3. A further problem makes the handling of the proportionality requirement of Art. 51, para. 5, lit. b AP I extremely difficult. In practice, the circumstances usually involve combatants and civilians, military objects or installations and civilian settlements; industrial plants, and infrastructure installations of dual use. Such a complicated mixture of categories, however, not only makes it difficult to meet the requirements of distinction, but also makes collateral damage inevitable, and often considerable. To prevent excessive losses and damage to the civilian population proves extremely difficult in such situations, unless the adversary takes it upon himself to ensure a certain minimum separation between military objectives and civilian population.[385] A particularly difficult problem is caused for the attacker if the opposing side illegally uses the civilian population to shield military activities,

---

[380] As to these problems see esp. Fenrick, *loc. cit.*, 126, and Solf, in Bothe/Partsch/Solf, 310.

[381] Doswald-Beck, in Meyer (Ed.), 156; see also Kalshoven, *Constraints*, 99–100.

[382] See BR-Drs. 64/90 of 2 Feb. 1990, 132 (Federal Republic of Germany), 125 (Belgium), 127 (Italy), 129 (Netherlands), 130 (Spain); see also Schindler/Toman, 707, 712, 714, 717.

[383] See BR-Drs. 64/90 of 2 Feb. 1990, 132; as to the background of the declaration see also Fenrick, in *Military Law Review* 98 (1982), 107; Parks, *Air Force Law Review* 32 (1990), 172; Solf, in Bothe/Partsch/Solf, 311, 325; Sassòli, 417; Doswald-Beck, in Meyer (Ed.), 156–7.

[384] See Sassòli, 414, with further references.

[385] See the critical observations by Parks, *Air Force Law Review* 32 (1990), 152–6.

whether by transferring parts of the civilian population deliberately to military installations, or by calculatedly establishing military objectives among the civilian population and civilian objects, a common example of which is sub-contracting in the armaments industry.[386] Art.51, para. 8 AP I now expressly confirms that the violation of international legal obligations by the adversary does not exempt the attacker from his legal obligations with regard to the civilian population.[387] The problem is obviously not solved by that new provision—quite the contrary. The attacker will face extreme difficulties of justification, without having the alternative of accepting a higher level of collateral damage, if he wants effectively to counter the moves of the other side.[388] Also, the role of civilians deliberately incorporated into the military organization of the belligerent, such as workers in arms factories or civilian drivers of munitions transports, has remained unclear in that regard.[389] Does the loss of thousands of workers in an attack on a munitions factory have the same relative value, in terms of the proportionality of collateral damage, as the predictable deaths of women and children caused by an attack on a military command centre located in the midst of a densely populated civilian quarter? Many would argue no, but it must be admitted that many questions are left open. The role of the commander responsible for the operation is not made easier by these uncertainties, although one should not exaggerate demands for exact detail in such a rule. What is required is no more than a sincere effort to cope with the problem of collateral damage, and a proper application of common sense. Humanitarian law in that regard is dependent on an inherent sense of and respect for humanity, whose impulse is to avoid attacks causing catastrophical collateral damage when the objective is of only marginal importance; in other words, which shuns blatant disproportionality.

4. Comparable elementary considerations underlie the third sub-category, the case of excessive injury and damage to civilians or civilian objects located outside the actual target area and its immediate vicinity. The pre-existing customary prohibition of such attacks results from the rule of distinction and the prohibition of attacks which are not directed against a specific objective, or the effects of which cannot be directed against a military objective (see Section 455). The damaging effects must not only be specifically directed (or directable) against the military objective; the planning and implementation of the attack must also ensure that the effects of the force employed are restricted to the military objective and do not result in the civilian population living nearby being damaged more than the military objective which was targeted.[390] At the same time proportionality must be observed, with the dictate that collateral damage may not exceed the direct military advantage achieved by the operation.

---

[386] See Parks, *Air Force Law Review* 32 (1990), 159–68.

[387] See Parks, *Air Force Law Review* 32 (1990), 163–4; Sassòli, 447–53; and Pilloud/Pictet, in ICRC *Commentary*, 627–8 (paras. 1989–93).

[388] See the critical remarks of Parks, *Air Force Law Review* 32 (1990), 164–5, on that point.

[389] Ibid., 174–9.

[390] As to the practical problems of such a rule see Doswald-Beck, *The Value of the Geneva Protocols*, 157.

Before engaging an objective, every responsible military leader shall :   457

—verify the military nature of the objective to be attacked (Art. 57, para. 2, lit a(i) AP I);

—choose means and methods minimizing incidental injury and damage to civilian life and objects (Art. 57, para. 2, lit a(ii) AP I);

—refrain from launching any attack which may be expected to cause incidental injury and damage to civilian life and objects which would be excessive in relation to the concrete and direct military advantage anticipated (Art. 57, para. 2, lit a(iii) AP I);

—give the civilian population advance warning of attacks which may affect it, unless circumstances do not permit this (Art. 57, para. 2, lit c AP I);

—when a choice is possible between several military objectives of equal importance, engage that objective the attack on which is likely to cause the least incidental injury or damage (Art. 57, para. 3 AP I).

An attack shall be suspended if it becomes apparent that the objective is not military or is subject to special protection or that the attack may be expected to cause excessive incidental loss of civilian life (Art. 57, para. 2, lit b AP I).

1. The rule repeats almost verbatim the content of Art. 57 AP I. By that article the international community drew its conclusions from the above explained rules on methods of warfare as to the precautions required by the attacking party in order to avoid or minimize civilian loss and damage. The military authorities responsible for preparing and implementing an attack are required by Art. 57 AP I to implement certain elementary safeguards and are subject to stringent standards in their attempts to protect the civilian population from collateral damage.[391] Paragraph 1 of the provision begins by stating the general principle underlying the whole provision, namely that the attacker shall take 'constant care' to spare the civilian population and civilian objects in the conduct of military operations, or—as formulated in the 1967 ICRC Memorandum—to reduce the damage inflicted upon non-combatants to a minimum.[392] This rule may be deduced from the general principle of military necessity provided by customary law.[393] With regard to non-international armed conflicts the same result is achieved by the humanitarian minimum standard laid down in common Article 3 of the Geneva Conventions.

2. Although the general rule requiring precautions is undisputed, one essential problem remains, namely as to which individuals are addressed by Art. 57. The obligations should be understood to address primarily commanders and staff officers who are directly responsible for specific operations, and only to a lesser degree the individual soldiers participating directly in the attack.[394] Due to the lack of

[391] As to the history and substance of Art. 57 AP I see Sassòli, 459–89; Solf, in Bothe/Partsch/Solf, 361–9; Pilloud/Pictet, in ICRC *Commentary*, 678–9 (paras. 2184–8).

[392] See Sassòli, 458.

[393] See Castrén, *The Present Law of War and Neutrality*, 202; Spetzler, 193; Sassòli, 456–64.

[394] As to the question of who is primarily affected by Art. 57 see Sassòli, 461, 463; Pilloud/Pictet, in ICRC *Commentary*, 681 (para.2197); Kalshoven, *Constraints*, 100.

Oeter

sufficient information, even non-commissioned officers and unit commanders up to the level of company commanders will not normally have the overview of the military situation which is required for an adequate evaluation of the legality of operations under Articles 48–57 AP I, in particular for the assessment of proportionality. Without an adequate idea of the operational framework and of the nature and importance of the target, however, the safeguard measures provided for in Art. 57 AP I cannot be implemented satisfactorily. Junior officers and soldiers in the field will thus have to rely on the assessment given by their superiors,[395] with the exception of obvious war crimes such as deliberate indiscriminate attacks. Only in so far as these officers and soldiers independently plan and carry out operations will comparable precautions be required of them. Some states have expressly recorded their understanding as to this point by filing corresponding declarations or reservations. Switzerland for example declared on the occasion of ratification: 'The provisions of Article 57(2) are binding only on batallion or group commanders and higher echelons. The determining factor shall be the information available to such commanders at the time of reaching a decision.'[396]

3. The point of reference of this declaration is the introductory formula of Art. 57, para. 2, lit. a AP I, which reads: 'Those who plan or decide upon an attack . . .' Such a restrictive clause is necessary since the specific precautions required by lit.a apply only to the planning staff and commanders who decide upon an attack. These persons bearing responsibility for operational decisions are required by point (i) of lit. a to 'do everything feasible to verify that the objectives to be attacked are neither civilians nor civilian objects and are not subject to special protection but are military objectives within the meaning of para. 2 of Art. 52, and that it is not prohibited by the provisions of this Protocol to attack them'. This is clearly intended primarily to impose a duty of verification, a duty to collect sufficient information to clarify the nature of the objective.[397] The command authorities responsible for planning and deciding upon an attack must employ all means of reconnaissance and intelligence available to them unless and until there is sufficient certainty of the military nature of the objective of an attack.[398] What is required is a subjective certainty: the standard of Art. 57 in that regard is relative, for there is no absolute obligation to employ all means until the ultimate attack. As soon as there are no longer any serious doubts concerning the military character of the objective (and the other requirements of lawfulness, such as proportionality have been observed), the duty of Art. 57 lit. a(i) is satisfied.[399] Where doubt remains, however, the situation is more problematic. For a military actor lacking elaborate means of gathering the necessary intelligence (a case not far from reality in most Third World conflicts), there is a simple alternative: refraining from attack or attacking without sufficient certainty as to the military character of the objective. Under Art. 57 AP I (and the corresponding

---

[395] Solf, in Bothe/Partsch/Solf, 366–7.

[396] Printed in Schindler/Toman, 716. See also Sassòli, 463; Solf, in Bothe/Partsch/Solf, 362–3.

[397] Sassòli, 464–70; Pilloud/Pictet, in ICRC *Commentary*, 680–1 (paras. 2194–6); Arrassen, 125–7.

[398] See Solf, in Bothe/Partsch/Solf, 363.

[399] See Pilloud/Pictet, in ICRC *Commentary*, 680 (para. 2195); see also as to corresponding problems in the course of the Kuwait War 1991 White/McCoubrey, 366.

customary rule in non-international conflicts) only the first option is legal; the second risks violating the principle of distinction. Although most military actors in internal conflict tend to an attack on the basis of mere suspicion in such cases,[400] they should be aware that this may constitute a war crime (or a crime against humanity in internal conflict), to which lack of information is no defence.

4. Sub-para. a(ii) calls upon commanders and planning staff officers to 'take all feasible precautions in the choice of means and methods of attack with a view to avoiding, and in any event to minimizing, incidental loss of civilian life, injury to civilians and damage to civilian objects'. The required measures relate in particular to the problems of so-called 'targeting' and to the choice of weapons and ammunition used in the attack.[401] How to select and locate the objective, and the linked question of selecting the weapons best suited for the attack, is probably the essential question in the practical implementation of the principles of distinction and proportionality.[402] Only if the target becomes, as far as possible, precisely demarcated and if, in selecting the means of attack and establishing the mission parameters, it is ensured that the effects of the use of force are as far as possible limited to the military objective, can the 'rule of proportionality' be realized in military practice.[403] Yet the logistics of such mission parameters are so complex and depend on so many factors that it is impossible to express the consequences of distinction and proportionality in a precise formula. The flexibility of the clauses contained in AP I reflect the recognition by the international community that it is not possible to regulate all the infinite variables affecting military operations in a stringent provision. The location and physical character of the objective, the configuration of the surrounding terrain, the presence of civilians in the vicinity of the objective and the adjacency of military and civilian objects, the degree to which the target is defended and the resulting risks for the attacker's personnel and equipment, the quality of the weaponry used by attacker and defender (in particular the relative accuracy of artillery, bombs, and missiles), the standards of technical training of combatants and their physical and psychological condition, meteorological conditions—all these may be factors decisive to the final result.[404] The list could easily be extended. Also the 'rules of engagement' governing the operating forces might play a key role in conforming with Art. 57, para. 2 lit. a(ii); to give one example, the principle included in the rules of engagement of the US Air Force in Vietnam and in the Kuwait War of 1991, according to which bomber aircraft must return home with the entire bomb load unless they are one hundred per cent certain of their target,[405] may have decisive importance in minimizing unnecessary collateral damage in aerial operations. In general, the weapon with most accurate delivery parameters should be employed to attack a military objective with

---

[400] See Goldman, *American University Journal of International Law and Policy* 1993, 67–8.

[401] Pilloud/Pictet, in ICRC *Commentary*, 682 (para. 2200).

[402] See Sassòli, 470; Fleck, *Rotkreuzentwurf*, 77–8, 114; Castrén, *The Present Law of War and Neutrality*, 202; Arrassen, 128; Kalshoven, *Constraints*, 99.

[403] Pilloud/Pictet, in ICRC *Commentary*, 682 (para. 2200).

[404] Solf, in Bothe/Partsch/Solf, 364.

[405] Concerning the United States practice in Vietnam see Carnahan, *American University Law Review* 31 (1992), 866 and Parks, *Air Force Law Review* 32 (1990), 154 n. 459.

Oeter

civilian objects in its vicinity. In some cases there may also be a requirement to use infantry operations in circumstances where firepower (air support or artillery) would traditionally have been employed. However, it is not to be expected that one could ever structure the whole question in a short and precise formula; the individual responsibility of the competent commander will therefore be sanctioned only in extreme cases, such as deliberate attacks on obviously civilian objects, because the above-mentioned uncertainties must be taken into account when assessing *ex post facto* the legality of an operation. What is required is a decision taken in good faith according to the standard of a 'reasonable military commander', and nothing more. However, some general safeguards will also apply in nearly every case at the level of high command. In order to avoid precipitate decisions being made without sufficient information, it is advisable to follow the example of the US forces during 'Operation Desert Storm' (Kuwait/Iraq 1991), which provided for the control of targeting decisions and operations plans by legal advisers to the armed forces who were specially trained for that task.[406] Admittedly such an additional precaution is not required by Art. 57, para. 2 lit. a(ii), but the mechanism is effective in assisting the competent commander in the exercize of his responsibilities, as long as the legal advice is properly taken into account.

5. Art. 57, para. 2 lit. a(iii) also reiterates the rule of proportionality. Command authorities and planning staff must ensure that operations remain within the bounds of proportionality, i.e. that they do not cause collateral damage which is excessive in relation to the expected military advantage.[407] Excessive attacks may result in criminal responsibility for the competent commander and staff officers responsible for their operation, since indiscriminate attacks in violation of the requirement of proportionality constitute 'grave breaches' as provided by Art. 85, para. 3 lit. b AP I, which must be sanctioned as war crimes by the criminal justice system.[408] Some military authors, particularly in the United States, have argued that an offence based on the principle of proportionality is too vague and uncertain to form the basis of a prosecution according to the rule of law.[409] It must be admitted that there is a debatable point here; war crime definitions in general, however, may not be equated with ordinary provisions in internal criminal codes, since war crimes are always dependent on imprecise rules of public international law, the violation of which is defined as a crime under international law. Since blatant violations of the principle of proportionality are traditionally considered to be unlawful indiscriminate attacks resulting in international responsibility, the objection is ultimately not convincing.

6. Art. 57, para. 2 lit. c also repeats the requirement of an effective advance warning prior to attacks which may cause damage to the civilian population, a rule which in

[406] See Keenan, *HuV-I* 4/1991, 36.

[407] As to background and legal effects of Art. 57 para. 2 lit. a(iii) AP I see Sassòli, 473–4; Solf, in Bothe/Partsch/ Solf, 364–5; Pilloud/Pictet, in ICRC *Commentary*, 683–5 (paras. 2204–19).

[408] See Pilloud/Pictet, in ICRC *Commentary*, 685 (para. 2216); Zimmermann, ibid., 995–6 (paras. 3477–81); Partsch, in Bothe/Partsch/Solf, 511–22 (esp. 516).

[409] See G.B. Roberts, *VaJIntL* 26 (1985), 161; Prugh, *RDMilG* 1992, 272–3.

principle was already binding on belligerents by virtue of Art. 26 Hague Regulations (for details, see Section 453).

7. Art. 57, para. 3 AP I stresses the self-evident consequence of the principle of proportionality and the corresponding general principle of optimal minimization of collateral civilian damage:[410] the need to choose, when several military objectives would provide equal military advantage, the objective 'the attack on which is likely to cause the least danger to civilian lives and objects'.[411] An example often cited is the option to attack, instead of a railway station inside a city, an equally important railway junction or line at a strategically important point outside a densely populated area, on the basis that the destruction of such a crucial point causes as much disruption to the enemy lines of communication as the destruction of an urban station.[412]

8. The duties of military leaders to take precautions in favour of the civilian population relates not only to the planning and preparation prior to an attack, but also to its implementation.[413] The officers responsible for carrying out each operation must minimize collateral damage to the civilian population even during the course of combat operations (Art. 57, para. 2 lit. b AP I). They must call off the attack immediately if it becomes clear that the attacked objective does not have the supposed military character, but constitutes a purely civilian object.[414] They must halt fire if it becomes apparent that the incidental danger to the civilian population is more serious than had been expected.[415] The commanders responsible for the attack must also call off the attack if the military advantage which can still be obtained from the operation becomes too small in relation to the probable collateral damage to the civilian population.[416] Military leaders therefore must ensure for the entire course of the operation that the attack remains inside the limits drawn by the rules of humanitarian law. All this relates primarily to military leaders, as was made clear by the wording of the preceding phrases. Whether a corresponding duty also affects the lower levels of hierarchy actually engaged in combat remains in doubt, however. On one hand, if there is a duty on ordinary soldiers to halt fire or break off an attack in the case of flagrant indiscriminate attack, this can relate only to the decisive phase of immediate combat.[417] Yet ordinary soldiers and junior officers have no authority to resist their superiors' orders and to break off an operation; they would risk sanction under domestic martial law if in following their personal judgment they refused to obey orders. Accordingly, the obligation in Art. 57, para. 2 lit. b AP I for ordinary cases cannot extend below the level of commanders with

---

[410] See Sassòli, 485; Solf, in Bothe/Partsch/Solf, 368; Kalshoven, *Law of Warfare*, 66.

[411] As to the interpretation of Art. 57, para. 3 AP I see Sassòli, 485–9, and Solf, in Bothe/Partsch/Solf, 368–9.

[412] See Pilloud/Pictet, in ICRC *Commentary*, 687 (para. 2227); Sassòli, 487; Fleck, *Rotkreuzentwurf*, 72–3.

[413] Pilloud/Pictet, in ICRC *Commentary*, 686 (para. 2220).

[414] See Solf, in Bothe/Partsch/Solf, 366; Sassóli, 474–7; Pilloud/Pictet, in ICRC *Commentary*, 686 (para. 2221); Kalshoven, *Constraints*, 99.

[415] See Sassòli, 474–6.   [416] Solf, in Bothe/Partsch/Solf, 366–7.

[417] See Roberts, *loc. cit.*, 160; Solf, in Bothe/Partsch/Solf, 366.

Oeter

authority to stop or modify an operation.[418] Only in extraordinary cases does there exist a counter-balance: an order to commit a war crime (which in this respect means the order to attack an obviously purely civilian object or to attack despite blatantly excessive collateral damage) must not be obeyed (see Section 1224); just to the contrary, in such cases a superior order is no defence to a combatant in criminal proceedings, who bears individual criminal responsibility.

458   The attack or bombardment of non-defended localities is prohibited (Art. 59, para. 1 AP I; Art. 25 HagueReg).

Traditional customary law recognized a distinction between defended localities, which by the fact of being defended become military objectives in their entirety,[419] and non-defended localities which may not be made the object of attack.[420] The Hague Peace Conferences had already codified this customary rule in Art. 25 of the Hague Regulations.[421] By declaring a city or village a non-defended locality, and thus ceding it to the adversary without resistance, the belligerent can exclude certain settlements from combat activity, in the interest of the civilian population, and to preserve important buildings or works of art; the adverse effects of warfare may be thus limited to the proper area of combat.[422] Non-defended localities *qua definitionem* cannot be military objectives, for the adversary has deliberately excluded them from his military activities, so that the intended military advantage could be achieved by mere occupation without combat activity, whereas a bombardment would be evidently unnecessary. Art. 59, para. 1 AP I restates this rule explicitly, although it follows logically from the general principles of distinction and necessity.[423] The same rules must apply also to non-international armed conflicts, since the fundamental principle of distinction between fighting troops and military objectives on one hand and the civilian population on the other is valid also for internal conflicts. The civilian population must be spared as far as possible even in domestic conflicts (Art. 13, para. 2 AP II), which leads to the conclusion that even for internal conflicts a prohibition against attacks on non-defended localities applies.[424]

459   A locality shall be considered non-defended if it has been so declared by its competent authorities, is open for occupation, and fulfils the following conditions:

[418] See Fleck, in Bothe/Kurzidem/Macalister, 192.

[419] As to the debate on the concept of 'defended locality' see Oppenheim/Lauterpacht, Vol.II, 421; Castrén, *The Present Law of War and Neutrality*, 201; Meyrowitz, 41 *ZaöRV* 28 (1981); Rauch, 19 *RDMilG* 234 (1980); Doswald-Beck, *The Value of the Geneva Protocols*, 158; Sassòli, 355–9.

[420] See Ipsen, *Die 'offene Stadt'*, 152–80; De Zayas, *EPIL* 4, 69–71; Solf, *American University Journal of International Law and Policy* 1 (1986), 135; see also the *US Field Manual* FM 27–10, para. 39b (ch.1, 15 July 1976) and the US Navy's *Annotated Supplement to the Commander's Handbook on the Law of Naval Operations*, NWP 9 (Rev.A)/FMFM 1–10, 8–26.

[421] As to the history and legal effects of Art. 25 Hague Reg, see Ipsen, *Die 'offene Stadt'*, 153–60.

[422] Concerning the declaration of an undefended locality see Ipsen, *Die 'offene Stadt'*, 160–6; Pilloud/Pictet, in ICRC *Commentary*, 703–4 (paras. 2282–6).

[423] As to background, history, and relevance of Art. 59 AP I see Solf, in Bothe/Partsch/Solf, 380–5.

[424] See De Zayas, 'Open Towns, *EPIL* 4, 69; Junod, in ICRC *Commentary*, 1449–50 (paras. 4766–72).

—all combatants, mobile weapons, and mobile military equipment must have been evacuated;

—no hostile use will be made of fixed military installations and establishments;

—no acts of hostility shall be committed by the authorities or the population; and

—no activities in support of military operations will be undertaken (Art. 59, para. 2 AP I).

1. The protection afforded by Art. 59, para. 1 AP I applies only if certain conditions are fulfilled.[425] In general: the locality must be totally excluded from the military activities of the belligerent hitherto exercising control, i.e. it must play no role in its operations; the locality must be open for occupation by the opposing side, and this fact must be declared to the adversary.

2. The declaration by the power responsible for the locality is intended to remove uncertainties, and binds the adversary to protect the 'open city' by formally announcing abandonment without resistance. The protection of Art. 59, para. 1 AP I then enters into force—unlike the provisions for demilitarized zones in Art. 60 AP I—*ipso jure*, as soon as the preconditions of Art. 59 are fulfilled. The declaration must define and describe the exact limits of the undefended locality.[426] The adverse party must acknowledge receipt of the declaration, and must protest immediately if it considers that the conditions laid down in Art. 59, para. 2 are not fulfilled.[427] Otherwise it is bound by the protective provisions of Art. 59 AP I. The non-defended locality must subsequently be marked by special signs, in order to enable the fighting troops of both sides to respect the protection of the locality at all times.[428]

3. For the purposes of Art. 59 AP I a non-defended locality must be situated in the immediate zone of combat or in its vicinity. The locality must be open to immediate entry by the adversary armed forces, and open to occupation without a fight, following its evacuation.[429] A city or town behind enemy lines, or even far in its hinterland, may not be a lawful target of military attack if there are no combatants or other military objectives in it; such a town, however, is not a 'non-defended locality', because the armed forces of the adverse party are prevented from entering it by the troops in between, at the line of combat.[430]

4. In order to enjoy the protection of Art. 59 AP I, the town or city must be free from all military activities. All combatants, mobile weapons, and mobile military equipment must be evacuated from the locality (Art. 59, para. 2 lit. a AP I). No hostile use may be made of fixed military installations and establishments (although it is not

---

[425] See Pilloud/Pictet, in ICRC *Commentary*, 701–2 (paras. 2267–74); Solf, in Bothe/Partsch/Solf, 383.

[426] See Pilloud/Pictet, in ICRC *Commentary*, 704 (para. 2284).

[427] Ibid. (paras. 2285–6).

[428] Ibid. 705–6 (paras. 2289–94).

[429] Solf, in Bothe/Partsch/Solf, 382; Pilloud/Pictet, in ICRC *Commentary*, 701–2 (para. 2268).

[430] Solf, in Bothe/Partsch/Solf, 382; see also the US Navy's *Annotated Supplement to the Commander's Handbook on the Law of Naval Operations*, NWP 9 (Rev.A)/FMFM 1–10, 8–26.

Oeter

necessary that they be made unfit for use or destroyed). Neither the authorities nor the population of the town or city shall participate in acts of hostility, nor may the town or specific installations or establishments in it be in any way involved in the military activities of any party to the conflict, whether by production of armaments or by provision of transport or telecommunications services with a military purpose.[431]

460   **A locality shall not on suspicion be deemed defended unless the behaviour of the adversary substantiates such a supposition.**

If by formal declaration a town or city has become an undefended locality, and if the adverse party has not transmitted a counter-declaration in accordance with Art. 59, para. 4, sentence 2 AP I, the advancing belligerent is bound by the declaration.[432] Even in other cases the attacker must, according to Art. 57, para. 2 lit. a(i) AP I (see Section 457), make sure that the town or city to be attacked constitutes a military objective. If there is no indication that combatants, military installations, or other military objectives are present in the town which serve to assist the combat activities of the adverse party, then such a town or city is by definition not a legitimate military objective, and thus may not be made an object of attack.

461   **It is prohibited to extend military operations to demilitarized zones. The prerequisites for establishing such a zone are the same as those applying to non-defended localities (Arts. 59, para. 2 and 60, para. 3 AP I). Demilitarized zones are created by agreement between the parties to the conflict either in peacetime or in the course of conflict. It is prohibited for any party to the conflict to attack or occupy such zones (Art. 60, para. 1 AP I).**

1. Unlike non-defended localities, the specific protection for demilitarized zones does not apply *ipso jure*, even when the conditions in Art. 60, para. 3 AP I are fulfilled.[433] A separate agreement between the parties to the conflict is required which establishes the specific modalities of demilitarization. The agreement may be concluded in peacetime, and may facilitate both disarmament and confidence building;[434] it can also be concluded *ad hoc* after the outbreak of a conflict in order to preserve certain areas from the effects of combat.[435] The requirement of an express agreement is sensible in this respect, since demilitarization of larger areas needs a whole series of complex and detailed provisions which cannot be deduced *in abstracto* from the general rules of humanitarian law.[436] Both the specific limits of the zone and the mechanisms of verification require a detailed legal framework, and these are only two examples of the many questions which require legal clarification

---

[431] See Pilloud/Pictet, in ICRC *Commentary*, 702 (paras. 2271–2).

[432] Solf, in Bothe/Partsch/Solf, 383–4.

[433] Pilloud/Pictet, in ICRC *Commentary*, 709–10 (para. 2304).

[434] As to the difference between demilitarized areas in peacetime international law and protected zones under Art. 60 AP I see ibid., 709 (paras. 2302–3).

[435] Ibid., 710–11 (paras. 2308–9).   [436] See Solf, in Bothe/Partsch/Solf, 388.

in such cases. Also, the question of any militarily relevant activities which may exceptionally be allowed should be regulated before it becomes a point of dispute.

2. The preconditions for establishing a demilitarized zone are nearly the same as those required for declaring a non-defended locality, i.e. the area must be entirely free from all military activities, and in principle also from all activities assisting the efforts of warfare.[437] Demilitarized zones, however, need not necessarily be situated in the combat zone. Even areas behind the enemy lines may be brought under the protection of Art. 60 in anticipation. By agreement, the zone becomes legally closed to military activities of both sides. No party to the conflict shall attack a demilitarized zone, or occupy it, or use it for military purposes in any other way.[438]

If a party to the conflict breaches these provisions, the non-defended localities,   462
open towns or cities, or demilitarized zones will lose their special protection. The
general provisions for the protection of the civilian population and civilian
objects shall, however, continue to apply (Arts. 59, para. 7 and 60, para. 7 AP I).

In paragraph 7 of both Art. 59 and Art. 60 Additional Protocol I contains one of the few express convention provisions concerning the consequences of violation of the treaty. If any party violates Art. 59 or 60 or an agreement concluded on the basis of these provisions, the non-defended locality or demilitarized zone automatically loses the protection accorded to it under these provisions.[439] This results from the basic logic behind these institutions, because by extending military operations to the respective localities or areas, the conditions required for protection are removed. The adverse party may then lawfully use force against the newly created military objective. As a matter of good policy, however, it should warn the party violating the demilitarization provisions that such practice endangers the protected status of the town or zone, to provide an opportunity to redress the grievance and to give the population time for precautions.[440] In the case of an attack, the attacker must still limit combat operations to the adverse armed forces and other military objectives. The civilian population continues to enjoy the protection afforded by the general principles of distinction and proportionality, with all the specific rules resulting from that body of law.[441]

It is further prohibited to attack: 463

—**safety zones and neutralized zones, i.e. zones designed to give shelter to**
   wounded and sick soldiers and to civilians who take no part in hostilities (Art.
   23 GC I; Arts. 14, 15 GC IV);

—**medical and religious personnel (Arts. 12, 15 AP I);**

—**hospital ships (Art. 22 GC II);**

---

[437] Concerning such activities there are possible (or even required) specific agreements: Art. 60, para. 2, last sentence; see Pilloud/Pictet, in ICRC *Commentary*, 711 (para. 2311); Solf, in Bothe/Partsch/Solf, 389.

[438] See Pilloud/Pictet, ibid., 710 (paras. 2305–6).

[439] Solf, in Bothe/Partsch/Solf, 384–5; Pilloud/Pictet, ibid., 706 (paras. 2295–7) and 712 (paras. 2315–18).

[440] Pilloud/Pictet, in ICRC *Commentary*, 712 (para. 2316).   [441] Ibid., (para. 2317).

Oeter

—hospitals and associated personnel (Art. 19 GC I; Arts. 18, 20 GC IV);

—objects indispensable to the survival of the civilian population (e.g. production of foodstuffs, clothing, drinking water installations) with intent to deprive the civilian population of their supply (Art. 54, para. 2 AP I; Art. 14 AP II); any deviations from this prohibition shall be permissible only on friendly territory if required by cogent military necessity (Art. 54, paras 3 and 5 AP I; Art. 14 AP II);

—coastal lifeboats and associated fixed coastal installations (Art. 27 GC II);

—cultural objects (Art. 53 AP I);

—aircraft protected by international law:
employed for the purpose of exchanging prisoners;
on the assurance of safe-conduct;
medical aircraft (Arts. 36, para. 1 and 37, para. 1 GC I; Art.39 GC II; Arts. 24 ff. AP I; Art. 17 AP II); and
civilian aircraft.

1. The system of the Geneva Conventions and Additional Protocols, supplemented by customary law, recognizes a whole series of specifically protected objects, against which the use of any form of force is prohibited. Such objects shall not be made the object of attack, and conversely they may not be used by belligerents for hostile purposes in the framework of military operations.

2. Comparable to demilitarized zones are the safety zones and neutralized zones provided for in Art. 23 Geneva Convention I and in Arts. 14 and 15 Geneva Convention IV (see also Sections 512–14 and 629–32). Specified localities may be declared safety zones to provide safe shelters for the wounded and sick, as well as for children, mothers, and the aged.[442] These zones shall serve only as lodging for protected persons (including the personnel taking care of them and the local population); they shall not contain any military objects and must be situated in areas which in all probability are not relevant for the conduct of hostilities. The agreement on a neutralized zone around the Anglican Cathedral in Port Stanley on the Falkland Islands, concluded between the Argentine and British authorities on 13 June 1982, is an example of such an arrangement in contemporary practice.[443]

3. Under the system of the First, Second, and Fourth Geneva Conventions and the Additional Protocols absolute protection is accorded to medical and religious personnel, to hospital ships, and to hospitals and personnel associated with them. The comprehensive standard of protection created by Articles 19 and 24 of the First Geneva Convention in regard to military hospitals, military medical personnel, and chaplains attached to the armed forces (and also that of Arts.18 and 20 Geneva Convention IV in regard to civilian hospitals and their personnel) was extended by

---

[442] As to the system of safety zones according to Arts. 23 GC I, 14 and 15 GC IV see Pictet, *Commentaire Convention de Genève* I, 227 *et seq.*; ibid. vol. IV, 129–37, 138–43.

[443] The case is mentioned in the US Navy's *Annotated Supplement to the Commander's Handbook on the Law of Naval Operations*, NWP 9 (Rev.A)/FMFM 1–10, 8–27n. 101.

Oeter

Articles 12 and 15 AP I to civilian medical and religious personnel (see Sections 620–8, 812–21). Even in non-international armed conflicts, Articles 9 and 11 AP II provide analogous protection for medical and religious personnel, as well as for medical units and their means of transport.[444] Hospital ships (as a special case) already enjoyed a certain protection from the Hague Convention on Hospital Ships of 21 December 1904.[445] Articles 22–35 Geneva Convention II consolidated the protected status of hospital ships (as to which, see Sections 1054–64). In the course of the new codification in Art. 27 AP I a specific regime of protection was accorded also to coastal lifeboats and associated fixed coastal installations (see Section 1054).

4. A new creation, in contrast, is the special category of protected objects, now codified in Art. 54 AP I and Art. 14 AP II, namely 'objects indispensable for the survival of the civilian population'.[446] In traditional customary law such a category was not recognized, even if the principle of proportionality had always set bounds on attacks on such objects, whose damage or destruction logically leads to particularly grave suffering for the civilian population.[447] As an expression of the general prohibition against the starvation of civilians as a method of warfare, laid down in Art. 54, para. 1 AP I, paragraph 2 of Art. 54 now prohibits any form of violence against 'objects indispensable for the survival of the civilian population'.[448] The most common examples of such protected objects are specifically listed as objects 'such as foodstuffs, agricultural areas for the production of foodstuffs, crops, livestock, drinking water installations and supplies, and irrigation works'. These examples clarify the core of the protection, but the list is not exhaustive. It is beyond doubt that the objects primarily protected under the provision are the food and water supply of the civilian population, being the basic means of subsistence;[449] this does not mean, however, that objects not directly linked to food and water supply are necessarily excluded from the category of 'objects indispensable for the survival of the civilian population'. It depends on the particular situation, and under certain circumstances (e.g. in climatically rough mountainous regions) other goods, such as the supply of clothing or the basic shelter of the civilian population, will undoubtedly be protected under Art. 54, para. 2 AP I.[450] It is prohibited 'to attack, destroy, remove, or render useless' such objects. 'Rendering useless' may include acts such as deliberate pollution, by chemical or other agents, of water reservoirs or the contamination of crops by defoliants.[451] The destruction, removal, or rendering useless of foodstuffs, water, or other 'indispensable' objects is only prohibited, however, in

---

[444] See Junod, in ICRC *Commentary*, 1417–2, 1431–6.

[445] Printed in Schindler/Toman, 295–7.

[446] See Pilloud/Pictet, in ICRC *Commentary*, 652–3 (paras. 2083, 2088, 2091); Solf, in Bothe/Partsch/Solf, 336–7.

[447] See Cassese, 3 *UCLA Pacific Basin Law Journal* 91 (1984).

[448] As to the history of Art. 54 AP I see Pilloud/Pictet, in ICRC *Commentary*, 652 (paras. 2083–5); Solf, in Bothe/Partsch/Solf, 336–40.

[449] Pilloud/Pictet, ibid., 655 (paras. 2102–3); Solf, in Bothe/Partsch/Solf, 339–40.

[450] Pilloud/Pictet, ibid., 655 (para. 2103); Solf, in Bothe/Partsch/Solf, 340.

[451] See Pilloud/Pictet, ibid., 655 (para. 2101).

Oeter

so far as it is committed deliberately for the purpose of depriving the civilian population of such objects 'because of their sustenance value'. By contrast, it is legitimate to damage the protected objects and installations by military operations if the impairment is only an incidental effect of the attack.[452] An irrigation channel, for example, shall not be destroyed deliberately in order to interrupt agricultural production; the same is true for the destruction of crops or gardens because of their importance to the sustenance of the civilian population. Nevertheless, the destruction of an irrigation channel may be permissible if the channel is used as a defensive position by the military forces in occupation and a field of crops may be burnt down in order to clear the field for artillery.[453] Installations for electric power supply have proved particularly problematic. To the extent that the power supply serves military purposes, in maintaining military installations, it undoubtedly constitutes a military objective (see Section 443). At the same time, however, electric power supply installations will often constitute an 'object indispensable for the survival of the civilian population'. The elimination of the power supply network will also cause considerable disruption to other elements of the civilian infrastructure, for example the drinking water supply system (as happened e.g. in the course of 'Operation Desert Storm' in 1991 in Iraq). Especially in arid regions, the breakdown of such vital sustenance systems may, albeit indirectly, expose the civilian population to the very risk that Art. 54 AP I was intended to prevent.

5. The protection of 'objects indispensable for the survival of the civilian population' is—as stated above—part of a far-reaching new approach underlying the provisions of Articles 54 AP I and 14 AP II. Art. 54, para. 1 AP I contains a new general prohibition against the starvation of civilians as a method of warfare. This rule completely outlaws traditional warfare methods, such as sieges of defended towns, or 'scorched earth' strategies.[454] Even in the course of the war crime trials after World War II, the deliberate devastation of occupied territories during operations of retreat, as well as the starvation of populations in besieged enemy towns, were still considered permissible.[455] In the wake of the reorientation effected by the general rules of Arts. 54, para. 1 AP I and Art.14 AP II, however, such practices must be reassessed.[456] The Fourth Geneva Convention already provided, in Art. 17, for evacuation of certain groups of persons from besieged territories, and in Art. 23 it called for the admission of humanitarian assistance deliveries into besieged localities for the assistance of specific groups of the population.[457] The general prohibition of starvation of the civilian population now implies that deliveries of foodstuffs, medicines, drinking water, and other goods indispensable for the survival of the civilian

[452] Solf, in Bothe/Partsch/Solf, 339.

[453] These examples are contained in the report of Committee III of the Diplomatic Conference—see Solf ibid.; Pilloud/Pictet, in ICRC *Commentary*, 656–7 (para. 2110).

[454] On the background of Art. 54, para. 1 see Pilloud/Pictet, in ICRC *Commentary*, 653 (paras. 2087–91); Solf, in Bothe/Partsch/ Solf, 336–8.

[455] See Solf, ibid., 337; Dinstein, in Delissen/Tanja (Eds.), 146–7.

[456] Solf, ibid., 338; Solf, 'Siege', *EPIL* 4, 227; Dinstein, *loc. cit.*, 148–52 (esp. 152); Macalister-Smith, 73 *RIC* 467–70 (1991); G.B. Roberts, *loc. cit.*, 153.

[457] See Solf, 'Siege', *EPIL* 4, 226; Dinstein, *loc. cit.*, 147–8; Pictet, *Convention de Commentaire Genève*, 148–51, 192–8.

Oeter

population must not be hindered by the adverse party, provided that they are delivered solely to the civilian population of the town under siege, and not to the military persons defending the town.[458] Art.70 now expressly requires the admission of humanitarian relief operations for the civilian population,[459] which completely outlaws siege strategies such as those still being used by the Serbian troops in Bosnia.

6. As a specific exception to Art. 54, para. 2 AP I, paragraph 5 of Art. 54 AP I provides that derogations from the prohibition of attacks on 'objects indispensable for the survival of the civilian population' may be made, 'in recognition of the vital requirements of any Party to the conflict in the defence of its national territory against invasion', where 'required by imperative military necessity'; such derogations are allowed, however, only within territory under a party's own control. The defender fulfilling this precondition may impede the advance of the enemy by deliberately devastating the areas from which he is retreating. In view of the fundamental interest of any defender in minimizing his own damage it was considered that in these exceptional circumstances the defender should be permitted to employ 'scorched earth' strategies.

7. Particular protection is granted to cultural objects. The Hague Convention of 14 May 1954 for the Protection of Cultural Property in the Event of Armed Conflict, and the supplementary provisions of Arts. 53 AP I and Art. 16 AP II, have developed an elaborate protective regime for historical monuments, works of art, and places of worship 'which constitute the cultural or spiritual heritage of peoples'. These specific safeguards are dealt with below; see Sections 901–33.

8. Aircraft are covered by specific regulation of mostly customary character. Civilian aircraft may not be attacked in peacetime and may not be shot down. For ordinary public international law this follows already from the fundamental rule of prohibition of the use of force and from the general rules of air law, now codified in the Chicago Convention on International Civil Aviation (Art. 3 bis); in an armed conflict such a prohibition can be inferred from the principle of distinction, since a civilian aircraft rarely constitutes a military objective in the sense of Art. 52, para. 2 AP I. In this respect problems arise mainly in respect of the practical implementation of the rule of distinction, for in situations of limited armed conflict the air space is normally used at the same time for both hostile military operations and civil aviation. The accidental downing of the Iranian civil aircraft (Airbus A300) over the Persian Gulf by the US Navy warship 'USS Vincennes' on 3 July 1988 was a telling example of the dangers inherent in such situations of confusion.[460] In addition to these general rules, particular protection is granted by customary law to: military aircraft employed for the purpose of exchanging prisoners; aircraft, whether civil-

---

[458] Dinstein, *loc. cit.*, 150.

[459] Cf. Solf, 'Siege', *EPIL* 4, 227; Macalister-Smith, *loc. cit.*, 471–3; and in great detail Sandoz, in ICRC *Commentary*, 816–29.

[460] See the report on the investigation undertaken by the International Civil Aviation Organization of November 1988, printed in 28 *ILM* 900–43 (1989), and the Iranian statement of claim filed in the ICJ of 17 May 1989, printed in 28 *ILM* 842–6 (1989).

Oeter

ian or military, which have been assured safe conduct,[461] and medical aircraft, the status of which has recently been exhaustively regulated by Articles 24–31 AP I (see Sections 1065–8).

3. *Protection of Works and Installations Containing Dangerous Forces*

464   **Works and installations containing dangerous forces, namely dams, dykes, and nuclear electricity generating stations (Art. 56, para. 1 AP I) shall not be made the object of attack, even where these objects are military objectives, if such attack could cause the release of dangerous forces and consequent severe damage to the civilian population (Art. 56 para. 1 AP I).**

1. Art. 56 AP I (and the analogous Art. 15 AP II concerning non-international armed conflicts) introduced a new category hitherto totally unknown, namely 'works and installations containing dangerous forces'.[462] According to the official definition of Art. 56 this category comprises three types of installation: dams, dykes, and nuclear power plants.[463] All three types of installation are potentially extremely dangerous, since in the event of their destruction uncontrollable forces are released that may cause immense damage to the civilian population.[464] The regulation of their status in warfare by a separate provision is undoubtedly justified by virtue of these risks. Although a considerable degree of caution was required under traditional customary law (because there was always a risk of excessive collateral damage in case of attacks on such objects),[465] there was no absolute prohibition of attack upon them in humanitarian law prior to the adoption of the Additional Protocols. In belligerent practice attacks had always occurred on such objects,[466] even if only under extreme precautions in recent times.[467]

2. The new rule of Art. 56 AP I must be understood in an overall perspective as an essential part of the general attempt to restrict the extent of permissible collateral damage. The evaluation of what constitutes admissible collateral damage has undergone a great change since World War II, a fact demonstrated with utmost clarity by US practice in the course of the last decades. An attack on a specifically dangerous installation in the sense of Art. 56 AP I would only be allowed—even without the special rule of Art. 56—under exceptional circumstances, given the strict precaution currently required to minimize loss of civilian lives and damage to civilian objects. The collateral damage likely to be caused by such an attack is so high that the deliberate acceptance of such a risk would in any event qualify as a blatant vio-

---

[461] See Oppenheim/Lauterpacht, Vol.II, 542; Castrén, *The Present Law of War and Neutrality*, 126–7; Greenspan, 397–9.

[462] Concerning the character of Art. 56 AP I as a completely novel creation see Cassese, 3 *UCLA Pacific Basin Law Journal* 94 (1984); on the drafting history of the rule see Solf, in Bothe/Partsch/Solf, 350–3; Pilloud/Pictet, in ICRC *Commentary*, 667–8 (para. 2145).

[463] Solf, ibid. 350; Pilloud/Pictet, ibid. 668–9 (paras. 2146–50).   [464] Solf, ibid., 350.

[465] See Parks, *Air Force Law Review* 32 (1990), 168–9.   [466] Ibid., 206–9.

[467] See esp. Parks, ibid., who gives the example of the attack by the US Air Force on the Lang Chi dam in Northern Vietnam in 1972.

lation of the prohibition against indiscriminate attack. Thus, even the undeniably novel rule of Art. 56 is arguably only an illustration of the standard of protection which is already provided for by customary law.

3. The installations referred to in Art. 56 will normally constitute military objectives, and accordingly would be admissible objects of attack under normal circumstances. The regulation of AP I, like that of AP II, has adopted a different yardstick, however, by providing a special degree of protection for these installations, in order to protect the civilian population against the catastrophic effects of damaging or destroying such objects.[468] Attacks are prohibited even if the installation obviously constitutes a military objective 'if such attack may cause the release of dangerous forces from the works or installations and consequent severe losses among the civilian population'.[469] The same considerations led to an expansion (by Art. 56, para. 1 second sentence) of the protection of 'other military objectives located at or in the vicinity of these works or installations', since comparably severe effects are likely to be caused by an attack on such objectives as from a direct attack on the dams, dykes or nuclear plants.[470] Hydroelectric facilities at the foot of dams, for example, fall into that category, since such electricity generating plants usually constitute a military objective, the destruction of which would necessarily risk the damage or destruction of the dam itself.[471]

4. Underlying the prohibition of Art. 56 AP I is a sort of 'worst case' analysis, an assessment which deems the serious risk of releasing dangerous forces to constitute an unacceptably high risk of collateral damage. In view of the risk potential inherent in the respective installations, that assessment is doubtless correct. It is nearly inconceivable that massive risks for the civilian population could ever be outweighed by military considerations so as to justify an attack on such installations used for purely civilian purposes. The attack is accordingly strictly prohibited and cannot be justified by any claim of military necessity, except under the exception of paragraph 2 of Art. 56.

This protection shall cease if these plants are used in regular, significant, and   465
direct support of military operations and such attack is the only feasible way to
terminate such use. (Art. 56, paras. 2 lit. a–b AP I). This shall also apply to other
military objectives located at or in the vicinity of these plants or installations (Art.
56, para. 2 lit. c AP I).

1. The mere fact that an installation which is protected under Art. 56 AP I constitutes, according to general criteria, a 'military objective' does not justify an attack on such an object. There exist, however, certain situations in which such an installation abandons its original purposes in favour of military concerns, when its use

---

[468] See Solf, in Bothe/Partsch/Solf, 350–7; Pilloud/Pictet, in ICRC *Commentary*, 666–70.
[469] As to the background of this rule see Solf, ibid., 351–2; Pilloud/Pictet, ibid., 669 (para. 2153).
[470] See Pilloud/Pictet, ibid., 670 (paras. 2155–7).
[471] See the example given by Parks, *Air Force Law Review* 32 (1990), 169.

exceeds its common contribution to military activities ('for other than its normal function') in order directly to support military operations.[472] This must be a form of use alien to its normal function, which does not result from its ordinary use, but which is given to it *ad hoc* in the framework of military activities. Dykes, for example, are often integrated in defence positions as a part of the system of fortifications. Roads on the top of a dam offer a strategic advantage for military transport, either for the movement of armed forces or logistical support for the combat troops. In such cases of immediate use for 'regular, significant and direct support of military operations' even dangerous installations in the sense of Art. 56 may be attacked and destroyed, 'if such attack is the only feasible way to terminate such support'.[473] There must, however, be no other objective which is not protected under Art. 56 but the destruction of which would achieve an equal military advantage to that gained by destroying the installation. For example, if a strategically important transport route includes a dyke and also another weak point, the destruction of which would prevent the use of the whole route for military transport, the other target must be chosen in preference to the dyke.

2. Art. 56, para. 2 AP I differentiates between dams and dykes (lit. a), in the case of which acts of regular, significant and direct support of military operations distinct from their normal function may lead to exclusion of the protection afforded by Art. 56, para. 1, and nuclear power plants (lit. b), in the case of which a different problem arises.[474] Nuclear electricity generating stations often constitute the central source of energy for modern electricity supply networks, and thus constitute—in contrast to dams and dykes—in their normal function a military objective of the first order.[475] Their contribution to military operations—i.e. the delivery of electric energy in 'regular, significant, and direct support of military operations'—can sometimes only be neutralized by destroying the power plant. In order to justify the extremely high risks of collateral damage resulting from such an attack, however, it is essential that the attack is absolutely necessary, which means that there must not exist any other 'feasible way' to terminate the support flowing from the nuclear plant. Accordingly, the exception of Art. 56, para. 2 lit. b requires that there must be no other way of neutralizing the power supply, for example by destroying the essential installations of the distribution network (transformer stations, or main circuit lines).[476]

3. Other military objectives located at or in the vicinity of these 'dangerous installations' (such as strategically important bridges or works of the defence industry) may also be destroyed only for compelling reasons of military necessity, and only if the objectives are used for 'regular, significant, and direct support of military operations', and then only if their contribution to military operations cannot be

[472] See Pilloud/Pictet, in ICRC *Commentary*, 671 (para. 2162).
[473] As to the interpretation of this clause see ibid., 671 (para. 2162); Solf, in Bothe/Partsch/Solf, 354–5.
[474] Solf, ibid., 354; Pilloud/Pictet, ibid., 670–1 (paras. 2161, 2164).
[475] See Pilloud/Pictet, in ICRC *Commentary*, 672 (para. 2165); Solf, in Bothe/Partsch/Solf, 355.
[476] See Pilloud/Pictet, ibid. (para. 2166).

neutralized in another way. After all, even for the cases excluded under Art. 56 para. 2 from the specific protection of Art. 56, para. 1 the rule still applies that, notwithstanding the special protection of Art. 56, the civilian population always enjoys the protection afforded by the general principles of distinction and proportionality.[477] Even in cases of exclusion from specific protection, due to direct contribution to warfare, all feasible precautions must be taken to prevent the release of dangerous forces (Art. 56, para. 3 AP I).

Regular, significant, and direct support of military operations (Art. 56, paras. 2 lit.   466
a-c AP I) includes, for instance, the manufacture of weapons, ammunition, and
defence materiel. The mere possibility of use by armed forces is not subject to
these provisions.

The definition of what constitutes 'regular, significant, and direct support of military operations' is extremely difficult. Problems of delimitation exist in particular concerning lit. b and c of Art. 56, para. 2 AP I. In the case of direct military appropriation of dams and dykes the identification of such support does not constitute a real problem. This is less clear-cut, however, as regards the directness of contributions from nuclear power plants and industrial works at or near installations containing dangerous forces. A power generating station which supplies electrical energy mainly for military installations undoubtedly delivers a direct contribution to warfare. As for a nuclear power plant delivering energy mainly for industrial works of the defence industry, the point is already debatable.[478] What directly supports warfare in such a case is the industry supplied with power, not the power station in itself. However, even such a primarily defence industry-related function should probably be regarded as a 'regular, significant, and direct contribution'. Only in cases where defence industry and genuinely civilian industry are intimately compounded will one have to conclude that immediacy is interrupted, even if the 'civilian' industrial installations produce goods with both civilian and military uses (so-called 'dual-use items').[479] Clearly excluded from the category of 'regular, significant, and direct support' is the case of normal power stations feeding electric energy into the normal electricity power grid, despite the fact that military installations may also be supplied by the same grid.

The decision to launch an attack shall be taken on the basis of all information   467
available at the time of action. The parties to a conflict shall be bound by the prin-
ciple of proportionality to refrain from launching an attack if the risk of releasing
dangerous forces is such that it is excessive to any military advantage.

Art. 56 AP I contains in paragraphs 1 and 2 a whole series of vague notions evidently needing some clarification. They preserve a considerable degree of discretion for

---

[477] Ibid. (paras. 2168–9).
[478] See on one hand Solf, in Bothe/Partsch/Solf, 355; on the other hand Pilloud/Pictet, in ICRC *Commentary*, 672 (para. 2165).
[479] Solf, *op. cit.*, 355; Pilloud/Pictet, *op. cit.*, 672 (para. 2165).

the military actors who are bound to apply the provision, but they also place on the military command authorities an enormous responsibility to assess the factual situation and apply the ill-defined notions of Art. 56. In particular, the prognostical requirements of the provision are extremely difficult to fulfil. Whether an attack on a protected installation will release dangerous forces, and thus risk severe damage to the civilian population; and whether the planned attack is the only feasible means of ending the military use; these are complex factual questions which require considerable technical expertise for their evaluation. However, all military actions involve an extremely high degree of factual uncertainty, which necessarily means that the decision of the responsible commander can only be judged on the basis of the information available to him at the time of the decision, and not on the basis of hindsight (see Section 446).

468   **Military objectives shall not be located in the vicinity of works and installations containing dangerous forces unless they are necessary for the defence of those works (Art. 56 para. 5 AP I).**

In paragraph 5 of Art. 56 AP I the Diplomatic Conference has included a concrete expression of the principle of 'passive precautions' as it applies to 'dangerous installations'. Military objects and other installations which qualify as military objectives (such as armaments and munitions factories) should be geographically clearly separate from installations containing dangerous forces, such as dams, dykes, and nuclear power stations; the state responsible for them should locate all potential military objectives at a considerable distance from such protected installations, in order to minimize the risks of attack on its 'dangerous installations'.[480] Only military installations erected for the sole purpose of defending the protected installations from attack are excluded from this rule. Since a military or police guard—even if of limited size—is always necessary to protect such installations against terrorists and saboteurs (at least in the case of nuclear power stations), one must accept as normal a certain minimum degree of military defence located at the installation itself. The character of the installation is not changed by such small-scale defence arrangements, and in particular such military defence does not render it an admissible target according to Art. 56, para. 2, as long as the military guard and their facilities (such as guarded enclosures, anti-aircraft guns etc.) serve the sole purpose of defending the installation against sabotage.[481]

469   **The parties to the conflict shall remain obliged to take all precautions to protect dangerous works from the effects of attack (e.g. by shutting down nuclear electricity generating stations).**

Besides the specific rule of Art. 56, para. 5 AP I, there apply also the general rules of Art. 58 AP I on 'passive precautions' (see Section 447, para. 4) concerning the pro-

---

[480] See Solf, in Bothe/Partsch/Solf, 356.
[481] See Solf, *op. cit.*, 356; Pilloud/Pictet, in ICRC *Commentary*, 673–4 (paras. 2173–6); a critical position towards this provision is taken by Kalshoven, *Constraints*, 102.

Oeter

tection of dams, dykes, and nuclear power stations. According to Art. 58, lit. c AP I the parties to the conflict shall take the 'necessary precautions to protect the civilian population, individual civilians, and civilian objects under their control against the dangers resulting from military operations'. In the case of 'dangerous installations' this could mean also that the party on whose territory, for example, an endangered dam lies, must drain the lake in order to mimimize the risk of collateral damage if the combat zone approaches the dam; a similar requirement is applicable to nuclear power stations, where the party responsible for the plant might even be obliged to switch off the reactor if imminent danger of combat in the vicinity of the nuclear installation arises.

Works and installations containing dangerous forces may be marked with a spe-   470
cial protective sign consisting of three bright orange circles on a horizontal axis
(Art. 56, para. 7 AP I).

The First Additional Protocol introduced in Art. 56, para. 7. lit. a, a protective sign (analogous to the system of the Hague Convention for the Protection of Cultural Property; see Sections 929–33), to be attached to protected objects. The lack of a protective sign, however, does not mean that the parties are exempted from the protective provisions of Art. 56; to the contrary, the obligations resulting from Art. 56 bind the parties irrespective of marking of the installations in accordance with Art. 56, para. 7.

4. Ruses of War and the Prohibition against Perfidy

471. Ruses of war and the employment of measures necessary for obtaining infor-   471
mation about the adverse party and the country are permissible (Art. 37, para. 2
AP I; Art. 24 HagueReg) (e.g. the use of enemy signals, passwords, signs, decoys,
etc.; to be distinguished from espionage, see Sections 321–4).

Deceiving the enemy about the military situation, in particular about the strength of one's own forces, their location, and one's own intentions and plans, has belonged to the common arsenal of warfare since time immemorial.[482] Since warfare has always been at least as much a psychological attempt to bring one's influence to bear on the adversary as it has necessarily comprised the use of physical violence against the enemy, deception is often better suited to achieve results than the blatant use of violence.[483] Camouflaging one's own defence positions and using them for ambushes, setting up surprise attacks from such camouflaged positions, simulating operations of retreat, as well as simulating operations of attack, using dummy weapons, transmitting misleading messages, *inter alia* by using the adversary's radio wavelengths, passwords, and codes, infiltrating the enemy's command chain in order to channel wrong orders, moving land-marks and route markers,

---

[482] See Ipsen, 'War, Ruses', *EPIL* 4, 330; Fleck, *RDMilG* 1974, 270; Furrer, 3–40; Krüger-Sprengel, *NZWehrr*, 164–8.
[483] See Fleck, *loc. cit.*, 298.

giving members of one military unit the signs of other units to persuade the enemy that one's force is larger than it really is—all these are established elements of traditional tactics.[484] The laws of war have never prohibited such measures of deception, or 'ruses of war'.[485] Art. 24 of the Hague Regulations states only the simple rule: 'Ruses of war and the employment of measures necessary for obtaining information about the enemy and the country are permissible.'[486] Art. 37, para. 2 AP I has added nothing new to this old rule, and is worded in terms reminiscent of Art. 24 HagueReg: 'Ruses of war are not prohibited. Such ruses are acts intended to mislead an adversary or to induce him to act recklessly but which infringe no rule of international law applicable in armed conflict and which are not perfidious because they do not invite the confidence of an adversary with respect to protection under that law. The following are examples of such ruses: the use of camouflage, decoys, mock operations, and misinformation.'

472   **Perfidy is prohibited. The term 'perfidy' refers to acts misleading the adverse party into the belief that there is a situation affording protection under international law (e.g. humanitarian agreement to suspend combat with the intention of attacking by surprise the adversary relying on the agreement, Art. 37 AP I).**

1. The real problem underlying Art. 37 AP I—already apparent from the wording of Art. 37, para. 2 AP I—is the threshold between a lawful ruse of war and an unlawful act of perfidy. What primarily distinguishes perfidy from ordinary ruses of war is, according to the definitional approach of Art. 37 AP I, the exploitation of deliberately induced trust on the part of the adversary in order to injure, kill, or capture him. There must be a deliberate attempt to instil confidence with an 'intent to betray'.[487] As it is expressed in Art. 37, para. 1: 'Acts inviting the confidence of an adversary to lead him to believe that he is entitled to, or is obliged to accord, protection under the rules of international law applicable in armed conflict, with intent to betray that confidence, shall constitute perfidy.'[488] Deception is not limited here to questions of general military interest, such as the disposition of forces, or potential strategic planning, but concerns the existence of a right to protection provided by international law.[489] Moral and legal duty requires the combatant in such situations to protect the adversary and the innocent civilian. Elementary rules of inter-

---

[484] See de Preux, in ICRC *Commentary*, 443–4 (para. 1521); Solf, in Bothe/Partsch/Solf, 207; Ipsen, *loc. cit.*, 331.

[485] Solf, in Bothe/Partsch/Solf, 202–3.

[486] Concerning Arts. 24 and 23 HagueReg see Ipsen, *loc. cit.*, 330; de Preux, in ICRC *Commentary*, 440 (para. 1513); Fleck, *loc. cit.*, 276–85; Furrer, 41–56.

[487] See the classical explanation given by Oppenheim/Lauterpacht: 'Stratagems must be carefully distinguished from perfidy, since the former are allowed, whereas the latter is prohibited. Halleck correctly formulates the distinction by laying down the principle that, whenever a belligerent has expressly or tacitly engaged, and is therefore bound by a moral obligation, to speak the truth to an enemy, it is perfidy to betray his confidence, because it constitutes a breach of good faith.'—Oppenheim/Lauterpacht, Vol. II, 430.

[488] As to the drafting history of the prohibition of perfidy in Art.37, para. 1 AP I see in particular Furrer, 62–80.

[489] Krüger-Sprengel, *loc. cit.*, 169; Furrer, 81–2; Kalshoven, *Constraints*, 82; Ipsen, 'Perfidy', *EPIL* 4, 130; Solf, in Bothe/Partsch/Solf, 204–5; de Preux, in ICRC *Commentary*, 435–6 (para. 1500); Fleck, *loc. cit.*, 284 *et seq.*

national law, the observance of which should be a matter of honour (and a product of a genuine sense of justice) are grossly abused by perfidy.[490] Accordingly, the old notion of breach of honour is still present in the notion of perfidy: the (dishonourable) violation of the rules of 'chivalry', which in medieval customs constituted the core of perfidy.[491]

2. Art. 37, para. 1 AP I illustrates the abstract definition of perfidy by examples—which, however, are not meant to be exhaustive, since the Diplomatic Conference in its drafting of Art. 37 limited itself to uncomplicated examples, avoiding debatable situations.[492] Prohibited as perfidy is *inter alia* (a) the abuse of a flag of truce by feigning an intent to negotiate or surrender, (b) the feigning of incapacity to fight due to wounds or sickness, (c) the feigning of civilian, non-combatant status, and (d) 'the feigning of protected status by the use of signs, emblems, or uniforms of the United Nations or of neutral or other States not Parties to the conflict'.[493] Of most importance in that respect is example (c), because the feigning of civilian, non-combatant status in order to attack the enemy by surprise constitutes the classic case of 'treacherous killing of an enemy combatant' which was already prohibited by Art. 23 lit. b HagueReg; it is the obvious case of disgraceful behaviour which can (and should) be sanctioned under criminal law as a killing not justified by the laws of war, making it a common crime of murder.[494] Obscuring the distinction between combatants and civilians is extremely prejudicial to the chances of serious implementation of the rules of humanitarian law; any tendency to blur the distinction must be sanctioned heavily by the international community; otherwise the whole system based on the concept of distinction will break down.[495] Art. 37, para. 1 lit. c AP I, has a parallel provision in Art. 44, para. 3 AP I, which signals (although only indirectly) attacks in violation of the conditions set out in Art. 44, para. 3 AP I as being perfidious (see Sections 309, 312). A problematic question has been how to distinguish permitted cases of operating in civilian clothes (guerilla fighters in occupied territories and in wars of national liberation) from cases of legally forbidden perfidy,[496] such as in the case of command units operating and attacking in civilian clothes, as was e.g. the concept of the former Soviet Spetsnaz troops (see Section 320).

3. The phrase: 'perfidy is prohibited' does not reproduce the entire current rule of international law. According to Art. 37 AP I, perfidy is prohibited only in so far as it intentionally wounds, kills or captures the enemy.[497] Perfidy as such, beyond this restrictive definition based on hostile intent, is not banned under international law; if it is used solely for combat against military objects, for example, without affecting

[490] Fleck, *loc. cit.*, 285.

[491] See de Preux, in ICRC *Commentary*, 434 (para. 1498); Solf, in Bothe/Partsch/Solf, 202.

[492] Solf, ibid., 205; Ipsen, 'Perfidy', *EPIL* 4, 131; Furrer, 85–6; de Preux, in ICRC *Commentary*, 436–7 (paras. 1502–3).

[493] As to the interpretation of these examples see de Preux, in ICRC *Commentary*, 439 (paras. 1508–11); Solf, in Bothe/Partsch/ Solf, 206; Ipsen, 'Perfidy', *EPIL* 4, 131.

[494] See de Preux, in ICRC *Commentary*, 438 (paras. 1506–7); see also Fleck, *loc. cit.*, 278.

[495] So argues convincingly de Preux, in ICRC *Commentary*, 438 (para. 1506).

[496] See Solf, in Bothe/Partsch/Solf, 205–6.

[497] See Ipsen, 'Perfidy', *EPIL* 4, 131–2; Solf, ibid., 203–4.

Oeter

any enemy combatant, it is permissible.[498] 'Perfidious' acts are also allowed in order to evade capture or to escape from a prisoner of war camp, as long as no attack is committed under cover of the disguise;[499] the same is true for all *attempts* to commit acts covered by Art. 37, para. 1.[500] To reiterate: only the commission of a treacherous attack on enemy personnel which wounds, kills or captures them is prohibited. That limitation of the prohibition on hostile attacks under cover of disguise has been heavily criticized,[501] but it corresponds to the general attitude of most states which were involved in drafting the provision. Accordingly, it was impossible to avoid such a limitation to the prohibition of perfidy, and one must accept that most acts committed under camouflage and feigning still constitute legitimate ruses of war, and not perfidy.

473 **It is prohibited to make improper use of flags of truce, enemy or neutral national flags, military insignia and uniforms, and internationally acknowledged protective emblems, e.g. the red cross or the red crescent (Art. 39 AP I; Art. 23, para. 1 lit. f HagueReg; Art. 17, para. 2 CultPropConv). (For peculiarities of naval warfare see Sections 1017 ff.)**

Apart from the basic rule of Art. 37, para. 1 AP I, the system of the Additional Protocols, Hague Regulations, and customary law contains a whole series of other prohibitions of various kinds of deception, i.e. prohibitions on specific ruses or stratagems. The prohibition of abuse of flags of truce (now expressly defined as perfidy by Art. 37, para. 1 lit. a AP I) was mentioned above; in Art. 38 AP I it is further enlarged to an all-embracing prohibition against any abuse of such signs.[502] In a parallel provision Art. 38 AP I prohibits the abuse of 'recognized emblems' such as the emblems of the red cross, of civil defence, the protective emblem of cultural property, or of 'other internationally recognized protective emblems, signs, or signals'.[503] Art. 39 AP I prohibits also the improper use of false flags, military insignia, emblems, or uniforms. Whereas according to Art. 39, para. 1 the use of the flags, military emblems, insignia, or uniforms of 'neutral or other States not Parties to the conflict' is generally prohibited,[504] paragraph 2 of the same Article imposes a different rule on the use of the flags, military emblems, insignia, or uniforms of adverse parties to the conflict. The use of such symbols of the opposing belligerent is prohibited only during attacks or if it serves 'to shield, favour, protect, or impede military operations'.[505] Although the use of enemy flags, insignia, or uniforms does

---

[498] See Ipsen, 'Perfidy', ibid., 132; Furrer, 82–3; Solf, *op. cit.*, 203–4.

[499] See Kalshoven, *Constraints*, 83.

[500] See Furrer, 82–3; Ipsen, 'Perfidy', ibid.; Kalshoven, *op. cit.*, 83.

[501] See Ipsen, 'Perfidy', ibid., 131–2.

[502] See de Preux, in ICRC *Commentary*, 437 (para. 1504), 457–8 (paras. 1551–6).

[503] See the detailed description of the rule by de Preux, in ICRC *Commentary*, 446–60; also Solf, in Bothe/Partsch/ Solf, 208–11; Furrer, 88–90; Ipsen, 'Perfidy', *EPIL* 4, 131.

[504] See Solf, in Bothe/Partsch/Solf, 213; Furrer, 90 and in great detail de Preux, in ICRC *Commentary*, 462–5; see also the US Navy's *Annotated Supplement to the Commander's Handbook on the Law of Naval Operations, NWP 9* (Rev.A)/FMFM 1–10, 12–7.

[505] As to Art. 39 para. 2 AP I, see de Preux, in ICRC *Commentary*, 465–9 (paras. 1572–9); Furrer, 91; Solf, in Bothe/Partsch/ Solf, 214.

Oeter

not constitute perfidy in the strict sense, since those items do not create a specific confidence (i.e. the confidence of protection demanded by the moral code of chivalry) state practice has nonetheless for centuries considered such deception to be dishonourable, and accordingly not permissible.[506] Art. 23(f) of the Hague Regulations puts the abuse of national flags, military emblems, insignia, and uniforms of the enemy on the same footing as abuses of flags of truce or the red cross emblem, and expressly prohibits such abuses as means of warfare;[507] military operations using false insignia or uniforms are not lawful under international law and may be prosecuted under criminal law as illegitimate acts of violence.[508] Apart from that, the mere fact of operating behind enemy lines in civilian clothes or false uniforms may be considered to be espionage and may be punished as such (see Sections 321–4) although such acts (if not accompanied by the use of force against the adversary) are not prohibited *per se* by Art. 39, para. 2 AP I.[509]

5. Psychological Warfare

It is permissible to engage in political and military propaganda by spreading false   474
information to undermine the adversary's will to resist and to influence the mili-
tary discipline of the adversary (e.g. instigation to defect).

Propaganda with intent to influence the adversary's civilian population and to work on the members of the opposing armed forces has been an important means of warfare throughout this century.[510] During World War I the issue arose for the first time and had led to a fierce debate on the legality of psychological warfare.[511] By the 1920s however, the use of propaganda was generally considered to be legally permissible (see Art. 21 of the Hague Rules of Air Warfare). In the course of World War II all sides made active use of the new weapon, as have the parties of all wars since 1945.[512] Classic forms of propaganda, often listed under the heading of (permissible) ruses of war, are the spreading of false rumours; the erosion of adverse armed forces' fighting morale by the dissemination of misleading information; the incitement of enemy combatants to rebel, mutiny, or desert; and the incitement of the entire enemy population to revolt against its government.[513]

---

[506] Fleck, *RDMilG* 1974, 276–85; de Preux, *loc. cit.*, 466 (para. 1573); the contrary position is taken, however, by the US Navy's *Annotated Supplement to the Commander's Handbook on the Law of Naval Operations, NWP 9* (Rev.A)/FMFM 1–10, 12–8.

[507] Concerning the much debated interpretation of Art. 23(f) HagueReg see Fleck, *loc. cit.*, 279 *et seq.*; Solf, in Bothe/Partsch/Solf, 212–13.

[508] See Solf, *op. cit.*, 206 n. 23 and de Preux, in ICRC *Commentary*, 467 n. 26. A US occupation tribunal came to the opposite conclusion in 1947 in the *Skorzeny* case: see Fleck, *loc. cit.*, 279 (with critical comments on that judgment ibid., 280 *et seq.*); the position taken in the *Skorzeny* judgment still seems to be the official US position today; see US Navy's *Annotated Supplement to the Commander's Handbook on the Law of Naval Operations, NWP 9* (Rev.A)/FMFM 1–10, 12–8.

[509] As to the discussion of this provision see Solf, *op. cit.*, 214–15 and de Preux, *op. cit.*, 469–71 (paras. 1580–1, 1583).

[510] Madders, *EPIL* 4, 334; Greenspan, 322–3.   [511] Cf. Madders, *op. cit.*, 334.   [512] Ibid.

[513] See Kunz, *Kriegsrecht*, 82; Castrèn, *The Present Law of War and Neutrality*, 208–10; Greenspan, 323; Solf, in Bothe/Partsch/ Solf, 206–7; Madders, *EPIL* 4, 334–5; de Preux, in ICRC *Commentary*, 443–4 (para. 1521).

Oeter

475   Incitement to commit crimes and breaches of international law is prohibited.

The expression of the rule in this Section is not totally correct, since it gives the impression that incitement to commit any crime is illegal. In fact, not all acts classified by the adversary as crimes are taboo for the power engaging in psychological warfare.[514] Many generally accepted forms of hostile propaganda are in essence incitement to commit crimes, e.g. to desert to the enemy, which is a crime sanctioned with severe penalties according to all legal systems, as are all acts of mutiny and treason.[515] Also, the common incitement to overthrow a 'war-mongering' regime clearly constitutes (from the perspective of the affected nation) incitement to commit high treason.[516] However, all these subversive activities may undoubtedly be lawfully encouraged (and assisted) by the opposing belligerent. What is generally recognized to be prohibited as disgraceful is incitement to commit common crimes such as murder, robbery, or rape,[517] and particularly incitement to commit war crimes or crimes against humanity, which would evidently constitute an illegal act leading to state responsibility.[518] The same would apply to elementary violations of rules of international law, although this seems to be a rather hypothetical question (the only case yet discussed is the dissemination of falsified banknotes in order to wreck the monetary order of the adverse power).[519]

6. Reprisals

476   Reprisals are coercive measures which would normally be contrary to international law but which are taken in retaliation by one party to a conflict in order to stop the adversary from violating international law.

1. The law of reprisals is one of the classic instruments to implement the rules of public international law (see also Section 1206). It must be seen as closely connected with the principle of reciprocity, since it allows one state illegally injured by another to react to the violation of the law by an action which itself would normally breach international legal obligations.[520] The underlying purpose of the law of reprisals is to induce a law-breaking state to abide by the law in future, and to respect the demands of law in its further conduct.[521]

2. The instrument of reprisal, however, involves serious difficulties. On one hand experience shows that reprisals are not necessarily effective in forcing the adverse party to respect the law, since reprisals often produce the contrary effect, tending to

---

[514] See Knackstedt, *WVR* II, 353.   [515] Ibid., 353; see also Kunz, *Kriegsrecht*, 82.

[516] The question of the legality of incitement to rebel against one's government was still disputed at the turn of the century, see Kunz, *Kriegsrecht*, 82; in the literature published after 1945, however, the question is generally considered to be solved; see Oppenheim/Lauterpacht, Vol.II, 426–8; Castrén, *The Present Law of War and Neutrality*, 209–10; Knackstedt, 353; de Preux, in ICRC *Commentary*, 444 (para. 1521).

[517] See Knackstedt, *loc. cit.*, 353.   [518] Madders, *EPIL* 4, 335; Greenspan, 324.

[519] Madders, ibid., 335–6.

[520] As to the institution of reprisals in general see Kalshoven, *Belligerent Reprisals*, 11–33 and Bierzanek, *Reprisals*, 232–40.

[521] Kalshoven, *Belligerent Reprisals*, 33.

prompt a harsher reaction to every new reprisal of the adverse side, thus setting up a process of escalation.[522] Also, on the other hand, the institution is prone to all kinds of abuse, because it offers an excuse serving merely to palliate breaches of law which would have been committed in any event—and this, in cases of reprisals concerning humanitarian law, to the detriment of innocent civilians or prisoners.[523] Accordingly, there has long existed a tendency which sought to bind the use of reprisals in a compelling legal framework, in order to make the use of reprisals dependent on strict observance of certain formalities.[524] At last, humanitarian law since the Geneva Conventions of 1949 has progressively developed a system with protective rules for specific groups of persons or objects who become immune from reprisals, in order to prevent any erosion of humanitarian rights under the guise of reprisal.[525]

Because of their political and military significance, reprisals shall be authorized by the highest political level. No individual soldier is authorized to order reprisals on his own accord.   477

Because of the extremely complex legal and political assessment which must precede any reprisal, it is necessary that the political leadership of a belligerent state decide on any possible use of reprisals. The exact legal nature of the adverse belligerent's actions may be extremely difficult to determine; even more importantly, a decision to use reprisals requires a genuine assessment of the political risks as well as the immediate dangers connected with use of a reprisal. It is not only uncertain whether the enemy will be forced to abide by the law, but under certain circumstances reprisals may even—particularly if at or near the limits of proportionality—set in motion an uncontrollable process of escalation which could expose one's own civilian population to considerable danger. Accordingly, it is not appropriate for individual military commanders to undertake reprisals on their own accord; this is the sole responsibility of the highest political authority, in the case of Germany: the Federal Government.

Reprisals shall not be excessive in relation to the offence committed by the adversary and shall be preceded by a warning. They must be the last resort, when all other means to stop the illegal behaviour have failed and the warning has not been heeded.   478

There are two basic preconditions of customary law for legal reprisals: the requirement of proportionality concerning the original breach of law and the reaction, and the duty to warn in advance that such a reaction is imminent.[526] These two limitations on the use of reprisals have proven to be the most efficient safeguards in preventing fundamental abuses of reprisals, or at least to reveal improper reliance on the law of reprisals.

---

[522] Ibid., 42.   [523] See Bierzanek, *Reprisals*, 237–40 and Kalshoven, *Belligerent Reprisals*, 367–70.
[524] Bierzanek, *op. cit.*, 241–3; Kalshoven, *op. cit.*, 5–10.
[525] Kalshoven, *op. cit.*, 263–77; Kalshoven, *NYIL* 21 (1990), 45–52.
[526] See Bierzanek, *Reprisals*, 241–3.

Oeter

479   **It is expressly prohibited by international agreement to take reprisals against:**
       —the wounded, sick, and shipwrecked; medical and religious personnel; medical
          facilities and supplies (Art. 46 GC I; Art. 47 GC II; Art. 33, para. 2 lit. b GC III; Art.
          20 AP I);
       —prisoners of war (Art. 13, para. 3 GC III);
       —civilians (Art. 33, para. 3 GC IV; Art. 51, para. 6 AP I);
       —private property of civilians on occupied territory or of enemy foreigners on
          friendly territory (Art. 33, para. 3 GC IV);
       —objects indispensable to the survival of the civilian population (Art. 55, para. 2
          AP I);
       —the natural environment (Art. 55, para. 2 AP I);
       —works and installations containing dangerous forces (Art. 56, para. 4 AP I); or
       —cultural objects (Art. 52, para. 1, 53 lit. c AP I; Art. 4, para. 4 CultPropConv).

1. In the course of the last decades humanitarian law was developed by a process which gradually excluded more and more groups of persons and protected objects from the scope of reprisals. The process was begun, after the Geneva Convention on Prisoners of War of 1929 which included a prohibition of reprisals,[527] by the provisions of Arts. 46 GC I, 47 GC II, 13, para. 3 GC III, and 33 GC IV, in which all reprisals were prohibited that prejudice the protection of the specific groups covered by the four Conventions (wounded, sick, and shipwrecked; medical and religious personnel; prisoners of war; civilians in occupied territories) and to the protection of certain objects (medical facilities and supplies, private property of civilians in occupied territories).[528] The Hague Convention on the Protection of Cultural Property of 1954 contains an analogous prohibition of reprisals in favour of objects protected under that Convention.[529]

2. The First Additional Protocol now enlarges the traditional prohibitions of reprisals considerably.[530] True, the comprehensively formulated proposal which sought to exclude all groups of persons and objects protected under the Convention from reprisals was rejected.[531] The final text of the Protocol, however, represented agreement on a whole catalogue of additional and specific prohibitions of reprisals. Reprisals in disregard of the protection of the natural environment (provided for in Art. 55) as well as reprisals to the detriment of objects indispensable for the survival of the civilian population (Art. 54, para. 4 AP I) and to the detriment of works and installations containing dangerous forces are now absolutely prohibited.

3. The most important of these safeguards, however, is the prohibition in the Additional Protocol, Art. 51, para. 6, namely the prohibition against attacks on a civilian population based on a justification of reprisal. Such reprisals had been

---

[527] See Kalshoven, *loc. cit.*, 45–6.
[528] See the detailed explanations given by Kalshoven, *Belligerent Reprisals*, 263–71.
[529] Ibid., 272–7.   [530] Ibid., 49–52; Bierzanek, *Reprisals*, 251–5.
[531] See Bierzanek, *Reprisals*, 249–50; Kalshoven, *loc. cit.*, 47–9.

Oeter

permitted under traditional customary law,[532] and they constituted the bulk of all measures declared to be reprisals. The prohibition set out in Art. 51, para. 6 AP I has been fiercely criticized in legal literature as well as in practice, since it almost completely prevents the taking of reprisals as a response to breaches of humanitarian law by the adverse side.[533] It also creates considerable difficulties in the legal justification of the dominant doctrines of nuclear deterrence, since even the planned inclusion of large-scale use of strategic nuclear weapons as a military option might be justified only in the framework of belligerent reprisals;[534] from this follows the immense importance of the nuclear declarations and of the resulting exclusion of the nuclear question from the applicability of all the new rules in AP I (and implicitly from the prohibition against reprisals contained in Art. 51, para. 6 AP I; see Section 430). Only by recourse to reprisal, which remains permissible under customary law, can current nuclear strategies be legitimated under international law. Apart from that, one must consider the prohibitions of reprisals included in Additional Protocol I to be one of the great achievements brought about by the development of humanitarian law, although it makes the entire system more dependent on an international system of implementation if decentralized reaction to breaches of law is to be excluded.

[532] Kalshoven, *Recueil des Cours* 191 (1985 II), 286; Kalshoven, *Belligerent Reprisals*, 353–61.
[533] As critical voices see in particular Greenwood, *NYIL* 20 (1989), 35–69; Hampson, *ICLQ* 37 (1988), 818–43; Roberts, *loc. cit.*, 143–4; as a (convincing) response see Kalshoven, *NYIL* 21 (1990), 53–63.
[534] See Kalshoven, *Belligerent Reprisals* 348–53.

5

Protection of the Civilian Population

I. GENERAL

Introductory Remarks

1. It is useful to divide the rules for the protection of the civilian population into two groups, which in turn can be understood as the response to two distinct situations: (a) protection of the civilian population or individual persons under the control of the adversary against violent or arbitrary acts; (b) protection of the civilian population against the effects of military operations and individual acts of hostility. The first case relates to the legal protection of human beings against the misuse of power. These rules are often called 'The Law of Geneva' or 'Red Cross Law'. Their affinity to international law on human rights is obvious. The second group of rules sets limits to the conduct of military operations themselves. This law is still called 'The Law of The Hague', since the Hague Conventions of 1907 were the first comprehensive codification in this area.

2. This commentary is based on the provisions of international law concerning the protection of civilians in international armed conflicts. This law is highly developed and extensively codified. Its application is limited to international conflicts, i.e. armed clashes between states. The written law dealing with non-international armed conflicts can be found in Article 3 common to the four Geneva Conventions and in AP II. Although these regulations are more summary in nature than the written law of international conflicts, AP II in particular contains important and, obviously, binding rules governing the protection of victims in a civil war. The codified law is supplemented by rules of customary law, which above all place limits on the conduct of military operations.[1]

3. Section 211 of this Manual makes clear that 'German soldiers . . . are required to comply with the rules of international humanitarian law in the conduct of military operations in all armed conflicts however such conflicts are characterized'. For this reason, the Manual makes no distinction between international and

---

[1] See Gasser in: Haller/Kölz/Müller/Thürer (Eds.); *International Institute for Humanitarian Law*, 'Declaration on the Rules of international humanitarian law governing the conduct of hostilities in non-international armed conflicts', *IRRC* 30 (1990), 404–8.

non-international armed conflicts with reference to the conduct of military operations. The same is true for the duty to treat humanely all those in the power of an opposing party, including those who have actively participated in hostilities. Since 1977 there is hardly any significant difference between the two legal regimes, since AP II protects individuals against the misuse of power just as clearly as the law of international armed conflicts (see in particular its Article 4). On the other hand, many of the remaining provisions of 'Geneva Law', for example the rules relating to the legal status of combatants or the law applying to occupation by a belligerent, are directed specifically towards international situations. By force of law, they do not apply in civil wars, and the Manual does not call for such application. It is to be hoped that, in any case, persons who have fought as combatants in a civil war will be treated in compliance with the legal rules dealing with prisoners of war.

501   **With the exception of the *levée en masse* (see Section 310) civilians shall not take part in hostilities.**

1. Civilians shall refrain from taking part in all military activities, since only combatants are permitted to participate in hostilities. Only members of the armed forces may be combatants (see Sections 301 ff., especially Section 304). They alone have the right to take part in military operations and to cause damage in the course of these without being held responsible for the consequences of their actions, provided they are lawful. On the other hand, they may also be opposed. The prohibition of civilians taking part in hostilities is not only the direct consequence but also the precondition of the principle by which the civilian population shall not be involved in military operations. Only if no attacks are feared from the adversary's civilian population will armed forces be prepared to spare that civilian population from attacks.

2. For the purpose of international humanitarian law, a civilian is a person who is not a member of the armed forces (Art. 50, para. 1 AP I). This (negative) definition, which is linked to the description of members of the armed forces, has the advantage of being conclusive. In a war it is usually clear who is a member of the opposing armed forces and who is not, and thus who is entitled to protection. This is true in any case for international armed conflicts, to which this legal differentiation alone applies. In internal armed conflicts also, it is generally evident who is in fact involved in acts of violence and who is not.

3. Civilians are under no obligation to identify themselves as such, e.g. by carrying an identity card, in order to claim the protection to which they are entitled. Rather, it is the duty of combatants to distinguish themselves from the civilian population by wearing uniform (see Section 308). In case of doubt, a person shall be treated as a civilian (Art. 50, para. 1, 2nd sentence). In doubtful cases, therefore, members of armed forces must first ascertain whether a person is a combatant or a civilian.

4. Persons accompanying the armed forces without being members thereof (e.g. war correspondents, members of labour units or of services responsible for the

Gasser

soldiers' welfare) are also considered civilians; they include civilian members of military aircraft crews and the crews of merchant ships (Art. 4a, paras. 4 and 5 GC III; Section 319). These persons may not take part in acts of war) The same is true for persons who—although undoubtedly civilians—are involved in the war effort in some other form, outside the armed forces, for example workers in armaments factories. Their work is not considered to be military activity, and they may not engage in actual military operations. Finally, civilians serving as military advisors to the armed forces are also prohibited from taking part in hostilities. They retain their civilian status, yet expose themselves, by their activities, to the risk of being called to account as irregular combatants.

5. What are the consequences if civilians do engage in combat, whether within (regular) military forces, within civilian groups, or as individuals? What does the status of combatant imply? Such persons do not lose their legal status as civilians (Art. 51, para. 8 AP I). However, for factual reasons they may not be able to claim the protection guaranteed to civilians, since anyone performing hostile acts may also be opposed, but in the case of civilians, only for so long as they take part directly in hostilities (Art. 51, para. 3, AP I). Any use of force against civilians must, in particular, conform to the general rule under which civilians are to be protected as far as possible and unavoidable losses among the civilian population are to be kept to a minimum (see Section 509). If such persons participating in combat fall into the power of the adversary, they shall be treated as civilians. They are entitled to all the rights due to civilians, particularly with regard to their treatment. They may, however, be held to account for their actions in conformity with applicable law and including judicial guarantees (see Sections 576 ff., 584). The mere fact of having engaged in hostilities does not confer the status of a combatant on a civilian, who remains a civilian with all corresponding rights and duties.

6. There is only one situation in which civilians have the right to take up arms and to engage in hostilities like combatants: the *levée en masse* (see Section 310). Under these circumstances, civilians may also be opposed. If captured, they shall be treated as prisoners of war (Art. 4a, para. 6 GC III).

7. In the law relating to non-international armed conflicts, the prohibition of civilians taking part in hostilities is implicit (see especially Art. 13, para. 3 AP II). A civilian disregarding this prohibition is nevertheless protected by international humanitarian law (Art. 3 GC I–IV; Arts. 4–6 AP II). This, however, does not prevent the prosecution under national law of persons who have engaged in hostilities. The legal guarantees of due process, embodied in common Article 3 of the Geneva Conventions and Article 6 AP II, must be observed under all circumstances.

Civilians who do not take part in hostilities shall be respected and protected. They   502
are entitled to respect for their persons, their honour, their family rights, their
religious convictions, and their manners and customs (Art. 27, para. 1 GC IV; Art.
46, para. 1 HagueReg). Their property is also protected (Art. 46, para. 2

HagueReg). **Neither the civilian population as such, nor individual civilians, shall be attacked, killed, wounded, or taken prisoner without sufficient reason (Art. 51, para. 2 AP I; Art. 13, para. 2 AP II).**

1. Persons who are not members of the armed forces and who may therefore not participate in hostilities shall under all circumstances be respected and protected. War shall not be waged against civilians. They shall at all times be treated humanely. The duty to protect and respect civilians forms part of binding customary international law. In treaty law, Article 27, para. 1 GC IV expresses this general obligation. The placing of this article within the text of the Convention makes clear that it includes all situations in which a party to a conflict comes into contact with civilians of the opposing side, i.e. for aliens in the territory of a party to the conflict, and for the inhabitants of occupied territories. Common Article 3 of the Geneva Conventions obliges the parties to a civil war to treat humanely all those not directly involved in hostilities.

2. The first sentence demands that civilians be 'respected' and 'protected'. The duty to 'respect' civilians demands conduct which is described in the negative: all acts that might unjustifiably cause harm to a civilian must be avoided. The duty to 'protect' civilians goes an important step further, since it calls for positive action. Everything necessary must be done to ward off or reduce harm. This means taking all measures required to ensure the safety of civilians, e.g. the establishment of safety zones or evacuation (see generally Sections 510, 512 ff., and 585). It also means guaranteeing the protection of the inhabitants of occupied territories against the effects of hostilities (see Sections 525 ff.). To leave the civilian population to its fate when danger arises from fighting would be a breach of this general duty to protect. It is self-evident that in the conditions of modern warfare such danger exists not only in the immediate vicinity of combat but also in areas far removed from the fighting.

3. The second sentence lists the interests and rights that must be respected and protected: the person, the person's honour, family rights, religious convictions, manners, and customs. This list is not exhaustive. It does however express very well that, even in the exceptional circumstances of war, human beings are entitled to protection and respect, together with all the immediate circumstances that determine their individual personality. This is the expression in humanitarian law of the duty to protect universal human rights.

4. In particular, the obligation of respect for persons includes the duty to protect and respect both their physical and mental or intellectual integrity. All physical or moral coercion, for example to obtain information, is prohibited from the outset (Art. 31, GC IV). For this reason, torture of any kind is prohibited and is punishable as a grave breach of the Conventions (or: a war crime) (Art. 147 GC IV).[2] Likewise, it

---

[2] See also the Convention against Torture and Other Cruel, Inhuman or Degrading Treatment or Punishment of 10 Dec. 1984.

Gasser

is prohibited to undertake medical and scientific experiments, or organ transplants that are not therapeutically justified, on such persons (see Sections 606 ff.). To sentence a civilian to death and to carry out the death penalty is allowed only in the cases permitted by GC IV (see Section 578, 2nd sentence). Other types of cruel treatment, such as mutilation or corporal punishment, are also prohibited (Art. 75, para. 2(a)iv AP I). International humanitarian law comprehensively prohibits outrages upon personal dignity, in particular humiliating and degrading treatment, enforced prostitution, and any form of indecent assault (Art. 75, para. 2(b) AP I).

5. Respect and protection of mental and intellectual integrity, which includes regard for personal honour, means that the person's uniqueness as an individual and as a member of social groups must be respected. In practical terms this means, for example, that his or her image may not be exposed to the curiosity of the public (e.g. in photographs or on television). Finally, the family's rights to protection include the right to continue to live within the family unit. The dispersion of families is prohibited.

6. The religious convictions of civilians in the power of the adversary shall be respected. They shall not be forced to profess any specific religion or belief. This prohibition protects first and foremost the persons concerned, especially against possible persecution on their return.

7. The reference to the manners and customs to be respected is a reminder that the individual is also part of the social fabric. Accordingly, the adversary has no right to tear a civilian out of his or her social surroundings or to destroy those surroundings through fundamental alteration. The conventions of international humanitarian law also expressly prohibit the forced removal of protected persons from their place of residence in order to settle them elsewhere (see especially Sections 544 ff.). The entire law governing occupation by a belligerent is based on the principle that the social order of the occupied territory shall not be altered by the occupying power (see Sections 525 ff.).

8. The third sentence stipulates that the personal property of civilians shall also be protected. The legal basis for this guarantee of property rights in the event of war is to be found not so much in the GCs as in the HagueReg (Art. 46, para. 2). As such, this guarantee has become part of customary law. The law governing occupation by a belligerent establishes in detail under what circumstances the occupying power may utilize private property (see Sections 557 ff.). On the other hand, GC IV comprehensively prohibits the occupying power from destroying movable or immovable property of inhabitants of the occupied territories (Art. 53). Unlawful and wanton destruction or appropriation of property on a large scale, which cannot be justified by military necessity, is a grave breach within the meaning of Article 147 GC IV.

9. The fourth sentence makes it perfectly clear that neither the civilian population as such nor individual civilians are legitimate objects of military operations (see in

detail Sections 451 ff.). Attacks against the civilian population or individual civilians resulting in death or serious injuries are punishable as grave breaches of AP I, i.e. as war crimes (Art. 85, para. 3(a) AP I). If the civilians are already in the power of the enemy, then any wilful killing constitutes a grave breach (Art. 147 GC IV).

10. The prohibition of the use of force against civilians is not absolute. For example, if a civilian is reasonably suspected of an offence for which an arrest would be a commensurate measure, then such arrest is permissible under international humanitarian law, and may involve the use of force if necessary. Under Section 501, para. 5 it has already been indicated that force may also be used against civilians taking part in hostilities. The limits on this permitted force are set by the rule of proportionality. Force against civilians is permitted as an act of self-defence, taking into account the limits imposed by the rule of proportionality. Finally, harm to civilians is lawful if it is an unavoidable and proportionate side-effect of lawful attacks on military objectives (see Sections 509 ff.).

11. A threat of violence shall be treated as an unlawful use of force if its primary purpose is to spread terror among the civilian population (Art. 51, para. 2, 2nd sentence AP I). Such threats, which may take the form of propaganda, verbal intimidation, or violence, are also prohibited.

12. It should also be recalled that civilians who disregard the obligations or prohibitions imposed upon them remain entitled to respect and protection (Art. 51, para. 8 AP I).

13. Certain particularly reprehensible attacks on a person's physical or mental integrity are considered grave breaches of international humanitarian law (see Art. 147 GC IV; Art. 85, para. 4(c) AP I; Sections 1207 ff.).

14. In cases of non-international armed conflict, 'persons taking no active part in the hostilities . . . shall in all circumstances be treated humanely' (Art. 3, para. 1 GC I–IV). This includes civilians. The use of disproportionate force against civilians is also prohibited in non-international armed conflicts. AP II confirms common Article 3 and extends the legal protection of civilians (Art. 4, para. 2 AP II). Article 13, para. 2 AP II expressly prohibits not only attacks against civilians but also threats of such attacks.

503   **If the civilian population of a party to the conflict is inadequately supplied with indispensable goods, relief actions by neutral states or humanitarian organizations shall be permitted. Every state, and in particular the adversary, is obliged to grant such relief actions free transit, subject to its right of control (Art. 23 GC IV; Art. 70 AP I).**

1. 'Starvation of civilians as a method of warfare is prohibited' (Art. 54, para. 1 AP I). Thus, deliberately to starve civilians is unlawful. The current law of armed

Gasser

conflict permits a blockade of enemy territory intended to prevent the shipment of goods of any sort (see Sections 1051 ff.). The siege of an enemy position can also result in the supply of goods for the civilian population being cut off. Section 503 is a reminder that sieges and blockades may not be aimed at starving the civilian population. Furthermore, hunger among the civilian population may not simply be accepted. Therefore, if the civilian population is inadequately supplied with indispensable goods as a result of the war, then relief actions intended for the needy population shall be allowed (Art. 23 GC IV; Art. 70 AP I).

2. GC IV contains specially detailed regulations about supplying the population of an occupied territory (see Section 569). At this point, only the situation of civilians in the territory of each of the belligerents will be examined, without considering the problems arising in occupied territories.

3. According to Article 70 AP I, relief actions intended for the civilian population shall be undertaken if it is not adequately provided with the supplies listed in Article 69. The civilian population meant here is that of a territory under the control of one or other party to the conflict. Such relief actions can be conducted only with the agreement of the relevant party to the conflict. If the civilian population of one party to the conflict is no longer adequately supplied, then the other party to the conflict is directly affected as soon as the relief action must pass through its territory or blockade. Since Article 54, AP I expressly prohibits starvation of the civilian population of the enemy, passage of the relief action must be allowed if refusal would in fact result in the starvation of those affected. Third states not involved in the conflict are bound by Article 23, GC IV, strengthened by Article 70, para. 2 AP I, to allow the free passage through their territory of relief actions intended for the civilian population of a party to the conflict.

4. Those states which allow a relief action must not only permit the passage of the actual relief supplies, but also of the relief personnel and the necessary equipment, such as means of transport. On the other hand, they are entitled to regulate the technical arrangements for the transport through their own territory, including search of the consignment for control purposes, and to require that distribution of the relief supplies be made under the supervision of the protecting power or of the ICRC. The relevant party to the conflict shall protect the relief action and facilitate distribution of the supplies. Such supplies may include, in particular, essential foodstuffs and medical supplies, but also other items essential for survival (clothing, bedding, etc.). Priorities shall be observed in the distribution. Article 70, para. 1, 3rd sentence AP I, names the following recipients in the order shown: children, expectant mothers, maternity cases, and nursing mothers.

5. The question arises of who should carry out relief actions destined for the civilian population of a party to the conflict. Article 70 AP I is addressed to all states parties, without expressly saying so. They are called upon to undertake or contribute to relief actions when the civilian population of any state is exposed to excessive

suffering as a result of war. Article 70 also lays down expressly that an offer of relief to a party to a conflict shall not be seen as interference in the armed conflict or as an unfriendly act. In practice, it is often international organizations that undertake relief actions. Traditionally, the ICRC has played an important role. Its 'humanitarian right of initiative', as laid down in Articles 9/9/9/10, GC I–IV, allows the ICRC to pursue negotiations proactively, even if a party to the conflict has a negative attitude.

6. The law applicable in non-international armed conflicts states similarly that relief actions are to be undertaken if the civilian population 'is suffering undue hardship owing to a lack of the supplies essential for its survival, such as foodstuffs and medical supplies' (Art. 18, para. 2 AP II). Impartial humanitarian organizations, especially the ICRC, are called upon where necessary to provide help to the population not taking part in the hostilities.

504 **Any attack on the honour of women, in particular rape, enforced prostitution, or any form of indecent assault, is prohibited (Art. 27, para. 2 GC IV; Art. 76, para. 1 AP I).**

1. The GCs contain different regulations intended to protect women. Article 76 AP I, which combines these and also extends the protection, provides for general protection to be observed under all circumstances. According to this article, women must be the object of special respect. They must be protected in particular against rape and enforced prostitution. It should be emphasized that this rule applies to all situations to which GC IV and AP I are applicable, i.e. in occupied territories and in the case of aliens in the territory of a belligerent. Serious contravention of this rule is punishable as a grave breach (GC IV, Art. 147; Section 1209).

2. If a pregnant woman or a mother with small children is detained on suspicion of an offence, then her case is to be treated with priority and particular dispatch (Art. 76, para. 2). In the case of an offence related to the armed conflict, pregnant women and mothers having small children shall not be sentenced to death. In no such case shall the death penalty be carried out (Art. 76, para. 3).

505 **Children shall be the object of special respect and protection. They shall be provided with the care and aid they require, whether because of their youth or for any other reason (Art 24 GC IV; Art. 77, para. 1 AP I). Children who have not attained the age of fifteen shall not take part in direct hostilities. They shall not be enlisted. If they fall into the power of an adverse party they shall be granted special protection (Art. 77, para. 3 AP I; see also Art. 38 of the 1989 Convention on the Rights of the Child).**

1. Children also deserve respect and special protection during war. They are entitled under all circumstances to be treated in accordance with their age. In particular, they must be protected against any form of indecent assault (Art. 77, para. 1 AP

I). Children who are orphaned and children separated from their families as a result of the war or for other reasons shall not be left to their own resources (Art. 24, para. 1 GC IV). With the consent of the protecting power, such children may be taken to a neutral country for the duration of the conflict (Art. 24, para. 2). In order to avoid abusive permanent evacuation to a foreign country, the effects of which are not in the child's interest, AP I permits evacuations only if they are temporary and necessary for compelling reasons relating to the children's health, medical treatment, or (except in occupied territories) the safety of the children (Art. 78 AP I). All measures shall be taken to make return to their country possible as soon as circumstances allow. Adoptions are therefore inadmissible on principle.

2. In the provisions described above, AP I does not define the term 'child', and in particular does not fix an age limit; this was a deliberate omission. In this way the varying views in different cultures are taken into consideration. It may be assumed, however, that from the point of view of international humanitarian law anyone who has not attained the age of fifteen is a child.[3]

3. A particularly tragic aspect of modern conflict is the active participation of children in hostilities. Section 505 states unambiguously that children under fifteen years of age are not permitted to take a direct part in hostilities. The relevant provision of AP I is unfortunately worded less clearly. It merely lays down that all parties to the conflict shall take 'all feasible measures' to ensure that children below the age of fifteen years take no direct part in hostilities; in particular, they shall refrain from recruiting them into their armed forces (Art. 77, para. 2, 1st sentence).[4] There is, however, no objectively justifiable reason for not establishing the age of fifteen years as the absolute lowest limit for recruiting youth into the armed forces. As further laid down on the subject by AP I, the oldest in the age group of fifteen- to eighteen-year-olds shall be recruited first, if at all (para. 2, 2nd sentence).

4. If children under the age of fifteen years are nonetheless inducted into the armed forces and take part in military operations, they shall, if captured, be guaranteed conditions of captivity which take their age into consideration. Such special conditions shall be afforded whether or not they are recognized as prisoners of war. In particular, such 'child soldiers' shall be held separately from adults (Art. 77, paras. 3 and 4).

5. If a person sentenced to death for an offence related to the armed conflict was below eighteen years of age at the time the offence was committed, then the sentence shall not be carried out (Art. 77, para. 5).

[3] ICRC *Commentary*, para. 3179.
[4] The Convention on the Rights of the Child of 20 Nov. 1989 confirms, in its Art. 38, para. 2, the age limit of fifteen years. In the declaration which it submitted upon ratification of the Convention, the German Federal Government regretted this and declared 'that it will not make use of the possibility provided by the Convention to set this age limit at fifteen years' (BGBl 1992 II 992).

6. The regulations for the protection of children in non-international armed conflicts are essentially identical to those applicable in international conflicts (Art. 4, para. 3, AP II).

506 **None of the parties to the conflict shall use civilians as a shield to render certain points or areas immune from military operations (Art. 28 GC IV; Art. 51, para. 7 AP I).**

1. This follows directly from the rule that neither the civilian population nor individual civilians shall be involved in hostilities. The immunity granted to the civilian population may not be abused for military purposes. Civilians may not be used in order to gain a military advantage or to deny the adversary such an advantage. The adversary would otherwise be in a position where he would have to choose between involving (protected) civilians in a (lawful) military attack and relinquishing a possible military advantage.

2. AP I differentiates between two situations. First, objects which may be military objectives must not be installed in a civilian area in order to gain protection for the military installation from the prohibition of attacks against the civilian population. This applies especially when the same military goal can be achieved at another location that does not lead to difficulties in terms of protecting the civilian population. Secondly, civilians may not be deliberately 'used' as a shield for a potential military objective. In the same way, civilians may not be misused to secure a military operation. The following examples illustrate the rule: the deployment of a military unit protected by a column of refugees; the movement of protected persons (prisoners of war, civilians) to strategically significant locations (weapon positions, communication centres, etc.), as happened in the Gulf War of 1990/91; sealing off a militarily important axis by causing a crowd of women and children to gather; and so on.

3. If one party to a conflict breaks this rule, this does not exempt the other side from the regulations applicable in military attacks (see especially Sections 502 and 509 ff.). The military commander must therefore take into account the column of refugees used by the adversary as a shield.

4. The prohibition of misusing civilians as a shield against the adversary's military actions may not be misunderstood to mean that international humanitarian law provides absolute immunity against attacks to the civilian population. Section 506 only prohibits the deployment of civilians as a shield against the adversary's military activities. The extent to which casualties among the civilian population as a result of military attacks may be tolerated is discussed in detail in Sections 509 ff.

507 **Collective penalties and measures of intimidation or terrorism (Art. 33, para. 1 GC IV; Art. 51, para. 2 AP I; Art. 13, para. 2 AP II), reprisals against the civilian popula-**

Gasser

tion and its property (Art. 33, para. 3 GC IV; Arts. 20 and 51, para. 6 AP I), and pillage (Art. 33, para. 2 GC IV; Art. 47 HagueReg) are all prohibited.

1. Collective penalties, terrorism, reprisals, and pillage are characterized by the use of force against the civilian population or individual civilians. They are prohibited without exception, as established in Article 27 GC IV. According to that provision, civilians shall 'at all times be humanely treated, and shall be protected especially against all acts of violence or threats thereof and against insults and public curiosity'.

2. With regard particularly to collective penalties, these clearly contradict the principle of individual penal responsibility, according to which no one may be convicted of or punished for an act which he or she did not personally commit. This rule is one aspect of the principle of fair trial which has been universally accepted. It is guaranteed in all international human rights conventions and in the four GCs (Art. 38 GC IV—with reference to the rules of general international law—and Art. 67 GC IV; Art. 75, para. 4(b) AP I).

3. For non-international armed conflicts, Article 6, para. 2(b) AP II also expressly lays down the principle of individual penal responsibility. It gives concrete form to common Article 3 of the GCs, which requires a fair trial by a regularly constituted court.

4. Collective penalties are also specifically and expressly prohibited, in both international (Art. 33, para. 1 GC IV; and Art. 75, para. 2(d) AP I) and non-international armed conflicts (Art. 4, para. 2(b) AP II).

5. According to Article 33, para. 1, 2nd sentence GC IV, every measure aimed at 'intimidating or terrorizing' civilians is prohibited. Such measures are already covered by the general prohibition in Article 27. Intimidation or terrorism is also prohibited if its declared purpose is to prevent the civilian population (e.g. of an occupied territory) from engaging in hostile or even illegal acts. The authorities or armed forces must adopt other measures, in conformity with human dignity and the rule of law, to ensure public security. Like collective penalties, intimidating and terrorist acts always affect the civilian population as a whole, without differentiating between potential trouble-makers and peaceful citizens.

6. Over and above the general prohibition of Article 33 GC IV, Article 51, para. 2, 2nd sentence AP I contains a rule drawn up specifically for military operations: 'Acts or threats of violence the primary purpose of which is to spread terror among the civilian population are prohibited.' This prohibits the use of terrorism as a weapon aimed deliberately against the civilian population. It should be pointed out that not every type of terrorization of the civilian population is prohibited by international law. Military operations against (lawful) military objectives in close proximity to a concentration of civilians will always arouse fear and terror, without the attack

Gasser

necessarily being rendered unlawful. The proportionality between the expected military advantage and harm to the civilian population must be the deciding factor in any specific case (see Section 509). In other words, it is not so much causing terror among the civilian population that is prohibited as the use of such measures with the primary intention of spreading terror. For non-international armed conflicts, AP II (Art. 13, para. 2, 2nd sentence) contains a similar ban on terrorism.

7. Reprisals against the civilian population, individual civilians, or their property are prohibited (Art. 33, para. 3 GC IV). AP I has extended the prohibition of reprisals to the provisions restricting the conduct of military operations themselves (Art. 51, para. 6; Art. 52, para. 1, etc.). Under current law, civilians and the civilian population as a whole are comprehensively protected against reprisals, at least during an international armed conflict. On the problem of reprisals in general, see Sections 476–9.

8. Finally, Article 33, para. 2 GC IV also prohibits pillage. A comprehensive prohibition of pillage is likewise to be found in the HagueReg (Art. 47).

508   The taking of hostages is prohibited (Art. 34 GC IV).

1. The term 'hostages' applies to persons who are held in the power of the adversary, whether voluntarily or by force, in order thereby to obtain specific actions (release of prisoners, cancellation of military operations, etc.) from the other party to the conflict or from particular individuals (e.g. partisans).

2. While in the past the taking of hostages to gain military advantage was considered lawful, since the GCs came into force the parties to a conflict are prohibited from taking hostages in any circumstances (Art. 34 GC IV). The taking of hostages is to be punished as a grave breach of GC IV, Art. 147. AP I reinforces this prohibition, so that there are no conceivable gaps in the legal protection (Art. 75, para. 2(c)). Common Article 3 of the GCs prohibits the taking of hostages in non-international armed conflicts.

509   Attacks on military objects must not cause loss of civilian life which is excessive in relation to the concrete and direct military advantage anticipated (Art. 51, para. 5 lit. b AP I; Art. 23, para. 1 lit. g HagueReg).

1. Attacks on the civilian population as such or on individual civilians are prohibited (see Sections 451 ff. and 502). The same applies to civilian objects (ibid.; see also Section 446). This does not mean, however, that in a war all casualties among civilians and any destruction of civilian objects are prohibited by international law. With pragmatic acceptance of reality, international humanitarian law takes into account losses and damage as incidental consequences of (lawful) military operations. Section 509 states the conditions in which such 'incidental damage' caused by attacks (collateral damage) may be acceptable. The criterion is the principle of proportionality.

Gasser

2. The requirement that the damage caused in the area surrounding a military operation shall not exceed a 'reasonable' proportion in relation to the military success strived for is probably as old as warfare itself. In the year 1907 the HagueReg introduced this principle into international treaty law in the following form '. . . it is especially forbidden: . . . to destroy or seize the enemy's property, unless such destruction or seizure be imperatively demanded by the necessities of war' (Art. 23, para. 1 (g)). Expanding on this, AP I conferred its present form on the principle of proportionality as applied to the assessment of expected collateral damage: losses among the civilian population and damage to civilian objects.

3. Under current law, an attack is prohibited 'which may be expected to cause incidental loss of civilian life, injury to civilians, damage to civilian objects, or a combination thereof, which would be excessive in relation to the concrete and direct military advantage anticipated' (Art. 51, para. 5(b) AP I). In this way—which admittedly is not simple—a balance must be found in practice between military considerations on one hand and the rules of humanity on the other.

4. This requires the military officers in charge of planning, preparation, and decision-making of a military operation to reflect on the possible damaging effects of the action on the civilian population and civilian objects. Incidentally, this rule is expressly laid down in Article 57 AP I, under the heading 'Precautions in attack', which urges persons in charge of an attack to take all feasible precautions to ensure that regulations dealing with the protection of the civilian population and civilian objects are observed as far as possible and that losses or destruction in the civilian domain are kept to a minimum (Section 510). This duty of military commanders to judge the situation from the point of view of international humanitarian law and to make decisions that also take into account the requirements of humanitarian law must be established and enforced within the armed forces through generally applicable instructions.

5. A reasoned decision on the losses to be anticipated among the civilian population or civilian objects as the result of a military attack can be reached only if information is available concerning not only the military value of the target but also any civilian environment that may be involved. The military commander is therefore obliged within the bounds of what is 'feasible' (Art. 57, para. 2(a)i AP I), to obtain information making possible a decision concerning the admissibility of the planned military operation. For further details, see Section 457.

6. Concerning the scale of the information-gathering required, the German Federal Government stated in the declaration of interpretation which it submitted upon ratification of AP I: 'feasible' is to be understood as 'that which is practicable or practically possible, taking into account all circumstances ruling at the time including humanitarian and military considerations'.[5] When the military

---

[5] See No. 2 of the declaration (BGBl 1991 II 968) in *IRRC* (1991), 234. Corresponding declarations were submitted upon ratification (as of 15 Dec. 1992) by: Australia, Belgium, Canada, Egypt, Italy, The

commander makes a decision, this must be based on the information obtained (by reconnaissance, etc.) in as far as it was obtained according to accepted standards. The commander's actions can be assessed only on the basis of the information available at the time, not on the basis of facts that only became known later or on the actual course of the military action. The German Federal Government has also stated its position on this question in its declaration of interpretation to AP I.[6]

7. However, if in the course of a military action facts become known making it obvious that the attack will cause casualties among civilians and/or destruction of civilian objects that can no longer be considered proportional, then the action shall be cancelled or suspended (Art. 57, para. 2(b) AP I).

8. The anticipated loss of civilian life and destruction must be measured against the 'concrete and direct military advantage' (Art. 51, para. 5(b) AP I). 'Military advantage' is to be understood as any advantage 'anticipated from the attack considered as a whole and not only from isolated or particular parts of the attack', as stated in the German declaration of interpretation.[7]

9. Civilians must be properly warned in advance of military actions that may affect them, 'unless circumstances do not permit' (Art. 57, para. 2(c) AP I).

10. Military decisions must be based on sound information, on military experience, and on the realization that respect for the civilian population is an absolute requirement in international law concerning the conduct of military operations. 'Anticipated military advantage' and 'possible losses of civilian life, which shall be avoided' are concepts tinged with subjectivity, giving those in charge of military operations a fairly wide range of discretion. Military considerations require this kind of latitude. Those making decisions, however, may not escape responsibility by claiming that they were not authorized or able to reach such decisions based on subjective considerations. Solf rightly stresses that most important decisions in all areas of life ultimately involve balancing factors which are not quantifiable.[8] International humanitarian law makes great demands on the judgement of military commanders, but it does not require them to do the impossible.

11. The rule discussed here sets no absolute limits to the acceptable level of damage, it expresses a ratio between two quantities. Under Article 51, para. 5(b) AP I, the greatest permissible potential losses among the civilian population during a

Netherlands, New Zealand, and Spain. No state party to Protocol I has raised any objection to these declarations.

[6] See No. 4 of the German declaration of interpretation (n. 5). Corresponding declarations were submitted by Australia, Belgium, Canada, Italy, The Netherlands, New Zealand, and Spain, with no objections raised.

[7] See No. 5 of the German declaration of interpretation (n. 5). Corresponding declarations were submitted upon ratification (as of 15 Dec. 1992) by Australia, Belgium, Canada, Italy, The Netherlands, New Zealand, and Spain with no objections being raised.

[8] Bothe/Partsch/Solf, 310.

Gasser

military action are measured in proportion to the extent of the anticipated military advantage. The greater this advantage, the greater the acceptable level of civilian casualties and destruction. Although the rule is silent on this point, it must be assumed that there is an upper limit to the extent of acceptable damage. It would be absurd if the rule governing collateral damage could completely nullify the fundamental prohibition of waging war against the civilian population (Art. 48 AP I).[9]

When launching an attack on a military objective, all feasible precautions shall be taken to avoid, and in any event to minimize, incidental loss of civilian life, injury to civilians, and damage to civilian objects (Art. 57, para. 2 lit. a ii AP I).   510

1. This rule stresses the obligation on all those responsible for planning or deciding on military operations to take all measures for the greatest possible protection of civilians and civilian objects, as well as other groups of persons entitled to respect and protection, e.g. wounded and sick military personnel, or protected objects such as military medical units, military hospitals, etc. Furthermore, an attacking party must respect any existing safety zones, undefended localities, and demilitarized or neutralized zones.

2. The precautionary measures to be taken when preparing and carrying out a military action are dealt with in detail in Sections 457 and 509. At this point it should be pointed out especially that the party to a conflict whose civilian population or civilian objects might suffer losses or damage in a (lawful) enemy attack also has specific obligations. In particular, the said party must enable the adversary to attack military objectives without excessive collateral damage in the civilian domain. This follows from the general rule under which a distinction must be made between a military objective and civilians or civilian objects. Each party to a conflict therefore has the duty to remove the civilian population, individual civilians, and civilian objects under its control from the vicinity of military objectives 'to the maximum extent feasible' (Art. 58(a), AP I). Moreover, military objectives should not be located within or near densely populated areas (Art. 58(b)). Finally, the said party to the conflict must take other precautions to protect the civilian population, individual civilians, and civilian objects as far as possible against the dangers associated with military operations (Art. 58(c)). Among these measures are civil defence activities (see Sections 519 ff.). The duty to take precautions against the effects of military actions applies to a party to the conflict not only with regard to its own population but also with regard to other civilians temporarily under its control, e.g. aliens, refugees, and others. It also applies to occupied territories (see Sections 543 ff.).

3. In the course of the discussions concerning these regulations, it was argued that particularly in modern states it would no longer be possible to make a distinction between potential military objectives on one hand and the civilian infrastructure

---

[9] Similarly ICRC *Commentary*, para. 1980; see also para. 1979.

on the other. It was reasoned that the prohibition of retaining or locating military objectives in civilian areas could make military defence measures impossible, and this would amount to an unacceptable breach of the right of self-defence.[10] Article 58 responds to this objection by expressing very pragmatically the duty to take precautions 'to the maximum extent feasible'. The precise meaning of 'feasible' was set down by the German Federal Government in its declaration of interpretation of AP I in the following manner: 'that which is practicable or practically possible, taking into account all circumstances ruling at the time including humanitarian and military considerations'.[11] According to this interpretation, it is also possible in defensive warfare to find an acceptable compromise between military arguments and humanitarian considerations, especially since in this case it is a question of protecting the civilian population of the defending party.

511   **Soldiers may, in principle, be employed for the protection of civilian objects. Since they may be attacked on account of their status, however, their presence is a factor endangering the object to be protected. Therefore, whenever soldiers are employed for the protection of civilian objects, the situation must be assessed by weighing the advantages and disadvantages.**

This rule is clear and does not require detailed commentary, simply a clarifying remark. The presence of members of armed forces on or at a civilian object does not *ipso facto* turn the object into a military objective which may legitimately be attacked. Only the soldiers employed for the protection of the object and the military equipment are lawful targets for a military attack. Such an attack is then subject to the usual obligation to weigh the military advantage aimed at against the expected loss of civilian life or the probable damage to civilian objects (see Section 509). If the anticipated damage is excessive in relation to the desired military success, then the attack must not be carried out; in any case, other methods to achieve the same aim must be found.

512   **Hospital and safety zones and localities shall be established by agreement so as to protect wounded, sick, and aged persons, children, expectant mothers, and mothers of children under seven from any attack (Art. 14 GC IV).**

513   **Military objects shall not be located within or in the vicinity of hospital and safety zones. These zones shall be neither used for military purposes nor defended.**

1. Hospital zones and hospital localities shall be understood as zones and localities intended for the accommodation and care of wounded and sick persons of military or civilian origin. International humanitarian law provides for hospital zones or

---

[10] Noted in Bothe/Partsch/Solf, 373. Austria and Switzerland submitted similarly worded declarations upon ratification, according to which Art. 58 can be applied only subject to the requirements of national defence.

[11] See no. 2 of the German declaration of interpretation (n. 5). Corresponding declarations were submitted (as of 15 Dec. 1992) by Belgium, Canada, Italy, The Netherlands, New Zealand, and Spain, with no objections raised.

Gasser

localities for members of the armed forces (Art. 23 GC I) and for civilians (Art. 14, GC IV; see Sections 629 ff.).

2. Safety zones or safety localities are zones or localities which provide safe accommodation for certain categories of especially vulnerable civilians, above all frail and elderly persons, children under fifteen, expectant mothers, and mothers of children under seven (Art. 14 GC IV; see Section 632).

3. Neutralized zones are specified areas within the combat zone which are set apart from the fighting by mutual agreement of the belligerents, so that wounded and sick combatants as well as civilians not taking part in the hostilities may be brought to safety (Art. 15 GC IV). There are also 'non-defended localities' and 'open cities', which likewise serve to protect the civilian population (Art. 59 AP I; Sections 458 ff.) and demilitarized zones (Art. 60 AP I; Sections 514 and 461 ff.).

4. In order that such zones and localities can fulfil their purpose, they must be secured as fully as possible against the effects of anticipated military operations. Refuges of the kind described are usually required most urgently within or in the vicinity of a zone where fighting is either taking place or likely to occur. On the question of safety, therefore, a difficult compromise must be reached between the need for a protected zone on one hand and the possibilities of the combat area on the other.

5. Only hospital and safety zones and localities serving humanitarian purposes are entitled to the protection of the GCs.

6. Hospital and safety zones or localities may be established in time of peace through agreements between states. After the outbreak of a conflict, they can also be determined by the parties through an agreement. This may mean the establishment of new zones or localities or the recognition of existing zones or localities established unilaterally by a party to the conflict before or during the hostilities. Hospital or safety zones can be set up in a party's own territory or in occupied territory. A draft agreement relating to hospital and safety zones and localities is provided in Annex I to GC IV.

7. In addition to the exact determination of the geographical position of the hospital and safety zones and localities in the agreement, such areas, in particular their boundaries, must be clearly and recognizably marked. Only in this way can their protection be ensured in practice.

8. The following categories of persons may find refuge in hospital zones or localities or in safety zones or localities:

—the wounded and sick of military or civilian origin,
—the frail and aged,
—children under fifteen, and
—expectant mothers and mothers of children under seven.

Gasser

In practice it is not always possible to differentiate between hospital zones or localities and safety zones or localities, for example because wounded persons have been admitted to a safety zone or children to a hospital locality. This is not a problem provided that the persons protected have not been or are no longer involved in hostilities or that, due to weakness, they present no danger to the enemy, in which case they are entitled unconditionally to respect and protection. AP I makes no distinction between the legal status of wounded or sick civilians and that of wounded and sick combatants (Art. 8 lit. a).

9. It is self-evident that no discrimination must be made based on irrelevant criteria when admitting persons seeking protection (for summary, see Art. 9 and Art. 75, para. 1 AP I). Only the need for protection counts.

10. In addition to the listed categories of persons, administrative personnel and persons who provide care are permitted to stay inside the zones. The original inhabitants of the territory where a zone is located or of the locality may also remain there, and they must abide by the rules applicable to the zone or the locality.

11. Hospital and safety zones or localities shall not be attacked. Section 512 lays down that they shall be protected against attacks. This means that measures shall be adopted to provide individual protection for those accommodated, in the sense of police protection of personal security against acts of violence. However, effective defence of the zone or locality with the aim of preventing enemy forces from taking it over is prohibited (Section 513). It must be handed over to the enemy without fighting, if possible in accordance with arrangements to avoid danger to the persons accommodated in the zone or locality. If the zone or locality is defended militarily against the advancing enemy it loses its special protection, although preliminary warning of this must be given. The persons within the zones or localities, however, remain entitled to protection as wounded or sick, or as civilians.

12. Objects which represent a legitimate military objective may not be brought into these zones or localities nor into the vicinity thereof. Particular care shall be taken that the special protection of the place of refuge is not nullified by dangers emanating from possible (lawful) attacks on nearby military objectives (collateral damage). Attackers must bear in mind the presence of a protected zone in the vicinity of a target objective (see Section 510).

13. It is the task of the protecting powers and the ICRC to offer their good offices to the parties to the conflict for the establishment or recognition of hospital and safety zones or localities (Art. 23, para. 3 GC I; Art. 14, para. 3 GC IV). Its extensive right of initiative in humanitarian questions, as laid down in the GCs, empowers the ICRC in particular to make suggestions to the parties to a conflict at any time and provide assistance in creating protective zones or localities (Art. 9 GC I–III; Art. 10 GC IV; see Section 1220).

Gasser

14. The law of non-international armed conflict does not include provisions dealing with protective zones. However, there is nothing to prevent parties to such conflicts from establishing such zones or localities through special agreements. An agreement of this kind would constitute an application of Article 3, para. 3 GC I–IV.

The parties to the conflict may agree to establish demilitarized (neutralized)   514
zones (Art. 15 GC IV; Art. 60 AP I). No military activities shall be carried out in these
zones. Their sole purpose is to provide shelter for wounded, sick, and other per-
sons not involved in the conflict.

1. Demilitarized zones are tracts of land which, according to an express and open-ended arrangement between two states, shall not be drawn into hostilities (Art. 60 AP I). In contrast, other rules apply to agreements concluded during a conflict, concerning hospital and safety zones in regions where fighting is taking place (see Sections 512 ff.) or concerning 'open cities' (see Sections 458–60).

2. The specifically humanitarian justification for demilitarized zones, i.e. the protection of civilians and civilian objects against the effects of hostilities, distinguishes them from similar institutions such as, in particular, regions that have been permanently neutralized or demilitarized by international treaty, e.g. the Antarctic[12] or the Åland Islands.[13]

3. The establishment of a demilitarized zone requires an explicit agreement between two or more states. To avoid misunderstanding, a tacit understanding is not sufficient. An agreement may be concluded either in time of peace or during a conflict. It is self-evident that the location and extent of the zone to be demilitarized must be precisely described. The zone must also be clearly marked, so that its boundaries can be recognized in all circumstances and at all times.

4. A region may be made into a demilitarized zone by agreement if the following conditions are met:

   a) Combatants, mobile weapons, and mobile military equipment must be removed from the zone. Military members of the medical service are not affected.

   b) No hostile use shall be made of fixed military installations or establishments.

   c) No acts of hostility shall be committed by the authorities or the population.

   d) No activities in support of military operations shall be undertaken. This point must be dealt with in detail in the agreement, providing expressly for any exceptions: for example, the further activities of industrial installations which could be used for arms production should be dealt with. Misunderstandings can be avoided through clear agreements.

---

[12] See Art. 1 of the Antarctic Treaty of 1 Dec. 1959.   [13] See Verdross/Simma, 991.

Gasser

5. A demilitarized zone is first and foremost open to the population already living there. In addition, other persons may be granted access, in particular civilian and military wounded and sick persons and civilians in need of special protection (see Sections 512 ff.). The local authorities may usually continue their work. In particular (civilian) police forces shall continue to maintain public order.

6. If enemy armed forces approach, the demilitarized zone must be handed over without resistance. It retains its status after passing to the other party to the conflict, if this was so determined in the agreement or if the occupying power unilaterally so decides. As before, it must not be used for military purposes, otherwise it loses its special status.

7. A breach by one of the parties to the conflict (usually the party controlling the zone) of the regulations applying to a demilitarized zone does not release the other party from its obligation to respect the zone unless it was a material breach (Art. 60, para. 7). It should be emphasized that only a material breach carries with it the extremely serious consequence of loss of immunity for the zone. What constitutes such a material breach must be interpreted through the practical application of this provision. The moving of heavy weapons into the zone on the decision of a higher level of military command would undoubtedly fall into this category, while the presence of a few scattered soldiers, even if armed, would not be regarded as a material breach. As a matter of principle, the removal of protected status must be preceded by a warning.

8. If a zone has lost its special status, military activities may be carried out there in compliance with the limits imposed by applicable international law. Accordingly, for example, the civilian population of the area in question or the displaced persons and refugees located there must be kept out of the hostilities and respected according to the general rules.

9. An attack against a demilitarized zone is a grave breach of AP I if it causes death or serious injury (Art. 85, para. 3(d) AP I).

515 **Journalists engaged in dangerous professional missions in areas of armed conflict are protected as civilians, provided that they take no action adversely affecting their status as civilians (Art. 79 AP I), and without prejudice to the right of war correspondents accredited to the armed forces to the status of persons accompanying the armed forces without being members thereof (Art. 4 lit. a iv, GC III). Journalists may obtain an identity card which attests to their status (Art. 79, para. 3 and Annex II of AP I).**

1. The term 'journalist' encompasses all occupations associated with the media, including reporters, cameramen, sound technicians, and photographers. International humanitarian law differentiates between 'war correspondents' on one hand and 'journalists engaged in dangerous professional missions' on

Gasser

the other. Both categories are treated as civilians by international humanitarian law.

2. **War correspondents** are representatives of the media who, in the case of an armed conflict, are accredited to and accompany the armed forces of a party to the conflict, without being members thereof (Art. 4a(iv), GC III). They accompany armed forces in the area of operations, or work in those locations to which the armed forces permit them to go. The armed forces shall provide them with a special identity card which confirms their status (see Annex IV A to GC III). Whether or not war correspondents are subject to censorship is not a question for international humanitarian law. War correspondents are and remain civilians. They work on their own responsibility or the responsibility of editors or an agency. They must therefore not be confused with persons working in the information services of the armed forces, who are members of the armed forces and have combatant status.

3. War correspondents are permitted to carry out all those activities in the area of operations which normally form part of their occupation, including 'looking around', taking notes, making visual and audio recordings, etc. Such activity is not considered as hostile behaviour permitting military attack against the person. On the other hand, as civilians who are not members of the armed forces, war correspondents must not under any circumstances take part in the hostilities. If they do so, they run the risk of being treated as unlawful combatants (see Section 501). In the area of military operations, war correspondents shall be respected and kept away from the fighting. This is possible, however, only if they are clearly recognizable as civilians, which is hardly the case, for example, for journalists wearing uniform-like clothing. If they happen to be close to an object which could be a military target, or if they accompany members of the armed forces, then they accept the risk of becoming victims of (lawful) side-effects (collateral damage) of an attack on the object or unit in question (see Section 509).

4. War correspondents who are injured or shipwrecked shall be treated in accordance with the provisions of GC I or GC II. If captured, they shall be entitled to the same treatment as a prisoner of war under the provisions of GC III (see Section 319), without however losing civilian status.

5. AP I devotes a special provision to journalists engaged in dangerous professional missions (Art. 79).[14] Originally it was intended that a special convention relating to journalists in war be prepared within the United Nations. When the above-mentioned Article 79 was included in AP I, however, work on the planned UN convention was abandoned, and the General Assembly of the United Nations explicitly stated that it was satisfied with the outcome obtained through AP I.[15]

6. Without creating new law and without changing the legal position of war correspondents (see para. 2 above), Article 79 clearly provides that journalists shall be

[14] See Gasser, *IRRC* 1983, 3–18.   [15] See ICRC *Commentary*, paras. 3250 ff.

Gasser

regarded as normal civilians. A special legal category was deliberately not created. Journalists enjoy the same rights and must abide by the same rules of conduct as all civilians. They may not be made the target of a military attack. They must, however, behave in such a way as to make themselves recognizable as civilians within the area of military operations; only in this way can their immunity as civilians be effective. Naturally, journalists may take no part in hostilities, and the exercise of their professional assignments is expressly not to be considered as hostile activities. In the area of operations they accept the risks associated with military actions against military objectives (collateral damage, see Section 509). If captured, they shall be treated as alien civilians who have fallen into the hands of a party to the conflict (see Sections 582 ff.).

7. Journalists who engage in dangerous professional missions in war zones must receive an identity card confirming their status. This identity card must resemble the model in Annex II of AP I. The authorities of the state in which journalists reside or of which they are nationals or in which the news agency employing them is located are responsible for issuing such an identity card (Art. 79, para. 3).

516 **Civilians may at any time seek help from a protecting power, the International Committee of the Red Cross (ICRC), or any other aid organization (Art. 30, para. 1 GC IV). Representatives of the protecting powers and the ICRC shall be entitled to visit protected persons at any place they like (Art. 143 GC IV).**

1. This provision must be seen in connection with Chapter 12, which gives more detail on the procedures and institutions for supervising the implementation of international humanitarian law. For the status and tasks of the protecting power, see Sections 1215 ff.; for the role of the ICRC see Section 1220. However, in this chapter dealing with the protection of the civilian population, it is useful to consider the institutions of the protecting power, the ICRC, and private relief organizations.

2. Under Article 30 GC IV, the civilian population is entitled to approach these institutions and organizations directly with requests at any time. The authorities concerned are obliged to make possible and facilitate such contacts. Indeed, the protecting power and the ICRC can only carry out their duties if they have direct contact with the population. In this way they obtain unimpeded access to information enabling them to form as true a picture as possible of the effects of breaches of international humanitarian law.

3. Of the relief societies also mentioned in Section 516, the most prominent are national Red Cross and Red Crescent societies.[16] As national societies 'duly recognized and authorized' by their government (Art. 26 GC I), they undertake wartime

[16] In many Islamic states this is a Red Crescent society. Except for the name and emblem, there is no difference between Red Cross and Red Crescent societies. In particular, they have the same tasks and the same status in the Movement.

duties in favour of the victims of hostilities. Those duties are embodied in part in the four GCs and otherwise are rooted in the free initiative of these oldest of all relief societies. The national Red Cross and Red Crescent societies are bound, by the Statutes of the International Red Cross and Red Crescent Movement, to carry out their activities on the basis of the seven fundamental principles of the movement, among which the principles of humanity, neutrality and impartiality should be specially noted in this context. The ICRC recognizes a national Red Cross or Red Crescent society if it fulfils the conditions laid down in the Statutes. The ICRC is charged with verifying that the principles are observed by the components of the Movement, while respecting the independence of individual national societies.[17]

4. The tasks of the Red Cross and Red Crescent societies are laid down in numerous provisions of the GCs.[18] In summary, Article 81, para. 2 AP I requires the parties to a conflict to grant to national Red Cross and Red Crescent societies facilities that they need for their humanitarian activities. These facilities undoubtedly include the ability of inhabitants to approach the societies freely and without hindrance. For the rights of national Red Cross and Red Crescent societies in occupied territories, see Section 571 and Article 63 GC IV. In addition to the Red Cross and Red Crescent societies, other relief organizations may work for the benefit of the population.

5. The population not only has the right to turn to the institutions named but must be granted facilities and freedom of movement by the authorities in order to exercise this right. Only military reasons or security requirements can justify temporary limitation of this right (Art. 30, para. 2 and Art. 63, para. 1 GC IV). It is self-evident that no disadvantage to a person may result from having approached one of the named institutions with a request for help or for any other reason.

6. GC IV contains a number of provisions making it obligatory for a party to a conflict to transmit to the protecting power, or in its absence to the ICRC, certain information concerning measures with respect to persons belonging to the other side. This is especially the case with respect to restrictions on personal freedom by court order or administrative decision (see Sections 577, 587, and 591). The ICRC has a Central Tracing Agency which processes and stores information and which permanently carries out the tasks set out in Article 140 for the Central Information Agency.

7. Representatives of the protecting power and delegates of the ICRC are entitled to go to all places where protected persons may be living, including places of detention and internment (Art. 143 GC IV). These visits serve to clarify whether and to what extent the rules of international humanitarian law are being observed. In this regard, see Sections 580, 592, 1215, and 1220.

---

[17] Statutes of the International Red Cross and Red Crescent Movement (1986), particularly Articles 3, 4, and 5, reprinted in *IRRC* (1987) 25–44. See Haug, esp. ch. 2, for a general introduction.

[18] See the comprehensive description in the *Guide for National Red Cross and Red Crescent Societies to Activities in the Event of Conflict*, published by the ICRC (1990).

Gasser

8. The law of non-international conflicts contains no corresponding provision. According to common Article 3 of the GCs, an impartial humanitarian organization, such as the ICRC, may offer its services to the parties to the conflict. If a party accepts this offer, this implies the entitlement to approach all the persons affected by the conflict. Conversely, the latter may freely turn to the delegates of the ICRC and no disadvantage shall accrue to them as a result thereof. If this were not possible, the ICRC would be unable to carry out its mandate and its delegates would withdraw.

517 **Persons taking a direct part in hostilities are not entitled to claim the rights accorded to civilians by international humanitarian law (Art. 51, para. 3 AP I; Art. 13, para. 3 AP II). The same applies if they are reasonably suspected of activities hostile to the security of the state (Art. 5, para. 1 GC IV).**

518 **The civilians concerned shall be treated humanely. They shall have the right to a regular and fair judicial procedure (Art. 5, para. 3 GC IV; Art. 75 AP I).**

1. Since only members of the armed forces have the right to participate in hostilities, civilians are prohibited from doing so (see Sections 301 ff., especially Section 302; also Section 501). Section 517 deals with the consequences in international law if civilians take part in hostilities.

2. In Article 51, para. 3 AP I for international armed conflicts, and in Article 13, para. 3 AP II for non-international armed conflicts, it is stipulated in identical terms that civilians are entitled to immunity 'unless and for such time as they take a direct part in hostilities'. Two questions should be dealt with in this connection: what constitutes taking a direct part in hostilities, and what are the consequences for civilians contravening this provision?[19]

a) Civilians who directly carry out a hostile act against the adversary may be resisted by force. A civilian who kills or takes prisoners, destroys military equipment, or gathers information in the area of operations may be made the object of attack. The same applies to civilians who operate a weapons system, supervise such operation, or service such equipment. The transmission of information concerning targets directly intended for the use of a weapon is also considered as taking part in hostilities. Furthermore, the logistics of military operations are among the activities prohibited to civilians.

b) It follows from the above that not only direct and personal involvement but also preparation for a military operation and intention to take part therein may suspend the immunity of a civilian. All these activities, however, must be proved to be directly related to hostilities or, in other words, to represent a direct threat to the enemy.

3. However, the term should not be understood too broadly. Not every activity carried out within a state at war is a hostile act. Employment in the armaments

---

[19] See esp. Solf, in Bothe/Partsch/Solf, 303–4.

industry for example, does not mean, that civilian workers are necessarily participating in hostilities (see Section 313). Since, on the other hand, factories of this
industry usually constitute lawful military objectives that may be attacked, the normal rules governing the assessment of possible collateral damage to civilians must
be observed (see Sections 509 ff.).

4. While civilians take a direct part in hostilities they may be resisted by all lawful
means of warfare for combating enemy armed forces. Once the civilians are *hors de
combat* they must once again be treated according to the rules applying to civilians,
since they have not lost their civilian status. They may be taken prisoner and subjected to criminal proceedings. Depending on the circumstances, either the provisions dealing with foreigners on the territory of a party to a conflict (Sections 582 ff.)
or the law of belligerent occupation (Sections 525 ff.) apply.

5. Civilians who have taken part in hostilities and are taken prisoner are, in particular, not entitled to prisoner of war status. The detaining power, however, may
decide to treat civilians who fought like 'real' combatants and in accordance with
the law of war as prisoners of war, applying the provisions of GC III accordingly.
Experience from several conflicts, especially civil wars with foreign intervention,
has shown that such a measure can be justified not only from the humanitarian
standpoint but also from the viewpoint of military considerations.

6. The situation described in the second sentence of Section 517 must be treated as
a special case. A foreigner detained in the territory of a party to a conflict who is reasonably suspected of being engaged in activities hostile to the security of the state
may not be entitled to claim all the rights granted under GC IV (Art. 5, para. 1 GC IV).
Although GC IV does not further specify, it can be assumed that this refers primarily to acts of espionage or sabotage.

7. If the above-mentioned conditions are fulfilled, then the detaining power is temporarily released from the obligation to respect the rights of GC IV in relation to this
person, although only to the extent that these rights 'would, if exercised in the
favour of such individual person, be prejudicial to the security of such State' (Art. 5,
para. 1 GC IV). This means only the right to have contact with the outside world.[20]
In contrast, the fundamental guarantees of international humanitarian law, as they
apply especially to detained persons, may never be questioned. To respect these
rights is in no circumstances 'prejudicial to the security of such State'. In close
alliance with international law on human rights,[21] Article 75 AP I has codified the
fundamental guarantees making up the minimum standard to which everyone,
without exception, is entitled. Even spies and saboteurs fall into this 'humanitarian
safety net'. The detaining power is bound to report the identity of captured civilians
to their state of origin no later than two weeks after their capture (Art. 136, para.
2, GC IV). The same applies for persons detained according to Art. 5 GC IV. The

---

[20] See Pictet, *Commentary*, Vol. IV, 56.
[21] In particular, Arts. 10 and 14 of the International Covenant on Civil and Political Rights of 19 Dec. 1966.

restrictions must be lifted as soon as the reason for their implementation ceases to exist, i.e. as soon as incommunicado detention is no longer justified by security considerations (Art. 5, para. 3, 2nd sentence).

II. CIVIL DEFENCE

Introductory Remarks

1. The purpose of civil defence is to protect the civilian population as far as possible from the effects of hostilities and to help it to survive during the war despite death, injuries, and destruction. As with medical facilities and personnel, the function of civil defence is to protect and to assist, exclusively the civilian population. Civil defence is not part of a country's war effort; civil defence organizations belong to the civilian sphere, even if military units are assigned to support them. This is the meaning of 'civil defence' as codified by AP I and recognized by international law.[22] The Federal Republic of Germany has also established its civil defence organization as a civilian institution.[23]

2. During negotiation of the new provisions, difficult questions had to be answered since numerous countries had already found different solutions for the organized protection of their civilian populations in the event of war. They differed, for example, as to whether and to what extent such an organization should also have defence responsibilities. The English expression 'civil defence' expresses a different concept from the German *Zivilschutz* which, literally, means 'civil protection'.

3. The solution chosen in 1977 is based on the concept of non-military protection of the civilian population. The organizations undertaking civil defence functions are civilian organizations. This does not mean that members of the armed forces or even entire military units cannot be assigned to a civil defence organization if the need arises (Art. 67).

4. On the other hand, it is quite possible for military units to bring aid to the civilian population, in coordination with the civil defence organization, while retaining their status as a part of the country's armed forces, i.e. being permitted to engage in military operations. Civil defence units, in contrast, may under no circumstances perform military duties.

---

[22] See, however, Art. 63, para. 2 GC IV (occupied territories).

[23] See Section 522 and generally the German Red Cross Manual: *Handbuch des Deutschen Roten Kreuzes zum IV. Genfer Rotkreuz-Abkommen und zu den Zusatzprotokollen: Zivilschutz* (1981).

Gasser

5. Each state is at liberty to decide whether and how it will guarantee the protection of the civilian population by a civil defence organization. AP I simply lays down the conditions under which a civil defence organization is entitled to the protection by international law and to privileged status. Similarly, it is for the state to determine whether it wishes to use its civil defence organization in disasters and emergencies other than those arising in armed conflict, for example in natural disasters. Such activities are not covered by international humanitarian law.

Civil defence organizations are protected in like manner as the medical service   519
(Arts. 61–67 AP I).

1. Like medical services, civil defence organizations and their personnel and equipment must not be involved in hostilities. They may not be attacked. Personnel and equipment must be kept safe so that civil defence is able to step in and carry out its duties when military operations have brought death, destruction, and despair to the civilian population. This rule prohibiting interference with the activities of the civil defence organization of the opposing side is an imperative duty of all parties to a conflict. Article 62, para. 1, 2nd sentence does, however, permit restriction of their tasks 'in case of imperative military necessity'. This exception must be interpreted restrictively and in any case may endure only for a limited period.

2. Civil defence personnel must not take part in hostilities, nor shall hostile acts be carried out under the protection of a civil defence organization. Here again, civil defence organizations and medical units are dealt with in the same way.

Civil defence tasks are particularly warning, rescue and maintenance, fire protec-   520
tion, medical service, NBC defence, construction of shelters, and other measures
to restore and maintain order (Art. 61 AP I).

1. The possible tasks of a civil defence organization are listed in Art. 61 (a) AP I. They are exclusively humanitarian tasks 'intended to protect the civilian population against the dangers, and to help it to recover from the immediate effects, of hostilities or disasters and also to provide the conditions necessary for its survival'. A civil defence organization may, according to this Article, carry out all or some of the following tasks:
'(i) warning;
(ii) evacuation;
(iii) management of shelters;
(iv) management of black-out measures;
(v) rescue;
(vi) medical services including first aid, and religious assistance;
(vii) fire-fighting;
(viii) detection and marking of danger areas;
(ix) decontamination and similar protective measures;
(x) provision of emergency accommodation and supplies;

Gasser

(xi) emergency assistance in the restoration and maintenance of order in distressed areas;

(xii) emergency repair of indispensable public utilities;

(xiii) emergency disposal of the dead;

(xiv) assistance in the preservation of objects essential for survival;

(xv) complementary activities necessary to carry out any of the tasks mentioned above, including, but not limited to, planning and organization'.

2. All these tasks are to be understood as being permitted exclusively for the protection of the civilian population and fulfilling a humanitarian purpose. Task (viii), 'detection and marking of danger areas', for example, may not be abused in order to seek information that can be used for military purposes, but must be performed solely to prevent the civilian population from entering dangerous areas (e.g. mined zones) and sustaining harm.

3. It may be asked whether the list in Art. 61(a) is an exhaustive description of the tasks of civil defence in wartime, or whether other tasks could be added, e.g. measures to protect the environment. The history of this provision in fact indicates that the list is final.[24] On the other hand, it seems reasonable to interpret the provision as meaning that a task not expressly included may also be allocated to civil defence, as long as it directly serves the well-being of the civilian population in a disaster situation caused by war. Measures to limit environmental disasters resulting from a war could, for example, be included, since it is almost inevitable that such disasters would cause loss or damage to the civilian population.

521 **Civil defence organizations, their personnel, buildings, and vehicles as well as shelters provided for the civilian population shall be especially respected and protected (Arts. 62–4 and 52, AP I).**

> *Example*: In the Federal Republic of Germany, the German Red Cross (*Deutsches Rotes Kreuz*), the St. John Rescue Service (*Johanniter-Unfallhilfe*), the Hospitaller Emergency Service (*Malteser-Hilfsdienst*), the Workers Samaritan Association (*Arbeiter-Samariterbund*), the Technical Relief Organization (*Technisches Hilfswerk*), the German Life-Guard Society (*Deutsche Lebensrettungsgesellschaft*), and the fire services have been recognized as relief societies.

1. Civil defence organizations are establishments and other units organized or authorized to perform the tasks enumerated in Section 520 'which are assigned and devoted exclusively to such tasks' (Art. 61(b)). Therefore there may be more than one organization. Private institutions, performing perhaps only some of the possible tasks of civil defence, may be employed in addition to a state-run service, provided that they are devoted exclusively to civil defence work. This does not mean that such institutions may not occasionally serve other purposes. However, while

---

[24] See Bothe, in Bothe/Partsch/Solf, 394–5.

they are employed in connection with civil defence they may only carry out civil defence duties.

2. Private organizations wishing to undertake civil defence duties must be authorized by the appropriate national authorities, in order to avoid abuse of the—protected—status of civil defence organizations by such private institutions.

3. The personnel of civil defence organizations must be respected and protected, and enabled to perform their tasks without hindrance (Art. 62). The personnel comprise all those persons who, as a part of such an institution, perform civil defence work, including administrative activities and not only permanent staff but also persons actually carrying out civil defence work under the supervision of such a recognized organization. Article 62, para. 2 also provides for the protection of all those who respond to an appeal from the competent authorities and perform civil defence work under their control.

4. Medical personnel working in civil defence have special status: they are protected as members of civilian medical services. They must be respected and protected and may not be hindered from carrying out their tasks (see Section 620). Their integration in a civil defence organization does not change this. Medical personnel may make themselves recognizable by means of the Red Cross (or Red Crescent) emblem or with the distinctive sign of civil defence (see Section 524), or both.

5. Civil defence organizations may employ, for medical duties, persons who either additionally or primarily also perform other tasks, which Article 8(c) AP I prohibits for medical personnel. This may for instance include persons trained in first aid. These persons may wear the distinctive sign of civil defence but not the red cross emblem.

6. Members of the armed forces permanently assigned to a civil defence organization in order to perform civil defence work occupy a position different from that of civilian personnel (Article 67). Such military personnel must be employed exclusively for civil defence and in particular may not have a combat task. Although they retain their position as members of the armed forces, they must be respected and protected. If they should fall into the power of the adversary they must be treated as prisoners of war.

7. It is self-evident that civil defence organizations require equipment, vehicles, buildings, etc. in order to carry out their tasks. These objects shall be respected and protected. They may not be diverted from their proper use (Art. 62, para. 3).

8. Of particular interest is the legal status of shelters provided for the civilian population. To the extent that such a structure serves solely to accommodate civilians, it is considered to be a civilian object within the meaning of Article 52 AP I. Attacks

Gasser

against civilian objects are prohibited (see Sections 451 ff.). This holds true whether the shelter formally belongs to a civil defence organization or not. If it does, then the actual protection can be increased by marking it with the distinctive sign of civil defence (Section 524). The integration of shelters into the sphere of responsibility of civil defence augments the degree of protection.

9. With the consent of the relevant party to the conflict, civil defence organizations of neutral or other states not parties to the conflict may be employed on its territory (Art. 64). They are subject to the same provisions and enjoy the same protection as the national organization. It should be noted that such assistance by a State not involved in the conflict shall not be considered as interference in the conflict.

10. The relevant party to the conflict must, when appropriate, facilitate the international coordination of civil defence measures through the relevant international organization (Art. 64, para. 2), namely the International Civil Defence Organization (ICDO), an intergovernmental organization for civil defence matters.

522 **The protection accorded to civilian civil defence organizations under international law shall cease if, in spite of a warning, such an organization continues to commit acts harmful to the enemy (Art. 65, para. 1 AP I). Co-operation with military authorities and the employment of some members of the armed forces shall not be considered as acts harmful to the enemy. The performance of civil defence tasks may benefit military victims (Art. 65, para. 2 lit. c AP I). Civilian civil defence organizations may be formed along military lines (Art. 65, para. 4 AP I). Their personnel may be enlisted for compulsory service (Art. 65, para. 4 AP I) and bear individual weapons for the purpose of maintaining internal order and for self-defence (Art. 65, para. 3 AP I).**

Example: In the Federal Republic of Germany, civil defence organizations are exclusively formed along civilian lines. The Federal Civil Defence Agency (*Bundesamt für Zivilschutz*) co-operates with the competent Federal and Land authorities and with relief societies. The personnel required may be enlisted for compulsory service under the Act on the Extension of Protection in Case of Disasters (*Gesetz über die Erweiterung des Katastrophenschutzes*) and the Labour Requisitioning Law (*Arbeitssicherstellungsgesetz*). The personnel of these organisations are not armed.

1. Under the heading 'Cessation of protection', Art. 65 AP I lays down the following principle: the special protection of civil defence ends only if acts harmful to the enemy are committed and if a warning setting a reasonable time-limit has remained unheeded. This applies to the organizations as such and also to their personnel, buildings, vehicles, and equipment. The statement of principle is followed by a description of acts not to be considered 'harmful to the enemy'. These are given in the text of Section 522 and require no further detailed comment, merely the

observation that civil defence personnel are permitted to carry light personal hand-guns (Art. 65, para. 3). Such weapons may be used only to maintain order and in self defence against violent attacks. This rule is modelled on the provisions governing medical personnel (see Section 627).

2. The significance of cessation of the legal protection of civil defence requires clar-ification. It is true that civil defence organizations on one hand and personnel and equipment on the other can no longer claim the protection of Articles 61 to 67 AP I. Since members of civil defence are necessarily civilians, however, they remain enti-tled to the general protection owed to all civilians (see Sections 502 ff.). Only if such persons take a direct part in hostilities do they lose the protection afforded to civil-ians (Art. 51, para. 3). The same holds true, *mutatis mutandis*, for their equipment, which is considered in principle to be a (protected) civilian object (Art. 52).

Civilian civil defence organizations may be permitted to continue their humani-tarian activities even in occupied territories (Art. 63 GC IV; Art. 63 AP I).   523

1. Article 63, para. 2 GC IV empowers relief societies to continue their activities in occupied territories. Article 63 AP I has enhanced the status of civil defence in occu-pied territories and increased its protection. Article 63, para. 2 GC IV remains in force as an independent rule.

2. Article 63 is to be understood in the context of Chapter VI of AP I (Arts. 61–7), on civil defence. The status, duties, entitlement to protection, and cessation of this protection for civil defence in occupied territories are determined by the general provisions of this chapter (see Sections 519–22). It is emphasized that the occupy-ing power must not only allow civil defence organizations of occupied territories to continue their work, but must also guarantee them 'the facilities necessary for the performance of their tasks' (Art. 63, para. 1). For this reason, the occupying power may not, for example, requisition buildings or equipment belonging to civil defence, unless and for so long as they are needed to meet other requirements of the population of the occupied territory.

3. As already noted, military personnel serving with civil defence become prisoners of war when captured. They may be employed for civil defence tasks in the occu-pied territories by the occupying power (Art. 67, para. 2 AP I).

4. The occupying power must allow civil defence organizations of neutral or other states not parties to the conflict to perform civil defence duties in occupied territo-ries, unless it can adequately carry out such work with its own resources (Art. 64, para. 3 AP I). The use in occupied territories of civil defence organizations from states not involved in the conflict always requires the consent of the occupying power.

The international distinctive sign of civil defence is an equilateral blue triangle on an orange ground (Art. 66, para. 4 AP I). It is shown in Appendix 1, No. 6. Civil   524 defence personnel shall be recognizable by this distinctive sign and by an identity card (Art. 66, para. 3 AP I). Aid organizations may also use their own traditional signs.

1. AP I establishes the equilateral blue triangle on an orange ground as the distinctive sign of civil defence (see Appendix 1, No. 6; Art. 66, and Art. 14 Annex I AP I). A special identity card for civil defence personnel was also introduced. The distinctive sign serves to make civil defence organizations as such, their personnel, buildings, vehicles, and other equipment recognizable. Shelters for the civilian population which are not under the control of a civil defence organization may also be marked with this sign. For the distinctive sign to serve its purpose, it must be sufficiently large to be recognizable from a distance.

2. The provisions relating to the civil defence sign have been modelled on the rules applicable to the distinctive sign of medical personnel and medical units and transports (see Sections 633 ff.). These may be consulted for guidance concerning display.

3. Abuse of the civil defence sign is forbidden and should be punished by the relevant parties to the conflict. Perfidious use of the sign is a grave breach of AP I (in other words, a war crime) when committed wilfully and causing death or serious injury (Art. 85, para. 3(f), AP I; see Section 1209).

4. The marking of all establishments, personnel, and equipment serving civil defence purposes is intended to enable the civilian population to survive during a war. The blue triangle on an orange ground alone can fulfil this task only to a very limited extent. What is decisive is that the civil defence establishments are kept as far as possible out of the firing line. In particular, shelters for the civilian population must be constructed in such a way that they have the greatest possible chance of being spared in the event of war. Effective civil defence helps to create the conditions necessary for international humanitarian law to be observed and for the civilian population to be respected and protected.

III. BELLIGERENT OCCUPATION

Introductory Remarks

1. The international law of belligerent occupation lays down the rights and obligations of the belligerent power in occupation of foreign territory. The law of belligerent occupation has undergone major development over the past two centuries: while the population of such territories originally had virtually no rights at all, their status and rights have now been greatly improved and are securely anchored in international law. The first codification of international rules relating to belligerent

Gasser

occupation can be found in the HagueReg, which themselves were built on custom-ary international law. As the Military Tribunal of Nuremberg laid down in its judg-ment, the contents of the HagueReg were already considered to be customary law during the Second World War.[25] This also covers the provisions relating to occupied territories. Many lessons drawn from the crimes committed in the occupied territo-ries of Europe and the Far East found their expression in GC IV, which codifies a major part of modern international law applicable to belligerent occupation.

2. The reformulation of the international law of belligerent occupation by GC IV has been accompanied by a strong upswing in the law on human rights. The treat-ment of the population of an occupied territory is thus in practice (e.g. by UN reso-lutions) increasingly measured against the standard of human rights. However, the provisions of GC IV and the relevant rules of customary law take precedence, as law specifically regulating belligerent occupation. It may be determined in each indi-vidual case whether a human rights rule offers greater protection to the inhabitants of an occupied territory.

3. The sources of the law of belligerent occupation are Articles 42–56 HagueReg; GC IV, especially Articles 27–34 and 47–78; and also general principles of interna-tional and customary law. Although Article 154 GC IV states that the new law of 1949 simply complements the HagueReg, Articles 27 ff. and 47 ff. GC IV are now seen to be a codification of the rights and duties of the occupying power.[26] The HagueReg, however, continue to be effective as international treaty law among the parties to HC IV, and, as pointed out in para. 1 above, in the form of customary law.

4. The law of belligerent occupation regulates the relationship between the occu-pying power on one hand and the—wholly or partially—occupied state or the inhabitants of the occupied territory (including refugees and stateless persons)[27] on the other. Not included in the category of protected persons are: nationals of the occupying power (excluding refugees), nationals of states not bound by GC IV, and nationals of a neutral state or a co-belligerent state, to the extent that their interests can be protected by diplomatic representatives accredited by the occupying power.

5. For foreigners not covered by international humanitarian law, the normal law applicable to foreigners within the power of another state remains valid. The state may, if necessary, take steps to protect its nationals. Under the heading 'General protection of populations against certain consequences of war', GC IV contains a number of provisions relating to the protection of all inhabitants (Arts. 13–26). They apply, in particular, also to foreigners who are not nationals of the occupied state and are present in the occupied territory. Finally, Article 75 AP I makes it obligatory for the occupying power to maintain a certain minimum standard of human rights which must be respected under all circumstances, i.e. also with respect to those

---

[25] Trial of the Major War Criminals before the International Military Tribunal, Nuremberg, Vol. XXII, 497.
[26] For a comparison of the provisions of GC IV and HagueReg see Pictet, *Commentary*, Vol. IV, 614 ff.
[27] See Art. 73 AP I.

categories of persons not covered by the protection of GC IV. Thus all persons are entitled to humane treatment and may be restricted in their freedom only by the decision of a court after a regular judicial procedure.

6. The law of belligerent occupation is applicable only in international armed conflicts. In a non-international conflict, the conquest by the government forces of territory held by the rebels does not constitute 'occupation' but the reestablishment of control which had been lost by government. Such forces are bound by the domestic legal order, if necessary taking into consideration international obligations, especially those concerning human rights. The rebels, on the other hand, must always abide by the provisions of common Article 3 of the GCs and AP II.

7. Belligerent occupation is a form of foreign domination. Its effects on the population are mitigated by the provisions of international law on belligerent occupation. Hence GC IV appears as a bill of rights with a catalogue of fundamental rights which, immediately upon occupation and without any further actions on the part of those affected, becomes applicable to the occupied territories and limits the authority of the occupying power.

1. General Provisions

525 **The occupying power shall assume responsibility for the occupied territory and its inhabitants (Arts. 29 and 47 ff. GC IV; Art. 43 HagueReg).**

1. The first step towards an understanding of the international legal consequences of the occupation of foreign territory is to recognize the general ban on acquiring foreign territory by force, derived from the prohibition of the use of force in the UN Charter.[28] The annexation of conquered territory is prohibited by international law. This necessarily means that if one state achieves power over parts of another state's territory by force or threat of force, the situation must be considered temporary by international law. The international law of belligerent occupation must therefore be understood as meaning that the occupying power is not sovereign, but exercises provisional and temporary control over foreign territory. The legal situation of the territory can be altered only through a peace treaty or *debellatio*. International law does not permit annexation of territory of another state. It follows from this that all measures taken by the occupying authorities should affect only the administration of the territory, avoiding far-reaching changes to the existing order. In this sense, the occupying power assumes 'responsibility for the occupied territory and its inhabitants'.

---

[28] See Declaration on Principles of International Law concerning Friendly Relations and Co-operation among States in accordance with the Charter of the United Nations, Resolution of the UN General Assembly No. 2625 (XXV) of 24 Oct. 1970.

2. Specific definitions of the rights and duties of the occupying power are given in detail in the following provisions.

Territory shall be considered occupied if it has actually come under the authority of hostile armed forces (Art. 42 HagueReg). The occupying power must be able to exercise its authority.   526

A force invading hostile territory will not be able to substantiate its occupational authority unless it is capable of enforcing directions issued to the civilian population.   527

1. These two provisions repeat the essential contents of Article 42 HagueReg, which is quoted here in its entirety because of its great significance. '(1) Territory is considered occupied when it is actually placed under the authority of the hostile army. (2) The occupation extends only to the territory where such authority has been established and can be exercised.' The question is whether in fact the armed forces that have invaded the adversary's territory have brought the area under their control through their physical presence, to the extent that they can actually assume the responsibilities which attach to an occupying power. This includes the ability to issue directives to the inhabitants of the conquered territory and to enforce them.

2. The British Manual suggests the following criteria for assessing a given situation: (1) due to the invasion of foreign armed forces, the national authorities are no longer in a position to enforce their authority in the territory concerned; (2) the invading forces, by contrast, are in a position to exercise control and to enforce their own authority.[29] This dual test should suffice in practice. If necessary, these criteria may be supplemented for special situations, e.g. for thinly-populated areas such as deserts. Supremacy in the air alone does not fulfil the requirements of actual occupation.

3. The law of occupation applies only to those parts of a foreign territory actually controlled by the occupying power and not to parts not occupied. The ability to exercise control over occupied territory is a prerequisite for the applicability of the international law of occupation, if only because total occupation may involve the international responsibility of the occupying power for the occupied territory.

4. It necessarily follows as a corollary of the rule described that any actual control by one state over the territory of another state brings with it the duty to respect the law of belligerent occupation. In other words, if the armed forces of a state actually become engaged in controlling foreign territory, then that state cannot evade its duties towards this territory and its inhabitants. The reason for the invasion of the foreign territory is irrelevant. Even if the stated strategic goal of an invasion of foreign territory is not to gain control of the area or its inhabitants, but 'merely' to secure against attacks on the invader's own territory close to the border, the

[29] Para. 503.

Gasser

invading power still bears responsibility for the parts of the territory actually controlled. Similarly, neither the (claimed) short duration of the occupation nor the absence of military administration for the occupied territory makes any difference.[30]

5. The occupation of part of the Kingdom of Jordan to the west of the River Jordan (the West Bank) and of the Gaza Strip by Israel in 1967 raised an interesting question concerning the applicability of the law of belligerent occupation. Having initially left unanswered the question of the applicability of GC IV to these territories, the Israeli government later took the view that this treaty was not applicable, since, *inter alia*, the international status of Western Jordan and Gaza was not clear. In any case, neither Jordan nor Egypt could claim territorial sovereignty, and thus Israel could not be seen as an occupant.[31] This reasoning is not acceptable since denying the existence of conditions for application of GC IV it relies upon a possible controversy regarding the legal status of that territory. The purpose of the law of belligerent occupation is to ensure protection for persons and objects no longer under the control of their own authorities but of a foreign power, as a result of war. There is no doubt that, from the viewpoint of the inhabitants of Western Jordan and the Gaza Strip, Israel is a foreign power. Furthermore, GC IV regulates only humanitarian issues resulting from the fact of occupation for the inhabitants of occupied territories. The legal fate of the territories is a question which must be kept distinct from the humanitarian purpose of Geneva Law. However, the Israeli authorities stated their determination to apply the humanitarian provisions of GC IV on a *de facto* basis.[32]

528 **Occupied territory does not include battle areas, i.e. areas which are still embattled and not subject to permanent occupational authority (area of invasion, withdrawal area). The general rules of international humanitarian law shall be applicable here.**

1. The law of occupation is not applicable until the armed forces invading a foreign country have established actual control over a certain territory (after invasion), and ceases to apply when they no longer have such control (after withdrawal). The rules are intended to apply in stable situations (see Section 527). This does not , however, create a legally unprotected period; all other provisions of international humanitarian law apply to the armed forces, especially those dealing with the conduct of military operations. In particular, this has the following consequences.

---

[30] The position of the Israel High Court of Justice, according to which the international law of occupation is not applicable to the presence of Israeli armed forces in Lebanon (in 1982 and later), can therefore not be agreed with. Decision reprinted in *IYHR* 13 (1983), 360 ff., 363.—The reason for dealing, in this and other notes to Section III, exclusively with legal problems associated with Israel's occupation of parts of neighbouring states is simply because the practice of the Israeli High Court of Justice has contributed greatly to clarification of the law relating to belligerent occupation.

[31] For the position of the Israeli government, see the standard work: Shamgar, *IYHR* 1 (1971), 262 ff. Shamgar was Israel's Attorney General and later a judge of the Israeli Supreme Court.

[32] Shamgar, ibid., 266.

Gasser

2. The armed forces shall under all circumstances observe the provisions relating to methods and means of warfare (see Sections 401 ff., 501–18). Accordingly, for example, attacks against civilians and civilian objects are always prohibited.

3. Under the heading 'General protection of populations against certain consequences of war', Part II of GC IV (Arts. 13–26) lays down a number of provisions that also apply in the situation described above. They cover:

—the establishment of hospital and safety zones (Art. 14) and neutralized zones (Art. 15);

—the protection of the wounded and sick, the infirm, and pregnant women (Art. 16);

—the conclusion of agreements for the evacuation of especially vulnerable categories of persons (Art. 17);

—the protection of civilian hospitals (Art. 18);

—the protection of medical personnel (Art. 20);

—the protection of transport of sick and wounded civilians and other especially vulnerable categories of persons on land, on sea, or by air (Arts. 21 and 22);

—allowing the free passage of aid consignments (Art. 23), especially the delivery of medical and hospital stores for the civilian population and essential foodstuffs for especially vulnerable categories of persons;

—the special protection of children (Art. 24);

—permission to exchange family news (Art. 25); and

—facilitation of enquiries relating to missing family members (Art. 26).

In occupied territory the sovereignty of the occupied state will be suspended. It shall be superseded by the factual authority of the occupying power.   **529**

Sovereignty—or the totality of sovereign rights—is suspended during belligerent occupation. Duties not related to physical control over the occupied territory may, if applicable, still be carried out by a government in exile or by authorities responsible for the unoccupied part of the state. For an understanding of the term 'factual authority', see Section 527.

The occupying power is not successor in right of the temporarily suspended national authority. It is prohibited from transferring its own sovereignty rights onto the occupied territory.   **530**

1. This provision is derived from the principle that the appropriation by force of foreign territory is prohibited and cannot result in a transfer of sovereignty to the conqueror (see Section 525). Annexation of foreign territory by the occupying power does not confer sovereign rights over the occupied territory. Under all circumstances the occupying power enjoys only the rights granted by international

Gasser

law relating to belligerent occupation. Through its acts, the occupying power in principle assumes obligations only for itself, not for the state whose territory it occupies, whether wholly or in part.

2. The international law on belligerent occupation imposes on the occupying power a duty, among others, to change the occupied territory as little as possible. Therefore it must not impose its own constitutional rules on the occupied territory. In this connection, mention should be made of Article 49, para. 6 GC IV, which provides that the occupying power 'shall not deport or transfer parts of its own civilian population into the territory it occupies'. Not only the legal institutions of the state but also the sociological structure of the population of an occupied territory shall be left as unchanged as possible. Article 49, para. 6 prohibits in particular the settlement of nationals of the occupying power in the occupied territory.[33]

3. The fact that the occupying power does not take over the rights and duties of the suspended national authority is made manifest, for example, in the fact that it is merely administrator and beneficiary of the public buildings and the remaining property of the state (Art. 55, HagueReg; see Section 556, para. 4).

531 **The occupying power is obliged to restore and maintain, as far as possible, public order and safety (Art. 43 HagueReg); it should declare a prospective date for the termination of occupation.**

1. Not only should the legal status of the territory remain unaltered by the occupying power, but its political institutions and public life in general should also be allowed to continue with as little disturbance as possible. The provisional and temporary character of the occupation naturally does not mean that the occupying authorities need not make arrangements to secure public order and safety. For further details see Section 532 (also Section 549).

2. Should belligerent occupation persist, certain measures which have a permanent effect on matters internal to the territory may prove necessary. The wellbeing of the inhabitants of an occupied territory must be the guiding principle. Examples are the introduction of new taxation (see Section 552) or the construction of a road, with requisitioning of property.[34]

532 **Civilians are entitled to respect for their persons, their honour, family rights, religious convictions, and manners and customs. Their private property is protected (Art. 27, para. 1 GC IV; Arts. 48 ff. and 75 AP I; Art. 46 HagueReg).**

---

[33] The settlement of civilians in the territories occupied by Israel therefore contravenes Article 49, para. 6. However, in its decision, reprinted in *IYHR* 9 (1979), 337 ff. (*Beth El* case), the Israeli High Court of Justice justifies the establishment of civilian settlements on the ground that they serve the military security of the occupying power.

[34] See the decision of the Israeli High Court of Justice dealing with the construction of a road in the West Bank, *IYHR* 14 (1984), 301 ff. On the question of longterm occupation in general, see Roberts, *AJIL* 84 (1990), 44 ff.

1. The protection to which the inhabitants of an occupied territory are entitled is laid down in general terms in Article 27 GC IV. This is a typical example of a rule with human rights content which has a central position in international humanitarian law. It must therefore be interpreted in the light of provisions for the protection of human rights. In addition to Article 27, numerous regulations in GC IV deal with individual aspects of the protection of the human person.

2. The general rule of humane treatment stated above is intended to guarantee for the inhabitants of occupied territory the enjoyment of individual human rights to which all persons are entitled. These fundamental rights include in particular the entitlement to respect for the person, also for honour, religious or other convictions, etc. The occupying power must respect these rights under all circumstances and without exception, although only to the extent permitted by the special conditions of belligerent occupation. Over and above individual rights, the occupying power must also respect and leave unchanged the social context in which the inhabitants of the occupied territories live. This results from the rule that manners and customs must be respected.

3. Under special circumstances, injury to physical or mental health may amount to a grave breach of GC IV, punishable as a war crime (Art. 147).

4. GC IV does not provide a universal guarantee of property rights. However, the provisions of the HagueReg dealing with occupied territories give extensive protection to private property. According to Article 46, para. 2 HagueReg: 'private property cannot be confiscated.' The protection of property in the event of occupation is thus now anchored in international customary law (see introductory remarks to Section III: Belligerent Occupation). Thus the permanent confiscation or requisition of private property by the occupying power during belligerent occupation is prohibited by international law (see Sections 557 ff.). The legal situation is the same, for example, if the occupying authorities wish to confiscate land for their own use or to benefit a third party.

5. According to Article 147 GC IV, 'extensive destruction and appropriation of property, not justified by military necessity and carried out unlawfully and wantonly' must be punished as a grave breach.

Any discrimination for reasons of race, nationality, language, religious convictions and practices, political opinion, social origin or position, or similar consideration is unlawful (Art. 27 GC IV; Art. 75 AP I).   533

1. This provision applies the general prohibition of discrimination, as contained in all codifications of human rights, to the special situation of occupied territories.[35] In addition to Article 27 GC IV, AP I has comprehensively restated the ban on

---

[35] See, for example, Art. 2 of the Universal Declaration of Human Rights.

discrimination in its Article 75. Due to its supplementary character, the new text applies to international humanitarian law as a whole. Accordingly, protected persons enjoy the protection provided in the conventions 'without any adverse distinction based upon race, colour, sex, language, religion or belief, political or other opinion, national or social origin, wealth, birth or other status, or on any other similar criteria' (Art. 75, para. 1).

2. According to Article 85, para. 4(c) AP I 'practices of apartheid and other inhuman and degrading practices involving outrages upon personal dignity, based on racial discrimination' shall be prosecuted as grave breaches of AP I.

534   **Civilians shall be protected from any acts of violence (Arts. 13 and 27 GC IV; Art. 46 HagueReg).**

1. The duty to protect the inhabitants of occupied territories against acts of violence acquires particular significance because of the tense situation which usually characterizes belligerent occupation. The occupying power must ensure that members of its own armed and police forces refrain from all use of force towards the inhabitants of the occupied territory, unless their orders and the prevailing situation make it necessary. In such a case, only absolutely necessary force may be used and only to the required extent, in accordance with the principle of proportionality.

2. The occupying power must also take all measures to protect the inhabitants of occupied territories from violence by third parties. This might be, chiefly, violence by private groups or individuals. The occupying authorities may under no circumstances tolerate the activities of such groups, much less support or use them to promote their own purposes. Moreover, in exceptional cases the inhabitants of occupied territories may even have to be protected from their own authorities. The occupying power bears ultimate responsibility for all events in the occupied territories.

535   **Reprisals against civilians and their property are prohibited (Art. 33, para. 3 GC IV; Arts. 20 and 51, para. 6 AP I).**

1. A reprisal is a form of self-help in response to a breach of international law. Reprisals should be understood as measures which are themselves normally prohibited, but which are allowed if certain preconditions are met. In particular, they must be aimed at causing the adversary to desist from unlawful behaviour (see Section 1206). If all the conditions are met, reprisal actions are permitted unless specifically prohibited, in the case of so-called 'reprisal-proof' rules. Reprisals are intended to secure the enforcement of international law, if necessary by way of threats with reprisal actions. Experience during wartime has shown, however, that their value as a means of enforcing humanitarian protection is not great.

2. Reprisals against inhabitants of occupied territories and their property are prohibited without exception. This comprehensive prohibition can be found in Article

33, para. 3 GC IV, which is among the common provisions relating to the protection of the civilian population. Threats with reprisals are also prohibited and considered to be an attempt to intimidate (see Section 536). The absolute prohibition of reprisals against civilians is an achievement of the codification of 1949, which outlawed the sort of terrible reprisal actions taken against civilians during the Second World War and replaced them by clear and specific prohibitions.

The same applies to collective penalties and to measures of intimidation and ter-   536
rorism (Art. 33, para. 1 GC IV). Pillage is prohibited (Art. 33, para. 2 GC IV; Art. 47
HagueReg).

1. Collective penalties and all measures of intimidation and terrorism carried out by the occupying power have only one purpose: to make the population of the occupied territory submissive. Such measures may take different forms, such as a curfew preventing the inhabitants from fulfilling their daily duties, punishment or detention of several members of a group or family for an alleged offence by one member, or the destruction of the house belonging to the family of an alleged offender. Such acts are prohibited, without exception, by Article 33, para. 1 GC IV.

2. While in earlier times pillage was considered a legitimate reward for the efforts of soldiering, it is now universally prohibited (Art. 33, para. 2 GC IV). This applies not only to occupied territories but also for the period immediately preceding occupation, i.e. during the military operations at the time of invasion. This is clearly shown by the inclusion of the prohibition of pillage among the common provisions of GC IV dealing with the status and treatment of civilians.

No one may be punished for an offence he or she has not personally committed.   537
The taking of hostages is prohibited (Arts. 33, para. 1 and 34 GC IV).

1. The principle that only personal responsibility for an alleged deed can lead to punishment is now undisputed. Article 33, para. 1 GC IV has fixed this principle in the law of belligerent occupation. Article 75, para. 4(b) AP I has placed the rule in the context of the generally recognized principles of regular judicial procedure to which all protected persons are entitled. Today it belongs beyond doubt to the *ius cogens* of international law.

2. Article 34 GC IV states: 'The taking of hostages is prohibited.' In earlier times hostages were taken or given in order to secure certain conduct from the inhabitants or from individual persons (e.g. members of the resistance) under enemy occupation. Hostages answered with their lives for the behaviour of other people. As recently as the Second World War, serious crimes were committed in this respect. Under present law, not only the execution but even the taking of hostages is prohibited. According to Article 147, any taking of hostages is to be punished as a grave breach of GC IV.

Gasser

3. A special case of hostage-taking is the use of human beings as a shield to ward off attacks by the enemy against important positions. This is expressly prohibited (see Section 506).

538   **Each of the Parties to the conflict is obliged to forward information regarding the fate of protected civilians who are in its power (Art. 136 GC IV), as well as of prisoners of war (Art. 122 GC III), the wounded, sick, shipwrecked, and dead (Art. 16 GC I; Art. 19 GC II; see below Sections 611, 708). For this purpose a National Information Bureau shall be instituted upon the outbreak of a conflict and in all cases of occupation (Arts. 136–41 GC IV). The Bureau shall cooperate with the Central Tracing Agency of the International Committee of the Red Cross (Art. 140 GC IV).**

Example: In the Federal Republic of Germany, in accordance with Article 2 of the Act on Additional Protocols I and II to the Geneva Conventions, the German Red Cross is responsible for planning and preparing for the National Information Bureau. The Federal Armed Forces Central Personnel Office's Information Bureau (*Personalstammamt der Bundeswehr—Bundeswehrauskunftsstelle*) is responsible for its implementation in the Federal Armed Forces.

1. The search for missing persons in wartime is a task whose overwhelming humanitarian significance needs no explanation. Article 15, para. 1 GC I obliges the parties to a conflict to search for the wounded, sick, and dead 'at all times, and particularly after an engagement'. This refers to the situation existing directly after a military engagement. Articles 32–4 AP I go significantly further. On the basis of 'the right of families to know the fate of their relatives', Article 33 lays down a number of obligations intended to achieve the location of, or at least information about, missing persons. Each party to the conflict must search 'as soon as circumstances permit, and at the latest from the end of active hostilities . . . for the persons who have been reported missing by an adverse Party' (Art. 33, para. 1).

2. The obligation to search for missing persons applies equally to both members of the armed forces and civilians. In the present context, only the fate of missing civilians is dealt with. Two situations are imaginable: first, on taking control of enemy territory an occupying power is obliged to search there for persons reported missing; second, a party to the conflict is obliged to search its own territory for members of an adverse party who may have been reported missing.

3. The establishment of a National Information Bureau is an international law obligation on every party to an armed conflict (Arts. 136–9 GC IV).[36] Although such a bureau need not be ready to operate until the outbreak of an armed conflict, the preparatory work must, for practical reasons, be undertaken in peacetime. The Information Bureau, operating at national level, collects all information regarding

---

[36] See Sassòli, *IRRC* (1987), 6-24.

the fate of protected persons, registers this information, undertakes searches, and transmits all information through the protecting power, the ICRC, or the national Red Cross or Red Crescent societies to the state concerned.

4. In practice, since it is permanently in operation, it is the Central Tracing Agency of the ICRC which collects, registers, processes, and transmits incoming data at international level (Art. 140 GC IV, Art. 33, para. 3 AP I).[37]

The period of occupation shall cease with the end of the state of war. An occupy-   539
ing power shall not order measures which will remain effective beyond the end of
the war. However, the cessation of military operations alone does not necessarily
lead to the termination of the state of occupation (Art. 6, para. 3, 1st sentence GC
IV).

Should the occupation continue, the occupying power shall remain bound by the   540
fundamental humanitarian provisions of the Fourth Geneva Convention (Art. 6,
para. 3, 2nd sentence).

1. Belligerent occupation means actual control by a state of territory not its own, usually by military coercion (see Section 525). Such occupation ends when control is no longer exercised, which may happen for a number of reasons, e.g. if control is regained by the party previously in control of the territory; if the occupying power retreats voluntarily from the occupied territory (for instance, in accordance with a decision by the Security Council or a peace treaty); or if there is *debellatio*. Annexation does not end the status of belligerent occupation, since international law does not recognize the validity of this act (see commentary to Section 525).

2. As long as the occupying power exercises actual control over an occupied territory, it is bound by international law relating to belligerent occupation. This law remains in force until the end of the occupation. Article 6, para. 3 GC IV lays down, somewhat unfortunately, that application of the provisions concerning belligerent occupation shall cease one year after the beginning of the occupation. Should occupation continue beyond this time, the occupying power is bound by a number of provisions of GC IV, enumerated specifically in Article 6.

3. The following explanation is clearer: the occupying power shall observe the rules of belligerent occupation until the end of the occupation. During the first twelve months, the entire body of the law of occupation applies. If the territory continues to be occupied after one year has passed, then the occupying power is bound only by the fundamental rules listed in Article 6, para. 3 GC IV, until the occupation ends. This permanently applicable 'hard core' of the law of belligerent occupation protects the vital rights of the inhabitants of an occupied territory.

---

[37] See Djurovic.

Gasser

4. The division of the law of occupation into one set of rules for the first year of occupation and a 'hard core' applicable during the remaining time is hardly satisfactory. There is no reason why the protection of the inhabitants of such territories should be reduced after twelve months have passed. The weakening of protection after the first year of occupation should be removed from international law.

2. Legal Status of the Population

541   **The legal status of the population shall not be infringed by any agreement concluded between the authorities of the occupied territories and the occupying power, nor by any annexation by the latter of the whole or part of the occupied territory (Art. 47 GC IV).**

1. According to Article 47 GC IV, the rights of the inhabitants of occupied territories shall not be curtailed by any agreement or other arrangement between the occupying power on one hand and the authorities of the occupied territory on the other. This provision is intended to prevent local authorities, under pressure from the occupying power, from making concessions to the detriment of the inhabitants of the territory which would impair their legal status. Any such agreement is void.

2. In particular, the annexation of foreign territory by the occupying power is prohibited by international law (see commentary to Section 525). Such annexation would be invalid even if 'concessions' in this respect were offered to the local authorities.

3. For the prohibition to abrogate individual rights under GC IV, see Section 542.

542   **Protected persons cannot abrogate their rights under the Fourth Geneva Convention (Art. 8).**

This principle applies to the entirety of international humanitarian law. In all circumstances it is prohibited for the inhabitants of an occupied territory to renounce their rights under GC IV. Whether on their own initiative or as a result of coercion, such a renunciation is null and void. This is to prevent the occupying authorities, acting from a position of strength, from exploiting the weak position of the subject population and to revoke, apparently legally, the protection guaranteed by international law.

543   **The occupying power shall as a matter of principle not detain protected persons in an area particularly exposed to the dangers of war (Art. 49, para. 5 GC IV).**

1. The occupying power must permit the inhabitants of an occupied territory or individuals to seek safety from the effects of military operations. Their freedom of movement may be curtailed and the affected persons detained in their place of residence for two reasons only: for the safety of the population itself, or for com-

pelling military requirements of the occupying power. This is chiefly to prevent panic-stricken and uncontrolled flight, which could not only endanger those fleeing but also make movement by the armed forces impossible.

2. In certain circumstances, however, the occupying power may be required to evacuate the inhabitants of occupied territories from dangerous zones (see Section 544).

A temporary evacuation of specific areas is permissible if the security of the pop-   544
ulation or compelling military reasons so demand. An evacuation of persons to
areas outside the bounds of the occupied territory shall be permitted only in case
of emergency (Art. 49, para. 2 GC IV).

1. Article 49 GC IV prohibits individuals or entire groups of an occupied territory being removed from this territory to that of the occupying power, to the unoccupied part of the country of origin, or to a third state. Forced resettlement within the occupied territory is also prohibited (for the two exceptions see para. 3 below). These prohibitions are among the most significant achievements of the codification of international humanitarian law in 1949. Such grave infringements of the rights of inhabitants of occupied territories have been wholly unlawful since then, regardless of the political reasons behind them. The alleged consent of those affected is immaterial (Art. 8 GC I–III; Art. 9 GC IV; see Section 542). Legitimate requests for resettlement—for example, by members of a minority—must be verified and confirmed by a neutral authority.

2. According to Article 147, the 'unlawful deportation or transfer' of inhabitants of an occupied territory to the territory of the occupying power, or to the unoccupied territory of the same state, or to a third state is a grave breach of GC IV.

3. If the safety of the population or imperative military reasons so demand, the occupying power may nevertheless undertake temporary evacuation of a specific area (Art. 49, para. 2 GC IV). The evacuated population may be provisionally accommodated in another part of the occupied territory, unless evacuation outside the occupied territory—to the territory of the occupying power or to a third state— is the only way to guarantee the safety of the evacuees. The authorities of the occupying power are responsible for their repatriation as soon as circumstances allow.

4. On the other hand, the parties to a conflict have a general obligation, under Article 58 AP I, to take precautionary measures to protect the civilian population against the effects of hostilities. This also applies to the population of occupied territories and means that the occupying power is not only authorized (under Art. 49, para. 2 GC IV; see para. 3 above) but also required to take protective measures in favour of endangered civilians. However, the restrictive provisions of Article 49, para. 2 GC IV discussed above, which specifically prohibit permanent evacuation of parts of the occupied territory, must be borne in mind.

Gasser

545   If evacuation is necessary, the occupying power shall provide sufficient accommodation and supply. Members of the same family shall not be separated (Art. 49, para. 3 GC IV).

Representatives of a protecting power or delegates of the ICRC must be given the opportunity to visit protected persons at the new place of accommodation (Art. 143 GC IV). For this reason, the protecting power and/or the ICRC must be informed in advance of such evacuation.

546   For imperative reasons of security, the occupying power may subject individual civilians to assigned residence or internment (Art. 78, para. 1 GC IV).

1. Under Article 27, para. 4 GC IV the parties to a conflict are entitled in general to 'take such measures of control and security in regard to protected persons as may be necessary as a result of the war'. This also applies in the case of occupation. Article 78, defining this right, states that occupying authorities may subject protected persons 'at the most' to assigned residence or to internment, but only if 'imperative reasons of security' so require. Such measures must not have a penal character. They may be justified only by security considerations of the occupying power.

2. Persons may be subjected to assigned residence in their place of residence or elsewhere. The restrictions imposed by Article 49 GC IV must be observed (see Section 544); in particular, a person may not be transferred outside the occupied territory.

3. For questions arising in connection with the internment of inhabitants of an occupied territory, see Sections 591–8.

3. *Rights and Duties of the Occupying Power*

547   The national laws applicable in the occupied territory shall, in principle, remain in force. Laws which serve the purpose of warfare in the territory now occupied, or which constitute a threat to security or an obstacle to the application of humanitarian law, may be repealed or suspended by the occupying power (Art. 64 GC IV; Art. 43 HagueReg).

1. The occupying power does not assume the rights of a sovereign state upon occupation of foreign territory (see Sections 529 ff.). Sovereign power rests with the lawful authorities of the state, even if they are temporarily unable to exercise control over the territory. The authority to pass laws is unquestionably an attribute of sovereignty. Thus the lawful authorities alone—even if absent from the country and in exile—can make laws for the occupied territory. The occupying power must administer the occupied territory within the context of its existing legislation. Exceptions to this principle are listed in the second sentence of Section 547 (see para. 3 below).

Gasser

That the occupying power is bound by the existing national system is clearly laid down in Article 43 HagueReg. Based on experiences in the Second World War, Article 64 GC IV has formulated this principle more specifically.

2. Although Article 64 speaks only of criminal law as remaining in force, the entire legal system must be taken into consideration here.[38] Incidentally, Article 43 HagueReg speaks unambiguously and without restriction of 'the laws in force in the country'. The express reference to criminal law in GC IV can be explained by the fact that during the Second World War, occupying powers interfered in a particularly scandalous manner with the criminal laws of occupied territories. Other areas of law, however, are not thereby excluded.

3. Of the three exceptions to the absolute binding power of national law described in Section 547, the first two should be understood as reservations justified by considerations of military necessity. Above all, the reservation based on the security of the occupying power is of great practical importance. Accordingly, occupying authorities do not have to observe national law if its application would directly prejudice their security. This reservation must be interpreted narrowly. It is not permissible to suspend all national legislation in the occupied territory by using a broad interpretation (see also Sections 548 and 572).

4. In addition, the occupying authorities should not observe provisions of the national law of the occupied territory which 'constitute . . . an obstacle to the application of humanitarian law' (see the similar wording of Art. 64, para. 1). This refers especially to national regulations not compatible with the provisions of international humanitarian law applicable to the occupying power during occupation, e.g. openly discriminatory measures ('race laws'). Further to this reasoning it may be concluded that in administering an occupied territory, the occupying power shall not apply national provisions that are contrary to international law. This applies especially if such domestic provisions violate the rules of *ius cogens* relating to international human rights protection.

5. Another view has consistently been taken by the Israeli authorities and courts, who maintain that the Jordanian Defence (Emergency) Regulations of 1945, in force in the West Bank in 1967, allow the destruction of the house of a suspected criminal or the deportation of inhabitants of the occupied territory. The reason given is that, since the occupying authorities are observing preexisting Jordanian law, international humanitarian law is not relevant.[39] For the reasons stated in para. 4, this position is untenable. According to Article 53 GC IV, such destructions are permitted only if absolutely necessary for military considerations (see also Section 532:

---

[38] See Pictet, *Commentary*, Vol. IV, 335; another view underlies the decision of the Israeli High Court of Justice, reprinted in *IYHR* 7 (1977), 257 ff.

[39] See the decisions of the Israeli High Court of Justice: *IYHR* 10 (1980), 345 ff. (destruction of houses); *IYHR* 9 (1979), 343 ff. and 11 (1981), 349 ff. (deportation).

Gasser

protection of private property). Deportation is a violation of Article 49, para. 1 GC IV (see Section 544).

548 **The occupying power may enact legal provisions of its own if military necessity or the obligation to maintain public order so demand (Art. 64, para. 2 GC IV; Art. 43 HagueReg).**

1. This results directly from the status and duties of the occupying power, which must be enabled to enforce the occupation regime. Consequently, it must be authorized to enact those provisions and undertake those organizational measures that appear necessary to maintain public order in the occupied territory. This includes all precautions necessary to ensure its own security. Obviously, such enactments may not contain provisions abrogating the responsibilities of the occupying power under international law, especially those of the HagueReg and GC IV.

2. On the other hand, the occupying authorities may not enact provisions other than those directly justified by considerations of military security or public order.

549 **The administration of the occupied territory shall be given the opportunity to carry on its activities. The jurisdiction of the occupied territory shall remain in force.**

1. The administration and judicial organization of the occupied territory may not be replaced by institutions of the occupying power.[40] This follows directly from Article 43 HagueReg, which underlies the entire law of belligerent occupation. It states that the public order of the occupied territory shall remain in place and that public life shall continue 'while respecting, unless absolutely prevented, the laws in force in the country' (see Sections 525 and 529–31). It is not the occupying authorities, but the administration and the courts of the country that must ensure the maintenance of public order, applying the law of the territory occupied. This definitely includes the duty to adapt the administrative system to new requirements, particularly if the occupation is long-lasting.

2. If the necessary administrative bodies or courts are not present at the time of occupation of the territory, or if they are unable or unwilling to perform their duties properly, then the occupying authorities must take measures to remedy this. In such a case, they are entitled to set up their own civilian administration and/or new courts for the occupied territories. There is usually no objection to this procedure if it is taken in order to fill a vacuum, e.g. because authorities, public officials, and judges have left the occupied territory. In no circumstances, however, may those newly in power simply sweep away the existing order and replace it with a new one without urgent reasons. According to the principle of subsidiarity, they may intervene and take their own decisions only to the extent that this is absolutely

---

[40] On questions relating to the organization of public administration of an occupied territory, see especially the papers edited by Playfair.

necessary in the interests of the population of the occupied territory. National administrative bodies or courts which are still functioning may not be altered. See also the commentary to Section 551.

The occupying power may set up administrative bodies of its own if military   550
necessity or the obligation to maintain public order so demand (Art. 64, para. 2 GC
IV).

In contrast to Section 549, the subject here is the right of the occupying authorities to set up administrative bodies and courts of their own in the occupied territories. These bodies exist alongside the existing national institutions and perform the duties of the occupying power as the power temporarily responsible for the occupied territory. These duties relate chiefly to maintaining security and public order (for instance, matters arising from the stationing of occupying troops and civilian members of the occupying authorities). The legal basis for this authority of the occupying power is Article 64, para. 2 GC IV. Section 550, which deals with enforcement, must be read together with Section 548, which describes the competence of the occupying authorities to make laws.

The status of judges and public officials shall not be altered. It is prohibited to   551
compel them to carry on their functions against their conscience (Art. 54, para. 1
GC IV). Public officials may be removed from their posts (Art. 54, para. 2 GC IV).

1. Under Article 54, para. 1 GC IV it is prohibited for the occupying power to 'alter the status of public officials or judges in the occupied territories'. This provision also stems directly from the general principle of the law of occupation that the public administration system in the occupied territory shall remain in place during belligerent occupation. Judges and public officials must be retained by the occupying authorities.

2. The status of members of the administration and the judiciary is guaranteed in international law but (as explained below) limited. That status can be justified on three grounds. First, it serves to ensure that central administrative functions, in particular, continue uninterrupted in the interests of the population of a territory after its occupation by a foreign power. Secondly, the population will be as undisturbed as possible by foreign control if day-to-day matters continue to be dealt with by familiar administrative bodies. Finally, public officials and judges should not suffer disadvantages or lose their posts because they have performed official duties in the past for the (conquered) authorities (guarantee of status).

3. This means specifically that judges and public officials may continue to carry out their activities in accordance with their obligations and without hindrance. In so doing, public officials shall follow directions from the occupying authorities which, even if only for a limited time, exercise control over the occupied territory. Officials could in such cases encounter difficult and contentious situations. However, these

Gasser

should be capable of solution if the occupying authorities observe international law, and if the government (in exile) of the occupied territory takes into account the delicate situation of its municipal authorities who must carry out their duties under the control of a foreign power.

4. The term 'public official' must be interpreted broadly. Elected officials, such as mayors or elected members of a municipal council, are included. It should be noted particularly that the civilian police must also be enabled to continue performing their duties of upholding law and order.

5. To guarantee essential public services, the occupying power may compel the inhabitants of occupied territories to work (see Sections 564–6). Such compulsory duties may be requried particularly of members of public services. Beyond this, however, the occupying power may not, in principle, force public officials or judges to remain in their positions. Officials may therefore resign if they do not wish to serve under the occupying authorities, without suffering disadvantage as a result.

6. On the other hand—and herein lies the important reservation to the guarantee of their status—public officials may be removed from their posts (Art. 54, para. 2 GC IV). This is permissible if a public official refuses to fulfil his or her tasks under the occupying authorities. In this case, the public interest in the performance of administrative functions has priority over the interests of the individual public official. Once dismissed, however, a public official may not be further sanctioned for his attitude. The occupying authorities may replace the public officials who resign or are dismissed to the extent required for the proper functioning of the administration.

7. Under Article 54, para. 2 GC IV the occupying power may remove public officials, but not judges, from their posts. The principle of the independence of the judiciary applies absolutely, even in the law of belligerent occupation. This can lead to difficult situations if judges collectively refuse to fulfil their tasks. Since the paralysis of justice cannot be in the interest of the population of an occupied territory, the occupying power is entitled in such a case to appoint new judges. On the question of jurisdiction in occupied territories, see Sections 572 ff.

8. Finally, it should be recalled that public officials and judges working in occupied territory are always protected civilians. As such, they are entitled to all the rights specifically granted by GC IV to civilians under the control of the enemy. This also applies to public officials and judges dismissed for any reason.

4. *Requisition of Civilian Resources by the occupying power*

552   **Within the purview of existing laws, the occupying power may itself impose taxes, tariffs, and dues, including an obligation to defray all administrative costs arising therefrom (Art. 48 HagueReg). Any additional money contributions shall only be**

Gasser

levied to meet the requirements of the occupational forces or to cover its administrative costs (Art. 49 HagueReg).

1. The reference to 'existing laws' means that taxes, tariffs, and tolls shall be imposed according to the national provisions in effect in the occupied territory.

2. The Israeli High Court of Justice has had occasion to pronounce on the question of whether new taxes may be introduced in occupied territories (in this case, the West Bank). The court answered the question affirmatively, adducing the necessity of integrating the occupied territories' economy into that of Israel.[41] That decision cannot be reconciled with the law of belligerent occupation, which is based on the assumption that foreign control will last only for a limited period of time. It may be assumed from the judgment, however, that the income from the new tax will go to the occupied territory.

**No extra charges (contributions) shall be collected except under a written order   553
issued by a commander-in-chief. For every contribution a receipt shall be given to
the contributors (Art. 51 HagueReg).**

Such extra charges shall also be collected according to the national laws.

**A local commander may demand contributions in kind and services (requisitions)   554
from the population and the authorities of the occupied territory to satisfy the
needs of the occupational forces (Art. 52, paras. 1 and 2 HagueReg). The requisitions shall be in proportion to the capabilities of the country. It is prohibited to
compel members of the population to take part in military operations against
their own country (Art. 52, para. 1 HagueReg).**

**Requisitions shall, on principle, be paid for in cash. If this is not possible a receipt   555
shall be given. Payment shall be effected as soon as possible (Art. 52, para. 3
HagueReg).**

1. The traditional right of the occupying power to demand contributions in kind and services from the population or from the local authorities is maintained in Art. 52 HagueReg. In practice this usually involves contributions in kind or services. Such services may be required only 'for the needs of the army of occupation' or 'for the public utility services, or for the feeding, sheltering, clothing, transportation, or health of the population of the occupied country', and then only in so far as they are indispensable for these purposes (Art. 51, para. 2 GC IV). Contributions in kind and services may never be demanded to benefit the occupying power's own population.

2. The right to demand contributions in kind and services for the needs of occupational forces is laid down in Article 52 HagueReg and customary law. Under GC IV

---

[41] Decision reprinted in *IYHR* 13 (1983), 348 ff.

Gasser

the occupying power may also introduce compulsory labour if it is required to meet essential needs of the population of the occupied territories (Art. 51, para. 2; see Sections 564 ff.).

3. Requisitions in kind or services benefiting the occupying power must 'be in proportion to the resources of the country' (Art. 52, para. 1 HagueReg), i.e. they may not exceed the capabilities of the occupied territory or its population. The occupied territory may not be bled dry by the occupying authorities. Similarly, provision for the population of the occupied territory always has priority over the needs of the occupying authorities and forces. As Article 55, para. 2 GC IV explicitly states, foodstuffs, articles, and medical supplies, in particular, may be requisitioned 'only if the requirements of the civilian population have been taken into account'. This is logical since, after all, the occupying power is obliged to guarantee the provision of foodstuffs and medical supplies for the occupied territories (Art. 55, para. 1 GC IV; Art. 69, para. 1 AP I; see Sections 567 ff.).

4. 'Such requisitions and services shall only be demanded on the authority of the commander in the locality occupied' (Art. 52, para. 2 HagueReg). The seizure of goods without the authority of the commanding officer or the occupying authority is pillage, which is prohibited in all circumstances (see Section 507). Contributions in kind shall be compensated (Art. 52, para. 3 HagueReg); Article 55, para. 2 GC IV stipulates that 'fair value' shall be paid. Work performed shall be remunerated by a fair wage (Art. 51, para. 3 GC IV; see Section 565). Sections 564–7 deal with the circumstances under which persons can be compelled to work.

556 Movable government property which may be used for military purposes shall become spoils of war (Art. 53, para. 1 HagueReg). Upon seizure it shall, without compensation, become the property of the occupying state. Such property includes, for instance, means of transport, weapons, and food supplies (Art. 53, para. 1 HagueReg). The latter shall not be requisitioned unless the requirements of the civilian population have been taken into account (Art. 55, para. 2 GC IV). The requirements of the civilian population shall be satisfied first (Art. 55, para. 1 GC IV).

1. By contrast to Sections 554 ff., these provisions deal with the fate of government property. Movable government property 'which may be used for military operations' (Art. 53, para. 1, HagueReg) is spoils of war, i.e. it can be freely requisitioned by the occupying power, and becomes its property without compensation. According to the HagueReg this may include, for example, cash, other funds, realizable securities, military equipment (weapons, ammunition, etc.), and means of transport.

2. Foodstuffs and other supplies, and particularly medical supplies, may be requisitioned only if the needs of the inhabitants of the occupied territory have been met, as clearly laid down by Article 55, para. 2 GC IV. This drastic restriction on the right

of seizure follows directly from the obligation of the occupying power to ensure 'to the fullest extent of the means available to it . . . the food and medical supplies of the population' (Art. 55, para. 1 GC IV).

3. The occupying power does not acquire ownership (in private law) of 'public buildings, real estate, forests, and agricultural estates' located in the occupied territory and belonging to the state whose territory is occupied (Art. 55 HagueReg). This list of types of fixed state assets is not exhaustive. It should also include, for example, common lands that are not private or community property. For the situation regarding the property of the community or public institutions, see Section 559.

4. The occupying authorities shall, however, manage the fixed assets of the state unless they transfer management to institutions of the territory occupied. They are in the position of a beneficiary owner, which includes the obligation to maintain the assets. The proceeds may be used only for the administration of the territory occupied. If the occupying power requires a piece of public land for military reasons (e.g. as a defence position or to construct accommodation for its forces), then it may requisition this land at most for the duration of the occupation. At the end of the war, movable state property shall be returned to the entitled state.

Movable private property which may be used for military purposes and immovable government property may only be requisitioned and not confiscated (Art. 53, para. 2; 55 HagueReg). Title to such property shall not pass to the occupying state. Upon termination of the war, the items and real estate seized shall be restored. 557

All private property shall be protected from permanent seizure (Art. 46, para. 2 HagueReg) except for commodities designed for consumption. 558

1. As is clearly laid down by Article 46, para. 2 HagueReg, movable private property is protected in the event of belligerent occupation. This rule has the character of customary law (see the introductory remarks to Section III, Belligerent Occupation, para. 1). Therefore the movable property of private persons may not as a rule be confiscated.

2. By contrast, Article 53, para. 2 HagueReg permits the occupying power to requisition the following, even if they belong to private persons: means of transport for persons or things by land, sea, or air; appliances for the transmission of news; and, in general, all war materials and ammunition. After the war has ended seized property must be returned and, if appropriate, compensation paid.

3. In the recent past the question of the significance of the proviso regarding military security in connection with the protection of the guarantee of property has come up in legal practice. The Israeli occupying authorities have repeatedly seized privately owned land in the occupied territories, and permitted the acquisition of

land by private persons, so that settlements for Israeli civilians could be established there. The Israeli High Court of Justice has approved these 'requisitions' with the explanation that such settlements increased the security of the occupying power and could thus be justified on the basis of military interests.[42] This extension of the concept of security as an exception to the guarantee of property should be rejected as excessive, since it nullifies the guarantee of property based in international law. Under existing law, seizure of land may be only temporary, which is incompatible with the construction of a residential settlement.

559 **The property of municipalities, of institutions dedicated to religion, charity, education, and arts and sciences shall be treated as private property (Art. 56, para. 1 HagueReg).**

Article 56 HagueReg, which protects the property of municipalities and certain public institutions, refers to the provisions of the HagueReg for the protection of private property. (See Sections 557 and 558.) The duty to protect institutions dedicated to religion also arises from Article 58 GC IV, which guarantees the continued spiritual sustenance of the population of occupied territories. Regarding the protection of 'institutions dedicated to . . . the arts and sciences', see also Section 561.

560 **Civilian hospitals may be requisitioned only temporarily and in cases of urgent necessity. The care and treatment of patients must be ensured (Art. 57, para. 1 GC IV). The material and stores of civilian hospitals cannot be requisitioned as long as they are needed for the civilian population (Art. 57, para. 2 GC IV; Art. 14, para. 2 AP I).**

1. Under Article 57, para. 1 GC IV, the occupying authorities may requisition hospitals for their own use only if and for as long as these are urgently needed for the care of injured and sick military personnel. The care of persons from the territory occupied must however be guaranteed elsewhere. AP I limits this right of the occupying power to use hospitals in occupied territories for its own purposes by giving absolute priority to the needs of the population of the territory occupied (Art. 14, para. 2). The same applies to the equipment, material, and personnel of such units. Thus it is made clear that the civilian hospitals of an occupied territory should primarily serve the same purpose as before the occupation: the care of the local population.

2. The provision regarding hospitals comes within the wider context of the occupying power's obligation to guarantee medical care for the civilian population in occupied territories (Art. 56 GC IV; Art. 14 AP I; see Section 570 below).

561 **It is prohibited to requisition, destroy or damage cultural property (Art. 56 HagueReg; Art. 5 CultPropConv).**

---

[42] '*Beth El* case', *IYHR* 9 (1979), 337 ff.

1. As to the protection of cultural property in armed conflicts see Chapter 9 (Sections 901 ff., especially 919–22).

2. The ban on requisitioning, destroying or damaging cultural property must be placed in a broader context. The occupying power is bound, under Article 5 CultPropConv, to 'support the competent national authorities of the occupied country in safeguarding and preserving its cultural property', although only to the extent possible. The occupying power should take measures to preserve cultural property, and in particular cultural property damaged as a result of the war.

The occupying power may not compel members of the population to serve in its armed forces (Art. 51, para. 1 GC IV). Any pressure or propaganda by the occupying power which aims at securing enlistment in the armed forces is also prohibited (Art. 51, para. 1 GC IV). 562

1. The prohibition against compelling members of the population of occupied territories to serve in the armed forces of the occupying power is absolute and admits of no exception (Art. 51, para. 1 GC IV). The recruitment of such persons for the auxiliary forces of the occupying power is likewise prohibited. This rule indirectly strengthens the prohibition in customary law against compelling persons to participate in military operations against their own country (Art. 23, para. 2 HagueReg). The prohibition in GC IV is expressed more broadly, however, than that of the HagueReg, since it prohibits not only participation in military operations but even mere recruitment into the forces of the occupying power, whether armed or auxiliary. Thus it is prohibited to use members of the population of occupied territories e.g. to fight against members of the resistance.

2. This prohibition does not cover service in the occupied territory's civilian police force, whose duty is to maintain public order. On the issue of compelling civilian members of local authorities see Section 564.

3. Pressure or propaganda aimed at encouraging inhabitants of the occupied territories to serve in the armed forces is also prohibited. In practice, it is hardly possible to distinguish pressure from propaganda; there is no clear line separating one from the other. Pressure and propaganda, both on the collective level and directed to individuals, are in any case covered by this prohibition.

4. To compel members of the population of an occupied territory to serve in the armed forces of the occupying power is a grave breach of GC IV, punishable as such (Art. 147 GC IV; see Sections 1207 ff.).

563. It is prohibited to exercise physical or moral coercion against members of the civilian population in order to obtain general (Art. 31 GC IV) or military (Art. 44 HagueReg) information from them. 563

Gasser

The HagueReg forbid the occupying power to coerce the population of occupied territories 'to furnish information about the army of the other belligerent, or about its means of defence' (Art. 44). Article 31 GC IV goes one step further by prohibiting any kind of coercion to obtain any kind of information.

564 **For the benefit of the occupational forces or for ensuring public utility services and the feeding, sheltering, clothing, transportation, and health of the population, the occupying power may compel civilians over eighteen years to work. Work which would oblige them to take part in military operations (Art. 51, para. 2 GC IV; Art. 52 HagueReg) or lead to the mobilization of workers in military or paramilitary organizations shall be excepted from this regulation (Art. 51, para. 4 GC IV).**

1. This rule must be read in conjunction with Section 564 and its commentary. Section 564 deals specifically with work assignments of members of the population of occupied territories. It permits compulsory labour only in two situations: to serve the immediate needs of the occupation forces, or for the benefit of the population of the occupied territory. It is emphasized that civilians compelled to work by the occupying authorities always retain their status as civilians.

2. Work for the benefit of the occupation forces is permitted only in very limited conditions. In particular, inhabitants of the occupied territory may not be ordered to carry out work to improve the state of readiness for war of the occupational forces, nor to contribute to military operations. According to Pictet's *Commentary*, work connected with e.g. public transportation, the reconstruction of roads, bridges, or harbours, or laying telephone lines, could be permitted.[43] It is difficult, however, not to see this type of work as a contribution to the state of readiness for war of the armed forces. It would probably be better to prohibit all work of benefit to the occupational forces.

3. Clearly, under current law the construction of trenches, fortifications, or airstrips should be considered as work that inhabitants of occupied territories may not be compelled to carry out. Work in the armaments industry is also prohibited. Article 51, para. 2 GC IV states explicitly that the inhabitants of occupied territories may not be compelled to do work 'which would involve them in the obligation of taking part in military operations'. This applies to military operations against their own country or against another state, also to actions against members of the resistance and partisans in the occupied territory.

4. The assignment of workers to projects the completion of which is in the immediate interests of the inhabitants of the occupied territory raises fewer questions. An example that springs to mind is work to reestablish public utility services following their destruction in the war, e.g. water supplies, electricity supply, transportation

---

[43] Pictet, *Commentary*, Vol. IV, 294.

lines, etc. Certain branches of industry, e.g. for the production of foodstuffs, fertilizers, or cement, must be set into motion again. Inhabitants of the occupied territory may be compelled to perform this kind of work. However, the work must always be in the occupied territory itself (Art. 51, para. 3 GC IV) and in the interests of its population. Persons under eighteen years of age may not be compelled to work in any circumstances (Art. 51, para. 2 GC IV).

5. Workers from occupied territories may not be grouped into 'an organization of a military or paramilitary character' (Art. 51, para. 4 GC IV). This provision is also aimed at barring practices employed during the Second World War.

6. The stringent interpretation of the kinds of work permitted as compulsory labour is intended to protect individuals against abuse and injury. It proscribes all types of modern slavery for the benefit of the occupying power. It is also intended to prevent the assignment of inhabitants of occupied territories to locations that might be military objectives, since they would then be exposed to the dangers associated with attacks against military targets. Moreover, it is absolutely forbidden to use civilians as shields (see Section 506).

**Civilians liable to work shall, as far as possible, be kept in their usual places of   565
employment to perform work for the occupying power. Existing working conditions (e.g. wages, working hours, labour protection) shall not be altered by the occupying power (Art. 51, para. 3 GC IV).**

1. Persons compelled to work shall, if possible, be employed where they already live and work. This again emphasizes the requirement to permit the inhabitants of occupied territories to continue their accustomed way of life as far as possible.

2. Article 51, para. 3 GC IV refers to the provisions on working conditions, in force at the moment of occupation and confirms that they shall remain in effect. This detailed and very useful regulation, which forms part of international labour law and of the law of war, was formulated jointly with the International Labour Organization (ILO). The relevant ILO agreements on the protection of workers remain in force in the occupied territories.[44]

**It is prohibited to employ protected persons for work outside the occupied terri-   566
tory (Art. 51, para. 3 GC IV).**

Persons may be ordered to carry out work only within the occupied territory. Work assignments in the country of origin of the occupying authorities are prohibited without exception. This prohibition, like others, is a response to a practice common during the Second World War.

---

[44] See Dugard, in Playfair (Ed.), 484.

Gasser

5. *Supplies to the Occupied Territory*

567   The occupying power is obliged to ensure the provision of supplies to the civilian population to the fullest extent of the means available to it. The resources of the occupied territory shall be used in the first place. If necessary, supplies shall be brought in by the occupying power (Art. 55, para. 1 GC IV; Art. 69, para. 1 AP I).

1. The old law, based on the HagueReg, required the occupying power simply to maintain public order in the occupied territories, and restricted its right to make use of their resources (Art. 43; Arts. 52 ff.). GC IV goes a significant step further and imposes on the occupying power the duty to ensure that the population of an occupied territory has all essential supplies to meet its basic needs (Arts. 55–63). AP I makes this obligation even more specific (Art. 69). Just as human rights law has developed from the simple obligation to ensure freedom for the individual— traditional human rights—to the obligation to implement economic and social rights, so international humanitarian law today includes a whole series of rules obliging the occupying power to undertake specific actions. Here we are considering the duty to ensure the survival of the population of occupied territories in humane conditions. This includes the supply of goods of urgent necessity.

2. Under Article 55 GC IV the occupying power must ensure that the population is provided with supplies 'to the fullest extent of the means available to it'. It is therefore not obliged to ensure the provision of all supplies to the occupied territories. First of all, the population of the occupied territories shall provide for itself as well as it can. Nevertheless it is the duty of the occupying power to make such self-help possible. Therefore the occupying authorities may make use of, for instance, the economic infrastructure of an occupied territory only to the extent permitted by the needs of the local population (see Sections 554 and 568).

3. If the supplies available in the occupied territories are not sufficient then the occupying power must take measures to guarantee such supplies. The representatives of a protecting power, where applicable, and the delegates of the ICRC have the right to verify the state of supplies on the spot at any time (Art. 55, para. 3 GC IV). They are bound to give an objective picture of the actual conditions.

4. If supplies are inadequate, the occupying power has a number of options. First, it shall permit authorities or private persons to import the goods that are lacking from a third state or from the unoccupied part of their own country. If this is not enough, then the occupying power must itself provide the required supplies. However, nothing impossible may be demanded: the occupying power must act 'to the fullest extent of the means available to it' (Art. 55, para. 1 GC IV; Art. 69, para. 1 AP I). Finally, if certain preliminary requirements are met, it must permit relief actions by other states (see Section 569).

Gasser

5. What categories of goods are involved here? Article 55 GC IV speaks of foodstuffs and medical supplies. Under the heading 'Basic needs in occupied territories', AP I adds clothing, bedding, means of shelter, and 'other supplies essential to the survival of the civilian population of the occupied territory' as well as objects necessary for religious worship (Art. 69). In this way the scope of the occupying power's obligation to supply the occupied territories was extended in 1977. The responsibility is now not only to supply basic food and medical supplies, but also other items indispensable for survival, such as clothing and shelter. How far this obligation goes in a particular case depends on the specific circumstances. In cold regions, for example, the delivery of fuel for heating purposes would be necessary. With regard to medical supplies, see Section 570.

6. It is self-evident that, in allocating and providing relief supplies, the occupying power is bound by the general prohibition of discrimination (Art. 27, para. 3 GC IV in association with Art. 75, para. 1 AP I). Special treatment is justified if the medical condition, age, or sex of the affected persons so require.

Stocks available in the occupied territory may be requisitioned for use by the occupying power only if the requirements of the civilian population have been taken into account and fair value is paid for the requisitioned goods (Art. 55, para. 2 GC IV). See also Sections 554 and 567.   568

If the whole or part of the population of an occupied territory is inadequately supplied, the occupying power shall agree to relief actions by other states or humanitarian organizations (Art. 59 GC IV; Arts. 69–71 AP I).   569

1. This provision, which is very important in practice, states that the occupying power is obliged, when preliminary conditions are met, to permit relief actions for the benefit of the population of the territory that it occupies. If the population of an occupied territory is suffering from hunger, that is no longer an 'internal matter' for the occupying power. The processes of international solidarity should then be set in motion, and the occupying power may not block them.

2. This provision applies only when the supplies to part or all of the population of the occupied territory are inadequate. It is a question of assessing, in an existing situation, whether or not supplies are inadequate. The occupying authorities are obliged to make such an assessment to the best of their knowledge and belief, taking only the interests of the population of the occupied territories into account and neglecting considerations of prestige. The representatives of a protecting power and delegates of the ICRC are bound to inform the occupying authorities of the true situation and to advise them on the measures to be taken (Art. 53, para. 3 GC IV).

3. If the population is adequately supplied, the occupying power is not obliged to accept any offers made by another state or by a humanitarian organization to deliver relief supplies. This also applies to offers from any unoccupied part of the

Gasser

country. However, the occupying power is well advised to accept such gestures from the unoccupied part for the benefit of the population of the occupied territory. The population of an occupied territory, on the other hand, is always permitted to receive private relief consignments, subject to compelling security considerations (Art. 62 GC IV).

4. If the population is inadequately supplied and cannot remedy this situation itself, then the occupying power is obliged under international law to allow aid by other states. This refers to relief for the population as a whole, not for individuals. The occupying power must not only allow such relief actions but must also facilitate these 'to the fullest extent of the means available to it' (Art. 55, para. 1 GC IV). This includes protecting relief actions. On the other hand, the occupying authorities may impose controls necessary for their own safety and that of the population. The contents of relief consignments are foodstuffs, medication, and articles of clothing. Recipients are the members of the population in need of help, including inmates of prisons. Internees have a specially detailed right to relief consignments (Arts. 108 ff. GC IV).

5. Other states are obliged to permit the free passage of relief consignments for the benefit of the population of occupied territories (Art. 59, para. 3) and must guarantee the protection of relief convoys. This applies in particular to states in conflict with the occupying power. Even in the event of a blockade, relief consignments for the benefit of the population of occupied territories, within the meaning of Article 59 GC IV, must also be permitted. In other words, supplies necessary to meet the basic needs of the population may not lawfully be blockaded. Such third states, however, always have the right to make sure that relief actions are carried out properly. They may check the contents of consignments in order to prevent, for example, the delivery of weapons. Such controls must not interfere with or delay the relief action excessively, as expressly laid down by AP I (Art. 69, para. 2).

6. Under Article 59 GC IV, relief actions can be carried out either by a state or by 'impartial humanitarian organizations such as the International Committee of the Red Cross'. In practice, neutrality is an important precondition, since only a neutral state or organization can convincingly guarantee, both for the occupying power and for the population of the occupied territory, a relief action that is impartial and free of political considerations. The GC specifically names the ICRC among the 'impartial humanitarian organizations'. Because of its neutral stance, recognized by all sides, and its extensive experience it is most often the ICRC which in practice carries out relief actions for the benefit of the needy civilian population. Its delegates stationed in the occupied territory are also best placed to distribute or supervise the distribution of relief supplies according to need and without discrimination based on irrelevant criteria.

7. The personnel involved in a relief action shall be respected and protected (Art. 71 AP I). The cooperation of technical and administrative personnel is indispens-

Gasser

able, especially for the transport and distribution of goods. The participation of such personnel in a relief action in occupied territory requires the permission of the occupying power. Obviously, such workers must keep strictly to their tasks and observe the security requirements of the occupying power. If a relief action is conducted or accompanied by representatives of the protecting power or by delegates of the ICRC, then these persons enjoy the rights and immunities due to the protecting power or the ICRC.

8. Relief actions by a third party do not release the occupying power from its obligation under international law to meet the needs of the population of the territory it occupies (Art. 60 GC IV).

The occupying power has the duty to ensure and maintain, in co-operation with 570
the appropriate authorities of the occupied territory, medical care for the civilian
population as well as public health and hygiene. Adequate prophylactic measures
shall be taken to prevent contagious diseases and epidemics (Art. 56, para. 1 GC
IV; Art. 14, para. 1 AP I).

1. Regarding the obligation of the occupying power to ensure and maintain medical care for the population of the occupied territory, the remarks in Sections 567 to 569 concerning general supplies again apply. As Article 56 explicitly states, the occupying power must guarantee medical care for the inhabitants of the occupied territory (see also Art. 14 AP I). It may and must rely in the first place on existing personnel and the material infrastructure. If medical supplies are lacking then the occupying power must either itself import them or accept relief consignments (see Section 569).

2. The medical infrastructure of an occupied territory must continue to serve the local population. According to Article 57, the occupying authorities are only permitted temporarily to requisition civilian hospitals if this is urgently and exclusively necessary for the treatment of injured and sick military personnel. This authorization is restricted by Article 14, para. 2 AP I, since in the case of belligerent occupation the existing hospitals would always be required for the local population. If the occupying authorities make use of such hospitals for the treatment of members of their own armed forces or of prisoners of war in the restrictive conditions of Article 14, para. 3, then they must guarantee medical care for the population of the occupied territory by other means. In no circumstances are they permitted to use the medical facilities of the occupied territory for the benefit of their own population.

3. Medical equipment and supplies may not be requisitioned as long as and to the extent that they are required for the population of the occupied territory (Art. 57, para. 2 GC IV).

571. The national Red Cross or Red Crescent society shall be permitted to pursue 571
its activities in accordance with Red Cross principles. Other relief societies shall

Gasser

be permitted to continue their humanitarian activities under equivalent conditions (Art. 63 GC IV).

1. This provision confirms the special status of national Red Cross and Red Crescent societies within the social organization of a country (see above, Section 516).[45] In the event of belligerent occupation of one state by the armed forces of another, the Red Cross society[46] remains at its post, to continue its traditional activities with voluntary helpers, and specialized personnel and equipment. Article 63 GC IV therefore places an explicit obligation on the occupying power to permit the local Red Cross society to continue its activities 'in accordance with Red Cross principles'. Article 81, para. 3 AP I confirms the role of the Red Cross societies and expressly stipulates that all parties to the conflict must facilitate the assistance that the societies provide to the victims of armed conflicts. The right of national societies to continue their activities for the benefit of the population in accordance with the fundamental principles of the Red Cross thus rests more on an obligation in international law than on the goodwill of the occupying power.

2. Only Red Cross societies recognized by the ICRC may rely on Article 63 GC IV. The ICRC grants recognition to a national society if it fulfils the requirements set out in the Statutes of the International Red Cross.[47] These include the obligation to respect the principles of the Red Cross as contained in the Statutes of the Movement, among them the principles of impartiality and neutrality. Once recognized, a society not only becomes a full partner in the worldwide Movement of the Red Cross and Red Crescent but is also obliged to abide by the Statutes of the Movement. In accordance with its authority, the ICRC must verify observance of the principles, while respecting the independent nature of national societies.[48] As an obligatory condition for recognition of a national society by the ICRC, it must be formally recognized by the government of its country as a voluntary humanitarian aid society.[49] For the position of Red Cross organizations that are not recognized, see below, para. 4.

3. If the entire territory of a state is occupied, then its national society also falls entirely under the control of the occupying power. In such circumstances it is entitled to continue its activities within the scope of its humanitarian objectives. Article 63 GC IV provides one exception: for urgent reasons of security, the occupying power may impose restrictive measures. These reasons may, in particular, concern the safety of the national society's workers. Yet it should also be borne in mind that the Red Cross was founded precisely in order to assist in conflict situations, which always involve danger. The traditional activities of the Red Cross may under no

---

[45] For an introduction to and overview of the tasks and organization of the Red Cross, see Haug (Ed.), also the practice-oriented description of the tasks of a National society: *Guide for National Red Cross and Red Crescent Societies to Activities in the Event of Conflict*, ICRC (1990).

[46] In many Islamic countries it is the Red Crescent society.

[47] See Art. 4, Statutes of the International Red Cross and Red Crescent Movement.

[48] Art. 5, para. 2 lit. a of the Statutes of the Movement.

[49] Art. 4 of the Statutes of the Movement, pursuant to Art. 26, GC I.

Gasser

circumstances be seen as a security risk for the occupying authorities or occupation forces. Restrictions imposed by the occupying power upon the National Society are justified only if, for example, by acting against the interests of the occupying authorities the society disregards its obligation to remain neutral.

4. If only parts of a state fall under the control of the adversary, then the part of the country's national society active in this territory may continue its work. It usually consists of local sections or chapters. A new Red Cross or Red Crescent organization may be formed in the occupied territories: recognition by the ICRC during a conflict is, however, not possible. With its general reference to 'organizations' of the Red Cross, Article 81 AP I leaves the door open to unrecognized societies, provided that they are guided in their activities by the Fundamental Principles of the Red Cross. At the very least, such groups are entitled to the same privileges as other relief societies (see para. 6 below).

5. The occupying authorities shall not interfere in the internal affairs of a Red Cross society. They may not change the internal structure of the society or replace the leadership or personnel (Art. 63, para. 1(b) GC IV). In the event of partial occupation of a state, the occupying power must take into account the legitimate desire of the parts of the national society under its control to maintain relations with the society's central bodies in the (unoccupied) capital.

6. Under Article 63 GC IV the occupying power shall also allow other relief societies to carry out their activities for the benefit of the population of the occupied territory. The article refers to existing or newly established non-military organizations performing the following activities: maintenance of essential public utility services, distribution of relief, and rescue.

7. Finally, mention should be made of the activities which the ICRC must undertake to implement international law relating to belligerent occupation. See in this regard Chapter 12 below: Enforcement of International Humanitarian Law, especially Section 1220. Under Article 143 GC IV, ICRC delegates have in particular the right, while carrying out their activities, to go to all places where inhabitants of the occupied territory may be living. This includes especially all establishments where detained persons may be found (prisons, detention camps, etc.—see Sections 580, 592 ff.).

6. *jurisdiction*

National laws relating to the prosecution of criminal offences shall, in principle,   572
remain in force. Penal laws of the occupied territory may be repealed by the occu-
pying power in cases where they constitute a threat to its security (Art. 64, para. 1
GC IV).

1. Belligerent occupation of a country does not invalidate its national legal system (see Section 547). This also applies to its penal laws. The general principle of the

international law of occupation, that the occupying power exercises its power over the foreign territory only temporarily (see Section 530), is of special significance for penal law. Penal law, of course, encroaches markedly upon the life of individuals. Even during the period of foreign rule, inhabitants of occupied territories are subject to the preexisting provisions of penal law with which they are familiar. Not only does the existing national legal system remain in effect in occupied territory, but the jurisdiction of the national courts continues to apply (Section 549).

2. The occupying power may repeal the penal laws of the occupied territory or suspend their effect 'in cases where they constitute a threat to its security or an obstacle to the application of the . . . Convention' (Art. 64, para. 1 GC IV). For the interpretation of this reservation see the commentary to Section 547, paras. 3–5.

573   **For these reasons, and particularly to maintain an orderly administration, the occupying power may enact penal provisions of its own (Art. 64, para. 2 GC IV). These penal provisions shall not come into force before they have been promulgated in the language of the inhabitants of the occupied territory (Art. 65 GC IV).**

1. See Section 548 and commentary.

2. Newly enacted penal provisions may not be retroactive. Occupying authorities are naturally also bound by this principle, without which there is no legal system deserving that name. The principle is now one of the generally recognized guarantees of a fair criminal trial, codified in human rights law.[50] Therefore, for example, an inhabitant of an occupied territory may not be prosecuted for an offence allegedly committed before the occupation and made punishable by the occupying power only after the fact.

3. The requirement that new penal provisions must be made known to the population of an occupied territory in its own language is more than a mere administrative regulation. Publication in the national language is a necessary condition for the effectiveness of such rules. The inhabitants of occupied territories must be able to understand a directive that affects them. Publication shall be accomplished in such a way that everyone is in fact enabled to become aware of it (notices, publication in the press, announcements in the other media, etc.).

574   **Courts of the occupying power may not prosecute criminal offences committed before the occupation unless they constitute violations of international humanitarian law (Art. 70, para. 1 GC IV).**

1. International humanitarian law does not confer on the occupying authorities competence to prosecute inhabitants of the occupied territory for offences com-

[49] No. 3, Art. 4 of the Statutes of the Movement, pursuant to Art. 26, GC I.
[50] See in particular Art. 15 of the International Covenant on Civil and Political Rights, and Art. 75, para. 4 lit. c AP I.

mitted prior to the occupation. For such offences, the normal rules governing the states' jurisdiction to prosecute apply. The same is true for offences committed during an interruption in the occupation.

2. According to Article 70, para. 1 GC IV, breaches of 'the laws and customs of war' are the only exception to this principle. These are breaches of the conventions applicable in armed conflicts, such as the GCs and AP I, and of general principles of law and rules of customary law. Such breaches may be prosecuted by the occupying authorities, including any breach of the conventions, not only those expressly defined as grave breaches. If a grave breach is suspected then the occupying power is, as stated, obliged to prosecute (see Sections 1208 ff.).

3. Further exceptions to the prohibition against prosecution are 'crimes against the peace and security of mankind'[51] and other breaches of international criminal law (e.g. genocide, torture, etc.). For both categories the occupying power's jurisdiction is unrelated to the belligerent occupation of foreign territory. These are offences against the law of the international community.[52]

4. In a non-international armed conflict, the legal situation is completely different. As a rule, offences are prosecuted by the state in whose territory the civil war is being waged, according to its domestic legislation. In some cases, a third state may also be competent to prosecute. International humanitarian law merely contains provisions regarding the conduct of criminal proceedings, which must be in accordance with the rule of law (Art. 3, para. 1 No. 1(d) GCs I–IV; Art. 6 AP II).

Breaches of the penal laws of the occupied territory shall continue to be prose- 575
cuted by local courts. Jurisdiction shall pass to a military court of the occupying
power only if local courts are not able to work.

This principle is also of great consequence for the inhabitants of occupied territories. It states that the ordinary courts of the country, which are familiar to them, are still competent to judge all criminal cases not having an immediate effect on the security of the occupying power (Art. 64, para. 1 2nd sentence GC IV). The local courts must apply national law and act in accordance with the rules of procedure in force prior to the occupation. Only if the national authorities or courts do not function may the occupying power replace them with its own institutions, with the sole purpose of ensuring the dispensation and administration of justice. This could be the case, for example, if the judges left the country at the time of the invasion. See also Sections 549 and 551 above.

576. Any breaches of penal provisions enacted by the occupying power may be 576
prosecuted by properly constituted military courts of the occupying power (Art.
66 GC IV).

[51] See Art. 6 of the Charter of the International Military Tribunal; further developed by the Draft Code of Crimes against the Peace and Security of Mankind; see also Ipsen, *Völkerrecht*, 536 ff.
[52] Ibid., 534 ff.

Gasser

1. For the right of the occupying power to enact its own provisions for the occupied territory, see Section 548.

2. The occupying authorities are competent to punish breaches of the laws which they have passed. The penal process may be assigned either to their own existing military tribunals or to special military courts created for the occupied territories. In either case it must be a military court, i.e. the judges must be members of the armed forces of the occupying power. In this way the responsibility of the armed forces for conducting belligerent occupation and enforcing the law of occupation is emphasized. The court, however, must be 'non-political' and 'properly constituted'. Special courts set up on an *ad hoc* basis are therefore not permitted. As Article 66 expressly states, military courts must sit within the occupied territories: the accused should be tried in his own surroundings.

3. With respect to the procedure of the courts of the occupying power, see Section 577.

4. The occupying authorities may provide or establish an appeal body; however, they are not obliged to do so (Art. 73, para. 2 GC IV; see Section 577).[53] Should a court of appeal exist, then it should preferably sit in the occupied territory (Art. 66, 2nd sentence).

577   Legal proceedings by military courts of the occupational power shall be conducted in accordance with the rule of law (Arts. 67 and 69–75, GC IV; Art. 75 AP I).

1. The courts of the occupying power must in all circumstances respect the provisions and procedural guarantees codified in Articles 67 and 69–75 GC IV and established in international law. As described in Article 71, para. 1 GC IV, no court of the occupying power may pass judgment without prior regular proceedings. The provisions of GC IV are supplemented by Article 75 AP I, which lists the minimum requirements of a regular and fair criminal procedure ('fair trial') against protected persons. In general, the courts of the occupying power must take into consideration that the accused are not nationals of the occupying power and therefore do not owe it allegiance.

2. The principles governing criminal proceedings before a military court of the occupying power include:

—the prohibition of retroactive effects of criminal provisions (*nullum crimen sine lege*) (Art. 67 GC IV),

—written notice of the charges in a language that the accused understands (Art. 71, para. 2 GC IV),

---

[53] See also to this effect: Judgment of the Israeli High Court of Justice, reprinted in 18 *IYHR* (1988), 255 ff.

—the right to representation by an advocate or counsel of the accused's choice (Art. 72, para. 1 GC IV); in serious cases, the right to defence counsel provided by the protecting power, or if necessary by the court (Art. 72, para. 2 GC IV),

—the right to present the necessary evidence for the defence, and in particular to call witnesses (Art. 72, para. 1),

—the right to an interpreter (Art. 72, para. 3),

—proportionality between the offence and any penalty imposed (Art. 67),

—deduction of the period spent awaiting trial (Art. 69 GC IV),

—the provision of information concerning any right of appeal or petition (Art. 73, para. 1 GC IV),

—rapid conclusion of the case (Art. 71, para. 2), and

—notification to the protecting power regarding the proceedings (Art. 71, paras. 2 and 3), representatives of which may attend the proceedings at any time and obtain information on their progress (Art. 74 GC IV).

3. As pointed out in para. 4 of Section 576, GC IV does not require that judgment be subject to review by appeal. If there is no possibility of appeal, then the person convicted must always be able to petition the occupying authorities (Art. 73, para. 2) who are obliged to review the finding and sentence of the judgment.

4. The protecting power has an important role to play in criminal proceedings against inhabitants of occupied territories. Where such a protecting power exists, it shall be informed of every criminal proceeding 'in respect of charges involving the death penalty or imprisonment for two years or more' (Art. 71, para. 2). Article 71, para. 3 gives details of the contents of the required notification, and stipulates that the protecting power must receive this information at least three weeks before the trial begins. The trial may begin only if it has been verified that these provisions have been met. The representatives of the protecting power have the right to attend the trial in person. Consequently, they must be informed in good time of the location and date of the trial. If any part of the proceedings is held in camera for security reasons then the court must so inform the representatives of the protecting power (Art. 74, para. 1).

5. The protecting power may at any time demand information concerning criminal proceedings against inhabitants of the occupied territory (Art. 71, para. 2). The occupying authorities are obliged, in particular, to communicate to the protecting power all judgments involving the death penalty or imprisonment for more than two years, and to state the reasons for the sentence. The period allowed for appeal does not begin until after this notification. The records of all other judgments shall be open to inspection by representatives of the protecting power (Art. 74, para. 2).

6. Under Article 136 the National Information Bureau must also be informed of every judgment. The Bureau passes this information on to the Central Tracing

Gasser

Agency of the ICRC (Art. 140 GC IV), which collects, transmits, and stores all information regarding protected persons. In this way, the country of origin, and if applicable the relatives, of the person accused or convicted can also be informed. In addition, every change in the relevant details must be reported. For general remarks on the National Information Bureau and the Central Information Agency, see Section 538.

578   **Minor offences shall only be punishable by internment or simple imprisonment (Art. 68, para. 1 GC IV). Serious offences (espionage, serious acts of sabotage, homicide) may be punishable by death if, in the occupied territory, such offences were likewise liable to death penalty before the occupation began (Art. 68, para. 2 GC IV; Arts. 76, para. 3 and 77, para. 5 AP I).**

1. A principle generally applicable in penal law also applies to occupying powers: the punishment must in all circumstances be proportionate to the gravity of the offence. The court must always bear in mind that inhabitants of the occupied territory convicted of criminal offences do not owe allegiance to the occupying power (Art. 67).

2. Under Article 68, para. 1 GC IV, a minor offence is a criminal act 'solely intended to harm the occupying power' and which does not cause bodily harm or serious damage to property. Such offences should be punished at most with imprisonment or 'internment'. The latter is not in itself a punishment (on internment generally, see Sections 591 ff.). If the criminal judge orders internment in place of imprisonment for less serious cases, that is to be seen as an alleviation of the penalty. In contrast to 'real' internment (within the meaning of Article 78), the extent of punishment must be determined by the judge when 'internment' is used as a penalty. The duration of 'internment' must consequently be established from the very beginning.

3. GC IV permits the death penalty in particularly serious cases. By doing so, international humanitarian law in no way expresses an opinion as to the controversial question of whether the death penalty is compatible with the guarantee of fundamental human rights. Provisions of GC IV regarding the death penalty place restrictions on those states which apply this penalty. According to Article 68, para. 2 GC IV, the occupying power may introduce or apply the death penalty for the following cases only:

—espionage,

—serious acts of sabotage against military installations of the occupying power, or

—intentional acts causing the death of one or more persons, in so far as the national law in effect prior to the occupation allows the death penalty for such acts.

4. As for the procedure, the death penalty may be pronounced only if the court's attention has been expressly called to the fact that, as an inhabitant of the occupied territory, the person sentenced does not have a duty of allegiance to the occupying

Gasser

power (Art. 68, para. 3 GC IV). In addition to a right of appeal, where applicable, persons sentenced to death always have the right to petition the authorities of the occupying power for pardon or reprieve (Art. 75, para. 1 GC IV), and must be given the opportunity to do so. Thus a death penalty may in no circumstances be executed for six months (Art. 75, para. 2). This period does not begin until the protecting power has received notification of the final judgment or of the denial of pardon or reprieve. Exceptions are only possible in strictly limited conditions (Art. 75, para. 3).

5. The death penalty may in no circumstances be pronounced on a person who was under eighteen years of age at the time of the offence (Art. 68, para. 4 GC IV). Article 76, para. 3 AP I calls upon the occupying power not to pronounce the death penalty on pregnant women and mothers with infants. If the death penalty is pronounced on such women, it may not be carried out in any circumstances.

Nationals of the occupying power who, before the occupation, sought refuge in the territory of the occupied state shall not be prosecuted on that account. Crimes and other punishable offences committed after the outbreak of hostilities which would have justified extradition in times of peace shall be liable to prosecution (Art. 70, para. 2 GC IV).   579

1. This rule addresses the special situation of nationals of the occupying power who left their country before the outbreak of hostilities and sought refuge in the territory subsequently occupied, possibly as refugees within the meaning of the law relating to refugees.54 With the conquest of the territory by the armed forces of their native state, they fell into the hands of the authorities from whom they had sought refuge. Article 70, para. 2 GC IV stipulates that such persons may not be prejudiced and, in particular, may not be taken out of the occupied territory. They may be prosecuted only for an offence punishable under domestic penal law and committed prior to the occupation, if the law of the occupied state would have allowed extradition for this offence. For offences committed after occupation, the general provisions relating to prosecution of inhabitants of the occupied territory apply.

2. See Section 588 below for the general position of refugees in international humanitarian law. According to Article 44 GC IV and (particularly) Article 73 AP I refugees and stateless persons are entitled to the same legal protection as nationals of the enemy party to the conflict.

Persons accused or convicted of offences shall be detained under humane conditions. All sentences passed must be executed in the occupied territory (Art. 76, para. 1 GC IV). Detainees have the right to be visited by delegates of the protecting power and of the International Committee of the Red Cross (Art. 76, para. 6 GC IV).   580

---

[54] See in particular the Convention on the Status of Refugees of 28 July 1951, and the Protocol thereto, of 31 Jan. 1967.

1. In contrast to Sections 591–8, which deal with internment as an administrative measure ordered for security reasons, Section 580 applies to the treatment of persons accused or lawfully convicted of having committed a criminal offence. With regard to the treatment of detainees persons, it is irrelevant whether the punishable act is a common law offence or a violation of an order for the protection of public security or the security of the occupying power.

2. The term 'persons accused of offences' as used here must be understood in a broad sense. It includes all persons deprived of their freedom because they are suspected of having committed a punishable offence. This means that a person is under the special protection of humanitarian law provisions regarding the treatment of prisoners from the moment that he or she is detained. This observation is particularly significant for the initial period of the investigation, which often takes place in complete isolation from the outside world. Article 5, para. 2 GC IV expressly states that any prisoners held incommunicado must always and without exception be treated humanely.[55]

3. Article 76 GC IV requires the following treatment for prisoners accused or convicted of offences:
—the conditions of detention must be at least equal to those of normal imprisonment;
—food and hygiene must enable good health;
—detainees shall receive the medical attention required by their state of health;
—women shall be confined in separate quarters and under the direct supervision of women;
—minors are entitled to special treatment;
—detainees have the right to maintain contact with the outside world (family, lawyer, etc.);
—they have the right to receive spiritual sustenance of their own choice;
—they have the right to receive at least one relief parcel monthly.

Moreover, the relevant international rules regarding detention must be respected.[56]

4. Under Article 76, para. 1 the persons sentenced to detention must be able to serve this sentence in a prison located in the occupied territory. The same applies for persons detained pending trial. This provision is a specific application of the general prohibition against displacement of persons from the occupied territories,

---

[55] Art. 5, para. 2 GC IV permits in certain conditions that persons suspected of having committed espionage, sabotage, or other offence directed against the security of the occupying power be cut off from any communication with the outside world for a limited period.

[56] See especially the Standard Minimum Rules for the Treatment of Offenders, adopted by ECOSOC on 31 July 1957 and 13 May 1977, and the Body of Principles for the Protection of All Persons under any Form of Detention or Imprisonment, Res. 43/173 (of 9 Dec. 1988) of the UN General Assembly.

Gasser

especially into the territory of the occupying power (Art. 49 GC IV; see Section 544). In addition, it is intended to facilitate contact between detainees and their families.

5. Under Article 143 GC IV, representatives of the protecting power and delegates of the ICRC have the right 'to go to all places where protected persons are found, particularly places of internment, detention, and work'. Regarding the protecting powers, see Sections 1215 ff.; on the task of the ICRC, see Section 1220. Prisons in which persons from the occupied territories accused or convicted of offences are held are indisputably such places. ICRC delegates in fact spend a great deal of their time visiting prisoners. The reason for detention is of no importance. The protecting power and the ICRC are interested above all in persons detained by the occupying authorities for reasons connected with the war, who are exposed to the greatest risks. Nevertheless, prisoners held under the ordinary law who are in the control of the occupying power are also visited.

6. Representatives of the protecting power and delegates of the ICRC have a duty to examine conditions of detention and, if necessary, to try to improve them. They concern themselves with the personal affairs of the detainees in so far as these require an outside and neutral institution. The visit to a prison by representatives of the protecting power or delegates of the ICRC includes inspection of all rooms and places where detainees may be, as well as private conversations with the detainees of their choice (Art. 143, para. 2). The conclusions following the visit are forwarded to the responsible authorities of the occupying power. Visits are repeated at intervals until all detainees have been released.

7. The occupying authorities may suspend visits to a prison only for imperative military reasons, and only for a limited period (Art. 143, para. 3).

At the close of occupation, all detainees and relevant records shall be handed over   **581**
to the authorities of the liberated territory (Art. 77 GC IV).

The handover to the authorities of the home state must be orderly, after suitable preparation and organization. The protecting power and/or the ICRC may be involved in the process. GC IV does not deal with the question of whether prisoners must remain in detention following the handover or whether they must be released.

IV. ALIENS IN THE TERRITORY OF A PARTY TO THE CONFLICT

Introductory Remarks

1. The fate of civilians present in the territory of the enemy at the outset of hostilities, either as residents or as persons travelling through, has changed greatly from

Gasser

enslavement to the securing of human rights through modern international humanitarian law.

2. Under the heading 'Aliens in the Territory of a Party to the Conflict', Section II of Part III of GC IV regulates a number of situations that arise when nationals of one party to a conflict, for whatever reasons, fall into the power of an adverse party. In contrast to the law of occupation (Arts. 47–78), this section is not intended to be a comprehensive codification of all the rights of such persons. That would be unnecessary, since the state of residence is already obliged to treat these persons in accordance with international law governing the treatment of nationals of other states. As such, in normal times aliens are entitled to all their rights under international customary law and, especially today, under the various human rights conventions.

3. The provisions of international law for the protection of aliens are applicable also in times of armed conflict, in accordance with Article 38 GC IV (on this point, see Section 584). This right has found expression in international conventions and in international customary law. The human rights conventions permit a state party, at the outbreak of an armed conflict, to suspend the guarantee of a number of human rights under certain conditions.[57] Such restriction of rights must be publicly announced, and then applies to citizens and resident aliens alike. GC IV goes one step further and expressly regulates a number of tricky questions that can arise during a war concerning the relationship between a party to the conflict and nationals of the opposing party. These provisions are the subject of this section.

4. Articles 13–26 GC IV formulate a number of provisions for the protection of the civilian population as such. All civilians, including the belligerent's own population, must be protected against the effects of the war. Articles 27–34 and 35–46 deal in particular with the position of alien civilians who find themselves in the hands of a party to the conflict. 'Aliens in the territory of a party to the conflict' are, first and foremost, nationals of the state with which their state of residence is in armed conflict. They also include nationals of a neutral state not involved in the conflict, who do not enjoy actual protection due to the absence of diplomatic representation in their state of residence (Art. 4, para. 2 GC IV). In practice, these persons would be nationals of a state which, although not taking part directly in the conflict, supports the cause of the 'other side', or is perceived as doing so by the state of residence. Finally, refugees and stateless persons are also aliens entitled to protection under the provisions of GC IV (Art. 73 AP I). These categories of persons are hereafter referred to as 'aliens'.

---

[57] International Covenant on Civil and Political Rights (Art. 4: 'In time of public emergency which threatens the life of the nation . . .'); European Convention for the Protection of Rights and Fundamental Freedoms (Art. 15: 'In time of war or other public emergency threatening the life of the nation . . .'); American Convention on Human Rights (Art. 27: 'In time of war, public danger, or other emergency that threatens the independence or security of a State Party . . .'). The African Charter of Human and People's Rights does not contain such a rule for conflict situations.

Gasser

5. The citizens of states with which their country of residence has normal diplomatic relations, who find themselves on the territory of a party to a conflict, are not 'protected persons' since they enjoy the usual diplomatic protection. They come under the provisions of international law effective in peacetime and have, for example, the unconditional right to leave the country. The consular representatives of their native state must be enabled to look after them. It should be noted, however, that the named category of persons does not fall entirely outside the protection of international humanitarian law. For example, Articles 13–26 GC IV, under the heading 'General Protection of Populations against Certain Consequences of War', apply to these persons. Also, Article 75 AP I acts as a 'legal safety net' guaranteeing a minimum standard of human rights for all persons who do not have protection on other grounds. Finally, it should be recalled also that such aliens are always protected by the provisions of international humanitarian law prohibiting military operations directed against civilians (see Sections 502 ff., especially Section 506).

6. This section deals only with international armed conflicts and the law applicable in such situations. In a non-international conflict, the members of the insurgent party who fall into the hands of the opposing side, i.e. of the government, are usually nationals of the same state. They are in any case entitled to the rights and guarantees owed to all nationals, including those deriving from human rights conventions.[58] Nationals of third party states must be dealt with according to the rules applicable to aliens. To these must be added the special provisions of common Article 3 of the GCs and of AP II. Members of the government faction in the power of insurgents are also protected under Article 3 of the GCs and AP II.

All civilians may leave the territory, unless their departure is contrary to the national interests of the State (Art. 35, para. 1 GC IV). The departure shall be carried out in humane conditions (Art. 36 GC IV).

If any such person is refused permission to leave, it shall be ensured that such refusal be reconsidered by an appropriate court or administrative board particularly designated for that purpose (Art. 35, para. 2 GC IV).

1. All aliens have the right to leave the territory, but are not obliged to leave their state of residence. Aliens who may have spent many years there already may be forced to leave the country against their will only in exceptional circumstances, as stipulated in GC IV (see Section 589).

2. The right to leave a state involved in an armed conflict is significantly restricted by GC IV. Under Article 35, para. 1 persons are entitled to leave the territory 'unless their departure is contrary to the national interests of the state'. This reference to the national interest of the state of residence is intended above all to enable this state to prohibit residents suitable for military service from leaving. Likewise, economic considerations may be adduced in order to prohibit persons from leaving on

---

[58] See, however, n. 57.

the grounds of 'national interest'.[59] The wide discretionary powers granted to the authorities by Article 35 may well be restricted today by Article 12 of the International Covenant on Civil and Political Rights of 19 December 1966 (although this Article is not guaranteed in a state of emergency),[60] which states that departure may be refused only on specific grounds.

3. Under Article 35, the application for departure must be dealt with by 'regularly established procedures'. This means, among other things, that the persons making an application must be heard and enabled to present evidence. As expressly laid down in Article 35, para. 1, the decision shall be made and the grounds given 'as rapidly as possible'. If the application is refused, then the applicant must be entitled to have the decision reconsidered by an ordinary court or by a specially created administrative board (para. 2). The protecting power must be notified of the names of all persons whose applications for departure have been rejected (para. 3). In addition, information concerning the reasons for rejection shall be provided.

4. Persons leaving the territory of a party to a conflict, with or without an explicit decision by the authorities, must be allowed to depart in an orderly manner. Article 35, para. 1 states in particular that they must be allowed to take with them the money necessary for the journey and 'a reasonable amount of their effects and articles of personal use'. The departure itself must take place 'in satisfactory conditions as regards safety, hygiene, sanitation, and food' (Art. 36). The costs are chargeable to the country of destination or, in the case of departure for a third country, to the state of origin. Collective repatriation, based on a special agreement between the states concerned, is also possible. The departure arrangements may be entrusted to the protecting power or the ICRC (see also Section 589).

584   **Aliens remaining in the territory of a party to the conflict shall, in principle, be treated in the same way as they would be in peacetime.**

1. Even a national of an adverse power is entitled to humane treatment by the authorities of the country of residence. In principle, such an alien may claim the protection of international human rights during an armed conflict, in the same way as in peacetime. As expressly laid down in Article 38 GC IV: 'the situation of [civilians belonging to the enemy state] shall continue to be regulated, in principle, by the provisions concerning aliens in time of peace.' This is subject only to the special provisions of GC IV. See in particular Section 585.

2. In wartime, the authorities of the state of residence may apply to aliens such measures of control and security as it deems necessary in the circumstances (Art. 27, para. 4). If it is absolutely necessary for security reasons, assigned residence or internment may be ordered (see Section 587).

[59] Pictet, *Commentary*, Vol. IV, 236.   [60] See n. 57.

3. As protected persons within the meaning of GC IV, aliens on the territory of a party to a conflict have the right at any time to approach the protecting power, if any, or the ICRC. They may also contact the national Red Cross or Red Crescent society or any other organization that may be able to assist them (Art. 30). Conversely, representatives of the protecting power and delegates of the ICRC have unrestricted access to all places where protected persons might be found, especially places of detention and internment camps (Arts. 30 and 143; see Section 592).

This implies *inter alia*:   585
—ensuring medical care and freedom of religion, and
—the right to exit from areas exposed to the dangers of the conflict.
Aliens shall be entitled to these rights to the same extent as the nationals of the state in which they are living (Art. 38 GC IV).

1. Article 27 GC IV, which applies to aliens on the territory of a party to a conflict, requires the authorities of the state in which they are living to 'respect . . . their persons, their honour, their family rights, their religious convictions and practices, and their manners and customs'. In the event of war, the nationals of an enemy state must be protected particularly from violence, intimidation, insults, and from public curiosity. If necessary, the authorities must order special measures for the protection of persons particularly at risk. Unjustified discrimination is expressly prohibited (Art. 27, para. 3).

2. The taking of hostages is prohibited (Art. 34 GC IV). Furthermore, aliens who have stayed in the country may not be taken to places of military importance and held there in order to prevent the adversary from attacking these objects. On the contrary, the authorities must protect aliens from harm by war in the same way as they protect their own citizens, i.e. as far as possible (see Sections 506, 510, and 585).

3. In addition to the fundamental rights guaranteed by Article 27, Article 38 guarantees to aliens additional rights:
—to receive individual and collective relief consignments;
—to receive medical attention if their state of health requires;
—to practise their religion and to receive spiritual sustenance;
—to protective measures against the dangers of war, especially the right to move away from a dangerous area;
—preferential treatment of children, pregnant women and mothers of small children.

4. The general prohibition against discrimination, which is given particular weight by Article 38, is intended to ensure that aliens remaining in the territory of a party to a conflict do not suffer from the immediate effects of war more than nationals of

Gasser

the state in question. On the other hand, aliens are not entitled to preferential treatment.

5. The guaranteed rights listed under paras. 1 and 3 above are examples only. As is clear from the reference in Article 38 to 'the provisions concerning aliens in time of peace', it is not an exhaustive list. A right not explicitly listed, but deserving special mention, is the guarantee of fair judicial proceedings. Aliens accused of having committed a criminal offence in connection with the conflict are entitled to penal proceedings in accordance with the international obligations of the state, in particular the human rights conventions. The prohibition of discrimination must be observed under all circumstances. Supplementary to this is the minimum standard codified by Article 75, para. 4 AP I, which all ordinary court proceedings must meet (see Section 518).

6. Detained persons accused or convicted of an offence shall be treated in accordance with the provisions applicable to all detainees in peacetime, and without discrimination. See also Section 580, paras. 3 and 4.

7. Article 5, para. 1 GC IV must be seen as an exceptional provision, which restricts the rights of persons suspected of being engaged in activities detrimental to the security of the state (see above, Sections 517 ff.).

586   **Aliens shall be given the opportunity to find a job. That opportunity shall be equal to that enjoyed by the nationals of the state in which they are living (Art. 39 GC IV). Aliens may be compelled to work only under the same conditions as nationals of the territory in which they are living (Art. 40, para. 1 GC IV).**

1. Persons remaining in the territory of the opposing party to the conflict must be given the opportunity to earn their own living, irrespective of whether they are in the hands of the adversary voluntarily or involuntarily. When looking for work, aliens may not be put in a worse situation than nationals of the state. The state retains the right to prevent aliens from being employed for certain types of work for security reasons (Art. 27, para. 4 GC IV; see Section 584).

2. If persons are prevented from earning their own living because of security measures applied to them, e.g. an order placing them in assigned residence, then the authorities must support them (Art. 39, para. 2).

3. Like nationals of the state, aliens may be compelled to work. They may be assigned only to work 'which is normally necessary to ensure the feeding, sheltering, clothing, transport, and health of human beings and which is not directly related to the conduct of military operations' (Art. 40, para. 2). Work connected with the armed forces or in weapons factories, for example, is prohibited. The obligation of equal treatment of aliens and nationals is applicable particularly with regard to safety at the workplace, protective measures to be taken, pay, and compensation for industrial accidents and occupational diseases.

Gasser

4. Article 40, para. 4, expressly provides that aliens may submit complaints to the protecting power (if any), to the ICRC, or to the national Red Cross or Red Crescent society if these provisions of labour law are not observed.

The placing in assigned residence or internment of aliens may be ordered only if   587
reasons of security make it absolutely necessary (Art. 42, para. 1 GC IV), or if it is
not possible to control these persons sufficiently (Art. 41, para. 1 GC IV). It shall
also be possible to have these measures reconsidered by an appropriate court or
administrative board (Art. 43, para. 1 GC IV).

1. Orders for assigned residence and internment are the severest security mea-sures that the authorities of the state of residence may take relating to nationals of the opposing side (Art. 41, para. 1). Regarding the legal questions associated with deportation of aliens to their own country or to a third state, see Section 589. Assigned residence restricts personal freedom of movement. Internment involves sending a person to a place of detention or a camp established for the purpose. Both measures may be ordered only if national security makes this 'absolutely necessary' (Art. 42, para. 1). Only reasons of general security of the state, therefore, can justify internment. On the reasons justifying internment, see in particular Section 591. Whether the order is for internment or for the less restrictive measure of assigned residence must be determined in accordance with the specific circumstances and the principle of proportionality, based on obligatory discretion.

2. GC IV says little about which institution should make decisions concerning assigned residence or internment, or about the procedure to be followed. It may be assumed that this will probably be an administrative body. In practice, proceedings must be rapid, so there is little alternative. By contrast, Article 43 expressly stipu-lates that such decisions may be reconsidered by a court or a special administrative board, either at the request of the person affected or on its own initiative. In partic-ular, this authority must review, at least twice yearly, the proportionality of every decision ordering assigned residence or internment. This control procedure is intended to safeguard the rights of persons affected. See also Section 591 regarding internment. In addition, the provisions in force in peacetime shall be applied (see Section 584).

3. GC IV has paid particular attention to the circumstances in which internment may be imposed and has described them in detail (see Part V, Internment of Civilians, Sections 592 ff.). Regarding assigned residence, with its less far-reaching restrictions, Article 41, para. 2 implies that the authorities must always take action if the persons affected can no longer support themselves or their dependants as a result of the assigned residence.

4. Finally, it should be noted that a person may request internment 'if his situation renders this step necessary' (Art. 42, para. 2), i.e. if he no longer feels safe. The state of residence must comply with this request.

Gasser

588   Refugees and stateless persons shall in all circumstances be treated as protected persons (Art. 44 GC IV; Art. 73 AP I).

1. Article 73 AP I provides unequivocally that refugees and stateless persons present in the territory of a party to a conflict have the same entitlement to protection as nationals of the adversary state. This applies particularly to refugees who are nationals of the adversary state, but who have left their country because they felt threatened. The term 'refugee' must be understood in a broad sense. A refugee in this connection is any person who does not in fact enjoy the protection of a government.[61]

2. Refugees and stateless persons shall be regarded as protected persons in every respect. As expressly laid down by Article 44 GC IV, refugees may not be regarded as enemy aliens on the mere basis of their nationality and thus automatically subject to the same control measures. This applies for instance to assigned residence or internment. The state of residence must always guarantee them at least equal treatment to nationals of the adversary, taking into consideration the special circumstances resulting from their status as refugees or stateless persons.

589   Enemy aliens may be transferred to a state party to the Fourth Geneva Convention if this does not cause any disadvantage for these persons (Art. 45 GC IV).

1. This provision relates to the handing over of civilians in the power of a party to the conflict to a third state, which may or may not be involved in the conflict. This action may well be in the interests of the persons affected, especially if living conditions in the accepting state are less difficult than those in the territory of the party to the conflict.

2. The actual and legal position of those affected may not be worsened by such a transfer. Under Article 45 certain conditions must therefore be met to ensure that transfer of civilians to another state is in the interests of the persons concerned and therefore permissible. Such persons may be transferred only to a state bound by GC IV, thus safeguarding their legal protection by GC IV. Moreover, the transferring state must ascertain that the accepting state is actually willing and able to treat the persons concerned according to the provisions of international humanitarian law. If these conditions are met, civilian nationals of the opposing party to the conflict[62] may be transferred to a third power, even against their own will, with the consequence that that state becomes responsible for fulfilling the obligations of GC IV, including the obligation to permit such persons to leave the country at any time (see Section 582).

---

[61] ICRC *Commentary*, para. 2942.

[62] This includes refugees, stateless persons, and members of third states with which there are no normal diplomatic relations. See introductory remarks to Section IV.

Gasser

3. In no circumstances may civilians be transferred to a country where they reasonably fear persecution on account of their political opinions or religious convictions (Art. 45, para. 4) or where they will not be afforded the protection guaranteed by Articles 27 ff. If, after the transfer the transferring state realizes that the accepting state does not meet the requirements of international humanitarian law on important matters, then it must find a remedy and if necessary take the persons back (Art. 45, para. 3). Extradition treaties concluded before the outbreak of the conflict continue to apply to persons accused of criminal offences under the ordinary law (Art. 45, para. 5).

4. If aliens, at the outbreak of a conflict, find themselves in the territory of a party to that conflict, is it permissible for the authorities simply to put them on an aircraft or to set them down at the border of the neighbouring state against their will? GC IV does not expressly regulate the conditions in which individual or collective deportation is permissible in such a situation. In this respect also the general rules applicable in peacetime apply (see Section 584). Certainly persons may not be deported to a country where they can expect to be persecuted because of their political opinions or religious convictions. Article 45, para. 4 GC IV contains a universally applicable principle of international law. In this connection, attention is drawn to Article 13 of the International Covenant on Civil and Political Rights, which stipulates an orderly procedure for expulsion of aliens and in particular a procedure enabling the persons concerned to present their own case. This rule should be applied generally. If these conditions are met, then nothing stands in the way of deportation from the point of view of international humanitarian law. Of course, it must be carried out humanely. See also Section 582, second sentence.

5. GC IV does not say whether members of one party to the conflict may be handed over or deported against their will to their native state, i.e. the other party to the conflict. Here again, the rule undoubtedly applies that persons may not forcibly be transferred to a country if they face persecution there for their political opinions or religious convictions. Apart from these special circumstances, repatriation must be considered as permissible. Special attention should be paid to the circumstances of such individual or collective deportation. In particular, the persons concerned may not be exposed to danger. An orderly, previously arranged transfer is essential.

All restrictions imposed on enemy aliens shall be cancelled as soon as possible   **590**
after the close of hostilities (Art. 46 GC IV).

This provision is clear. For interpretation of the term 'close of hostilities', see Section 221. If necessary, the return of assets or compensation, for instance for the benefit of interned persons, shall be regulated by treaty.

Gasser

V. INTERNMENT OF CIVILIANS

Introductory Remarks

1. Section 591 below is a reminder that a person may be interned only if this is absolutely necessary for security reasons (Arts. 42 and 78 GC IV). Section 546 describes the conditions in which an inhabitant of an occupied territory may be interned, while Section 587 states the circumstances in which the internment of aliens present in the territory of a party to the conflict is permissible.

2. Sections 592–8 deal with the treatment of internees. They apply both to the occupied territories and to the internment of aliens present in the territory of a party to the conflict.

3. The internment of a belligerent's own national during wartime is not covered by international humanitarian law. The international provisions concerning the protection of human rights, however, are applicable.

591 **Internment of civilians shall be permissible only in exceptional cases:**

   —if, in specific cases, it is necessary for imperative reasons of security (Arts. 41–3 and 78, para. 1 GC IV); or

   —as a penalty to be imposed on civilians (Art. 68 GC IV).

   Decisions regarding such internment shall be made according to a regular procedure and subject to regular review (Arts. 43 and 78, para. 2 GC IV).

1. Internment is a drastic restriction of personal freedom. It is permitted only as *ultima ratio*, i.e. only if security requirements cannot be met by less severe measures, such as an obligation to register with the police, or an order for assigned residence. Internment is permissible solely as a measure to ensure public order. It is not a form of punishment. The reasons allowing internment of a civilian who is a national of the adverse party are listed definitively in GC IV.

2. Civilians present in the territory of the other party may be interned 'if the security of the detaining power makes it absolutely necessary' (Art. 42, para. 1). In the event of belligerent occupation, the occupying power may intern a person if it regards it as necessary 'for imperative reasons of security' (Art. 78, para. 1). In both situations there must be a threat to public security linked with the person in question. GC IV allows the authorities a great deal of latitude. In exercising the discretion they must take into account the personal situation of the person concerned. Internment should be ordered only if other control measures are not sufficient.

3. GC IV regulates the procedure by which the decision about the internment of a person shall be made in the event of belligerent occupation and in relation to aliens

present in the territory of the adverse party to the conflict (Arts. 42 ff. and Art. 78, para. 2). In particular, in the event of occupation Article 78, para. 2 requires a 'regular procedure'. This includes the right of the person concerned to be heard. The same must unquestionably apply to the internment of aliens in the hands of the opposing side, although Articles 42 ff. remain silent on this point. This idea is supported by Article 38, with its reference to 'provisions . . . in time of peace' (see Section 584). Moreover, without 'regular procedure' no proper decision which takes into account the provisions of international humanitarian law is possible. It is clear, however, that under GC IV it is the administration and not necessarily a court, that may deal with and reach decisions concerning internment. The convention does not prescribe anything else.

4. In both situations the competent authorities must establish procedures permitting the examination of internment orders (Art. 43; Art. 78, para. 2). On one hand the person concerned must be able to have the decision reconsidered by a court or administrative board set up specially for the purpose; it must reach a decision within the shortest possible time. On the other hand this authority, whether a court or an administrative board, must on its own initiative periodically, and at least every six months, review all decisions regarding internment and decide whether the conditions for internment are still met. This supervision by a special, independent body is extremely important and should be capable of ending abusive internment.

The treatment of internees basically corresponds to the treatment of prisoners of war (Arts. 79–141 GC IV). Representatives of the protecting power and delegates of the ICRC may visit internees in their camps at any time and talk to them individually and without witnesses.   592

The place of internment shall be placed under the authority of a responsible officer or a public official chosen from the civil administration of the detaining power (Art. 99, para. 1 GC IV). The detaining power shall, as far as possible, accommodate the internees according to their nationality, language, and customs (Art. 82, para. 1 GC IV). The detaining power shall ensure that members of the same family are lodged together in the same place of internment. Separation of a temporary nature may be necessitated for reasons of employment or health or for the purpose of executing penal or disciplinary measures (Art. 82, para. 2 GC IV).   593

Internees shall always be accommodated separately from prisoners of war and from persons detained for any other reason (e.g. convicts) (Art. 84 GC IV).   594

Internees shall be treated humanely. In particular, any victimization, punishment drill, military drill, or reduction of food rations is prohibited (Art. 100 GC IV). Contact with the exterior shall be permitted (Arts. 105–16 GC IV).   595

In principle, internees are not obliged to work (Art. 95, para. 1 GC IV). Internees may, however, be employed for work within places of internment or for activities   596

Gasser

serving their own interests (Art. 95, para. 3 GC IV). Internees shall not do voluntary work connected with the conduct of military operations.

597 Internees who commit offences shall be subject to the laws in force in the territory
in which they are detained (Art. 117, para. 1 GC IV).

1. Section IV of Part III of GC IV, entitled 'Regulations for the Treatment of
Internees', contains its own code of laws, with detailed provisions regulating the
organization of places of internment and the treatment of internees. These are
closely modelled on the arrangements applicable to prisoners of war (Arts. 21–108
GC III; see Chapter 7 below).

2. Articles 79–135 GC IV regulate the following matters (according to the headings
of the individual chapter of Section IV):
—General provisions (Arts. 79–82)
—Places of internment (Arts. 83–8)
—Food and clothing (Arts. 89 ff.)
—Hygiene and medical attention (Arts. 91 ff.)
—Religious, intellectual, and physical activities (Arts. 93–6)
—Personal property and financial resources (Arts. 97 ff.)
—Administration and discipline (Arts. 99–104)
—Contacts with the exterior (Arts. 105–16), including provisions dealing with relief
  consignments
—Penal and disciplinary sanctions (Arts. 117–26)
—Transfers of internees (Arts. 127 ff.)
—Deaths (Arts. 129–31)
—Release, repatriation, and accommodation in neutral countries (Arts. 132–5).
Sections 592–7 describe the essential contents of the regulations concerning the
treatment of interned civilians. For further information, refer to Articles 79–135 GC
IV.[63]

3. Certain provisions deserve closer attention:

a) The party to the conflict that interns civilians must inform the internees themselves, the authorities of their state of origin and the protecting power (if any) of the
measures taken in connection with the internment (Art. 105). In practice, this
means particularly that the Central Tracing Service of the ICRC is to be informed of
every decision regarding internment and of any change in the condition of an
internee, through the National Information Bureau.

---

[63] See also Pictet, *Commentary*, Vol. IV, 370 ff.

b) Directly following their internment, in the event of transfer to another place of internment, or in the case of illness, internees must be given the opportunity personally to inform their families (Art. 106).

c) Internees must be given detailed information about their rights and obligations through notices posted in the place of internment. The full text of GC IV shall also be available in the place of internment, in a language that the internees can understand (Art. 99).

d) Representatives of protecting powers and delegates of the ICRC have the right to visit interned civilians and places of internment at will (Art. 143). The purpose of these visits is to check that the provisions of GC IV are observed by the detaining power and to deal with any personal requests by the internees requiring the involvement of a neutral authority. During such visits, relief supplies may also be distributed to the internees.

Upon the close of hostilities or occupation, the belligerent parties shall ensure the   598
return of all internees to their last place of residence or facilitate their repatriation
(Art. 134 GC IV).

1. As civilians can be interned only for so long as is necessary for security reasons (see Sections 591, 546, and 587), the measure must be abolished and the internees released when the motive for internment ceases to exist. This is plainly indicated in Article 132, para. 1. The periodical review of decisions regarding internment by the responsible court or the administrative body established for this purpose (see Section 591 and commentary) is intended to ensure that the release is ordered when necessary, even without being requested by the person concerned.

2. Article 132, para. 2 calls upon the parties to the conflict to attempt, through agreement and while the conflict is in progress, to find alternative solutions to internment for detained persons. The following categories of persons are here considered: children, pregnant women, mothers with infants or small children, the injured and sick, and in general any persons who have been interned for a long time. Other categories are naturally not excluded from such agreements; Article 132, para. 2 merely states an order of priority.

3. The following measures are possible: release, repatriation, return to the place of residence, or accommodation in a neutral country (Art. 132, para. 2). Every release or return must be carried out in orderly conditions. The protecting power and the ICRC are willing to assist in the release of internees and in particular in transfers to a third state.

4. When repatriation or transfer to a third state is ordered during the conflict, to what extent should the wishes of the persons affected be taken into consideration? Their refusal to allow themselves to be transferred to a specific country must at all times be respected if they can expect serious persecution there; this principle is

Gasser

rooted in the general rules of international law (see Section 589). For occupied territories, the following is also expressly stipulated: any transfer against their will of inhabitants of an occupied territory from such territory to the territory of the occupying power, to the unoccupied part of their native state, or to a third state is prohibited (see Section 544), even with the consent of the person concerned. The general provision of Article 49, para. 2 GC IV undoubtedly applies also to internees.

5. After the conclusion of hostilities, internment shall be revoked and the internees released as quickly as possible. Article 133, para. 1 makes clear that this is an absolute obligation. The release must be carried out in an orderly way and must take account of the state of health of the internees. The states involved must guarantee and facilitate the return of the internees to their last place of residence (Art. 134). They are also required to search for dispersed internees (Art. 133, para. 3). Aliens repatriated from the territory of a party to the conflict must have their wishes taken into consideration, in that they shall not be transferred to a country in which they may fear persecution (see para. 4 above). Upon the return of occupied territory, a solution must be found, justified by human rights considerations, for those persons who would face serious persecution if transferred to the lawful authorities.

6. With the close of hostilities the detaining power may detain those internees against whom criminal proceedings have been initiated or who have a sentence to serve (Art. 133, para. 2). They shall be released at latest once the sentence has been served or the trial has ended.

6

Protection of the Wounded, Sick, and Shipwrecked

I. GENERAL

Preliminary note

The principles of the humanitarian protection of the wounded, sick, and ship-wrecked were laid down in the first, semi-official, international conference of the Red Cross in Geneva, October 1863.[1] The sixteen states, which had assembled on initiatives of Genevan citizens—the *Comité des Cinq*, later the *Comité international et permanent de secours aux blessés militaires*[2]—and the ICRC decided to establish national commissions. These should support the army medical corps in times of war. A red cross on white ground should serve as a distinctive emblem and should be worn by soldiers in the army medical corps on their uniform. Since then the steps toward the creation of an organization and the maintenance of neutrality for the aid for wounded soldiers have been further developed.[3]

The wounded, sick, and shipwrecked shall be respected and protected in all cir-cumstances (Arts. 12, para. 1 and 35, para. 1 GC I; Art. 12, para. 1 GC II; Art. 3, para. 1 No. 2 GC III; Art. 10, para. 1 AP I; Art. 7, para. 1 AP II). Any attempts upon their lives, or violence to their persons, are prohibited. They shall be treated humanely and cared for (Art. 12, para. 2 GC I; Art. 12, para. 2 GC II; Art. 10, para. 2 AP I; Art. 7, para. 2 AP II).   601

1. The history of the 'Law of Geneva' shows that the sick and wounded of the armies and navies of belligerent states were the first object of humanitarian care. The Geneva Convention of 1864, for instance, considered the army's wounded. After supplementary provisions added in 1868 were not ratified, the Third Hague Convention of 1899[4] decided that the principles of the existing treaties should also apply to members of the navy. The development from two- to three-dimensional warfare brought the need to place members of the air force also under

---

[1] Schindler Toman, 275.   [2] Ruegger, *Recueil des Cours* 1953 I 82, 381, 383.
[3] For an historical survey of existing law in detail see Baccino-Astrada, 9 *et seq.*
[4] Convention of 29 July 1899 for the Adaptation of the principles of the Geneva Convention of 22 Aug. 1864 to Maritime Warfare, Schindler Toman, 289.

the protection of the humanitarian agreements. GC I, whose dispositions are supplemented in AP I, Part I, states in Art. 12 that the wounded and sick shall be respected and protected in all circumstances. Art. 13 then defines those wounded and sick persons who are subject to the convention's protection. Art. 14 GC I provides that those persons shall be prisoners of war when captured by the opponent. On that point the content of Art. 13 GC I corresponds with that of Art. 4 GC III.

2. AP I expands the categories of sick, wounded, or shipwrecked persons who are to be protected. Art. 6 describes the persons who, whether or not they are members of the armed forces, are subject to the protection of the Protocol. The regulations for the wounded, sick, and shipwrecked start with a list of definitions. Art. 8 lit. a AP I makes clear that the provisions concerning the 'wounded' and 'sick' are no longer applicable only to combatants, but extend to civilians who on account of injury or disease need aid and assistance. In addition, women in childbirth and pregnant women are protected as well as new-born babies, and infirm persons. The need for medical assistance is therefore the essential criterion for the application of the term 'wounded' or 'sick'.[5] Such persons must refrain from any hostile act; persons who continue fighting despite their wounds or disease cannot expect protection or indulgence.[6]

3. Arts. 12 and 13 GC I are based upon the principle of equality. Members of the armed forces, as well as the other wounded and sick persons named in Art. 13, have to be treated with care and protected by all means. Only urgent medical reasons justify, according to Art. 12, para. 3 GC I, a preference in order of treatment.[7] According to the wording, preference on the basis of the adolescent age of a wounded person would not be legitimate. In the event of a sudden increase in the numbers of wounded, of both one's own and enemy forces, priority may be given to the more heavily wounded. That the adolescent age of a wounded soldier is then also taken into account probably does not contradict the spirit of GC I. This view also results from Art. 12, para. 4 GC I: as in Art. 3 of the Geneva Convention for Prisoners of War of 1929[8] the specific position of women is pointed out in paragraph 4. Such a provision in favour of women is omitted from the Convention for Wounded of 1929.[9] It was not considered necessary, since special respect for wounded and sick female combatants was believed to be a constituent part of the Convention.[10] Only the experience of World War Two with the increasing involvement of female soldiers made it necessary that in GC I the protection of the women should receive special emphasis. The equal treatment of military and civilian sick, wounded, and shipwrecked is underlined in Art. 10 AP I: 'All the wounded, sick, and shipwrecked, to whichever party they belong , shall be respected and protected'.

---

[5] Bothe/Ipsen/Partsch, *ZaöRV* 38 (1978), 1–85 (15).   [6] Bothe/Partsch/Solf, 96.

[7] Pictet, Vol. I 149 ff.

[8] Convention of 27 July 1929 Concerning the Improvement of the Fate of Wounded and Sick on the Battlefield.

[9] Convention of 27 July 1929 Concerning the Treatment of Prisoners of War.   [10] Pictet, Vol. I 140.

Rabus

4. In addition to GC I, Art. 12, para. 1 GC II determines that those persons shall be protected who are at sea and are victims of any sort of shipwreck, no matter how this occurred, including forced landings on water or the crash of aircraft into the sea. The regulations for the protection of the wounded, sick, and shipwrecked at sea are mostly identical with those effective on land. Some differences result from the special circumstances of naval warfare. There are, however, no special regulations for the sick and wounded in the air above the sea. Depending on the battle's circumstances they are sick, wounded or shipwrecked in the sense of the respective GCs and AP I. For example, the term 'shipwrecked' includes those who are forced to land on sea because their aeroplane crashes there (Art. 12 GC II, Art. 8 lit. b AP I). The categories of persons to which the regulations of GC II for shipwrecked, sick, or wounded at sea are to be applied concur with those stated in Art. 13 GC I. AP I expands the categories to include, beside those of the armed forces, wounded, sick, and shipwrecked civilians who are subject to the scope of the Protocol (Art. 8 lit. a and b AP I).

5. There are no comparable regulations for members of air forces. Depending on the combat situation, their protection is regulated by the specific regulations for land or naval warfare. The governmental experts who presented the HRAW in 1922/23 considered the crews of 'military aircraft' to be members of the armed forces. To those, as well as to flying ambulances, the principles in respect of protection in war on land of the Geneva Convention of 1906,[11] and the regulations of the X Hague Convention of 1907[12] for protection in naval warfare should be applied. That the combatant status of pilots and crews was not always accepted is shown, for example, by trials after World War II, in which the lack of protection against attacks on the crews of crashed aircraft by the population was condemned.[13] The attempts to treat captured American and allied pilots as war criminals due to their actions in the Vietnam and the Gulf War aimed at depriving those servicemen of their rights under humanitarian law.[14] Under such circumstances the possibility of direct repatriation of crew members in accordance with Arts. 109–17 GC III, for example, would be removed. Also, the medical assistance for convicted prisoners of war required by Art. 108 GC III is less detailed than for those not yet convicted.[15]

6. Art. 42 AP I deals with the protection of persons in distress in the air. They must not be attacked while bailing out. This regulation resembles Art. 20 HRAW which determined that crew members of an aircraft must not be attacked during their descent.[16] In the course of the negotiations for AP I it was not clear whether an air

---

[11] Convention of 6 July 1906 Concerning the Improvement of the Fate of Wounded and Sick of the Armies.

[12] X Hague Convention of 18 Oct. 1907 Concerning the Application of the Principles of the Geneva Convention to Maritime Warfare.

[13] Cf. The *Essen Lynching* case, Trial of *Erich Heyer and Six Others*, Law Reports, London 1947, Vol. I, 88–92, Case No. 8.

[14] Cf. Rosas, 179, 180; Hailbronner, 81, 92.   [15] Cf. Jescheck, *EPIL* 4, 296 ff.; Pictet, Vol. III 477.

[16] Cf. Hailbronner, 86–8.

Rabus

crew bailing out in distress might be attacked when landing in an area controlled by their own military forces. In the end, the compromise stated in Art. 42, paras. 1 and 2 AP I was reached. The content of this article cannot be applied to airborne troops, even if they jump from an aircraft in distress (Art. 42, para. 3 AP I).

602 **The protection of the wounded and sick ceases if they commit any act of hostility (Art. 8 lit. a AP I).**

1. In order to avoid abuse, the regulations of GCs and AP I contain detailed prohibitions against medical units giving support to hostilities. It is therefore inadmissible to use medical units for military purposes. Another danger which results from army medical corps' immunity from military offences is that a commanding officer may be tempted to abuse the medical units for camouflage. On the basis that a special protection granted can also be withdrawn, Art. 21 GC I determines that medical units lose their particular protection if they are abused for actions, beyond their humanitarian mission, which inflict loss on the opponent. Medical units must not, for example, be used for the accommodation of healthy soldiers or for the establishment of observation posts. Art. 12, para. 4 AP I adds that medical units must not be used as a shield for military objects. They must also not be situated where they are likely to be endangered by military actions.

2. The protection granted to medical units may cease only after a warning and after the expiration of an appropriate time limit (Art. 21 GC I; concerning civilian medical units see Art. 13, para. 1 AP I). Abuse justifying the suspension of protection for medical units includes abuse of the distinctive emblem which is considered to be a grave breach of humanitarian law (Art. 53, lit. f GC I; Art. 23, lit. f HagueReg). It is a standard reproach in war propaganda that medical units are abused for military purposes by the adversary, and it is therefore useful that those situations in which protection for medical units cannot be suspended are defined, as in Art. 22 GC I and Art. 13, para. 2 AP I. The regulations of GC I and AP I on the whole correspond. The definition in AP I has been adapted to recent developments. Art. 22, para. 5 GC I, for example, allows medical units to care for sick and wounded civilians, while Art. 13, para. 2 lit. d AP I additionally allows combatants to be treated in civilian medical establishments.[17] Art. 22 , para. 5 GC I became unnecessary when the scope of AP I was expanded; for that reason it was not included in Art. 13 AP I.

603 **'Shipwrecked' persons are those in peril at sea or in other waters and who refrain from all acts of hostility (Art. 13 GC II; Art. 8 lit. b AP I).**

604 **Reprisals against the wounded, sick, and shipwrecked are prohibited (Art. 46 GC I; Art. 47 GC II; Art. 20 AP I).**

---

[17] McCoubrey, 56, notes the case of a military messenger sent out by the military commander to make inquiries respecting the situation of the sick and wounded. Such a consolidation exercise is necessary for the service of the medical units.

All possible measures shall be taken at all times to collect the wounded, sick, and   605
shipwrecked and to ensure their adequate medical assistance. They shall be pro-
tected against pillage and ill-treatment (Art. 15 GC I; Art. 18, para. 1 GC II; Art. 11,
para. 1 AP I; Art. 8 AP II).

1. The wounded, sick, and shipwrecked shall be rescued, cared for, and protected against pillage and ill-treatment. Prisoners of war shall be quartered at safe places. The detaining power is obliged to remove prisoners of war as fast as possible from the combat zone and to transfer them to safe camps. Prisoners may only be left temporarily in a danger zone if their transport would be prejudicial on account of their injuries or diseases, Art. 19, para. 2 GC III. Article 47 GC III contains a similar provision. The transfer of sick or wounded prisoners of war after their arrival in a prison camp, for example if the combat zone shifts closer, is inadmissible if the transfer could impair their physical condition. Only immediate danger to their security justifies their removal. In order to treat wounded and sick effectively, accomodation in medical centres is essential. Art. 15, para. 2 GC I encourages the parties to the conflict to reach agreements for armistices and cease-fires in order to facilitate the rescue of the wounded and sick. Additionally, local arrangements can be made to evacuate the sick and wounded from areas under siege. It must also be possible for medical and religious personnel to enter the areas under siege.

2. The obligation to search for and collect victims after each battle, stated in Art. 18 GC II, corresponds with Art. 15 GC I. In naval warfare, however, the task of searching for and rescuing victims is far more complicated than in a land war. While in former times hospital and other medical ships were expected to search for and collect the shipwrecked, in modern naval battles rescue activities are carried out by the ships engaged in the conflict. Hospital ships are employed to treat the wounded and sick and for medical transport only. The search for and rescue of shipwrecked persons is perilous to the extent that warships have no particular protection and are therefore vulnerable in such a situation.[18] Even though the search for and rescue of shipwrecked persons by warships is subject to the conditions of military necessity, an attack on the shipwrecked is a war crime.[19]

3. Military authorities can take advantage of the population's willingness to help, or call for volunteers to collect and care for the sick and wounded. The authorities shall ensure protection for these volunteers. Spontaneous aid is also allowed, without being threatened by attack. This also applies to the activities of private relief organizations, for example the national Red Cross and Red Crescent societies (Art. 17 AP I). These regulations refer to the International Red Cross as a source of spontaneous and voluntary assistance.

---

[18] McCoubrey, 65, points to the risks of submarine warfare and the cessation of the search for survivors of the *Bismarck* by the British warships *Dorsetshire* and *Maori* in 1941.

[19] McCoubrey, 65–7, refers to the trial of *Dönitz*. Cf. the *Peleus* case, the incidents during the rescue of the survivors of the *Laconia* and the following '*Laconia* order', de Zayas, 259 ff.

Rabus

4. If wounded and sick persons fall into the hands of the civilian population of the adverse party, dangerous situations may develop, since the civilian population will not always demonstrate a benevolent attitude toward captured enemies, whether wounded or not. In World War II pilots lost their lives through lynch-law. On account of such incidents it was determined by the Conventions that the civilian population must respect the sick and wounded who are *hors de combat* and may not use force against them. Each state is obliged to protect the wounded in its territory against pillage and ill-treatment (Art. 15 GC I; Art. 17 AP I).

606   It is prohibited to subject wounded, sick, and shipwrecked persons to any medical procedure not consistent with generally accepted medical standards (Art. 12, para. 2 GC II; Art. 11, para. 1 AP I). In particular it is prohibited to carry out physical mutilation, medical or other scientific experiment, or removal of tissue or organs for transplantation.

1. Art. 11 AP I determines that the physical and mental condition and safety of persons who have fallen into the hands of the enemy must not be endangered. Similar regulations can be found in Art. 12 GC I and II, Arts. 13 and 17 GC III, and Arts. 31 and 32 GC IV.

2. Art. 16 AP I regulates medical procedure in accordance with the medical code of honour. A physician who acts according to this code must not be punished (para. 1). Physicians must not be forced to contravene this code. Art. 16, para. 3 refers to medical discretion. Physicians must not give details of medical records to the enemy. It is, on the other hand, permissible to supply such information to one's own forces, if national law so permits.

607   Exceptions to the prohibition of the removal of tissue or organs may be made only if donations are given voluntarily. This applies in particular to donations of blood. Such operations shall only serve therapeutic purposes and shall be consistent with generally accepted medical standards (Art. 11, para. 3 AP I).

608   Wounded, sick, and shipwrecked persons have the right to refuse any surgical operation or similar treatment. In such cases, medical personnel shall request a written statement to that effect, signed or acknowledged by the patient (Art. 11, para. 5 AP I). Simple diagnostic measures, such as the taking of blood, shall be permitted. The same applies to measures necessary to prevent, combat, and cure contagious diseases, such as epidemics.

609   Each party to the conflict has the duty to keep and retain medical records, and to make them available at all times for inspection by the protecting power (Art. 11, para. 6 AP I).

610   Each wounded, sick, shipwrecked, or dead person shall be identified. All pertinent information shall be forwarded to the appropriate information bureau (Art. 16 GC I; Art. 19 GC II; see below Section 708).

Rabus

The power detaining the wounded, sick, or shipwrecked is obliged to identify them. The data to be supplied to the information bureau by the parties detaining such persons is stipulated in Art. 16, para. 1 lit. a-h GC I. It includes surname, military rank, nationality, date of birth, and date and place of capture or decease, as well as all available information about the person's wounds, disease, or death. If personal data cannot be obtained by inquiry, for example on account of a person's wounds, it should be obtained from the identity disks. Tags contain duplicated data, so that one half always remains with the person or corpse to facilitate an identification (Art. 17 GC I).

The dead are to be collected and prevented from being despoiled (Art. 15, para. 1   611
**GC I). Burial or cremation of the dead shall be preceded by a documented exami-
nation of the bodies (Art. 17, para. 1 GC I; Art. 20, para. 1 GC II).**

1. While the GCs refer only to the wounded, sick, and dead on the battlefield (Arts. 16 and 17 GC I; Arts. 19 and 20 GC II), Art. 33 AP I also covers persons reported missing in action by any opposing party. Art. 32 AP I states the principle that family members have the right to be informed about the fate of their relatives. The regulation does not however grant to the dependants the right of information from and investigation by the parties to the conflict.[20] As soon as the circumstances of the combat permit, each party to the conflict shall search for missing persons (Art. 33 AP I). In order to facilitate the search for missing persons the adverse party shall give all information in their possession concerning those persons. The necessary contacts between the parties to the conflict can be established by the protecting power, the central information bureau at the ICRC, or by the national information bureaux (cf. Sections 538, 708).

2. Art. 17 GC I and Arts. 32–4 AP I regulate the collection and burial of the dead. Art. 33, para. 4 AP I determines the co-operation required between the conflicting parties to allow persons in charge of the collection of the dead to carry out their assignment. The parties to the conflict shall see to it that special units search for the dead on the battlefield and identify them. These units shall be respected and protected. To achieve complete documentation of the search for missing persons the parties shall also collect information about those persons who are not subject to any favourable treatment under the Conventions and the Protocol.

a) The dead are generally to be interred in graves, unless religious reasons or the demands of hygiene require that other measures be taken. In any case, funerals must take place in an honourable manner and in accordance with the religious customs of the deceased. The treatment of persons killed in naval warfare as described in Art. 20 GC II, corresponds for the most part with GC I. As long as no funeral at sea takes place the regulations of the GC I shall be applied.

---

[20] Bothe/Ipsen/Partsch, *ZaöRV* 38 (1978), 1–85 (19).

Rabus

b) Art. 17, para. 3 GC I regulates the establishment of cemeteries and war graves. If possible these should be arranged according to the nationality of the dead. Cemeteries and graves shall be marked. The parties shall establish an official War Graves Commission after the outbreak of hostilities. The conflicting parties must, as far as practically possible, inform the central information bureau about the place and identity of the war graves. Arts. 16, para. 2 and 17 GC I refer on that matter to the national information bureaux (cf. Sections 538, 708). These shall contact the central information bureau.

c) The parties on whose territory cemeteries and war graves are situated shall, if circumstances permit, reach agreement concerning the maintenance of the graves, maintenance costs, and access to them for relatives and representatives of the official record offices. Here reference must be made to the compromise between those states which demanded an individual right of access to war graves and those which wanted a treaty to govern such questions: the states agreed upon a *pactum de contrahendo*, which means that the parties are obliged to reach necessary agreements about access to war graves. Nevertheless, the circumstances and the relationship between the parties must render agreement possible.[21]

d) An exhumation of the dead is permitted unless urgent reasons, such as public health requirements, dictate otherwise (Art. 34, para. 4 AP I). The repatriation of corpses and their personal possessions to the native country on application by relatives should be facilitated as far as possible (Art. 34, para. 2 AP I).[22]

e) Following the principle that the dead shall be treated with respect and that their graves shall be maintained, protected, and marked,[23] warships sunk with their crews are considered to be war graves.[24] Examples from World War I are the British warships *Royal Oak, Edinburgh,* and *Repulse,* and also the *Hampshire* which sank with Lord Kitchener aboard.[25] It is of importance whether those ships sank in international or national waters. Wrecks in national waters can be protected by regulations of national law.

II. MEDICAL ESTABLISHMENTS AND TRANSPORT

612   Fixed medical establishments, vehicles, and mobile units of the medical service shall under no circumstances be attacked (Art. 19, para. 1 GC I; Art. 18 paras. 1 and

---

[21] During the conflict, access to the graves is hardly possible. The remark that the relations between the parties to the conflict must render the conclusion of such a treaty possible was included in AP I with regard to Arab–Israel relations, cf. Bothe/Ipsen/Partsch, *ZaöRV* 38 (1978), 1–85 (20); Bothe/Partsch/Solf, 177.

[22] After the Falklands conflict in 1982 difficulties occurred regarding the visit by relatives to war graves of the Argentine soldiers killed on the Falkland Islands. Art. 34, para. 2 lit. a AP I provides that such visits must be permitted as soon as possible. Among the British some suspected that the visits were designed to further Argentine territorial claims, cf. McCoubrey, 48.

[23] According to Bothe, *EPIL* 4, 315 ff., with reference to the German Law of 22 Dec. 1922 referring to the War Graves of World War I and the German War Graves Law of 27 May 1952.

[24] O'Connell, Vol. II, 912.   [25] McCoubrey, 48 n. 16.

Rabus

5 GC IV; Art. 12, para. 1 AP I; Art. 11, para. 1 AP II). Their unhampered employment shall be ensured at all times. As far as possible, medical establishments and units shall be sited or employed at an adequate distance from military objectives (Art. 19, para. 2 GC I; Art. 18, para. 5 GC II; Art. 12, para. 4 AP I).

Art. 8 lit. e AP I enlarges the definition of medical units stated in Art. 19 GC I. Medical units now include all military or civilian establishments organized for medical purposes, for example military hospitals, blood banks, medical precaution services, and medical and pharmaceutical commissaries. Such establishments can be either fixed or mobile, permanent or temporary. Of importance is that the definition of AP I includes also civilian establishments; GC I refers only to military medical units. However, civilian establishments only receive the protection of GCs and AP I if they are acknowledged by an act of state (Art. 12, para. 2 AP I).

They shall not be used to commit acts harmful to the enemy (Art. 21 GC I; Art. 34   613
GC II; Art. 19, para. 1 GC IV; Art. 13, para. 1 AP I; Art. 11, para. 2 AP II).

Should medical establishments or units fall into the hands of the adversary, the   614
latter shall allow them to pursue their activities until the adversary itself has
ensured necessary medical care (Art. 19, para. 1 GC I; Art. 57, para. 1 GC IV; Art. 14
AP I).

Art. 19 GC I confirms that medical establishments shall be respected and protected. Should they fall into the hands of the adversary they can pursue their activities until the opposing party has established its own appropriate medical service for the treatment of the sick and wounded. The special protection is also effective for the equipment of medical units. Should this fall into the hands of the adversary it may be used only for the treatment of the sick and wounded (Art. 33 GC I). There are similar regulations for the facilities of aid societies which may be seized by the opponent only if medical care for the wounded and sick is ensured (Art. 34 GC I).

The material of the mobile medical units of the armed forces (stretchers, medi-   615
cine, surgical dressings, vehicles, etc.) shall remain available to the medical per-
sonnel to enable them to perform their functions (Arts. 33 and 35, para. 2 GC I; Art.
57, para. 2 GC IV; Art. 14 AP I). Hospital ships and medical aircraft are subject to
special regulations (see below Sections 1054 ff., 1065 ff.).

The property (buildings, materials, stores, etc.) of aid societies shall be protected.   616
In case of urgent necessity, it may be requisitioned provided that the welfare of the
wounded and sick has been ensured (Arts. 33 and 34 GC I; Arts. 14, paras. 2 and 3
and 21 AP I; Art. 53, para. 2 HagueReg).

1. In occupied areas the occupying power is responsible for supplies to the population and for the maintenance of public health (Arts. 55 and 56 GC IV; Art. 14 AP I). In co-operation with the local authorities it must ensure that the civilian population

is provided with medical supplies and equipment. Moreover, the establishments and services of hospitals and medical care shall be continued. Stores must not be requisitioned by the occupying power. Should this happen, compensation must be paid. Aid activities for the civilian population—for example by the ICRC—shall be permitted by the occupying power (Arts. 59 and 61 GC IV). Problems occur if it is uncertain which authority is in fact in control of an area. In such situations much depends on the humanitarian diplomacy of the ICRC.

2. Personal or public property generally may be destroyed if combat action so requires. By contrast, Art. 12 AP I determines that civilian medical units and civilian health establishments shall *always* be respected and protected. In contrast to the prohibition of the destruction of other property (Art. 53 GC IV) there is no exception for military necessity. Art. 14 AP I supplements the regulations on medical supply for the civilian population in occupied areas, in so far as the occupying power is as a matter of principle not permitted to requisition medical establishments as long as they are needed by the civilian population.

617 **All vehicles transporting wounded and sick persons, or medical equipment shall be respected and protected. They shall be marked by clearly visible (Arts. 36, paras. 2 and 42, paras. 2 and 4 GC I; Art. 21 GC IV; Art. 18, para. 4 AP I; Art. 12 AP II) distinctive emblems (red cross on a white ground or related emblems) (Arts. 38, 39 and 44 GC I; Art. 18 AP I).**

1. The protection of medical transport is similar to the protection of medical units. Means of transportation can be military or civilian, permanent or temporary (Art. 8 lit. f and g AP I). Different problems result from land, sea, or air transport.

2. Medical transport vehicles are subject to martial law (Art. 35 GC I). This means that they can legally fall into the hands of the adversary. If ambulances or other medical vehicles are captured by the opposing party the continuing protection of the wounded and sick being transported must be ensured and the opposing party must care for captured sick and wounded.

3. Being medical units, medical vehicles must not be used to harm the enemy. If, for example, ambulances are employed to transport healthy troops in order to promote war efforts, then this ends the protection in the same way as abuse of other medical units (Arts. 21 and 22 GC I ; Art. 13 AP I).

4. Medical vehicles on land must be marked, as other medical installations and equipment, with a distinctive emblem. On trucks or ambulances the emblem is normally placed on large surfaces and, if possible, also on the roof to facilitate identification from above by aircraft. Vehicles should also carry a flag bearing the distinctive emblem. The obligation to carry the distinctive emblem applies even if the vehicle is only used temporarily to transport the sick and wounded.

Rabus

5. Medical aircraft and helicopters gained importance in conflicts after 1949. Art. 36 GC I regulates the protection of ambulance planes. They must display both national and distinctive emblems on their top, bottom, and lateral surfaces. Hostile territory may be flown over only by a prior agreement. Orders to land for the purpose of inspection must be followed. Even when flying over territory controlled by their own side, agreements with the adverse party on flight routes, altitude, and time are required. Since the regulations concerning medical vehicles on land cannot be applied fully to air transport, above all because of problems of identification, AP I includes only one paragraph concerning air transport.

a) Art. 24 AP I determines the basic principle that medical aircraft shall be respected and protected. Their employment, however, is subject to certain restrictions designed to prevent abuse (Art. 28 AP I). Medical aircraft, like all other medical vehicles, must not be used to gain military advantage or to protect legitimate military objectives against attack. A medical aircraft must also not be used for the collection and transfer of information and must therefore not be equipped for such purposes; instruments for navigation and communication, however, are of course permitted (Art. 28, para. 2 AP I). With the exception of small-arms for the self-defence of medical personnel and for the defence of the patients in their charge, medical aircraft must not carry weapons. In addition, Art. 24, para. 5 AP I prohibits the use of medical aircraft to search for the sick, wounded, or shipwrecked except with the prior consent of the adverse party. This serves to avoid misunderstandings, so that aircraft thus employed are not suspected of hostile intentions and treated as military objectives.

b) The conditions in which medical aircraft are protected depend on the situation of the territory flown over. Arts. 24–31 AP I distinguish four situations which are regulated differently. First, transport over land areas controlled by own and allied forces, and over sea areas not controlled by the adversary (Art. 26 AP I); second, transport in contact zones or similar zones controlled by own party or the control over which is uncertain (Art. 27 AP I); third, medical transport over territory controlled by the opposing party (Art. 27 AP I); and fourth, air transport over the territory of states not involved in the conflict (Art. 31 AP I). Medical transport over areas controlled by the adversary and flights over neutral territory require the permission of the state the territory of which is flown over. In contact zones medical aircraft can only be protected effectively if agreement between the opponents is reached. Although no formalities for medical flights over own territory are required, it seems sensible to inform the adverse party of such flights. The formal aspects of the notification of medical aircraft flights are stated in Art. 29 AP I. Among other things notification must include the number of aircraft, flight plans, and aircraft marks. A party to the conflict which receives such notification may propose alternative or modified flight plans (Art. 29, para. 3 lit. c AP I). Medical aircraft crossing an area controlled by the adversary can be ordered to land for the purpose of inspection (Art. 30 AP I). Such inspection shall be carried out as fast as possible, and the wounded and sick must not be ordered to leave the plane unless necessary to achieve inspection. Persons aboard medical aircraft who belong to the inspecting party may be retained. If the aircraft does not comply

Rabus

with the Protocol it can be requisitioned. The persons aboard then shall be treated according to the Conventions and the Protocol. Medical aircraft seized may only be used by the requisitioning party for medical purposes.

c) If medical aircraft fly over enemy territory because of a miscalculation in navigation, an emergency, or for security reasons the adversary must be informed of its presence and the reasons therefor. The opposing party may then arrange for inspection or allow the medical aircraft to leave adverse air space without hostile action. This regulation corresponds with that concerning civilian aircraft in peacetime in Art. 3 of the Convention on International Civil Aviation of 1944, which prohibits the use of weapons against civilian aircraft.[26] There is no specific difference between medical aircraft operating over sea and those operating above land (Art. 36 AP I ; Arts. 24, 25, and 27–30 AP I). Medical helicopters assigned to hospital ships may be employed to transport and evacuate the wounded, sick, or shipwrecked.[27]

6. Medical transport at sea is usually carried out by hospital ships. Medical helicopters can be employed to search for and rescue the shipwrecked; in this case the regulations of GC I and AP I for missions on land apply. Hospital ships (or medical ships) are defined in Art. 22 GC II and Art. 8 lit. f AP I.

a) The status of hospital ship can be given to any vessel, irrespective of its tonnage. However, the parties must endeavour to use only vessels of over 2000 gross register tons for the transport of the sick and wounded (Art. 26 GC II). Hospital ships can be equipped and supplied by both the military forces and the national societies of the Red Cross and Red Crescent, as well as by other unofficial humanitarian organizations, or by neutral states (Arts. 24 and 25 GC II).

b) The parties to the conflict shall notify which vessels are used as hospital ships. Hospital ships shall be clearly marked with the distinctive emblem. All outward surfaces shall be painted white (Art. 43 GC II). (The former regulation that the hull of hospital ships had to be marked also by a green belt has been abandoned.) In addition ships shall fly, besides their national flag, a white flag displaying the red cross or crescent. If the hospital ship belongs to a third state, it shall also carry the flag of the party for whom it is acting. Hospital ships' lifeboats must be marked in the same way. The regulations for limiting the use and preventing abuse of the red cross and crescent correspond with those of land and air warfare (Arts. 44 and 45 GC II). Hospital ships shall always be respected and protected; they shall under no circumstances be attacked or captured (Arts. 22, 24, 25, and 27 GC II).

c) GCs and AP I no longer contain the former discussion as to whether hospital ships were allowed to transport the wounded and sick of land warfare.[28] Common Art. 13 GC I and II explains that it is irrelevant which part of the armed forces the

---

[26] This prohibition was reinforced in 1973; see 12 *ILM* 1983, McCoubrey, 61 n. 62.

[27] Ibid., 76.

[28] HC X corresponds with GC II on that matter, see McCoubrey, 70, with reference to the sinking of the *Dover Castle* by the German submarine *UC67*; cf. the trial at the *Reichsgericht* in Leipzig, *AJIL* 16 (1922) 704–8; also Higgins, *BYIL* 2 (1921–2), 177–8.

sick and wounded belong to, or where they sustained injuries; thus they can be transported by hospital ships.

d) Although hospital ships are entitled to immunity from attacks and requisition, the parties to the conflict have the right to inspect and search them (Art. 31 GC II). They can also demand that the wounded, sick, or shipwrecked of any nationality on board the ship be surrendered to them. However, this right may only be exercised if the physical condition of the wounded, sick, and shipwrecked is such that the transfer can be safely carried out and if the warship is capable of providing adequate medical care (Art. 14 GC II).

e) Art. 21 GC II provides that parties to a conflict can ask the captain of a neutral ship to take wounded, sick, shipwrecked, or dead aboard. Neutral ships may also do so of their own accord. Such assistance does not justify the capture of neutral vessels.

f) Hospital ships, like infirmaries, lose their special protection only if they act contrary to their humanitarian assignments or carry out acts harmful to the enemy. As in land warfare, protection shall cease only after prior warning and adequate reprieve have been given (Art. 34 GC II).[29] Parallel to the regulations concerning medical units on land, Art. 35 GC II determines certain circumstances in which a hospital ship does not lose its protected status. Art. 35, para. 4 provides that wounded, sick or shipwrecked civilians may be cared for aboard hospital ships. This regulation is elaborated in AP I. The personnel of hospital ships and infirmaries may carry small-arms to maintain order, for their own protection, and to protect the wounded, sick, and shipwrecked in their charge (Art. 35, para. 1 GC II). In addition, means of navigation and communication are permitted aboard hospital ships (Art. 35, para. 2 GC II).[30]

g) Sick-bays aboard warships are entitled to protection (Art. 28 GC II). In case of fighting on board a warship they shall be respected as far as possible. Should the ship be captured by the adversary, the sick-bay shall not be used for other than medical purposes unless urgent military necessity so requires.

Medical establishments which contrary to their intended purpose are used to carry out acts harmful to the enemy may lose their protection after prior warning has been given (Art. 21 GC I; Art. 34 GC II; Art. 19, para. 1 GC IV; Art. 13, para. 1 AP I; Art. 11, para. 2 AP II).   618

In that regard, the following shall not be considered as acts of war (Art. 22, para. 2 GC I; Art. 35, para. 3 GC II; Art. 13, para. 2 AP I):   619

---

[29] An example of the forfeiture of protection is the 1944 case of the German hospital ship *Rostock*: the *Rostock* tried to reach a Spanish harbour starting from Bordeaux but was captured by Allied naval forces. It was discovered that the *Rostock* had the order to transfer weather reports which were of military importance by the means of secret codes; see McCoubrey, 72.

[30] McCoubrey, 73, expounds that hospital ships, although provided with special protection, are not immune from the general dangers of war.

Rabus

—that medical personnel use arms for their own protection, or that of the wounded and sick;

—that medical personnel and medical establishments are protected by sentries or an escort;

—that medical personnel are employed as sentries for the protection of their own medical establishments; and

—that war material taken from the wounded and sick is retained.

III. MEDICAL AIRCRAFT

620　Medical aircraft are military or civilian aircraft, designed exclusively for medical transport on a permanent or *ad hoc* basis and subordinate to a competent authority of a party to the conflict. As well as the national emblem they must carry the distinctive emblem on their wings and hull and may not be attacked (Art. 39 GC II; Arts. 26, para. 1 and 29 AP I).

1. The concept of protection. It follows from the definition of medical aircraft (Art. 39, para. 1 GC II and Art. 8(j) and (g) AP I) that they may be used for the removal of wounded, sick, and shipwrecked as well as for the transport of medical personnel and equipment. They may either be owned by the armed forces, requisitioned, or belong to a relief society.[31] If they are indefinitely assigned exclusively to medical transportation they are permanent medical aircraft. In all other cases they are temporary medical aircraft.

Medical aircraft are accorded protected status only if they are flying at the altitude and time and on the route specifically agreed upon between the parties to the conflict.[32] In the absence of such agreement they may not fly over enemy or enemy occupied territories.[33] The respect and protection of medical aircraft is not dependent upon any agreement in and over land areas physically controlled by friendly forces, or in and over sea areas not physically controlled by an adverse party (Art. 25 AP I). Still, for greater safety in these areas, according to the second sentence of Art. 25 AP I, a party to the conflict is advised to notify the adverse party, particularly when such aircraft will come within range of surface-to-air weapons systems of the adverse party. In and over those parts of the contact zone (i.e. any area on land where the forward elements of opposing forces are in contact with each other)[34] which are physically controlled by friendly forces and in and over those areas where control is not clearly established, protection for medical aircraft can be fully effective only by prior agreement between the competent military authorities of the parties to the conflict.[35] Although, in the absence of such an agreement, medical aircraft operate at their own risk, they shall nevertheless be respected after they have been recognized as such.

---

[31] See Pictet, *Commentary* GC II, 216.　　[32] Art. 39, para. 1 GC II.
[33] Art. 39, para. 3 GC II; Art. 27 AP I.　　[34] Art. 26, para. 2 AP I.
[35] Art. 26, para. 1 AP I. See also Bothe, in Bothe/Partsch/Solf, 149 ff.

A medical aircraft which flies over an area physically controlled by the enemy without, or in breach of the terms of, an agreement, either through navigational error or because of an emergency affecting the safety of the flight, shall make every effort to identify itself and to inform the enemy of the circumstances. As soon as such medical aircraft has been recognized, the enemy is obliged to undertake all reasonable efforts which enable it to land or alight on water, or to take other measures to safeguard its own interests, and, in either case, to allow the aircraft time for compliance before resorting to attack.[36]

Upon alighting involuntarily on land or water in enemy or enemy occupied territory, the wounded, sick, and shipwrecked, as well as the crew of the aircraft, shall be prisoners of war. The medical personnel continue to be protected.[37]

2. Markings. According to Art. 39, para. 2 GC II, medical aircraft shall be clearly marked with the distinctive emblem, together with their national colours, on their lower, upper, and lateral surfaces. They shall also be provided with any other markings or means of identification which may be agreed upon between the parties to the conflict. Such technical means of identification, according to the regulations of Annex I to AP I, may include the flashing blue light,[38] the radio signal,[39] and the Secondary Surveillance Radar (SSR) system.[40, 41] As in the case of hospital ships and other medical vessels, markings are merely intended to facilitate identification and do not themselves confer protected status.[42]

The parties to a conflict are prohibited from using their medical aircraft to gain   621 any military advantage over an adversary. The presence of medical aircraft shall not be used in an attempt to render military objectives immune from attack (Art. 28 AP I).

Medical aircraft, like hospital ships and other protected vessels, must not be used to commit acts harmful to the enemy. This customary principle has now been codified in Art. 28 AP I.[43] They lose their protected status if they carry any equipment intended to collect or transmit intelligence data. They shall not be armed, except for small-arms for self-defence, and shall carry only medical personnel and equipment.[44]

A medical aircraft which loses its exemption as described above is liable to capture. It may be attacked only if:[45] (a) diversion for landing, inspection and search, and possible capture, is not feasible; (b) no other method is available for exercising military control; (c) the non-compliance is sufficiently grave that the aircraft has become, or may reasonably be assumed to be, a military objective; and (d) the collateral casualties or damage will not be disproportionate to the military advantage gained or anticipated.

[36] Art. 27, para. 2 AP I.   [37] Art. 39, para. 5 GC II.   [38] Art. 6, Annex I to AP I.
[39] Art. 7, Annex I to AP I.   [40] Art. 8, Annex I to AP I.
[41] See also the recommendations in *ICRC Manual for the Use of Technical Means of Identification*.
[42] See also *San Remo Manual*, para. 176.
[43] See also Bothe, in Bothe/Partsch/Solf, 157 ff.; *San Remo Manual*, para. 178.
[44] Art. 28, para. 3 AP I; *San Remo Manual*, para. 178.   [45] Ibid., para. 57.

In cases of doubt as to whether a medical aircraft is being used to make an effective contribution to military action, it shall be presumed not to be so used.[46]

622　**Medical aircraft may be ordered to land, whether on land or on water, to permit inspection. The inspection shall be commenced without delay and shall be conducted expeditiously. The inspecting party shall not require the wounded and sick to be taken off the aircraft unless this is essential for inspection. In any event the inspecting party shall ensure that the condition of the wounded and sick is not adversely affected (Art. 30, para. 2 AP I).**

The right to order a medical aircraft to alight on land or water is expressed in Art. 39, para. 4 GC II and Art. 30, paras. 1 and 2 AP I. Its purpose is to enable belligerents to verify whether such aircraft are in fact innocently employed in their normal role. In any event, the condition of the wounded and sick on board shall not be adversely affected.

623　**If inspection discloses that the aircraft does not meet the requirements for special protection or has acted in breach of its obligations, it may be seized. An aircraft which has been assigned as a permanent medical aircraft and is seized may be used thereafter only as a medical aircraft (Art. 30, para. 4 AP I).**

As in the case of protected vessels, any breach of the requirements for protection set out in the preceding paragraphs leads to loss of exemption of medical aircraft. They may then be captured and used for the captor's own purposes.[47] However, any aircraft captured which had been assigned as a permanent medical aircraft may be used thereafter only as a medical aircraft.[48]

IV. MEDICAL PERSONNEL

624　**Civilian and military medical personnel are entitled to special protection. They shall neither be made the object of attack nor prevented from exercising their functions (Arts. 23, para. 1 and 24 GC I; Art. 37 GC II; Art. 14 GC IV; Art. 15 AP I; Arts. 9–11 AP II).**

625　**Military medical personnel are military non-combatants. They include:**

　　—persons exclusively engaged in the care or the collection and transport of the wounded, sick, and shipwrecked, and in the treatment and prevention of disease, including physicians, nurses, etc., and the hospital personnel of hospital ships (Art. 24 GC I; Art. 30 GC II; Arts. 22 and 23 AP I);

---

[46] *San Remo Manual*, para. 58.

[47] As regards attacks on medical aircraft which have lost their protected status see the commentary on Section 621.

[48] Art. 40, para. 4 AP I.

Rabus

—administrative personnel of medical units and establishments, such as managers, clerks, mess personnel, etc. (Art. 26 GC I; Arts. 36 and 37 GC II);

—medical personnel of aid societies of the medical service (Art. 26 GC I; Art. 8 lit. c. ii AP I);

—medical personnel assigned to civil defence organizations (e.g. the Technical Relief Organization in the Federal Republic of Germany) of the parties to a conflict (Art. 3, para. 2 GC I; Art. 8 lit. c. i AP I); and

—non-permanent medical personnel (including attendants in the medical service who have been adequately trained) (Art. 25 GC I).

1. Members of the medical service are also members of the military forces, although they are not authorized to harm the enemy and are therefore not legitimate combatants. On account of the special protection to which they are entitled, they shall not be made the object of attack while performing their duties according to the GCs and AP. GC I defines three categories of protected persons: permanent medical personnel and army chaplains; medical support personnel; and personnel of aid societies (Art. 24–6 GC I). Complete protection is given to those who are exclusively engaged in the humanitarian functions stated in Art. 24 GC I. Those persons shall be respected and protected under all circumstances (cf. Art. 8 lit. c AP I). Military personnel who have been trained as assistant nurses or ambulance men in addition to their military function equally shall be respected and protected while discharging their medical duties (Art. 25 GC I). The personnel of the Red Cross or Red Crescent or other authorized aid societies, for example the Order of Malta or the Order of St. John, are treated in the same way as the personnel listed in Art. 24, provided that the personnel of these aid societies is subject to military laws and regulations. Other contracting parties shall be informed about which aid societies are authorized to co-operate with the medical services of the armed forces (Art. 26 GC I). The notification may be given in peacetime, at the outbreak of, or even during hostilities, but not before those aid societies actually take up duty.

2. Art. 22, para. 4 GC I provides that personnel and equipment of the military veterinary service may be present at medical units. That service however is not part of the medical service.[49] Its origins are connected with the employment of the cavalry. The veterinary service can be of importance for example for pack horses of mountain troops. Yet the veterinary service is not subject to humanitarian law. Even if the veterinary service is in a medical unit, its role is as the technical service of a military unit.

3. A national society of the Red Cross or the Red Crescent or an aid society of a neutral state may participate in medical efforts provided that both the government of that neutral state and the government of the party to the conflict for which the society shall be employed agree (Art. 27 GC I). The government of the neutral state shall notify the adversary of the state which is supported that the national aid society is

---

[49] See McCoubrey, 56.

Rabus

performing its protective functions abroad. The personnel of the neutral state's aid society engaged in the conflict area shall be supervised by the party to the conflict, and thus become subject to the protection of Art. 26 GC I.

626 **Permanent medical personnel who have been captured shall be free to pursue their duties under the direction of the detaining party until the latter has ensured the necessary care of the wounded and sick (Art. 19 GC I). They are not deemed prisoners of war; nevertheless they shall at least benefit from all the provisions of GC III. They shall preferably be engaged in the care of the wounded and sick of the party to which they themselves belong (Art. 30 GC I).**

1. The personnel named in Arts. 24 and 26 GC I cannot be captured but only retained and obliged to pursue their functions (Art. 28 GC I). This is a remnant of the Convention of 1864.[50] At that time it was determined that medical personnel were entitled to immunity and that they should be protected against capture (Art. 3 GC 1864). In the course of time this generous position was abandoned. Art. 28 GC I provides that protected personnel who fall into the hands of the adversary may be retained if the treatment of prisoners of war detained by the opponent so requires. The medical personnel retained shall continue their functions, preferably in relation to prisoners of war belonging to their own military forces. They are subject to the direction of the competent authorities. The care of prisoners of war is the responsibility of the detaining party.

2. In each camp the senior officer is answerable to the camp authorities for the work of medical personnel. In order to avoid uncertainty about the rank of medical personnel the parties shall reach agreement at the beginning of the conflict (Art. 28, para. 2 lit. b GC I ; Art. 33, para. 2 lit. b GC III). The medical personnel retained must be permitted to visit prisoners of war in camps, infirmaries, work units, and medical establishments outside the camp in which the medical personnel is detained, by appropriate means of transportation, to fulfil their duties there. During their presence in the camp medical personnel are subject to the internal discipline of the camp. They cannot, however, be forced to do work other than provide medical care (Art. 28, para. 2 lit. c GC I, Art. 33, para. 2 lit. c GC III). Although retained personnel are not prisoners of war, they are entitled to the protection defined in GC III (Arts. 28 and 30 GC I).

3. The personnel of hospital ships are subject to more extensive protection than their colleagues on land. During service aboard a hospital ship they must not be captured, even if there are no sick or wounded aboard (Art. 36 GC II; cf. Art. 28 GC I). The immunity from capture does not include the term 'retention' developed in land warfare. However, retention is treated in Art. 37 GC II. Medical and religious personnel of infirmaries aboard ships other than hospital ships can continue to perform their duties if care of the wounded and sick is required. They shall be sent

[50] Convention of 22 Aug. 1864 for the Amelioration of the Condition of the Wounded in Armies in the Field (Schindler-Toman, 279).

Rabus

back thereafter (Art. 37 GC II). On the other hand Art. 28 GC I determines that the adversary is permitted to retain medical personnel, even against their will. The religious and medical personnel aboard hospital ships and other vessels shall wear armlets displaying the distinctive emblem; additionally they can identify themselves by the water-resistant identity card (Art. 42 GC II; cf. Art. 40 GC I).

4. In so far as civilian medical assistance is restricted due to hostilities, either party can provide necessary assistance. An occupying power shall not force civilian medical personnel to perform duties contrary to their intended humanitarian functions. The occupying power also shall not demand that the treatment of certain persons should have precedence over others unless this is for medical reasons.

Medical personnel whose retention is not indispensable for the care of prisoners of war shall be repatriated (Art. 30 GC I; Art. 37 GC II).   627

As soon as the retention of medical personnel for the treatment of prisoners of war is no longer required they shall be repatriated. The choice of the persons to be repatriated must not be discriminatory. As far as possible those who were retained first should be allowed to return first. An agreement on gradual repatriation between the parties to the conflict may also be reached (Arts. 30 and 31 GC I).The regulations for repatriation of medical personnel are more theoretical than practical, because for the most part medical personnel retained will pursue their duties for the benefit of prisoners for the entire duration of the conflict. Since the enactment of GC I there have been no known cases where the regulations for repatriation were exercised in favour of the medical personnel. Art. 32 GC I provides that the personnel of aid societies of neutral states shall not be retained if they fall into the hands of the adverse party.

Captured irregular military medical personnel become prisoners of war, but shall be employed in their medical duties in so far as the need arises (Art. 5, 29 GC I).   628

The employment of medical personnel of the aid societies of a state not party to a conflict requires the consent of the government of that state and the authorization of the party to the conflict for which the personnel shall be employed (Art. 27 GC I).   629

Medical personnel who fall into the hands of the adverse party may only be detained as long as the state of health and the number of prisoners of war so require (Art. 28, paras. 1 and 2 GC I; Art. 37, paras. 2 and 3 GC II). This shall not apply to the personnel of a state which is not a party to the conflict (Art. 27 and 32 GC I; Art. 9, para. 2 AP I).   630

Medical personnel may be equipped with small-arms weapons for the protection of the wounded, sick, and shipwrecked in their charge and for their own protection (Art. 22 GC I; Art. 35 GC II; Art. 13 AP I). Small-arms are pistols, sub-machine-guns and rifles.   631

Rabus

1. Medical personnel are authorized to use small-arms for their own protection or for the protection of the sick and wounded. It is also permitted that a medical unit be protected by sentries against pillage and theft. It is also provided that the presence of small-arms and ammunition, taken from the sick and wounded in the medical unit and which are stored there, does not constitute a violation of the Convention or the Protocol. The weapons and ammunition shall, nevertheless, be handed to the competent officers.

2. Art. 15 AP I protects civilian medical personnel; paragraph 4 determines that they shall have access to all localities where their services are required. Art. 13, para. 2 lit. a AP I authorizes members of civilian medical units to carry small-arms for the protection of their patients as well as for their own protection.

632   **Civilians must respect the wounded, sick, and shipwrecked, even if they belong to the opposite party. They must not use violence against them. Civilians and help organizations such as national Red Cross or Red Crescent societies are permitted to collect and care for the wounded, sick, and shipwrecked. No one should be attacked, pursued, or punished for such humanitarian actions (Art. 18 GC I; Art. 17 AP I).**

V. HOSPITAL ZONES AND LOCALITIES

633   **The parties to an armed conflict may agree to establish hospital zones and localities to protect the wounded and sick as well as medical personnel from the effects of the conflict (Art. 3 and Annex I GC I; Annex I GC IV).**

1. HC IX prohibits the bombardment of undefended sea-ports, towns, villages, habitations, and buildings (Art. 1, para. 1). Art. 25 HagueReg also prohibits the bombardment or attack of undefended towns within the theatre of operations.[51] Art. 23 GC I provides that states, whether involved in a conflict or not, may establish hospital zones and localities for the protection of the wounded and sick within their territory or in an occupied area, therefore also outside the theatre of operations. During the armed conflict the parties may be assisted by the good offices of the ICRC or the protecting power to reach agreement for the mutual respect of these zones and localities. A draft for such an agreement is contained in Annex I of GC I. It sets down that hospital zones comprise only a small part of the territory of a state and that they must be situated as far as possible from any military object, industrial centre, or administrative institution. It is not necessary to evacuate the population living in that area, but the hospital zones and localities must not be abused to protect military objects.

---

[51] See Ipsen, *Offene Stadt und Schutzzonen des Genfer Rechts*, 151 *et seq.*

2. Hospital and security zones are also important for the protection of the civilian population. On the basis of GC IV, states can establish, either in peacetime or by agreement with the adversary after the opening of hostilities, hospital and security zones as well as security localities in their own or, if necessary, in occupied territory. The creation of such zones and localities will enable the protection of the wounded, sick, and old, children under the age of fifteen, pregnant women, and mothers of children up to the age of seven from the effects of the war. For the establishment of hospital and security zones the protecting power and the ICRC may offer their good offices (Art. 14 GC IV). The draft of an agreement for the establishment of hospital and security zones can be found in Annex I GC IV.

3. In the course of an armed conflict each party to the conflict may propose to the adversary, either directly or by intercession of a neutral state or humanitarian organization, the creation of neutralized zones within the combat theatre (Art. 15 GC IV). These zones shall protect the wounded and sick during their presence in the zones, be they combatants, non-combatants, or members of the civilian population not engaged in the conflict and not fulfilling military tasks.

4. Persons who do not participate in armed operations or are *hors de combat* shall not be made the object of attack. The largest group against which no armed operations may be carried out is the civilian population. This tenet is extended by the principle that these persons must be protected and victims of violence adequately cared for (Art. 51 AP I). In order to realize this principle it is prohibited to attack certain areas and the persons residing there. Art. 25 HagueReg prohibits, for example, the attack on undefended towns and villages, which can be occupied without fighting. The Protocol elaborates this principle of towns and zones entitled to special protection. Art. 59 AP I concerns undefended towns, Art. 60 AP I deals with the establishment of demilitarized zones, which are established by agreement between the parties to the conflict. Both establishments serve to protect victims of war.

5. 'Non-defended localities' in the sense of Art. 59 AP I must be in the combat theatre. It is therefore possible that undefended localities may be subject to infringement by the adversary. Undefended localities can be established by the unilateral declaration of a party to the conflict (Art. 59, para. 2). It is also possible for the parties to create non-defended localities by agreement (Art. 59, para. 5 AP I). All mobile military units have to be removed from these zones and permanent installations must not be used for hostile actions. The presence of police does not impair the status of these villages (Art. 59, paras. 2 and 3 AP I). The establishment of undefended localities is intended to prevent losses for the civilian population.

6. By contrast, demilitarized zones, according to Art. 60 AP I, are always based (as a development of the neutralized zone, Art. 15 GC IV) on agreement between the parties to the conflict, although this can be reached in different ways. Unlike undefended localities, demilitarized zones are not necessarily in or near the combat theatre. Agreements for the creation of demilitarized zones must refer to four matters:

Rabus

no combatants or weapons are permitted in the zone; permanent military installations must not be used to commit any act of hostility; the authorities and the population must refrain from all hostile actions and activity related to military efforts. A demilitarized zone comes into existence by agreement between the party controlling the relevant territory and the adverse party, either directly or by negotiation through a protecting power or neutral humanitarian organization, for example the ICRC (Art. 60, para. 2 AP I). As in non-defended localities, all mobile military installations must be removed from the demilitarized zone and permanent fixtures must not be used for hostile operations. It is permitted for police forces to remain in the zone to maintain public order. A demilitarized zone must be marked by signs accepted by the parties to the conflict (Art. 60, paras. 3–5 AP I). Military operations, for example the occupation of non-defended localities, must not affect the demilitarized zone (Art. 60, para. 1 AP I). A protecting power or humanitarian organisation may help to establish a demilitarized zone and agreement as to this may be reached in peacetime. Nevertheless it is unlikely that states will, on account of the political reactions to be expected, make use of such a possibility.

7. Although hospital ships are entitled to immunity from military offences they must not impede the operations of the combatants (Art. 30 GC II). In order to ensure their safe and unhindered operation, agreements were reached during the Falklands conflict between Great Britain and Argentina for the establishment of a neutralized maritime zone with a diameter of 130 sea-miles to the north of the Falkland Islands. This zone became known as the 'Red Cross Box',[52] where hospital ships of both parties could treat the sick and wounded. It is notable that this maritime security zone came into existence in the huge expanse of South Atlantic waters. In enclosed waters, for example in the Gulf War, the establishment of such zones would be far more complicated. On the other hand, the precedent of the 'Red Cross Box' could have a positive effect on future cases.

634 **These zones and localities shall be situated as far as possible from any military object and shall not be situated in areas which are important for the conduct of military operations (Art. 4 lit. c and d, Annex I, GC I). They shall not be made the object of any military operation (Art. 11, Annex I, GC I). They shall comprise only a small part of the territory governed by a party to the conflict and shall be only thinly populated (Art. 4 lit. a and b, Annex I, GC I).**

635 **Hospital zones and localities shall be clearly marked with the red cross or red crescent emblem on a white ground being displayed on buildings and outer precincts (Art. 6, para. 2, Annex I, GC IV).**

636 **Hospital zones and localities shall, as far as possible by agreement, also be set up for civilians (Art. 23 GC I; Art. 13, Annex I, GC I; Art. 14 GC IV; Art. 1, para. 1, Annex I, GC IV).**

---

[52] McCoubrey, 76.

Rabus

VI. THE DISTINCTIVE EMBLEM

1. *General*

The distinctive emblem of medical and religious personnel as well as that of med-   637
ical establishments (including hospital ships), medical transports, medical materials, and hospital zones is the red cross on a white ground. Countries may use the
red crescent in place of the red cross.

1. The International Red Cross plays a decisive role in the development and application of humanitarian law. The reasons for this lie in the historical development of
this branch of law since the nineteenth century. Nowadays the Red Cross consists
of four elements: the International Committee of the Red Cross (ICRC); the
National Red Cross or Red Crescent societies; the International Federation of Red
Cross and Red Crescent Societies; and the International Conference of the Red
Cross and Red Crescent.[53]

2. With the development of the Red Cross, it was acknowledged that establishments and persons who devote themselves to the neutral humanitarian aims of the
Red Cross should distinguish themselves from the belligerents.[54] The recognized
distinctive emblems are described in Art. 38 GC I, which refers to the emblem of the
red cross (the reversal of the Swiss national flag), the red crescent, and the red lion
with red sun.[55] Designs of these three distinctive emblems are presented in Art. 3
with illustration 2 of Annex II AP I. Art. 3 also requires the distinctive emblem to be
of appropriate size. At night or in times of reduced visibility the emblem shall be
illuminated; moreover it should be made of material that facilitates the recognition
of the emblem. Art. 4 Annex II AP I adds that the emblem must be displayed on plain
surfaces or flags, clearly visible from different directions and from the greatest possible distance.

3. The diversity of the distinctive emblems could have a negative influence on their
protective and identificatory function. It is important that this emblem should be as
simple as possible so that it can be easily identified to prevent the risk of mistake. A
controversy still exists in respect of the Star of David, which has been used since
1930 by the Israeli Red Star of David Society. Israeli representatives regularly
pointed out that the Christian cross could not be used as a symbol of charity for
Jews for historical reasons; for political reasons the red crescent is not acceptable
either. The compromise reached is that the Star of David, though not acknowledged
as a fourth official emblem, is *de facto* accepted; the Israeli medical service has used

---

[53] Cf. Bindschedler, *EPIL* 5, 248–54; Willemin/Heacock, 19 *et seq.*
[54] Cf. Bugnion; Macalister-Smith, *EPIL* 9, 113–19.
[55] The emblem of the red lion with the red sun introduced by the Shah of Persia has not been used since
1980, namely since the Iranian revolution. During the Gulf War between Iran and Iraq both sides used the
distinctive emblem of the red crescent.

Rabus

this emblem in several Arab–Israeli conflicts and its use was not challenged by the Arab states.[56]

638 **The distinctive emblem shall be displayed on armlets worn by medical and religious personnel who shall also carry a special identity card (Arts. 40 and 41 GC I; Art. 42 GC II; Art. 20, paras, 2 and 3 GC IV; Art. 18, para. 3 AP I; Art. 12 AP II) as well as on flags and signs used for medical units and their equipment (Arts. 39, 42, and 43 GC I; Art. 2, para. 1 GC II; Art. 18, paras. 3 and 4 GC IV; Art. 18, para. 4 AP I; Art. 12 AP II). It shall only be used for the intended purposes and shall be large and clearly visible from a distance.**

1. The special status of medical personnel is shown by the fact that they wear an armlet displaying the distinctive emblem of the Red Cross or the Red Crescent affixed to the left arm. This armlet is stamped and issued by the competent military authorities. Protected persons are additionally obliged to carry an identity card on which the distinctive emblem is displayed. The form of this identity card is described in Annex II GC I. Attendants in the medical service employed in the maintenance of the sick and wounded also wear a white armlet with the distinctive emblem, although smaller in size. Attendants shall carry service passes that show what medical training they have received and that they are entitled to wear the armlet with the distinctive emblem (Art. 41 GC I). The identification card is of importance, since unauthorized use of an armlet with the distinctive emblem constitutes a grave breach of GC I.

2. Medical units protected by the GCs and AP I shall be marked by a flag displaying the distinctive emblem (Art. 42 GC I). The flag of the state to which the medical unit belongs may also be flown, but if a medical unit falls into the hands of the adversary, the flag of the Conventions alone shall be displayed. The same rule applies to medical units of neutral states which are authorized to assist the belligerent parties. In addition to the flag of the state under the control of which they pursue their duties they may carry the flag of their own state (Art. 43 GC I).

639 **The red cross and the red crescent are, in times of peace, also the emblems of the national Red Cross and Red Crescent societies as well as of their establishments and members. As long as they are only used for the purpose of identification, and protection is not being provided by the Geneva Conventions (Art. 44 GC I), the emblems shall be smaller in size and may not be displayed on armlets or on the roofs of buildings (Art. 44, para. 2 GC I).**

While in peacetime the emblem of the red cross frequently serves for the purpose of identification, for example when used legally by Red Cross aides ('indicative sign'),

---

[56] Agreement on a single distinctive emblem probably cannot be realized. McCoubrey, 38, refers as an example for possible difficulties to the symbol of the extended hand. Although the humanitarian meaning of this sign is acknowledged, it would be unsuitable as a distinctive emblem since it is the national emblem of Ulster/Northern Ireland.

Rabus

in war-time the protective function is paramount. The emblem marks the personnel, equipment, and establishments that are entitled to the special protection of the
Conventions and Protocols ('protective sign'). Together with the military medical
service, the national Red Cross and Red Crescent societies assume important
responsibilities for the treatment of the sick, wounded, and shipwrecked. During
the exercise of these functions, the personnel are entitled to protection.

The perfidious use of the distinctive emblems is explicitly prohibited and consti-   640
tutes a grave breach of international law (Arts. 49, 53, and 54 GC I; Art. 44 GC II;
Arts. 37, 38, and 85, para. 3 lit. f AP I; Art. 12 AP II; Art. 23 lit. f HagueReg).

1. The distinctive emblem shall be protected against abuse. If a distinctive emblem
is abused during an armed conflict its protection can cease. Art. 53 GC I prohibits—
for whatever purpose—the use of the emblem or any imitation of it, literal or picto-
rial, by persons or societies not authorized to display it. The Conventions also
require states to take necessary steps to enable compliance with the Conventions in
the domestic sphere and to enact the necessary national legislation. A model are the
national regulations for the protection of the distinctive emblem (Art. 53 GC I; Art.
45 GC II; cf. para. 638). This obligation was also stated in Art. 28 of the Geneva
Convention for Wounded of 1929.[57]

2. Art. 37 AP I formulates the prohibition of perfidy. This prohibition, also provided
by Art. 23 HagueReg, finds its ultimate expression in AP I concerning the killing,
wounding, and capture of the adversary. Unlike Art. 23 HagueReg, Art. 37 AP I
includes a definition of the term 'perfidy'. Whoever abuses the trust of the adversary
by taking advantage of the humanitarian protective standards in order to inflict on
the enemy the losses mentioned in Art. 37 commits perfidy. Art. 37, para. 1 then lists
some examples of perfidious acts. Of interest for the treatment of the sick and
wounded are examples (b), (c) and (d). These are: (b) the feigning of incapacity by
wounds or sickness; (c) the feigning of civilian or non-combatant status by, *inter
alia* (d) the use of signs, emblems, or uniforms of the United Nations.[58]

3. Art. 38 AP I prohibits without exception the abuse of the distinctive emblem of
the red cross or red crescent or of other signs, emblems, and marks named in the
Conventions or in Protocol I. This regulation echoes Art. 23 lit. f HagueReg. The prohibition of the abuse of the distinctive emblem of the red cross and related signs
allows no exception. The fact that the emblems introduced in other contracts (para.
1, clause 2) are not forbidden as absolutely as those of the GCs and AP I is explained
by the fact that not all parties to AP I are parties to those treaties in which the protective effect of the other signs is determined, for example the sign of the blue and

---

[57] In one case a laundry plant in the Netherlands used the sign of the red cross for its commercial purposes. Since the Dutch Government did not meet the liability to enact a law according to Art. 28 of the
Convention for Wounded of 1929, years passed before this violation was prosecuted; see *Annual Digest*
1933–34, Case No. 220; *Annual Digest* 1952, Case No. 128 (19 ILR, 598).

[58] Fleck, *RDMilG* XIII–2 (1974), 269.

Rabus

white arms of the CultPropConv. However, the strictness of the prohibition of abuse is not relaxed.[59]

4. Modern warfare poses the problem that the emblem may not in practice achieve the intended protective effect. For example, the range of modern weapons can render the 'clearly visible' emblem insignificant. This problem besets particularly the identification of medical aircraft. AP I stipulates detailed regulations in this regard. Arts. 5–8 Annex I AP I provides for light, radio, and electronic signals to be used as signs of identification. These signals are determined in detail with the co-operation of the competent international organizations, for example the International Telecommunications Organization and the International Civil Aviation Organization.[60] Medical aircraft can, for example, identify themselves by means of a blue flashing light. This signal can also be used by medical vehicles and hospital ships if the parties to the conflict specifically so agree.

5. The concept of military necessity is referred to for example in Art. 12, para. 5 GC I. Should a party be forced to hand over sick and wounded to the adversary, the latter will, as far as the military necessities allow, provide medical personnel for their treatment. Military medical personnel can be ordered to stay with the wounded and sick, and then have no choice but to do so.[61]

6. Each party to an armed conflict should nominate a neutral protecting power to take care of the interests of the respective party and its sick, wounded, and shipwrecked. Objections that a nominated protecting power is unacceptable to the adverse party have in a number of cases led to dispute. If no agreement can be reached, the ICRC can take the function of a protecting power upon itself, in fulfilment of humanitarian purposes. Concerning the treatment of the sick, wounded, and shipwrecked GCs I and II refer to the function of the protecting power as a mediator and representative of its nominating party's interests in any disagreement concerning the application and interpretation of the Conventions (Art. 11 GC I; Art. 11 GC II). The protecting power can also offer its good offices for the establishment of hospital zones and localities (Art. 23 GC I). In addition, the protecting power verifies reports of the death of prisoners of war, whether they died from natural causes or otherwise (Art. 121 GC III). In conflicts since 1949 protecting powers have occasionally been nominated. In the Falklands conflict, Great Britain nominated Switzerland and Argentina Brazil. On the other hand there was no protecting power in the Vietnam conflict or in the war between Iraq and Iran. During the latter, in particular, the ICRC frequently tried to fulfil this function in favour of the wounded and sick, but in vain.

641 **The use of a distinctive emblem by persons and organizations other than those entitled thereto is prohibited. To this end, the Parties to the Geneva Conventions shall take the precautions necessary for the prevention or repression of any abuse**

---

[59] Fleck, *RDMilG* XIII-2 (1974), 285–90.   [60] Cf. Bothe/Partsch/Solf, 18.
[61] Baccino-Astrada, 59.

of the distinctive emblems and signs (Arts. 53, 54 GC I; Art. 45 GC II; Art. 18, para. 8 AP I; Art. 12 AP II).

In the Federal Republic of Germany, the abuse of certain distinctive emblems may be liable to prosecution as an administrative offence under paragraph 125 of the Administrative Offences Act (*Ordnungswidrigkeitengesetz*).   642
    This paragraph provides as follows:

—(1) Any person who without authority uses the emblem of the red cross on a white ground or the word 'Red Cross' or 'Geneva Cross' commits an adminis-trative offence.

—(2) Any person who without authority uses the emblem of the Swiss Confederation also commits an administrative offence.

—(3) The emblems, names, and heraldic figures designated in paras. 1 and 2 are on an equal status with those that may be mistaken for them.

—(4) Paras. 1 and 3 shall apply by analogy to those emblems or names which, under international law, are on an equal status with the emblem of the red cross on a white ground or the words 'Red Cross'.

—(5) This administrative offence is punishable by a fine.

2. Camouflage of Medical Establishments

Camouflage of medical establishments in order to protect them against discovery by the enemy shall exceptionally be permitted without prejudice to Section 640 above when military reasons so require.   643

The basic requirement of Art. 42, para. 4 GC I is distinct marking of medical estab-lishments by day and night. Military reasons may, however, require that a black-out be imposed to conceal landmarks from the adversary, and particularly from its air force. In such a situation the military commander may lawfully order the camou-flage of medical establishments; in an attack this camouflage must be suspended.[62]

Camouflage of the distinctive emblem may only be ordered by brigade comman-ders and comparable and superior officers. The senior medical officer in charge and the legal adviser shall previously be consulted. The camouflage must be lim-ited in space and time. Movable medical establishments which are assigned to the treatment of the wounded and medical establishments shall not be camouflaged.   644

Camouflage does not deprive medical establishments of the protection accorded to them by international law. They are, however, exposed to the danger that the enemy—not recognizing them—might consider them to be military objectives and attack them.   645

---

[62] Pictet, Vol. I 321–2.

Rabus

7

Protection of Prisoners of War

Introductory Remarks

1. *Framework for the protection of prisoners of war.* The development and application of the international humanitarian law provisions for the protection of prisoners of war contain ethical, military, and political elements. The humane treatment of prisoners of war is rooted in the realization that captured combatants no longer pose any threat to the lives of the persons who capture them nor to their army. This is the basis for the humane treatment of prisoners required in armed conflict. The treatment may in specific cases be influenced by the former conduct of the prisoner during the combat, e.g. the use of prohibited weapons, attacks against protected persons, or perfidious conduct.

Military considerations also play an important role in the treatment of prisoners of war. In principle, every prisoner is of military value to the adversary. They can be used as sources of information or to influence their comrades who are still fighting. On the other hand, taking and detaining prisoners can impede the detaining power's military operations. Prisoners must be taken care of and guarded, and they may even have to be protected from the angry population of the detaining power. In order to remove prisoners from forward positions, transport facilities must be available. These few examples show that the humane treatment of prisoners of war is embedded in a moral, military, and political framework that is likely to influence the development and application of protective provisions of international humanitarian law. Conversely, these protective provisions have to take this field into account in order to fulfil their purpose and also to be practicable. To be effective, the protective provisions of international humanitarian law must resolve four questions:

—Who is a prisoner of war?

—How should prisoners of war be treated?

—For how long and under what circumstances shall this treatment be guaranteed?

— Which institutions or organizations supervise this treatment and thereby contribute to the enforcement of the protective provisions?

Fischer

2. *The treatment of prisoners of war until the end of the nineteenth century.* The treatment of prisoners of war until the end of the nineteenth century varied depending on the conflict, its geographical area, and the parties involved.[1] Prisoners were usually either killed or enslaved. This treatment mainly resulted from the lack of distinction between combatants and non-combatants. It was not until the end of the eighteenth century and after Jean-Jacques Rousseau had established the basis for this distinction in *Du Contrat Social* in 1762, that attempts were made to draft protective provisions for prisoners of war. The treaty of friendship between Prussia and the United States of 1785 contains the obligation of the contracting parties to protect prisoners of war. The Lieber Code of 24 April 1863 embodies the first detailed attempts to establish protection for prisoners of war. Although the American Civil War would today be classified as a non-international armed conflict, the Code had a significant influence on European attempts to protect prisoners of war. Art. 56 of the Lieber Code, which prohibits the inhumane treatment of prisoners of war, had an important impact on the European attempts in the nineteenth century. Following its establishment in 1863, the International Committee of the Red Cross played an important role in this development. A report dealing with general questions concerning the treatment of prisoners of war was presented at the first international Red Cross Conference in Paris in 1867. Henri Dunant finally put international negotiations on a new basis with his speech on 'A proposal for introducing uniformity into the condition of prisoners of war' in London in 1872. The Brussels Conference of 27 August 1874 resulted in the first twelve articles on the protection of prisoners of war during armed conflict.[2] Although the final document of the Brussels Conference did not enter into force, it formed the basis for the first protective provisions contained in the multilateral treaties of the Hague of 1899 and 1907.

3. *The Hague Rules.* The Hague Convention Concerning the Laws and Customs of War of 1899 contained in its Annex a chapter on the treatment of prisoners of war. It covered the first three of the four key areas identified above. It identified the groups of persons to be considered as prisoners of war and postulated the principle of 'humane treatment'. Art. 20 stipulated that following the conclusion of peace, prisoners of war were to be repatriated as quickly as possible. Although the provisions of 1899 were expanded at the second Hague Peace Conference, the First World War revealed the inadequacy of the Hague Rules. For this reason, Germany concluded bilateral treaties for the regulation of questions relating to prisoners of war first with Great Britain on 2 July 1917 and then with France on 26 April 1918.

4. *The Geneva Conventions of 1929.* In 1921 the International Committee of the Red Cross organized a conference which adopted a draft convention on the treatment of prisoners of war. This draft separated the question of prisoners of war from the Hague Law, which contained rules for warfare. The draft served as the basis for the

---

[1] On the development of the law in this area before the twentieth century see Scheidl; Bluntschli, 339–51; F. von Martens, Vol. 2, 499–505.

[2] Cf. Boissier, 286–93.

Fischer

discussions between the ICRC and the states parties in the 1920s. These resulted in the Geneva Convention of 1929 on Treatment of Prisoners of War, which was negotiated by forty-seven states. Although the Geneva Convention was based on the Hague Rules, it should be regarded as the beginning of a new era of protection for prisoners of war. A number of the provisions of the Hague Rules were adopted, e.g. the principle of humane treatment; the 1929 Convention lays down that prisoners must at all times be treated humanely and be protected, particularly against acts of violence, insults, and public curiosity. Other provisions contain new principles, e.g. the prohibition of reprisals against prisoners of war. One of the most widely known provisions of the Convention on Treatment of Prisoners of War, namely the right of prisoners of war to give only certain information when questioned, was introduced by the Geneva Convention of 1929. Obvious deficiencies of the Hague Rules, like the repatriation provision required on the conclusion of peace, were removed by the Geneva Convention of 1929. Necessary additions to the existing rules were also made. The Geneva Convention was the first to provide for a control mechanism.

5. *The Second World War.* By 1929, forty-six states had signed the Convention on the Treatment of Prisoners of War. Most of them, including Germany, Great Britain, France and the United States of America, ratified the Geneva Convention prior to the outbreak of World War II. The Soviet Union, however, did not ratify it. As a result, during the Second World War there were different legal requirements concerning the protection of prisoners of war among the main parties to the conflict. The Convention of 1929 was the basis of the legal relationship between Germany and its western adversaries. However, between Germany and the Soviet Union, the applicable provisions were those of the Hague Conventions of 1907 and the subsequent rules of customary law.

a) During the Second World War, there were violations of the existing rules in all the areas identified at the beginning. Small violations, as well as complete disregard for the humanitarian foundations of the provisions of the Geneva Convention of 1929, had to be ascertained. The so-called *Kommissar-Dekret* of 1941, for instance, was not even compatible with the Hague Rules of 1907. The denial of prisoner of war status for the political commissars of the Red Army and the order to execute them had no basis in international law. A further gross violation of international law by Germany in its treatment of prisoners of war was the so-called *Kommando-Befehl*, which ordered the execution of commando units operating behind German lines, wearing uniforms, who were taken captive.[3] There were also problems on the side of the Allies concerning the recognition of prisoner of war status of persons engaged in combat, which have been reappraised in recent years. For instance, members of the *Wehrmacht* who surrendered to Allied armed forces following the capitulation of 8 May 1945 were denied prisoner of war status. Instead, these German prisoners were given the so-called 'Surrendered Enemy Personnel Status'. The SEP prisoners were denied the guarantees for prisoners of war of the Geneva Convention of 1929, e.g. supervisory control by the ICRC in camp visits. Similarly,

---

[3] Cf. Kalshoven, *Belligerent Reprisals*, 184–93.

the Soviet army refused to grant prisoner of war status to Germans whom they considered to be war criminals.

b) In addition to the status problem, there were also violations of fundamental guarantees for the treatment of prisoners of war, especially on the German and Soviet sides. For example, Soviet prisoners of war in German camps were not provided with necessary food rations nor, in some cases, with any food at all. Many of them were transferred to concentration camps or forced to do dangerous work in industries important for the war effort. It is believed that of the 5.7 million Soviet prisoners of war in German captivity, 3.3 million died. Of the 3 million German prisoners of war in Soviet camps, approximately 1 million died during captivity.[4] The large number of deaths among German prisoners of war in Soviet camps was especially due to lack of care, the so-called death marches from the battle fields to the final place of internment, and forced labour under life-threatening conditions. Besides the insufficient care given to prisoners of war during the Second World War, especially in German and Soviet camps, reports were published after the war that medical experiments had been carried out on captured Allied soldiers in German and Japanese camps. While in camps of the western Allies the treatment of German and Japanese prisoners of war was far more positive, the SEP prisoners were subjected to hard conditions for weeks or even months after 8 May 1945.

c) In addition to the insufficient care provided during the Second World War, prisoners were often executed for violations of the laws of war or of laws of the detaining power. Although the Geneva Convention of 1929 permitted the death penalty for certain actions of prisoners of war, a fair trial for accused prisoners was rare. For example, prisoners were not permitted to defend themselves or to present evidence in their defence.

d) A further threat to prisoners of war during the Second World War was that the parties to the conflict exercised reprisals against them. Although the Convention of 1929 expressly prohibited reprisals against prisoners of war, even between parties to the Convention violations of protective rules were claimed to be justified as reprisals. Thus, for example, eighty German prisoners of war were executed by French authorities as a reprisal after the occupying German authority executed eighty French hostages near Lyon in 1944.[5]

e) From 1945 to 1955, the unresolved question concerning the repatriation of prisoners of war proved to be a major stumbling block in the restoration of a peaceful relationship between Germany and the Soviet Union. In 1950 the Soviet Union stated that 12,000 German prisoners of war were held in captivity. Of these, 9,000 were regarded as war criminals. In contrast to the American repatriation policy, which led to the termination of prisoner of war exchange in July 1946, it took until 1955 to resolve the German–Soviet prisoner of war problem. Among the numerous reasons why the Soviet Union held prisoners of war for so long, the labour provided by the prisoners for post-war reconstruction played a crucial role. Other wartime

---

[4] Rousseau, 100, bases his observations on similar figures.
[5] ICRC, *Report on Activities during the Second World War*, Vol. I, 522–3; Hinz, 58–9.

adversaries of Germany also used German prisoners of war for reconstruction work. For example, in 1947 there were still 630,000 German prisoners of war being held in France, many of whom were so employed.

6. *Development of the law after the Second World War.* The numerous violations of the rules of the Geneva Convention of 1929 had revealed the necessity for extension and clarification of the provisions for prisoner of war protection. As after the First World War, the ICRC took the initiative for the improvement of prisoner of war protection. Between 1946 and 1948 a number of drafts were discussed with the representatives of national Red Cross societies and official representatives of the parties to the Convention of 1929. After the Red Cross Conference in Stockholm in 1948, at which the ICRC's draft for an improved convention for the protection of prisoners of war was discussed, Switzerland convened the Diplomatic Conference of Geneva in 1949, in which sixty-two states participated. This diplomatic conference adopted the Four Geneva Conventions of 12 August 1949. The Third Convention (GC III) expands and improves the provisions of the Convention on Treatment of Prisoners of War of 1929. GC III is one of the most extensive codifications of international humanitarian law. Based on experiences of violations of the humanitarian rules of the 1929 Convention, important fundamental rules for the protection of prisoners of war were clarified, expanded, or completely revised. New provisions were added and existing ones were set in a different order so as to increase their significance.

In virtually all armed conflicts since 1949 violations, and sometimes grave breaches, of the provisions of GC III of 1949 were ascertainable. As in the Second World War, violations of fundamental provisions for the protection of prisoners of war were at the forefront. The community of states did not respond to these violations by attempting further codification. GC III establishes such a detailed regime that further attempts to improve the protection of prisoners of war would merely clarify individual rules. Such a clarifying addition is contained in Arts. 43 and 44 of the First Protocol (AP I) of 12 December 1977 Additional to the Geneva Conventions of 12 August 1949. Both these articles reflect the efforts of the community of states to deal with the problems—which arose particularly during the Vietnam War—relating to the treatment of guerrillas as combatants and prisoners of war. More far-reaching provisions supplementary to GC III are contained in a few parts of AP I, e.g. in Art. 41, although without altering the character of GC III as the most important basis of the protection of prisoners of war.

7. *Protection of prisoners of war and customary law.* It is generally agreed by the community of states and most international lawyers that the fundamental provisions of GC III of 1949 are valid as customary law. In addition, some provisions are accepted as *ius cogens.* Due to the large number of parties, the qualification of the fundamental provisions of GC III as rules of customary law is only of minor significance for their application in armed conflicts. The question as to which violations of GC III should constitute war crimes and should thus be internationally punishable becomes increasingly important. Art. 130 GC III lists those acts which are

Fischer

,

regarded by the parties as grave breaches of the Convention. These include wilful killing and torture or inhumane treatment of, including biological experiments on, prisoners of war. During the Second Gulf War and the war in the former Yugoslavia the states of the European Community made statements and the Security Council of the United Nations issued resolutions confirming the content of Art. 130 GC III.[6] The Statute of the International Tribunal for the Prosecution of Persons Responsible for Serious Violations of International Humanitarian Law Committed in the Territory of the Former Yugoslavia since 1991 expressly refers to 'grave breaches' of the Geneva Conventions. *Inter alia* they underlie the prosecution of war crimes in the former Yugoslavia.[7]

I. GENERAL

701   **The purpose of captivity is to exclude enemy soldiers from further military operations. Since soldiers are permitted to participate in lawful military operations, prisoners of war shall only be considered as captives detained for reasons of security, not as criminals.**

The purpose of captivity is not defined in GC III. It is in the interest of the detaining power to prevent enemy combatants from taking part in further military operations. The group of persons liable to being taken prisoner goes beyond the narrow term of 'soldiers'. All persons considered in Art. 43 AP I or Art. 4 GC III to be members of the armed forces or prisoners of war belong to this group if they fall into the hands of the enemy. War correspondents, for example, in so far as they are authorized to carry out their activities by the armed forces which they accompany, shall also be considered prisoners of war if they are in possession of the identity card required for their activities.

Leaving aside the question of responsibility for waging aggressive war, lawful military operations in armed conflict are not contrary to international law. Thus, attacks against military objectives of the adversary are permitted if carried out by lawful methods of warfare. International law does not provide sanctions for such conduct. Taking an enemy combatant prisoner can therefore never serve as a punishment but only to prevent further participation in military operations against the detaining power. Because of this fundamental perception of lawful operations during an armed conflict, the internment conditions of prisoners of war must differ from those of convicts. GC III only permits prisoners of war to be interned in prisons in exceptional cases. If prisoners of war are e.g. sentenced to imprisonment for acts committed prior to their capture, they may be held in prisons if members of the armed forces of the detaining power would also be treated in this manner.

---

[6] Cf. the statement of the EC of 22 Jan. 1991, reprinted in *European Journal of International Law*, Vol. 4 (1993), No. 1, 146/147.

[7] UN Doc. S/25704 of 23 May 1993, 10.

However, the benefits of Arts. 78 and 126 GC III still apply in the case of such punishment.

Prisoners of war are not prisoners of the capturing unit but prisoners of the government to whose armed forces the capturing unit belongs (detaining power). The detaining power is responsible for the treatment of prisoners of war (Art. 12, para. 1 GC III). 702

That prisoners of war are to be regarded as prisoners of a state, the detaining power, is linked to the fact that armed conflicts have since the eighteenth century no longer been considered as a struggle of man against man, but rather as a conflict between one state and another. In practice, the effect of this principle is twofold: first, it serves to protect prisoners of war, who must not be subjected to arbitrary acts by the adversary's soldiers who take them captive. Even if their lives were in danger only a few minutes prior to the capture, the captors are not permitted to view the captives as their personal prisoners, nor therefore to subject them to arbitrary acts. The principle that prisoners of war are considered to be prisoners of the state also constitutes the basis of the responsibility for their treatment: it is the detaining power's obligation to require its organs to abide by the rules of international law on the treatment of prisoners of war, and to ensure the application of these rules. Irrespective of any improper conduct by individual soldiers when capturing or dealing with prisoners of war, the detaining power is responsible in international law for the treatment of prisoners of war. Claims relating to the improper conduct of its organs can therefore be directed against the detaining power under the principles of international responsibility.

A detaining power may transfer prisoners of war to another power only if it has satisfied itself of the willingness and ability of the latter to apply the rules of international law as to the protection of prisoners of war (Art. 12, para. 2 GC III). 703

1. *Transfer.* In international armed conflicts of previous decades the transfer of prisoners of war was common practice. The reasons for transfer differed. In most cases the feasibility of interning and taking care of a large number of prisoners of war played the decisive role in the transfer. However, transfers have also been decided on the basis of considerations of alliance policy. Following the Second World War, for example, the United States transferred a large number of the aforementioned German 'SEP' to France and Great Britain.[8] During the Second Gulf War, the United States transferred Iraqi prisoners of war to Saudi Arabia.[9]

Before a transfer can take place, three requirements must be met. First, the detaining power may only transfer prisoners of war to a state party to GC III. In addition, the other power's willingness to apply GC III must have been subjectively ascertained, and the preconditions for the application of the provisions must be

[8] See Introductory para. 5a above.
[9] Department of Defense, *Conduct of the Persian Gulf War, Final Report to Congress*, Washington April 1992, Appendix L–3.

objectively fulfilled. Therefore, a transfer may not take place if the transferee power, for instance, has indicated that it will refrain—wholly or in part—from applying GC III. Inadequate camps, no available camps, or predictably inadequate supplies for the prisoners of war prevent the transfer of prisoners of war.

The conditions for transfers are usually determined in treaties concluded by the states involved. In the Second Gulf War, the United States concluded transfer agreements with Saudi Arabia, Great Britain, and France.[10] These treaties dealt with every aspect of the transfer procedure, starting with the capture of Iraqi soldiers, through their questioning and medical treatment, and up to their transfer to Saudi prison camps.

2. *Extent of preconditions.* The aforementioned preconditions apply to the transfer of prisoners of war from the detaining power to another power. There are no further requirements. GC III does not, for example, specify whether the 'transferee power' must be a party to the conflict. In the absence of a contrary provision, it can be assumed that every state which is a party to GC III can be a receiving state if the conditions described are met. During the Afghanistan conflict, for example, Switzerland agreed to receive Soviet soldiers who had been captured by Afghan rebels.[11]

3. *Permanent responsibility.* By transferring prisoners of war to another power, the detaining power does not entirely shed its responsibility for the prisoners. The transfer is only effective as long as the receiving state applies GC III in all its important respects. In the event of violation of these rules, the transferring power has not only a right but, as the wording of Art. 12, para. 3 suggests, also an obligation to take effective measures in order to provide a remedy. For instance, the USA changed their practice of transferring prisoners of war to South Vietnam during the Vietnam War when violations of the provisions of GC III by South Vietnam during the phase following the transfer were made public.[12] The transferring state can also request the return of prisoners of war. The receiving state cannot refuse such a request.

The Statute of the International Tribunal for the Prosecution of Persons Responsible for Serious Violations of International Humanitarian Law Committed in the Territory of the Former Yugoslavia since 1991 raises problems as to the obligations under GC III. According to the statute, states with suspected war criminals under their control are obliged to transfer these persons to the tribunal.[13] As the United Nations is not a party to the Geneva Conventions, this statutory obligation contradicts Art. 12, para. 2 GC III. Further problems arise as to imprisonment: the statute lays down that imprisonment shall be served according to the law of the state which has agreed to accept the convicted war criminal.[14] No reference is made

---

[10] Department of Defense, *Conduct of the Persian Gulf War, Final Report to Congress*, Washington April 1992, Appendix L–3.

[11] Hess, 202.   [12] Levie, *Procedures*, 212.   [13] UN Doc. S/25704 of 23 May 1993, 32.

[14] Ibid., 31.

here to the guarantees of GC III. Hence the transfer of prisoners of war to the tribunal, as required by the statute, causes considerable problems for the detaining power in respect of its responsibilities under GC III.

Fundamental rules for the treatment of prisoners of war are:

—It is prohibited to treat prisoners of war inhumanely or dishonourably (Arts. 13 and 14 GC III).

—Any discrimination on the grounds of race, nationality, religious belief or political opinions, or similar criteria is unlawful (Art. 16 GC III).

—Reprisals against prisoners of war are prohibited (Art. 13, para. 3 GC III).

Representatives of the protecting power and delegates of the ICRC may visit internees in their camps at any time and talk to them individually and without witnesses.

1. *Humane treatment.* Section 704 contains the fundamental provisions on the treatment of prisoners of war. Prisoners of war must be treated humanely *at all times*. The wording of Section 704 reiterates the prohibitive part of the basic provision already contained in the Hague Conventions of 1899.

It is not specified in Section 704 what constitutes inhumane treatment of prisoners of war. Neither the Hague Regulations of 1899 and 1907 nor the Geneva Conventions of 1929 contained specific definitions. For this reason, problems of interpretation emerged during the Second World War, which the wording of Art. 13 GC III—especially by stressing certain examples of inhumane treatment—had intended to avoid. For example, acts or omissions causing death or seriously endangering the health of the prisoners of war are a violation of the principle of humane treatment. The same is true for physical mutilation or medical or scientific experiments. However, these acts may be carried out if they are justified by the medical treatment of the prisoners of war and are carried out in their interest. This formulation leaves open the possibility of providing sick prisoners with medical treatment, which is in their interest and might save them.

2. *'At all times'.* It is emphasized that the principle of humane treatment applies 'at all times'. In contrast to the Convention of 1929, GC III expressly includes this term. The experiences of the wars of the first half of the twentieth century, especially the Second World War, were the reason for introducing this terminology at the Geneva Conference of 1949. Thus it is no longer possible for the detaining power to justify inhumane treatment by reference to the circumstances of the hostilities, causes of the conflict, and so forth.

3. *Obligation to protect.* Humane treatment requires not only that the detaining power desist from inhumane acts, but also as expressly emphasized in Art. 13, para. 2, that the detaining power prevent such acts by any other party. In particular, prisoners of war shall be protected against violence and intimidation, insults and public curiosity (see Section 711). Following incidents during the Second World War,

Fischer

e.g. the so-called *Essen Lynching* case,[15] express reference was made to this in 1949. Thus, prisoners of war may not, for example, be transported through the streets of a town in order to subject them to acts of violence or intimidation. Incidents of this type have occurred in all conflicts in this century. During the Second World War, for instance, French prisoners of war were paraded through German towns. During the Vietnam War, Allied pilots were put on display in Hanoi. Also, during the Second Gulf War, captured Allied pilots were publicly displayed in the streets of Baghdad.[16]

Even if there are no acts of violence or intimidation, it has to be asked whether there is a violation of the prohibition of exposing the prisoners of war to public curiosity. Pictures of prisoners of war[17] can be broadcast world-wide almost instantaneously due to modern technology, as happened on a number of occasions during the Second Gulf War. Broadcasts by Iraqi television, in which Allied pilots were coerced to denounce their own countries, and also television broadcasts of interviews with Iraqi prisoners of war directly following their capture were correctly deemed to be violations of Art. 13 GC III.[18]

Even if such cases were not anticipated during the negotiations for GC III in 1949, the underlying purpose of rules on humane treatment prohibits the transmission of pictures of prisoners of war by the detaining power. Only two types of case may be considered permissible.[19] First, photographic reports about prisoners of war do not violate the principle of humane treatment if the photographs do not enable the identification of individual prisoners. The other permitted case applies to reporting on prisoners and their conditions of captivity by the protecting power, the International Committee of the Red Cross, or other internationally recognized organizations. Although in such cases the prisoners are exposed to public curiosity, reporting about them serves to enforce international humanitarian law and to improve their conditions in captivity. The examples of reports on prisoner of war camps in the former Yugoslavia illustrate the requirement to weigh the need to preserve prisoners' lives against the rule prohibiting their exposure to public curiosity. In the case of reporting by international observers, preservation of the prisoners' lives must prevail.

4. *Prohibition of discrimination.* GC III takes a clear stance on equality of treatment of prisoners of war (referred to in Section 704). Equal treatment of prisoners of war must be guaranteed by the detaining power even if the prisoners can be classified according to race, nationality, religious belief, and the other aforementioned characteristics. However, Art. 22, para. 3 GC III contains a rule on positive discrimination. It might be advantageous for prisoners of war to be grouped together in camps

---

[15] *The Essen Lynching Case, Trial of Erich Heyer and Six Others Before British Military Court*, reprinted in Friedman, Vol. II, 1482–6.

[16] On this problem see Fischer/Wallenfels, Bildberichterstattung, 28–46 with further references.

[17] The admissibility of pictures was also recognized as a problem by the American side, Keenan, *HUV-I* 4/1991, 37.

[18] Ipsen, *Auswirkungen*, 44. The report of the US Department of Defense about the Gulf War mentions the problem of reporting and refers to measures adopted to avoid placing the prisoners of war in danger, without listing in detail the actions of the Allies: Department of Defense, *Conduct of the Persian Gulf War*, Appendix O–18.

[19] Fischer/Wallenfels, *Bildberichterstattung*, 28–46.

on the basis of their nationality, language, and customs. Such grouping is only possible if the prisoners are not thereby separated from the armed forces in which they were serving at the time of their capture, unless with their consent.

GC III contains further positive obligations in terms of the treatment of women, who are afforded special protection during their internment.[20]

5. *Prohibition of reprisals.* GC III lays down an absolute prohibition of reprisals against prisoners of war. There is no exception whatsoever to this principle. Even the most severe violations of GC III by the opposing side do not entitle the detaining power to contravene the prohibition of reprisals. Unlike other international conventions, GC III is not governed by the principle of reciprocity. This is made clear in Art. 1, in which the High Contracting Parties commit themselves to respect GC III in all circumstances. Violations of the provisions of the convention therefore cannot be justified by reference to violations by the adversary. The clear and express prohibition of reprisals has, however, been repeatedly disregarded in conflicts since 1949. For example, in the war between Iran and Iraq both states sought to justify certain operations by reference to violations by the adversary. Obviously the conduct of the parties to the conflict was based on notions of reciprocity and reprisals.[21] On the other hand, the Second Gulf War proved that the provisions of GC III can be respected even in the face of the most severe violations. Following the obvious maltreatment of Allied pilots and their presentation on Iraqi television, the Allied headquarters expressly confirmed that Allied troops would abide by GC III. During the course of the war on land the Iraqi prisoners were therefore treated in accordance with GC III by the Allies.[22]

During the Second World War, it was often said that violations of the provisions of the law on prisoners of war were justified because the prisoner consented. In addition to the prohibition of reprisals, Art. 7 GC III prevents the detaining power from relying on consent by the prisoner. Prisoners cannot, even partially, renounce their rights under GC III. Thus it is impossible for a detaining power to justify violations of GC III by claiming that a prisoner of war consented. If the rights of prisoners are being limited in their effect or tailored to certain groups, e.g. the rules on work by prisoners of war, then the Geneva Convention contains express stipulations for these cases. The highly detailed character of GC III is therefore an additional safeguard against a claim that prisoners of war had renounced certain rights.

6. *Protecting powers.* The detaining power is responsible for respecting the provisions of GC III. In order to fulfil this responsibility, GC III contains obligations for the High Contracting Parties, applicable in peace as well as in wartime. According to Art. 127, the text of GC III is to be disseminated as widely as possible and in particular its study is to be included in military training programmes and, if possible, in civil instruction. All armed forces of the High Contracting Parties and their

---

[20] During the Second Gulf War two female American soldiers were taken prisoner by Iraqi armed forces: Department of Defense, *Conduct of the Persian Gulf War*, Appendix R–2.

[21] Tavernier, 132.

[22] Department of Defense, *Conduct of the Persian Gulf War*, Appendix L–12.

Fischer

civilian populations are thereby to be made familiar with the principles of GC III. The system of the 'protecting power' was introduced by the Third Geneva Convention of 1949 to ensure compliance with the provisions of GC III.

7. *Definition of the protecting power.* A protecting power is any state instructed by one of the parties to a conflict to safeguard its interests. The protecting power appoints delegates to carry out its tasks. These can be chosen from among its diplomatic or consular representatives, its nationals or the nationals of other neutral powers. The party to the conflict must approve the delegates appointed. GC III enables an organization to act as a protecting power if it is clearly impartial and effective. The organization can be either international or non-international. It is a precondition, however, that the High Contracting Parties agree that the duties of a protecting power may be conferred on that organization.

It is a fundamental weakness of the system under GC III that approval is necessary from the party detaining prisoners before the delegates appointed by the protecting power can carry out their activities. As there is no general obligation to accept the appointed delegates, and furthermore there are no procedures for the selection of protecting powers by the parties to a conflict, detaining powers can paralyse the system of protecting powers completely by refusing to approve the delegates. With the adoption of AP I in 1977 this situation changed considerably. Under this Protocol the parties to a conflict are obliged to ensure the implementation of GC III and AP I by applying the system of protecting powers from the beginning of the conflict. Each party to the conflict shall without delay designate a protecting power at the outbreak of an armed conflict. The commencement of activities by this protecting power depends, however, on its acceptance by the adverse party. In contrast to Art. 9 GC III, Art. 5 AP I provides a procedure intended to facilitate the selection of a substitute protecting power in the event of non-acceptance of the appointed protecting powers. According to Art. 5, para. 4, the substitute protecting power must also be accepted by the parties to the conflict before it can commence its services.

8. *Tasks.* The main task of the delegates of the protecting powers is to visit prisoners of war and to question them without witnesses. In order that delegates can obtain a comprehensive and clear idea of the extent to which the provisions of GC III are being met, they can, as a rule, visit any place where prisoners of war are held. This applies first to the camps mentioned in Section 704, but also to places of detention and work as well as points of departure, transit and arrival of transferred prisoners of war. The right to visit is not subject to temporal restrictions. The length and frequency of visits is left for the delegates of the protecting powers to determine. The planning of visits by the delegates in terms of their location and timing may only be restricted by the detaining power for imperative military reasons, and then only temporarily. It will not be possible regularly to claim such military necessity for camps falling under Art. 21. Visits shall be permitted even in transit camps as long as the delegates do not interfere with military operations of the detaining power and are not endangered by their visit.

Fischer

A further function of the protecting powers is their participation in the settlement of disputes. According to Art. 11 GC III, the protecting powers offer their good offices particularly in cases of disagreement between the parties to the conflict regarding the application or interpretation of GC III, if they consider it necessary in the interest of the protected persons. The protecting powers' mediation services are not confined to these cases.

9. *Practice.* The system of protecting powers has only rarely been used since the Second World War. During the Suez crisis in 1956, protecting powers were designated by Israel, but Egypt did not authorize them to perform any duties. In the Falklands war, Switzerland assumed the function of protecting power for Great Britain and Brazil did likewise for Argentina. Thus the Falklands war is one of the few cases in which protecting power functions were utilized. Protecting powers were appointed neither in the conflicts in Korea and Vietnam nor in the war between Iraq and Iran. The fact that the consent of the detaining power—also required by Art. 5 AP I—is a prerequisite to the protecting power's delegates commencing their activities continues to be a considerable restriction on the functioning of the system of protecting powers in international humanitarian law.

10. *The role of the ICRC.* The system of protecting powers in GC III and AP I is not limited to the functions of the High Contracting Parties. In those cases in which the parties to a conflict are unable to reach an agreement on protecting powers, GC III allocates tasks to humanitarian organizations such as the International Committee of the Red Cross. These organizations can assume the same humanitarian duties which can be assigned to protecting powers in two cases. First, the detaining power can request the ICRC or another humanitarian organization to carry out protecting power duties. A second possibility is for the International Committee of the Red Cross, for instance, to offer the detaining power their humanitarian services under the system of protecting powers; the detaining power must accept this offer before such services can be performed. As in the case of a High Contracting Party who adopts protecting power tasks, ICRC activities within the system of protecting powers also depend on invitation or acceptance by the detaining power.

In this respect, it should be kept in mind that recent practice of supervising compliance with GC III has certain distinctive features. First, in its Resolution 771 of 13 August 1992, the United Nations Security Council called on all parties to the conflict in Bosnia-Herzegovina to grant all responsible international humanitarian organizations, and particularly the International Committee of the Red Cross, access to camps, prisons, and detention centres on the territory of the former Yugoslavia.[23] Although the Security Council's primary concern in this resolution was the facilitation of humanitarian assistance operations of the International Committee of the Red Cross and other international humanitarian organizations, the obligation to grant access necessarily affects the ICRC's function in the system of protecting powers. Obviously the Security Council does not consider the approval of the

---

[23] Reprinted in *Vereinte Nationen*, 6/1992, 216.

Fischer

International Committee's activities by the detaining power as necessary in cases of gross violations of international humanitarian law. The fact that the resolution does not distinguish clearly between humanitarian assistance and the functions of protecting powers also hints at an expansion of the latter.

Following the response of the international community to the conflicts in the former Yugoslavia, one may also assume a further change in the understanding of the function of the protecting power. In these conflicts the functions of protecting powers were carried out by international organizations and special organs. For instance, delegations of the Conference for Security and Co-operation in Europe visited prisoner of war camps in the former Yugoslavia.[24] The former Polish Prime Minister Mazowiecki, appointed by the Human Rights Commission of the United Nations, also visited camps in the former Yugoslavia on several occasions and reported violations against international humanitarian law.[25] These activities, and particularly the international debate on the findings of the investigations and its influence on the parties to the conflict, seem to indicate that in the future international organizations and organs created especially for this purpose will increasingly be in a position to carry out the functions of protecting powers.

II. BEGINNING OF CAPTIVITY

705   The status of prisoner of war begins as soon as a combatant (Arts. 4A paras. 1–3 and 6 GC III; Art. 44 AP I) or other person with equal status (Arts. 4A paras. 4 and 5, 4B para. 1, and 5, para. 2 GC III; Art. 45, para. 1 AP I) and *hors de combat* (Art. 41, para. 2 AP I) falls into the hands of the adversary. An adversary who, having laid down his arms, or no longer having means of defence, surrenders or is otherwise unable to fight or defend himself shall no longer be made the object of attack (Art. 41, para. 1 AP I; Art. 23, para. 1 HagueReg). He shall be taken prisoner of war.

1. *The connection between combatant and prisoner of war status.* The definite linkage between combatant and prisoner of war status is one of the fundamental principles of international humanitarian law. Art. 44 AP I has confirmed this by categorically linking the status of prisoner of war with that of combatant. Only one precondition is laid down for the applicability of prisoner of war protection: the combatant must be captured by the adverse party to the conflict. The definitions of combatants in AP I, the Geneva Conventions, and the Hague Regulations therefore determine which group of persons is entitled to claim protection as prisoner of war (Sections 301 ff.). The relations established through treaties and by customary law between the parties to the conflict are the foundation for granting combatant status. If Art. 43 AP I is seen as a further development of humanitarian law (cf. Sections

[24] The suggestion of the Committee of Senior Officials of the CSCE of 9 Feb. 1993 concerning an international criminal court refers to the various CSCE missions; *Proposal for an International War Crimes Tribunal for the Former Yugoslavia*, 30–3.

[25] See *Report on the situation of human rights in the territory of the former Yugoslavia*, E/CN.4/1993/50.

Fischer

304 ff.) which also changed the constitutive preconditions for the classification as a combatant, then problems may arise in the uniform application of international humanitarian law in a mixed conflict where several states are involved but only some of them are bound by AP I. For instance, if one party to the conflict is bound by AP I, members of its armed forces shall be treated as prisoners of war even if they only carry their weapons openly prior to an attack. For soldiers acting likewise who belong to parties to the conflict only bound by GC III, the situation is different. If the carrying of weapons openly is regarded as a constitutive element of combatant status, in this case one of the necessary conditions for combatant status is not fulfilled. Hence prisoner of war status cannot be claimed.[26]

Since the Gulf War, a new problem has emerged as to the point in time and the act by which persons become members of the armed forces. During the Second Gulf War, Great Britain interned Iraqi students studying in London as prisoners of war. The reason stated was that the students were registered on a list of Iraqi reserve forces. Great Britain's position was criticized because the mere inclusion on a reserve list does not prove membership of the armed forces. Instead, passive and active reservists have to be distinguished.[27] As every state determines autonomously the composition of its armed forces, the commencement and termination of service in the armed forces must be ascertained according to the national law of the state involved.

In contrast to what the term suggests, non-combatants also enjoy prisoner of war status. They do not belong to the civilian population. Non-combatants are members of the armed forces who have been assigned special non-combatant functions by a national statute. Despite these different functions in armed conflicts, non-combatants, as members of the armed forces, shall be treated as prisoners of war on capture.

2. *Capture.* Combatants become prisoners of war at the moment of their capture. It has to be clarified when and by which act a combatant 'falls into the hands of' the adversary. The definition of *hors de combat* in Art. 41, para. 2 AP I presumes that the detaining power has established its power over the adversary's combatant. On the battlefield this usually means that soldiers either surrender to the enemy or fall under the enemy's power after becoming unable to fight through injury.

During the Second Gulf War, for example, Iraqi soldiers surrendered to journalists in the desert.[28] As Art. 12, para. 2 GC III lays down that the detaining power is responsible for prisoners of war, 'falling into the hands' can only occur if the combatants are captured or taken into custody by the competent state organs. The Iraqi soldiers did not attain prisoner of war status until they were handed over to the Allied armed forces. Being on the adversary's territory does not fulfil the condition of 'falling into the hands'. Custody of a prisoner of war only commences with an act by a competent state organ corresponding to capture on the battlefield. It is immaterial whether the prisoners of war surrender to the enemy following the cessation of their state's military operations. Persons captured after the surrender of their

---

[26] Rosas, 342, 343.   [27] Hampson, 515.   [28] *Süddeutsche Zeitung*, 28 Feb. 1991.

power are also considered to be in the hands of the enemy. They shall also be treated as prisoners of war.[29]

3. *Denial of prisoner of war status.* The Convention of 1929 contained no clear provisions about the status of captured war criminals. After the Second World War Allied courts denied German and Japanese soldiers the status of prisoner of war because of the uncertain legal situation.[30] GC III determines in Art. 85 that prisoners of war do not lose the benefits of the Convention because of acts committed prior to their capture. A detaining power is therefore not permitted to deny prisoner of war status to enemy combatants with the justification that they were involved in unlawful war activities. Nonetheless, in numerous conflicts since the Second World War persons have been denied prisoner of war status for this reason.[31] After ratification of GC III, the Soviet Union and a number of other states made a reservation with regard to Art. 85 aimed at changing the legal effect of that article. Properly construed, the reservation[32] means that persons convicted of war crimes or crimes against humanity should not receive the protection of GC III.[33] The reservation is considered today to be impermissible.[34] The majority of authors argue that even combatants who have obviously committed a war crime before being taken prisoner are entitled to the benefits of GC III. Art. 44 AP I of 1977 strengthens this rule by stipulating that, in principle, uncertainties about the status of prisoners must be interpreted in their favour. On a correct application of the provisions on the legal effect of inadmissible reservations and the treatment of prisoners of war after their conviction, the relevance of Art. 85 GA III is reduced in cases involving a reservation of the Soviet type.[35]

During the Second Gulf War in 1991 Iraq initially refused to grant prisoner of war status to the Allied pilots in their hands, who were wrongfully denied prisoner of war status on the ground that they were war criminals. Furthermore, combatants may not be denied prisoner of war status on the grounds that the state for which they were fighting no longer exists or that its territory belongs to the state which is taking the soldiers prisoner. This latter was claimed by Iraq following the invasion of Kuwait in 1990 in order to deny Kuwaiti soldiers the status of prisoner of war.[36]

706 **Prisoners of war shall be disarmed and searched. Their military equipment and military documents shall be taken away from them (Art. 18, para. 1 GC III).**

1. *Disarming and search.* The wording of Section 706 provides for the classification of prisoners of war as security prisoners. At the same time, the section takes into account the security requirements of the troops of the detaining power. Thus the

---

[29] Levie, *Prisoners of War*, 35; on the problem of the treatment of Germans captured following their surrender after 8 May 1945 cf. H. Fischer, *HUV-I* 1/1990, 117.

[30] Cf. in this respect Levie, 384, 385; Spinnler, 90, 91.

[31] On the cases in North Vietnam cf. Levie, in Falk (Ed.), Vol. 2, 383.

[32] The text of the reservation is reprinted in Levie, *loc. cit.*, 386.

[33] On the assessment of the North Vietnamese reservation and the debate thereon during the Vietnam War see Meyrowitz, in Falk (Ed.), Vol. 2, 565–6.

[34] McCoubrey, 105.   [35] As correctly argued by Hinz, 171.   [36] Meron, 104.

disarming and search of prisoners of war is a precondition for the detaining power to ensure that their detention is a security detention. The detaining power's right to search is not restricted: the detaining power is entitled to find out what objects the prisoners of war are carrying with them. However, the authority to remove items is limited to arms, military equipment, and objects other than those listed in Section 707.

2. *Tying up prisoners of war.* It is not expressly laid down in GC III whether or not prisoners of war may be tied up following their capture. In 1942 German soldiers were captured and bound by British and Canadian task forces near Dieppe at the French Channel coast.[37] The German soldiers were shackled order to prevent them from destroying military documents. By way of reprisal for the incident at Dieppe both Allied prisoners of war in German camps and German prisoners of war in Allied camps were bound. Tying of prisoners of war as a security measure also occurred during the Second Gulf War. Pictures of Iraqi soldiers in the Saudi desert with their hands tied behind their backs and waiting to be transported were seen world-wide.

There is no doubt that, as a general rule, binding prisoners of war in camps is prohibited.[38] Other standards might be applicable to tying on the battlefield, because the first goal of the detaining soldiers must be to prevent the prisoners of war from escaping or—as in Dieppe in 1942—to prevent the destruction of information. If it is permissible to shoot at prisoners of war in order to prevent them from escaping, then it is argued that the less drastic measure of tying them also complies with GC III.

The decisive argument against the permissibility of tying prisoners of war on the battlefield can be found in the detaining power's obligation to provide care for prisoners of war. As prisoners of war generally require freedom of movement on the battlefield in order to escape from danger, e.g. to seek cover from the use of weapons, tying them can be seen as a violation of the rule that prisoners of war shall not be subjected to unnecessary dangers prior to being moved from the battlefield.[39] Practices such as those seen occasionally during the Second Gulf War must therefore be regarded as violations of GC III.[40]

Prisoners of war shall keep all effects and articles of personal use, their metal helmets, and NBC protective equipment as well as all effects and articles used for their clothing and feeding (Art. 18, para. 1 GC III). They shall also keep their badges of rank and nationality, their decorations, and articles of mainly personal or sentimental value, e.g. pictures of family members (Art. 18, para. 3, 40 GC III).   707

For centuries, an important component of the law of war was the right to booty. Art. 18 restricts this right with regard to the effects of prisoners of war. Above all, this

---

[37] Cf. the description of the incident, ICRC, *Report*, 368–70.

[38] On the shackling of American prisoners of war in Vietnamese camps see Miller, 172.

[39] Kalshoven, *Belligerent Reprisals*, 182.

[40] Ipsen, *Auswirkungen*, 43. The report of the US Department of Defense about the Gulf War does not refer to these practices, Department of Defense, *Conduct of the Persian Gulf War*, Appendix L.

Fischer

takes into account the security interests of the prisoners of war and of the detaining power as well as the special circumstances of captivity. Thus the rule in Art. 18 is based not on ownership of items carried by prisoners but on the use of the objects to the prisoner. Articles of personal use, regardless of whether they are owned by the prisoners of war or were provided by the home state, may not be confiscated. Thus the scope of Art. 18 exceeds the scope indicated in Section 707. Even clothing and items of food which are part of the prisoner's military equipment may not be taken away. It is essential for the safety of prisoners of war that helmets, gas masks, and similar items used for personal protection are not permitted to be removed from them.

Art. 18, para. 3 lists items of personal or sentimental value separately. Their significance to the well-being of the prisoner of war is obvious. Wedding rings or keepsakes shall therefore not be confiscated. Not all articles of value are exempt from seizure by the detaining power. In this respect, the GC III is less restrictive than the Convention of 1929 which did not permit any objects of value to be taken away. Because during the Second World War prisoners of war used articles of value which they had been permitted to keep for their escape, GC III contains a special rule applicable to articles of value and money in Art. 18, paras. 4 and 5 (see Section 709). Confiscation of arms, military equipment, horses and military documents is permitted, even if these items are the personal property of the prisoner of war.

Another question is whether prisoners of war must be permitted to keep objects which could be used for escape. In these circumstances, both the security interest of the detaining power and the interest of protecting the prisoner of war, both of which find expression in Art. 18 GC III, must be taken into consideration. Confiscation is only permitted if two conditions are met: the objects must be essential to the escape and they must be replaceable by other objects provided by the detaining power. For instance, if the prisoners' clothing resembles that of the civilian population, the detaining power may replace it with other clothing.

708   **The detaining power is obliged to forward information regarding the fate of prisoners of war (Art. 122 GC III) as well as of wounded, sick, shipwrecked, and dead (Art. 16 GC I; Art. 19 GC II, see above Sections 538, 611), and of protected civilians (Arts. 136–41 GC IV). For this purpose, each of the parties to the conflict shall institute an official Information Bureau on the outbreak of a conflict and in all cases of occupation (Art. 122, para. 1 GC III). The Bureau shall co-operate with the Central Prisoners of War Information Agency of the International Committee of the Red Cross (Arts. 122, para. 3 and 123 GC III).**

Example: In the Federal Republic of Germany, the Federal Minister of the Interior, acting in accordance with Art. 2 of the Act on the Protocols I and II Additional to the Geneva Conventions, has given to the German Red Cross the responsibility to plan and prepare for the National Information Bureau. The German Armed Forces Personnel Office's Information Bureau (*Personalstammamt der Bundeswehr—Bundeswehrauskunftsstelle*) is tasked with the implementation in the German Armed Forces.

Fischer

1. *Obligation and organizational consequences.* Informing the relatives of prisoners of war would be impossible without imposing an obligation on the detaining power to provide information about the fate of prisoners of war. Art. 122 GC III lists the details concerning prisoners of war and their well-being which the detaining power shall pass on. It covers personal data such as first name, rank, etc.; information about the medical condition of seriously ill prisoners; and notification of release, repatriation, escape, etc. The degree of fulfilment by the detaining power of the obligation regarding personal data depends on the conduct of the prisoners of war. The detaining power can pass this information on only if they give details beyond those required by Art. 17, e.g. their place of birth. If the prisoners of war fail to give such details, the context of the GC III rules implies that the non-fulfilment of the obligation under Art. 122 cannot be held against the detaining power.[41]

The obligation of the detaining power to provide information is not limited to the establishment of an official Information Bureau. The organizational structure of the Information Bureau has to ensure its effective functioning. The detaining power may employ prisoners of war to work in the bureau, taking into account the rules of GC III. The main task of the bureau is to forward the information gathered to the home state of the prisoners of war. This shall be done as quickly as possible. Thus in all conflicts during this century the question of the burden of costs for forwarding such communications by international mail and telegraph service has played a crucial role.[42] The wording of Art. 124 GC III indicates a general exemption from charges for communications by the national Information Bureaux and the Central Prisoners of War Information Agency. However, state practice since the Second World War has shown a need for separate regulations to cover the question of costs, e.g. in connection with the International Telecommunications Union.[43]

The information is forwarded to the home state either by the protecting power or by the Central Prisoners of War Information Agency. This agency, set up by the ICRC under Art. 123 GC III, not only deals with the forwarding of information received from the national Information Bureaux; the Central Prisoners of War Information Agency also collects all available information and often assumes the role of a mediator. In the spring and summer of 1993 the ICRC dealt with about 3,000 prisoners in the former Yugoslavia.[44] The Central Prisoners of War Information Agency played an important part in this.

2. *Registration and special agreements.* In conflicts since the Second World War parties have often violated their obligations under Art. 122 GC III to collect and forward information. Severe violations occurred during the Korean War, the border conflict between India and China in 1962, and the Vietnam War.[45] In order to rectify violations of the obligation to report states often conclude agreements, once conflicts are settled, about the joint search for missing war victims and prisoners of war. The Vietnamese–American agreement of October 1992 on the opening of

---

[41] Cf. also Levie, *Prisoners of War*, 155.
[42] By 30 June 1947 the Central Tracing Agency of the ICRC had received 347,892 telegrams, de Preux, 592.
[43] de Preux, 591.   [44] *Süddeutsche Zeitung*, 4 June 1993.
[45] See Levie, *Prisoners of War*, 156, 157, fn. 221; on the development in Vietnam, Miller, 182–5.

Fischer

Vietnamese military archives is the most recent example.[46] In some conflicts the parties did not even meet the basic precondition for gathering information, namely the registration of prisoners of war. The Iraq–Iran war is a typical example.[47]

709   **Sums of money and articles of value carried by prisoners of war may not be taken away from them except by order of an officer of the detaining power and after a receipt has been given. Such money and objects shall be returned to prisoners of war at the end of their captivity (Art. 18, paras. 4–6 GC III).**

The express regulation concerning sums of money and articles of value constitutes an exception to the prohibition of Art. 18, para. 1 GC III. However, it provides only for temporary removal of money and articles of value. Thus the security of the prisoner of war's personal articles of value under the 1929 Convention remains intact in GC III,[48] although it is now permitted to take away money from prisoners of war in the prescribed manner at all times. In contrast, articles of value may only be taken away from the prisoners of war for security reasons. The detaining power must decide whether or not articles of value, such as jewellery, could be used for an escape. In this case the same procedure must be followed as for taking away money.

The application of Art. 18, para. 4 GC III involves two main problems which have not been dealt with satisfactorily to date. The first is connected with the actual securing of the money and articles of value, the issuing of a receipt, the registration, and the return at the end of captivity. Although the prescribed procedure is appropriate in principle for enabling the return of money and articles of value after the end of the conflict, the actual observation of the rule in practice, particularly when larger sums are involved, depends on the honesty of the officers and lower ranks. Furthermore, the detaining power must be able to administer and allocate the money to accounts. This is doubtful during the first phase of a conflict as well as in cases of great financial need of the parties to the conflict.

If the prisoners of war have in their possession money in the currency of the detaining power or of a neutral state, it is questionable whether this money is subject to Art. 18 GC III. Art. 18 GC III does not differentiate between currencies. This is criticized by legal scholars, because prisoners of war could have acquired money through pillage, keeping money belonging to prisoners of war from the detaining power illegally, or receiving it from their home state in order to facilitate their escape. By applying Art. 18 GC III in these cases and crediting their account with money attained in these ways, the prisoners of war might be rewarded for an illegal act.[49]

In a war, it will be nearly impossible to determine the origin of money and it will be difficult for all prisoners of war to prove the origin if special information is not available. For example, the involvement of prisoners of war in capturing soldiers of the detaining power could indicate illegal acquisition. The burden of proof in

---

[46] *Amerika Dienst* 44, 4 Nov. 1992, 1.   [47] Cf. Tavernier, 132.

[48] It was considered as early as last century to prohibit taking away sums of money from prisoners of war, Bluntschli, 370.

[49] Levie, *Prisoners of War*, 114, 115.

Fischer

respect of the origin of money cannot, however, be imposed on the prisoners of war.[50] This would mean that the prisoners of war would also have to provide proof of ownership of their articles of value. Only if there are clear indications that the money has been obtained illegally is the detaining power permitted to deviate from its obligations under Art. 18 GC III.

Prisoners of war shall be evacuated as soon as possible to camps situated in an area far enough from the area of operations for them to be out of danger. Prisoners of war shall not be unnecessarily exposed to danger while awaiting evacuation (Art. 19 GC III).   710

1. Obligation to evacuate and provide care.

a) *Aim of the evacuation.* From the beginning of their captivity the detaining power is responsible for the lives of the prisoners of war. This not only implies obligations to refrain from certain acts, as in the fundamental rules in Section 704 and Sections 714 ff., but also imposes a positive duty to act in order to protect the lives of prisoners of war. The obligation to evacuate is one element of this duty to act. The geographical location of the camps to which prisoners may be taken (see Section 714) shall ensure that prisoners of war are not exposed to the effects of action on the battlefield. The basic duty to evacuate is complemented by the obligation to provide care intended to protect the lives of the prisoners of war, from the time of their capture until they are evacuated. This does not mean, however, that the detaining power has to plan and execute its hostilities solely with the protection of the prisoners of war in mind. It is merely expected that the dangers which already exist for the prisoners of war are minimized following their capture.

b) *Distance from the area of operations.* Section 710 refers to 'distance from the area of operations'. This involves a term not used in GC III. In specifying the obligation to evacuate and to provide assistance prior to evacuation, Art. 19 GC III uses the three terms 'combat zone', 'danger zone', and 'fighting zone'. According to the NATO glossary ZDv 65/351, the area of operations should be construed as referring to that part of the area of war 'which is required for offensive or defensive military operations under a task assigned and for administrative measures in connection with these military operations'. Comparing the wording of the terms shows that the area of operations includes, first, the combat or fighting zone and the danger zone, as offensive or defensive military operations undoubtedly occur there. Secondly, the obligation under Art. 19 GC III is extended to those areas necessary for administrative measures. The term 'area of operations' in Section 710 is therefore consistent with international law even though the feasibility of fulfilling the obligation in a conflict is doubtful.

The evacuation of prisoners of war from the combat zone does not guarantee complete and absolute safety from the effects of hostilities. During the Second Gulf War, Allied air raids as well as the use of long-range missiles turned the entire

---

[50] Taking the point too far, Levie, ibid.

territory of the opposing state into a combat zone. In view of this, it is questionable whether the term 'combat zone' in Art. 19 GC III reflects the standards of modern warfare. For example, was the accommodation of Allied pilots in hotels in Baghdad during the Second Gulf War equivalent to an internment in camps as required by Art. 19 GC III? Baghdad could at any time be attacked, for instance, by sea-launched cruise missiles from Allied ships. *De Preux* defines the combat zone by reference to the range of land- and sea-launched weapons. The camps would have to be situated beyond their range to comply with Art. 19.[51] Obviously, this provision requires amendment, as no party to a modern conflict can fulfil its obligations.

Nevertheless, warfare employing modern long-range weapons is already taken into account on three levels by GC III: first, Art. 23 provides prisoners of war with the same protection against air bombardment and other hazards of war as the civilian population. Secondly, through the protecting powers, the detaining powers can exchange information about the geographical location of prisoner of war camps. Thirdly, camps can be marked with the letters PG or PW. In addition, a detaining power is not permitted to use prisoners of war camps in order to shield certain points from military operations.

The terms combat and fighting zone used in Art. 19 GC III must therefore today be construed as being confined to the area of military ground operations and tactical measures supporting them from air or sea. This interpretation is also in line with the object of Art. 47, para. 2 GC III concerning the transfer of prisoners of war when the front line draws closer, which may only occur under certain conditions.

2. *Timing.* The detaining power does not have an unlimited discretion regarding the evacuation, which must be carried out as soon as possible. This temporal requirement is not defined any more specifically in GC III. It depends on the circumstances of the individual capture and the tactical and strategic battle situation. GC III undoubtedly permits a waiting period for prisoners of war following their capture, as is made clear by Art. 19, para. 3 GC III which imposes a duty on the detaining power to prevent unnecessary dangers prior to evacuation. It should also be kept in mind that the detaining power has an interest in questioning the prisoners of war on the battlefield in order to obtain information which can be of military use (see Section 713).

What transportation facilities have to be maintained in an armed conflict by the detaining power in order to fulfil the obligation under Art. 19 GC III? During the Second Gulf War, the unpredictably large number of Iraqi soldiers who surrendered sometimes caused unavoidable delays in their evacuation from the front line and from temporary camps. The shortfalls in transport capacities were classified as a shortcoming in the report of the US Department of Defense on the Gulf War.[52] This cannot be called a violation of GC III, as the number of Iraqi prisoners of war was unforeseeable.

The detaining power violates the obligation to evacuate if it makes available no, or obviously insufficient, transportation for prisoners of war. What constitutes as

---

[51] De Preux, 172.   [52] Department of Defense, *Conduct of the Persian Gulf War*, Appendix L–18.

insufficient capacity depends on the circumstances of the conflict. No detaining power can avoid its obligation under Art. 19 GC III by claiming that available transport vehicles were required for its military operations. If no transport is available or if the detaining power cannot ensure a timely evacuation, it has a duty under Art. 41 AP I to release the prisoners of war (cf. Section 712).[53]

The evacuation of prisoners of war shall be effected in humane conditions, simi-   711
lar to those for the forces of the detaining power in their changes of station.
Prisoners of war shall be supplied with sufficient food, clothing, and medical care.
The civilian population shall be prevented from attacking prisoners of war (Art. 20
GC III).

1. *Transport conditions.*

   a) *Humane treatment.* During the Second World War, transport conditions were one of the greatest difficulties in the treatment of prisoners of war. Prisoners of war died on the way from their place of capture to the camps because of insufficient care. As a result of these experiences, Section 711 refers to Art. 20 GC III, which requires humane treatment and sets express and absolute restrictions on the treatment of prisoners of war during transportation. In this sense, Art. 20 is a specific instance of the general principle of humane treatment laid down by Art. 13 GC III. The reference to sufficient food, clothing, and medical care exemplifies three areas essential to humane treatment. The connection between Art. 13 and Art. 20 GC III shows that all inhumane treatment generally prohibited by Art. 13 is also prohibited during transportation.

   In an armed conflict, it cannot realistically be expected that the transport of prisoners of war will be carried out in a way similar to the transfer of forces of the detaining power,[54] although this standard is required by the wording of Art. 20 GC III. The conditions for the transport of own troops are inevitably different from those for the transport of prisoners of war. Transferring units might have a decisive impact on the hostilities, whereas these considerations are immaterial in the case of transporting prisoners of war. The reference to the conditions of transport of the detaining power's troops can therefore only be understood as strengthening the requirement of humane treatment. On the other hand, such reference can by no means justify a violation of the principle of humane treatment. Even if the detaining power transports its own troops with insufficient care, this cannot be used as a justification for inhumane treatment of prisoners of war.

   b) *Marches.* Apart from insufficient care, excessively long daily marches also caused the death of many prisoners of war on the way from the place of capture to their camps, both in the Second World War and the Korean War. Although Art. 7 of the Convention of 1929 prohibited marches longer than 20 km. per day, prisoners of war were forced to march much greater distances.[55] Those responsible for these

---

[53] On the obligations from GC III, see Castrén, 161.   [54] Levie, *Prisoners of War*, 101.
[55] On the most famous example of the 'death marches' of the Second World War and in the Korean war: Levie, *Prisoners of War*, 102; on the observations of the United States Military Tribunal in Nuremberg of 14 April 1949: Verzijl, Vol. IX, 115.

Fischer

so-called 'death marches' in the Pacific theatre of war were found guilty of war crimes.[56] Despite the means of transportation available to every army, marches still play an important role in the evacuation and transfer of prisoners of war. In contrast to the 1929 Convention, Art. 20 GC III does not specify a maximum number of kilometres the prisoners of war can be made to march per day. This obvious gap has been criticized,[57] and today a limit for prisoners of war of about 20 km. or 12 miles per day is suggested for marches,[58] which was the figure stated in the 1929 Convention.

The reference to a specific distance in kilometres should not detract from the fact that in practice, it is the physical condition of the prisoners of war, their clothing, mental state, the climate and geographical conditions which have to determine the required marching distance. For soldiers who fall into the hands of the detaining power in a weakened state of health, marches of 20 km. per day can mean certain death. On the other hand, troops in good physical condition with sufficient supplies and favourable climatic conditions can cover considerably greater distances. The commander responsible must, in the light of all of the circumstances, determine the distance which can be expected from the prisoners of war within the bounds of humane treatment. Hence the distances suggested by international lawyers can only serve as guidelines for the decision-makers of the detaining power.

2. *Transit camps.* Section 711 implies that the detaining power is also obliged to treat prisoners of war humanely in transit camps. Two types of transit camps are dealt with in GC III. First, there are those which the detaining power is permitted to establish under Art. 20, para. 3 GC III for the temporary accommodation of prisoners of war being transferred to their permanent camps. Secondly, there are the permanent transit camps mentioned in Art. 24. These camps are permanent establishments, accommodating prisoners of war before they are relocated to other camps. The permanent transit camps shall meet the standards set out in Arts. 20 ff. GC III for all camps (see Section 714). Due to the conditions of transport and the temporary nature of the transit camps regulated by Art. 20, para. 3 GC III, the more detailed rules do not apply there.[59] However, it must be guaranteed that they are not used as permanent camps, as was the case in the Second World War.

3. *Protection against attacks on prisoners.* The duty to protect prisoners of war from attacks by the civilian population is a general principle of the treatment of prisoners of war. Therefore it also applies to the transport phase, during which the prisoners may come into contact with the civilian population. This holds true for cases in which the transport of prisoners involves driving through localities as well as situations in which they are deliberately paraded before the civilian population. Attacks on prisoners include actual attacks, insults, and defamations. The parading of prisoners of war shall also be regarded as a prohibited infringement, as it is not permitted to expose prisoners of war to public curiosity (see Section 704).

---

[56] Hingorani, 117.   [57] Levie, *Prisoners of War*, 104.   [58] Hingorani, 132, n. 42.
[59] De Preux, 176.

Fischer

Prisoners of war who, under unusual conditions of combat, cannot b(
shall be released; in this case, too, all feasible precautions shall be tak
their safety (Art. 41, para. 3 AP I).

1. *Duty to release.* A significant addition to GC III concerning the treatment of prisoners of war is stipulated in Art. 41 AP I. The obligation to release or repatriate during an armed conflict in GC III is limited to cases of injury and sickness and thus
depends on the physical condition of the prisoners of war. In contrast, Art. 41 AP I
applies irrespective of the physical condition of the prisoners of war. If the lives of
prisoners cannot be guaranteed because evacuation is impossible, they must be
released. Art. 41 AP I thus adds a further responsibility to the duty to evacuate and
care for prisoners under Art. 19 GC III. At the Diplomatic Conference where the
Additional Protocols (see Section 127) were negotiated, the capture of soldiers by
commandos operating behind enemy lines was mentioned as a typical example of
situations with unusual conditions of combat to which Art. 41 AP I might apply.[60]
Neither the wording nor the object and purpose of Art. 41 AP I indicate that its scope
is limited to this type of situation. It is true that Art. 41 AP I must be regarded as an
exceptional rule. However, whenever an evacuation is impossible because of the
circumstances of combat, prisoners must be released. The term 'unusual conditions of combat' can include situations resulting from a normal battle situation,
where climatic circumstances render it impossible to care for or to evacuate the
prisoners of war over a longer period of time.

2. *Safety measures.* The duty arising out of Art. 41 AP I is not fulfilled simply through
the act of release. The safety of the prisoners of war following their release shall also
be taken into consideration. This requires positive action on the part of the releasing party. It is not clear which particular acts can be expected. Rowe points out that
international customary law requires that the prisoners of war are provided with
sufficient amounts of food and water to ensure their survival.[61] However, if the food
supplies of a commando unit are necessary for a long operation, Art. 41, para. 3 AP
I should not be construed as requiring that some of these supplies be given to the
prisoners of war being released.[62]

Every prisoner of war, when questioned on the subject, is entitled to give only his   713
surname, first names, rank, date of birth, and army, regimental, personal, or ser-
ial number (in the German Armed Forces: service number). The exercise of this
right shall not cause him any disadvantage (Art. 17, para. 4 GC III). The question-
ing of prisoners of war shall be carried out in a language which they understand
(Art. 17, para. 6 GC III). No physical or mental torture, nor any other form of coer-
cion, may be inflicted on prisoners of war to secure from them information of any
kind whatsoever. Prisoners of war who refuse to answer may not be threatened,

---

[60] De Preux, 489.   [61] Rowe, *Gulf War,* 164.
[62] According to the report of the Committee at the diplomatic conference, reprinted in Solf, *New Rules,*
224.

insulted, or exposed to unpleasant or disadvantageous treatment of any kind (Art. 17, para. 4 GC III).

1. *The right to question and its limits.* The Hague Conventions laid down the right of the detaining power to question prisoners of war and the corresponding rights of the prisoners. This is one of the reasons why the right to question and the limits imposed on this right are among the best known rules of GC III. The characteristics of questioning prisoners of war is another reason for the special public awareness in this respect.

Among other things, the detaining power has a substantial interest in obtaining information about military planning of the enemy. As they are in the hands of the detaining power, the prisoners of war, on the other hand, cannot usually estimate how the interrogating officer would react if refused information. If they give information about military actions of their units and armed forces, they infringe the obligation of loyalty owed to their state. However, providing information on their name, army, regiment, personal or serial number etc. permits the detaining power to identify the prisoner of war and to pass on information to the official Information Bureau in accordance with Art. 122 GC III.

Art. 17 first of all lays down that, when questioned, prisoners of war only have to provide the information expressly specified therein. The prisoner of war's obligation to provide information is thus limited. Yet the provision implies that the detaining power has a right to question prisoners. The questioning procedure is regulated particularly as to the mode of questioning, the duties of the prisoner of war to co-operate, and possible reactions of the detaining power.

The questioning must be carried out in such a manner that the prisoner of war is able to respond to the questions posed. Therefore, a language which the prisoner understands must be chosen for the questioning. This has to be the native tongue of the prisoner of war if he does not speak and understand any other language. All types of coercion on the part of those questioning in order to secure information from prisoners of war are prohibited. Art. 17 expressly forbids the use of physical and mental torture as coercive measures. Physical coercion falling short of torture is also generally prohibited. The beating of Allied pilots held as prisoners of war by the Iraqis in the Gulf War in 1991 was therefore correctly judged to be a violation of Art. 17 GC III.[63]

Art. 17 does not mention any other kinds of influence apart from coercing prisoners of war in order to obtain information. According to international lawyers, the promise of privileges or the use of psychological tricks do not breach Art. 17 GC III.[64] This interpretation of the law reflects the reality of armed conflicts, in which parties continue to try to obtain information from prisoners of war. As was demonstrated by the preparation and operation of the Allied forces' land warfare in the Gulf War against Iraq in 1991, information about the morale of enemy troops, for instance, plays an important part in the conduct of hostilities. Reliable information about morale can only be obtained through the questioning of prisoners of war.

[63] Department of Defense, *Conduct of the Persian Gulf War*, Appendix O–19.
[64] Levie, *Prisoners of War*, 108 with further references.

The general permissibility of questioning should not obscure the
questioning procedure must be strictly observed in order to fulfil the
purpose of Art. 17. Prisoners of war are in danger of being punished by
state for giving information to the detaining power, even if this infor
obtained by adopting skilful methods of questioning, rewards and
addition, other prisoners in the same camps may punish them for the information
disclosed, if they find out about it.

2. *Prohibition of disadvantageous treatment and prosecution.* The prohibition
against coercing prisoners of war does not restrict the detaining power's ability to
prosecute prisoners of war for acts committed prior to their capture. The wording
of Art. 85 is clear in this respect (see Section 725). The repatriation of the Argentine
Captain Astiz by Great Britain following the Falklands war can therefore not be justified on the basis of the prohibition against coercion during questioning under Art.
17, para. 4 GC III.[65]

III. CONDITIONS OF CAPTIVITY

The detaining power may subject prisoners of war to internment, i.e. put them   714
into camps and guard them (Art. 21, para. 1 GC III). These camps shall not be sit-
uated in danger zones (Arts. 19, para. 1 and 23, para. 1 GC III). They shall not be
used to render certain areas immune from military operations (Art. 23, para. 1 GC
III).

1. *The right of internment.* Art. 23 confirms the traditional right of the detaining
power to intern prisoners of war in order to preclude them from participating further in hostilities against the detaining power. The detaining power may restrict the
movement of the prisoners, depending on the organization of individual prisoner
of war camps. This can, but need not necessarily, coincide with the enclosure of the
camp. Prisoners of war may be granted greater freedom of movement. They may
only be locked up in a cell as a disciplinary or penal measure under Chapter VI GC
III. Tying up prisoners of war in the camps is prohibited.[66]

2. *The use of weapons.* The right of internment implies that the detaining power
also has a right—as a last resort—to use weapons against prisoners of war. This is
expressly laid down in Art. 42 GC III, listing escape and attempted escape as examples. With the purpose of internment and the detaining power's general obligations
towards the prisoners of war in mind, it can be concluded that the use of weapons
against rioting prisoners of war is also permitted. Weapons may only be used if
actually *necessary*. This means that the use of force by a single prisoner of war

[65] This was expressly argued by Rowe, *Defence*, 164; similarly, though not as unambiguously, with further
references to the Astiz affair, McCoubrey, 104.
[66] Cf. Miller, n. 35.

against guards does not necessarily entitle them to use weapons. Only if the guards are in serious danger may prisoners of war be shot at.[67] A prisoner of war who surrenders while fleeing may not be fired at, as the reason for using arms has ceased to exist.

The use of weapons must always be preceded by an appropriate warning to the prisoner of war. A warning shot qualifies as reasonable warning. Other forms of acoustic or visual signals might also meet the requirement. The crucial point is that the prisoner of war can recognise the warning for what it is. The establishment of so-called death lines, the crossing of which leads to the immediate shooting of the prisoner of war without warning, is therefore not permitted.[68]

3. *Prisoners of war as shields.* The obligation carefully to choose the location for camps entails two consequences for the detaining power. The distance from the combat zone is the first factor in determining the position of prisoner of war camps (see Section 710). Additionally, the detaining power shall not use camps in order to secure a military advantage. Art. 23, para. 1 does not define the meaning of 'certain points or areas' which can be rendered immune from military operations by the presence of prisoner of war camps. A reference to the definition of military objectives in Art. 52 AP I undoubtedly indicates that only military objectives of the detaining power are included, as attacks against other, civilian, objects are already prohibited by international humanitarian law. The use of prisoner of war camps as a shield for civilian objects can be eliminated by definition. As the headquarters of the Iraqi secret service in Baghdad is a military objective, the internment of US prisoners of war in that building was a violation of Art. 23 GC III.[69]

715   **The camps shall meet certain minimum requirements of hygiene and health (Art. 22, para. 1 GC III). They shall be provided with shelters against air raids and other hazards of war (Art. 23, para. 2 GC III). Whenever the military situation permits, prisoner of war camps shall be marked by the letters PG (*prisonniers de guerre*) or PW (prisoners of war), clearly visible from the air (Art. 23, para. 4 GC III).**

1. *Minimum requirements.* Corresponding with the general requirement of keeping prisoners of war alive, Section 715 refers to the required conditions of hygiene for prisoner of war camps. In contrast to the conclusion that can be drawn from the wording of Section 715, Art. 22, para. 1 GC III does not refer to the hygiene conditions *in* the camps. This follows from the wording of Art. 22, para. 1 GC III, which refers to localities affording every guarantee of hygiene and health. The relation between Arts. 22, para. 1, 22, para. 2 and 29 GC III also shows that Art. 22 refers to the location of the camp. The reference to the climatic conditions in Art. 22, para. 2 GC III elucidates the connection between the minimum requirements and the geographical location of the camp. In addition, the requirements for camps

---

[67] Taking the point too far: Greenspan, 104; see also Levie, *Prisoners of War*, 403.
[68] Harvey, *RDMilG* 1963, 137.
[69] Department of Defense, *Conduct of the Persian Gulf War*, Appendix O–19.

concerning cleanliness and health are dealt with explicitly in Art. 29 GC III.[70] Hence Section 715 should be conceived of as a summary and combination of Art. 22 GC III and 29 GC III. The following situations are practical examples of violations of Art. 22, para. 1 GC III:

—the construction of a camp in a region in which water is not available and to which sufficient amounts of water cannot be brought;

—the construction of a camp in an area which is chemically contaminated.

In contrast, the obligation from Art. 29 GC III is not met in cases where the detaining power, for example, does not provide any or enough facilities for personal hygiene within prisoner of war camps. Art. 29, para. 2 GC III also lays down that separate conveniences shall be provided for female prisoners of war.

2. *Protection against air raids.* In all conflicts since air warfare began, the protection of prisoners of war against air raids has caused great difficulties. The Convention of 1929 contained neither a rule about the protection of prisoners of war against air raids nor about the marking of prisoner of war camps. Art. 23, para. 2 GC III does not impose an absolute duty on the detaining power to provide the camps with air raid shelters. The detaining power's duty to provide protection for prisoners of war is linked to the protection provided to the civilian population. Shelters shall be provided for prisoners of war only 'to the same extent' as that afforded to the civilian population. Thus there are two possible scenarios for prisoners of war in camps which are located near towns. Either the same shelters must be built for prisoners of war as for the civilian population or the existing shelters for the civilian population must also be made available to the prisoners of war.[71] The second alternative is expressed in Art. 23, para. 2, second sentence GC III.

In respect of camps located close to inhabited areas, Section 715 exceeds the obligations imposed by GC III. GC III does not require the construction of any shelters in prisoner of war camps separate from residential areas of the civilian population. The protection of prisoners of war against attacks in these cases can be achieved through the marking of the camps. The detaining power has, however, no choice as to other protective measures, as these are for the benefit of the prisoners of war as much as for the civilian population. The distribution of gas masks, for example, may not be limited only to the civilian population.

3. *Obligation to mark.* In the Second World War approximately 1,000 prisoners of war died as a result of air raids. In view of the dangers of air warfare, Art. 23, para. 4 GC III introduced the duty to mark prisoner of war camps with the letters PG or PW. However, the detaining power need only meet this obligation 'when the military situation permits'. The question arises as to whether marking is therefore left to the unrestricted discretion of the detaining power. De Preux has correctly stated that marking does not depend on criteria to be determined by the detaining power

---

[70] On the conditions in Iraqi and Iranian prisoner of war camps during the war between Iraq and Iran cf. Lamar, *Emory International Law Review* 5 (1991), 270–273.

[71] De Preux, 188.

alone.[72] Concerns that enemy air forces could use the marks as a navigation aid[73] are no longer a convincing argument in the age of satellite reconnaissance. As a rule, the detaining power will not be able to avoid marking the camps. In practice since the Second World War, however, the marking of prisoner of war camps has caused difficulties despite the rule in GC III. In the Korean War, American aircraft bombarded prisoner of war camps killing US soldiers.[74] North Vietnam marked virtually none of its prisoner of war camps during the Vietnam War, and US soldiers who attempted to mark the camps themselves were punished.[75]

716   **As far as possible, prisoners of war shall be assembled according to their nationality, language, and customs (Art. 22, para. 3 GC III).**

The obligations binding the detaining power as to the treatment of and supplies for prisoners of war in camps includes their accommodation according to nationality, language and customs. Art. 22 GC III is of practical importance particularly in cases in which several allied parties fight in an armed conflict. Under Art. 22, para. 3 GC III, there is no discretion for the detaining power as to the internment, although Section 716 suggests this. Both the German and the English wording indicate an absolute obligation which the detaining power must fulfil.

The assembling of prisoners of war according to language serves primarily to improve their conditions of captivity. It also helps the detaining power to meet its obligations in respect of the dietary needs of prisoners from different cultures and with different customs and to meet their religious requirements. To alleviate the special psychological problems of prisoners of war, grouping under Art. 22 GC III also serves to maintain the emotional ties between the individual prisoners.

The grouping together of prisoners of war is irrelevant to maintaining discipline.[76] GC III presupposes the separate internment of officers; this practice during the Second World War was generally accepted.

717   **Prisoners of war shall receive sufficient food (Art. 26 GC III) and clothing (Art. 27 GC III) as well as necessary medical attention (Arts. 29–31 GC III).**

1. *Sufficient food.* This section specifies the general obligation of the detaining power to protect the lives of the prisoners of war in terms of providing food, clothing, and medical care. In contrast to Art. 11 of the Convention of 1929, Art. 26 GC III does not link the amount and quality of food required to the supplies of the troops of the detaining power. During the Second World War, parties to the conflict limited or altogether denied the provision of food to prisoners of war and referred to the poor food supplies of their own troops in order to justify their actions by referring to the wording of the Convention of 1929.

GC III has not left the decision of what is considered to be sufficient up to the

---

[72] De Preux, 190.

[73] This concern was expressed by some states at the diplomatic conference of 1949, *Final Record of the Diplomatic Conference of Geneva*, Vol. II, Section A, *Report of Committee* II, 564.

[74] Spinnler, 51.   [75] Miller, 287.   [76] Spinnler, 70–3.

detaining power, although Section 711 could be construed in this way. According to Art. 26 the food must be sufficient to keep prisoners of war in good health and to avoid weight loss and deficiency symptoms. This rule sets out an objective standard which must be applied to each individual prisoner of war. GC III does not allow exceptions to the obligation to provide care. Prisoners of war may not receive insufficient care because of their religion or association with an aggressor state. If GC III is considered to be applicable to the war in Bosnia,[77] then the insufficient care for the prisoners in the so-called starvation camps, such as Omarska near Banja Luka in 1992,[78] was a flagrant violation of Art. 26 GC III. This is also true of the insufficient nutrition given to some American prisoners of war held captive in Iraq during the Second Gulf War in 1991.[79]

The wording of Art. 26 GC III raises two problems. First, it is possible that weight loss occurs not as a result of insufficient food but due to the psychological condition of prisoners of war. In this case the detaining power would have to prove that the weight loss could not be due to poor nutrition. More important in practice is the situation where prisoners of war receive insufficient food because the detaining power is also unable to provide its own troops with sufficient food. Levie refers to this problem.[80] Since GC III states an express obligation to provide the prisoners of war with sufficient food, with no exceptions, prisoners of war must be released if the detaining power is unable to fulfil its obligations.[81]

The significance which GC III gives to the nutrition of the prisoners of war is also illustrated by Art. 26, para. 6. According to this provision, the detaining power is not permitted to impose collective disciplinary measures by withholding food from prisoners of war. Prisoners are thus protected against reductions of food rations for disciplinary reasons, which are a reaction to the misconduct of some prisoners but affect other members of the group. Furthermore, the link between Art. 26 GC III and 89 GC III clearly shows that disciplinary punishments must not, as a rule, affect the provision of food as required under Art. 26 to the extent that the health of the prisoners of war is endangered.[82] Only special privileges going beyond the scope of Art. 26, e.g. special rations, may be affected by disciplinary punishments.

It is disputed whether food may be used to enforce order in the camp. Is it permitted, for instance, to provide rioting prisoners of war with food only in certain areas of a camp in order to induce them to return to those areas? This measure may be less detrimental to the health of prisoners of war than, for example, the lawful use of weapons by guards under Art. 42 to maintain order in the camps in the event of revolt (see Section 714). However, danger of abuse of such measures should not be underestimated. If a detaining power permits visits to the camps by ICRC

---

[77] See in this respect and with further references H. Fischer, *Humanitäres Völkerrecht und Humanitäre Hilfe*, 27 ff.; the Commission of the Security Council of the United Nations to examine war crimes in the former Yugoslavia bases its findings on the GC III, see *Interim Report of the Commission of Experts Established pursuant to Security Council Resolution 780* (1992) 26 Jan. 1993, UN Doc. S/25274, 14.

[78] The Canadian report to the Secretary General of 10 Mar. 1992 contains a comprehensive overview of the conditions in the camps in the former Yugoslavia, UN Doc. S/25392, 10 ff.

[79] Department of Defense, *Conduct of the Persian Gulf War*, Appendix O–19.

[80] Levie, *Prisoners of War*, 127.

[81] Dinstein appears to reach the same conclusion in 'Prisoners of War', *EPIL* 4, 147.

[82] De Preux, 200.

delegates under Art. 122, the reasons for such measures are still relatively easy to ascertain. Harvey is therefore correct in arguing for the lawfulness of such actions.[83]

2. *Sufficient clothing.* In contrast to the provision of food, the obligation to provide clothing is not expressly linked to the medical condition of the prisoners of war. Qualifications, such as preventing the prisoners from freezing to death, burning, etc. are not included in the wording of Art. 27 GC III. The purpose behind the provisions for the treatment of prisoners of war in captivity is to keep them alive. Clothing must correspond to this purpose. This holds true generally, and particularly in areas with harsh climatic conditions. The greater the dangers of the climate to the health of prisoners of war, the stricter the requirements are for the detaining power to provide prisoners of war with adequate clothing.

3. *Medical attention.* The fundamental duty to provide prisoners of war with medical attention is stipulated in Art. 15 GC III and complemented by the special duties for preventing and treating illness in Arts. 29–31 GC III. The provisions of Chapter III GC III concern both the prevention of sickness and its treatment. The required medical attention stated in Section 717 applies to the treatment of sick prisoners of war. They should primarily be treated by doctors of their own state. The treatment by doctors of the detaining power is secondary to this.

Art. 31 GC III is directly connected with Art. 13 GC III, which specifies the obligation of humane treatment in terms of providing medical treatment. Generally, the treatment of sick prisoners of war required by Art. 31 GC III prohibits medical or scientific experiments. Such experimentation is permitted only if justified by the medical treatment of the prisoners of war and is in their interest. In practice, this leads to the complicated clause that, as a rule, medical experiments of any kind are prohibited unless they are required to keep a certain prisoner of war alive. This formula prevents any type of experimentation on prisoners of war being carried out, as was the case during the Second World War in German and Japanese prisoner of war camps. On the other hand, there is enough latitude to enable doctors to use all possible treatments for prisoners of war without running the risk of being found guilty of a war crime.

718   **Latitude in the exercise of religious duties shall be ensured (Art. 34 GC III).**

1. *Religious practice.* The guarantee of freedom of worship touches on one of the most important preconditions for the mental well-being of prisoners of war. This guarantee is of particular importance during conflicts in which soldiers of different religions fight against one another. The practice of religion is subject only to the disciplinary routine prescribed by the military authorities. The interpretation of the term disciplinary routine and its contents may cause problems in individual cases. Under no circumstances may the disciplinary routine render the practice of religion impossible or substantially impede it. On the other hand, the practice of

---

[83] Harvey, 143; the different position of the ICRC is also cited.

Fischer

religion must not interfere with the maintenance of discipline in the camps. It is in the interest of both the prisoners of war and the detaining power that the camp commander arranges the disciplinary order of the camp so as to enable prisoners of war to carry out their religious customs. This is particularly important because under Art. 34, para. 2 GC III, the detaining power must provide adequate premises for religious services.

2. *Chaplains.* Complementary to the freedom of worship of prisoners of war, Art. 35 GC III contains special provisions regarding the work of chaplains. They are permitted to minister to the prisoners of war and the detaining power shall permit them to have access to the necessary facilities. If chaplains care for prisoners of war located outside the camps, the detaining power must provide them with the means of transportation required for these visits. Chaplains also have a special privilege in respect of communication. Subject to permitted censorship by the detaining power they are allowed to correspond with the ecclesiastical authorities of the detaining power and with international religious organizations and to send letters and cards in addition to the usual quota laid down in Art. 71 GC III.

The detaining power may utilize the labour of able-bodied enlisted men for cer-   719
tain non-military works (Arts. 49, para. 1 and 50 GC III). Non-commissioned offi-
cers shall only be required to do supervisory work. Officers are exempted from
compulsory work (Art. 49, paras. 2 and 3 GC III).

1. *Obligation and right to work.* The Hague Regulations already permitted prisoners of war to be employed for work. Both the Convention of 1929 and GC III have maintained this right of the detaining power. As is made clear by Art. 49, para. 3 GC III, the detaining power is entitled to compel prisoners of war to work. The disciplinary measures under Art. 89 GC III may be used as a means of enforcement of the work.

Originally, work was regarded from the point of view of its importance to the health of prisoners of war. In both world wars the value of the labour of prisoners of war to the detaining power's economy also became apparent. The wording of Art. 49 GC III is based on the entitlement of the detaining power.[84] There is no express duty for the detaining power to provide work. According to Art. 49, para. 1 GC III, a special purpose of work can be to maintain the prisoners of war in a good state of physical and mental health. From this addition to the general right to employ prisoners, a right of prisoners of war to be given work can be derived.[85] Section III of GC III, concerning the labour of prisoners of war, contains no further definition of any such a right of prisoners of war to work. The general obligations of the detaining power under Arts. 29 and 38 GC III do not refer to a right of prisoners of war to work either. This right is merely hinted at by the general purpose of GC III, i.e. to guarantee the protection of prisoners of war as far as possible. In practice, this

---

[84] De Preux does not give effect to the wording when he sees the purpose of Art. 48 only in maintaining the health of prisoners of war: 260.
[85] Hinz acknowledges this duty to a certain extent ('*in gewissem Umfang*'), 98.

Fischer

can only be relevant if the health of prisoners of war is likely to suffer if they do not work.

2. *Conditions and limitations.* The detaining power's right to utilize the labour of prisoners of war is not unlimited. The obligation to work only applies to healthy prisoners of war. Their age, sex, rank, and physical aptitude must all be taken into consideration. The employment of sick prisoners of war for labour is prohibited, as is the use of physically weak prisoners of war for hard physical work. In this respect, special protection is provided to women.

The categories of work permitted and the working conditions of prisoners of war are laid down in much greater detail than in the Convention of 1929. Work in agriculture, domestic service, and in commercial arts and crafts areas are permitted without restriction. Employment in metallurgical, chemical, and machinery industries is absolutely excluded because these industries play an important role in the production of weapons in wartime.[86] The employment of prisoners of war in industries of military importance, which was required of prisoners during the Second World War in Germany, is thus prohibited.[87]

Work involving the transport and handling of stores, public works, and building operations is permissible if this work has a civilian character and purpose. The detaining power shall ensure working conditions equal to those for nationals of the detaining power.

3. *Exceptions to the duty to work.* First, GC III sets down exemptions from the duty to work for non-commissioned officers and officers, thereby preserving the differential treatment which has been accepted since the nineteenth century. GC III does not define what is meant by 'supervisory work'. It is generally agreed that manual labour does not qualify. Both groups may ask for suitable work and may also give it up without restriction. The special rules concerning officers were for the most part complied with during the Second World War.[88]

Prisoners of war carrying out certain special functions are also exempt from the duty to work. Enlisted men fall under this category if they are assigned to officers' camps under Art. 44, para. 2 GC III. If doctors and nurses who are prisoners of war and do not belong to the medical service of their armed forces are assigned by the detaining power to care for other prisoners, then they are also exempt from the duty.

720 **No prisoner of war shall be employed against his will on labour which is of an unhealthy or otherwise dangerous nature (e.g. mine-clearing), or which is humiliating; nevertheless, he may volunteer to do dangerous or unhealthy work (Art. 52 GC III).**

---

[86] De Preux, 266.

[87] Rousseau, 92, 93; on the employment of Vietcong in South Vietnamese military projects, see Meyrowitz, in Falk (Ed.), Vol. 2, 560.

[88] Levie, *Prisoners of War*, however, mentions violations of this rule by the Japanese, 224 n. 39.

Fischer

Art. 52 GC III contains a special qualification to the detaining power's general right to employ prisoners in labour. The general right is limited in three cases. First, the prisoner of war may not be used for unhealthy or dangerous work; GC III repeats the words of the 1929 Convention. The conference of 1949, however, was unable to agree on which types of work should be regarded as unhealthy or dangerous. Art. 52, para. 3 GC III mentions only the removal of mines or similar devices as dangerous work. This express reference to mine-clearing combined with the possibility of voluntarily carrying out such work is the result of intense debates at the diplomatic conference of 1949. There were considerable differences of opinion as to the employment of prisoners of war in mine-clearing operations. On one hand, there was the opinion that prisoners of war should not be used for mine-clearing on the basis of humanitarian considerations. On the other hand, the fact that some of the mines were likely to have been laid by the prisoners themselves was put forward. Furthermore, it was suggested that prisoners of war were better trained for mine-clearing than the civilian population who would be adversely affected by clearing operations. The conference eventually agreed the provision on mine-clearing, because in the final phase of the Second World War German prisoners of war were employed in France on such work, resulting in numerous deaths.[89]

Types of work classified as unhealthy or dangerous are limited to the permitted types expressly identified by Art. 50. Work in agriculture, if it is connected with unhealthy conditions, can be prohibited work within the meaning of Art. 50.[90] This also applies to work in industries that could endanger the lives of the prisoners of war. There is an exception to the prohibition of dangerous labour. If prisoners of war volunteer to do unhealthy or dangerous work the detaining power may employ them in this way. Positive action by the prisoners of war is required to ensure that the preconditions of Art. 52 GC III are fulfilled. The act of volunteering meets these requirements. Thus the detaining power may not impute consent to employment in unhealthy or dangerous work. On acceptance the prisoner of war must be aware of the danger or health risks involved; the detaining power must inform the prisoner of war about the risks involved in the work.

As far as unhealthy and dangerous labour is concerned, the quality of the work has to be weighed against the physical condition of the prisoner of war. This is not required for humiliating work. In this respect, the application of the prohibition depends on how the work is classified by the detaining power if it is to be done by the members of its own armed forces. If in these cases the work is considered to be humiliating, then prisoners of war may not be employed to do it either. In contrast to unhealthy or dangerous work, prisoners of war cannot validly consent to do humiliating work. In combination with Art. 14 GC III, Art. 52, para. 2 GC III secures the principle of the inalienability of rights also contained in Art. 7 GC III. Under no circumstances may the detaining power circumvent the limits imposed by GC III by giving the prisoners of war a partially civilian status. The French practice of

---

[89] ICRC *Report on Activities*, Vol. I, 333–4.

[90] The ICRC, for instance, protested during the Second World War against the work of German prisoners of war in sugar plantations in the USA because the prisoners were subjected to the sun in the tropical climate all day long without protection, ibid.

Fischer

giving prisoners of war the status of 'travailleur civil' violated the 1929 Convention.[91]

721 **Not more than one week after arrival at a camp, every prisoner of war shall be enabled to write direct to his family and the Central Prisoners of War Agency, informing them of his captivity (Arts. 70 and 123 GC III), and to correspond regularly with his relatives thereafter.**

Contact with the outside world is very important for the well-being of prisoners of war. Such contact also allows the protecting power or the ICRC to ensure that GC III is enforced. As a rule, therefore, prisoners of war are permitted to send and receive correspondence. Although the detaining power is entitled to limit the number of letters and postcards sent, at least two letters and four postcards per month must be permitted.

The notification to the family and the Central Prisoners of War Agency about the capture as expressly provided in Art. 70 GC III does not count as part of the permitted quota of letters and postcards. With this card the prisoners of war are given the opportunity to communicate with their relatives and also with the central information agency established by the ICRC. The detaining power cannot prevent or delay this communication. This message must be permitted to be sent after one week and, as laid down in Art. 71, para. 1, fifth sentence GC III, shall be forwarded by the fastest method available. Neither the initial message to families and the information agency nor normal correspondence may be prevented for disciplinary reasons. This applies to both incoming and outgoing post. The conduct of North Korea and China during the Korean war was a clear violation of this obligation.[92] Since correspondence provides contact between prisoners of war and their relatives, the protecting power, and so forth, it is unlawful for the detaining power to misuse the post for propaganda purposes.

722 **Regarding inadequate conditions of captivity, prisoners of war may apply to the authorities of the detaining power or to a protecting power (Art. 78, paras. 1 and 2 GC III). The exercise of the right to make complaints shall not give rise to any punishment (Art. 78, para. 3 GC III).**

One of the prerequisites for observing the provisions of GC III is the detaining power's awareness of the conditions in the prisoner of war camps. Art. 78, para. 1 GC III gives prisoners of war the right to appeal to the detaining power in respect of all matters relating to the conditions of captivity. As pointed out in Section 722, it especially includes those cases concerning poor camp conditions. GC III is based on the idea that prisoners of war apply in writing to the military authorities detaining them. Art. 78, para. 3 GC III expressly sets out that requests and complaints may not be limited and must be transmitted immediately. In particular, inspection visits by representatives of the protecting power serve to check compliance with GC

---

[91] Rousseau, 93.   [92] Spinnler, 74.

III. Under Art. 78, para. 2 GC III the right of prisoners of war to present requests and complaints also exists *vis-à-vis* representatives of the protecting power. Prisoners of war can apply to the representative of the protecting power with their complaints either directly of through their representative. Art. 78, para. 2 GC III names the representative of the protecting power as the contact person. The International Committee of the Red Cross and its delegates are not separately mentioned. An analogous application of Art. 78 GC III to the representatives of the ICRC follows from Art. 126, para. 4 GC III, which gives the delegates of the International Committee the same privileges as representatives of the protecting powers. This is especially important for prisoners of war, as the system of protecting powers has not functioned to date.

The detaining power is not permitted to punish requests and complaints by prisoners of war. Even if their assertions prove unfounded, the requests and complaints may not give rise to any punishment. Thus both disciplinary punishments and penal measures of the detaining power against prisoners of war for exercising their right under Art. 78 are prohibited.

The prisoners of war shall elect representatives to represent their interests; where   723
officers are among the prisoners of war, the senior officer shall be recognized as
the camp prisoners' representative (Arts. 79–81 GC III).

Communication by prisoners of war with the organs of the detaining power and with the delegates of the protecting power or of the International Committee of the Red Cross can be difficult due to the large number of prisoners of war in camps. In addition, it might sometimes be difficult for prisoners of war to make their needs clear. GC III provides for the election of prisoners' representatives whose task it is to promote the physical, moral, and mental well-being of the prisoners of war. Representatives are elected every six months by free and secret ballot. Art. 79 GC III lays down two conditions for the election of prisoners' representatives. First, Art. 79, para. 2 GC III stipulates that in officers' camps and mixed camps the most senior officer who is a prisoner of war is automatically the prisoners' representative. In mixed camps the representative's assistant shall be elected from among the prisoners of war who are not officers. This preference for officers serves to improve communication between the detaining power and the protecting power since officers have more experience in negotiating than other prisoners of war. Both elected and recognized representatives must be approved by the detaining power. The detaining power therefore has the right to decide on the commencement of duties of the prisoners' representatives. If they do not approve they must inform the protecting power of the reason. If prisoners of war of different nationalities, languages, and customs live in the same camp a separate representative shall be elected for each of these groups.

A prisoner of war shall be subject to the laws, regulations, and orders effective in   724
the armed forces of the detaining power. The detaining power shall be justified in
taking judicial or disciplinary measures in respect of any offence committed by a
prisoner of war against these provisions (Art. 82, para. 1 GC III).

Fischer

1. *Applicability of the detaining power's legal order.* The special situation of prisoners of war in camps becomes especially clear in Chapter III of GC III. During captivity prisoners of war, who are normally subject to the national law of their home state, are subject to those legal rules of the detaining power which also apply to its armed forces. This subjection lasts until captivity ends, either by escape or release. This rule also applies if a prisoner of war is transferred from one detaining power to another under Art. 12, para. 2 GC III. On transfer, the law applicable to the armed forces of the new detaining power automatically applies to the prisoners of war. GC III reiterates the rule already laid down in the HagueReg and the Convention of 1929, although following the Second World War intensive debates took place about other rules which would more appropriately take into account the interests of prisoners of war.[93]

The application to prisoners of war of the law governing the armed forces of the detaining power requires that the prisoners be aware of the applicable rules. The detaining power has an obligation under Art. 41, para. 2 GC III to inform prisoners of war of the rules governing their conduct. Two conditions must be met in this respect: the information must be given in a language understood by the prisoners of war, and displayed in locations in the camp where all prisoners of war can read them.

2. *Restrictions on the choice of procedure.* As with its own troops, the detaining power can choose between two types of punishment for violations of the aforesaid provisions. Due to the special situation of prisoners of war, Art. 83 GC III directs the authorities of the detaining power to choose disciplinary rather than judicial measures whenever possible. For two types of offences judicial measures are expressly prohibited and disciplinary measures prescribed. Certain offences committed by prisoners of war while attempting to escape are subject exclusively to disciplinary measures (see Section 728). Violations of national laws, regulations etc. of the detaining power which are only punishable if committed by prisoners of war, under Art. 82 GC III, entail only disciplinary punishment. An act violating administrative rules of a prisoner of war camp for example, which of course do not apply to the detaining power's own troops, may only result in disciplinary punishment by the camp commanders.

3. *Prosecution of war crimes and criminal offences.* Art. 85 GC III provides a special ground for prosecution. The detaining power is permitted to prosecute prisoners of war for acts committed prior to capture. Thus prisoners of war can be held responsible by the detaining power for both war crimes and for criminal offences. The GC III does not, however, resolve any of the fundamental problems about the responsibility of individual persons in international criminal law.[94] Thus it remains unanswered, for example, whether a prisoner of war may be convicted for a war crime if the sentence for the act had not been set out at the time the act was committed. The Statute of the International Tribunal for the Prosecution of Persons Responsible for

---

[93] Hinz, 144, 145.   [94] See in this respect Ipsen, *Völkerrecht*, 532–43.

Serious Violations of International Humanitarian Law Committed in the Territory of the Former Yugoslavia since 1991 avoids this difficulty by referring to the respective sentence under Yugoslav criminal law.[95]

The application of Art. 85 GC III raises two particular problems. Some former socialist states made a reservation on ratification of GC III, rendering inapplicable the provisions of GC III on the treatment of convicted war criminals (see Section 705). Although there should be no disagreement today as to the correct interpretation of these reservations, it should still be asked, in the face of the ethnic conflicts in Eastern Europe, whether the effect of the reservations is still current.

The right to prosecute other acts as war crimes under Art. 85 GC III only exists if the act in question was a crime in the detaining power's legal order at the time it was committed. This is problematic if, for instance, the prisoner of war committed the act in another state. Usually the national criminal law of the detaining power indicates whether prosecution is possible in such cases. This was taken into account at the trial of the Panamanian General Noriega for drug trafficking by an American court in 1992.[96] The question remains, however, if Noriega, as the head of state of Panama, retained his immunity despite the invasion by the USA, thus making his prosecution under Art. 85 GC III a violation of international law.[97]

Penal and disciplinary sanctions are governed by the following rules: 725

—**No prisoner of war may be punished or disciplined more than once for the same act (Art. 86 GC III).**

—**Prisoners of war may not be sentenced to any penalties except those provided for in respect of members of the armed forces of the detaining power for the same acts (Art. 87, para. 1 GC III).**

—**Prisoners of war shall be given an opportunity to present their defence (Arts. 96, para. 4 and 99, para. 3 GC III).**

—**Collective punishment for individual acts and cruel punishment are forbidden (Art. 87, para. 3 GC III).**

Without procedural guarantees, the detaining power would be in a position to endanger the life and health of prisoners of war on the basis of judicial decisions. As a result of the experiences of the Second World War, during which numerous violations of the Convention of 1929 occurred in respect of the punishment of prisoners of war, GC III established procedural rules for both disciplinary and juridical procedures. This is of particular importance with regard to disciplinary procedures, because in 1949 the rights of the defendant in disciplinary procedures varied greatly in the different national legal orders. With the often limited possibilities for camp commanders to determine who is responsible for violations of camp rules, the prohibition of collective penalties is an important restatement of the rule in the Convention of 1929. It protects the innocent and prevents arbitrary punishment by the camp authorities.

[95] Fn. 6, 29.   [96] See in this respect *Archiv der Gegenwart*, 36791 A.
[97] Sticher, *HUV-I* 2/1990, 65, 66.

Fischer

In addition to the fundamental guarantees of criminal law, Art. 84 GC III determines the composition of the trial court. As a rule, this shall be a military court. Civil courts may only try prisoners of war in exceptional cases where they would also have jurisdiction had the alleged offence been committed by a member of the detaining power's armed forces. Under no circumstances shall a prisoner of war be tried by a court which does not guarantee independence and impartiality.

726 **Acts which constitute offences against discipline shall be investigated immediately (Art. 96, para. 1 GC III). Disciplinary punishment may be ordered only by appropriate courts of law, military commanders, camp commanders, and their representatives who have been assigned disciplinary powers (Art. 96, para. 2 GC III). In no case may prisoners of war themselves exercise disciplinary powers (Art. 96, para. 3 GC III).**

1. *Responsible organs.* Usually, prisoner of war violations of disciplinary rules occur more frequently than offences against criminal law. This is why GC III sets out not only general procedural rules for disciplinary punishment, but also who may order such punishment, what form the punishment may take, and how it shall be implemented. In view of the special circumstances particularly of large prisoner of war camps, GC III requires an immediate examination of offences against discipline. This rule promotes the safety of prisoners of war from arbitrary treatment by camp commanders or fellow prisoners. Despite the possibility of punishment being ordered by subordinates of the camp commander, it is always the commander's responsibility to ensure compliance with GC III. The practice during the Second World War of permitting prisoners of war to punish violations of the rules of the camp, e.g. theft from fellow prisoners, is clearly prohibited by the wording of Art. 96, para. 3 GC III.

2. *Disciplinary punishments.* The organs of the detaining power are not free to choose any disciplinary punishment. Art. 89 GC III contains an exhaustive list of permissible disciplinary punishments. By stating that disciplinary punishments shall not be inhumane, Art. 89 GC III does not open the door to punishments not mentioned in GC III, but instead imposes a further restriction on the execution of the prescribed disciplinary punishments.[98] The punishment of a prisoner of war by sentencing him to a permitted form of work can be inhumane if the prisoner is in no physical condition for it. The serving of a disciplinary punishment in penal establishments is also not permitted. As a rule, food and correspondence by mail may not be withheld as a disciplinary punishment from prisoners of war.

The restriction in GC III on the types of permissible disciplinary punishment could make it difficult to maintain order in a prisoner of war camp if the prisoners break the rules of the camp frequently and severely. The camp commander can take all measures necessary to prevent such violations, provided that none of the guarantees for prisoners of war in GC III are infringed. Usually, severe violations of camp

---

[98] De Preux, 440.

rules are also included in the criminal law of the detaining power. Criminal prosecution is therefore possible in these cases.[99]

IV. ESCAPE OF PRISONERS OF WAR

Prisoners of war who have made good their escape and who are recaptured shall   727
not be liable to any punishment in respect of their escape (Art. 91, para. 2 GC III).
The escape of a prisoner of war shall be deemed to have succeeded when (Art. 91,
para. 1 GC III):
—he has joined friendly or allied armed forces;
—he has entered neutral territory or otherwise left the territory under control of
the adversary; or
—he has joined a ship in the territorial waters but not under the control of the
detaining power.

The regime governing prisoners of war is based on the detaining powers exercise of control over them. If this is no longer possible, captivity in the sense of international law ceases. The Brussels Declaration as early as 1874 contained a rule about the termination of captivity by escape. Since 1874 this general principle has not been the subject of any serious discussion. Only defining a successful escape proved to be difficult. The rules of GC III for the most part do not raise any problems from a legal point of view. The definition of a successful escape is based on the possibility of the actual exercise of control, either on land or at sea. An escape can therefore not be considered successful simply because the prisoner of war has reached the high seas with a rowing boat. On the other hand, captivity ends if the detaining power cannot exercise its territorial sovereignty on its own territory, as is the case when foreign ships are in its territorial waters or when part of its territory is occupied. If several escaped prisoners of war continue their escape jointly or if they join a unit of their own armed forces which is about to be captured, the conditions of Art. 91, para. 1 GC III are not fulfilled as there is no actual interruption, not even a brief moment of being beyond the detaining power's reach.[100] The question of whether the preconditions of Art. 91 GC III are in fact fulfilled will only be relevant if prisoners of war are recaptured by troops of the detaining power and penal or disciplinary punishment is considered for acts committed during the escape.

728. A prisoner of war who has been captured in his attempt to escape shall be   728
liable only to disciplinary punishment in respect of his act (Art. 92, para. 1 GC III);
this shall also apply to a repeated offence.

Art. 92 GC III imposes an absolute prohibition on the punishment of prisoners of war in cases of attempted escape. One of the reasons why penal and other

[99] Harvey, *RDMilG* 1963, 147.   [100] Inferring from de Preux, 446.

non-disciplinary punishments are categorically prohibited is that particularly during the Second World War prisoners of war who attempted to escape were subjected to draconian punishment and even killed. It is a prerequisite for the imposition of disciplinary punishment that the prisoner of war is caught. Art. 92 GC III does not exclude the use of weapons under the circumstances described above (see Section 714) in order to prevent escape. In order to avoid the use of weapons once the escape has been discovered, and in order to qualify for the privilege of Art. 92 GC III, prisoners of war should indicate unequivocally that they will not continue with their attempt to escape.

729   **A prisoner of war shall not be liable to judicial prosecution even if he has committed offences to facilitate his escape, e.g. theft of food or clothing, or the drawing up and use of false papers. This shall not apply to cases in which the escapee has used violence against life or limb during his escape (Art. 93, para. 2 GC III).**

Art. 92, para. 2 GC III singles out a special case of disciplinary punishment of prisoners of war following an attempted escape. Punishable acts, with the exception of violent acts against life or limb, shall merely lead to the disciplinary punishment of prisoners of war because the other listed acts do not involve criminal intent. However, the privilege concerning punishment only applies if the acts were committed in order to facilitate an escape. Judicial prosecution is not permitted in these cases. Facilitating the escape must have been the primary and only reason for committing the offence.

In the case of theft, the prisoner of war loses the privilege if he also has the intent to enrich himself. For example, if prisoners of war steal an automobile in order to help them to escape with the intention of selling it after escaping, then Art. 93 GC III does not prohibit their criminal prosecution.[101] It is difficult to ascertain their intention if prisoners of war destroy public property possibly impeding their escape. The demolition of a bridge or the destruction of a telephone switchboard can make it more difficult to trace the escapee and thus facilitate the escape.[102] Such acts could also be seen as unnecessary acts of destruction. In the second case punishment according to the criminal law of the detaining power is possible. The fact that as combatants they are permitted to carry out legal acts of war cannot be used by prisoners of war as a defence. Until the termination of captivity either by release or escape, prisoners are subject to the legal order of the detaining power to the same extent as the detaining power's own troops. The detaining power may try prisoners for sabotage in connection with acts of destruction.

There is no privilege if the acts carried out involved violence against life or limb. This is particularly important if escaped prisoners of war are recaptured. It is true that the detaining power's right of disciplinary punishment for acts connected to the escape is not revived following recapture.[103] For all other offences, however, the

---

[101] Examples of the punishment of prisoners of war for theft of automobiles and other articles during the Second World War are given by Frey, 95–7.

[102] Harvey, *loc. cit.*, 146, considers such acts or destruction to be permitted.

[103] Apparently de Preux concurs, 454.

detaining power's right to punish persists. A murder which was committed during an escape, for instance, can be prosecuted following recapture.

V. TERMINATION OF CAPTIVITY

Save by a successful escape, captivity shall cease with the release of the prisoner   730
from the custody of the detaining power.

GC III provides two possibilities for the termination of captivity. The successful escape mentioned in Section 730 terminates captivity. In this case, the detaining power is released from all obligations under GC III concerning the captivity. The term release includes both the repatriation of seriously sick and seriously wounded prisoners of war during the conflict and the release and repatriation of prisoners of war after the conflict has ended. In both cases the duties of the detaining power are not fulfilled by merely releasing the prisoners, but the release is linked with the repatriation of the prisoners of war.

Captivity is also formally terminated by the death of a prisoner of war. In view of the detaining power's fundamental duty to care for prisoners of war, Art. 121 GC III requires an enquiry and report, for example that the cause of death is unknown or the death was caused by a sentry. In fulfilment of the duty to carry out an official enquiry into deaths of prisoners of war and in order to inform the protecting power, the United States forwarded enquiry reports about three deaths in Saudi Arabian prisoner of war camps to the ICRC following the Gulf War.[104]

Seriously wounded and seriously sick prisoners of war who are fit to travel and   731
whose mental or physical fitness has been incurably or permanently diminished
or whose recovery may not be expected within one year shall be repatriated dur-
ing the armed conflict. No prisoner of war however, may, be repatriated against
his will during hostilities (Arts. 109, 110 GC III).

1. *Duty to repatriate during the conflict.* Art. 109 GC III is an exception to the detaining power's right to intern prisoners of war for the duration of the conflict. Art. 110, para. 1 GC III lays down an obligation to repatriate for the three categories of wounded and sick prisoners of war named in Section 731. The reason for imposing this duty on the detaining power can be found in the state of health of the prisoner of war. The detaining power has to send these prisoners of war back to their own country without delay. For other wounded and sick prisoners of war whose physical condition is less critical, the detaining power has a discretion to transfer them to neutral states for hospitalization.[105] The precondition for such transfer is the

---

[104] Department of Defense, *Conduct of the Persian Gulf War*, Appendix O–18.
[105] During the First World War many prisoners of war were interned in Switzerland under an agreement between the parties to the conflict, Garner, 55, 56.

Fischer

expectation that through internment in a neutral country the prisoners of war will recover, or recover more quickly, or that a threat to health from continued captivity can be avoided.

2. *Renewed involvement in hostilities.* One aim of captivity is to prevent the prisoners from taking further part in hostilities against the detaining power. The repatriation prescribed in Art. 109 GC III for prisoners of war during a conflict increases the risk that, after recovering, the prisoners will once again take part in hostilities on the side of their own country. For this reason Art. 117 GC III prohibits the employment of repatriated persons in active military service. The United States expressly fulfilled this obligation under Art. 117 GC III following the repatriation of three pilots by North Vietnam during the Vietnam War in 1972.[106]

Since this obligation is addressed to the home state, it is generally assumed that the prisoners of war cannot be held responsible for violations of Art. 117 if recaptured by the detaining power.[107] Prisoners of war may not be charged with a war crime for their renewed involvement in hostilities.[108] The list of grave breaches in Art. 130 GC III does not refer to Art. 117 GC III. Neither has a recognition that breaches of Art. 117 GC III constitute war crimes emerged in customary law.

732   **All prisoners of war shall be released and repatriated without delay after the cessation of active hostilities (Art. 118 GC III). This requires neither a formal armistice agreement nor the conclusion of a peace treaty. What matters is the actual cessation of hostilities—provided that, according to a reasonable estimate, they are unlikely to resume. Repatriation is carried out in an orderly manner, in accordance with a plan agreed by all parties, working with and under the control of the protecting powers and the International Committee of the Red Cross (Arts. 8–10 GC III).**

1. *Duty to release.* Art. 118 GC III stipulates the general duty of the detaining power to release prisoners of war. This duty is qualified in a number of respects. First, in terms of timing, the prisoners shall be released after the cessation of active hostilities. Furthermore, this Article prohibits every detaining power from determining a time for the release. The phrase 'without delay' clarifies that the obligation to release is in force directly after the cessation of active hostilities. The duty to repatriate is not affected by peace negotiations.[109] Under international law the obligation to release is not dependent on corresponding conduct of the enemy.[110] Practice has shown, however, that states do base their conduct on such reciprocity.

The duty to release is interwoven with the duty to repatriate. These terms are linked by the wording of Art. 118, para. 1 GC III so that the mere release of prisoners of war after the cessation of active hostilities does not fulfil the obligation. Repatriation requires a plan which may either be concluded by agreement among

---

[106] Falk, *AJIL* 67 (1973), 470.   [107] De Preux, 539.

[108] Cf. in this respect the comments of Dinstein, *Release*, 39.

[109] H. Fischer, *HUV-I* 3/1991, 15.

[110] Quigley, *The American Journal of International Law and Policy* 5 (1989), 80.

the parties to the conflict or, failing such agreement, may be set up by the detaining power. Art. 118 GC III does not allow for repatriation without a plan. The release of Kuwaiti prisoners of war following the Second Gulf War, when Iraq sent prisoners of war on their way home through the desert, constituted a breach of Art. 118 GC III.[111]

A repatriation plan must stipulate the type of repatriation, the time schedule, and the persons involved. Furthermore the requirements laid down in Art. 119 GC III shall be taken into consideration. Thus articles of value shall be returned to the prisoners of war. They are permitted to take with them their personal effects, their money, and parcels they received during detention.

The possibility of exchanging prisoners of war during a conflict is not expressly mentioned. In twentieth century wars such exchanges have almost never occurred. In the conflict between Croatia and Serbia in 1991, however, the parties concluded an agreement on the release of 1,600 prisoners through the mediation of the ICRC.[112]

2. *Cessation.* Unlike the Hague Regulations and the Geneva Convention of 1929, the obligation to release does not arise only by agreement between the parties to the conflict. While the Hague Regulations considered a peace treaty to be such an agreement, the first Convention on Treatment of Prisoners of War of 1929 stipulated that an armistice agreement effected the obligation to release. The practice of wars after 1907, particularly the two World Wars, demonstrated that linking the duty to release to the international treaty provided the detaining powers with a means of keeping prisoners of war under their power for as long as possible. This is now precluded by the wording of Art. 118 GC III. The actual cessation of hostilities automatically effects the obligation to release prisoners of war.

What is meant by cessation of hostilities and who decides when this actually occurs? The formulation of Schwarzenberger is frequently adopted, according to which hostilities have ceased if 'neither side expects a resumption of hostilities'.[113] This definition permits parties to a conflict to estimate subjectively the intention of the adversary. In particular, states which are ideologically on hostile terms may always claim that a resumption of hostilities forms a part of the other party's politics. The term 'active' makes clear that the mere expectation of parties to the conflict that hostilities *could* be resumed does not justify retaining prisoners of war.

In order to protect prisoners of war it is more appropriate to refer to the military circumstances accompanying the cessation of hostilities and to choose an objective approach. An armistice agreement is not necessarily a cessation within the meaning of Art. 118 GC III. The circumstances of the individual case indicate whether an armistice appears to be a return to lasting peace or merely an interruption of the hostilities.[114] If the armistice is monitored by UN Blue Helmets, for instance, this is a good indication of a lasting cessation of hostilities if it involves the demobilization

---

[111] See Gasser, *IKRK im Golfkrieg*, 15.

[112] On the assessment of these agreements in the former Yugoslavia from the point of view of international law see Jakovljevic, *HUV-I* 3/1992, 108–11.

[113] Schwarzenberger, *International Law*, 134.   [114] Too critical: Dinstein, *Release*, 45.

Fischer

of the parties to the conflict. General demobilization of the enemy parties, withdrawal of troops from the front line, compliance with demands, and resolution of disputed questions can also be indications of the cessation of active hostilities. If the fighting has stopped, then despite the continued occupation of territory a cessation of hostilities might still have been achieved.[115] All attempts to define the term of cessation of hostilities more clearly[116] depend on the geographic and military circumstances of the conflict and its historic-political causes. In future, regional organizations of the UN Security Council might assist in determining a cessation under Art. 118 GC III.

3. *The duty to repatriate.* After almost every conflict since 1945, especially the Korean, Vietnam, Iran–Iraq, and Second Gulf Wars, some prisoners of war have refused repatriation. For political, economic, or humanitarian reasons large numbers of prisoners of war have requested to stay in the territory of the detaining power or in another state not involved in the conflict. Approximately 15,000 Iraqi prisoners of war declined to return to Iraq following the Second Gulf War,[117] about an eighth of the total number of Iraqi prisoners of war. Thus the question arises whether Art. 118 GC III imposes a duty on the detaining power to repatriate in these circumstances.[118] The wording indicates this duty through the formulation that prisoners of war shall be released *and* repatriated. The option of leaving prisoners of war with the detaining power after the conflict cannot be derived from the wording. International lawyers have repeatedly claimed that any discretion for the detaining power in whether or not to repatriate would considerably increase the risks to prisoners of war. Such an option would give the detaining power the opportunity to breach the duty to repatriate under Art. 188 GC III by referring to the will of the prisoner of war.

On the other hand, the humanitarian problems resulting from forced repatriation of prisoners of war are also relevant. Art. 109, para. 3 GC III, which prohibits the repatriation of sick or wounded prisoners of war against their will during a conflict, has been referred to in this respect. The problem of fulfilling the requests of the prisoners of war and at the same time preventing abuse by the detaining power has not been solved in a satisfactory manner to date.[119] State practice in this respect is inconsistent.[120] The report of the Pentagon to Congress on the Second Gulf War presumes a right of the prisoners to decide about being repatriated. It is expressly stated that since the entry into force of GC III 'this principle has become conditional: each POW must consent to repatriation rather than being forced to return'.[121]

---

[115] Schneider, *HUV-I* 2/1989, 14.

[116] Shields-Delessert, 111 *et seq.*, suggests a differentiation which takes into account the various categories of prisoners of war.

[117] Gasser, *IKRK im Golfkrieg*, 15.

[118] On the organization of the mass flight of North Korean prisoners of war by the Allies in order to avoid the problem of repatriation see Kunz, *Kriegsgefangenenfrage*, 416–19.

[119] Kunz, *The Laws*, 336, proposed a revision of Art. 118 as early as 1956 on the basis of experiences of the Korean War.

[120] Sassòli, *Status*, 32.

[121] Department of Defense, *Conduct of the Persian Gulf War*, Appendix O–20.

Fischer

Gasser correctly refers to the importance of the role of ICRC delegates.[122] They alone are in a position to determine whether prisoners of war in fact prefer to remain in the state of the detaining power, or in another state, rather than returning to their home country. In this respect the detaining power's duty to repatriate under Art. 118 GC III cannot be limited. The duty is absolute. In individual cases exceptions can be made for humanitarian reasons if the life of the prisoner of war might be endangered by the repatriation. However, this goal can only be achieved on a case-by-case basis taking into account the supervision by the ICRC. After the Second Gulf War the United States provided the ICRC with the names of prisoners of war who were not willing to be repatriated. Prior to repatriation, the ICRC delegates asked all Iraqi prisoners of war about their willingness to return. Those prisoners of war who refused to return to Iraq were transferred back to the detaining power.[123]

Prisoners of war who have committed an indictable offence and against whom   733
criminal proceedings are pending or who have yet to complete a punishment may
be detained beyond the cessation of active hostilities (Art. 119, para. 5 GC III).

Art. 119, para. 5 GC III provides an exception to the duty to release. Those prisoners of war against whom criminal proceedings for an indictable offence are pending may be detained until the end of such proceedings, and if necessary until the completion of the punishment. As is expressly laid down, the same applies to prisoners of war already convicted of an indictable offence. The first alternative requires that proceedings are already afoot. Prisoners of war cannot be retained on mere suspicion until evidence can be found which allows proceedings to be initiated. As a rule, the detaining power has a power to delay the release until the completion of the punishment imposed if proceedings have been issued or if prisoners of war are already serving a sentence. In this case the requirements for their internment are set out in Art. 88 GC III.

---

[122] Gasser, *Das humanitäre Völkerrecht*, 538.
[123] Department of Defense, *Conduct of the Persian Gulf War, Appendix* O–20; this report is confirmed by Gasser, ICRC, 20.

8

Religious Personnel

Preliminary remarks

1. The military 'chaplains assigned to the armed forces' are, in accordance with Art. 24 GC I, protected in the same way as medical personnel. In contrast to GC I, Art. 8 lit. d AP I uses the term 'religious personnel' as more neutral than the Christian term of 'chaplain'. (Art. 36 GC II speaks of 'spiritual' personnel).[1] These military or civilian persons are exclusively engaged in religious duties. They are assigned to the armed forces of a party to the conflict either permanently or temporarily (Art. 8 lit. d i-iii AP I). In case of temporary assignment, protection is also limited in time (Art. 8 lit. k AP I). The regulations mentioned imply that religious personnel shall not be the object of discrimination by the adversary with regard to their particular religion. Moreover, religious personnel must not be hindered in pursuing their religious duties among their own citizens, even if the national regulations of the state in which they are working prohibit it. These protections are applicable only to genuine religious personnel. The content of GC I and AP I shows that the term 'religious' has to be interpreted in a restricted sense. 'Political commissaries', for example, are excluded from this definition.

2. Modern conflicts often have religious motives. In such cases it is questionable whether in practice religious personnel and medical personnel will be treated equally.[2]

I. GENERAL

Chaplains are ministers of faith assigned to the armed forces of a state to provide spiritual care to the persons in their charge (Art. 24 GC I; Art. 37 GC II; Art. 23, para. 5 AP I).   801

The status of chaplains is accorded to: 802

---

[1] Bothe/Partsch/Solf, 99.   [2] McCoubrey, 53 n. 37.

—ministers who belong to a militia not forming part of the regular armed forces, a volunteer corps, or an organized resistance movement whose members are combatants (Art. 13, para. 2 GC I);

—ministers who have been charged by the appropriate military authority to care for the personnel accompanying the armed forces (Art. 13, para. 4 GC I);

—ministers assigned to hospital ships (Art. 36 GC II), even if they are not chaplains; and

—religious personnel of merchant ships (Arts. 37 and 13, para. 5 GC II).

803 Under international law, non-permanent military chaplains are not accorded the same status as permanent military chaplains. They are protected as civilians by Geneva Convention IV.

804 The auxiliaries of the chaplains (chaplain's assistants and drivers) assigned to the Federal Armed Forces shall be accorded the status of soldiers in a state of defence. It is, however, in keeping with the principles of international humanitarian law to respect and protect these persons, too, as far as possible.

805 The groups of persons to be attended by chaplains include:

—members of the armed forces to which they themselves belong;

—for chaplains who fall into the hands of the adversary, also prisoners of war belonging to allied armed forces (Arts. 33, para. 2 and 35, first sentence GC III);

—in exceptional cases, members of the opposing armed forces who have been taken prisoner (Art. 37 GC III);

—in case of need, wounded, sick, and shipwrecked members of opposing armed forces; and

—for the duration of an occupation, the civilian population in particular children (Arts. 13, 24, 27, para. 1, 38, para. 3, 50, para. 3 and 58, para. 1 GC IV), protected persons accused of offences (Art. 6, para. 3 GC IV), and internees (Arts. 93 and 94 GC IV).

806 Chaplains shall exercise their functions within the scope of the laws and regulations of the detaining power and in accordance with their religious doctrine (Art. 33, para. 2 and 35, first sentence GC III). They shall, however, not be confined to their religious duties and may particularly:

—perform the functions of a personal adviser;

—receive and forward the last wishes of dying soldiers; and

—provide material assistance.

807 Wherever possible, the dead shall be interred by chaplains of the same denomination. The states concerned have the duty to assist the chaplains, within the means available to them, in fulfilling this task (Art. 17, para. 3 GC I).

Rabus

Chaplains shall wear, affixed to the left arm, an armlet displaying the red cross or   808
red cresent on a white ground (Art. 40, para. 1 GC I; Art. 42, para. 1 GC II; Art. 18,
paras. 1 and 3 AP I; Art. 12 AP II). The armlet shall be issued and stamped by the
appropriate authority (Art. 40, para. 1 GC I; Art. 42, para. 1 GC II).

In addition to this armlet and the identity disk to be worn by all members of the   809
armed forces, chaplains shall also carry a special identity card (Art. 40, para. 2 GC
I; Art. 42, para. 2 GC II).

Chaplains may not be deprived of their special insignia, armlets, or identity cards.   810
In case of loss or destruction, they have the right to replacements (Art. 40, para. 4
GC I; Art. 42, para. 4 GC II). Should chaplains fall into the hands of the adversary,
the latter shall be obliged to allow new identity cards or armlets to be forwarded
to retained chaplains (Art. 40, para. 4 GC I; Art. 42, para. 4 GC II).

II. PROTECTION OF CHAPLAINS

Chaplains shall be respected and protected in all circumstances (Art. 24 GC I; Arts.   811
36 and 37 GC II; Art. 15, para. 5 AP I). This shall apply:

—at any time throughout the duration of an armed conflict;

—at any place; and

—in any case in which chaplains are retained by the adversary, whether temporarily or for a prolonged period of time.

Chaplains are entitled to the protection provided by international law. Direct par-   812
ticipation in rendering assistance to the victims of war (wounded, sick, shipwrecked, prisoners of war, protected civilians) is not required.

Unlike medical supplies, the articles used for religious purposes are not explicitly   813
protected by international law. It is, however, in keeping with the spirit of the
Geneva Conventions to respect the material required for religious purposes and
not to use it for alien ends.

Reprisals against chaplains are prohibited (Art. 46 GC I; Art. 47 GC II). This prohi-   814
bition shall protect chaplains from any restriction of the rights assigned to them.
They may, however, be deprived of privileges exceeding the statutory minimum of
protection provided to them by the Geneva Conventions.

Chaplains may in no circumstances renounce the rights secured to them by inter-   815
national humanitarian law (Art. 7 GC I; Art. 7 GC II).

Any attack directed against chaplains and any infringement of their rights   816
constitutes a grave breach of international law, which shall be liable to criminal
prosecution (Art. 49 GC I; Art. 50 GC II).

Rabus

817   The fact that chaplains may be armed, and that they may use the arms in their own defence or in that of the wounded, sick, and shipwrecked shall not deprive them of the protection accorded to them by international law (Art. 22 GC I; Art. 35 GC II). They may use the arms only to repel attacks violating international law, but not to prevent capture.

818   The protection accorded to chaplains shall cease if they use their arms for any other purpose than that of self-defence and defence of protected persons.

819   The only arms which may be used are weapons suited for self-defence and emergency aid (individual weapons).

820   In the Federal Republic of Germany chaplains may not be armed.

III. LEGAL STATUS OF CHAPLAINS RETAINED BY A FOREIGN POWER

821   Chaplains who are retained by an adverse party shall not be considered as prisoners of war (Art. 28, para. 2 GC I; Art. 36 GC II; Art. 33, para. 1 GC III).

822   Chaplains may be retained to assist prisoners of war of the armed forces to which they themselves belong in so far as the state of health, spiritual needs, and number of prisoners require (Art. 28 GC I; Arts. 36 and 37 GC II; Art. 33 GC III).

823   The provisions of Geneva Conventions I and III apply to the treatment of the retained chaplains as minimum requirements for protection. As a consequence, chaplains shall receive at least the benefits accorded to prisoners of war by these conventions (Art. 30 GC I; Art. 33 GC III). Like prisoners of war, chaplains shall be released and repatriated without delay after the cessation of active hostilities (Arts. 33, para. 1 and 118, para. 1 GC III).

824   In particular, the detaining power shall ensure the representatives of religious organizations a proper reception. The detaining power shall provide the duly accredited agents of these organizations with all necessary facilities for:

—visiting prisoners of war and chaplains in their camps;

—distributing relief supplies and material intended for religious, educational, or recreative purposes; and

—assisting prisoners of war and chaplains in organizing their leisure time (Art. 125 GC III).

825   The provisions of the Geneva Conventions apply by analogy to chaplains received or interned in neutral territory (Art. 4 GC I; Art. 5 GC II).

Rabus

Chaplains who are not retained shall be returned (Arts. 28 and 30 GC I; Art. 37 GC   826
II).

Chaplains shall be returned to the party to the conflict to which they belong. A   827
detaining power which merely releases a person into the territory of his home
state which the said power still occupies does not fulfil its duty to return this person.

The repatriation of chaplains depends on the condition that a means is open for   828
their return and that military requirements permit (Art. 30, para. 3 GC I; Art. 37 GC
II).

Chaplains who are repatriated may take with them the effects, personal belong-   829
ings, valuables and ritual objects belonging to them (Art. 30, para. 3 GC I; Art. 37
GC II).

Retained chaplains shall continue to exercise their spiritual functions for the ben-   830
efit of prisoners of war, preferably those belonging to the armed forces upon
which they depend. They shall perform their duties within the scope of the military laws and regulations of the detaining power and in accordance with their professional etiquette and their religious conscience. Their work shall be subject to
the control of the competent services (Art. 28, para. 2 GC I; Art. 37 GC II; Arts. 33,
para. 2 and 35 GC III).

The spiritual functions to be exercised for the benefit of prisoners of war particu-   831
larly include:
—holding religious services (Art. 34 GC III);
—ministering to prisoners of war of the same religion (Art. 35 GC III); and
—burying prisoners of war who have died according to the rites of the religion to
   which they belong (Art. 120, para. 4 GC III).

In order to ensure a uniform level of assistance for prisoners of war, chaplains will   832
be allocated to camps and labour detachments containing prisoners of war
belonging to the same forces, speaking the same language, or practising the same
religion (Art. 35 second sentence GC III).

The detaining power shall provide chaplains with all facilities necessary for the   833
exercise of their spiritual functions.

In particular, they shall be accorded the following facilities: 834
—They shall be provided with adequate premises where religious services may be
   held (Art. 34, para. 2 GC III).
—They shall be authorized to visit periodically prisoners of war situated outside
   the camp (e.g. in working detachments or hospitals). For this purpose, the

Rabus

detaining power shall place at their disposal the necessary means of transport (Arts. 33, para. 2 lit. a and 35, third sentence GC III).

—They shall have the right to deal with the competent authorities of the camp on all questions relating to their duties (Art. 33, para. 2 lit. b, third sentence GC III).

—They shall enjoy all facilities for correspondence on matters concerning their duties. They shall be free to correspond, subject to censorship, with the ecclesiastical authorities in the country of detention and with international religious organizations. Letters and cards which they send for this purpose shall be in addition to the quota provided for prisoners of war (Arts. 35, fourth and fifth sentences, and 71 GC III).

—They shall be allowed to receive by any means whatsoever individual parcels or collective shipments containing devotional articles (e.g. bibles, prayer and service books, hymnals, ritual articles, sacramental wine, crucifixes, and rosaries Arts. 33 and 72, para. 1 GC III).

835   Retained chaplains shall be subject to the disciplinary authority of the detaining power (Art. 28, para. 2 GC I; Art. 33, para. 2 GC III). They shall therefore be subordinate to the general orders of the camp commander. This shall not apply to the exercise of their religious duties.

836   Chaplains may not be compelled to carry out any work other than that concerned with their religious duties (Art. 28, para. 2 GC I; Art. 33, para. 2 lit. c GC III).

837   Prisoners of war who are ministers but not chaplains e.g. ministers who serve in the armed forces as soldiers only, shall be at liberty to minister freely to the members of their community (Art. 36, first sentence GC III). The detaining power has the duty to give them an appropriate authority if prisoners of war of the same faith are to be ministered. Ministers who have been accorded this authority shall enjoy the same privileges and facilities as retained chaplains. They shall also not be compelled to carry out any work (Art. 36 GC III). Nevertheless, they shall remain prisoners of war, although endowed with special rights.

838   When prisoners of war do not have the assistance of a chaplain or of a prisoner of war minister, another minister belonging to the prisoners' or a similar denomination, or alternatively, a qualified layman, shall be appointed if such a course is feasible from the confessional point of view, at the request of the prisoners concerned (Art. 37 GC III). These persons will normally be selected from among the prisoners of war, but they may also be members of the civilian population of the detaining power.

839   Subject to the approval of the detaining power, these ministers and laymen shall regularly be appointed by the appropriate local religious authorities of the respective faith with the agreement of the community of prisoners concerned (Art. 37 GC III).

Rabus

The ministers and laymen thus appointed shall enjoy the same privileges and   840
facilities as chaplains. They are subject to the discipline of the camp as well as to
all regulations established by the detaining power in the interests of discipline
and military security (Art. 37, third sentence GC III). If these persons are selected
from the prisoner of war community their status will not change.

Rabus

9

Protection of Cultural Property

Preliminary Remarks

1. Historical development of the protection of cultural property. It has been out-lined above (Sections 105–24) how the international humanitarian law of war was developed gradually and only recently led to the rules now in force as the 'rules of armed conflict'. There follow some remarks on the way in which protection of cul-tural property has developed. The necessity for such protection was recognized rel-atively early, but strong incentives were needed before special rules on this subject were established.

As early as the eighteenth century it was regarded as a violation of civilized man-ners and reasonable behaviour wantonly to destroy items of cultural value or to loot such items from occupied territories. The systematic destruction of the Palatinate by Louis XIV met with general disapproval as did the terrible incursions by Napoleon. The congress of Vienna therefore decided that works of art had to be restored by Paris to their lawful owners.

It took several decades until legally binding general rules were created. The ear-liest regulations were contained in the Lieber Code of 1863 (see Section 116) and the Declaration of Brussels of 1874 (see Section 120). Both exercised remarkable influ-ence on the work of the Hague Peace conferences in 1899 and 1907.[1]

During earlier periods rather cautious rules of protection were provided. Not only hospitals, but also works of classical art and similar objects had to be secured against all avoidable injury (Lieber Code, Art. 35). It was generally forbidden to destroy or seize the enemy's property unless imperatively demanded by the neces-sities of war (Art. 23 lit. g HagueReg). In sieges and bombardments hospitals and buildings dedicated to art and science had to be spared as far as possible, provided that they were not being used for military purposes. Since 1907 'historic monu-ments' have also been protected. Similar provisions were introduced concerning bombardments by naval forces (Art. 5 HC IX). The inhabitants of the regions affected had to mark such protected objects by visible signs and to communicate such measures to the opponents. In case of enemy occupation any intentional

---

[1] See the comparison of texts, *ZaöRV* 16 (1955/56), 76–7 (documents concerning the protection of cul-tural property in armed conflicts). For the history until the Second World War see Verri, *Acts of the Symposion of the Istituto Internazionale di Diritto Umanitario* (IIDU), 1986, 41–68; for later events Makagiansar, ibid., 27–31.

destruction of or damage to such institutions, was prohibited and liable to proceedings (Art. 56 HagueReg). No reservations for military necessity were apparently considered necessary.

These provisions are regarded as binding customary international law. They are relevant in practice primarily for those states which are not bound by conventions for the protection of cultural property concluded later (such as the UK).

A regional treaty concluded under the auspices of the Pan-American Union in 1935 (the Treaty on the Protection of Artistic and Scientific Institutions and Historic Monuments, or the Roerich Pact)[2] was signed by twenty-one American states and ratified by eleven. It considerably influenced further development in this field, and proved an inspiration for further agreements. The standard of protection of the Hague Regulations was improved. An obligation to register the protected objects with the Union and the use of distinctive emblems were introduced. The 1935 Treaty was also discussed in the International Museum Council of the League of Nations. This organ aimed to introduce similar binding obligations on all members of the League of Nations, and found the support of the Netherlands. Its initiative was, however, suppressed by World War II and renewed only in 1948. Following a suggestion by the Netherlands, UNESCO called a diplomatic conference at The Hague in 1954 where forty-five states concluded the Cultural Property Convention together with RegEx and a Protocol. By 1991 the CultPropConv had been ratified by seventy-five states, but not by Ireland, Japan, New Zealand, the Philippines, Portugal, Uruguay, the United Kingdom and the USA, although these states had participated in the conference.

There were differences from the Hague Regulations. The protected objects were defined in greater detail; the distinction was made between general protection (Sections 905–9) and special protection (Sections 910–18); the use of distinctive emblems was made mandatory for cultural property under special protection (Sections 929–36); more detailed rules were introduced concerning protection in occupied territories (Sections 919–22), during transport (Sections 913–15), and concerning the position of personnel entrusted with protective functions (Sections 926–8). These matters are dealt with below.

When AP I and II were negotiated in the 1970s, the need was felt to include this matter dealt with in the HagueReg. This was due to the fact that the CultPropConv was not yet binding worldwide; it had been ratified by only half of the ten UN members with the largest populations. A broader field of application seemed necessary. Thus, Arts. 53 and 85, para. 4 lit. d AP I and Art. 16 AP II deal with the protection of cultural property.

Such provisions were inserted not only in AP I but also in AP II, since the CultPropConv covers also non-international conflicts, without indicating where the high threshold required according to AP II lies. It is presupposed that rebels have conquered a territory permitting planned military operations and an effective

---

[2] *LNTS* Vol. CLXVII 290–5, No. 5874 (1936); the Pact is regarded as still in force, though for all practical purposes it has been superseded. Registration of monuments and institutions in accordance with its Art. 4 has never taken place. In view of its historic importance, mainly its influence on the conclusion of the Hague Convention of 1954, some references to the Pact appear in the following commentaries.

application of AP II. According to Art. 3, common to GCs I–IV, this is not required. Certain minimal requirements are also valid for its application. Mere internal unrest, tension, or sporadic acts of violence do not suffice, even if the police are unable to master the situation and the employment of armed forces becomes necessary.

In all cases of non-international conflict there exists a common problem: whether the conflict fulfils the requirements of AP II or only of common Art. 3. The insurgent opponents are not contracting parties to the conventional instruments. The provisions of protection are only binding on the contracting parties, while to the rebels they constitute no more than a request to respect them.

The ICRC has developed the thesis that all inhabitants of a country in which a conflict takes place are obliged to respect the humanitarian instruments on the basis of their ratification by the competent government. This thesis is, however, not universally applicable.[3] It may apply only in those states where obligations under international law are declared to be applicable also in the internal legal order as in Germany and Italy, but not in some common law countries.

2. *The relationship between the legal norms.* The protection of cultural property is governed by legal instruments created in different periods and effective in different states. The law of the Hague Peace Conferences of 1899 and 1907 is binding as customary law on the whole international community of states; the CultPropConv, exclusively dedicated to this matter, binds only a limited number of contracting parties; the provisions of AP I and AP II on this matter are applicable to a larger number of states. Even if a state orders that its soldiers are required to comply with the rules of international humanitarian law in the conduct of military operations in all armed conflicts, however such conflicts are characterized (see Section 211 sentence 2), it is nevertheless sometimes legally relevant which of these treaties is binding on the adversary or an ally of that state.

a) First, the relationship between the customary law of the Hague and the new rules established by APs has to be defined. The new rules are convention law and are not yet accepted as customary law. Can these new rules of convention law be regarded as special protection for a limited class of objects not intended to replace the existing customary law prohibitions? Several contracting parties declared when accepting Art. 53 AP I (then Arts. 47 ff.) that its provisions establish a regime of special protection as *lex specialis* without replacing customary rules.[4] This opinion can be based on several arguments. Art. 27 HagueReg covers a broader field of application, including charitable and medical institutions as well as objects of cultural value. It does not require that cultural values belong to the cultural or spiritual heritage of peoples. The definition of cultural property and its protection will be analyzed in detail together with the respective provisions (see Sections 901 and 902).

---

[3] See Bothe/Partsch/Solf, 608, 628.

[4] See the declaratory explanations of Canada, Federal Republic of Germany, United Kingdom, and USA, annexed to CDDH/SR. 42, official records VI, 224 to 241.

b) The relationship between the customary law of the Hague Conferences and the convention law of the CultPropConv can be defined in a similar way. The latter extends protection to several objects not mentioned in Art. 27 HagueReg. Such protection is, however, limited to cultural values 'of great importance to the cultural heritage of every people' (Art. 1, lit. a) or of 'very great importance' (Art. 8, para. 1). It is not required that they 'belong to' such heritage (as according to Art. 53 lit. a AP I) which may afford less protection but still brings responsibilities.

c) The relationship between the CultPropConv and the new law of the APs is not easily definable. The introductory words 'without prejudice to the provisions of the Hague Convention . . . of 14 May 1954' establish a bridge between the two instruments. The CultPropConv must be respected when the two Protocols are applied by those states which have ratified both of them. The Diplomatic Conference emphasized in its Resolution 20[5] the paramount importance of the CultPropConv. Its application will by no means be prejudiced by the adoption of new Articles. States which had not yet done so were urged to become parties.

The CultPropConv can certainly be used when the provisions of the Protocols are correctly interpreted (see Sections 901, 902). Art. 53 of Protocol I protects certain specified objects absolutely and without exception. The CultPropConv, however, recognizes two important exceptions which apply even to cultural property under special protection: if the cultural property or its surroundings are used for military purposes (Art. 11, para. 1) or if in exceptional cases of unavoidable military necessity the immunity is withdrawn from cultural property under special conditions (Art. 11, para. 2). The obligation to respect cultural property under general protection may also be waived in cases where military necessity imperatively requires such waiver (Art. 4, para. 2).

There is no unanimity on whether these exceptions can be applied under AP I and AP II. As this problem is clearly connected with the protection established for cultural property (see Sections 903, 906, 917, and 918 below), it is dealt with in this connection. The situation of non-contracting parties of the 1954 Convention also deserves discussion.

3. *General and Special Protection.* The CultPropConv distinguishes between cultural property under general protection (Chapter I, Arts. 1–7; see Sections 905–9) and that under special protection (Chapter II, Arts. 8–11; see Sections 910–18). The broad definition of cultural property in Art. 1 CultPropConv states that objects under general or special protection are exclusively objects of 'great importance to the cultural heritage of every people'. A selection is made from the objects mentioned under the aspect of their artistic and historic quality. Objects mentioned in Article 1 CultPropConv which do not fulfil this requirement are not deprived of all protection; they are civilian objects to be treated in accordance with the disposition valid for them. In any case they should not be attacked as military targets but must be spared to the greatest possible extent (see Section 904).

Special protection is provided for a very limited category of cultural property,

[5] Schindler/Toman, 645.

namely shelters for movable cultural property, centres containing monuments, and other immovable cultural property of very great importance (Art. 8, para. 1). Between the cultural property defined in Art. 1 particularly qualified objects are selected for this purpose.

The following distinctions exist between the regimes of general and special protection under the CultPropConv.[6]

a) All objects defined as cultural property are automatically under general protection. Cultural objects under special protection must be entered in the international register. Their immunity will only begin on registration (see Section 912).

b) Even in peacetime cultural property under special protection shall not be used for military purposes.

c) Cultural property under general protection may bear a distinctive emblem (Art. 6 CultPropConv). Items under special protection must be marked with the distinctive emblem during an armed conflict and shall be subject to international control (Art. 10 CultPropConv).

d) The obligation to respect cultural property under general protection may be waived in cases where military necessity 'imperatively so requires' (Art. 4, para. 2); with respect to objects under special protection, such waiver is permitted only in exceptional cases of unavoidable military necessity. Its applicability is controlled by national and international organs (Art. 11, para. 2 CultPropConv. and Section 918).

e) For cultural property under special protection additional measures apply (Art. 11 CultPropConv and Section 918).

f) Some authors are of the opinion that the protection accorded by Art. 53 AP I and Art. 16 AP II is similar to the regime of special protection in Chapter II CultPropConv.[7] There are differences in terminology between APs I and II and a definition of an extension of the CultPropConv. They do not allow, however, for a definition of the protection under the Protocols as going further than the general protection under the Convention. According to both instruments no registration is required. The definitions of the protected objects do not differ widely (see para. 3 of Section 901). If the protection under the Protocols were to be regarded as special protection according to the CultPropConv, the field of application of APs I and II would be disproportionately reduced.

g) Control measures, according to the regulations for the execution of the CultPropConv, are valid for objects under both general and special protection.

---

[6] De Breucker, 534.

[7] Solf, 68; the ICRC *Commentary*, para. 2067, also uses the term 'special protection', as does Chapter II of the Convention.

I. GENERAL

901   **The term 'cultural property' means movable or immovable objects of great importance to the cultural heritage of all peoples irrespective of origin or ownership (e.g. monuments of architecture, art, or history, (whether of secular or religious nature), archeological sites, and collections) (Art. 53 lit. a AP I; Art. 16 AP II; Art. 1 CultPropConv).**

1. This definition is modelled on Art. 1 lit. a CultPropConv, although it does not contain all the same elements. The provision also lists 'groups of buildings which, as a whole, are of historical or artistic interest; works of art; manuscripts, books and other objects of artistic, historical, or archeological interest as well as scientific collections and important collections of books or archives or reproductions of the property defined above'. Objects in brackets are cited merely as examples. This list is not exhaustive.

2. This broad paraphrase has to be read with the reservation that the objects mentioned are of *great importance* to the cultural heritage of *every people*, not only of national or regional significance.

3. The relevant articles of the two Protocols (Art. 53 AP I and Art. 16 AP II) cover only objects 'which belong to the cultural or spiritual heritage of peoples'. They mention only historic monuments, works of art, or places of worship. In view of the reference to the CultPropConv it has to be assumed that the designation of objects in AP I and II are examples of the broader collective category intended to be covered by the Convention. Thus, groups of buildings may be understood as historic monuments; books and other objects of artistic, historical or archeological interest as 'works of art'. It is doubtful, however, how archives and reproductions are to be treated. Their close connection with a work of art may justify treating them as their accessories. Examples are the drawings enabling the completion of Cologne Cathedral, or reproductions kept in shelters to enable the reconstruction of any damaged works of art.

4. However, it should not be concluded from the differences in the two instruments between the selection of protected objects that Art. 53 AP I concentrates on objects requiring special protection by excluding others. The main difference between the objects mentioned in Art. 1 lit. a CultPropConv and in APs I and II lies in their qualification as being of 'great importance' on one hand and belonging to the cultural or spiritual heritage of peoples on the other hand.[8] According to the CultPropConv ecclesiastical buildings and works of art are only covered as cultural property if they are of great importance to the cultural heritage. When the Protocols were elabo-

---

[8] This was expressed by several participants in the Diplomatic Conference when Article 53 AP had been accepted *in plenum*. See the explanations of the Netherlands vote CDDH/SR 43 paragraph 14 and in the annexes of Canada (224), the Federal Republic of Germany (225), Italy (230), the United Kingdom, and the USA (240).

Partsch

rated there was criticism of the fact that ecclesiastical treasures were only to be included on the basis of their artistic value. Their qualities as religious objects should also be taken into account. For this reason, beside the cultural heritage, the Protocols refer also to the 'spiritual' heritage. No one will deny that the windows of the Cathedral of Chartres, the frescoes of Assisi, or the mosques of Fez belong to the cultural heritage; however, it may come as a surprise that the spiritual inspiration for the creation of these works had not been given due consideration.[9] The result of such inspiration may well be a work that belongs neither to the cultural nor to the spiritual heritage.

5. The Roerich Pact of 15 April 1935 (see para. 1 of the Preliminary Remarks above) states as its purpose the protection of 'all nationally or privately owned immovable monuments which form the cultural treasure of peoples' (Preamble). It lists in detail 'the historic monuments, museums, scientific, artistic, educational, and cultural institutions' as well as 'the personnel of such institutions in time of peace and war' (Art. 1).

The pact does not expressly mention the objects preserved in such institutions. Apparently they enjoy only indirect protection. Religious institutions are protected only if they fulfil educational purposes; churches only if they can be regarded as 'historic monuments'. On the basis of the Preamble they should also belong to the cultural treasures of peoples. Spiritual treasures are not included.

A comparison between the Roerich Pact and the CultPropConv shows that the protection guaranteed by the Pact goes further in certain respects. It applies also in time of peace, as well as in international or non-international conflicts. The protection presupposes that the monuments and institutions are internationally registered. Dispositions concerning distinctive emblems do not vary substantially between the Pact and general protection under the Convention, although different emblems are provided.

On the other hand a larger number of objects enjoy protection under the CultPropConv. The form of protection is also defined in greater detail and goes further than to declare the protected objects as neutral. States have positive duties of conservation (Art. 3). In addition, there exist special provisions concerning the protection of objects in occupied territories (see Sections 919–22). There are no such provisions in the Roerich Pact.

Both treaties provide that the objects shall cease to enjoy privileges if they are used for military purposes (Art. 4, para. 1 CultPropConv; Art. 5 Roerich Pact). The convention goes even further by providing for a withdrawal of the immunity in cases where military necessity imperatively requires such a waiver (Art. 4, para. 2 for property under general protection, Art. 11, para. 2 for property under special protection). These provisions were included after demands by the United Kingdom and the United States of America, against strong opposition from other members of the diplomatic conference, although they are not contained in the Roerich Pact.

---

[9] Declaration by the Holy See, CDDH/SR 42 Annex, 227.

902   Apart from this actual cultural property, a number of indirect cultural objects shall also be protected. These indirect cultural objects include:

—buildings for preserving or exhibiting cultural property (museums, archives, etc.);

—shelters for cultural objects; and

—centres containing monuments, i.e. containing a large amount of cultural property (Art. 1, Cultural Property Convention).

Protected cultural objects in the Federal Republic of Germany are documented in regional lists of cultural objects which are available with the territorial command authorities.

1. The distinction between 'actual cultural property' and 'indirect cultural objects' does not involve different evaluation. Art. 27 HagueReg named 'buildings dedicated to religion, art, science, or charitable purposes' and other centres, whose objects were called 'indirect cultural objects'. From 'actual cultural property' only historic monuments were added. Works of art and science preserved in such buildings constituting 'actual cultural property' were protected against seizure and destruction (Art. 56, para. 2). The CultPropConv establishes only two categories of objects, which in general enjoy the same protection. Notably, two categories of 'indirect cultural objects' together with immovable cultural property of very great importance can be placed under 'special protection' (see para. 3 of the Preliminary Remarks and Sections 910–18).

2. Lists of cultural objects are established in Germany on a regional basis by the competent territorial command authorities in collaboration with the civilian land directorates of monuments. The objects are marked on regional maps. They contain several thousand objects (see Section 929, para. 2). These maps are regularly updated and are available to all military units.

3. The objects protected under the Roerich Pact are dealt with above (Section 901, para. 5). Two additional remarks are necessary. A limitation to objects in territories 'subject to the sovereignty of signatory and acceding states' (Art. 2) seems to exclude territories occupied by them during military operations. They are included in Art. 5 CultPropConv. The prohibition of 'any discrimination as to the state allegiance of said monuments and institutions' (also in Art. 2) apparently refers to the requirement that the protected objects 'form the cultural treasure of peoples', mentioned only in the Preamble. According to Art. 4, states should include in their lists objects regarded as 'treasures of peoples' in accordance with international standards. Whether they are appreciated by public opinion in the country itself is irrelevant. A rigorous Christian faith dominating a country should not lead to the refusal to demand protection of treasures from the pre-Columbian period.

903   Cultural property shall not be used either directly or indirectly in support of military efforts. All acts of hostility directed against cultural property shall be avoided (Art. 4, para. 1 CultPropConv).

Partsch

1. This sketches concisely the principles valid for the protection of cultural property in the two preceding Sections. They are explained further in the following Sections. These principles bind the contracting party in whose territory or under whose factual jurisdiction the cultural object exists as well as the adversary. They oblige the parties to respect and safeguard these objects even in times of peace, not only during armed conflict.

2. The first sentence takes up an idea already expressed in Art. 27 HagueReg. Protection of these objects presupposes that they will not be used for military purposes. Such use is absolutely forbidden. It is not only unlawful to use protected objects directly for military purposes; indirect use is also illegal. The immediate surroundings of the protected objects and the appliances in use for their protection shall not be used for purposes which are likely to expose them to destruction or damage. For instance, the safe cellars of a museum shall not be used to store ammunitions nor shall a church tower serve as a military observation post.

3. The second sentence is clearly addressed to all parties of armed conflicts. The HagueReg expressly mention the adversary who destroys (Art. 25, para. 1 lit. g), attacks, bombards, or besieges (Arts. 25 and 27). Here, however, the neutral expression 'acts of hostility' is used. It also covers the neglect of protective measures or the exposure to vandalism by the forces of the state in whose territory the cultural property is situated. It has correctly been stated that the attitude of the attacker is influenced by the attitude of the owner.[10] The adversary commits an act of hostility not only by deliberately attacking the protected object, but also by taking action against its immediate surroundings.

4. The conditions for a legitimate deviation from these two principles result from the rules for general (Sections 905–9) and special protection (Sections 910–18, see also Sections 130–2).

5. The Roerich Pact uses a different method of defining the character of protection from that used in Art. 4, para. 1 CultPropConv. Cultural treasures 'shall be considered as neutral' (Arts. 1 and 2). This method of defining the legal situation of relevant objects and their protection against attacks, destruction, and requisition has been used mainly in the rules concerning naval warfare.[11] It does not oblige the possessor to safeguard the objects under its jurisdiction to the same extent.

In addition, civilian objects such as churches, theatres, universities, museums, 904
orphanages, homes for the elderly, and other objects shall also be spared as far as
possible, even if they are of no historic or artistic value (Art. 27, para. 1 HagueReg;
Art. 5 HC IX).

---

[10] Nahlik, 124.
[11] Cf. Declaration respecting Maritime Law, signed at Paris, 16 Apr. 1856, Roberts/Guelff, 23; Schindler/Toman, 787.

Partsch

1. For a great number of buildings the HagueReg provide a modest protection. They cover more objects than the CultPropConv (see Sections 901–3). Their protection is, however, on a lower level.

2. These civilian objects are determined exclusively by their purpose, not by their historic or artistic value. This includes even churches constructed by means of mass production or a local history museum of limited importance, all of which shall be spared from bombardments to the greatest possible extent.[12]

3. The list of buildings contains only examples, mainly taken from the instruments of the Hague Peace Conferences of 1899 and 1907. Civilian objects are also protected under Art. 52 AP I. They shall not be the object of attack or reprisal. In the Protocol only military objects are defined by their nature, location, purpose, or use in order to distinguish them from civilian objects. In this definition of military objects there appears an important element which may help to understand what is meant by civilian objects. Only those objects whose destruction offers a definite military advantage (para. 2) are regarded as military. This should not be the case with civilian objects. In addition an important presumption is expressed in cases of doubt. Objects formally dedicated to civilian purposes shall be presumed not to make an effective contribution to military action (para. 3). The examples cited are places of worship, houses or other dwellings, and schools. Such presumption should also be extended to other buildings dedicated to art and science and to monuments.

4. Art. 27, para. 1 HagueReg provides only that such buildings and monuments 'should be spared as far as possible'. This does not exclude all possibility of attack. Art. 52 AP I goes further. It prohibits attacks and reprisals against civilian objects. This provision is applicable to all civilian objects including cultural treasures in a broad sense not fulfilling all the conditions specified in Sections 901 and 902: for instance, objects not of great importance to the cultural or spiritual heritage of all peoples.[13]

5. The High Contracting Parties of the Roerich Pact are bound by the customary law contained in Art. 27, para. 1 HagueReg. Objects not protected under the Pact are treated as civilian objects.

---

[12] Art. 3 lit. d of the Statute for the International *Ad-hoc* Tribunal on War Crimes in the former Yugoslavia (UN Doc S/25704 of 3 May 1993) describes as punishable the seizure, destruction, or wilful damage of similar objects.

[13] Cf. the interpretation of Art. 52 AP I by Solf in Bothe/Partsch/Solf, 320–7.

Partsch

II. SPECIFIC PROVISIONS FOR THE PROTECTION OF CULTURAL PROPERTY

1. General Protection

General protection shall be granted to all cultural objects and does not require   **905**
any special registration. Cultural property placed under general protection shall
neither be attacked nor otherwise damaged (Art. 53 AP I; Art. 16 AP II; Art. 4, para.
1 CultPropConv). It is also prohibited to expose cultural property, its immediate
surroundings, or appliances in use for its protection to the danger of destruction
or damage by using them for other purposes than those originally intended (Art.
4, para. 1 CultPropConv).

1. The relationship between general protection and special protection was explained in para. 3 of the Preliminary Remarks.

2. The phrase 'all cultural objects' refers exclusively to those objects mentioned in Sections 901 and 902. Those protected only as 'civilian objects' (see Section 904) are not included.

3. The rule concerning general protection (see sentence 2) prohibits both attacks and other damage. Art. 4, para. 1 CultPropConv and Art. 53 lit. a AP I prefer the term 'acts of hostility', to cover actions from both sides (see Section 903). There is no difference between the terminology used here and that of the instruments quoted. The High Contracting Party which administers cultural property causes 'other damage' if the protection is neglected. This is confirmed by Art. 4, para. 3 of the CultPropConv.

4. The Roerich Pact does not distinguish between general and special protection. For all objects protected under this treaty registration with the Pan American Union (now the Organization of American States, or OAS) is required (Art. 4).

An exception to this rule shall be permissible only in cases of imperative military   **906**
necessity (Art. 4, para. 2 CultPropConv). The decision is to be taken by the com-
petent military commander. Cultural property which the enemy uses for military
purposes shall also be spared as far as possible.

1. The instruments of the Hague Peace Conferences of 1899 and 1907 introduced the idea that humanitarian protection of civilian objects had to recede in cases of military necessity.[14]

It was only against the opposition of several great powers that this idea was carried through by Germany.[15] The UNESCO draft for the CultPropConv made no such

[14] Para. 6 of the Preamble to HC II of 1899; para. 5 of the Preamble to HC III; Art. 23 lit. g HagueReg.
[15] Nahlik, *Deficiencies*, 103 (with ample documentation).

Partsch

provision. It was, however, tabled by the USA and supported by the United Kingdom. Socialist and romanic countries opposed the introduction of such a provision into a convention intended to protect cultural property, but finally gave in when both Anglo Saxon powers made their ratification of the whole convention conditional on this exception. In the same way as Art. 23 lit. g HagueReg, the text of Art. 4, para. 2 CultPropConv also requires 'imperative' military necessity.

In contrast to the rules for special protection (Section 917) no special conditions are required for the application of this exception in respect of property under general protection. It has, however, to be accepted that an imperative necessity presupposes that the military objective cannot be reached in any other manner. It is not sufficient that the objective could be more easily attained by endangering the protected object. 'Imperative' necessity requires a careful evaluation of the items which could be affected, taking into account the fact that not all works of art or places of worship are protected. They must be of great importance for the cultural or spiritual heritage of mankind.

2. The decision is taken by the responsible military commander. Under the rules for special protection (Section 917) this competence can only be exercised by officers of the rank of division commander or higher. Doubts have, rightly, been expressed as to whether rank is a guarantee of expertise in art.[16] A captain or even a reserve sergeant who in civilian life is an historian of art or an artist may be more expert than his superior.

3. The first two sentences are also binding on states which have ratified the Protocols but not the CultPropConv. The relevant provisions of both Protocols refer not only to the CultPropConv but also to other relevant international agreements, such as the Hague Conventions, which required that regard be had to imperative military necessities when attacking civilian objects (see Art. 23 lit. g HagueReg).[17]

4. The third sentence appears in neither the HagueReg nor the CultPropConv, but may be derived from the requirements of imperative military necessity.

5. As mentioned above (Section 903, para. 5) no waiver for cases of military necessity is contained in the Roerich Pact. This is remarkable in view of the active role of the United States delegation in favour of inserting such a clause in the CultPropConv.

907   **The parties to the conflict shall take sufficient precautions to prevent cultural property from being used for military purposes.**

1. It may be asked whether states parties are free to decide on such precautions. According to Art. 3 CultPropConv they undertake to safeguard cultural property situated in their own territory against the foreseeable effects of armed conflict. Which

---

[16] Nahlik, *Deficiencies*, 104.   [17] Solf, in Bothe/Partsch/Solf, 333 ff.

Partsch

measures are appropriate is decided by them. They are, however, obliged to act by Art. 4, para. 1.

2. The following measure serves as an example. On 19 June 1944 all military installations were removed from the city of Florence by order of the German authorities so as to prevent this city, abundant in artistic treasures, from becoming a theatre of war. The broad avenues surrounding the city of Florence on its former fortifications were regarded as a boundary which was not to be crossed by military transport.

3. Since the Roerich Pact obliges states parties to prevent the military use of cultural objects, internal legislation may have to be enacted to ensure protection and respect (Art. 2, sentence 2).

All acts of theft, pillage, misappropriation, confiscation, or vandalism directed   908
against cultural property are prohibited (Art. 4, para. 3 CultPropConv).

This provision is mainly addressed to the powers with custody of objects in their jurisdiction or in territories occupied by them. In such territories they may not confiscate cultural property (Art. 4, para. 3, sentence 2). Violations of these duties must be prosecuted and are liable to penal or disciplinary sanctions (Art. 28).

It is prohibited to make cultural property the object of reprisals (Arts. 52, para. 1   909
and 53 lit. c AP I; Art. 4, para. 4 CultPropConv).

1. Numerous prohibitions of reprisals are contained in AP I (see above Sections 476–9), including a general prohibition of reprisals directed against civilian objects in international conflicts (Art. 52, para. 1).

2. This prohibition applies to cultural property under both general and special protection. It is repeated especially for cultural property in Art. 53, lit. c AP I, which was not absolutely necessary. Reprisals remain prohibited even if exceptions to general (Section 906) or special protection (Section 917) are permitted.[18] Though both provisions are closely connected with the idea of reciprocity, the above mentioned exceptions only define the content of the contractual obligations.

2. Special Protection[19]

The contracting parties may place a limited number of cultural objects under spe-   910
cial protection (Art. 9 CultPropConv).

Special protection may be considered only for the following cultural objects (Art.   911
8, para. 1 CultPropConv):

---

[18] Doubtful: Nahlik, IIDU Symposium (note 1), 93.
[19] See Preliminary Remarks para. 2 on the distinction between general and special protection.

Partsch

—shelters for cultural property in the event of armed conflict;

—centres containing monuments; and

—immovable cultural property of very great importance.

1. Cultural property determined for special protection is first selected by the states parties. It is their decision which property to protect, which involves arrangements requiring considerable expense and administrative effort (diversions of traffic, Section 915; custody, Section 916; eventually the provision of information to the adverse party or the Commissioner General, Section 917). Only if they are ready to take such steps shall a motion be carried to enter the objects in the International Register of specially protected items (Section 912).

2. Not all cultural property listed in Section 902 can be put under special protection. Buildings for preserving or exhibiting cultural property (such as museums, libraries, and archives) are mostly situated in the centres of cities. They only rarely fulfil the conditions required in Section 912 for their location.

3. The creation of shelters constitutes a measure for the safeguarding of cultural property which can be undertaken in time of peace (Art. 3 CultPropConv). It is, however, up to the states parties to do this. They may prefer to safeguard such objects in a different way in order to keep them accessible to the larger public and to avoid the dangers of transport under precarious conditions. Shelters shall, as a rule, be situated in remote places such as those provided for in Sections 912 and 913.

4. The Regulations for the Execution of the Convention, which constitute an integral part thereof and come into force together with it (Art. 20 CultPropConv), provide for the setting up of 'improvised refuges' by the states parties after the beginning of an armed conflict. They can be entered in the register for cultural property (Section 912 and Art. 11 RegEx) in agreement with the respective Commissioner General (Section 928) and the delegates of protecting powers. No such possibility is provided for centres containing monuments and for immovable cultural property of very great importance.

912   Special protection shall be subject to the following conditions:

—the property to be protected shall be situated at an adequate distance from any large industrial centre or other important military objective which is particularly vulnerable (aerodrome, broadcasting station, armament plant, major port or railway station, critical river crossing, or main line of communication) (Art. 8, para. 1 lit. a CultPropConv);

—the property to be protected shall not be used for military purposes (Art. 53 lit. b AP I; Art. 16 AP II; Art. 8, para. 1 lit. b CultPropConv);

—the property to be protected shall be entered in the International Register of Cultural Property under Special Protection (Art. 8, para. 6 CultPropConv)

Partsch

which is maintained by the Director General of UNESCO (Arts. 12–16 RegEx CultPropConv).

At the request of the Federal Republic of Germany, the Oberrieder Stollen located in the Breisgau (Schwarzwald) district has been entered in this register as the central refuge for cultural property.

1. The first condition creates problems; for example it renders it impossible to put the historic centre of Cologne with its famous Cathedral under special protection because of the proximity of the railway station. As it serves one of the most heavily used railways in Europe it cannot be expected that the traffic be diverted as provided in Art. 8, para. 5 CultPropConv (Section 913). In order to put the Vatican City under special protection, the Italian Government declared on 18 September 1959 that it would not use the Via Aurelia for military purposes. This street runs along the southern frontier of the Vatican City. It is doubted whether this declaration constitutes an authentic interpretation of the term 'adequate distance' (as Nahlik meant at the Florence Symposium (note 1), 96). When the Convention was drafted a delegate expressed the opinion that only some of the pyramids in Egypt would really fulfil this strict condition[20].

2. Cultural property must not be used for military purposes. For objects under special protection the same terminology is used as in Art. 27, para. 1. HagueReg. For general protection, however, the same idea is expressed indirectly (Art. 4, para. 1 and Section 903) describing the effects of illegitimate use. Apparently no substantial difference exists between these different methods of expression.[21] This is confirmed by the definition in Art. 8, para. 3 of the use of a centre containing monuments for military purposes (see Section 915). Objects under special protection should certainly not enjoy a weaker protection than those under general rules.

3. The third condition requires registration with UNESCO. The state party has to file an application with the Director General of UNESCO for objects in its territory or in a territory occupied by it. Registration is ordered only after notification of the application to all other states parties, who may object to registration if the necessary conditions are not fulfilled. The procedure, including an eventual arbitration, is defined in Arts. 12–16 RegEx. Only after it has been concluded can registration take place. A preliminary registration is possible only if a state party has already filed an application and is involved in an armed conflict before registration has taken place (Art. 14, para. 5 RegEx). This proviso applies for all three categories of cultural property mentioned in Section 911. Objections can be raised by all other state parties until the property is actually registered.

4. In view of the strict conditions for placing property under special protection only a few applications have been filed by state parties. As a centre containing monuments the entire Vatican City has been put under special protection; in addition

---

[20] Nahlik, *Deficiencies*, 90.   [21] Toman concurs; 335.

some refuges have been registered in the Netherlands and in Austria together with Oberrieder Stollen in Germany. A zone of 3 kilometers around the entrance to Oberrieder Stollen has been declared as a prohibited area not to be used for military purposes. Members of the armed forces are not allowed to enter it to fulfil official duties. In the case of an armed conflict they are not allowed to enter this area in uniform even for private purposes. A refuge is to be marked with distinctive emblems (see Section 931) and denoted on military maps.

5. UNESCO not only keeps an International Register for cultural property under special protection in accordance with Art. 12 RegEx but also a 'World Heritage List' under the Convention Concerning the Protection of the World Cultural and Natural Heritage of 16 November 1972. The list contains 359 monuments in eighty states. They are selected according to less strict criteria than those for cultural property under special protection. The World Heritage List has the general merit of offering a measure of protection, without demanding compliance with the extensive conditions for special protection required under the CultPropConv.[22]

6. According to Art. 4 of the Roerich Pact a list of all cultural property protected under this treaty shall be notified by the High Contracting Parties (HCP) to the Pan American Union, now the Organization of American States (OAS). Other governments shall be informed of these lists and of any changes to them.

913 **A refuge for movable cultural property may also be placed under special protection, whatever its location, if it is so designed that it will in all probability not be damaged in the event of attack. The same applies to cases in which the party asking for special protection undertakes, in the event of armed conflict, to make no use of a military object located in the vicinity of cultural property and particularly, in the case of a port, railway station, or aerodrome, to divert all traffic away from there (Art. 8, paras. 2 and 5 CultPropConv).**

1. As mentioned above (Section 911) it seemed necessary to enable states parties to place refuges for movable cultural property under special protection in case their locations should not fulfil the severe conditions required. The first item of Section 912 (Art. 8, para. 2) may be applicable to bomb-proof shelters which are not at a sufficient distance from an endangered objective. 'Attacks' apparently include bombardments with conventional, but not with atomic, weapons.

2. The second sentence applies not only to shelters but also to the two other properties mentioned in Section 911, centres containing monuments and immovable cultural property of very great importance. In practice it may be relevant mainly for shelters whose location can be freely determined. This is not the case for centres

---

[22] For details see Rudolf, 853; Nahlik proposed in 1984 to put all cultural objects from the list under special protection (Florence Symposium (note 1), 97 ff.). This proposal seems to have little chance of acceptance by the states parties of the CultPropConv. It has also not been included in the Final Conclusions of the Symposium (10).

containing monuments or for immovable cultural property of very great importance. It does not seem likely that a state will renounce the right to use a harbour, railway station, or airfield important for supplies, if such object is not already replaced by a newer one.

Neither cultural property placed under special protection nor its surroundings shall be used for military purposes (Art. 9 CultPropConv).   914

Special protection only applies if the protected object is not used for military purposes (Section 912). It is only added here that the requirement is also valid for the immediate surroundings of the property. Their use constitutes a form of indirect use excluded by Section 903.

A centre containing monuments shall also be deemed to be used for military purposes whenever it is used for the movement of armed forces or military material, even in transit. The same shall apply whenever activities are carried on within the centre which are directly connected with military operations, the stationing of armed forces, or the production of military material (Art. 8, para. 3 CultPropConv).   915

This rule explains the meaning of 'use for military purposes'. This definition can also be applied to other cultural property under special protection. During the Second World War former mines were used as shelters for works of art from museums and at the same time also for the production of war material. For objects under special protection this is now forbidden.

The guarding of cultural property by specially empowered armed custodians, or the presence of police forces responsible for the maintenance of public order, shall not be deemed to be use for military purposes (Art. 8, para. 4 CultPropConv).   916

The safeguarding of cultural property even under general protection is a duty under the CultPropConv (Arts. 2 and 3). Nevertheless adequate custody of cultural property under special protection is not mandatory under the Convention. If armed military personnel are employed for this purpose, or if police maintain public order in the neighbourhood of cultural objects, this is not regarded as a violation of the prohibition of military use. In view of the broad definition of military objectives (Section 915) it was necessary to clarify this point.

It shall be permissible, by way of exception, to make cultural property under special protection the object of attack if reasons of unavoidable military necessity so require. Unavoidable military necessity can be determined only by the commander of a division or higher rank. The competent legal adviser shall previously be consulted. When circumstances permit, the adversary shall also be notified a reasonable time in advance of the decision (Art. 11, para. 2 CultPropConv). If a Commissioner General for Cultural Property is nominated (Arts. 2–10 RegEx   917

Partsch

CultPropConv), he shall be informed in writing, with reasons (Art. 11, para. 3 CultPropConv).

1. It was already highly controversial during the drafting of the CultPropConv whether attacks on cultural objects under general protection should be permitted in cases of 'imperative military necessities' (Section 906). It is understandable that such an exception applicable to objects under special protection met with stronger opposition.[23] Only carefully selected objects enjoy this higher form of protection and very few of them now have its benefits: besides the Vatican City only a few refuges in three European states.

2. It is also doubted whether the experience of World War II justifies such an exception. It is true that in 1943 the workshop for mosaics in the Vatican was hit by an American bomb. This attack may have been committed erroneously.

3. The exception is subject to strict conditions. Not only 'imperative military necessities' are required but 'unavoidable' ones. It is open to doubt whether a real difference exists between these two requirements. Not any commander shall be entitled to order the attack but only the commander of a division or larger unit. Apparently it was expected that an officer in charge of an operation might hesitate to demand an authorization for such awkward action from a higher commander.[24] This argument met with the objections described above (Section 906). For the procedural requirements (consultation of the legal adviser, notification to the adversary and to the Commissioner General, stating the reasons) were apparently imposed with the hardly realistic idea that such an order would be planned in advance and that the officer in charge of the operation would to able to fulfil all these requirements and therefore abstain from the whole operation.[25]

4. In addition, it is also questionable whether such exceptions have to be applied under the rules of the two Protocols (I/53 and II/16). The HagueReg (Section 906) do not provide for special protection and are therefore not applicable. A state party to the CultPropConv may base its action on Art. 11, para. 2 thereof, but a non-party cannot.[26]

5. The Roerich Pact does not provide for similar exceptions (see Section 906 and para. 4 following).

918 **If one of the parties to the conflict violates its obligation to protect cultural property under special protection, the other party shall, as long as this violation persists, be released from the obligation to ensure the immunity of the property**

[23] Nahlik, *Deficiencies*, 103–6.

[24] Nahlik at the Florence Symposium (note 1), p. 92, expressed the opinion that a superior commander was more easily identifiable and could thus be held responsible at a later date.

[25] According to de Breucker this could also happen in the case of use of nuclear weapons.

[26] Toman, 334, agrees; Solf treats both exceptions under Art. 11, paras. 1 and 2 together (p. 68) and therefore does not exclude this different treatment.

Partsch

concerned. Nevertheless, whenever possible, the latter party shall first request the adversary to cease such violation within a reasonable time (Art. 11, para. 1 CultPropConv). In addition, only those measures shall be taken which are necessary to ward off the danger arising from such violation.

1. By contrast to the matter dealt with in Section 917, here one party, namely the adversary of the acting party, has violated the obligation to respect cultural property under special protection. This party has used such objects for the support of military operations, contrary also to the rules under the two Protocols. In this case an exception to protection under the two Protocols can be deduced on the rules of those Protocols themselves. The prohibition of acts of hostility presupposes that the relevant objects are not used for the support of military efforts. Lit. a and b of Art. 53 AP I must be read together. At the diplomatic conference not only the United States but also delegations from several other states agreed with this opinion.[27] Here also Art. 85, para. 4(d) of AP I confirms this interpretation. A violation is punishable under this provision only if 'there is no evidence of the violation by the adverse party of Art. 53, subpara. (b)'. If protected property is abused its protection is at least diminished.[28] It is, however, not required that the property be made a military objective in the sense of Art. 52, para. 2 AP I[29].

2. If an object only contributes to support the military effort it does not necessarily constitute a military objective whose destruction offers a definite military advantage. This criterion can hardly be applied to cultural property.[30]

3. A state not party to the CultPropConv is not obliged to request from the adversary the cessation of the violations within a reasonable time (Art. 11, para. 1), although this would seem advisable. The other conditions for suspension of the immunity mentioned in Section 918 are applicable. Only so long as the violation by the adversary persists may the dangers created by the violation be repulsed. This results from the principle of proportionality. The legal situation concerning the different elements of Art. 4, paras. 1 and 2 is not identical. In the case of a provoked attack on cultural property (Art. 11, para. 1) the same misgivings explained in Section 917 concerning military necessities do not apply.

III. PROTECTION OF CULTURAL PROPERTY DURING OCCUPATION

Preliminary Remarks The following rules contained in Sections 919 to 922 are applicable if one state party occupies the territory of another state party (Art. 5,

---

[27] The Netherlands in plenary CDDH/SR 42 para. 17; in explanation of vote CDDH/SR 42 Annex, Off. Records Vol. VI, 241 (USA), 224 (Canada), 225 (Germany), 239 (UK); similar Bosly, Symposium (note 1), 86.
[28] Also Solf, 68.
[29] As declared by the Federal Republic of Germany, (n. 27 above) and ICRC *Commentary* para. 2072.
[30] Rightly: Solf, 68.

Partsch

para. 1 CultPropConv). Non-international conflicts are taken into account as far as resistance movements recognize the government of a state party as their legitimate government. In this case the government shall draw the attention of members of such movements to the obligation to respect cultural property. If a resistance movement exercises control over a part of the territory of a state party, in which it is based itself, this shall not be regarded as 'occupation' in the sense of Art. 5 of the Convention.

919   **The protection of cultural property also extends to a period of occupation. This implies that a party which keeps a territory occupied shall be bound to prohibit, prevent, and if necessary put a stop to any theft, pillage, confiscation, or other misappropriation of, and any acts of vandalism directed against, cultural property (Art. 4, para. 3 CultPropConv).**

1. The special rules concerning occupation of the territory of another state party apply to cultural property under general or special protection. No distinction is made between legal and illegal occupation.

2. No exceptions in the interest of military necessity were deemed appropriate for property under the control of the occupying force. Such property is, however, possibly exposed to 'acts of hostility'. This should be emphasized.

3. The official German version of Art. 4, para. 3 CultPropConv translates the English 'acts of vandalism' to read literally 'senseless destruction'. Such acts are certainly 'senseless', but the phrase tends to suggest 'harmless'. Apparently this term was used in order not to impugn the German tribe of Vandals.

920   **It is prohibited to seize, wilfully destroy, or damage institutions dedicated to religion, charity and education, and the arts and sciences; the same shall apply to historic monuments and other works of art and science (Art. 56 HagueReg; Arts. 52 and 53 lit. a AP I; Art. 16 AP II).**

Section 920 extends rule 919 to institutions serving a number of purposes. Such institutions are already covered by the HagueReg (Art. 56) to whose principles the Preamble of the CultPropConv refers.

921   **The occupying power shall as far as possible support the authorities of the occupied country in safeguarding and preserving cultural property (Art. 5, para. 1 CultPropConv). Should the national authorities be unable to take such measures of preservation for cultural property already damaged, the occupying power itself shall, in close co-operation with these authorities, initiate the necessary measures (Art. 5, para. 2 CultPropConv).**

The safeguarding and preserving of cultural property remains in principle within the competence of the authorities of an occupied country. The occupying power

Partsch

should support them as far as possible and should, in particular, not prevent them from discharging their duties. If support is required only 'as far as possible', this limitation seems to be relevant to active support (e.g. by the supply of material). In one special case the occupying power itself has to take necessary measures, namely if cultural property has been damaged by military operations. When such damage occurs during a period of occupation, the responsibility of the occupying power is apparently greater. Its collaboration in this case, however, is limited to the most necessary measures.

Each party to the conflict shall be bound to prevent the export of cultural property   922
from a territory which it occupies during an international armed conflict (Art. I,
para. 1 Protocol CultPropConv). If, in spite of this prohibition, cultural property
should be transferred from the occupied territory into the territory of another
party, the latter shall be bound to place such property under its protection. This
shall be effected either immediately upon the importation of the property or fail-
ing this at a later date, at the request of the authorities of the occupied territory
concerned (Art. I, paras. 2 and 3 Protocol CultPropConv).

These obligations result from the Protocol, ratified separately but at the same time as the CultPropConv, and now in force.[31] It provides, *inter alia*, that:

a. Cultural property illegally exported into the territory of another state party shall be returned by it at the close of hostilities to the competent authorities of the country previously occupied (Art. I/3 of the Protocol).

b. The former occupying power shall pay an indemnity to those who hold such property in good faith (Art. I/4 of the Protocol);

c. Cultural property deposited by one state party with another state party shall be returned by the latter at the close of hostilities (Art. II/5 of the Protocol).

These undertakings may be excluded when the Protocol is ratified (Art. III/9 of the Protocol).

IV. TRANSPORT OF CULTURAL PROPERTY

Preliminary Remark: This Section brings together the rules for cultural property under special protection (Section 923) and for that under general protection (Sections 924–5). The model for Arts. 12–14 CultPropConv and Arts. 17 and 18 of the regulations were the provisions on medical transport in the GCs. Mainly at the beginning of an armed conflict such transport is not recommended by experts on the conservation of monuments and of civilian protection.

---

[31] See below, sub-chapter VII, para. 2.

923   **Authorized transport of exclusively cultural property may be placed under special protection. Any acts of hostility directed against such transport are prohibited (Art. 12 CultPropConv). It is also prohibited to seize such property in transport (Art. 14 CultPropConv).**

This rule is valid for transport both within one territory or into another. The latter must not be under the jurisdiction of another state party to the CultPropConv. Such transport needs to be authorized by the Commissioner General for cultural property. The RegEx contain rules on the procedure to obtain immunity and on other legal questions for transport within the territory (Art. 17), for export (Art. 18), and transport within an occupied territory (Art. 19). According to these rules the Commissioner General acts in agreement with the delegates of protecting powers, with the support of inspectors, for the organization of the transport. The latter accompany the property moved. The transport vehicles are marked with distinctive emblems (Section 931). The means of transport enjoy immunity from seizure according to Art. 14 CultPropConv. There are unlimited rights to inspect and search.

924   **Transport of cultural property which must, in urgent cases, be effected to safeguard specially valuable cultural property, with no opportunity to apply the procedure for granting special protection, shall be spared as far as possible. If possible, the adversary shall previously be notified of such transport (Art. 13 CultPropConv).**

This rule does not apply to transport abroad nor in cases where an application for immunity has been refused (Art. 13, para. 1 CultPropConv).

925   **Whenever cultural property is transferred to the territory of another state, that state shall deposit such property with the same care which it bestows upon its own cultural property (Art. 18 lit. a RegEx CultPropConv).**

The other state shall return the cultural property not later than six months after the end of the conflict (Art. 18 lit. b RegEx). It is protected against seizure (ibid. lit. c) if the respective state has accepted these conditions. Special rules regulate the transfer of cultural property within an occupied territory (ibid. Art. 19).

V. PERSONNEL ENGAGED IN THE PROTECTION OF CULTURAL PROPERTY

Preliminary Remark: It is necessary to distinguish between:

a. Personnel engaged by the state in which cultural property is situated:

—services or specialized personnel of the armed forces already organized in times of peace (Art. 7, para. 2 CultPropConv and Section 926);

Partsch

—representatives appointed after the beginning of an armed conflict for cultural property, eventually also for occupied territories (Art. 2(a) RegEx);

b. Personnel appointed in order to take care of the interests of opposing parties:

—protecting powers acting on their behalf (Art. 4, para. 1 RegEx);

—delegates appointed by protecting powers with the parties of the conflict (Art. 3 RegEx);

—experts employed by those delegates with the state in which cultural property is situated (Art. 7, para. 2 RegEx);

—personnel of neutral states fulfilling the functions of a protecting power (ibid. Art. 9).

c. Personnel engaged in international control:

—the Commissioner General for Cultural Property appointed by the Director General of UNESCO (Arts. 2–10 RegEx);

—inspectors of cultural property (Art. 7, para. 1 and Art. 9, second sentence RegEx);

—experts engaged by the Commissioner General (Art. 7, para. 2 RegEx).

Personnel engaged in the protection of cultural property shall be respected (Art.   926
15 CultPropConv).

1. According to the text of Art. 15, this rule covers only personnel engaged by the state where cultural property is situated. It is subject to a reservation concerning the interests of security. The principle of respect should, however, also be applied to personnel acting in the interests of opposing parties (above lit. b), or engaged in international control (above lit. c). The general reservation concerning security would not apply to personnel engaged in international control; their collaboration with the state where the cultural property is situated is assured by special provisions.

2. The personnel of the state in which cultural property is situated shall wear an armlet and carry a special identity card (Art. 17, para. 2 lit. (b) and (c) CultPropConv; Art 21, paras. 1 and 2 RegEx; see Section 930).

3. The Roerich Pact provides that personnel of the protected institutions shall be re. ected and protected in the same way as the institutions themselves. No provision is made for international personnel controlling the implementation of the Treaty.

Should such protective personnel fall into the hands of the adversary, they shall   927
be allowed to continue to carry out their duties (Art. 15 CultPropConv).

This rule only applies if the cultural property entrusted to them also falls into the hands of the adversary. If these personnel have the status of combatants, further

Partsch

activity for the protection of cultural property is compatible with the status of prisoner of war (see Sections 701–33).

928 **At the beginning of an armed conflict the Director-General of UNESCO shall nominate a Commissioner General for Cultural Property who, together with inspectors, monitors compliance with the Cultural Property Convention (Arts. 2–10 RegEx CultPropConv).**

1. An international list of all persons regarded as qualified to carry out such functions by the state parties is compiled by UNESCO in time of peace (Art. 1 RegEx). A candidate shall be choosen from this list by the party to which he will be accredited and by the protecting powers acting on behalf of opposing parties (see below Sections 1215–17). Should they fail to reach agreement within three weeks, the President of the International Court of Justice shall be requested to appoint a Commissioner General who is also approved by the party to whom he shall be accredited (Art. 4, para. 2 RegEx). If no protecting power is available, a neutral state may be asked to replace it for the appointment of the Commissioner General (Art. 9, sentence 1 RegEx).

2. The Commissioner General shall deal with all matters (see Art. 6 RegEx) in conjunction with the state to which he is accredited (Art. 6, paras. 1 and 3–5; Art. 7, para. 1 RegEx) or with the protecting powers of the opposing party (Art. 6, para. 1; Art. 7, para. 1 RegEx) which nominate delegates for this purpose. This is also necessary upon the appointment of inspectors for specific missions (Art. 7, para. 1 and Art. 9, sentence 2 RegEx). The expenses of the Commissioner General shall be met by the party to which he is accredited (Art. 10, sentence 1 RegEx).

3. During the conflict in the Middle East in 1967 Commissioners General were appointed. The complicated and clumsy system of control created some difficulties.[32] Since that time no further Commissioners General have apparently been appointed.

4. In case of a non-international conflict occurring in the territory of one of the states parties, each party to the conflict, including a resistance movement, shall be bound to apply at least those provisions concerning the respect of cultural property (Art. 19, para. 1 CultPropConv). This provision does not constitute the basis for the appointment of a Commissioner General accredited to a resistance movement. He has functions of 'control', resulting from Art. I of the RegEx.[33] This result is confirmed by Art. 19, para. 3 of the Convention. In such cases UNESCO may offer its services to the parties to the conflict. Such offer is not provided if a Commissioner General is appointed. In 1968 such an offer was made in the Biafran conflict. It was

---

[32] See Landolt, 58 *et seq.*, based on ample information from the Swiss Commissioner General accredited with Arab countries; see also de Breucker, 546.
[33] Toman, 324, agrees with reference to Art. 2 RegEx.

not accepted by Nigeria, which gave an assurance that it would itself ensure respect for the Convention.[34]

VI. DISTINCTIVE MARKING OF CULTURAL PROPERTY

Preliminary Remark: Marking makes sense in so far as the emblems can be seen in a modern armed conflict. This may be problematic not only if nuclear weapons are used but also of long-range conventional weapons. Notification of property under special protection to the adversary (above Sections 912, 917, 918) may be effective as a precautionary measure. If territories of a state party are under occupation marking of objects is of special importance.

The CultPropConv does not establish a duty to place distinctive emblems on items in peacetime, even for objects under special protection which must be marked in conflicts (Art. 10). Some states parties have nevertheless done so. Others prefer to furnish the emblems to the holders of protected objects who are to display them only in the case of an armed conflict. Early marking creates the danger that emblems are damaged or destroyed. In the critical situation of the outbreak of a conflict, however, the emblems may not be found, or the need to display them may be overlooked. The German *Länder* do not follow a uniform practice.[35]

The Roerich Pact (Art. 3) provides for identification of protected objects by the use of a distinctive flag (a red ring around three circles on a white background, see Appendix 1, para. 10). Such identification is, however, not mandatory.   **929**

Cultural property placed under general protection shall be identified by a blue and white shield with a point at its base (Arts. 6 and 16 CultPropConv). This distinctive emblem may also be displayed on the armlets and identity cards of personnel engaged in the protection of cultural property (Art. 17, para. 2 lit. c CultPropConv; Art. 21, para. 1 RegEx CultPropConv).

1. The distinctive emblem is shown in Appendix 1, para. 7.

2. The only obligation to mark objects arises during armed conflicts for cultural property under special protection (Art. 10). It is debatable which other cultural property may be marked. On one hand the term 'cultural property' is defined in Art. 1 CultPropConv with binding force. On the other hand, it is argued, this definition could not be regarded as strictly binding in view of the merely voluntary nature of the marking (see Art. 6). Also, other cultural objects (for instance those of minor importance) could be marked with a distinctive emblem. A further argument is that the competent authority must issue written authorization (Art. 17, para. 2).[36]

---

[34] Makagiansar, 36.
[35] At the beginning of the 1980s in Germany 610 historians, curators of monuments, and architects protested against the marking of cultural objects. They denied any effectivity in a modern war and objected to an official selection of treasures. Peace researchers even regarded this measure as a preparation for war.
[36] Thus Hönes, in *Die Öffentliche Verwaltung* 1988, 538–47.

Partsch

The first argument is not entirely unconvincing, though it is scarcely compatible with the goal of the Convention to formulate uniform rules for marking. States parties would have to apply such rules with a certain legitimate discretion.

The second argument is not convincing. Art. 17, para. 4 concerns the application of the Convention and does not authorize states parties to adopt alternative solutions. If the state exceeds the authorization of Art. 6 it assumes additional responsibilities. The competent authority, when issuing the authorization, has to explore whether it is ready to accept additional duties and able to fulfil the financial burdens.

930   **Protective personnel may not, without legitimate reason, be deprived either of their identity card or of their armlets (Art. 21, para. 4 RegEx CultPropConv).**

1. The term 'protective personnel' has to be regarded as extending to persons responsible for control (Art. 17, para. 2(b) CultPropConv). While they are *authorized* to wear armlets, they are *obliged* always to carry their identity cards. Both armlets and identity cards may be confiscated if used by non-authorized persons.

2. It is not expressly provided that identity cards must be issued in several languages. Their text in all four official languages of the Convention—English, French, Russian and Spanish—is reproduced in the Official Federal Gazette (BGBl. 1967 II, 1290–1).

931   **Cultural property (Art. 10 CultPropConv) and vehicles transporting it under special protection—as authorized and as emergency transport (Arts. 12 and 13 CultPropConv)—as well as improvised refuges (Art. 11 RegEx CultPropConv) shall display three depictions of the distinctive emblem (Art. 17, para. 1 CultPropConv). The emblem shall be arranged in a triangular form, with one shield below and two shields above (Art. 16, para. 2 CultPropConv).**

1. During an armed conflict the distinctive marking of cultural property under special protection is obligatory, including during internal emergency transport (Art. 13 CultPropConv) and on improvised refuges (Art. 11 RegEx). That the distinctive emblem is shown threefold indicates the high level of protection that these treasures enjoy. (See Appendix 1, para. 8.)

2. Arts. 16 and 17 CultPropConv and Art. 20 RegEx indicate further technical details concerning the form of the emblem, its placement, and visibility. The data required on the identity card are indicated in Art. 21 RegEx.

932   **During an international armed conflict, the use of the distinctive emblem for any other purpose than to protect cultural property is forbidden (Art. 17, para. 3 CultPropConv).**

Illegitimate use of the distinctive emblem is only prohibited during an armed conflict, not before. In prctice these emblems are displayed extensively for the propaganda of tourism. Such use should be prohibited, and it is regrettable that Art. 17, para. 3 fails to provide for this.

In general it shall be in the discretion of the competent authorities to select a   933
proper place for affixing the distinctive emblem to cultural property.

There are, however, rules for their placement on vehicles of transport (Art. 20, para. 2 RegEx), for indicating the perimeter or the entrance of centres containing monuments under special protection (lit. a), and for immovable cultural property.

Distinctive emblems placed on transport vehicles must be clearly visible in day-   934
light from the air as well as from the ground (Art. 20, para. 2 RegEx CultPropConv).

This is a further exception to Section 933.

In the case of immovable cultural property under special protection the emblem   935
shall be placed at the entrance of the building concerned (Art. 20, para. 2 lit. b
RegEx CultPropConv).

Another exception to Section 933.

In the case of a centre containing monuments under special protection emblems   936
shall be placed at regular intervals around the perimeter of the centre (Art. 20,
para. 2 lit. a RegEx CultPropConv).

Not only the treasures, but also their perimeters are protected (Art. 9 CultProp-Conv); sentence 2 provides for this.

VII. FINAL REMARKS

1. The CultPropConv suffers from a substantial omission. None of the violations are designated grave breaches justifying penal sanctions. It is only provided in Art. 28 that all necessary steps must be taken in national legislation to prosecute and to impose penal or disciplinary sanctions upon persons who commit or order relevant breaches.[37] If international treaties provide only for penalizing violations of such duties without precisely defining the elements of specific crimes, an excessive margin of discretion is left to the states parties.[38] To a certain extent this gap is filled by Art. 85, para. 4 lit. d AP I, which classifies as 'grave breaches' extensive destruction caused by attacks against clearly recognized historic monuments, works of art, or places of worship (as defined in Art. 53) if committed wilfully and under certain

---

[37] Nahlik, 105.
[38] An example is Art. 4 of the Convention for the Elimination of Racial Discrimination of 1965, see Partsch, *GYIL* 20 (1977), 119–38.

Partsch

additional conditions. An international duty to extradite offenders, as practised by the Nürnberg International Military Tribunal, has, however, not been included in this Protocol.[39]

2. It is likewise regarded as a weakness[40] that the provisions for the restitution of cultural items illegally exported from occupied territories during an armed conflict (see Section 922) are located not in the Convention itself but in a separate Protocol, requiring separate ratification. The intention was to take into account the different private law systems, particularly in respect of the acquisition of property in good faith. This Protocol has been in force for many years although it is not ratified by all the states parties to the Convention.

3. Art. 26, para. 2 CultPropConv provides that states parties should, at least every four years, report to the Director General of UNESCO on the measures taken in order to implement the Convention. Such reports serve as a basis for discussions during common sessions of these states on the realization of its principles (Art. 27). They would be even more useful if these reports were examined by experts beforehand, as has been done for many years in the Committee on Conventions and Recommendations of the Executive Council of UNESCO for reports on the implementation of the Convention on discrimination in education, and also in organs of the International Labour Organization and the United Nations in the field of human rights. This has, however, not been implemented, although it was requested by a conference of experts in October 1983 through the rapporteur Mr. Toman from Geneva, and despite the fact that the majority of those present agreed. Here too a gap exists in the implementation of this important Convention.[41]

---

[39] See Art. 88 AP I which refers to the municipal law of extradition; Partsch in Bothe/Partsch/Solf, 518 ff.; 531 ff.; Nahlik, *Deficiencies*, 105 ff. expresses regret; Bosly, IIDU Symposium Florence (note 1), 82, regards Art. 85 AP I as generally strengthening the penal protection.

[40] Nahlik, *Deficiencies*, 105 ff.

[41] This was again discussed at the experts' meeting in The Hague in July 1993 (see final report, *HuV-I* 4/1993, 233).

Partsch

10

The Law of Armed Conflict at Sea

Preliminary Remarks. Naval warfare has never been limited to the military subjugation of the enemy. Its overall aim is sea denial and sea control. Methods necessary for sea control do not merely affect the parties to an international armed conflict but also states which are neutral or states not parties to the conflict. If the weakening of the enemy's economy is considered a legitimate goal, the law would be incomplete if it lacked rules relating to measures taken against neutral merchant shipping. Such rules are necessary since a state party to the conflict could otherwise shift its sea trade to third states' merchant shipping, and the adversary would be unable to prevent the supply of arms and war material to its opponent. However, measures against neutral merchant shipping are not dealt with in the present chapter, which is restricted to the legal relationship between the parties to an armed conflict at sea. The rules governing the relationship between belligerents and states not parties to the conflict or their vessels are contained in Chapter 11 on the law of neutrality. However, in the present chapter the laws of neutrality cannot be ignored completely. They are relevant for the delimitation of areas of naval warfare and for the determination of the enemy character of vessels.

I. GENERAL

1. Definitions

**'Ship' means manned surface and submarine vessels. 'Aircraft' means all manned   1001
means of transport that are or can be used in the air above sea or land.**

The qualification that vessels must be manned is meant to exclude from the definition surface and submarine vehicles that have no personnel on board and are remotely controlled, such as 'drones' employed in mine countermeasures. Similar considerations are valid for aircraft. Vessels exclusively employed in inland navigation are not 'ships' within the meaning of this definition. They are governed not by the rules of naval warfare but by those of land warfare. However, if such vessels are seaworthy and employed, e.g., in coastal navigation they are to be considered 'ships' in the sense of Section 1001.

Heintschel von Heinegg

1002 'Warships' are ships belonging to the (naval) armed forces of a state and bearing the external marks distinguishing warships of its nationality, under the command of an officer duly commissioned by the government and whose name appears in the appropriate service list or its equivalent, and manned by a crew which is under regular armed forces discipline. Warships need not be armed.

1. *Warships.* The definition of these[1] has its legal basis in Art. 29 of the 1982 United Nations Convention on the Law of the Sea.[2] It differs from the definition in Art. 8, para. 2 of the 1958 Convention on the High Seas[3] in that it also covers ships not belonging to the naval forces of a state. A further difference is that the name of the commanding officer need not necessarily appear in the Navy List. While it is generally agreed that the 1958 definition is customary in character it is open to doubt whether this is also true as regards the 1982 definition.[4] Still, the latter is here taken as the legal basis because it better meets the practical requirements of naval armed forces who then need not distinguish between warships operated by the enemy's naval forces and those belonging to other units. According to the present definition a vessel need not be armed in order to qualify as a warship. Hence tenders, troop transporters, and supply ships are covered as soon as they meet the requirements.[5] Merchant vessels converted into warships in accordance with the 1907 Hague Convention No. VII are also covered.[6]

2. *Submarines.* It follows from the inclusion of submarine vessels in Section 1001 that submarines are warships in the sense of Section 1002. Although especially Great Britain, at the beginning of the twentieth century,[7] endeavoured to outlaw submarines, today they are generally considered legitimate means of naval warfare.

1003 'Government ships' are ships owned or operated by a state and used only in governmental non-commercial service (e.g. customs and police vessels, state yachts).

1. *Government ships.* There is at present no generally accepted definition of government ships or of state ships. However, the elements contained in Section 1003 should not give rise to objections.[8] In times of peace, the vessels covered by this definition, e.g. customs and police vessels or state yachts, enjoy complete immunity from the jurisdiction of any state other than the flag state. This follows from Art. 9 HSC 1958. They must, however, be employed in public or government service. It

---

[1] See Geck, *EPIL* 4, 346 ff. The same definition is used in the *San Remo Manual*, para. 13(g).
[2] Signed on 10 Dec. 1982, UN Doc. A/CONF.62/122 (hereinafter: UNCLOS). On 16 Nov. 1993 Guyana, as the sixtieth state, ratified the Convention, which according to Art. 308, para. 1 entered into force on 16 Nov. 1994.
[3] Signed on 29 Apr. 1958, UN Doc. A/CONF.13/L.53 (hereinafter: HSC 1958). The Federal Republic of Germany is a party to HSC 1958 (BGBl. 1972 II, 1089). Since the Federal Republic will accede to UNCLOS the HSC 1958 will, however, become obsolete, at least in so far as states parties to UNCLOS are concerned.
[4] Even though UNCLOS entered into force on 16 Nov. 1994, at present only sixty states are bound by it.
[5] Cf. Colombos, paras. 530 ff.; O'Connell, Vol. II, 1106 ff.   [6] See Section 1005.
[7] Cf. Colombos, paras. 531 ff.; O'Connell, Vol. II, 1131 ff.; Anderson, *USNIP* Vol. 53 (Jan. 1927), 50 ff.
[8] See *inter alia* Rodriguez Iglesias, *EPIL* 11, 320 ff.

Heintschel von Heinegg

goes without saying that in times of armed conflict, belligerent government ships are not immune or specially protected against measures by the enemy.

2. *Government ships operated for commercial purposes.* It follows from Section 1003, as well as from the Brussels Convention on the Unification of Rules on the Determination of the Immunity of Government Ships of 10 April 1926,[9] that government ships operated for commercial purposes are to be treated in the same manner as privately owned merchant vessels and their cargoes.[10]

'Merchant vessels' are ships other than warships as defined in Section 1002 and   1004
used exclusively for commercial or fishery purposes or profit passenger transport
(whether private or owned or controlled by the state) or private ships of non-com-
mercial character (e.g. yachts). The mere fact that a merchant vessel is armed does
not change its legal status, unless it fulfils the conditions described in Section
1025.

1. *Merchant vessels.* In international law there exists no generally accepted definition of 'merchant vessel'. This term can, however, be defined negatively, i.e. in contradistinction to other vessels. In order for a vessel to qualify as a merchant vessel it needs to be exclusively employed for commercial or fishery purposes or transporting passengers for profit.[11] The attribute 'commercial' means that the use of such vessels has to be aimed at obtaining profits.[12] Hence, government ships operated for commercial purposes, and deep-sea and coastal fishing vessels and passenger liners, are merchant vessels within the meaning of Section 1004. In this context it is, however, important to emphasize that vessels used exclusively for fishing along the coast, small boats employed in local trade, and passenger liners enjoy protected status under the law of naval warfare.[13] Also covered by the present definition are seagoing private vessels not used for commercial purposes, e.g. yachts and pleasure boats.

2. *Arming.* Traditionally, scholars differentiated between offensively and defensively armed merchant vessels, but were unable to agree on the relevant criteria.[14] Altogether, there never existed a generally accepted prohibition of arming merchant vessels.[15] Still, according to the US *Manual* and the Canadian *Draft Manual* merchant vessels qualify as legitimate military objectives as soon as they are armed.[16] In view of the various difficulties involved, the German Manual has taken a different approach. Hence, it is stressed in the last sentence that the mere

---

[9] This Convention never entered into force but, on 24 May 1934, was amended by an additional protocol. Cf. Beckert/Breuer, para. 428.

[10] Rodriguez Iglesias, *EPIL* 11, 320 ff.

[11] Cf. Lagoni, *EPIL* 11, 228 ff. See also *San Remo Manual*, para. 13(i) defining merchant vessel as 'a vessel, other than a warship, an auxiliary vessel, or a State vessel such as a customs or police vessel, that is engaged in commercial or private service'.

[12] A similar definition of 'merchant vessel' is used in the Canadian *Draft Manual*, para. 702.

[13] See Section 1034 and the accompanying commentary.

[14] Cf. Zemanek, *EPIL* 3, 258 ff.; Knackstedt, *Marine Rundschau* 56 (1959), 69 ff.

[15] Colombos, para. 548.   [16] *NWP 9*, para. 8.2.2.2; Canadian *Draft Manual*, para. 716 (5).

Heintschel von Heinegg

fact that a merchant vessel is armed does not change its legal status. It may only be attacked if it meets the conditions of the definition of 'military objectives' in Section 1025.

1005 **Merchant ships converted into warships in accordance with the VIIth Hague Convention of 1907, thus fulfilling the conditions of the definition of warships described in Section 1002, have the same status as warships. The state which converts a merchant ship into a warship has to notify this as soon as possible on its list of warships.**

The conversion of merchant vessels into warships is governed by the rules laid down in the 1907 Hague Convention VII.[17] The commanding officer must be duly commissioned by the government and his name must appear in the Navy List (Art. 3). The crew must be under regular armed forces' discipline (Art. 4). The conversion must as soon as possible be notified on the list of warships (Art. 5). Hence, all those conditions must be fulfilled that are contained in the definition of warships proper. However, the rules of Hague Convention VII leave a number of unresolved problems. On one hand, it is silent on the question of whether a merchant vessel may be converted only in the flag state's territorial waters or also on the high seas. On the other hand, it lacks rules on the reconversion of warships to merchant vessels. In the legal literature those questions are hotly disputed.[18] In the absence of any express prohibitions, conversion on the high seas as well as reconversion should be considered permissible.[19]

1006 **'Support ships' are ships with civilian crew owned or operated by the government—i.e. government ships as defined in Section 1003—and which perform support services for the naval forces without being warships.**

The domestic legislation of the majority of western states provides for the incorporation of their merchant fleets into the naval armed forces in times of armed conflict or a state of emergency.[20] It is sometimes difficult to distinguish such support ships from converted merchant vessels.[21] For example, during the Falklands/ Malvinas conflict Great Britain, in accordance with the Requisitioning of Ships Order 1982[22] requisitioned a number of merchant vessels. Their masters and crews were subject to armed forces' discipline and to instructions by the Royal Navy. Thus, it was open to doubt whether those ships were converted merchant vessels, i.e. warships proper, or civilian.[23] In any event, however, even if supply ships do not

---

[17] For an overview see Venturini, *Commentary*, 120 ff.

[18] See, *inter alia*, Schramm, *Marine Rundschau* 22 (1911), 1255 ff., 1539 ff.

[19] See only Venturini, *Commentary*, 122 ff.

[20] Note, however, that according to s. 5, para. 2 no. 4 of the Federal Law on Performances (*Bundesleistungsgesetz*) sea-going and inland merchant vessels and maritime fishing vessels may not be required so to act.

[21] Cf. Helm, *Marine Rundschau* 54 (1957), 152 ff.

[22] Order in Council of 4 April 1982, reprinted in Villar, 8.

[23] Lagoni, *Gladisch*, 66.   [24] See Section 1025.

qualify as warships because of their function (supplying naval forces) they meet the requirements of the definition of military objectives and may be attacked without prior warning.[24]

'Military aircraft' are all aircraft belonging to the armed forces of a state and bearing external marks distinguishing such aircraft of their nationality. The commanding soldier must be a member of the armed forces, and the crew must be subject to military discipline. Military aircraft need not be armed.   1007

As regards the details of this definition reference is made to the commentary on Section 1002.[25] Military aircraft are state or government aircraft within the meaning of Section 1008.

'State aircraft' are all aircraft belonging to or used by the state and serving exclusively state functions (e.g. in customs or police service).   1008

Although there exists no generally accepted definition of state or government aircraft in international law[26] it is agreed that aircraft employed in customs and police services as well as those transporting heads of state are to be considered as state or government aircraft.[27]

'Civilian aircraft' are all aircraft other than military aircraft as described in Section 1007 and state aircraft as described in Section 1008, serving the exclusively civilian transport of passengers or cargo.   1009

Again, there is no definition of civilian aircraft in international law. Hence, they have to be distinguished negatively from military and other government aircraft.[28]

2. Scope of Application

The scope of application of the law of armed conflict at sea, i.e. the area in which acts of naval warfare within the meaning of Section 1014 may be performed, comprises: 1010

—the territory of the parties to the conflict accessible to naval forces,

—inland waters, archipelagic waters, and territorial sea of the parties to the conflict,

—the high seas including exclusive economic zones (except the areas mentioned in Section 219) and

—the airspace over these land and sea areas.

[25] A similar definition of military aircraft is given in the Canadian *Draft Manual*, para. 702(4); and in the *San Remo Manual*, para. 13(j).
[26] See, however, Art. 3(b) of the 1944 Chicago Convention on Civil Aviation (15 *UNTS* 295; BGBl. 1956 II, 411 ff.).
[27] Fischer, in Ipsen, s. 51, para. 29.
[28] See also the Canadian *Draft Manual*, para. 702(2); *San Remo Manual*, para. 13(l); Fischer, in Ipsen, s. 51, para. 29.

Heintschel von Heinegg

1. *Preliminary Remarks.* In contrast to earlier times, it is now difficult to determine the scope of application of the law of naval warfare, or the areas of naval warfare. The Third United Nations Conference on the Law of the Sea has progressively developed the law and contributed to the emergence of multiple differing regimes, some of which are now customary in character. Problems arise not so much in relation to the sea areas of the belligerents as to those sea areas which traditionally belonged to the high seas (and thus to the area of naval warfare) and in which states not parties to the conflict now enjoy certain sovereign rights. While the laws of neutrality are not dealt with in detail in the present chapter it is necessary to describe the principles of the international law of the sea governing neutral coastal states' rights in order to explain the delimitation of areas of naval warfare.[29]

2. *Neutral territory and neutral territorial waters.* The land territory, inland waters, archipelagic waters, and the territorial sea of states neutral or not parties to the conflict are, in principle, excluded from the area of naval warfare. Belligerents are obliged to respect the inviolability of these areas. Special rules apply to neutral states' rights in their archipelagic waters and in international straits. These matters are, however, dealt with in Chapter 11. With regard to exclusive economic zones and continental shelves of neutral states see Sections 1012 and 1013 and the accompanying commentaries. With regard to other sea areas exempt from acts of naval warfare, see Section 219. It should be noted in this context that the Montreux Convention of 20 July 1936 provides special restrictions for the Dardanelles in times of armed conflict.[30]

1011 'Internal waters' are waters on the landward side of the baseline of the territorial sea. 'Archipelagic' waters are waters on the landward side of archipelagic baselines. The 'territorial sea' comprises the waters on the seaward side of the baseline or archipelagic baseline in a breadth not exceeding twelve nautical miles. The so-called 'contiguous zone' does not belong to the territorial sea.

1. *Baselines.* In order to be legally effective baselines must be drawn in accordance with Arts. 3 ff. of the Geneva Convention on the Territorial Sea and the Contiguous Zone of 29 April 1958 (hereinafter: TSC 1958) and Arts. 5 ff. UNCLOS. According to these provisions, which are customary in character, the normal baseline is the low-tide line along the coast. In localities where the coastline is deeply indented and cut into, or if there is a fringe of islands along the coast in its immediate vicinity, the method of straight baselines joining appropriate points may be employed in drawing the baseline. Straight baselines may also be drawn in mouths of rivers and to and from low-tide elevations if lighthouses or similar installations have been built on them which are permanently above sea level. The drawing of straight baselines must not depart to any appreciable extent from the general direction of the coast,

---

[29] For an overview see O'Connell, Vols. I and II. In the context of naval warfare see Rauch, *Protocol Additional*, 31 ff.; Robertson, *Theatre of Operations*, in Heintschel v. Heinegg (Ed.), Ottawa, 1 ff.; *San Remo Manual*, paras. 10, 14 ff.

[30] Text in *AJIL* Vol. 31 (1937), Suppl., 1–18; see also Vignes, *Commentary*, 468–82.

and the areas lying within the lines must be sufficiently closely linked to the land to be subject to the regime of internal waters.[31]

2. *Internal waters.* Waters on the landward side of the baselines form part of the internal waters of a state.[32] Also included are mouths of rivers where a straight baseline is drawn across the mouth between points in the low-water line of the river's banks.[33] Bays are internal waters only if they belong to a single state and if further qualifications are met.[34] According to UNCLOS a bay is a well-marked indentation whose penetration is in such proportion to the width of its mouth as to contain land-locked waters and constitute more than a mere curvature of the coast. An indentation shall not, however, be regarded as a bay unless its area is as large as, or larger than, that of the semi-circle whose diameter is a line drawn across the mouth of that indentation. If the distance between the low-water marks of the natural entrance points of a bay does not exceed twenty-four nautical miles, a closing line may be drawn between these two low-water marks, and the waters enclosed thereby shall be considered as internal waters. From this it follows that, for example, the Gulf of Sirte is not a bay in the legal sense. Nor can it—despite Libya's assertions—be considered an 'historic' bay.[35] Outermost permanent harbour works which form an integral part of the harbour system are regarded as forming part of the coast. Off-shore installations and artificial islands shall not, however, be considered as permanent harbour works.[36]

3. *Territorial sea.* The breadth of territorial seas was the subject of a number of international conferences, all of which failed to agree upon a concrete rule. Now, according to Art. 3 UNCLOS, every state has the right to establish the breadth of its territorial sea up to a limit not exceeding twelve nautical miles. Some states claim a territorial sea of less than 12 nautical miles (e.g. the Federal Republic of Germany claims—in most parts of the North Sea—a three-mile territorial sea), others claim a territorial sea of up to 200 nautical miles (e.g. some South American states). Still, in view of more than 110 states claiming a territorial sea of twelve nautical miles [37] the rule laid down in Art. 3 UNCLOS can be considered as declaratory of a corresponding rule of customary international law.[38] Roadsteads which are normally used for the loading, unloading, and anchoring of ships, and which would otherwise be situated wholly or partly outside the outer limit of the territorial sea, are included in

---

[31] Cf. O'Connell, Vol. I, 171 ff.; Gloria, in Ipsen, s. 47 paras. 2 *et seq.* For allegedly excessive baseline claims see US Dept. of State, Limits in the Seas No. 112, *United States Responses to Excessive National Maritime Claims*, 17 ff. (Washington DC, 9 Mar. 1992).

[32] Art. 5 TSC 1958; Art. 8 UNCLOS. See also Gloria, in Ipsen, s. 47, paras. 3 ff.

[33] Art. 9 UNCLOS.

[34] Art. 7 TSC 1958; Art. 10 UNCLOS. Note, however, that the following rules do not apply to so-called 'historic' bays.

[35] For a general overview see Bouchez, *EPIL* 11, 45 ff.; O'Connell, Vol. I, 353 ff., 389 ff. With regard to the Gulf of Sirte see Francioni, *Ital YBIL* 5 (1980/81), 85 ff., and *Syracuse Journal of International Law & Commmerce* 11 (1984), 311 ff.

[36] Art. 8 TSC 1958; Art. 11 UNCLOS.

[37] See the references in United Nations, *Law of the Sea Bulletin* No. 15 (May 1990), 39; United Nations, *National Claims to Maritime Jurisdiction*, New York 1992.

[38] Gloria, in Ipsen, s. 48, paras. 3 ff.; O'Connell, Vol. I, 165 ff.

Heintschel von Heinegg

the territorial sea.[39] Within the territorial sea ships of all states enjoy rights of peaceful passage.[40]

4. *The contiguous zone* is the sea area bordering the territorial sea. It may not extend beyond twenty-four nautical miles from the baselines from which the territorial sea is measured. The sovereignty of the coastal state does not extend to the contiguous zone. Rather, the coastal state's rights are limited to the control necessary to prevent infringement of its customs, fiscal, immigration, or health and safety laws and regulations within its territory or territorial sea, and to punish infringements of such laws and regulations committed within its territory or territorial sea.[41]

5. *Archipelagic waters.*[42] An 'archipelagic state' is a state comprised entirely of one or more archipelagos and may include other islands. An 'archipelago' is a group of islands, including parts of islands, interconnecting waters, and other natural features which are so closely interrelated that such islands, waters, and other natural features form an intrinsic geographical, economic, and political entity, or which historically have been regarded as such. An archipelagic state may draw straight archipelagic baselines joining the outermost points of the outermost islands and drying reefs of the archipelago provided that within such baselines are included the main islands and an area in which the ratio of the area of the water to the area of the land, including atolls, is between 1 : 1 and 9 : 1. Only a few countries, such as the Philippines and Indonesia, qualify as archipelagic states. Within such archipelagic waters the archipelagic state exercises full sovereignty. Third states enjoy the right of peaceful passage. The right of peaceful passage may only be suspended temporarily in specified areas if such suspension is essential for the security of the archipelagic state. Furthermore, all states enjoy the right of archipelagic sea lanes passage in sea- and air-routes designated by the archipelagic state.[43]

1012   Exclusive economic zones may not be extended more than 200 nautical miles from the baselines which are relevant for the landward limitation of the territorial sea. While coastal states and archipelagic states exercise full sovereignty within their internal waters, archipelagic waters, and territorial sea, they have only certain sovereign rights in exclusive economic zones. The latter do not belong to the high seas, but third states also enjoy freedom of navigation and overflight and certain other freedoms within them. Hence as a matter of principle for naval warfare

---

[39] Art. 9 TSC 1958; Art. 12 UNCLOS.

[40] As regards the right of peaceful passage in general, see Arts. 17 ff. UNCLOS; O'Connell, Vol. II, 867 ff., 959 ff. In times of armed conflict the right of passage of belligerent warships and prizes through a neutral territorial sea is restricted to 24 hours. It may even, on a non-discriminatory basis, be restricted or suspended. With regard to the right of peaceful passage in cases where a belligerents mines its territorial sea, see Section 1041 and accompanying para. 2.

[41] Art. 24 TSC 1958; Art. 33 UNCLOS. For a general overview see Gloria, in Ipsen, s. 48 paras. 32 ff.

[42] For the exclusion of neutral archipelagic waters from the area of naval warfare see *San Remo Manual*, paras. 14 ff. Special rules apply where third states enjoy the right of archipelagic sea passage. See *ibid.*, paras. 23 ff.

[43] UNCLOS Arts. 46 ff. See also O'Connell, Vol. I, 237 ff.; Rajan, *GYIL* 1986, 137 ff.

purposes, the exclusive economic zones of neutral or non-belligerent states belong to the high seas. The rights of coastal and archipelagic states must, however, be taken into due consideration.

1. *Legal basis of the exclusive economic zone.* The right to proclaim an exclusive economic zone (EEZ) was for the first time laid down in Articles 55 ff. UNCLOS. Although that Treaty entered into force only on 16 November 1994, at the time of writing eighty-six states have already proclaimed such a zone with a breadth of 200 nautical miles.[44] Despite some doubts with regard to the customary character of the right to proclaim an EEZ there have so far been no significant protests against such proclamations. Hence, it follows that it has at least become a customary right in the making.[45]

2. *Rights in the EEZ.* In the EEZ the coastal state has sovereign rights to explore and exploit, conserve and manage the natural resources, whether living or non-living, of the waters superjacent to the sea bed and of the sea bed, and its subsoil, and to undertake other activities for the economic exploitation and exploration of the zone, such as the production of energy from the water, currents and wind. For these purposes the coastal state may establish and use artificial islands, installations, and structures.[46]

3. *Neutral EEZ.* The EEZ of states not parties to the conflict is not excluded from areas of naval warfare *per se*. However, it cannot be ignored that those states enjoy certain sovereign and exclusive rights in their economic zones. Hence, even though the belligerents are not barred from taking naval warfare measures within a neutral EEZ they are obliged to pay due regard to the coastal state's sovereign rights. Accordingly, if hostile actions are conducted within the exclusive economic zone of a neutral state, belligerent states shall, in particular, have due regard for artificial islands, installations, structures, and safety zones established by the coastal state.[47] The duty to pay due regard to the coastal states' rights in their EEZs is, however, subject to considerations of military necessity.

The 'high seas' comprise all parts of the sea which do not belong to the exclusive   1013 economic zone, the territorial sea, the internal waters, or archipelagic waters. The high seas also comprise the continental shelf of neutral or non-belligerent states.

---

[44] See the references in United Nations, *National Legislation on the Exclusive Economic Zone*, New York 1993.

[45] Attard; Wolfrum, *NYIL* 1987, 121 ff. See also O'Connell, Vol. I, 553 ff.

[46] Art. 56 UNCLOS. For a general overview see Gloria, in Ipsen, s. 50; O'Connell, Vol. I, 553 ff.

[47] For a provision to the same effect see para. 34 of the *San Remo Manual*. The *San Remo Manual*, in para. 35, provides for the laying of mines in a neutral EEZ: 'If a belligerent considers it necessary to lay mines in the exclusive economic zone . . . of a neutral state, the belligerent shall notify that state, and shall ensure, *inter alia*, that the size of the minefield and the type of mines used do not endanger artificial islands, installations, and structures, nor interfere with access thereto, and shall avoid so far as practicable interference with the exploration or exploitation of the zone by the neutral state. Due regard shall also be given to the protection of the marine environment.'

Heintschel von Heinegg

The rights of coastal and archipelagic states must, however, be taken into due consideration.

1. *Belligerent rights on the high seas.* Traditionally the high seas belong to the areas of naval warfare.[48] In view of the practice of the parties to the Israeli–Egyptian, Korean, and Vietnam conflicts some international lawyers endeavoured to restrict the areas of naval warfare to the territorial waters of the belligerents.[49] They argued that under the UN Charter the freedoms of the high seas, especially the freedom of navigation and overflight of states not parties to the conflict, may not be interfered with by states that were either unwilling or unable to refrain from the use of armed force. This position has never been generally shared by the international community. The freedom of the high seas has always been subject to the law of naval warfare. Hence, it is not seriously disputed that on the high seas belligerents are entitled to visit and search neutral merchant vessels or to attack enemy forces.[50] Of course, in the above-mentioned conflicts the belligerents restricted their measures to their respective territorial waters. This practice, however, does not meet the qualifications required for a rule of customary law to come into being ('widespread', 'uniform', 'duration'). Moreover, it is not reflective of an *opinio juris* to the effect that those states felt obliged to refrain from committing acts of naval warfare on the high seas. Rather, those abstentions were merely deliberate self-limitations due to the special circumstances ruling at those times.[51] This is the sole possible understanding. Nothing else follows from the fact that according to Art. 136 UNCLOS the so-called 'Area', i.e. the sea bed and ocean floor and subsoil thereof beyond the limits of national jurisdiction,[52] and its resources are 'the common heritage of mankind'. The resulting rights and duties of states do not apply to the water column or the air space above the 'area'.[53] However, hostile actions on the high seas shall be conducted with due regard for the exercise by neutral states of rights of exploration and exploitation of the natural resources of the sea bed, the ocean floor, and the subsoil thereof.[54] Finally, the reservation of the high seas for peaceful purposes in Arts. 88 and 301 UNCLOS is also without prejudice to the legality of acts of naval warfare. These provisions merely repeat the fundamental prohibition of the threat or use of force in Art. 2(4) UN Charter.

2. *The continental shelf* of a coastal state comprises the sea bed and the subsoil of the submarine areas that extend beyond its territorial sea; it does not comprise the superjacent water column.[55] According to the 1958 Geneva provisions the term 'continental shelf' is used as referring to the sea bed and subsoil of the submarine areas adjacent to the coast but outside the area of the territorial sea, to a depth of 200 metres or, beyond that limit, to where the depth of the superjacent waters

---

[48] See, *inter alia*, Colombos, para. 558.   [49] O'Connell, *BYIL* 1970, 28 *et seq.*
[50] With regard to state practice since the end of World War II see Ottmüller, 47 ff.
[51] Fenrick, *CYIL* XXIV (1986), 115.   [52] Art. 1, para.1(1) UNCLOS.
[53] Rauch, *The Protocol Additional*, 53 ff.   [54] To the same effect: *San Remo Manual*, para. 36.
[55] Geneva Convention on the Continental Shelf of 29 April 1958 (hereinafter: CSC 1958); Arts. 76 ff., UNCLOS. See also O'Connell, Vol. I, 467 ff.; Gloria, in Ipsen, s. 50 paras. 12 ff.

Heintschel von Heinegg

admits of the exploitation of the natural resources of the said areas.[56] According to UNCLOS the continental shelf comprises the said submarine areas throughout the natural prolongation of the land territory to the outer edge of the continental margin, or to a distance of 200 nautical miles where the outer edge of the continental margin does not extend up to that distance.[57] The coastal state exercises exclusive sovereign rights over the continental shelf for the purpose of exploring it and exploiting its natural resources. Hence, the same considerations apply here as with regard to neutral EEZs. Belligerents are obliged to pay due regard to those rights, subject to military necessity.

3. Acts of Naval Warfare, Competences, and Principles

a) Acts of Naval Warfare, Competences

Acts of naval warfare within the meaning of this chapter are the use of weapons   1014
including the (special) methods of naval warfare and the following measures of
economic warfare at sea:

— visiting and searching,

— ordering to take a specific course,

— capture of ships,

— requisitioning of cargo,

— bringing in,

— confiscation, and

— blockade.

1. *Preliminary Remarks.* This enumeration of acts of naval warfare is rather general and far from exhaustive. It is meant to supplement the provisions of Sections 1015 and 1016 on competences. Hence, for the present purposes it is sufficient to give a short overview of the different acts of naval warfare and merely to refer to the use of weapons generally. Special legal aspects relating to the use of certain methods of naval warfare are dealt with in Sections 1039 ff.[58] Further legal restrictions on the use of weapons follow from the principles laid down in Sections 1017 ff. and 1021 ff. As regards the so-called 'prize measures' the following should be taken into consideration: prize measures and measures of economic warfare at sea are respectively aimed at cutting off the enemy's supplies by sea and rendering impossible, or at least difficult, further enemy war efforts.[59] As long as these measures affect

---

[56] Art. 1(a) CSC 1958.

[57] Art. 76. para. 1 UNCLOS. See also Heintschel v. Heinegg, *Ägäis-Konflikt*, 135 ff. According to Art. 76, paras. 5 and 6 UNCLOS, under certain conditions the breadth of the continental shelf may extend to 350 nautical miles.

[58] Those methods and means comprise blockades even though a blockade is generally considered a measure of economic warfare at sea.

[59] With respect to economic warfare at sea see Tucker, 74 ff.; Colombos, paras. 635 ff.; Johnson, *EPIL* 4, 154 ff.; Rabus, *EPIL* 3, 68 ff.; Scheuner, *WVR* I, 199 ff., and *WVR* II, 794 ff.; Heintschel v. Heinegg, *CYIL* 29 (1991), 292 ff.

Heintschel von Heinegg

enemy merchant vessels and their cargoes the mentioning of prize measures in the present chapter seems to be reasonable. However, legal problems only arise with regard to specially protected vehicles and goods. Of far more practical relevance are, of course, prize measures taken against neutral merchant vessels and their cargoes. Visit, search, diversion, and capture of neutral vessels and goods are dealt with in Chapter 11. Accordingly the commentaries on the following Sections are restricted to those rules that apply to the relationship between the parties to the conflict (including their respective merchant shipping). It may be added, however, that the competences dealt with in Sections 1015 and 1016 are also valid if prize measures are taken against neutral merchant vessels and their cargoes.

2. *Prize measures in detail.* National implementation of international law rules on prize measures is effected in so-called Prize Rules or Prize Ordinances. As regards the Federal Republic of Germany one may argue that the Prize Ordinance of 28 August 1939[60] is of continuing validity as pre-constitution law. In view of the many difficulties and uncertainties involved, the Federal Ministry of Defence issued Standing Order No. 10 which was to remain in force until a formal revision of the law. Even though Standing Order No. 10 has now been superseded by the present Manual it is worthwhile referring to the following definitions on prize measures given therein.[61]

—Visit comprises the procedure of ordering a vessel to stop and of examining the ship's papers.[62]

—Search means the interrogation of a ship's master, its crew, and its passengers as well as the examination of a ship and its cargo.[63]

—Diversion is an order to take a specific course in order to be visited and searched in an appropriate area or port.[64]

—Capture is exercised by sending a prize crew on board another vessel and assuming command over the ship.[65]

—Seizure of cargo is effected by the capture of a vessel. However, cargo may be seized independently, i.e. without capture of the vessel.

—Bringing in means to escort a vessel to a port of the captor or of an ally. This includes ports under the captor's or its allies' power.

—Confiscation of captured vessels is effected by a prize court decision. With the prize court's decision ownership of the vessel and its equipment passes to the captor state.

1015 **The following vessels and units are competent to perform acts of naval warfare:**
—warships and other units of naval forces,

—military aircraft, and

—units of land and air forces.

---

[60] RGBl. 1939 I, 1585.
[62] See also Rojahn, *EPIL* 4, 224 ff.
[64] See also Scheuner, *WVR* II, 385; Wolf, *EPIL* 4, 223 ff.
[65] See also Phillips, in *USNIP* 91 (Apr. 1965), 60 ff.

[61] Blockade is dealt with in Sections 1051 ff.
[63] Ibid.

Section 1015 clarifies that only lawful 'combatants' are allowed to take the measures enumerated in Section 1014. It is self-evident that methods of naval warfare (including the use of weapons) may only be employed by units under military command and subject to military discipline. Section 1015 is of particular importance with regard to measures of economic warfare at sea. According to the 1856 Declaration of Paris[66] and customary international law 'privateering is, and remains, abolished'. Hence, such measures may be ordered by commanders of warships and of military aircraft as well as by other units of armed forces. They may also be ordered and carried out by other departments if specially authorized. However, in view of the abolition of privateering, private individuals or entities are never authorized to take prize measures at sea.

The following vessels and persons may not perform acts of naval warfare: 1016

—**state ships other than warships, even when carrying out support services for the naval forces,**

—**state aircraft other than military aircraft,**

—**merchant ships,**

—**fishing boats and other civil ships,**

—**civil aircraft, and**

—**prize crews of captured ships.**

The crews of all ships and aircraft are, however, entitled to defend themselves against attacks by enemy forces.

Section 1016 re-emphasizes the rule laid down in Section 1015 that the categories of persons entitled to take measures of naval warfare are limited. In view of the characteristics of naval warfare it is important to refer expressly to those units that, on one hand, are particularly affected but, on the other hand, are not allowed to take such measures. Of course Section 1016 is without prejudice to the right to convert merchant vessels into warships.[67] In this context it should be stressed that according to Section 1025 merchant vessels visiting, searching, or attacking enemy merchant vessels are legitimate military objectives, and thus liable to attack on sight, without prior warning. To a certain extent, therefore, Section 1025 formulates the consequences resulting from a breach of Section 1016. Although the vessels and aircraft enumerated here are not entitled to take measures of naval warfare, they may defend themselves against enemy attacks.[68] This is a well-founded principle of customary international law. However, such self-defence measures may legitimately be countered by the enemy. If, e.g., a merchant vessel resists capture the enemy warship may either break that resistance by force or, if the resisting merchant vessel qualifies as a legitimate military objective, it may even be attacked and sunk.

---

[66] *Declaration Respecting Maritime Law*, Paris, 16 Apr. 1856. For a general overview see Fujita, *Commentary*, 68.

[67] Colombos, paras. 536 ff.   [68] O'Connell, Vol. II, 1108; Colombos, para. 553.

b) Principles of Naval Warfare

1017 Without prejudice to other conditions described in this chapter the following principles shall be observed in all acts of naval warfare, in particular those involving the use of arms:

—The right of the parties to the conflict to adopt methods of warfare is not unlimited.

—Neither the civilian population nor individual civilians may be the object of attacks.

—The parties to the conflict shall at all times distinguish between combatants and non-combatants.

—Attacks shall be limited strictly to military objectives. The definition of military objectives described in Chapter 4 is applicable also in naval warfare.

—In planning or deciding upon acts of war at sea or in the air all parties to the conflict shall ensure that all feasible precautions are taken in accordance with international law applicable in armed conflicts to avoid losses of civilian lives and damage to civilian objects.

—Ships and aircraft which surrender, e.g. by turning down the flag or by any other means of clear surrender, shall not be attacked any longer.

—After each battle the parties to the conflict shall without delay take all feasible action to search for and rescue the shipwrecked, wounded, and sick, to protect them against deprivation and maltreatment, to ensure necessary care, as well as to search for the dead and to protect them from pillage.

1. *Preliminary Remarks.* The validity of the principles enumerated in Section 1017 follows from international treaty and customary law.[69] Despite the heading of this section these principles are not peculiar to naval warfare. They are expressly mentioned in the present chapter to stress that the fundamental principles of the laws of armed conflict apply equally in naval warfare. The principles are not absolute in character but have to be weighed against considerations of military necessity.[70] However, such considerations do not render these principles obsolete. Such considerations justify deviations only if the norm in question expressly refers to military necessity. On the other hand, the principles are rather general in character. It is, therefore, difficult to determine specific duties beforehand and in the abstract. Such duties can be formulated only if the said principles are applied to a concrete case.[71]

2. *The problem of the applicability of AP I to naval warfare.* According to Art. 49, para. 3 AP I the provisions of Part IV Section I (Arts. 48–67) 'apply to any land, air or

---

[69] Evidence of the respective legal basis will be given in the commentaries to the individual principles. For a first overview see van Hegelsom, *Methods*, 11 ff.; Robertson, *Technology*, 363 ff.; NWP 9, ch. 8; Canadian *Draft Manual*, paras. 701, 707.

[70] Cf. Draper, *RDMilG* 1973, 129 ff.

[71] O'Connell, Vol. II, 1105 ff.; Colombos, paras. 524 ff.

sea warfare which may affect the civilian population, individual civilians or civilian objects on land. They further apply to all attacks from the sea or from the air against objectives on land but do not otherwise affect the rules of international law applicable in armed conflict at sea or in the air.' As regards the applicability to naval warfare of the rules of AP I dealing with the civilian population, this provision as well as Art. 49, para. 4 AP I have been cited in support of contradictory positions.[72] Today, there is general agreement on the following solution: Art. 49, para. 3 AP I merely excludes the application of Arts. 48–67 AP I to naval warfare proper. The other provisions of AP I, especially Arts. 35–41, are applicable. Section I governs methods of naval warfare 'which may affect the civilian population on land' and is moreover applicable to attacks from the sea against objectives on land. The second sentence of Art. 49, para. 3 AP I is restricted to attacks against military objectives on land. Attacks against civilian objects are already dealt with in the first sentence. Hence, section I is applicable to ship-to-ship, ship-to air, or air-to-ship operations only if the civilian population, individual civilians, or civilian objects may be affected. In other words: those operations are covered by section I if there is or may be collateral damage to human beings or civilian objects on land. Therefore, Arts. 51 and 52 AP I are not applicable to attacks on merchant vessels or to mine warfare. These operations are subject to 'the rules of international law applicable in armed conflict at sea'. That is made clear by the second sentence of Art. 49, para. 3 and by Art. 49, para. 4 AP I.[73] It follows from the preceding that the provisions of AP I may also be taken into consideration when it comes to the identification of principles and rules applicable in armed conflicts at sea.

3. *No unlimited right to choose methods of warfare.* This fundamental principle, first codified in Art. 22 of the 1907 Hague Regulations, was reaffirmed in Art. 35 AP I. As concerns the latter provision its applicability to naval warfare as part of Section I Part III follows from the interpretation of Art. 49, para. 3 AP I favoured here. Moreover, it is applicable to all methods of naval warfare *qua* customary law.[74] The fact that the wording of the Hague Regulations differs from that of AP I is without prejudice to the principle's customary character as codified in Art. 35, para. 1 AP I. The formulation in AP I is merely an adaptation to modern conditions.[75] In view of its relatively abstract wording this principle, as such, allows no conclusions as to the extent of the limitations on the right to choose methods of warfare. These limitations are specified in the following principles as well as in the other rules laid down in the present chapter.

4. The customary prohibition of making the civilian population or individual civilians the object of attack is for the first time codified in Art. 51, para. 2 AP I.[76] This

---

[72] See, on the one hand, Rauch, *The Protocol Additional*, 57 ff.; cf. Meyrowitz, *Revue Générale de Droit International Public* 89 (1985), 243 ff.

[73] For the applicability of AP I to naval warfare and for further references see Bothe, *Commentary*, 761 ff.

[74] Solf, in Bothe/Partsch/Solf, 193 ff.; Robertson, *Technology*, 363. See also *San Remo Manual*, para. 38.

[75] Cf. van Hegelsom, *Methods*, 11.   [76] Solf, in Bothe/Partsch/Solf, 299 ff.

Heintschel von Heinegg

provision is directly applicable to measures of naval warfare 'which may affect the civilian population, individual civilians, or civilian objects on land'.

5. *The principle of distinction.* Also customary in character, and thus valid in naval warfare, is the principle of distinction, now codified in Art. 48 AP I. Of course, Art. 48 AP I as such is applicable to naval warfare only within the limits mentioned above. Still, the applicability of the principle of distinction to naval warfare *qua* customary law is undisputed.[77] Hence, it is prohibited to employ in naval warfare methods that are not, or cannot be, directed against a specific military objective or whose effects cannot be limited to such objectives. However, the principle does not prohibit attacks that result in collateral damage which has to be tolerated in the light of the principle of proportionality.

6. *The definition of military objectives.*

a) *Validity.* In view of Art. 49, para. 3 AP I the definition of military objectives laid down in Art. 52, para. 2 AP I is not directly applicable to naval warfare. Despite the differences between land and naval warfare there is, however, general agreement that this definition is also valid in the context of naval warfare *qua* customary law. For example, the Round Table of Experts of International Law Applicable to Armed Conflicts at Sea, at its Bochum session (1989), affirmed its applicability to naval warfare.[78] Accordingly, in land as well as in naval warfare, only military objectives may be attacked. The fact that the 1974–77 Diplomatic Conference agreed on excluding naval warfare proper from the applicability of Part III Section I does not justify a position to the contrary. In their military manuals, Canada[79] and the United States[80] expressly acknowledge the validity of the definition of military objectives for naval warfare. As concerns the United States, this is of particular significance since they have, so far, felt unable to ratify AP I.

b) *Legal consequences arising from the validity of the definition of military objectives.* It follows from the validity of the definition of military objectives that, in naval warfare too, military objectives are not merely those which, according to present day language, qualify as genuinely 'military'. A contribution to military action is 'effective' not only if there is a direct connection between action and object; indirect contributions are also sufficient as long as they conduce to (specific) military actions. Moreover, the total or partial destruction, capture, or neutralization of such an object must offer a definite military advantage. It is impossible to determine in advance and in the abstract when an attack will offer such a definite military advantage. Accordingly, multiple military considerations will have to be taken account of, especially the object of the military operation in question. 'Definite'

---

[77] See *NWP* 9, para. 8.1; *San Remo Manual*, para. 39.

[78] For the commentaries, the discussions, and the Bochum results see Heintschel v. Heinegg (Ed.), *Military Objective*, 45 ff., 141 ff., 170 ff. The 1994 *San Remo Manual*, in para. 40, now states: 'In so far as objects are concerned, military objectives are limited to those objects which by their nature, location, purpose or use make an effective contribution to military action and whose total or partial destruction, capture or neutralization, in the circumstances ruling at the time, offers a definite military advantage.'

[79] Canadian *Draft Manual*, para. 714. [80] *NWP* 9, para. 8.1.1.

does not mean that the advantage anticipated must be obvious or that it has to be effected directly. It means rather that the advantage must be not merely hypothetical but concrete and discernible. 'In the circumstances ruling at the time' is meant to exclude advantages that materialize sometime during the course of hostilities; they must be ascertainable at the time of the attack. This presupposes the ability to base the selection of targets upon reliable and up-to-date information. If there remain doubts as to the military character of an objective non-military character must be presumed unless the omission to take military measures would entail significant dangers.[81]

7. *Precautions in attack.* The obligation to take appropriate precautions before launching or ordering an attack is codified in Art. 57 AP I. However, its validity *qua* customary law follows implicity from the preceding principles.[82] If belligerents are obliged to limit attacks strictly to military objectives and to spare, as far as possible, civilians and civilian objects they are also obliged to take the appropriate precautions. Otherwise the definition of military objectives and the principle of distinction are meaningless.

8. *No attacks on ships and aircraft that have surrendered.* The obligation to suspend attacks upon vehicles that have surrendered follows from the customary rules codified in Art. 41 AP I and Art. 23 lit. (c) of the 1907 Hague Regulations.[83] The protective scope of this prohibition is limited to the people on board such vehicles. Consequently, a ship that has surrendered may, for example, be sunk after its passengers and crew have been taken to a place of safety.[84]

9. *Search for and rescue of survivors.* After each engagement the parties to the conflict shall take all possible measures to search for and collect the shipwrecked, wounded, and sick. This obligation is codified in Art. 18, para. 1 GC II. It follows from the principle of humanity and is applicable to naval warfare *qua* customary law.[85] It needs to be stressed that, in contrast to land warfare, the parties to an armed conflict at sea are not obliged to search for and collect survivors 'at all times, and particularly after an engagement'[86] but only 'after each engagement'. Thus, the special circumstances of naval warfare, especially the vulnerability of ships engaged in rescue operations, is taken into account.[87] Of course, an omission to search for and collect the shipwrecked, wounded, and sick is justified only if such measures, in view of considerations of military necessity or of the circumstances ruling at the time, are not feasible. The formulation 'after each engagement' is, therefore, not restricted to major naval hostilities but covers all situations of hostilities at sea that have caused victims.[88]

---

[81] For this and the preceding commentaries see Solf, in Bothe/Partsch/Solf, 323 *et seq.*; Heintschel v. Heinegg, *HuV-I* 3/1989, 51. For legitimate military objectives in naval warfare see Sections 1021 *et seq.*

[82] See also Canadian *Draft Manual*, para. 707; *San Remo Manual*, para. 46.

[83] See, *inter alia*, Colombos, para. 519.

[84] Note, in this context, that special rules apply for the destruction of captured merchant vessels.

[85] For further references see Mallison, *Submarines*, 134 *et seq.*

[86] This is the wording of Art. 15, para. 1 GC I.   [87] Pictet, *Commentary* GC II, 132.   [88] Ibid.

Heintschel von Heinegg

1018   Ruses of war are permissible also in naval warfare. Unlike land and aerial warfare, naval warfare permits the use of false flags or military emblems (Art. 39, para. 3 AP I). Before opening fire, however, the true flag shall always be displayed.

1. *State practice.* A famous example of flying false flags in naval warfare is the case of the German cruiser *Emden*. In 1914, the *Emden* while flying the Japanese flag entered the port of Penang. Before attacking the Russian cruiser *Shemtshug* the *Emden* displayed the German Navy's war flag. Another example is the case of the German ship *Kormoran*. After it had been stopped by the Australian destroyer *HMS Sydney* the *Kormoran* pretended to be registered in the Netherlands. Before the *Sydney* could verify the true character the *Kormoran* displayed the German flag and sank the Australian warship.[89] No cases of ruses are reported from state practice during the post-World War II conflicts.

2. *Legitimate ruses in naval warfare.* In contrast to land warfare, the use of false flags and markings has always been considered a legitimate ruse in naval warfare. This has been expressly reaffirmed by Art. 39, para. 3 AP I. It should be noted, however, that such ruses may be performed only by warships and the other ships and aircraft enumerated in Section 1015. It is hotly disputed whether merchant vessels are also entitled to fly false flags.[90] Be that as it may; for the present purposes this problem needs no further consideration. Its relevance is restricted to the determination of the enemy character of merchant vessels. As will be shown, the flag flown by a merchant vessel is only *prima facie* evidence of its true character.[91] In view of the technological development (over-the-horizon targeting, etc.) the use of false flags has almost become a negligible issue. The true character of a vessel will only in rare cases be determined by visual means. It is more likely that in future the use of civilian radar equipment by warships will be of practical relevance. Other electronic means of misleading the enemy may also be taken into consideration in the present context. For example, a transponder with an 'identification of friend or foe' (IFF) code whose use is intended to make the enemy believe that the ship or aircraft in question belongs to his allies. As regards their legitimacy, these and other ruses are legally restricted only by the prohibition of perfidy. Other legitimate ruses are, for example, the use of camouflage, decoys, mock operations, and misinformation.[92]

1019   Perfidy is prohibited also in naval warfare. In particular, it is prohibited to misuse the emblem of the Red Cross or to give a ship, in any other way, the appearance of a hospital ship for the purpose of camouflage. It is also prohibited to make improper use of other distinctive signs equal in status with that of the Red Cross (Art. 45 GC II; Art. 37 AP I) and of the flag of truce, or to feign surrender or distress

---

[89] For further cases that occurred during the World Wars see Colombos, paras. 520 ff.

[90] Cf. Colombos, para. 522.   [91] See Section 1022.

[92] Art. 37, para. 2 AP I. See also *San Remo Manual*, paras. 109 *et seq.* For an overview of ruses and perfidy in naval warfare see Gimmerthal, 54 *et seq.*, 173 *et seq.*; Politakis, *Austrian Journal of Public International Law* 45 (1993), 253 *et seq.* For a general overview see Fleck, *RDMilG* 1974, 269 *et seq.*; Ipsen, *EPIL* 4, 330–1.

Heintschel von Heinegg

by sending a distress signal or by the crew taking to life-rafts. In addition, the principles described in Section 472 apply.

As regards the prohibition of perfidy see first Arts. 37, para. 1 and 38 AP I as well as the commentary in Chapter 4 above. The example of the use of a transponder in the commentary to Section 1018 is to be considered an act of perfidy if, e.g., one of the electronic means of identification for medical aircraft (Art. 8 Annex I to AP I) is used. It would also be perfidious to use one of the other internationally recognized marks, signs, or signals which indicate a right to special protection.[93]

It is prohibited to employ weapons or warfare which are intended, or may be   1020
expected, to cause widespread, long-term and severe damage to the natural envi-
ronment (Art. 35, para. 3 AP I).

This provision hardly allows conclusions as to concrete obligations, nor legal evaluation of specific behaviour. In view of the obscure meaning of the terms used in Art. 35, para. 3 AP I, like 'natural environment', 'widespread' and 'long-term', one can only think of extreme and exceptional cases in which this prohibition would cover the use of methods of naval warfare. That would, presumably, be the case if the belligerents massively employed weapons in an enclosed or semi-enclosed sea (like the Baltic Sea) and if the resulting damage to the flora and fauna in the entire ecosystem would last for decades. The events during the second Gulf War (Kuwait–Iraq)[94] have made evident the difficulties of a proper legal evaluation of the effects of the use of methods of naval warfare on the natural environment.[95] In any event it is incorrect to characterize the Iraqi conduct as war crimes or 'ecological terrorism'.

Similar difficulties of interpretation are involved when it comes to the application of the Convention on the Prohibition of Military or any other Hostile Use of Environmental Modification Techniques, signed at Geneva on 18 May 1977 (ENMOD Convention). However, the ENMOD Convention has to be strictly distinguished from Art. 35, para. 3 AP I. The prohibition of using the modified environment as a means of warfare does not seem to reflect existing technologies. Obviously, only in exceptional cases will states dispose of the technical means massively to modify the natural environment.[96]

Finally, it is noted that at least those states bound by AP I are obliged to take into consideration the natural environment when it comes to the use of methods of

---

[93] e.g. those agreed upon in the International Telecommunication Convention of 25 Oct. 1973 (BGBl. 1976 II, 1089); see also Solf, in Bothe/Partsch/Solf, 207 *et seq.*; Gimmerthal, 173 *et seq.*; Ipsen, *EPIL* 4, 130–3.

[94] Iraq had set fire to oil wells in Kuwait, and parts of the Persian Gulf had been polluted by oil. See US Deptartment of Defense, *Conduct of the Persian Gulf War*—Appendix on the Role of the Law of War, in *ILM* 31 (1992), 636; Robinson, *Environmental Policy & Law* 21 (1991), 216 *et seq.*

[95] It should be noted in this context that the reports and articles published either during the conflict or in its aftermath were highly exaggerated and, in many cases, based on deliberate misinformation. For a recent legal evaluation of the law applicable to the protection of the environment in naval armed conflicts see Heintschel v. Heinegg/Donner, *GYIL* 37 (1994).

[96] For an evaluation of the ENMOD Convention see Sánchez Rodríguez, *Commentary*, 661 ff.

naval warfare.[97] Measures which may be expected to have an impact on the natural environment should not be taken if the resulting damage would be disproportionate to the military advantage anticipated.[98] In any event, damage to, or destruction of, the natural environment not justified by military necessity, or carried out wantonly, is prohibited.[99] However, the mere fact that the use of methods and means of warfare may have an impact on the natural environment, whether marine or terrestrial, does not imply a legal duty on the parties of the conflict to refrain from their employment.[100]

II. MILITARY OBJECTIVES AND PROTECTED OBJECTS IN ARMED CONFLICTS AT SEA

1. Enemy Warships and Military Aircraft

1021 **Without prejudice to the principles applicable in the law of armed conflict at sea, enemy warships and military aircraft may be attacked, sunk, or seized at any time without warning. Such ships should, as far as circumstances permit, be sunk only after the crews and ships' papers have been brought to a safe place. Upon seizure such ships and the cargo on board become war booty and property of the seizing state, since they do not fall under prize law. Members of the crew falling into the hands of the adversary become prisoners of war. The same applies to persons on board who accompany the armed forces.**

1. *Military objectives.* Enemy warships, including converted merchant ships, and military aircraft are entitled to perform acts of naval warfare. They are, thus, military objectives that may be attacked, sunk, or captured without prior warning anywhere and at any time in the areas of naval warfare.[101]

2. *The principles of naval warfare,* i.e. those peculiar to naval warfare as well as the general principles of the laws of armed conflict, may, however, in specific cases oblige belligerents to refrain from destroying or sinking such ships and aircraft. This would be the case, for example, if in relation to the military advantage anticipated sinking or destruction were unnecessary or disproportionate.[102] A geographical

---

[97] It is questionable if there already exists a corresponding duty in customary international law, especially because some states have expressly excluded the applicability of Art. 35, para. 3 AP I. Note, however, that para. 44 of the *San Remo Manual* states: 'Methods and means of warfare should be employed with due regard for the natural environment taking into account the relevant rules of international law.'

[98] This follows from the fundamental principles of the laws of war.

[99] See also *San Remo Manual*, para. 44.

[100] One possible way of protecting the natural environment is an agreement of the parties to the conflict to this effect. Accordingly, para. 11 of the *San Remo Manual* encourages them 'to agree that no hostile actions will be conducted in marine areas containing . . . rare or fragile ecosystems or . . . the habitat of depleted, threatened or endangered species or other forms of marine life.'

[101] See only Fenrick, *CYIL* 24 (1986), 91 ff.

[102] For this reason the definition of military objectives refers not only to destruction but also to capture.

limitation of the conflict may also be of significance in so far as hostilities beyond a certain area may not take place even if directed at military objectives.[103] This is made clear by the introductory part of the first sentence of Section 1021. The second sentence according to which such ships 'should be sunk only after the crews and ships' papers have been brought to a safe place' is, therefore, restricted to the cases just mentioned. There is no general legal obligation to this effect. The 1936 London Protocol is restricted to merchant vessels and does not apply to the sinking of warships. It should be noted that, even if enemy warships and military aircraft are not attacked, they are still subject to capture and the laws of booty.

3. *Prisoners of war.* The crews of warships, converted merchant vessels, and military aircraft are combatants within the meaning of Art. 43 AP I. They therefore become prisoners of war as soon as they fall into the power of an adverse party according to Art. 4A No. 1 GC III and Art. 44, para. 1 AP I. As regards persons who accompany the armed forces, this follows from Art. 4A No. 4 GC III.

4. *Booty of war.* According to customary international law enemy warships and military aircraft, as well as other state ships not merchant vessels, are not subject to the law of prize. As soon as capture is completed they are to be considered as war booty. Property upon capture automatically passes to the captor state.[104] Cargo on board such vehicles owned by the enemy state is also considered to be booty of war. Private property is subject to the laws of prize.[105]

2. Enemy Merchant Ships, their Cargo, Passengers, and Crew

a) Enemy Merchant Ships

**In principle, the enemy character of a merchant ship is determined by the flag   1022
which the ship is entitled to fly (Art. 57 LondonDecl 1909).**

Flying the enemy's flag has always been considered sufficient proof of the enemy character of merchant vessels.[106] Hence, in such cases the commander of a warship need not bother with questions of proper registration or ownership. This does not mean, however, that only those merchant vessels flying the enemy's flag have enemy character. The fact that a merchant vessel is flying the flag of a neutral state or a state not party to the conflict is only *prima facie* evidence of its neutral character.[107] If search of the ship's papers, or other information available to the

---

[103] On 2 May 1982 the Argentine war ship *General Belgrano* was sunk by the British submarine *Conqueror* outside the British exclusion zone. 368 Argentine seamen died. Despite some allegations to the contrary, the attack on the *Belgrano* was not illegal. The reactions in state practice as well as in legal writings show, however, that in geographically limited conflicts even the sinking of warships is subject to more legal restrictions than in a conflict of a global nature. See Jacobson, *Submarine Warfare*, 221. As regards the *Belgrano* incident and for further references see Rice/Gavshon and Zuppi.

[104] Oppenheim/Lauterpacht, 474 ff.; Downey Jr., *AJIL* 1950, 488 *et seq.*; Rabus, *EPIL* 3, 68 *et seq.*; A. P. Higgins, *BYIL* 1925, 103 *et seq.*

[105] See the provisions on capture and seizure of enemy and neutral cargoes in Sections 1027 ff.

[106] Heintschel v. Heinegg, *CYIL* 29 (1991), 300. See also *San Remo Manual*, para. 112.

[107] Heintschel v. Heinegg, *CYIL* 29 (1991), 301; *San Remo Manual*, para. 113.

Heintschel von Heinegg

commander, reveal that there has been a transfer of flag in order to evade the consequences to which an enemy vessel is exposed, then a vessel flying a neutral flag may be treated as an enemy merchant vessel.[108] If, however, there has been a transfer of one neutral flag to another neutral flag the vessel concerned may not be considered as enemy in character even if the transfer was made because of the ongoing hostilities.[109] Moreover, according to the international laws of armed conflict, the enemy character of merchant vessels flying neutral flags may be presumed if there exist certain reasons for suspicion.[110] These cases are, however, of no relevance for the naval commander. He may regularly rely upon the information made available to him by higher authorities. The final determination of the enemy character of vessels lies with the competent prize court which has to decide on the legality of capture and other acts in any event.

1023   **In relation to enemy merchant ships all acts of economic warfare at sea may be performed, without consideration of the cargo and its owner. The same applies in principle to other seagoing private vessels, such as yachts and pleasure-boats, subject to particular provisions of protection. Prize law also applies to wrecks and to ships still in construction. After the capture of an enemy merchant vessel it must be decided in a prize court procedure whether the capture was lawful. Upon confirmation by the prize court the ship becomes property of the capturing state.**

1. *Protection of enemy private property in naval warfare.* In contrast to the position in land warfare, enemy private property is not exempt from capture in naval warfare.[111] The traditional rule according to which enemy private property is liable to capture and confiscation has not been modified by the definition of military objectives that is also applicable in naval warfare. According to that definition, the capture of objects is permissible only if capture 'offers a definite military advantage' and if the objects concerned 'make an effective contribution to military action'.

---

[108] Art. 55 of the—unratified—London Declaration of 1909. According to this provision there is, however, a rebuttable 'presumption, if the bill of sale is not on board a vessel which has lost her belligerent nationality less than six days before outbreak of hostilities, that the transfer is void. . . . Where the transfer was effected more than thirty days before the outbreak of hostilities, there is an absolute presumption that it is valid if it is unconditional, complete, and in conformity with the laws of the countries concerned, and if its effect is such that neither the control of, nor the profits arising from the employment of the vessel remain in the same hands as before the transfer.' According to Art. 56 of the 1909 London Declaration the 'transfer of an enemy vessel to a neutral flag, effected after the outbreak of hostilities, is void unless it is proved that such transfer was not made in order to evade the consequences to which an enemy vessel, as such, is exposed. There is, however, an absolute presumption that a transfer is void: (1) if the transfer has been made during a voyage or in a blockaded port; (2) if a right to repurchase or recover the vessel is reserved to the vendor; (3) if the requirements of the municipal law governing the right to fly the flag under which the vessel is sailing, have not been fulfilled.'

[109] That was the case when, during the Iran–Iraq conflict Kuwaiti tankers were reflagged by the United States of America. See Nordquist/Wachenfeld, *GYIL* 1988, 138 ff.

[110] For further details see Heintschel v. Heinegg, *CYIL* XXIX (1991), 301. No sufficient reason for suspicion exists if a merchant vessel is flying a flag of convenience.

[111] During the nineteenth and early twentieth centuries the USA persistently endeavoured to exempt, with the exception of contraband and breach of blockade, private property from capture. Although they were supported by a number of other states, proposals to this effect were rejected by the respective majorities. See Arts. 33 *et seq.* of the *Oxford Manual*; O'Connell, Vol. II, 1112 ff.; Heintschel v. Heinegg, *CYIL* 29 (1991), 305 ff.

Heintschel von Heinegg

This does not, however, imply that according to the law of prize only objects qualifying as military objectives are liable to capture. The laws of prize on capture and confiscation of enemy private goods have not been altered by the validity of the definition of military objectives. The reference to 'capture' in that definition is merely a clarification of the principle of proportionality, as set out in Section 1021.[112]

2. *Procedure.* Whereas neutral merchant vessels may, in principle, be captured only after prior visit and search, that is not the case for enemy merchant vessels.[113] That does not mean that they may not be visited and searched. Visit and search should be exercised in order to verify whether a vessel belongs to a category of specially protected vessels. Property of a captured enemy merchant vessel does not pass to the captor automatically on assuming command over the ship. It only passes if the competent prize court decides upon confiscation.[114] The decision of the prize court on confiscation is without prejudice to the legality of capture.[115]

A merchant ship belonging to one of the parties to the conflict located in an enemy port at the commencement of the hostilities shall be allowed to depart freely within a reasonable time. It may be furnished with a pass permitting it to proceed to its port of destination or any other port indicated (Art. 1 HC VI). Merchant ships unable, owing to circumstances of *force majeure*, to leave the enemy port within the period fixed, or which have not been allowed to leave, cannot be confiscated. The belligerent may only detain such ships subject to the obligation to return them after the armed conflict or requisition them on payment of compensation (Art. 2 HC VI). These rules do not affect merchant ships whose design shows that they are intended for conversion into warships (Art. 5 HC VI). 1024

During the Crimean War it was common practice to capture and confiscate, upon the declaration of war, enemy merchant vessels in one's own port.[116] Hague Convention VI of 1907 then took into account the practice of states during the second half of the nineteenth century. During the two World Wars Hague Convention VI was of no practical relevance whatsoever.[117] On 14 November 1925, Great Britain and, on 13 July 1939, France denounced that Convention. Germany took the Convention into consideration when it passed its Prize Ordinance of 1939, whose applicability was, however, made subject to strict reciprocity. The United States never ratified Hague VI. Today the provisions of Hague VI, probably apart from those referring to *force majeure*, are of even less practical relevance. Only in rare

---

[112] See commentary to Section 1021, para. 2. According to para. 135 of the *San Remo Manual* 'enemy vessels, whether merchant or otherwise, and goods on board such vessels may be captured outside neutral waters', unless they are exempt from capture.

[113] According to the traditional law this also applies to wrecks. See Terfloth.

[114] Colombos, para. 925; Oppenheim/Lauterpacht, 474 ff.; Berber, Vol. II, 195 ff.

[115] Capture is permissible and legal if there are sufficient reasons for suspecting that the vessel concerned is either enemy or has committed acts rendering it a legitimate military objective. Confiscation is legal only if the facts justifying such confiscation have been proved in prize court proceedings.

[116] O'Connell, Vol. II, 1124 ff.

[117] De Guttry, *Commentary*, 108; A. P. Higgins, *BYIL* (1922/23), 55 ff.

and exceptional cases will merchant vessels travel to an enemy port without knowledge of the outbreak of hostilities. Moreover, in modern armed conflicts at sea the belligerents will certainly not wish to release ships likely to make an effective contribution to the enemy's war efforts. For these and other reasons the exception in the last sentence of Section 1024 will be interpreted widely.

1025   **Without prejudice to the principles applicable in the law of armed conflict at sea enemy merchant ships are military objectives and may be attacked at any time without warning, if they are:**

—**engaging in acts of war (e.g. laying mines, mine-sweeping, cutting submarine cables and pipelines, visiting, searching or attacking other merchant ships);**

—**making an effective contribution to military action (e.g. by carrying military material, troop-carrying or replenishing);**

—**incorporated into or assisting the enemy's intelligence system, subject to, where necessary, a prior political determination;**

—**sailing in convoy with enemy warships or military aircraft;**

—**refusing an order to stop or actively resisting visit, search, or capture;**

—**armed to an extent that they could inflict damage on a warship; or**

—**engaging in any other activity bringing them within the definition of a military objective.**

1. *Preliminary Remarks.* According to the 1936 London Protocol warships are allowed to sink merchant vessels whether enemy or neutral only if certain preconditions are fulfilled.[118] At first sight the provisions of that agreement could be interpreted restrictively. The sinking of a merchant vessel without prior warning and without first taking passengers, crews, and ship's papers to a place of safety would be permissible only if the vessel concerned persistently refused to stop on being duly summoned or if it actively resisted visit and search. However, this would be a too simplistic way of looking at the 1936 Protocol. The rules laid down in that document formed part of the 1922 Washington Treaty and were reaffirmed by the 1930 London Conference. During that conference a committee of legal experts presented a report in which the matter was clarified as follows: 'The Committee wish to place it on record that the expression "merchant vessel", where it is employed in the declaration, is not to be understood as including a merchant vessel which is at the moment participating in hostilities in such a manner as to cause her to lose her right to the immunities of a merchant vessel.' Whereas it remains unclear what is meant by 'participating in hostilities' it is obvious that merchant vessels are not in all circumstances protected by the 1936 London Protocol. This was confirmed by the judgment of the Nuremberg Tribunal.[119] Hence, enemy merchant vessels that,

---

[118] As regards the continuing validity of the 1936 London Protocol see the preliminary remarks in the commentary on Sections 1046 ff.

[119] For details see the commentary on Section 1047.

by their conduct, qualify as legitimate military objectives[120] are not protected by the 1936 London Protocol and may—as an exceptional measure—be attacked and sunk.[121] As made clear above, this applies only if sinking offers a definite military advantage and there are no other means available. The last sentence shows that the enumeration in Section 1025 is not exhaustive. Hence, enemy merchant vessels may also be attacked if they commit acts other than those mentioned here.[122] Such cases should, however, be treated with utmost care. If an enemy merchant vessel does *not* commit one of the acts expressly enumerated in Section 1025, the responsible commander will have to prove that the vessel in question did effectively contribute to military action and that destruction was the only possible reaction.

2. *Engagement in acts of war*, especially the exercise of visit, search, and capture, is a breach of the prohibition laid down in Section 1016. In this context, it is stressed that measures of self-defence against attacks of enemy forces are not considered to be engagement in acts of war. On the other hand, under the laws of armed conflicts at sea warships are not prohibited from breaking resistance by force. Self-defence by an enemy merchant vessel is, therefore, not prohibited but entails considerable risks because it conflicts with the warship's right of capture. The distinction between permissible measures of self-defence and illegal engagement in hostilities is not always an easy task. For example, in 1916 Charles Fryatt, captain of the unarmed British merchant vessel *Brussels*, tried to ram the German submarine *U 23*. Captain Fryatt was sentenced to death and executed.[123]

3. *Effective contribution to military action* is regularly fulfilled by the acts enumerated.[124] Since Section 1025, as an exceptional provision, has to be interpreted narrowly the term 'war material' may not be understood as comprising goods which have some tenuous relevance for the enemy's war efforts. Rather, the objects concerned must be directly apt for use by the enemy's armed forces. If that is not the case, enemy merchant vessels and goods on board such vessels are subject to the laws of prize only. With regard to the exceptional permissibility of the destruction of captured enemy merchant vessels[125] see Section 1026.

4. *Incorporation into or assisting the enemy's intelligence system*. Even during the World Wars this was considered sufficient ground for attack without prior warning. In its sentence against Admiral Dönitz the Nuremberg Tribunal ruled that such

---

[120] Note that mere arming is not a sufficient reason for rendering a merchant vessel a military objective. See para. 2 of the commentary on Section 1004.

[121] Cf. Fenrick, *CYIL* 24 (1986), 105 ff.; Mallison, *Submarines*, 106 ff.

[122] e.g. breach of blockade. See also *San Remo Manual*, para. 60, but note that, according to the position taken here, mere arming does not render an enemy merchant vessel a military objective.

[123] The sentence of the German War Tribunal of 27 July 1916 was considered in conformity with the law by a commission chaired by Schücking. Others characterized it as 'simple murder, bare of any military necessity', as a 'violation of the fundamental right of self-defence' and as 'inconsistent with the rules of the laws of war'. See, *inter alia*, Garner, Vol. 1, 413; Colombos, para. 557. For the *Fryatt* case generally see Dischler, *WVR* I, 606 ff.

[124] See also *NWP* 9, para. 8.2.2; Canadian *Draft Manual*, para. 716(5); *San Remo Manual*, para. 60(b).

[125] Cf. Mallison, *Submarines*, 122 ff.

vessels lose the protection of the 1936 London Protocol.[126] Attacks on vessels incorporated into the enemy's intelligence system may, however, be undertaken only after a prior political decision to that effect. This reservation was deemed necessary to avoid an escalation of relatively low-scale conflicts.

5. *Convoy.* Sailing in convoy with enemy warships and military aircraft, too, has always been considered a sufficient justification for attacking enemy merchant vessels on sight. By travelling under convoy the merchant vessel concerned manifests its readiness to resist—with the help of the accompanying warship—visit, search, and capture.[127]

6. *Refusal to stop on being duly summoned or active resistance to visit, search, and capture.* These exceptions were acknowledged in the 1936 London Protocol. It is emphasized that resistance to visit, search, and capture must be 'active'. Enemy merchant ships are under no legal obligation to facilitate such measures.[128] The legitimacy of attack in such cases is in no way affected by the right of self-defence of enemy merchant vessels against attacks or other belligerent acts of the enemy, as laid down in Section 1016. The right of self-defence conflicts with the warship's right of capture and right to enforce capture whenever necessary.

1026   **Enemy merchant ships may only be destroyed if it is impossible to bring them into a port of one's own or that of an ally, and without having first brought the passengers, crews, and ships' papers to a safe place (Art. 2 LondonProt 1936). The ship's boats are not regarded as a safe place unless the safety of the passengers and crew is assured, in the existing sea and weather conditions, by the proximity of land, or the presence of another vessel which is in a position to take them on board (Art. 2 LondonProt 1936). Where possible, the personal belongings of the passengers and crew shall also be recovered.**

Enemy merchant vessels are often not legitimate military objectives because they do not commit any of the acts enumerated in Section 1025. However, they are always subject to capture according to the laws of prize. If military circumstances preclude taking or sending an enemy merchant vessel for adjudication as an enemy prize it may become necessary to destroy it. This situation is covered in Section 1026. The legality of the destruction of a (captured) enemy merchant vessel as an exceptional belligerent right follows from the 1936 London Protocol.[129] However, before destruction passengers, crew, and ship's papers must be taken to a place of safety. The 1936 London Protocol contains no further restrictions on the right of

---

[126] See commentary on Section 1047, including the references given. Further: Mallison, *Submarines*, 122 ff.; *NWP* 9, para. 8.2.2; Canadian *Draft Manual*, para. 716(5); *San Remo Manual*, para. 60(c). In the *San Remo Manual* the following examples are given: engaging in reconnaissance, early warning, surveillance, or command, control, and communications missions.

[127] Stödter, *EPIL* 3, 128 ff.; *NWP* 9, para. 8.2.2; Canadian *Draft Manual*, para. 716(5); *San Remo Manual*, para. 60(d).

[128] Cf. Rojahn, *EPIL* 4, 224 ff.; Schönborn, *Archiv für öffentliches Recht* 1918, 161 ff.

[129] For its continuing validity and for further details see the preliminary remarks to Sections 1046 ff.

Heintschel von Heinegg

destroying enemy prizes.[130] However, such destruction may never take place for its own sake. It is an exceptional right, to be strictly distinguished from the destruction of enemy merchant vessels qualifying as legitimate military objectives. In the majority of cases it will suffice to destroy the cargo or simply to divert the vessel.[131] The destruction of passenger vessels carrying only civilian passengers is prohibited at sea. For the safety of the passengers, such vessels must be diverted to an appropriate area or port in order to complete capture.[132]

b) Cargo of Enemy Merchant Ships

The enemy or neutral character of cargo is determined by the nationality of the   1027
owner or, if the owner is a stateless person, by his residence (Art. 57 LondonDecl
1909). In the case of corporations and companies, their registered office is rele-
vant. Where after the outbreak of hostilities enemy ownership of goods is trans-
ferred in transit they retain their enemy character until they reach their
destination (Art. 60 LondonDecl 1909).

This provision stems from the 1909 London Declaration which never entered into force. As far as the rules laid down in that treaty are here taken into consideration they are, however, reflective of customary international law. Many of the provisions of the 1909 London Declaration have been implemented in national legislation and in prize regulations. The enemy character of the cargo's[133] owner is determined by his nationality.[134] Contrary to Anglo-American doctrine and jurisprudence, his residence is of relevance only if he is a stateless person. If cargo is owned by a corporation its head or registered office is decisive. The nationality of owners and/or shareholders is irrelevant unless the so-called 'control test' applies.[135] If, according to the preceding criteria, a determination of enemy or neutral character is impossible there is a rebuttable presumption that goods on board enemy vessels are of enemy character.[136] Transfers of title effected in the course of the vessel's journey do not have to be recognized. If, however, such transfer has been effected before the commencement of a journey, neutral cargo of enemy origin remains immune from seizure.[137]

[130] See, however, para. 139 of the *San Remo Manual* which is more specific.

[131] It is interesting to note in this context that para. 138 of the *San Remo Manual* provides that 'as an alternative to capture, an enemy merchant vessel may be diverted from its declared destination.'

[132] *San Remo Manual*, para. 140. See also commentary on Section 1034.

[133] Note that the ship's equipment does not belong to its cargo but is an integral part of and shares the sa. destiny as the ship. Personal belongings of passengers and crews are also not part of the cargo.

[134] Nationality is, however, only one criterion. Anglo-American prize courts always based their decisions on the owner's residence. Thus, even British or US nationals could be characterized as enemies if their residence was in enemy or enemy occupied territory. See Heintschel v. Heinegg, *CYIL* 29 (1991), 305 ff.

[135] According to the 'control test' a corporation not based in enemy or enemy-controlled territory may be deemed enemy in character if it is controlled by individuals who are enemy subjects. See Berber, Vol. II, 200; Domke, *WVR* I, 509 ff.

[136] This is the well known maxim '*robe d'ennemi confisque robe d'ami*'. It can be traced back to Hugo Grotius (*De jure belli ac pacis*, Lib. III, ch. VI, para. VI) and was acknowledged in Art. 59 of the 1909 London Declaration. During the World Wars it was the basis of a significant number of prize court decisions. See Colombos, para. 616.

[137] Art. 60, para. 1 of the 1909 London Declaration. See also Tucker, 86.

1028   Enemy cargo on board enemy ships may be requisitioned and confiscated no matter whether such cargo is contraband or whether it is state or private property.

In international treaties or drafts there is no express rule that enemy cargo on board enemy vessels is liable to capture and confiscation. The validity of the rule follows, however, from international customary law[138] and, indirectly, from the 1856 Paris Declaration. According to that Declaration only neutral goods and enemy goods on board neutral merchant vessels are exempt from capture. In principle, seizure of goods is effected by capturing the vessel carrying them. If the vessel's master consents or if the vessel concerned can neither be captured nor diverted or destroyed, only its cargo may be seized. Confiscation of seized cargo is subject to a confirmatory prize court decision.

1029   Neutral cargo on board enemy ships is exempt. Such cargo may, however, be requisitioned and confiscated if:

—it is contraband, e.g. goods designated for the adversary and apt to be used for war purposes;

—the ship is breaching a blockade, unless the shipper proves that at the time of loading he neither knew nor should have known of the intention to breach the blockade; or

—its carrier is sailing in convoy with enemy warships or engaging in any other activity bringing it within the definition of a military objective.

1. According to the 1856 Paris Declaration and international customary law neutral goods are exempt from seizure.[139] The exceptions to that principle enumerated in the present Section are also part of customary law.[140]

2. Neutral goods are not exempt from seizure if they are contraband. If contraband goods on board neutral merchant vessels are not exempt, *a fortiori* they are not protected when on board enemy merchant vessels. The classification of goods as contraband is closely related with prize measures taken against neutral shipping. Therefore, reference is made to the commentaries on Sections 1142 and 1143. In the present context it suffices if the goods in question are contained in a belligerent's contraband list.[141]

3. The provision on breach of blockade is based upon Art. 21 of the 1909 London Declaration which—despite doubts as to the continuing validity of the Declaration—is generally accepted as customary law.[142]

---

[138] Tucker, 74 ff.; Oppenheim/Lauterpacht, 462 ff.; Dinstein, *IYHR* 1980, 40.

[139] See, *inter alia*, Heintschel v. Heinegg, *CYIL* 29 (1991), 306 ff.

[140] Arts. 21 and 63 of the 1909 London Declaration.

[141] *San Remo Manual*, para. 148, defines contraband as 'goods which are ultimately destined for territory under the control of the enemy and which may be susceptible for use in armed conflict.' Note that under the present law of prize contraband lists may vary according to the particular circumstances of the armed conflict.

[142] See, *inter alia*, Kalshoven, *Commentary*, 262, 269 ff.

4. Neutral cargo on board enemy merchant vessels travelling in convoy or qualifying in some other way as a legitimate military objective is liable to seizure and confiscation. This is consistent with the legality of attacking such vessels without prior warning. In such cases the cargo shares the destiny of the vessel.

Private and official postal correspondence found on board enemy ships is inviolable. If a ship conveying such postal correspondence is captured the captor shall ensure that the correspondence is forwarded without delay (Art. 1 HC XI). Before sinking a ship postal correspondence shall as far as possible be recovered and forwarded. The enemy ship itself, even a mail ship, shall be liable to capture. The prohibition relating to the seizure of postal correspondence does not apply to postal consignments destined for or proceeding from a blockaded port. Parcels are exempt from seizure if they are destined for neutral persons and do not contain any contraband. The captor shall be entitled to open mail bags and inspect their contents. Inviolability shall not apply to contraband contained in letter post. 1030

The inviolability of postal correspondence (except parcels) and the captor's duty to forward it if the ship is detained follow from Art. 1 of the 1907 Hague Convention XI.[143] In view of the practice of the two World Wars and of modern military manuals the continuing validity of Hague XI is open to severe doubt. Still, for practical reasons its provisions should be maintained.[144]

The following objects shall not be confiscated: 1031

— **objects belonging to the passengers or crew of a captured ship and intended for their personal use;**

— **material exclusively intended for the treatment of the wounded and sick, the prevention of disease, or religious purposes, provided that the transport of such materiel has been approved by the capturing party (Art. 35 GC I; Art. 38 GC II);**

— **instruments and other material belonging to relief societies;**

— **cultural property;**

— **postal correspondence of the national Prisoner of War Information Bureaux (Art. 122 GC III) and the Central Prisoners of War Information Agency (Art. 123 GC III);**

— **postal consignments and relief shipments destined for prisoners of war and civilian internees as well as postal consignments dispatched by these persons;**

— **relief shipments intended for the population of occupied territory, provided that the conditions attached by the capturing party to the conveyance of such shipments are observed (Art. 59 GC IV); and**

— **relief shipments intended for the population of any territory under the control of a party to the conflict other than occupied territory (Art. 70 AP I).**

---

[143] Cf. Shearer, *Commentary*, 183 ff.   [144] Ibid., 189.

Heintschel von Heinegg

1. *Personal effects.* According to customary international law, personal effects of the passengers and crew of captured vessels are not liable to seizure. Such personal effects are objects, including money, of the type usually taken on a voyage. Other objects or large amounts of money that do not serve personal needs may be seized.

2. *Medical and religious equipment.* Equipment intended exclusively for the treatment of wounded and sick, for the prevention of disease, or for religious purposes are exempt from seizure if their shipment has been approved by the belligerents. It should be noted that such equipment is regularly shipped on ships specially chartered for that purpose.[145] If their voyage has been approved by the belligerents then their cargo has the same protected status as the ship in question.

3. *Equipment of relief societies.* Instruments and other equipment of recognized relief societies are also exempt from capture. Otherwise such societies would be unable to fulfil their tasks.

4. *Cultural property.* The specially protected status of cultural property follows from Art. 53 AP I and from the Hague Convention for the Protection of Cultural Property in the Event of Armed Conflict of 14 May 1954.[146]

5. *Postal correspondence* of the national Prisoner of War Information Bureaux and the Central Prisoners of War Information Agency are specially protected under Arts. 122 and 123 GC III. Such postal correspondence continues to be exempt from capture even if it contains goods covered by a belligerent's contraband list. It is irrelevant whether the sender is a relative, a third person, or an organization.

6. *Relief shipments intended for the population of occupied territory or intended for the population of any territory under the control of a party to the conflict other than occupied territory.* The exemption from capture of relief shipments intended for the population of occupied territory follows from Art. 59 GC IV. As regards relief shipments intended for the population of any territory under the control of a party to the conflict other than occupied territory, their protected status follows from Art. 70 AP I. The 1977 AP I contains no provisions on contraband. However, in view of its applicability to acts of naval warfare affecting the civilian population on land, such relief shipments may neither be declared contraband nor seized.[147]

c) *Crews and Passengers of Enemy Merchant Ships*

1032 The captains, officers, and crews of enemy merchant ships, if they are nationals of the enemy state, become prisoners of war (Art. 4A No. 5 GC III) unless they promise in writing not to undertake, while hostilities last, any service connected with the armed conflict (Art. 6 HC XI). If they prove that they are nationals of a neutral state, they do not become prisoners of war (Art. 5 HC XI). The provisions

[145] See Art. 38 GC II. [146] See the commentary in Chapter 9.
[147] Bothe, *Commentary*, 764 ff.

on releasing crew members do not apply if the ship has been engaging in any activity bringing it within the definition of a military objective.

In principle, members of crews, including masters, pilots, and apprentices of a merchant navy, according to Art. 4A No. 5 GC III, become prisoners of war if they fall into the power of the enemy. Art. 4A No. 5 GC III, however, prevents such persons from becoming prisoners of war if they would 'benefit by more favourable treatment under any other provisions of international law'. This is a clear reference to Art. 6 of the 1907 Hague Convention XI.[148] Since release of those persons on the high seas will in most cases not be feasible they will normally be released in the port to which their vessel has been diverted or taken. It may, however, be doubted whether Art. 6 Hague XI can still be considered as according with the realities of modern armed conflicts. Hence, this provision will prevail over Art. 4A No. 5 GC III only if reciprocity is guaranteed. In any event, release must in fact result in 'more favourable treatment'.

Passengers of enemy merchant ships shall, in general, be released. Passengers who have taken part in hostilities or are travelling to join the enemy armed forces may be detained. They become prisoners of war if they belong to one of the categories enumerated in Article 4 of the Third Geneva Convention. Should any doubt arise as to whether they belong to any of these categories, they enjoy the protection of prisoners of war until such time as their status has been determined by the competent tribunal (Art. 5 GC III). Passengers who are members of enemy armed forces shall become prisoners of war.   **1033**

Passengers on board enemy merchant vessels may only be made prisoners of war if they meet the conditions in Art. 4A GC III. This is the case if they are members of the enemy's armed forces.[149] If they belong to none of the categories enumerated in that provision they must, in principle, be released. The practical relevance of this rule is of minor interest since passengers of enemy nationality may be interned after they have been taken to an enemy port.[150]

3. Protected Enemy Vessels (except hospital ships and ships under similar protection)

The following enemy ships enjoying special protection may neither be attacked nor seized: **1034**

— **vessels carrying material intended exclusively for the treatment of wounded and sick or for the prevention of disease, provided that the particulars regarding the consignment have been approved (Art. 38 GC II),**

— **vessels carrying relief goods for the civilian population of an occupied territory, provided that the conditions connected with the transport are fulfilled (Art. 23 GC IV),**

---

[148] Cf. Shearer, *Commentary*, 187.   [149] Art. 4A No. 1 GC III.
[150] Cf., *inter alia*, O'Connell, Vol. II, 1117.

— vessels that, with the consent of the belligerent parties, are carrying relief consignments for the civilian population of territory under the control of a party to the conflict other than occupied territory (Art. 70 AP I),

— vessels used exclusively for fishing along the coast or small boats employed in local trade (Art. 3 HC XI),

— vessels charged with religious, non-military scientific, or philanthropic missions (Art. 4 HC XI),

— vessels engaged exclusively in the transfer of cultural property (Art. 14 CultPropConv),

— vessels used exclusively for the transport of parlementaires or exchanging prisoners of war (cartel ships),

— vessels furnished with an acknowledged letter of safe conduct, provided that they observe the restrictions imposed on them, and

— without prejudice to the right of capture, passenger ships on the high seas used exclusively for the transport of civilians while engaged in such transport.

The right to stop and search such ships remains unaffected.

1. *Transport of certain material and goods.* A precondition for the special protection accorded to the first three categories of vessels enumerated in Section 1034 is that the material and goods they carry must exclusively serve humanitarian purposes. However, the particulars regarding their voyage must either be notified to and approved by the enemy or there must be an agreement to this effect.[151]

2. *Coastal fishing vessels and small boats engaged in local trade.* The exemption from capture of such vessels and boats, including their appliances, rigging, tackle, and cargo,[152] was codified in Art. 3 of the 1907 Hague Convention XI. According to customary international law they are exempt not only from capture but also from attack.[153] High seas fishing vessels are not protected by this provision.[154] The object and purpose of exemption is to guarantee sufficient supply of fish for the popula-

---

[151] See Art. 38 GC II; Art. 23 GC IV; Arts. 69 and 70 AP I; *San Remo Manual*, paras. 47(c)(ii) and 136(c)(ii). With regard to the famous case of the Japanese ship *Awa Maru* see the references in Whiteman, Digest 10, 628 *et seq.*; Mallison, *Submarines*, 126. In the case of relief shipments for the civilian population according to Art. 70 AP I the adversary is not free to deny approval. See Bothe, in Bothe/Partsch/Solf, 434 ff.

[152] Cf. O'Connell, Vol. II, 1122 ff.

[153] For the famous case of the *Paquete Habana* see v. Münch, *WVR* II, 736 ff. For state practice during the World Wars see Oppenheim/Lauterpacht, 478; Rousseau, 291. With regard to the Korean conflict see the references in Cagle/Manson, 296 ff.; Mallison, *Submarines*, 127. During the Vietnam conflict the US Navy respected Vietnamese coastal fishing boats although Vietnam was not bound by Hague XI. The US attitude only changed after those boats had been abused for the transport of ammunition etc. Still, naval commanders were obliged to verify such abuse before taking measures. See O'Connell, *Influence*, 177. For the general protection of coastal fishing boats see also *NWP 9*, para. 8.2.3; Canadian *Draft Manual*, para. 718; *San Remo Manual*, para. 47(g) and para. 136(f); Colombos, paras. 656, 658; Shearer, *Commentary*, 185 ff.; Tucker, 96.

[154] Cf. Schramm, *Prisenrecht*, 145; Shearer, *Commentary*, 186; Oppenheim/Lauterpacht, 477; Colombos, para. 657.

Heintschel von Heinegg

tion.[155] This does not, however, mean that the activities of coastal fishing boats have to be limited to the enemy's territorial sea. Fishing may also take place off the coasts of a third state.[156] As regards small boats engaged in local trade it is widely agreed that it is not the boats' size but the extent of the economic factors involved, i.e. the trade, which determines their right to protection.[157] Hence, vessels engaged in general coastal trade are not exempt from attack and capture.[158]

3. *Vessels charged with religious, scientific, or philanthropic missions.* According to Art. 4 Hague XI and customary law, these are likewise exempt from capture and attack.[159] In contrast to the wording of Art. 4 Hague XI, today vessels charged with scientific missions are specially protected only if those missions do not serve military purposes.[160] It will not always be easy to distinguish between military and non-military scientific research. Hence in practice such vessels should commence their voyage only after notifying and obtaining approval from the adversary.[161] Vessels charged with philanthropic missions will usually already be protected by GC II and AP I or as one of the other categories enumerated in the present Section. Today this category is, therefore, of minor practical relevance.[162] This also holds true for vessels on religious missions. Formerly, missionary vessels would have fallen into that category.[163] Vessels transporting pilgrims will be classified as passenger ships.

4. *Transfer of cultural property.* Vessels engaged in this task are protected in accordance with Articles 12, 13, and 14 of the 1954 Convention.[164] This presupposes that the transfer has been approved by the adversary in advance. In the absence of such approval, vessels may carry the protective emblem only if the transfer of cultural property takes place within the territory of one single state.

5. *Cartel vessels and vessels granted safe conduct.* Cartel vessels are usually designated for and engaged in the exchange of prisoners of war, or in the transport of parlamentaires and of certain messages. As the term 'cartel' implies, agreement between the parties to the conflict is a precondition for their special protection. In

[155] At the 1907 Hague Conference the Fourth Committee gave the following explanation in its report: '*La raison d'être de cette exemption est, et a toujours été, une raison d'humanité. Le régime de faveur est fait non pas à l'industrie de la pêche, mais aux pauvres gens qui s'y adonnent; il n'a pas pour but de protéger un commerce maritime particulier, plus qu'un autre, mais seulement d'éviter de causer à des individus pauvres, spécialement dignes s'intérêt, un dommage sans utilité pour le belligérant.*'
[156] Cf. Schramm, *Prisenrecht*, 144 ff.; Colombos, para. 657; Castrén, 339.
[157] Colombos, para. 658; Shearer, *Commentary*, 186 ff.; Stone, 586; Castrén, 340 ff. For the opposing view see Oppenheim/Lauterpacht, 478, who regard the boats' size as relevant. Rousseau, 292, merely states: '*Quant à la notion de petite navigation locale, c'est une question d'espèce à déterminer dans chaque cas.*'
[158] See references given by Whiteman, *Digest* 10, 642 ff.
[159] NWP 9, para. 8.2.3; Canadian *Draft Manual*, para. 718; *San Remo Manual*, paras. 47(f) and 136(e); Shearer, *Commentary*, 189 ff.
[160] NWP 9, para. 8.2.3; *San Remo Manual*, paras. 47(f) and 136(e).
[161] Cf. Mallison, *Submarines*, 128; Tucker, 97.
[162] As regards state practice during World War I see Rousseau, 292 ff.; Oppenheim/Lauterpacht, 476; Tucker, 96 ff.
[163] With regard to the Prussian missionary ship *Palme* captured during the Franco-Prussian War of 1870/71 see references in Oppenheim/Lauterpacht, 476 n. 2; Rousseau, 292.
[164] Cf. Prott, *Commentary*, 582 ff.; *San Remo Manual*, paras. 47(d) and 136(d).

Heintschel von Heinegg

the majority of cases they are then granted safe conduct. Hence, the difference between cartel vessels and vessels granted safe conduct is in the special mission for which those ships are designated.[165] The document granting safe conduct may always be examined. In case of falsification the special protection ceases, according to Section 1035.

6. *Passenger vessels.* According to Section 1004, these are merchant vessels. Hence, they are subject to visit, search, and capture. However, if such vessels are exclusively engaged in carrying civilian passengers a warship will only in rare cases be in a position to take passengers to a place of safety. They may, therefore, neither be attacked nor destroyed as prize in accordance with Section 1026 unless they lose their protected status because not innocently employed in their normal role.[166]

7. *Visit and search.* It is made clear in the last sentence of Section 1034 that the vessels enumerated are only exempt from attack and capture. Outside of neutral waters they may therefore be visited and searched any time. This follows from the restricted scope of protection. Especially, belligerents must be able to verify whether the vessels concerned are innocently employed in their normal role and that they comply with the conditions for exemption. Belligerents should, however, refrain from exercising the right of visit and search if it is provided for otherwise that such vessels are not abused (e.g. by the presence of neutral observers on board).

1035   **The special protection ends if such vessels do not comply with conditions lawfully imposed upon them, if they abuse their mission, or engage in any other activity bringing them within the definition of a military objective.**

According to Art. 3 Hague XI the vessels protected 'cease to be exempt as soon as they take any part whatever in hostilities'. Under customary international law the same applies to the other vessels enumerated in Section 1034.[167] They are all protected because of the special functions they serve. Hence, as soon as they are no longer innocently employed in their normal role, or if they are in some other way employed for purposes unrelated with their original function, they may be subject to measures of naval warfare. This is also the case if they do not submit to identification and inspection or to orders to stop or move out of the way. After loss of exemption they may be captured and confiscated. Moreover, if they make a direct

---

[165] Cf. Schramm, *Prisenrecht*, 151 ff.; Colombos, para. 660; Oppenheim/Lauterpacht, 542; Tucker 97 ff.; Castrén, 339; *NWP* 9, para. 8.2.3; Canadian *Draft Manual*, para. 718; *San Remo Manual*, paras. 47(c) and 136(c).

[166] Besides the well known but still disputed case of the *Lusitania*, the case of the *Athenia* is worth mentioning. The Nuremberg Tribunal characterized the sinking of the unarmed *Athenia* by the German submarine *U 30* on 3 Sept. 1939 as a war crime; see Zemanek, *EPIL* 3, 41. See also *NWP* 9, para. 8.2.3 (6); *San Remo Manual*, para. 47(e).

[167] See, *inter alia*, *San Remo Manual*, para. 48: 'Vessels listed in Section 47 are exempt from attack only if they: (a) are innocently employed in their normal role; (b) submit to identification and inspection when required; and (c) do not intentionally hamper the movement of combatants and obey orders to stop or move out of the way when required.' A rule to the same effect (para. 137) applies to vessels exempt from capture.

contribution to military action, e.g. by participating in hostilities, they may be attacked on sight and sunk, provided that destruction offers a definite military advantage. In any event, the abuse must be clearly established before attack. Passenger vessels engaged in carrying civilian passengers as well as members of the enemy armed forces, contraband, or war material lose exemption and may be captured. Destruction is permissible only if the safety of passengers, crews, and ship's papers is ensured. If that is impossible the ship must be diverted to an appropriate port. The special protection of passenger vessels is, however, restricted to those cases in which they are carrying civilian passengers. In other cases they may be attacked and sunk if they meet the criteria laid down in the definition of military objectives.

4. *Protected Enemy Aircraft (except medical aircraft)*

The provisions of Sections 1034 and 1035 are also relevant for enemy aircraft serv-   1036
ing the enumerated purposes and operating exclusively in established corridors.
Such aircraft may be requested to put down on land or water to be searched.

1. *General.* The special status of the vessels listed in Section 1034 results from the functions they serve. Aircraft serving the same functions are similarly exempted from attack and capture. In view of the manifold difficulties involved in the identification of aircraft they are, however, obliged to operate exclusively in established corridors. In order to verify whether such aircraft are innocently employed in their normal role and whether they comply with conditions legitimately imposed upon them they may be requested to put down on land or water for the purpose of inspection.[168] If it is clearly established that exempt aircraft do not comply with the conditions imposed upon them or that they are not innocently employed in their normal role they lose their special status and may be captured. Also, if they commit acts rendering them legitimate military objectives they may be attacked.

2. *Civil airliners.* These are civil aircraft, clearly marked, and engaged in carrying civilian passengers in scheduled or non-scheduled services along air traffic routes.[169] Civil airliners are exempt from attack only if they are innocently employed in their normal role, do not intentionally hamper the movements of combatants, and operate exclusively along air traffic routes. The fact that a clearly identifiable civil airliner does not operate within a designated corridor does not in itself justify an attack. It may, however, be intercepted and forced to land. The prohibition of destruction does not apply to civil airliners on the ground, unless there is good reason to believe that there are civilian passengers on board. They are even then liable to capture, and may be intercepted and forced to land. As regards crews and passengers Sections 1032 and 1033 apply. Identification is one of the major problems involved in the implementation of the rules protecting civil airliners. The *Vincennes* incident during the Gulf War between Iran and Iraq made that evident.

---

[168] See also *San Remo Manual*, paras. 53 ff.
[169] This definition is taken from para. 13(m), *San Remo Manual*.

Heintschel von Heinegg

Even the use of transponders identifying an aircraft as a civil airliner does not guarantee absolute protection. It is therefore crucial that the parties to the conflict promulgate and adhere to safe procedures for identifying and intercepting civil aircraft. The Recommendations issued by the ICAO can in this regard prove helpful.[170] According to the *San Remo Manual* 'civil aircraft should file the required flight plan with the cognizant Air Traffic Service, complete with information as to registration, destination, passengers, cargo, emergency communication channels, identification codes and modes, updates en route, and carry certificates as to registration, airworthiness, passengers and cargo. They should not deviate from a designated Air Traffic Service Route or flight plan without Air Traffic Control clearance unless unforeseen conditions arise, for example, safety or distress, in which case, appropriate notification should be made immediately.'[171] Moreover, 'belligerents and neutrals concerned, and authorities providing air traffic services, should establish procedures whereby commanders of warships and military aircraft are continuously aware of designated routes assigned and flight plans filed by civil aircraft in the area of military operations, including information on communication channels, identification modes and codes, destination, passengers, and cargo.'[172]

5. Other Protected Objects

1037 **Submarine cables and pipelines connecting occupied territory with neutral territory shall not be seized or destroyed. Submarine cables and pipelines connecting different parts of the territory of one party to the conflict, or connecting the territories of parties to the conflict and neutrals, may be interrupted within the law of naval warfare in case of military necessity.**

Submarine cables were internationally protected by the Convention on the Protection of Submarine Cables of 14 March 1884.[173] Today the laying of submarine cables and pipelines, according to Art. 2 HSC 1958 and Art. 87 para. 1(c) UNCLOS, is one of the freedoms of the high seas generally recognized as customary law. Hence, submarine cables and pipelines connecting neutral states may not be interfered with in naval armed conflict. As regards the laws of armed conflict at sea, there is no express prohibition on the destruction of submarine cables and pipelines.[174] The 1884 Convention, in Art. 15, expressly excludes war situations from its scope of application. Therefore, in case of military necessity submarine cables connecting enemy territory with neutral territory may be cut outside of neutral territorial waters.[175] This does not mean, as mentioned above, that considerations of military necessity alone justify such action.

---

[170] Printed in *AJIL* 1989, 335. [171] *San Remo Manual*, para. 129.
[172] *San Remo Manual*, para. 130. [173] 75 *BFSP* 356.
[174] According to Art. 54 of the 1907 Hague Regulations, submarine cables connecting occupied territories with neutral territories are protected. The scope of this provision is, however, restricted to land warfare.
[175] Lagoni, *EPIL* 11, 50.

6. Targets on Land

The following rules apply to targets on land subject to the provisions on the protection of the civilian population and the general principles of the law of naval
warfare. The bombardment of defended localities, ports, and buildings situated
on hostile coasts is permitted. The mining of ports and coastal installations alone
does not justify bombardment (Art. 1 HC IX). Military objectives located within
undefended localities or ports may be bombarded if there are no other means
available to destroy these objectives and when the local authorities have not complied with a summons within a reasonable period of time (Art. 2 HC IX). The
absence of such summons may be justified by urgent military reasons. If there is
a possibility that these objectives could be destroyed by landing forces, bombardment shall not be permissible.

1. *The relevance of the 1907 Hague Convention IX.*[176] In view of the progressive
development and the reaffirmation of international humanitarian law by the 1977
Additional Protocol I, the provisions of Hague IX concerning bombardment by
naval forces in time of war have become largely obsolete. The obligations in the latter can easily be derived from the provisions of Part IV, Section I of AP I.[177] However,
especially because not all states are bound by the Protocol, those provisions of
Hague IX which are recognized as customary law, Articles 1, 2, and 5, are relevant.

2. *Specific obligations.* The introductory sentence clarifies that, when attacking targets on land, naval forces are obliged to ensure the protection of the civilian population as laid down in AP I.[178] Accordingly, 'without prejudice to the provisions of
the Hague Convention for the Protection of Cultural Property in Event of Armed
Conflict of 14 May 1954 . . . it is prohibited . . . to commit any acts of hostility
directed against historic monuments, works of art or places of worship'.[179]
Moreover, when attacking land targets, naval forces shall take care 'to protect the
natural environment against widespread, long-term, and severe damage'.[180]
'Works or installations containing dangerous forces, namely dams, dykes and
nuclear electrical generating stations, shall not be made the object of attack, even
where these objects are military objectives, if such attack may cause the release of
dangerous forces and consequent severe losses among the civilian population'.[181]
Also worth mentioning are the provisions of Art. 59 (non-defended localities) and of
Art. 60 (demilitarized zones) AP I.[182]

*

---

[176] Cf. Robertson, *Commentary*, 161 ff.   [177] Cf. Ipsen, *Die 'offene Stadt'*, 149 ff.
[178] Other conventions of relevance are: the 1925 Geneva Protocol, ENMOD, and Protocols I to III of the
1980 UN Weapons Convention.
[179] For further details see Art. 53 AP I.   [180] Art. 55, para. 1 AP I.
[181] Ibid.
[182] As regards the so-called 'hunger blockade' and relief shipments for the civilian population, see para.
4 of the commentary on Section 1051.

Heintschel von Heinegg

III. SPECIAL PROVISIONS CONCERNING METHODS OF NAVAL WARFARE

1. Mine Warfare

Preliminary Remarks

1. *Hague Convention VIII as the basis for legal evaluation of mine warfare at sea.* The extensive use of mines during the Russo-Japanese War (1904–5) and the damage caused to innocent shipping even after the end of hostilities led to the inclusion of naval mines in the agenda of the Second Hague Peace Conference.[183] Even by 1907 Hague Convention VIII, which resulted from the Conference's deliberations, was considered a meagre compromise between the interests of the great sea powers on one hand, and of states with only small naval forces on the other.[184] Great Britain had urged the prohibition of automatic contact mines in sea areas beyond the belligerents' territorial seas.[185] The reason was that it considered their use in the high seas as prejudicial to its naval supremacy. The majority of states represented at the Hague, however, were unwilling to refrain from the use of this most effective means of naval warfare.[186]

Hence, Hague Convention VIII contains neither a general prohibition nor a specific geographical limitation of the use of automatic contact mines. Especially, it lacks a rule on mining of international straits which are overlapped by the territorial seas of the belligerents. Despite several proposals on the prohibition of mining such straits submitted by the Netherlands,[187] the majority held that questions related to straits were not covered by the mandates of either the Committee or of

---

[183] See Verzijl, *International Law in Historical Perspective* Vol. IX, 297.

[184] Hence, in the Preamble, the contracting parties deplored that 'the existing state of affairs makes it impossible to forbid the employment of automatic submarine contact mines'. They also expressed their hope that, in the future, it would be possible 'to formulate rules on the subject which shall ensure to the interests involved all the guarantees desirable'.

[185] Article 4 of the British proposal which served as a basis for discussion, (Annex 9) provided: '*Les belligérants ne pourront se servir de mines sous-marines automatiques de contact que dans leurs eaux territoriales ou celles de leurs ennemis.*'

[186] Especially the United States and Germany were in favour of an explicit rule on the use of mines in the high seas. Hence, Germany proposed the following amendment to Article 4 of the British proposal: '*La pose des mines automatiques de contact sera aussi permise sur le théâtre de la guerre; sera considéré comme théâtre de la guerre l'espace de mer sur lequel se fait ou vient de se faire une opération de guerre ou sur lequel une pareille opération pourra avoir lieu par suite de la présence ou de l'approche des forces armées des deux belligérants.*' At first, the *Comité d'Examen*, in Article 2 of its draft, had been in favour of the British proposal. After the US delegate Sperry had made clear the US standpoint, the Third Committee dispensed with any spatial limitation of the use of mines. In its report of 9 Oct. 1907, the Third Committee explained this as follows: '*Cette solution n'a pas obtenu, devant la Commission, la majorité absolue des suffrages. L'alinéa 2 de l'article 4, qui établissait la différence mentionnée entre l'attaque et la défense, fut même rejeté, n'ayant obtenu que 10 voix contre 12 et 10 abstentions.*'

[187] The proposals by the Netherlands (Annex 12 and 22) provided: '*En tous cas les détroits qui unissent deux mers libres ne peuvent pas être barrés.*' '*Dans aucun cas la communication entre deux mers libres ne peut être barrée entièrement et le passage ne sera permis qu'aux conditions qui seront indiquées par les autorités compétentes.*'

the Conference.[188] The existing treaty regimes for certain straits was not to be jeopardized by general rules on mining. Hence, the Netherlands' proposals were rejected.[189] The only provision referring to the area of minelaying is Article 2, which prohibits the laying of automatic contact mines 'off the coast and ports of the enemy, with the sole object of intercepting commercial shipping.'[190] The material scope of Hague Convention VIII is limited to automatic submarine contact mines (and torpedos).[191] To this effect the Convention differentiates between anchored and unanchored mines. According to Article 1, para. 1 the latter may not be laid 'except when they are so constructed as to become harmless one hour after the person who laid them ceases to control them'. The one-hour limit is designed to enable warships to escape pursuing enemy units by planting mines.[192] According to Article 1 para. 2, anchored mines must 'become harmless as soon as they have broken loose from their moorings'. Furthermore, the belligerents must take 'every possible precaution . . . for the security of peaceful', i.e. neutral,[193] shipping (Article 3, para. 1). Finally, they should 'undertake to do their utmost to render these mines harmless within a limited time, and, should they cease to be under surveillance, to notify the danger zones as soon as military exigencies permit, by a notice addressed to

---

[188] Thus, the Third Committee in its report to the plenary stated: '*Après discussion, il fut jugé préférable de ne rien ajouter au texte du Règlement, mais de modifier le passage du Rapport qui parle de la résolution prise sur cette question par le Comité d'Examen.; on établirait dans le Rapport que les détroits sont restés en dehors les délibérations de la présente Conférence et, tout en réservant expressément les déclarations faites au sein du Comité par les Délégations des Etats-Unis d'Amérique, du Japon, de la Russie et de la Turquie, on indiquerait la conviction de voir appliquer sur les mines dont on pourrait se servir dans les détroits les conditions techniques adoptées par le présent Règlement.*'

[189] In the report of the Comité d'Examen these statements are summarized as follows: '. . . *la Délégation du Japon [. . .] qui, tout en déclarant qu'il n'avait pas d'objection, si la règle s'appliquait seulement aux pays neutres, avait fait observer . . . que l'amendement néerlandais . . . lui paraissait pouvoir s'adapter peut-être aux conditions géographiques des Etats continentaux mais pas toujours à celles des Puissances insulaires. En raison de la configuration particulière du Japon . . . détroits qui sont partie intégrante de son territoire, mais qui tomberaient néanmoins sous le coup de la définition inscrite dans le dit amendement, la Délégation japonaise ne pourrait adhérer à cette disposition. . . . le Contre-Admiral Sperrry déclara, au nom de la Délégation des Etats-Unies d'Amérique, que "prenant en considération le grand nombre d'îles qui composent le groupe des Philippines, et l'incertitude des résultats que pourrait avoir la stipulation en question, envisageant en outre les stipulations de traités comprises dans l'alinéa ajouté, il ne pourrait pas prendre part à la discussion comme, à son avis, la matière sort des limites de ses instructions". . . . la Délégation ottomane . . . exposa que: "La Délégation Impériale Ottomane croit de son devoir de déclarer qu'étant donné la situation exceptionnelle créé par les traités en vigueur aux détroits des Dardanelles et du Bosphore, détroits qui sont partie intégrante du territoire, le Gouvernement Impérial ne saurait, d'aucune façon, prendre un engagement quelconque tendant à limiter les moyens de défense qu'il pourrait juger nécessaire d'employer pour ces détroits, en cas de guerre ou dans le but de faire respecter sa neutralité". . . . La Délégation de Russie estime que le régime de certains détroits étant réglé par les traités spéciaux, basés sur des considérations politiques, ces stipulations concernant ces détroits ne peuvent faire l'objet d'une discussion. Quant à créer un régime spécial pour une partie des détroits en exceptant les autres, ce procédé lui paraîtrait inconséquent et très dangereux. La diversité du régime qui en résulterait tant pour les neutres que pour les belligérants, serait inévitablement une nouvelle source de conflits entre eux.*'

[190] With regard to the difficulties in establishing the subjective element see Dinstein, *IYHR* 45 (1980), 38–69, 45. Stone, *Legal Controls*, 583 ff. states: 'The escape from this prohibition provided by the reference to the *object* of the operation largely frustrated it from the start.'

[191] The use of torpedoes is regulated by Article 1, para. 3. Originally, the Conference's agenda was restricted to torpedoes. 'Torpedo' used to be the general designation that also covered mines. However, in view of the existence of self-propelling destructive devices, as early as 1907 the Conference agreed on the notion of 'mines'.

[192] See Dinstein, *IYHR* 45 (1980), 44; Cowie, 170. [193] See Dinstein, *IYHR* 45; Cowie, 175.

Heintschel von Heinegg

ship owners, which must also be communicated to the Governments through the diplomatic channel' (Article 3, para. 2).

In view of the unrestricted mine warfare of the two World Wars and of the technical development of naval mines,[194] the continued legal relevance of Hague Convention VIII has become a matter of dispute.[195] Indeed, it is open to doubt whether its provisions are applicable to bottom mines, modern anchored mines,[196] or to remote-controlled minefields activated by means of, e.g., VLF transmissions. These sophisticated and highly accurate mines are not covered by the wording of the Convention because they react to magnetic and acoustic signals or to changes in water pressure, not to mere physical contact.[197] However, it should not be overlooked that the old automatic contact mine is still used by most of the world's navies.[198] During armed conflicts since 1945, the belligerents only in rare cases employed modern sophisticated mines.[199] Hence, apart from the problem of whether Hague Convention VIII is of significance for modern mines, it seems to be the correct view that Hague Convention VIII *qua* customary law remains a valid legal yardstick for the use of automatic contact mines.[200]

Hague Convention VIII has therefore acquired the status of customary international law governing the use of automatic contact mines. However, its provisions are not applicable as such to other modern mines. These are, it is submitted, governed by rules and principles of customary international law, which also provide norms regulating the area where naval mines—whether antiquated or sophisticated—may be employed. These principles are elaborated in Sections 1040 and 1043.

2. *'Mines'*. International law still lacks a generally agreed definition of naval mines. The Hague Conference at first used the term 'torpedo' to include mines. In the course of the deliberations, mines were distinguished from torpedoes.[201] Still, the delegates did not agree on a definition. It merely follows from the wording that Hague VIII is applicable to 'submarine automatic contact mines', which explode on physical contact. The present Manual also lacks a definition of mines. Hence, its provisions on mining are applicable to contact mines as well as to more modern

---

[194] See Levie, *Mine Warfare*, 97 *et seq*. With regard to the current technological state see Blake (Ed.), *Jane's Underwater Warfare Systems*, 43; Hartmann, *Weapons That Wait*, 106 ff.; Griffiths, *Hidden Menace*, 60 ff., 144 ff.

[195] Especially Baxter considers Hague Convention VIII to have become obsolete by desuetude; Baxter, *Recueil des Cours* 129 (1970 I), 25–104, 97. See also Stone, *Legal Controls*, 584 ff.

[196] Since modern anchored mines may be employed at greater depths than bottom mines, they are a highly effective means of naval warfare.

[197] According to a minority opinion, Hague Convention VIII may be applied to modern mines by analogy. See E. Rauch, *Protocol Additional*, 116. However, according to the view taken here, it is not possible to apply an international treaty by way of analogy to subjects not expressly regulated therein.

[198] Allegedly, the former Soviet Union still disposes of a vast number of automatic contact mines of the World War II type. Other states, such as Iraq, were supplied with these mines.

[199] See Levie, *Mine Warfare*, 135 ff.

[200] e.g. during the Iraq–Kuwait conflict the US expressly referred to Hague Convention VIII. See U.S. Dept. of Defense, *Conduct*, Appendix O. With regard to the customary status of the Convention see also Levie, *Mine Warfare*, 177 ff.; Bock, 75 ff.; *NWP* 9, paras. 9.2 and 9.2.3; Canadian *Draft Manual*, para. 710 (1).

[201] Cf. Levie, *Mine Warfare*, 24 ff.

mines. Thus, the difficulties involved with regard to the applicability of Hague VIII to modern mines are avoided. For a better understanding it is, however, useful to refer to NATO practice according to which naval mines are defined as 'an explosive device laid in the water, on the seabed or in the subsoil thereof, with the intention of damaging or sinking ships or of deterring shipping from entering an area.'[202]

Since that definition is also employed in Article 2 of the Swedish proposal for amending the 1980 Conventional Weapons Convention[203] it can be taken as a basis for the present Manual. Hence, the following means of naval warfare are not, or not exclusively, covered by the provisions on mining:

—anti-aircraft systems launched from submarines, such as the French *SM Polyphem*;

—devices attached to the bottom of ships or to harbour installations by personnel operating underwater;[204] and

—devices like the 'encapsulated torpedo' (CAPTOR) that are usually designated as mines[205] but are in fact torpedoes.

3. *Special Treaty Provisions.* Before elaborating the rules and principles of international law governing modern conventional mines, brief reference to two important treaties is necessary. The use of nuclear mines is subject to the 1971 Sea-bed Treaty.[206] Although an arms control treaty, its provisions are binding not only in peacetime but also in times of armed conflict.[207] Accordingly, a belligerent may not, in sea areas beyond its own 12 nm. territorial sea,[208] 'emplant or emplace on the sea bed and the ocean floor and in the subsoil thereof . . . any nuclear weapons', including nuclear mines.[209] This prohibition also covers tethered[210] tactical low yield nuclear mines used for anti-submarine purposes.[211] The contrary view taken by Professor O'Connell[212] is incompatible with the wording ('nuclear weapons') as well as with the object and purpose of the Sea-bed Treaty.[213] Article 1 Protocol II of the 1980 Conventional Weapons Convention[214] refers *inter alia* to 'mines laid to interdict beaches'. In some cases such mines are laid in waters less than 5 metres

---

[202] See van Hegelsom, *Methods*, 27.
[203] U.N. Doc. A/CN.10/141 of 8 May 1990.
[204] Cf. van Hegelsom, *Methods*, 28.
[205] See, e.g., *Jane's Underwater Warfare Systems*, 56.
[206] Treaty on the Prohibition of the Emplacement of Nuclear Weapons and Other Weapons of Mass Destruction on the Sea bed and the Ocean Floor and in the Subsoil Thereof, London, Moscow, Washington, 11 Feb. 1971. For the text see UN Juridical Yearbook 121–4 (1970).
[207] See *NWP* 9, para. 10.2.2; Migliorino, *Commentary*, 615–22, 620.
[208] According to Article II the 12 nm. limit applies even when the breadth of the territorial sea is less than 12 nm.
[209] On 7 Oct. 1969, the US delegate declared: 'The Treaty would therefore prohibit, *inter alia*, mines that were anchored to or emplaced on the sea bed.'; *Documents on Disarmament* 479 (1969). See also Thorpe, *Ocean Development and International Law* 18 (1987), 255–78, 262.
[210] Drifting or floating mines are neither 'emplanted' nor 'emplaced' in the sense of Article I. See Rauch, *Protocol Additional*, 131; Thorpe, *loc. cit.*, 262.
[211] Ibid.
[212] O'Connell, *Influence*, 157.
[213] See Clingan, *Submarine Mines*, 354 ff.; Thorpe, *loc. cit.*, 262.
[214] Convention on Prohibitions or Restrictions on the Use of Certain Conventional Weapons Which May Be Deemed to Be Excessively Injurious or to Have Indiscriminate Effects, Geneva, 10 Oct. 1980; Protocol on Prohibitions or Restrictions on the Use of Mines, Booby Traps and Other Devices (Protocol II). For the text see Schindler/Toman (Eds.), 179 ff.

Heintschel von Heinegg

deep. However, Protocol II does not apply to naval warfare. The scope of that Protocol is restricted to anti-personnel mines and to land warfare.[215]

4. *Minelaying in times of crisis prior to the outbreak of hostilities.* The provisions of the present section are not restricted to the employment of naval mines in times of armed conflict. Sections 1041 and 1042 deal with minelaying prior to the outbreak of an international armed conflict. This is justified by the following consideration. In view of a possible escalation of a given situation it may become necessary to secure one's territorial sea and ports in times of crisis. However, the minelaying state must respect a number of legal restrictions stricter than the rules applicable in times of armed conflict.

a) Types of Mine Warfare: Principles

1039   In laying mines the following purposes are distinguished:

— protective mining, i.e. in friendly territorial and internal waters;

— defensive mining, i.e. in international waters for the protection of passages, ports and their entrances; and

— offensive mining, i.e. in hostile territorial and internal waters or in waters predominantly controlled by the adversary.

The distinction between different types of minelaying laid down in Section 1039 is not reflective of customary international law. It does, however, reflect the practice of the Federal Republic of Germany and its NATO allies.[216] Hence, it is taken as a basis for the purposes of the present Manual.

1040   Any mode of minelaying, whether before or after the beginning of an armed conflict, shall be subject to the principles of effective surveillance, risk control, and warning (HC VIII). In particular, all feasible measures of precaution shall be observed for the safety of peaceful navigation.

1. *Legal basis.* As stated above, the provisions of Hague Convention VIII are applicable neither as such nor by analogy to mines other than automatic contact mines. Nevertheless, there is a general consensus, in practice as well as in the literature, that the customary principles derived from Articles 1, 2, 3, and 5 of the Convention must be taken into account when laying modern naval mines.[217] The duties derived from these principles may vary according to the circumstances of each case.

[215] See Levie, *Mine Warfare*, 138.

[216] Cf. Ide, *Europäische Wehrkunde* 7/89, 447 ff.; Hoffmann, *USNIP* 103 (May 1977), 142 ff.

[217] Thus, *NWP* 9, para. 9.2, provides: 'the general principles of law embodied in the 1907 Convention continue to serve as a guide to lawful employment of naval mines.' See also Canadian *Draft Manual*, para. 710(2); Dinstein, *IYHR* 45 (1980), 46; Thorpe, *loc. cit.*, 259 ff.; Rowe, *Defence*, 128; Clingan, *Submarine Mines*, 353; Bring, *Journal of Peace Research* 24 (1987), 275–86, 283; O'Connell, *Influence*, 157.

2. *Legal obligations of minelaying states.*

a) *Basic considerations.* The provisions of Section 1040 should not be considered an exhaustive enumeration of the duties incumbent on the minelaying state. The general principles of the (maritime) *jus in bello* also apply;[218] in particular the principle of distinction.[219] Any indiscriminate use of mines, i.e. that are not or cannot be directed against a military objective, is contrary to international law. Moreover, naval mines may in principle only be employed against military objectives.

b) *The Principle of Effective Surveillance.* This is designed to secure the principle of warning and the duty of clearing mined areas after the cessation of hostilities. It can therefore be deduced from Articles 3 and 5 of Hague Convention VIII. In particular, it implies that the minelaying belligerent is obliged carefully to record the location of minefields.[220] Otherwise the duties on warning and mine-clearance would be rendered obsolete. Moreover, belligerents are obliged to ensure, e.g. by random tests, that their mines are programmed correctly and will not react to other than the anticipated stimuli.

c) *Risk Control.* Closely related to the foregoing is the principle of risk control, which can be deduced from Articles 1 and 3 of Hague Convention VIII. Risk control does not mean that the minelaying party is obliged permanently to exercise surveillance over a minefield; it is sufficient if that party is able effectively to manage the dangers which minefields constitute for peaceful shipping. The concrete duties resulting from the principle of risk control may, therefore, vary according to the type of mine used. Controlled mines, and especially remote-controlled minefields designed for anti-submarine warfare purposes, do not generally pose much threat to peaceful surface shipping.[221] Therefore, the minelaying state will normally comply with the principle of risk control by equipping the minefield with a remote control device. It needs to be stressed that in practice remotely controlled minefields will only be laid if the control system is nearly infallible. Otherwise the military advantage envisaged (long duration, flexibility) cannot be achieved. The control systems depending on VLF transmissions from land require a considerable amount

---

[218] See *NWP* 9, para. 9.2; Rauch, *Protocol Additional*, 130.

[219] Article 3 of the Swedish proposal provides: 'The indiscriminate use of mines is prohibited. Indiscriminate use is (a) any use of mines which is not or cannot be directed against a military objective; (b) any laying of mines which may be expected to cause incidental loss of civilian life, injury to civilians, or a combination thereof which would be excessive in relation to the concrete and direct military advantage anticipated.'

[220] *NWP* 9, para. 9.2.3 provides: 'The location of minefields must be carefully recorded to ensure accurate notification and to facilitate subsequent removal and/or deactivation.' See also para. 84 of the *San Remo Manual*: 'Belligerents shall record the locations where they have laid mines.' Also Article 7, para. 1 of the Swedish proposal: 'The parties to a conflict shall record all zones where they have laid mines.'

[221] In *NWP* 9, para. 9.2.1, the differences between controlled and armed mines is explained as follows: 'Armed mines are either emplaced with all safety devices withdrawn or are armed following emplacement, so as to detonate when preset parameters (if any) are satisfied. Controlled mines (including mines possessing remote control activation devices) have no destructive capability until affirmatively activated by some form of controlled arming order (whereupon they become armed mines).' See also Dinstein, *IYHR* 45 (1980), at 46.

Heintschel von Heinegg

of energy and will probably not be absolutely immune from failure.[222] Hence, additionally, the mines must be equipped with a deactivation device. If the control system breaks down the belligerent is of course obliged to issue an appropriate warning. If other than (remotely) controlled mines are used, anchored mines must become harmless as soon as they break loose from their moorings.[223] They must be equipped with a self-destruction or deactivation device.[224] If Article 1, para. 1 Hague Convention VIII applied to bottom mines, designed to explode upon magnetic, acoustic signatures and/or changes in water pressure, then they would have to become harmless 'one hour at most after the person who laid them ceases to control them'.[225] Customary international law, however, has not developed in that direction. Modern bottom mines are highly sophisticated weapons systems that can be programmed to react to specific types of ships or even to one single ship only if sufficient data are available.[226] Hence, these mines need not become harmless within one hour after they have reached their position on the ocean floor. Only when it is not possible to ensure by programming that the mine will be directed at military objectives alone must it be equipped with some kind of deactivation device.[227] However, if drifting or floating mines are used the dangers which they pose to peaceful shipping (sometimes overestimated)[228] mean that they still have to be made harmless within one hour.[229]

---

[222] See *Jane's Underwater Warfare Systems*, ('Jane's') 43.

[223] Art. 1, para. 2 Hague Convention VIII; *NWP* 9, para. 9.2.3; Article 4 of the Swedish proposal: 'It is prohibited to lay anchored mines which do not become harmless as soon as they have broken loose from their moorings.'

[224] While the mines used for the blockade of Haiphong were equipped with such devices, the mines laid by Iran in the Gulf war (1980–88) did not become harmless after they had broken loose from their moorings.

[225] Professor Dinstein seems to be in favour of a rule to that effect: 'The rule must be that the use of any mine—antiquated or sophisticated—is permissible only if they are anchored (even though the anchor may enable them to home in on a ship within a given range), and on condition that they become harmless as soon as they are disconnected from their moorings'; Dinstein, *IYHR* 45 (1980), 46. For the contrary view see Levie, *Syracuse Journal of International Law and Commerce* 14 (1988), 727–39, 732 ff.; Thorpe, *loc. cit.*, 260 ff.

[226] See *Jane's*, 43.

[227] *NWP* 9, para. 9.2.3: 'Unanchored mines otherwise affixed or imbedded in the bottom must become harmless within an hour after loss of control over them.' Article 4, para. 3 of the Swedish proposal provides: 'It is prohibited to lay mines, unless an effective neutralizing mechanism is used on each mine, that is to say, a self-actuating or remotely controlled mechanism which is designed to render a mine harmless or cause it to destroy itself when it is anticipated that the mine will no longer serve the military purpose for which it was placed in position, or at the latest 2 years after such emplacement.'

[228] In the course of the proceedings of the *Corfu Channel* case it became evident that drifting automatic contact mines were less dangerous than generally believed. Cowie states: 'Incidentally, the legend has grown up that all drifting mines are dangerous to shipping, but this is by no means the case. When moored, mines are normally kept dangerous due to the tension in the mooring rope, and if they break adrift the tension is relaxed and a strong spring takes charge, so opening a switch in the circuit between the firing battery and the detonator. If a mine breaks adrift with a length of mooring trailing from it, that mooring may get caught up on rocks, pier structures, and so forth; the mine in effect becomes moored once more and so liable to detonate if one of the horns is struck. . . . Finally, it is extremely difficult to ram a mine or any small object floating freely on the surface of the sea. The chances of a ship being sunk or damaged by a mine which has broken adrift from its moorings are in fact remote, but none the less the prudent seaman will give them a clear berth.'; Cowie, 188 ff.

[229] *San Remo Manual*, para. 82 provides: 'It is forbidden to use free-floating mines unless: (a) they are directed against a military objective; and (b) they become harmless within an hour after loss of control over them.' See also Art. 4, para. 4 of the Swedish proposal: 'It is prohibited to use drifting mines.'

Heintschel von Heinegg

d) *Warning*. The duty to warn arises as soon as effective control of the risk involved is lost. The duty to issue warnings of armed or dangerous minefields is not, however, absolute. The belligerent is obligated to notify danger zones or the position of a minefield only if 'military exigencies permit'.[230] This does not mean that the belligerent may refrain from issuing effective warnings only because there is still a potential military advantage. Rather, according to the general principles of the (maritime) *jus in bello*, the military advantage anticipated must, in the circumstances ruling at the time, be definite.[231] In case of doubt, the limits of the mined areas must be notified at least roughly. Judge Schwebel in his dissenting opinion to the *Nicaragua* judgment has summarized these duties in a way that may also be applied in times of armed conflict: 'However, as against third states whose shipping was damaged or whose nationals were injured by mines laid by or on behalf of the United States, the international responsibility of the United States may arise. Third States were and are entitled to carry on commerce with Nicaragua and their ships are entitled to make use of Nicaraguan ports. If the United States were to be justified in taking blockade-like measures against Nicaraguan ports, as by mining, it could only be so if its mining of Nicaraguan ports were publicly and officially announced by it and if international shipping were duly warned by it about the fact that mines would be or had been laid in specified waters; international shipping was not duly warned by it in a timely, official manner.'[232] The form in which these warnings must be issued depends on the circumstances of each case. In general, it will suffice to inform international shipping by the usual means, e.g. the 'Notices to Mariners'. If, however, a vessel that may not legitimately be considered a military objective is about to enter a mined sea area, the belligerent must use all means to prevent it from proceeding, *inter alia* by making use of internationally recognized emergency frequencies. Article 3, para. 2 Hague Convention VIII obliges the belligerents also to communicate danger zones to the 'Governments through the diplomatic channel'. In view of the technical state of modern means of communication it is, however, doubtful whether such formal notification is still necessary.[233]

e) *Precautionary Measures*. In principle, a belligerent is required to allow peaceful shipping to leave the sea area that is, or is about to be, mined.[234] Since this is not

[230] Art. 3, para. 2 Hague Convention VIII; *NWP* 9, para. 9.2.3 (1). Art. 6, para. 1 of the Swedish proposal provides: 'Effective warning, through notification of danger zones, of any use of activated mines which may affect neutral or non-belligerent shipping or vessels protected under Article 4, shall be given as soon as military considerations permit.' Para. 83 of the *San Remo Manual* reads: 'The laying of armed mines or the arming of prelaid mines must be notified unless the mines can only be exploded by ships which are military objectives.' This implies that sophisticated and discriminating mines need not be notified.

[231] This formulation stems from Art. 52, para. 2 AP I. The definition of military objectives contained in that provision is today generally accepted as customary international law and thus applicable in naval warfare. See commentary on Section 1017; *NWP* 9, para. 8.1.1.; Canadian *Draft Manual*, para. 714(1).

[232] ICJ Reports 1986, 379 ff.

[233] According to the judgment of the ICJ in the *Nicaragua* case obviously any form of information may be considered sufficient as long as it is effective; see ICJ Reports 1986, para. 292.

[234] The US, when mining Haiphong, employed mines that were activated three days after they had been laid. Thus, innocent shipping was able to leave Haiphong unmolested; see Levie, *Mine Warfare*, 147. Para. 85, *San Remo Manual* provides: 'Mining operations in the internal waters, territorial sea or archipelagic waters of a belligerent State should provide, when the mining is first executed, for free exit of shipping of neutral States.'

Heintschel von Heinegg

an absolute duty the belligerent may refrain from granting such a period of grace if the military advantage anticipated would thereby be jeopardized. If the safety of peaceful shipping cannot be ensured by any of the means described above the belligerent is obliged to take additional precautionary measures.[235] This may include the duty to designate safe passages or to provide piloting.

b) Mine Laying Prior to the Beginning of an Armed Conflict

1041 **Protective mining is permissible even in times of crisis, subject to the right of innocent passage of foreign ships through territorial waters. If it is indispensable for the protection of its security and if the ships have been appropriately warned, the coastal state may temporarily prohibit innocent passage through specific parts of its territorial waters. In the case of straits serving international navigation there is no right of protective mining in times of crisis.**

1. *Prior to the outbreak of an international armed conflict.* Only protective minelaying is permissible. It is self-evident that prior to the outbreak of an international armed conflict it is prohibited to lay mines in the territorial waters of a foreign state.[236] Rights and duties of states are governed by the law of peace. They are, therefore, obliged to respect the freedom of navigation beyond their territorial sea[237] and to use the high seas (including EEZs) for peaceful purposes only.[238] Violation of these obligations by the use of mines may be justified as self-defence, according to Art. 51 UN Charter.[239] This presupposes an armed attack. If, however, an armed attack occurs then Section 1042 on wartime mining comes into operation. In such cases the question of mining prior to the outbreak of an international armed conflict is no longer of relevance. The question remains whether it is also prohibited to lay mines in sea areas beyond the outer limit of the territorial sea. According to the position taken in the present Manual the laying of mines in international waters, whether armed or remotely controlled, is contrary to international law. According to the US *Manual,* mining of international waters is considered legitimate under the following conditions: 'Controlled mines . . . may be emplaced in international waters beyond the territorial sea subject only to the requirement that they do not unreasonably interfere with other lawful uses of the oceans. The determination of what constitutes an "unreasonable interference" involves a balancing of a number of factors including the rationale for their emplacement (i.e., the self-defense requirements of the emplacing nation), the extent of the area to be mined, the hazard (if any) to other lawful ocean uses, and the duration of their emplacement. Because controlled mines do not constitute a hazard to navigation,

---

[235] Art. 6, para. 2 of the Swedish proposal provides: 'When mines are employed, all feasible precautions shall be taken for the safety of vessels and shipping protected under Article 4. Feasible precautions are those precautions which are practicable or practically possible taking into account all circumstances ruling at the time, including humanitarian and military considerations.'

[236] See *NWP* 9, para. 9.2.2. In the *Nicaragua* case the ICJ held: 'In peacetime for one state to lay mines in the internal or territorial waters of another is an unlawful act'; ICJ Reports 1986, 112.

[237] See Arts. 87 and 58 UNCLOS.   [238] See, *inter alia,* Clingan, *Mines,* 356.

[239] *NWP* 9, para. 9.2.2. See also Thorpe, *loc.cit.,* 267.

Heintschel von Heinegg

international notice of their emplacement is not required. Armed mines may not be emplaced in international waters prior to the outbreak of armed conflict, except under the most demanding requirements of individual or collective self-defense. Should armed mines be emplaced in international waters under such circumstances, prior notification of their location must be provided and the anticipated date of their complete removal must be clearly stated. The nation emplacing armed mines in international waters during peacetime also assumes the responsibility to maintain an on-scene presence in the area sufficient to ensure that appropriate warning is provided to ships approaching the danger area. All armed mines must be expeditiously removed or rendered harmless when the imminent danger that prompted their emplacement has passed.'[240] Even though there is some support in the literature for the US position, especially by those who acknowledge a right of preventive self-defence,[241] the rules laid down in *NWP* 9 are not covered by existing international law. Prior to the outbreak of an international armed conflict, the rights and duties of states are exclusively governed by the law of peace: in the present context, by the international law of the sea. Hence, the freedom of navigation as well as the duty of peaceful use of the high seas have to be observed. An infringement of these rules and principles is only justified if an armed attack occurs. It may be that according to *NWP* 9 the scope of self-defence is broader. Even then it is open to doubt whether a case of 'most demanding requirements of individual or collective self-defence' is still governed by the law of peace.[242]

2. *Minelaying in one's own territorial waters.* In times of crisis the laying of mines is permissible in the territorial sea, in the internal waters, and in the archipelagic waters of the minelaying state. The question arises whether and to what extent these rules are compatible with the international law of the sea, as far as the territorial sea is concerned. Even though the coastal state's sovereignty extends to the territorial sea it is not free to suspend the right of innocent passage.[243] Innocent passage may—temporarily—be suspended in exceptional cases only.[244] The ICJ in the *Nicaragua* case emphasized that 'if a State lays mines in any waters whatever in which the vessels of another State have rights of access or passage, and fails to give any warning or notification whatsoever, in disregard of the security of peaceful shipping, it commits a breach of the principles of humanitarian law underlying the specific provisions of Convention No. VIII of 1907'.[245] Hence, if mines are laid in the territorial sea peaceful shipping must be effectively warned if the mines form a threat. The rules laid down in the US Manual do, however, comply with these principles. Mining of one's own territorial waters is said to be permissible only when

---

[240] *NWP* 9, para. 9.2.2.

[241] See, *inter alia*, Thorpe, *loc. cit.*, 267 ff.; Rowe, *Defence*, 128. Bowett, *Self Defence*, 71, states: 'It can scarcely be contemplated that a state must remain passive while a serious menace to its security mounts on the high seas beyond its territorial sea. It is accordingly maintained that it is still permissible for a state to assume a protective jurisdiction, within the limits circumscribing every exercise of the right of self defence on the high seas in order to protect its ships, its aircraft and its right to territorial integrity and political independence from an imminent danger or actual attack'.

[242] See Clingan, *Submarine Mines*, 356.   [243] Ibid., 355 ff.

[244] See Art. 25, UNCLOS.   [245] ICJ Reports 1986, 112.

either peaceful shipping remains unaffected or when it is demanded by fundamental security considerations.[246] If states, like Sweden, lay controlled minefields in their territorial waters in peacetime, they are not obliged to give notice of the minefield, nor are they obliged to issue warnings.[247] Only when the minefield is activated does the right temporarily to suspend innocent passage presuppose a prior warning.[248]

3. *International straits.* Prior to the outbreak of an international armed conflict the coastal state is not entitled to suspend the right of transit passage through international straits. In the *Corfu Channel* case the ICJ held that 'unless otherwise prescribed in an international convention, there is no right for a coastal state to prohibit such passage through straits in time of peace'.[249] Since controlled minefields do not interfere with transit passage there is no reason for denying the coastal state the right to employ them within international straits. The foregoing commentary applies *mutatis mutandis* to archipelagic shipping lanes.

c) *Minelaying During Armed Conflicts*

1042   During an armed conflict protective mining is permissible without the limitations applicable before it begins. As a matter of principle, defensive mining is permissible only after the beginning of the armed conflict; the shipping lanes of neutral and non-belligerent states shall be kept open to an appropriate extent, if military circumstances so permit. Offensive mining is permissible only in the exercise of the right of individual or collective self-defence (Article 51, UN Charter), which presupposes an armed attack. Acts of aggression not amounting to armed attacks do not suffice as a motive. Offensive mining may not be undertaken solely to interdict merchant shipping.

1. *Protective mining.* In the course of an international armed conflict this is a generally acknowledged belligerent right.[250] With the outbreak of hostilities the relationship between the belligerents is no longer governed by the rules of the international law of the sea concerning innocent passage, transit passage, or archipelagic shipping lane passage. The relationship of the parties to the conflict with neutral states or those not parties to the conflict must be differentiated. Whereas, for security reasons, the right of innocent passage may be denied to neutral shipping at least temporarily, this is not the case with regard to transit (and archipelagic shipping lanes) passage. In view of the provisions of UNCLOS III guaranteeing an inalienable right of transit passage, such mining constitutes a violation of inter-

---

[246] *NWP* 9, para. 9.2.2.

[247] *NWP* 9, para. 9.2.2 provides: 'Emplacement of controlled mines in a nation's own archipelagic waters or territorial sea is not subject to such notification or removal requirements.'

[248] *NWP* 9, para. 9.2.2: 'If armed mines are emplaced in archipelagic waters or the territorial sea, appropriate international notification of the existence and location of such mines is required.'

[249] ICJ Reports 1949, 28. See also Baxter, *BYIL* 31 (1954), 187–216.

[250] Oppenheim/Lauterpacht, 471 ff.; Colombos, paras. 562 ff.; *NWP* 9, para. 9.2.3; Canadian *Draft Manual*, para. 710.

Heintschel von Heinegg

national law if the belligerents do not provide for safe alternative routes of similar convenience.[251] It may be added in this context that at least in the first months of World War II free passage through international straits as well as piloting services were provided by the belligerents.[252] The conditions under which the right of transit passage may be exercised will depend on the circumstances ruling at the time. Probably, vital security interests will entitle a belligerent temporarily to close an international strait. This question is, however, far from settled. In any event such closure will only be legitimate in exceptional cases and may not last indefinitely.

2. *Defensive mining.* This presupposes the existence of an international armed conflict. The admissibility of mining international waters follows from the fact that the high seas belong to the areas of naval warfare. Mines may only be laid within the general area of naval operations.[253] Accordingly, the territorial seas[254] and internal waters of states not parties to the conflict are exempt. This is also true of archipelagic waters[255] since they are covered by the sovereignty of the archipelagic state. In addition, mining must not have the practical effect of preventing passage between neutral waters and international waters. In principle, the Exclusive Economic Zones (EEZs) and continental shelf areas of neutral states are part of the general area of naval operations.[256] However, the belligerents shall have due regard for the rights of the coastal state concerning the exploration and exploitation of the natural resources in such sea areas. In particular, artificial islands, installations, structures, and safety zones may not be interfered with. In any event, if mines are laid within the EEZ or on the continental shelf of a neutral state the belligerent is obliged to give notice of the mined areas.[257]

As regards the mining of high seas areas there seem to exist no significant restrictions. Especially Article 3 of Hague Convention VIII suggest that 'belligerents may

[251] *NWP* 9, para. 9.2.3 (6) provides: 'Naval mines may be employed to channelize neutral shipping, but not in a manner to impede the transit passage of international straits or archipelagic sea lanes passage of archipelagic waters by such shipping.' Para. 89, *San Remo Manual* reads as follows: 'Transit passage through international straits and passage through waters subject to the right of archipelagic sea lanes passage shall not be impeded unless safe and convenient alternative routes are provided.' See also Hoog, *EPIL* 3, 284; Alexander, *International Straits*, 91–108, 94 ff.

[252] According to secret documents prepared by the German Naval High Command, in the following straits free passages and piloting services were provided by the belligerents: Skagerrak, the Sound and the Great Belt, the Kattegat, the Dover Strait, and the Firth of Forth. See Oberkommando der Kriegsmarine, *Urkundenbuch zum Seekriegsrecht* (1 Sept. 1939 to 31 Aug. 1940), document Nos. 340, 345, 346, 348, 354, 361. See also Levie, *Mine Warfare*, 77 ff.

[253] For the 'general area of naval operations' see Sections 1010 ff.; Robertson, *Theatre of Operations*; Colombos, paras. 558 ff.

[254] It may be added that according to military manuals the 12 nm. territorial sea is generally accepted as in accordance with international law and has to be respected in times of armed conflict. See *NWP* 9, para. 7.3.4.2; Canadian *Draft Manual*, para. 706.

[255] See *NWP* 9, para. 7.3.6; Canadian *Draft Manual*, para. 1509.

[256] Canadian *Draft Manual*, para. 1509.

[257] Ibid., para. 1509 (1). See also para. 35, *San Remo Manual* which provides: 'If a belligerent considers it necessary to lay mines in the exclusive economic zone or the continental shelf of a neutral State, the belligerent shall notify that State, and shall ensure, *inter alia*, that the size of the minefield and the type of mines used do not endanger artificial islands, installations and structures, nor interfere with access thereto, and shall avoid so far as practicable interference with the exploration or exploitation of the zone by the neutral State. Due regard shall also be given to the protection and preservation of the marine environment.'

sow anchored automatic contact mines anywhere upon the high seas.'[258] It should, however, not be overlooked that according to the Preamble the contracting states were '[i]nspired by the principle of the freedom of sea routes, the common highway of all nations'. The generally accepted rules on treaty interpretation laid down in Article 31 of the Vienna Convention on the Law of Treaties would allow the Preamble to be taken into consideration. It would therefore be possible to deduce a prohibition of unrestricted mining in the high seas. On the other hand, this result may be doubted in view of the practice of the two World Wars.[259] If, however, recent statements on the law of naval warfare are taken into account it becomes obvious that even though international law still lacks a general and comprehensive prohibition, the right of belligerents to lay mines in the high seas is not unlimited.[260] *NWP* 9, for example, expressly states: 'Mining of areas of indefinite extent in international waters is prohibited. Reasonably limited barred areas may be established by naval mines, provided neutral shipping retains an alternate route around or through such an area with reasonable assurance of safety.'[261] Hence, unless free and safe passages for peaceful shipping are provided for, the mining of the high seas is contrary to international law.[262] Of course, during an international armed conflict at sea the freedom of navigation is not absolute.[263] Still, the parties to the conflict are not entitled to treat it as obsolete.

3. *Offensive mining.* During an international armed conflict this is also legitimate as long as the principles laid down in Section 1040 are observed. Its admissibility also follows from the provisions on the areas of naval warfare. Still, as is shown by paragraphs 3 to 5 of the present Section, the mere existence of (armed) hostilities is not considered sufficient to justify the mining of enemy territorial waters. In accordance with the right of individual or collective self-defence of Art. 51 UN Charter it is made subject to an 'armed attack'.[264] These provisions are, however, of minor

[258] Tucker, 303.

[259] Tucker states: 'Indeed, the severe condemnation of war zones from which neutral shipping is barred under threat of destruction from submarines and aircraft has not infrequently been accompanied by the acquiescence to zones from which neutral shipping is barred by means almost equally destructive'; Tucker, 303.

[260] See Thorpe, *loc. cit.*, 264.   [261] *NWP* 9, para. 9.2.3 (8).

[262] See Levie, *Mine Warfare*, 41 ff., 177; Hoog, *EPIL* 3, 283–5. The corresponding *opinio juris* can also be deduced from the practice of states during the Iran–Iraq war. States not parties to that conflict, by deploying naval units in the Persian Gulf, made abundantly clear that they were not willing to acquiesce in a restriction of the freedom of navigation by unrestricted mine warfare. *San Remo Manual*, para. 88, provides: 'The minelaying States shall pay due regard to the legitimate uses of the high seas by, *inter alia*, providing safe alternative routes for shipping of neutral States.'

[263] See Thorpe, *loc. cit.*, 257. Schwarzenberger, *International Law* II, 417, holds: 'On the high seas, fields of anchored automatic contact mines, even if announced and supervised, amount to a purported occupation of a portion of the high seas of indefinite duration. It appears impossible to square pretensions of this character with the rules underlying the principles of the freedom of the seas; for they deny the free use of the mined area of the high seas not only to the enemy, but also to neutral shipping at large'. However, this position finds no foundation in state practice.

[264] For the term 'armed attack' see, *inter alia*, Ipsen, s. 57 Rn. 28 *et seq.* 'Aggression' is defined in UN GA Res. 3314 (XXIX) of 14 Dec. 1974 that is meant to help the UN Security Council in determining the existence of such aggression. Certain kinds of direct force (open military attack, occupation of foreign territory, blockade, and attacks on foreign armed forces, ships, aircraft etc.) are declared acts of aggression. That enumeration is not exhaustive; see Verdross/Simma, s. 233; Ipsen, s. 57 Rn. 10 *et seq.* Despite the non-binding

Heintschel von Heinegg

relevance for the naval commander. They are rather addressed to political and high military decision makers. On the justification of mining enemy territorial waters as an act of collective self-defence, the judgment of the ICJ in the *Nicaragua* Case is of considerable significance. The ICJ ruled that the use of force, including the mining of another state's territorial waters, is to be considered a legitimate act of collective self-defence only if the following criteria are met: 'At all events, the Court finds that in customary international law, whether of a general kind or that particular to the inter-American legal system, there is no rule permitting the exercise of collective self-defence in the absence of a request by the State which regards itself as the victim of an armed attack. The Court concludes that the requirement of a request by the State which is the victim of the alleged attack is additional to the requirement that such a State should have declared itself to have been attacked.'[265] If there is no such declaration and request offensive mining is not justified by the right of collective self-defence.

4. *The prohibition against laying mines with the sole object of intercepting commercial shipping.* According to a widely held view the prohibition of Article 2 Hague Convention VIII also applies to modern mines.[266] It is thus forbidden to lay mines 'off the coast and ports of the enemy, with the sole object of intercepting commercial shipping'. In practice, a violation of this prohibition is unlikely to be established. In any event, mining activities will only in exceptional cases be exclusively motivated by considerations of economic warfare.[267] However, even under conditions of modern naval warfare this prohibition is not meaningless. It implies that the offensive use of mines for the sole object of conducting economic warfare at sea is strictly forbidden.[268] Of course, mines may be employed for establishing and enforcing a naval blockade. Mines may not, however, be the only means employed for that purpose. If mines are used for blockade purposes the belligerent is obliged to deploy warships or other units of its armed forces near the blockaded area. The rationale behind that obligation is to ensure that ships in distress can reach a place of safety.

d) Duties after the Cessation of Hostilities

At the close of hostilities the conflicting parties must do their utmost to remove,   1043
for the sake of safe shipping, the mines they have laid (Art. 5 HC VIII).

1. *Removal of mines by the former belligerents.* At the close of the armed conflict the former belligerents must make every effort to remove the mines which they have

character of UN GA Resolutions, Res. 3314 (XXIX) is widely considered as declaratory of customary international law.

[265] ICJ Rep. 1986, 105.
[266] See *NWP* 9, para. 9.2.3 (7); Canadian *Draft Manual*, para. 710; Dinstein, *IYHR* 45 (1980), 45.
[267] See Levie, *Mine Warfare*, 32 ff.; Dinstein, *IYHR* 45 (1980), 45; Stone, *Legal Controls*, 583–4. For an evaluation of Article 2 from a purely military point of view see Heintschel v. Heinegg, in Fleck (Ed.), *Gladisch Committee*, 46 ff.
[268] See *NWP* 9, paras. 7.7.5. and 9.2.3; Dinstein, *IYHR* 45 (1980), 45.

laid.[269] This duty is generally accepted as a rule of customary international law.[270] Accordingly, each belligerent is obliged to remove the mines it has laid in its own territorial waters and in the high seas. As regards those mines laid in a belligerent's own territorial waters, it is sufficient merely to render them harmless. Remotely controlled minefields must only be switched off. Mines laid in the territorial waters of the (former) adversary may be removed only with the latter's express consent. A mine-clearing operation within the territorial sea without permission by the coastal state is a violation of its territorial sovereignty.[271] If the coastal state is unwilling to permit mine-clearing operations by the other state the latter is, in principle, obliged to notify the former of the position of the mines.[272] In practice the performance of this duty may cause considerable difficulties. The mine-laying state may, for security reasons, not be willing to provide its former adversary with information on the construction of the mines it uses. International law provides no rules for such cases except for the general duty to resolve international disputes by peaceful means. Finally, if a state is unable to remove the mines it has laid because it does not have the necessary technical means it shall ask other states for assistance.[273]

2. *Removal of mines by neutrals.* The parties to an ongoing international armed conflict at sea do not, of course, always comply with the above requirements.

---

[269] Art. 5, para. 1 Hague Convention VIII; *NWP* 9, para. 9.2.3; Canadian *Draft Manual*, para. 710. Para. 90, *San Remo Manual* provides: 'After the cessation of active hostilities, parties to the conflict shall do their utmost to remove or render harmless the mines they have laid, each party removing its own mines. With regard to mines laid in the territorial seas of the enemy, each party shall notify their position and shall proceed with the least possible delay to remove the mines in its territorial sea or otherwise render the territorial sea safe for navigation.'

[270] In one of the Protocols of the US–North Vietnamese Agreement of 27 Jan. 1973, the US accepted international responsibility for the removal of approximately 8,000 mines it had laid in North Vietnamese coastal waters. 'Operation End Sweep' started in Feb. 1973 and was completed in July 1973.

Egypt, after the end of the Yom Kippur War (1973) also accepted its responsibility for the removal of mines it had laid in the Suez Canal and in the Red Sea.

During the Gulf War (1980–88) Iran, on 13 Aug. 1987, announced it would sweep mines in international waters of the Persian Gulf; *The Times* (London) 1 Sept. 1987, 6.

For further references see Levie, *Mine Warfare*, 49 ff., 75, 88, 122, 149 ff.

[271] This follows from the judgment of the ICJ in the *Corfu Channel* case, ICJ Reports 1949, 4 ff.

[272] See Art. 7, para. 2 of the Swedish proposal:

'All such records shall be retained by the parties who shall:

(a) as soon as possible, by mutual agreement, provide for the release of information concerning the location of activated mines, particularly in agreements governing the cessation of hostilities;

(b) immediately after the cessation of active hostilities take all necessary and appropriate measures, including the use of such records, to protect civilians from the effects of mines; and make available to each other and to the Secretary-General of the United Nations all information in their possession concerning the location of activated mines.'

[273] e.g. after the end of the Yom Kippur War Egypt asked the US for assistance. Within three months (April to June 1973) the waters were cleared of the mines. See Levie, *Mine Warfare*, 157 ff.; Kowark/Taylor, *Marine-Rundschau* 71 (1974), 724–36.

India, after the close of the 1971 conflict with Pakistan, removed the mines it had laid with the assistance of the former Soviet Union. See Petersen, *Marine Rundschau* 72 (1975), 665–76.

Art. 8 of the Swedish proposal provides: 'After the cessation of active hostilities, the parties shall endeavour to reach agreement both among themselves and, where appropriate, with other States and with international organizations, on the provision of information and technical and material assistance—including, in appropriate circumstances, joint operations—necessary to remove or otherwise render ineffective mines placed in position during the conflict.' An identical rule is laid down in para. 91, *San Remo Manual.*

Heintschel von Heinegg

Drifting mines are laid in sea areas with a high traffic density. In many cases the mines used can neither be directed at military objectives nor are they equipped with effective deactivation devices. In such cases the question arises whether neutral states are entitled to protect their shipping by removing the illegally laid mines. The practice of states during the Iran–Iraq War has, it is submitted, contributed to the emergence of a confirmatory rule of international law. On 24 July 1987 the reflagged tanker *Bridgeton* hit a mine 18 nm. off the Iranian island of Farsi. Almost immediately the US sent mine experts to assist Saudi Arabia and Kuwait in removing the mines off their respective coasts and ports. It soon became clear, however, that the mines could be removed only if the necessary equipment was available. Therefore, the US started deploying its 'airborne mine countermeasure units' (AMCM) in the area.[274] At the request of the US, Great Britain and France also deployed naval units in the Gulf region to protect peaceful shipping and to remove mines in international shipping lanes.[275] On 21 September 1987 two US helicopters detected an Iranian landing craft, the *Iran Ajr*, approximately 50 nm. to the northeast of Bahrain. After they had verified that the *Iran Ajr* was engaged in mining activities they opened fire. Five members of the Iranian crew were killed, the other twenty-six were captured.[276] While the Iranian government accused the US of having killed innocent seamen the Legal Adviser of the Department of State, Judge A. Sofaer, justified the attack on the *Iran Ajr* as follows: 'Where, as here, a government engages in manifestly illegal use of armed force, international law entitles the victim to act in self-defense. The response must be necessary and proportionate. The United States' action plainly comported with these requirements. The United States acted to stop the unlawful act itself, and an imminent threat to US shipping was thereby avoided. The US immediately reported this action to the Security Council pursuant to Article 51 of the UN Charter and stated its hope and intention that the incident not be followed by additional hostilities.'[277]

As regards the removal of mines in areas beyond the territorial seas of the belligerents, there is unanimous agreement in the literature that the activities were in compliance with international law.[278] State practice supports this view since even the parties to the conflict in the Gulf War acquiesced in the removal of mines by neutral states.[279] Possible justifications are either the inherent right of self-defence[280] or the right to enforce the freedom of navigation against illegal interference by belligerent mining.[281]

[274] See Levie, *Mine Warfare*, 167 ff.
[275] See Gioia/Ronzitti, *Third States' Commercial Rights and Duties*, 223 ff., 237 ff.); Levie, *Mine Warfare*, 168.
[276] See Peace, *Proceedings of the American Society of International Law* 82 (1988), 151; Magnusson, *Time Magazine* 10 (5 Oct. 1987).
[277] Quoted in Meron, *Proceedings of the American Society of International Law* 82 (1988), 164–9.
[278] See Ronzitti, *Annuaire Francais de Droit International* XXXIII (1987), 647–62, 651; Nordquist/Wachenfeld, *GYIL* 31 (1988), 138–64, 162 ff.; Gioia/Ronzitti, in Dekker/Post (Eds.), 237; Meron, *loc. cit.*, 168.
[279] Originally, Iran had denied having laid mines for other purposes than coastal defence against US (!) attacks. When mines were detected in Omani waters, however, Iran proposed to remove them from Omani territorial waters. See Levie, *Mine Warfare*, 168.
[280] Nordquist/Wachenfeld, *GYIL* 31 (1988), 162 ff.; Meron, *loc. cit.*, 167 ff.   [281] Ronzitti, *loc. cit.*, 651.

Heintschel von Heinegg

A far more difficult question is whether neutral states are entitled to remove mines illegally laid in international straits. So far the only precedent is the *Corfu Channel* case.[282] The facts are well known. On 13 Nov. 1946 Great Britain removed twenty-two mines from the Corfu Channel because Albania had refused to clear the mines itself or give permission to Great Britain. The ICJ held Albania responsible for damage caused to two British warships that struck mines when passing through the Corfu Channel.[283] The British action, however, was also considered illegal because it constituted a violation of Albania's sovereignty. The Court was not prepared to accept any justification for the British action. If the Corfu Channel decision were still considered as valid law the removal of mines in international straits overlapped by the territorial sea of a coastal state would be contrary to international law. Whether the mines were laid in accordance with the maritime *jus in bello* would make no difference. In view of the new rules on non-suspendable transit passage and of the importance of international straits for international commerce it is open to doubt whether the mere reference to the sovereignty of the belligerent coastal state suffices to render the removal of illegally laid mines by neutral states a violation of international law. The right of transit passage may only be infringed by measures that comply with the maritime *jus in bello*. Therefore, if the belligerents are not willing to observe these rules and if there exist no alternative routes of similar convenience, third states are entitled to remove mines in international straits in order to enforce their right of transit passage.[284]

2. Torpedoes

1044   **Torpedoes which have missed their mark must become harmless (Art. 1 HC VIII). When using torpedoes, action shall be taken in accordance with the principles of naval warfare to ensure that only military objectives and not other ships and objects are damaged.**

This provision stems from Art. 1, para. 3 Hague Convention VIII[285] and is today generally accepted as part of customary international law.[286] In general, torpedoes presently in use by naval armed forces meet the requirements laid down in the first sentence. The provisions of the second sentence, in view of the accuracy of modern torpedoes[287], pose no serious problems either. In this regard it makes no difference whether torpedoes are employed against surface or against subsurface vessels. However, torpedoes guided by wire during the initial phase seek their target independently during the final phase of their run. Hence they may hit other targets than those originally aimed at. It is the object and purpose of the second sentence to

---

[282] ICJ Reports 1949, 4 ff.   [283] Ibid., 22.

[284] Accordingly, para. 92, *San Remo Manual* provides: 'Neutral States do not commit an act inconsistent with the laws of neutrality by clearing mines laid in violation of international law.'

[285] Cf., *inter alia*, Levie, *Commentary*, 143 with further references.

[286] See *NWP* 9, para. 9.3; Canadian *Draft Manual*, para. 710. *San Remo Manual*, para. 79 provides: 'It is prohibited to use torpedoes which do not sink or otherwise become harmless when they have completed their run.'

[287] For the technical aspects see *Jane's*, 3 ff.

remind naval commanders of their duty to ensure that only military objectives are attacked.

3. Missiles

**For the use of missiles at sea, including cruise missiles, the general principles of   1045
the law of naval warfare apply.**

The inclusion of a special provision on missiles is meant to take account of modern naval warfare. Short-range missiles were successfully employed during the 1967 Arab–Israeli conflict,[288] the Falklands/Malvinas conflict,[289] and during the two Gulf Wars.[290] No specific rules on the use of cruise or other missiles have yet been included in the law of naval armed conflict. Hence, Section 1045 clarifies that when belligerents employ missiles (cruise or other) they are obliged to ensure that they are directed exclusively at military objectives.[291] In general, the technical state of modern missiles enables belligerents to conform with the fundamental principles of the laws of naval armed conflicts, especially with the principle of distinction. However, there still exist problems with regard to identification and targeting.[292] If the use of missiles and projectiles depends upon over-the-horizon targeting belligerents are obliged to take precautionary measures to ensure that anything other than military objectives is spared.[293] Provided that, if necessary, such measures are taken the legality of the use of missiles cannot be doubted.[294] Modern missiles are highly discriminate weapons that will not usually miss their targets. In the light of the fundamental principles of naval armed conflict, it is, therefore, not necessary to equip them with self-destruction or similar devices.[295]

4. Submarine Warfare

Preliminary Remarks. The rules on submarine warfare result from a development beginning in 1899. This development was to a considerable extent influenced by Great Britain's endeavours to outlaw the submarine as a legitimate means of naval warfare.[296] These endeavours (made during international codification and

---

[288] Cf. O'Connell, *Influence*, 86 ff.   [289] Cf. Zuppi, 200 ff.

[290] For the Iran–Iraq conflict (1980–88) see Danziger, *USNIP* 111 (May 1985), 160 ff. An excellent description of the employment of Tomahawk cruise missiles during the Iraq–Kuwait conflict (1991) is given in *Frankfurter Allgemeine Zeitung*, 23 Jan. 1991.

[291] *San Remo Manual*, para. 78 provides: 'Missiles and projectiles, including those with over-the-horizon capabilities, shall be used in conformity with the principles of target discrimination as set out in Sections 38–46.'

[292] Cf. Robertson, *Technology*, 371 ff.; van Hegelsom, *Methods*, 35.   [93] See also *NWP* 9, para. 9.7.

[294] van Hegelsom, *Methods*, 36; Truver, *USNIP* Vol. 103 (Aug. 1977), 82 *et seq.*; Parks, *USNIP* Vol. 103 (Sept. 1977), 120 *et seq.* For the opposing view see O'Connell, *AJIL* 1972, 785 ff.

[295] In any event a self-destruction device would not mean any improvement. The time period between launching and reaching the target is too short to achieve any modifications. The flight time of the missile fired by *USS Vincennes* against the Iranian Airbus took only 17 seconds from launching to impact. Cf. Friedman, *USNIP* Vol. 115 (May 1989), 76.

[296] For a general overview of the law of submarine warfare see Mallison, *Submarines*, 12 ff.; Jacobson, *Submarine Warfare*, 205 ff.; Gilliland, *Georgetown LJ* 1985, 976 ff.; Sohler, *Marine Rundschau* (Sept. 1956), 1.

Heintschel von Heinegg

disarmament conferences) failed in the face of resistance by other states, especially of France.[297] Already during World War I the principal legitimacy of the submarine as a means of naval warfare was not seriously doubted. It became evident, however, that it would be at least difficult to reconcile the use of submarines with the rules of naval warfare. Despite allegations to the contrary, submarines, because of their poor speed, could only be employed to a limited extent against enemy warships. Hence from the very beginning their importance lay with measures against enemy merchant shipping. However, if submarines were to capture a merchant vessel they had to comply with the regular procedure of visit and search. This exposed them to serious dangers since, once surfaced, they could be rammed or otherwise attacked. Moreover, during World War I, for example Great Britain had armed its merchant shipping and ordered it to fly false flags and to ram German submarines if possible. Hence, after initial compliance with the rule on visit, search, and capture, Germany turned to a policy of 'unrestricted submarine warfare'. Vessels encountered within the limits of a pre-declared so-called 'war zone' were sunk without prior warning.[298] A further difficulty resulting from compliance with the rules of naval warfare was the lack of space on board submarines. They were unable to take crews, passengers, and ship's papers to a place of safety if a captured merchant vessel had to be destroyed. It was also nearly impossible to take shipwrecked and wounded on board. In addition, rescue operations, in view of the vulnerability of surfaced submarines, caused severe problems. Still, it was agreed at the 1922 Washington Conference that submarines were subject to the same rules of naval warfare as surface vessels and that non-compliance constituted an act of piracy. The Washington Treaty never entered into force but the same rules concerning the use of submarines were laid down in the 1930 London Agreement on Naval Armaments. When that Treaty expired the same rules were reaffirmed in the 1936 London Protocol[299] that became binding law for the majority of the belligerent states of World War II. State practice during World War II, however, did not differ from that of World War I.[300] From the beginning all belligerents, including the USA, conducted unrestricted submarine warfare directed at enemy merchant shipping and caused tremendous losses.

Shortly after its adoption the provisions of the 1936 London Protocol were criticized on the ground that they disregarded the differences between surface and subsurface vessels, and overlooked the impossibility for submarines to comply with the rules on visit and search.[301] Still, in its judgment on Admiral Dönitz, the Nuremberg Tribunal affirmed the continuing validity of the Protocol. The Tribunal did not, however, find Dönitz guilty of unrestricted submarine warfare against British merchant shipping.[302] In its reasoning the Tribunal did not refer to the dangers involved in the compliance with the procedure of visit and search. Rather, it considered British merchant vessels that had been incorporated into Britain's war

---

[297] Cf., *inter alia*, Mallison, *Submarines*, 31 ff.　　　　　　　　　　　　　　　[298] Ibid., 62 ff.

[299] Worth mentioning are also the so-called Nyon Arrangements of 1937 that contain similar provisions; cf. Goldie, *Commentary*, 489 ff.

[300] Cf. Mallison, *Submarines*, 75 ff.; Sohler, *loc. cit.*

[301] Cf. the references given by Gilliland, *Georgetown Law Journal* 1985, 978–9.

[302] Judgment of 1 Oct. 1946, Vol. I, 350 ff.

Heintschel von Heinegg

efforts to have lost the protection of the 1936 London Protocol.[303] Neither was Dönitz sentenced for having ordered attacks on neutral merchant vessels, especially within 'war zones'. The Tribunal qualified those attacks as violations of the 1936 London Protocol but refrained from a sentence in view of the similar practice of the Allies, especially of the USA in the Pacific.

International lawyers have drawn quite different conclusions from practice during World War II and from the Nuremberg judgment. Whereas some consider the 1936 London Protocol to have been abrogated on grounds of desuetude,[304] others emphasize its continuing and unmodified validity.[305] The view according to which the 1936 London Protocol has been abrogated, according to the position taken here is not tenable. The conduct of states during World War II can hardly be considered a practice based upon an *opinio juris* that has contributed to the development of a new rule of customary international law. In the vast majority of cases states justified their conduct by reference to reprisals.[306] Hence, they were convinced of the basic illegality of their measures. Therefore, state practice and the fact that measures of unrestricted submarine warfare were characterized as violations of the law are evidence of the *opinio juris* of states that they have continuously been bound by the 1936 London Protocol. Of course, post-World War II practice gives less testimony. The only known case of an employment of submarines during an international armed conflict was the attack by the British submarine *HMS Conqueror* on the Argentine *General Belgrano* that is of no relevance as regards the continuing validity of the 1936 Protocol. However, the provisions of the Protocol are referred to in recent military manuals[307] (even though the rules on submarine warfare sometimes differ from those on surface warfare[308]). Neither is the Nuremberg judgment authority for the abrogation of the 1936 London Protocol. Rather, it has contributed to a clarification of the law in so far as enemy merchant vessels participating in hostilities are not covered by the Protocol's protective scope and may therefore be attacked and sunk without prior warning or prior exercise of visit and search. It needs to be emphasized in this context that, according to the Nuremberg Judgment, an attack may not take place in cases of doubt as to the qualification of a merchant vessel as a legitimate military objective. The Nuremberg judgment merely lacks clarification of the status of neutral merchant vessels. According to the Tribunal all neutral merchant vessels are protected by the Protocol regardless of the fact that under certain circumstances they become legitimate military objectives (e.g. if they are transporting enemy troops or if they are integrated into the enemy's

---

[303] See also Nwogugu, *Commentary*, 358.

[304] This view is especially taken by O'Connell, *BYIL* (1970), 52. See also Gilliland, *loc. cit.*, 978–9.

[305] Cf. Fleck, in Delissen/Tanja (Eds.), 420; Jacobson, *Submarine Warfare*, 214 ff.

[306] Cf. *inter alia*, Whiteman, Vol. X, 660 ff.

[307] The Canadian *Draft Manual*, para. 709, expressly repeats the wording of the Protocol. In a footnote there is a clarification to the effect that merchant vessels meeting the requirements of the definition of military objectives are not protected.

[308] In *NWP 9*, para. 8.3.1, there is an enumeration of those conditions relieving submarines of the obligation to first, i.e. before attack, take crews, passengers and ship's papers to a place of safety. Those conditions, however, do not differ from those applicable to surface ships. There are, for mere practical reasons, different provisions in order to differentiate between surface and subsurface warfare.

Heintschel von Heinegg

intelligence system).[309] Attacks on neutral merchant vessels are, however, not the subject of the present chapter.

Finally, the continuing validity of the 1936 London Protocol is questioned because it allegedly does not meet the practical requirements of naval armed forces engaged in active hostilities. Its provisions would, therefore, not be observed during armed conflict. Submarines, by using their sonar equipment, could distinguish between different types of vessels but could not verify their respective functions. (One may add that communication with operational control is almost impossible because of the danger of detection). A naval commander would not expose his submarine to the dangers involved in visit and search merely to realize after surfacing that the supposed merchant vessel is really a warship in disguise.[310] Such practical difficulties, however, are not sufficient proof for the validity of the allegation that, under international law, there are only two types of ships: submarines and targets. On one hand, the effective employment of submarines in modern armed conflict is not jeopardized by the continuing validity and applicability of the Protocol. Its protective scope only covers merchant vessels proper. It does not cover warships and merchant vessels that are legitimate military objectives. Today, submarines are neither exclusively nor predominantly employed against merchant shipping. Because of the technological development since the end of World War II their velocity and operability have increased considerably. They can thus be entrusted with specific military tasks, like protective mining for coastal defence purposes, and attacks on enemy warships and enemy territory.[311] In view of the fundamental principles of naval armed conflict and the overall principle of humanity, it would, on the other hand, be difficult to justify the existence of different sets of rules for surface and subsurface forces by mere reference to practical considerations. In any event attacks by submarines as well as by surface vessels must be restricted to military objectives. Only if an object is clearly identified as of military character may it be attacked. In cases of doubt there is a presumption of the non-military character of an object and attacks must be terminated. If, in such cases, the commander is unwilling to expose his submarine to the dangers involved in visit and search he can only leave the vessel concerned to pass unmolested above his periscope. It may be added that many of the concerns raised against the continuing validity of the 1936 London Protocol lose much of their weight in view of the endorsement of maritime exclusion zones in the present manual.[312]

1046 **Submarines are subject to the same rules of international law as surface vessels (Art. 1 LondonProt 1936).**

As stated in the preliminary remarks, in view of the continuing validity of the 1936 London Protocol and since no rule of customary law to the contrary has developed,

---

[309] See, *inter alia*, Mallison, *Submarines*, 80 ff.; *San Remo Manual*, paras. 67 ff.
[310] This position is taken by esp. Gilliland, *loc. cit.*, 987.
[311] Cf. Lautenschläger, *International Security* Vol. 11 (1986–87), 94 ff.
[312] The same view is taken by Gilliland, *loc. cit.*, 991 ff.

submarines are subject to the same rules as surface ships.[313] Apart from measures against enemy merchant vessels (dealt with in the commentary on Section 1047) this implies that when a submarine launches attacks on targets at sea, in the air, or on land, the fundamental principles of the law of naval armed conflict, as well as the rules on specific methods of naval warfare, must be strictly observed. Hence, despite their restricted technical capabilities, submarines are also subject to the rules on target discrimination. In principle, submarines are equally obliged to res-cue shipwrecked and wounded. As already mentioned,[314] this obligation is subject to considerations of military necessity and to the circumstances prevailing at the time.[315] Hence, a submarine may refrain from rescue operations if the risks involved are too high. This will be the case e.g. if the submarine, after surfacing, could be attacked by aircraft. Nor will rescue be feasible if there is not sufficient space available to take shipwrecked and wounded on board. However, the com-mander is obliged to transmit the position of those who need help as long as this is possible without exposing his ship to attacks.

Merchant ships which meet the requirements of a military objective may also be   1047
attacked and sunk by submarines without prior warning. A submarine intending
to capture a hostile merchant ship which does not meet the requirements of a mil-
itary objective must first surface. It may not sink a merchant ship without having
first brought the passengers, crew, and ship's papers to a safe place (Art. 2
LondonProt 1936). If the merchant ship refuses to stop on being duly summoned
or puts up active resistance to visit or search, the submarine shall be allowed to
attack without warning.

1. *Merchant vessels meeting the requirements of the definition of military objectives.* These may be attacked anywhere within the areas of naval warfare, without prior warning. This is reaffirmed in the first sentence of the present Section. Still, sub-marines are bound by the same rules as surface ships. Hence they may not attack if under the prevailing circumstances the sinking of an enemy merchant vessel offers no definite military advantage, if less severe means are available, or if the military character of the vessel concerned cannot be clearly established.[316]

2. *Capture and destruction of other enemy merchant vessels.* The dangers con-nected with surfacing do not release a submarine from compliance with the oblig-ations laid down in the 1936 London Protocol. Enemy merchant vessels not qualifying as legitimate military objectives may therefore only be destroyed if after capture passengers, crews, and ship's papers have been taken to a place of safety. If this is not feasible, destruction is illegal.

---

[313] *San Remo Manual,* para. 45, provides: 'Surface ships, submarines and aircraft are bound by the same principles and rules.'
[314] See para. 8 of the commentary on Section 1017.   [315] See also *NWP* 9, para. 8.3.1.
[316] See para. 1 of the commentary on Section 1025.

Heintschel von Heinegg

5. *Maritime Exclusion Zones*

1048 A maritime exclusion zone is a distinct area of sea and the air space above in which a party to the conflict exercises extensive rights of control and prohibits access to ships and aircraft. Its purpose is to facilitate identification of military objectives and defence against hostile acts, but not to attack the war economy of the adversary. A difference is made between static and movable exclusion zones. A static exclusion zone comprises a space in three dimensions designated by co-ordinates, i.e. a distinct area of the sea and the air space above that area. A movable exclusion zone comprises the space in three dimensions around units of the naval forces, thus it changes its position when the unit moves.

Example: During World War II both England—in the Skagerrak—and Germany—around the British Isles—established maritime exclusion zones.

1. *Preliminary Remarks*. The validity of the term 'exclusion zone' as well as the particular rules laid down in the present Section can only to a limited extent be based upon state practice. Rather, the provisions of Sections 1048 *et seq.* have to be considered a contribution to the progressive development of international law. It will be seen whether they will meet the general acceptance of the community of states necessary for a rule of customary international law to come into existence.

2. *'Exclusion zones'*. The extent of these is limited by the first two sentences of Section 1048.[317] They do not include either so-called 'war zones' (*Sperrgebiete*),[318] as established during the two World Wars, or areas of a naval blockade. The latter differ from exclusion zones in that they are primarily a method of naval economic warfare, aimed at the enemy's economy and ability to sustain his war efforts by capturing vessels and goods. Blockades neither facilitate the identification of military objectives nor directly assist in defence against enemy measures. An exclusion zone has also to be distinguished from the *cordon sanitaire* used in times of crisis or tension.[319] Finally, exclusion zones differ from areas of actual naval combat.[320] It is generally acknowledged that, according to international law, naval units engaged in combat operations are entitled to prevent neutral and protected enemy vessels from approaching or entering the area of actual naval operations. If such vessels are already present in the vicinity of naval operations they may be ordered to leave the area. Thus, international law takes account of the practical and security needs of naval units engaged in hostilities.

3. *Movable exclusion zones*. In Anglo-American parlance these are sometimes called 'defence bubbles'. In general they serve the same purposes as stationary exclusion zones. Thus, naval units are enabled to minimize the risks resulting

---

[317] For an excellent overview of the development of this method of naval warfare see Fenrick, *CYIL* 24 (1986), 91 ff.; Goldie, *Maritime War Zones*, 156 ff.

[318] See para. 1(a) of the commentary on Section 1049.

[319] Cf. *Gilchrist, Naval War College Review* 35 (1982), 60 ff.   [320] Cf. Fenrick, *CYIL* 24 (1986), 93.

Heintschel von Heinegg

from short reaction times. In addition, identification of submarine vessels is facilitated.

The establishment of static maritime exclusion zones as an exception under inter-   1049
national law is permissible only under the following circumstances:

— The establishment of the maritime exclusion zone must be effective. Hence
sufficient units of air forces and naval forces must be charged to enforce the
exclusion zone so that there is a reasonable chance of meeting all vessels entering that zone.

— The size and duration of, as well as the rights claimed in, exclusion zones shall
by no means exceed legitimate national security and defence requirements.
Vessels in the exclusion zone must be allowed an appropriate time to leave it.

— The boundaries of exclusion zones, the restrictions to be placed on sea and air
traffic within and above these areas, and the control measures to be taken shall
be determined according to the principles of military necessity and proportionality. As far as military considerations permit, particular routes on which
only the right to stop and search is exercised shall be held free for neutral vessels.

— The size, exact boundary lines, and duration of the exclusion zone shall be
announced in public. If an exclusion zone is divided into subzones, it is necessary to define the extent of restrictions and the boundaries of each individual
subzone.

1. *Exclusion zones as new methods of naval warfare.* As stated, the establishment of
exclusion zones is not yet a method of naval warfare generally accepted by international law. It will be shown that the practice of the two World Wars does not fulfil
the criteria for a rule of customary international law. The fact that, as a contribution
to the progressive development of international law, the exclusion zone device has
been adopted in the present Manual is, however, justified both by recent state practice and in the legal literature.

  a) *State practice until 1945.* Before and during the two World Wars exclusion/war
zones were established primarily to attack any vehicle encountered there, without
prior warning. Exclusion zones for merely defensive purposes were for the first time
proclaimed during the Russo-Japanese War of 1904/5.[321] As regards World War I,
Great Britain established a war/exclusion zone on 2 November 1914;[322] followed by
Germany on 4 February 1915.[323] Because of the inferiority of its surface forces
Germany felt compelled steadily to increase the areas covered by its war zones.[324]
Great Britain could confine itself to the originally proclaimed areas because it had
already conducted a very successful economic war by means of a long-distance

---

[321] Cf. Garner, Vol. I, 351 ff.; Goldie, *Maritime War Zones*, 158 ff.; Schmitt, 15.
[322] Cf. Garner, Vol. I, 333 ff.
[323] The *Kriegsgebietserklärung* is printed in *Reichs-Marine-Amt, Seekriegsrecht im Weltkriege*, Nos. 117, 135.
[324] Garner, *AJIL* (1915), 594; Fenrick, *CYIL* 24 (1986), 94 ff.

Heintschel von Heinegg

blockade.[325] In view of the fact that the belligerents justified their zones as reprisals and of the severe impact upon neutral merchant shipping, international lawyers in the aftermath of World War I almost unanimously agreed on the illegality of such war/exclusion zones.[326] During World War II Great Britain established a war/exclusion zone in the Skagerrak: by day all German vessels and by night all vessels regardless of their nationality were liable to attack on sight.[327] At the beginning of hostilities the German naval forces were obliged to comply with the rules of the 1936 London Protocol, as implemented in the Prize Ordinance of 28 August 1939. Soon, however, they were released from those restrictions. Consequently, a comprehensive war zone around the British Isles was proclaimed. It was gradually increased in the course of the war.[328] In the Pacific Ocean the USA also made use of the exclusion zone device and conducted unrestricted submarine warfare against Japan.[329] After the end of World War II the Nuremberg Tribunal characterized the establishment of war/exclusion zones as a violation of the 1936 London Protocol. The Tribunal held that the Treaty had been ratified in knowledge of the practice of World War I. However, there were no exceptions on war/exclusion zones in the Protocol.[330] In this context, it is emphasized that the Tribunal reached its decision merely upon the ground that, within the German war zones, neutral merchant vessels had been sunk without prior warning. The Tribunal did not base its judgment upon attacks on enemy merchant vessels that had lost the protection of the Protocol by having been integrated into Great Britain's war efforts. Nevertheless, Admiral Dönitz was not sentenced for that violation of the Protocol, because Great Britain (in the Skagerrak) and the USA (in the Pacific) had also established war zones in which neutral merchant vessels had been attacked on sight. It therefore remained an open question whether and to what extent neutral merchant vessels—whether within or outside exclusion zones—could be attacked. Obviously, the Nuremberg Tribunal did not take that possibility into consideration in order not to divest itself of the only legal yardstick available: the 1936 London Protocol.[331] Hence, from the reasons given one may draw the conclusion that maritime exclusion zones are probably not illegal if measures taken there either serve purely defensive purposes or are directed solely at enemy military objectives. Still, state practice of the two World Wars is without prejudice to the legality of exclusion zones as laid down in the present Section. The World War zones had a quite different object and purpose.

b) *State practice since 1945.* This also does not justify the conclusion that, under customary international law, maritime exclusion zones as described in the present

[325] For British economic warfare during World War I see Guichard, *Blockade*, 22 ff.

[326] For this and further references see Hall, *Naval Warfare*, 246 ff.

[327] Cf. Mallison, *Submarines*, 36 ff.

[328] Cf. Fenrick, *CYIL* 24 (1986), 100. The order to attack all enemy vessels in the Channel was issued on 4 and 17 Oct. 1939. On 24 Nov. 1939 neutral merchant shipping was advised to refrain from travelling in the sea areas around the British Isles.

[329] This is evidenced by the statement of Admiral Nimitz before the Nuremberg Tribunal; see Vol. 17, 414 ff.

It should be added that other states participating in World War II proclaimed similar zones often labelled 'danger zones'.

[330] Vol. I, 350 ff.

Heintschel von Heinegg

Manual are a legitimate method of naval warfare. The number of precedents—the Falklands/Malvinas conflict[332] and the first Gulf War[333]—is far from sufficient.[334] Moreover, there are considerable differences between the exclusion zones established in the South Atlantic and those established in the Persian Gulf. However, the reactions of third states as well as statements in the legal literature justify the conclusion that the exclusion zone device may become a generally accepted method of naval warfare if certain criteria are met. On 28 April 1982 Great Britain proclaimed a 'Total Exclusion Zone' (TEZ) in the South Atlantic.[335] Beside deterring the Argentine naval forces from leaving their ports, its main purpose was to facilitate the early identification of military objectives and to prevent vessels flying neutral flags from conveying information to Argentina. Argentina, on 11 May 1982, proclaimed a war zone covering the whole South Atlantic and announced that any British vessel would be attacked. On one hand, the British TEZ covered an area of 200 nautical miles measured from the centre of the main island.[336] On the other hand, the TEZ was situated far from any main shipping lanes. Moreover, its duration was comparatively short. It did not serve economic warfare purposes but was aimed at facilitating military operations, including identification. Vessels and aircraft flying flags of states not parties to the conflict suffered no damage whatsoever.[337] For these reasons, only the former USSR officially protested against the British TEZ. During the 1980–88 Gulf Conflict neither Iran nor Iraq seem to have been led by legal considerations when establishing their respective exclusion zones.[338] Iraq mainly concentrated on shipping (largely neutral) serving Kharg Island. It made no difference whether those tankers were travelling in convoy, armed or unarmed. Iraq's measures were generally condemned, as were similar

---

[331] See also O'Connell, *BYIL* 1970, 52.   [332] Cf. Zuppi, 190 ff.

[333] Cf. Leckow, *ICLQ* 1988, 629 ff.; Fenrick, *CYIL* XXIV (1986), 116 ff.

[334] During the Korean conflict the US Navy proclaimed something similar to an exclusion zone. According to the Rules of Engagement the 7th Fleet was entitled to attack any submarine contact in certain specified sea areas. Cf. O'Connell, *Influence*, 167.

[335] *BYIL* 53 (1982), 542. Already on 7 April 1982 Great Britain had proclaimed a 200 nautical miles 'Maritime Exclusion Zone' around the Falklands to the effect that 'any Argentine warship and Argentine naval auxiliaries found within this zone will be treated as hostile and are liable to attack by British forces' (*BYIL* LIII [1982], 556). In its proclamation of the TEZ the British government declared: 'The exclusion zone will apply not only to Argentine warships and naval auxiliaries but also to any other ship, whether naval or merchant vessel, which is operating in support of the illegal occupation of the Falkland Islands by Argentine forces. The zone will also apply to any aircraft, whether military or civil, which is operating in support of the Argentine occupation. Any ship and any aircraft, whether military or civil, which is found within the zone without authority from the Ministry of Defence in London will be regarded as operating in support of the illegal occupation and will therefore be regarded as hostile and will be liable to be attacked by British forces.'

[336] On 7 May 1982 Great Britain extended the TEZ to all sea areas 12 nautical miles off the Argentine coast. Consequently, 'any Argentine warship or military aircraft which is found more than 12 nautical miles from the Argentine coast will be regarded as hostile and is liable to be dealt with accordingly'; *BYIL* LIII (1982), 549; Barston/Birnie, *Marine Policy* 7 (1983), 21.

[337] However, in June 1982 the tanker *Hercules* flying the Liberian flag was attacked by Argentine aircraft outside the British TEZ and was severely damaged. Cf. *ILR* Vol. 79, 1 ff.

[338] For the belligerents' practice see Danziger, *USNIP* 111 (May 1985), 162 ff.; Leckow, *ICLQ* 37 (1988), 636 *et seq.*; Fenrick, *CYIL* 24 (1986), 118 ff.; Politakis, *Netherlands International Law Review* 1991, 148; Peace, *Proceedings of the American Society of International Law* 82 (1988), 147.

Heintschel von Heinegg

measures taken by Iran against neutral merchant vessels travelling to and from other coastal states of the Persian Gulf.[339]

c) *Statements in the legal literature.* In the post-World War II era the issue of the legality of exclusion zones is addressed in a far more differentiated way than in the post-World War I period.[340] There seems to be a tendency to acknowledge the legality of exclusion zones in principle if the interests of neutral shipping are duly taken account of and if they are not intended to serve as 'free-fire zones', where all vessels are attacked indiscriminately, regardless of the fundamental principles of the law of naval warfare, and without prior warning.[341]

2. *Exceptional right.* The wording of Section 1049, especially the emphasis on the exceptional character of the right to establish an exclusion zone, makes it clear that belligerents are not entitled to use such zones as they will. Rather, an exclusion zone may only be established if necessary for legitimate reasons of national security and of military necessity. Its geographical scope, its duration, and the restrictions imposed upon neutral shipping and air traffic must be kept within the limits of proportionality. It is, therefore, not possible to state in advance and in the abstract the legal limitations which the belligerents will have to observe. It will depend upon the circumstances of each case whether an exclusion zone is acceptable under international law.[342] Accordingly, a zone established in remote sea areas may be legal; a zone in areas of high marine traffic density may not, because of its greater interference with neutral shipping. Subject to the prevailing circumstances, the interests of neutral shipping and air traffic must be taken into due consideration by providing safe passage through the zone. Reasons of military convenience alone do not justify the establishment of an exclusion zone. In any event they may not be made 'free-fire zones' where all objects are indiscriminately attacked. The proclaiming belligerent is obliged to take all militarily feasible precautions to ensure that the use of weapons is confined to the minimum necessary for self-defence. E.g. if prize measures can be expected to be equally effective, the use of weapons is prohibited. Moreover, naval armed forces are not released from the duty to ensure proper target identification. Within exclusion zones, too, only legitimate military objectives may be attacked. However, the demands resulting from the principle of distinction are less strict than outside an exclusion zone. In sum, exclusion zones exclusively serving economic warfare purposes or where the proclaiming belligerent disregards the principle of distinction are illegal.

3. *Effectiveness.* Since the establishment of an exclusion zone is an exceptional belligerent right, it has to meet strict legal requirements. It cannot be expected that so-called 'paper exclusion zones', not enforced by a sufficient number of naval and air

---

[339] See the references given by Fenrick, *CYIL* 24 (1986), 121 ff.

[340] Cf. Colombos, paras. 559 ff.; Tucker, 302; Mallison, *Submarines*, 91 *et seq.*; Whiteman, Vol. X, 607 ff.; Goldie, *Maritime War Zones*, 156 ff.; Gilliland, *loc. cit.*, 991 ff.; Fenrick, *CYIL* 24 (1986), 91 ff.

[341] Gilliland, *loc. cit.*, 991 ff.; Fenrick, *CYIL* 24 (1986), 91 ff.

[342] A similar approach is taken in paras. 105 ff., *San Remo Manual.*

forces, will be accepted by the international community.[343] This, however, does not mean that a large number of armed forces must be present in the area concerned. It is sufficient if the area is surveyed by radar and if naval and air forces units are able to reach any point situated within the zone quickly.

4. *Time limits and notification.* A grace period sufficient for all interested vessels and aircraft to leave the area covered by a proclamation is as essential for a zone's legality as the official notification of its commencement, duration, location and extent, and the restrictions imposed. Restrictions on neutral air and sea traffic must be confined to what is necessary to serve the proclaiming state's security interests.

The establishment of movable maritime exclusion zones is permissible only if   1050
they are announced in public in general form. In the announcement the requested rights shall be determined. The size of movable maritime exclusion zones, the limitations of sea and air traffic in and above them, and the measures to be enforced are to be determined according to the principles of military necessity and proportionality. The use of weapons in such zones shall be limited to military objectives.

1. *Preliminary Remarks.* Neutral sea and air traffic are affected by the proclamation of a movable exclusion zone only to a relatively minor extent. Hence and in view of recent state practice, it is to be expected that such zones will become part of the generally accepted body of international law. During the Falklands/Malvinas conflict Great Britain established 'defence bubbles' around its naval units.[344] Defensive measures were to be restricted to cases in which the approach of vessels or aircraft constituted a threat.[345] There were no protests by third states. Legal commentators apparently did not question their legality.[346]

2. *Admissibility.* It is self-evident that in the case of the proclamation of a movable exclusion zone the belligerent is not obliged publicly to notify the unit's course and/or destination. Otherwise, the units concerned would be too easy a target for, e.g., over-the-horizon attacks by the enemy. It is, therefore, sufficient if the declaration contains information about the extent of the zone and about what will be perceived as hostile intent. The permissible extent will depend upon the defence needs in the prevailing circumstances. It may be up to 5 nautical miles[347] but may also exceed that limit if otherwise the approach of vessels or aircraft would constitute an unbearable risk. The restrictions imposed and measures to be taken must be limited to that degree of force necessary to ensure effective self-defence. The use

[343] Even though the term 'paper exclusion zone' is an allusion to the term 'paper blockade' it is emphasized that the legal basis of exclusion zones is not the law of blockade.

[344] See the declaration of 23 Apr. 1982 in *The Times*, 26 Apr. 1982; Fenrick, *CYIL* XXIV (1986), 110.

[345] A similar 'defence bubble' was proclaimed by the US Navy during the Iran–Iraq war. However, the US were not a party to that conflict.

[346] Cf. Gilliland, *loc. cit.*, 991 ff.; Fenrick, *CYIL* 24 (1986), 110 ff.

[347] During the Iran–Iraq war the US Navy considered 5 nm. as sufficient because the main threat was expected from the Iranian *Pasdaran.*

Heintschel von Heinegg

of weapons will be permissible if an approaching vessel or aircraft qualifies as a legitimate military objective and if less severe means are not available.

6. *Blockade*

1051 **A blockade is a means of obstructing an enemy coast or port so that vessels and aircraft are prevented from entering and departing. The purpose of blockades is to block supplies to an enemy coast without directly meaning to conquer this coast. Starvation of the civilian population as a method of warfare is prohibited (Art. 49, para. 3 in connection with Art. 54, para. 1 AP I). It is also prohibited to hinder relief shipments for the civilian population (Art. 70 AP I).**

1. *Introduction.* Blockade is one of the oldest methods of naval economic warfare. The conditions for its legality were laid down in the 1856 Paris Declaration. The fact that none of the 1907 Hague Conventions contains provisions on blockade is due to the fact that the time then available was limited. In 1909, blockade was regulated in the London Declaration.[348] Although the 1909 London Declaration never entered into force the main features of its provisions on blockade are today generally recognized as customary in character.[349] However, the practice of the two World Wars made evident that only in exceptional cases can naval armed forces maintain a blockade in accordance with the relatively strict preconditions of the traditional law. Today the maintenance of a naval blockade in accordance with the traditional law will only be feasible if the sea area in question is almost completely under the control of the blockading power.[350] Often the blockaded state will have intermediate or long-range missiles and will, thus, be able to keep its enemy forces far away from its coastline.[351] Hence, today the preconditions for a legal blockade are less strict, as will be shown in the commentary on Section 1053.

2. *Impartiality.* In principle, a blockade must be applied impartially to the vessels and aircraft of all nations.[352] This duty also applies to vessels flying the flag of the blockading power. Apart from relief shipments, only in exceptional cases is it permissible to exempt neutral warships and military aircraft by permitting them to enter and leave a blockaded port or coastline.[353] Neutral merchant vessels and civil aircraft in distress may also be allowed to enter and leave the blockade area, provided they have neither discharged nor loaded any cargo there.[354]

---

[348] For these provisions see Böhmert, *WVR* II, 428 ff.; de Zayas, *EPIL* 3, 249 ff.; Kalshoven, *Commentary*, 257 ff.

[349] Cf. Colombos, *Revue Héllenique de Droit International* 12 (1959), 10 ff.; *NWP* 9, para. 7.7.5; Canadian *Draft Manual*, para. 722.

[350] This was the case during the Iraq–Kuwait conflict in which the Allied forces were able to cut off all imports by sea and air destined for Iraq.

[351] See also O'Connell, Vol. II, 1154 ff.

[352] Art. 5, 1909 London Declaration.

[353] Ibid., Art. 6.

[354] Ibid., Art. 7. See also *NWP* 9, para. 7.7.3.

3. *Free access to neutral ports and coastlines.* A blockade must not extend beyond the ports and coasts belonging to or controlled or occupied by the enemy.[355] It must not prevent access to ports or coasts of neutral states since this would violate their neutrality.[356]

4. *'Hunger blockade' and relief actions.* If a blockade has the effect of starving the civilian population it becomes illegal according to Art. 49, para. 3 and Art. 54, para. 1 AP I. During the Diplomatic Conference the Third Committee took the view that Art. 54 AP I had no impact on naval blockades.[357] That view, it is argued here, is untenable. Art. 54 AP I applies to naval blockades if they 'may affect the civilian population, individual civilians, or civilian objects on land' (Art. 49, para. 3 AP I).[358] If the establishment of a blockade causes the civilian population to be inadequately provided with food and other objects essential for its survival, the blockading party must provide for free passage for such essential supplies.[359] It is questionable in this context whether the blockading power is to be considered a 'party concerned' whose permission is necessary. In any event, the blockading power is under an obligation to provide for and permit free passage of goods essential for the survival of the civilian population.[360] That permission may be denied only temporarily for the reason of overwhelming security concerns.[361] Of course, the obligation to provide for and to permit free passage of relief shipments is subject to the right to prescribe the technical arrangements, including search, under which such passage is permitted.[362]

A blockade shall be declared and notified by the government of the party to the conflict concerned or by a commander authorized by that government (Art. 8 LondonDecl 1909). It shall also be notified to the neutral powers (Art. 11 LondonDecl 1909). Any extension and lifting of the blockade shall be declared and announced in the same manner (Art. 12 LondonDecl 1909). A declaration of blockade shall contain the following details: 1052

— the date on which the blockade begins;

— geographical boundaries of the blockaded coastal strip;

— the period granted to neutral ships for departure (Art. 9 LondonDecl 1909).

---

[355] Art. 1, 1909 London Declaration.
[356] Art. 18, 1909 London Declaration. See also para. 99, *San Remo Manual.*
[357] CDDH/215/Rev. 1, para. 73.
[358] See also Bothe, *Commentary*, 764. *San Remo Manual*, para. 102, provides: 'The declaration or establishment of a blockade is prohibited if (a) it has the sole purpose of starving the civilian population or denying it other objects essential for its survival; or (b) the damage to the civilian population is, or may be expected to be, excessive in relation to the concrete and direct military advantage anticipated from the blockade.'
[359] Art. 70 AP I. See also *San Remo Manual*, para. 103.
[360] According to para. 104, *San Remo Manual* the 'blockading belligerent shall [also] allow the passage of medical supplies for the civilian population or for the wounded and sick members of armed forces, subject to the right to prescribe technical arrangements, including search, under which such passage is permitted.'
[361] Bothe, *Commentary*, 764. For the opposite view see Rauch, *Protocol Additional*, 91 ff.
[362] *San Remo Manual*, para. 103.

Heintschel von Heinegg

The provisions on notification, competences, content, and announcement follow from Arts. 8, 9, 11, 12 and 13 of the 1909 London Declaration, which are generally recognized as customary law.[363] The requirement to inform neutral powers, i.e. states not parties to the conflict, is justified by the fact that, according to the principle of impartiality, a blockade must be applied to all vessels and aircraft regardless of their nationality. The declaration must contain the details enumerated in order to enable vessels of neutral states to leave the blockaded coastline in time or to refrain from entering it.

1053 **A blockade, in order to be binding, must be effective (Art. 4 ParisDecl 1856). It must be maintained by armed forces sufficient to prevent access to the blockaded coast. Long-distance blockades are also permissible, i.e. the obstruction and control of the enemy coast by armed forces keeping a longer distance from the blockaded coast. A blockade shall be considered to be effective if ship-to-shore supplies are cut off. Air transport need not be stopped. A barricade achieved by other means, e.g. by ships scuttled in the entrance, does not constitute a blockade. Neither will the mining of coasts and ports compensate for the absence of warships even if all movements are temporarily stopped by the mines. The effectiveness of a blockade is not suspended if the blockading force is temporarily withdrawn on account of bad weather (Art. 4 LondonDecl 1909) or in pursuit of a blockade-runner. A blockade which ceases to be effective is no longer binding. The blockade shall end with the repulse of the blockading forces by the enemy or with their complete or partial destruction, even if new forces are charged with this task without delay. In this case the blockade must be declared and notified anew (Art. 12 LondonDecl 1909).**

1. *Traditional law.* Originally, blockades were applied to coastal forts, never to a coastline as a whole. Hence, the former rules on blockade were taken from the law of siege. During the Dutch–Spanish War the purpose of a blockade changed for the first time from siege to obstruction of traffic to and from the enemy's coastline.[364] Since then blockades, in order to be legal, have to be effective. This means, according to the 1856 Paris Declaration, they must be maintained by a force sufficient to prevent access to the enemy coastline.[365] Hence, naval forces had to be stationed within sight of the blockaded port or coastline.

2. *Effectiveness.*

a) Shortly after the adoption of the 1909 London Declaration many realized that, in view of the probable employment of submarines, mines, and aircraft, the establishment of an effective blockade was nearly impossible. This is one of the reasons why Great Britain was not prepared to ratify the Declaration. During the two World Wars the principle of effectiveness was generally disregarded. Instead of effective blockades in the traditional sense Great Britain proclaimed so-called 'long-

---

[363] *NWP* 9, para. 7.7.2; Canadian *Draft Manual*, para. 722; *San Remo Manual*, paras. 93, 94, and 101.
[364] Cf. O'Connell, Vol. II, 1150.   [365] See also Art. 2, 1909 London Declaration.

distances blockades'. Germany declared a number of 'war zones'. However, the principle of effectiveness was never officially declared void. Rather, the belligerents justified their excessive methods as reprisals.[366]

b) In view of the practice of the World Wars and of the technological development of modern weapons systems the principle of effectiveness had been modified. It is, therefore, now sufficient that within the area specified in the declaration any import of goods is cut off. It makes no difference if the blockade is maintained by air or by naval forces stationed at a distance determined by military requirements or by both.[367] It must, however, be probable that vessels (and aircraft) will be prevented from entering or leaving the blockaded area.[368] A blockade may be restricted to vessels. Its effectiveness is not negated on the sole ground that it does not apply to aircraft.

c) It is a matter of dispute whether during the maintenance of a blockade the presence of surface naval forces or other units of the armed forces is an indispensable condition for its legality. The USA, in particular, has taken the view that a blockade may also be established merely by mining the enemy's ports and coasts,[369] as was done in the case of Haiphong. The following considerations, however, speak against that approach: on one hand, it is still forbidden to lay mines off the coast and ports of the enemy with the sole object of attacking commercial shipping.[370] The mining of Haiphong can hardly be considered a sufficient practice to give rise to the development of a rule of customary law to the contrary. On the other hand, it must be recalled that certain vessels may or even must be exempted from the restrictions imposed by a blockade.[371] That is especially true for vessels in distress. The provisions on the protected status of such vessels would not make much sense if the rule on the compulsory presence of surface naval forces or other units were renounced. Hence, it is not forbidden to enforce and maintain a blockade *also* by naval mines. In any event units of naval or other forces must be present in the vicinity of the blockaded areas in order to ensure that protected vessels and aircraft, especially those in distress, can reach a place of safety.

d) In spite of many technological improvements naval forces may still be forced to leave the blockade area temporarily because of bad weather. Since vessels intending to enter the blockade area will also be affected, the temporary withdrawal of the blockading force does not prejudice the blockade's effectiveness.[372] The

---

[366] Cf. O'Connell, Vol. II, 1153 ff.   [367] *San Remo Manual*, para. 96.

[368] This result can—to a certain extent—be founded upon Art. 3 of the 1909 London Declaration according to which the 'question whether a blockade is effective is a question of fact.' See also para. 95, *San Remo Manual*. Effectiveness is, therefore, dependent upon the circumstances of each case. See also Kalshoven, *Commentary*, 260.

[369] Cf. *NWP 9*, para. 7.7.5. See also van Hegelsom, *Methods*, 46. A more cautious approach is taken in the *San Remo Manual*, para. 97: 'A blockade may be enforced and maintained by a combination of legitimate methods and means of warfare provided this combination does not result in acts inconsistent with the rules set out in this document.'

[370] Art. 2 Hague Convention VIII. See also para. 3 of the commentary on Section 1042.

[371] See para. 2 of the commentary on Section 1051.

[372] Art. 4 of the 1909 London Declaration.

Heintschel von Heinegg

same holds true with regard to a temporary absence due to pursuit of a blockade-runner. If, however, entry and exit are no longer generally prevented the blockade becomes ineffective. Measures connected with the enforcement of a blockade then automatically become illegal. In particular, neutral merchant vessels entering the area may no longer be captured or attacked. The blockading party must confine itself to visit and search.

IV. HOSPITAL SHIPS

1. *General*

1054   The following ships and boats enjoy special protection in naval warfare in accordance with the following provisions, so that they shall not be attacked, sunk, or captured under any circumstances:

— military hospital ships (Art. 22 GC II),

— hospital ships operated by national Red Cross and Red Crescent societies, officially recognized relief societies, or private persons, whether or not they are members of a party to the conflict, or citizens of a state not party to the conflict (Arts. 24, 26 GC II),

— coastal rescue craft operated by a state or by officially recognized relief societies, as far as military necessity permits (Art. 22, 24 GC II), and

— ships specially designed to transport wounded and sick civilians (Art. 21 GC IV; Art. 22 AP I).

1. *Legal basis.* Hospital ships were dealt with at the Hague Peace Conferences of 1899 and 1907. The results of these conferences, the provisions of Hague Convention X, were revised in 1949.[373] The treaty law forming the basis of the present section is to be found in Chapter III of the Second Geneva Convention of 1949, as amended by Arts. 21 ff. AP I.

2. *Protected vessels.*

a) *Military hospital ships.* The protected status of military hospital ships[374] is closely linked to the protection of wounded, sick, and shipwrecked according to Art. 12 GC II. However, their special status remains unchanged whether or not such persons are in fact on board. It is not the transport of wounded, sick, and shipwrecked that is decisive but the ship's function, whose fulfilment must be guaranteed. The protection of military hospital ships, including their lifeboats,[375] does not cease

---

[373] As to the minor modifications of Hague Convention X by GC II, see Pictet, *Commentary* GC II, 156.

[374] Note that the German Federal Navy has no hospital ships.

[375] Art. 26 GC II; Art. 22, para. 1(b) AP I.

simply because they are transporting wounded, sick, and shipwrecked civilians.[376] Protected status means that such vessels 'may in no circumstances be attacked or captured'. In view of their special functions, however, that alone would not suffice. They must at all times be respected and protected. Hence, hospital ships may not be hampered in fulfilling their tasks. This may amount to an obligation on the part of belligerents actively to support hospital ships.[377]

b) *Other hospital ships.* Hospital ships utilized by national Red Cross societies, officially recognized relief societies, or private persons, and their lifeboats,[378] are accorded the same protection as military hospital ships by Art. 24 GC II. This presupposes that 'the Party to the conflict on which they depend has given them an official commission',[379] that they are 'provided with certificates from the responsible authorities, stating that the vessels have been under their control while fitting out and on departure',[380] and that 'their names and descriptions have been notified to the Parties to the conflict ten days before those ships are employed'.[381] Subject to those requirements, the protection provided by Arts. 22 and 24 GC II also extends to hospital ships made available for humanitarian purposes to a party to the conflict by either a neutral state or other state not party to the conflict[382] or by an impartial international humanitarian organization.[383]

c) *Tonnage.* In principle, the specially protected status of all hospital ships, including military hospital ships, is not dependent upon the ships' tonnage.[384] However, during the Second World War smaller vessels were not recognized as legitimate hospital ships.[385] The delegates of the 1949 Geneva Conference, while unable to agree upon a minimum tonnage, therefore laid down in the second sentence of Art. 26 GC II that the parties to the conflict 'shall endeavour to utilize . . . only hospital ships of over 2,000 tons gross'.

d) *Coastal rescue craft.* Under the conditions laid down in Arts. 22 and 24 GC II small coastal rescue craft employed by the state or by officially recognized lifeboat institutions enjoy the same protection as hospital ships.[386] The notification envisaged in Arts. 27 and 22 GC II is not necessary for their protection. Art. 22, para. 3 AP I now provides that they 'shall be protected even if the notification . . . has not been made'. Nevertheless, the parties to the conflict are 'invited to inform each other of any details of such craft which will facilitate their identification and recognition'. The area of operation of small coastal rescue craft need not be confined to waters near the coast.[387] The special status of such craft is subject to 'operational requirements'. This restriction is due to the fact that such craft travel at high speed, cannot easily be identified, and are often perceived as dangerous.

---

[376] Art. 22, para. 1 AP I.
[378] Arts. 24 and 26 GC II.
[380] Art. 24, para. 2 GC II.
[382] Art. 22, para. 2(a) AP I.
[384] Art. 26, first sentence GC II.
[385] Cf. Mossop, *BYIL* XXIV (1947), 160 ff., 398 ff., 403 ff.; Tucker, 125 n. 92.
[387] Cf. Pictet, *Commentary* GC II, 173.

[377] Pictet, *Commentary* GC II, 157.
[379] Art. 24, para. 1 GC II.
[381] Art. 24, para. 2 in conjunction with Art. 22 GC II.
[383] Art. 22, para. 2(b) AP I.

[386] Art. 27 GC II.

e) *Other medical ships and craft.* The protection of vessels designed for the transport of wounded, sick, and shipwrecked civilians can be derived from Art. 21 GC IV. It is now made clear in Art. 22, para. 1 AP I that the protected status of hospital ships is not prejudiced if they carry 'civilian wounded, sick and shipwrecked who do not belong to any of the categories mentioned in Article 13 of the Second Convention'. A well known example of such a hospital ship is the case of the '*Helgoland*' which operated in the waters off Vietnam from August 1966 until January 1972. The German Red Cross sent the *Helgoland* to Vietnamese waters in order to care for wounded and sick civilians after the Federal Republic of Germany and Vietnam, on 28 March 1966, concluded an agreement[388] to this effect.[389] Medical ships and craft other than those referred to in Art. 22 AP I and Art. 38 GC II now enjoy special protection under Art. 23 AP I. This provision covers all means of transportation by water fulfilling the following conditions:[390]

— they must be exclusively assigned, for the duration of their assignment (which may be short), to medical transportation;

— they must be placed under the control of a party to the conflict.

They do, however, remain subject to the laws of war, which means that they are subject to capture unless one of the exceptions of Art. 23, para. 2 applies.

3. *'In accordance with the following provisions'.* The following provisions of Sections 1055 to 1064, according to their wording, refer to hospital ships. Unless there is an express reservation, those provisions also apply to the other vessels referred to above.

2. Conditions for Protection and Identification

1055 **Hospital ships are ships exclusively designed to assist, treat, and transport the wounded, sick, and shipwrecked. Their names and descriptions shall be notified to the parties to the conflict not later than ten days before they are employed for the first time (Art. 22 GC II).**

1. *Function.* The function of hospital ships and the other vessels dealt with in the present section is the essential condition of their protected status. This does not mean that they must have been specially built solely for the purpose of assisting the wounded, sick, and shipwrecked.[391] All vessels solely and definitely assigned to service as hospital ships or to serve one of the other functions mentioned above are protected. Thus it is permissible to transform a merchant vessel or a passenger vessel into a hospital ship. Transformed vessels may not, however, be put to any other use throughout the duration of hostilities.[392]

---

[388] BGBl. 1966 II, 323. [389] Cf. Schlögel, in *Jahrbuch für Internationales Recht* 1973, 92 ff.
[390] Cf. Sandoz, in ICRC, *Commentary*, para. 885. [391] Cf. Pictet, *Commentary* GC II, 159.
[392] Art. 33 GC II.

Heintschel von Heinegg

2. *Notification.* The notification shall include details of registered gross tonnage, length from stem to stern, and numbers of masts and funnels.[393] The parties to the conflict are, of course, free to notify further details. According to Art. 23, para. 4 AP I a party to the conflict 'may notify any adverse Party as far in advance of sailing as possible of the name, description, expected time of sailing, course and estimated speed of the medical ship or craft, particularly in the case of ships of over 2,000 gross tons, and may provide other information which would facilitate identification and recognition'. The notification according to Art. 22 GC II must be made ten days before those ships are employed.[394] The object and purpose of that time limit is to increase the safety of hospital ships (and of small coastal rescue craft) by enabling the adverse party to pass the information to armed forces. In peacetime the notification will normally be transmitted directly. After the outbreak of hostilities the parties to the conflict will usually make use of the assistance of protecting powers.

Hospital ships shall be distinctively marked as follows: 1056

— all exterior surfaces shall be white;

— the distinctive emblem of the Red Cross shall be painted once or several times on each side of the hull and on the horizontal surfaces, as large as possible, so as to be clearly visible from sea and air;

— a white flag with a red cross shall be flown as high as possible, visible from all sides.

In addition, all hospital ships shall fly their national flags; neutral ships shall further hoist the flag of the party to the conflict whose direction they have accepted (Art. 43 GC II). As far as possible, their painting and distinctive emblems shall be rendered visible at night. Other identification systems, e.g. internationally recognized light, radio, and electronic signals, are also permissible (Arts. 5–6 Annex I AP I). Lifeboats of hospital ships, coastal rescue boats, and all small craft used by the medical service shall be marked in the same manner as hospital ships (Art. 43, paras. 3 and 4 GC II; Art. 23, para. 1 AP I).

1. *Visual marking.* For hospital ships and small coastal rescue craft these are not an essential condition of their special protection. Such markings do not, of themselves, confer protected status but are intended only to facilitate identification.[395] In place of the red cross on a white ground the parties to the conflict can use the red crescent or the red lion and sun on a white ground.[396] In principle, the distinctive emblem as well as the national flag must be hoisted permanently.[397] Only hospital ships temporarily detained in accordance with Section 1061 lower the flag of the state in whose service they are employed or under whose control they have placed themselves. The obligation to fly the distinctive emblem at the mainmast as high as

---

[393] Art. 22, para. 2 GC II.
[394] Originally, a period of 30 days was envisaged. After a proposal of the ICRC to this effect that period was reduced to 10 days which was considered sufficient. Cf. Pictet, *Commentary* GC II, 161.
[395] See also para. 173, *San Remo Manual.*
[396] Art. 43, para. 7 and Art. 41 para. 2 GC II.   [397] Art. 43, para. 2 GC II.

Heintschel von Heinegg

possible[398] is because that part of the ship will first be visible on the horizon. There are no specific obligations as to visual marking at night. Hence, all means appropriate to facilitate identification, especially lights, are permissible. Visual means of identification also include flashing lights.

2. *Other kinds of identification.* Already in 1949 the delegates of the 1949 Geneva Conference were aware of the insufficiency of visual signs and markings in modern naval wars. Hence, Art. 43, para. 8 GC II provides that 'parties to the conflict shall at all times endeavour to conclude mutual agreements, in order to use the most modern methods available to facilitate the identification of hospital ships.' There was, however, no agreement on specific and universally binding methods. A first improvement was then brought about by the regulations concerning identification in Annex I to AP I. Now the parties to the conflict can, by agreement, supplement visual methods of identification of hospital ships and other medical transports by light signals,[399] radio signals,[400] or electronic identification.[401] In modern warfare, which is characterized by the use of electronic means of warfare, these additional technical means of identification are essential for minimizing the danger of mistaken attacks.[402] Provisions on special means of underwater acoustic identification of hospital ships[403] have now been included in the revised Annex I to AP I. In 1990 the ICRC tried to optimize the provisions of Annex I by publishing its *Manual for the Use of Technical Means of Identification.*[404] In view of modern weapons technology the methods recommended therein are, however, only a first step in the right direction.[405]

3. Rights and Obligations

1057   **Hospital ships shall afford assistance to all wounded, sick, and shipwrecked without distinction of nationality (Art. 30 GC II). They shall by no means be employed for any military purposes.**

1. *Obligation to afford relief and assistance impartially.* This is laid down in Art. 30, para. 1 GC II, but also follows from Arts. 12 and 22 GC II. Nationality is not the only unlawful criterion for discrimination. Others are sex, race, religion, and political opinion.[406]

2. *The prohibition against using these vessels for any military purpose.* (Art. 30, para. 2 GC II.) Prohibited purposes include intelligence activities and transport of troops, weapons, and ammunition.[407] This provision is closely linked to Section 1062 con-

---

[398] Art. 43, para. 2 GC II.   [399] Art. 6, Annex I to AP I.   [400] Art. 7, Annex I to AP I.
[401] Art. 8, Annex I to AP I.   [402] Cf. Feist, *HuV-I* 1990, 212.
[403] Cf. Eberlin, *IRRC* 267 (Nov.–Dec. 1988), 505–28.   [404] Geneva 1990.
[405] Feist, *HuV-I* 1990, 212, states: '*Der eigentliche Nutzen des Handbuchs ist darin zu sehen, daß es das Problem der Identifizierung und des Schutzes von militärischen Konflikt nicht betroffener oder besonders geschützter Fahrzeuge mit der Kompetenz des Roten Kreuzes international thematisiert*'.
[406] Cf. Pictet, *Commentary* GC II, 179.   [407] Cf. O'Connell, Vol. II, 1120.

cerning loss of protection. It is self-explanatory, and was inspired by the experience of the World Wars.[408]

Hospital ships may be equipped with radio systems. They may not, however, possess or use a secret code for their wireless or other means of communication (Art. 34 GC II). Also permissible is (Art. 35 GC II):

—the use of apparatus designed to facilitate navigation or communication;

—the transport of medical supplies and personnel over and above the ship's requirements (Art. 35 GC II);

—the use of portable arms by the personnel of a hospital ship for the maintenance of order, for their own defence, or for that of the wounded and sick;

—the carrying of portable arms and ammunitions taken from the wounded, sick, or shipwrecked and not yet handed over to the proper service; and

—the taking on board of wounded, sick, or shipwrecked civilians (Art. 22, para. 1 AP I).

1. *Radio and communications systems.* In contrast to some delegates of the 1907 Hague Conference, the delegates of the 1949 Geneva Conference considered the equipment of hospital ships necessarily to include a radio. This is made evident by Art. 35, para. 2 GC II. According to Art. 34, para. 2 GC II hospital ships may not, however, 'possess or use a secret code for their wireless or other means of communication'. Despite the differences between the French (*pour leurs émissions*) and the English wordings of that provision it is a widely held view that hospital ships may neither send nor receive messages in other than generally known codes. This is without doubt true as regards the emission of messages in encrypted form. In that case a hospital ship will lose its protected status. It is questionable, however, whether they are also forbidden to receive encrypted messages. In order to fulfil their humanitarian mission most effectively, hospital ships should—it is submitted here—be permitted to use cryptographic equipment.[409] Otherwise a belligerent will refrain from informing its hospital ships of possible areas of operation.[410]

2. *Other permissible equipment and actions.* Apparatus intended exclusively to facilitate navigation is nowadays part of the essential equipment of modern vessels. Hence, its presence on board will not prejudice the protected status of hospital and other ships.[411] Also permissible is the transport of equipment and personnel intended exclusively for medical duties above the normal requirements.[412] This helps avoid the difficulties arising from the transport of equipment and personnel

---

[408] e.g. in World War I the German hospital ship *Ophelia* was condemned because it had not afforded assistance and because it had transmitted encrypted messages that had not been properly documented. Moreover, the *Ophelia* was equipped with a radio system; then unusual for a hospital ship. The radio installations were destroyed by the crew prior to capture. Cf. O'Connell, Vol. II, 1120.

[409] Also provided in para. 171, *San Remo Manual.*

[410] As was the case during the Falklands/Malvinas conflict. Instead hospital ships were made to stay in a so-called 'Red Cross Box' established by *ad hoc* agreement between the belligerents.

[411] Art. 35, No. 2 GC II.   [412] Art. 35, No. 5 GC II.

Heintschel von Heinegg

that do not belong to the usual equipment and personnel of a hospital ship but are intended for a specific area of operations. The crews of hospital ships, according to Art. 35 No. 1 GC II, are entitled to carry small ('portable') arms and to use them either for the maintenance of order, for their own defence, or for that of the sick and wounded. Military hospital ships and infirmaries are usually subject to military discipline. Guards are necessary to prevent patients from leaving without permission. They must also be in a position to hinder unauthorized persons from entering. For these purposes small-arms are necessary but also sufficient. Weapons and weapons systems with the capability of repulsing a military attack may not be placed on board the vessels protected under the present Section. If such an (illegal!) attack occurs the crews of a hospital ship can and must make all efforts to warn the attacking ship or aircraft. It is not uncommon that wounded, sick, and shipwrecked at the time of their rescue still possess weapons and ammunition. Such weapons and ammunitions must be taken away and delivered to the competent authority. Delivery, however, will take some time because the competent authority is situated on land. Therefore, the presence of such weapons and ammunition on board a hospital ship does not jeopardize its protected status. Finally, as stated above, the mere fact that a hospital ship is carrying wounded, sick, and shipwrecked civilians does not deprive it of its special protection.[413]

1059   **Any hospital ship in a port which falls into the hands of the adversary shall be authorized to leave the said port (Art. 29 GC II). During and after an engagement, hospital ships will act at their own risk. Hospital ships shall not hamper the movements of the combatants (Art. 30 GC II).**

1. *The right to leave a port.* The ability to leave a port which is in the hands of the enemy (Art. 29 GC II) is a consequence of the general protection of hospital ships. It also follows indirectly from the provisions on the exceptional and temporary detention of hospital ships. However, it was considered necessary to restate that principle in a separate provision.

2. *Acting at their own risk.* This refers to the entering of areas of operation in order to assist the victims of armed conflict. Hospital ships may not be attacked. However, belligerents cannot be held responsible for accidentally hitting a hospital ship. This also holds true for damage suffered during entrance to the area of naval operations shortly after the cessation of active hostilities.[414]

3. *The prohibition against hampering the movements of combatants.* (Art. 30 para. 3 GC II.) This corresponds with the basic rule that hospital ships may not be employed for any military purpose (Art. 30, para. 2 GC II). The exemption from attack ceases according to Section 1062 if a hospital ship breaches these conditions. Otherwise a party to the conflict could position its hospital ships in such a way as to render impossible any self-defence measures by the enemy.

---

[413] Art. 35, No. 4 GC II; Art. 22, para. 1 AP I.   [414] See also Pictet, *Commentary* GC II, 180.

While hospital ships are not liable to capture, they are subject to the right of con- 1060
trol and visit accorded to the parties to the conflict (Art. 31 GC II). Any warship
may request the handing over of the wounded, sick, and shipwrecked by hospital
or other ships, no matter which nationality such ships have, provided that the
state of health of the wounded and sick allows such action and that the receiving
warship can provide the facilities necessary for medical treatment (Art. 14 GC II;
Art. 30 AP I).

1. *Control and search.* According to Art. 31, para. 1 GC II the parties to the conflict
are entitled to control the vessels protected under this Section. Control and search
serve to verify whether the adverse party is complying with its duty not to use hospital and other vessels for military purposes. Control and search may also be conducted in order to examine the condition of the wounded on board. This right
comprises search of the whole ship, its equipment, and cargo, as well as control of
the list of patients and the establishment of the identity of the members of the crew.

2. *Handing over.* All warships of a belligerent are entitled to demand that wounded,
sick, or shipwrecked persons on board hospital and other ships shall be surrendered, whatever their nationality.[415] This right is conferred on the belligerents to
meet their interest in preventing those persons from joining the hostilities after
recovery. If they are members of the armed forces or if they belong to any of the categories of Art. 4A GC III they become prisoners of war as soon as they fall into the
enemy's hands.[416] If they are not in a fit state to be moved and if the warship cannot provide adequate facilities for necessary medical treatment, surrender of those
persons may not be demanded. Surrender of merchant vessel crew members who
have promised in writing not to undertake any service connected with the armed
conflict while hostilities last may not be required.

The belligerents are not obliged to accept assistance from hospital ships. They 1061
may order them off, make them follow a certain course, control the use of their
means of communication, and, if the gravity of the circumstances requires, detain
them for a period of up to seven days (Art. 31, para. 1 GC II). A commissioner may
temporarily be put on board to monitor the execution of such orders (Art. 31, para.
2 GC II). For the purpose of control, the parties to the conflict may also send neutral observers on board (Art. 31, para. 4 GC II).

1. *Orders of belligerents to hospital ships.* For reasons of military security the parties
to the conflict may refuse assistance from hospital ships, order them off, or make
them take a certain course.[417] The right to control the use of their radio or of other
means of communication is to ensure that a hospital ship is not abused for military
purposes.

2. *Detention of hospital ships.* According to Art. 31 para. 1 GC II this is an exceptional right. It may be exercised only if necessary, e.g. to ensure the secrecy of

[415] Art. 14 GC II.   [416] Art. 16 GC II.   [417] Art. 31. para. 1 GC II.

important military operations that have come to the knowledge of the hospital ship.[418] The time limit of seven days runs from the detention order. Even if the reasons for detention continue to exist, that time limit may not be extended. This is meant to prevent belligerents from effectively capturing hospital ships. If the reasons for detention cease to exist before seven days have passed, the hospital ship must be released immediately.

3. *Commissioners and neutral observers.* The sole task of commissioners temporarily put on board a hospital ship is to see that legitimate orders are carried out. If the commissioner is a naval officer he may be captured by enemy armed forces, not by the hospital ship's crew and personnel. If he is also a member of the medical or hospital personnel he continues to be protected.[419] The sending of a non-neutral commissioner has often led to problems. According to Art. 31, para. 4 GC II it is, therefore, also possible to place (either unilaterally or by particular agreements) neutral observers on board hospital ships who shall verify the strict observation of the provisions of GC II.

4. Discontinuance of Protection

1062 **If such ships are misused for military purposes or act in any other way contrary to their obligations, in particular by clearly resisting an order to stop, to turn away, or to follow a distinct course, they lose their protected status, after due warning has been given (Art. 34 GC II).**

Art. 34 GC II provides that the 'protection to which hospital ships . . . are entitled shall not cease unless they are used to commit, outside their humanitarian duties, acts harmful to the enemy'. The following acts, *inter alia*, constitute an abuse for military purposes: transmission of military/intelligence information to the enemy,[420] transport of military material or enemy troops, intentionally hampering the movements of naval forces, or any of the acts rendering a vessel a legitimate military objective.[421] It is emphasized in the present context that, in view of modern weapons technology, hospital ships may be equipped with purely deflective means of defence, such as chaff and flares. The presence of such equipment should, however, be notified.[422] Abuse does not automatically lead to loss of exemption. In view of the humanitarian function of such vessels their protection may cease only after due warning has been given, allowing in all appropriate cases a reasonable time limit, and after such warning has remained unheeded. The extent of the time limit will depend upon the circumstances prevailing at the time. The aggrieved belligerent is not obliged to name a time limit if that would be inappropriate, e.g. if the

---

[418] Cf. Pictet, *Commentary* GC II, 183.　　　　　[419] Cf. Pictet, *Commentary* GC II, 185.

[420] Art. 34, para. 2 GC II.

[421] According to para. 49, *San Remo Manual* hospital ships and other protected vessels lose their exemption if they (a) are not innocently employed in their normal role; (b) do not submit to identification and inspection when required; and (c) intentionally hamper the movements of combatants and do not obey orders to stop or move out of the way when required.

[422] *San Remo Manual*, para. 170.

Heintschel von Heinegg

hospital ship participates in the hostilities or if its crew fires at the warship. If after due warning a hospital ship persists in breaking a condition of its exemption, it renders itself liable to capture or other necessary measures to enforce compliance.[423] It may only be attacked as a last resort if: (a) diversion or capture is not feasible; (b) no other method is available for exercising military control; (c) the circumstances of non-compliance are sufficiently grave that the hospital ship has become, or may reasonably be assumed to be, a military objective; and (d) collateral casualties or damage will be proportionate to the military advantage gained or expected.[424] If feasible, before destruction the wounded, sick, and shipwrecked shall be taken to a place of safety.

5. Personnel and Crew

**The religious, medical, and hospital personnel of hospital ships and their crews   1063
shall be respected and protected; they may not be captured during the time they
are in the service of the hospital ship, whether there are wounded and sick on
board or not (Art. 36 GC II).**

This provision guarantees a far-reaching protection because it also covers crew members. This is justified because hospital ships will only be able to fulfil their humanitarian function if they are equipped with a crew able to handle the ship. 'During the time they are in service' does not mean that the personnel must be actively engaged in the assistance and care of wounded, sick, and shipwrecked. It is sufficient if they are assigned such duties. Therefore, it makes no difference whether there are wounded and sick on board or not. A temporary absence of patients from the ship does not prejudice their protected status. It is emphasized that personnel and crew on board coastal rescue craft, according to Art. 37 GC II, are protected only while engaged in rescue operations.[425]

**The personnel of hospital ships, including the crew, shall wear a white armlet   1064
bearing the distinctive emblem. Their armlets or identity cards may not be taken
away from them (Art. 42 GC II).**

The obligation of personnel on board hospital ships to wear an armlet bearing the distinctive emblem follows from Art. 42, para. 1 GC II. According to Art. 42, para. 2 GC II the identity card shall be worded in the national language, shall mention at least the full name, date of birth, rank, and service number of the bearer, and shall state in what capacity he is entitled to the protection of GC II. The card shall bear the photograph of the owner and also his signature or finger-prints or both. The prohibition in Art. 42, para. 4 GC II of depriving said personnel of their insignia, identity cards or armlets is intended to guarantee permanent protection for such personnel. In case of loss the owner is entitled to receive duplicate or replacement cards and insignia.

---

[423] Ibid., para. 50.   [424] Ibid., para. 51.
[425] See also *San Remo Manual*, para. 162; Pictet, *Commentary* GC II, 205.

Heintschel von Heinegg

11

The Law of Neutrality

I. GENERAL

Neutrality (derived from the Latin *neuter*: neither of both) is defined in interna- 1101
tional law as the status of a state which is not participating in an armed conflict
between other states. Neutral status gives rise to rights and duties in the relationship between the neutral state on one hand and the parties to the conflict on the
other.

'Neutrality' describes the particular status, as defined by international law, of a
state not party to an armed conflict.[1] This status entails specific rights and duties in
the relationship between the neutral and the belligerent states. On one hand, there
is the right of the neutral state to remain apart from, and not to be adversely affected
by, the conflict. On the other hand there is the duty of non-participation and impartiality.

The right not to be adversely affected means that the relationship between the
neutral and belligerent states is governed by the law of peace, which is modified
only in certain respects by the law of neutrality. In particular, the neutral state must
tolerate certain controls in the area of maritime commerce. The duty of non-participation and impartiality are a necessary corollary to the right not to be adversely
affected. The duty of non-participation means, above all, that the state must
abstain from supporting a party to the conflict. This duty not to support also means
that the neutral state is under a duty not to allow one party to the conflict to use the
resources of the neutral state against the will of the opponent. Therefore, the
defence of neutrality is part of the duty of non-participation. The scope of those
duties is described in more detail in the following provisions.

The duty of impartiality does not mean that the state is bound to treat the belligerents in exactly the same way. It entails a prohibition of discrimination, i.e. it
forbids only differential treatment of the belligerents which in view of the specific
problem of the armed conflict is not justified. This duty of impartiality, too, will be
defined more precisely below.

As impartiality does not entail a duty of exactly equal treatment, a neutral state is

---

[1] Bindschedler, *EPIL*, 4, 9 ff.; Kussbach, *RDMilG* 17 (1979); Seidl-Hohenveldern, *Festschrift für Friedrich
August Freiherr von der Heydte* (1977) Vol. 1, 593–613; Köpfer.

Bothe

under no duty to eliminate differences in the commercial relations between itself and each of the parties to the conflict at the time of the outbreak of the armed conflict. The neutral state is entitled to continue existing commercial relations (the principle of the so-called *courant normal*). A change in commercial relationships favouring one of the belliegerents would, however, constitute taking sides in a manner incompatible with the status of neutrality. In more general terms, impartiality means that the neutral state must apply the specific measures it takes on the basis of the rights and duties deriving from its neutral status in a substantially equal way as between the parties to the conflict (Art. 9 HC V, Art. 9 HC XIII). This regime of rights and duties of the neutral state is an important international legal tool for restraining conflicts. By establishing a clear distinction between neutral states and states parties to the conflict, international law prevents more states from being drawn into the conflict. Neutral states may help parties to a conflict to maintain or establish relations which may mitigate the suffering of victims (e.g. by conducting relief operations or exchanging information) and which may finally smooth the path to peace (e.g. by arranging cease-fires). It is incompatible with this conflict-restraining function of neutrality that states should try to evade the duties flowing from their neutral status by styling themselves non-belligerents.[2] This, however, has often happened in the past.

The USA considered itself as a non-belligerent before entering the Second World War, but not as neutral because it supported Great Britain in a way which was incompatible with the duty of non-participation under the law of neutrality. Although there are a number of cases of declared or undeclared non-belligerency, there is no sufficiently uniform general practice which would justify the conclusion that non-belligerency has become a notion recognized by customary international law. The cases of non-belligerency either arose in the absence of a conflict of sufficient scope to require the application of the law of neutrality (or in a conflict which was not considered as such) or were simply violations of the law of neutrality. If a 'non-belligerent' state violates the law of neutrality it must bear the consequences, for instance reprisals. A claim of non-belligerent status may not be used as a justification. The consequences of such violations are discussed below.[3] Violations of the law of neutrality occur even where support is given to the victim of aggression, and even when it does not amount to participation in the conflict. It may, thus, be answered by countermeasures.[4] Neutrality is not optional, in the sense that each state is free to violate single duties of the law of neutrality as it will, or to declare them irrelevant, without having to fear a countermeasure taken by the adversely affected state.

The situation, however, is different where the law of neutrality is modified by the Charter of the United Nations or by a binding decision of the Security Council (see Section 1103). To that extent, it is meaningful and correct that newer treaties use the term 'neutral or other states not party to the conflict' (Art. 2(c) AP 1). Such a formulation clarifies that a provision is to be applied to any state not participating in the conflict, without the need to enter into any controversy over the status of

---

[2] Bindschedler, *EPIL* 4, 13.   [3] See commentary to Section 1107.
[4] Schindler, in *Essays in Honour of Frits Kalshoven* (1991), 373.

Bothe

neutrality, and also where there is a conflict not sufficiently great in scope to trigger the application of the law of neutrality.[5]

The sources of the international law of neutrality are customary law and, for cer-   1102
tain questions, international treaties (HC V; HC XIII).

The essential aspects of neutrality have been developed through state practice in modern times.[6] As a legal status of non-participation, its basic scope was fixed by the end of the eighteenth century. The development continued during the nineteenth century in two ways. On one hand, greater protection of neutral commerce from belligerent acts was achieved. On the other hand, a legal duty of permanent neutrality as an essential element of the maintenance of peace and the balance of powers in Europe was established (by the recognition of the neutrality of Switzerland, Belgium, and Luxembourg). During the First and Second World Wars, and also in a number of later conflicts, the law of neutrality retained its significance. The development of the international legal prohibition of the use of force, however, offered reasons to differentiate between the aggressor and the victim of aggression, a fact which calls into question the classical principle of the impartiality of the neutral state. In addition, the political polarization after the Second World War, which had an impact on many conflicts, made the impartiality of the neutral state a politically doubtful rule. Some details of this development are discussed below. The development of the earlier state practice gave rise to customary law which is still an essential source of the law of neutrality. Following a modification of state practice, this customary law too underwent changes and introduced distinctions. This change, however, has produced only modifications of single specific rules of the law of neutrality, not a general revocation of this whole body of law.

Essential parts of the law of neutrality were codified during the nineteenth and the early twentieth centuries. Important steps in this development were the Paris Declaration of 1856[7] and the Hague Conventions of 1907, namely Convention V respecting the rights and duties of neutral powers and persons in case of war on land and XIII concerning the rights and duties of neutral powers in naval warfare. Other treaties relating to the laws of war contain specific provisions concerning the rights and duties of neutral states, in particular the four Geneva Conventions of 1949 and Protocol I Additional thereto of 8 June 1977. There has, however, been no comprehensive codification of the law of neutrality since the Hague Conventions of 1907. These rules of 1907 have in part been rendered obsolete by later practice. The need for a new codification is urgent. The different bases of the rules of the law of neutrality will be indicated in the commentaries below.

The Charter of the United Nations and decisions of the Security Council based on   1103
the Charter may in certain circumstances modify the traditional law of neutrality.
Therefore enforcement measures taken by the United Nations are governed
by particular rules different from the traditional law of neutrality. The general law

---

[5] See commentary to Section 1106.   [6] Bindschedler, *EPIL* 4, 10 ff.; Castrén, 421 et seq.
[7] Schindler/Toman, 787 et seq.

of neutrality, however, has not been revoked by the Charter of the United Nations.

The Charter of the United Nations completed the development of the international legal prohibition of the use of force and established a system of collective security, by the reaction of the international community against breaches of peace. The traditional law of neutrality with its duty of impartiality, i.e. the prohibition of discrimination between the parties to the conflict, seems to be incompatible with this development which outlaws the aggressor. However, this is not generally the case. Also under the Charter of the United Nations, neutrality during international armed conflicts is permissible and possible.[8] States expressly rely on the law of neutrality.[9] The impartiality of the neutral state retains its important functions at least as long as there is no possibility of a binding decision concerning the question of who in a given conflict is the aggressor and who is the victim. Although the Charter of the United Nations provides for a binding decision by the Security Council on the question of whether there has been an armed attack and which state is the aggressor, decisions of this kind have long been politically impossible in view of the polarization between the super-powers. Whether and to what extent the Security Council has gained a new capacity to act due to the developments of the most recent past remains to be seen. The details of this development cannot be discussed in the present context. However, it cannot be taken for granted that the Security Council will always exercise its powers in this respect.

Furthermore, it is stressed that the Charter of the United Nations provides a right of collective self-defence, i.e. a right of all states to assist a victim of aggression, but not a duty to do so. Thus, it is by no means unlawful if a state abstains from supporting a victim of aggression, i.e. remains impartial and neutral.[10] The situation is different only if and to the extent that the Security Council uses its powers under Chapter VII of the Charter to oblige states to conduct enforcement measures (Art. 41, 42, 43, and 48 of the Charter of the United Nations). This means that the traditional duty of non-participation and impartiality has not in a general way been revoked by the Charter, but only that it may in particular cases be suspended by a binding decision of the Security Council. When taking such a decision, the Security Council may also differentiate the supporting duties imposed upon particular states.[11]

In the future, it will probably be necessary to distinguish between enforcement measures *stricto sensu* undertaken by the United Nations under the direction of the Security Council and military operations undertaken by one or more states and authorized by the Security Council. The military operation to liberate Kuwait was not an enforcement action undertaken by the United Nations. This operation is considered by many as simply constituting collective self-defence authorized by the Security Council. A distinction must be made, however, between the authorization to conduct military operations against Iraq, an authorization given only to the

---

[8] Ipsen, in Ipsen, *Völkerrecht*, 1056.   [9] Schindler, in Delissen/Tanja (Eds.), 367 ff.
[10] Schindler, *loc. cit.*, 373.
[11] See Torrelli, *Annales de droit international médical* 35 (1991), 38 ff.

states 'co-operating with the government of Kuwait', which clearly implies the legal admissibility of non-participation, and non-military enforcement measures against Iraq, in particular the interruption of commercial relations and of monetary transactions imposed as a duty on all members of the United Nations. In this case, states were clearly under a duty to deviate from the principle of *courant normal*,[12] to that extent there was a modification of the rules of neutrality.

More generally, the duty of non-participation as well as that of impartiality may be restricted by decisions of the Security Council.[13]

Under general international law every state is free to participate in an armed con-   1104
flict or not. A state may, however, in accordance with current law, participate only
on the side of the victim of an armed attack (collective self-defence), not on the
side of the aggressor.

Traditional international law left to each state the sovereign decision of whether, at the outbreak of a conflict between other states, it would participate or remain neutral. Thus neutrality, as a matter of principle, was a question to be decided *ad hoc* by each state when a conflict broke out. Therefore, there was a practice of pronouncing 'declarations of neutrality' at the outbreak of a conflict.

As explained above, this is still true but only in a limited sense. At the outbreak of a conflict between two other states, a state is still free to participate or to remain neutral. Modern international law, however, limits the freedom of decision as to the side on which a state may become involved. Support granted to an aggressor is illegal, participation on the side of the victim of aggression, being collective self-defence, is permissible.

The distinction between participation and neutrality is a political, not military, decision. Where the law of neutrality requires decisions to be taken by military command, the government concerned must give political guidance and clarify the position which it takes in relation to a particular conflict.

Permanent neutrality is a status under which a state undertakes in peacetime a   1105
legal obligation to remain neutral in case of an armed conflict between two other
states. This status requires the neutral state in peacetime not to accept any mili-
tary obligations and to abstain from acts which would render the fulfilment of its
obligations of neutrality impossible should the armed conflict occur. A distinction
must be made between such a *legal obligation* to remain neutral and a neutrality
policy.

The legal neutralization of certain states was one of the political tools used to maintain a balance of power in Europe under the European Concert during the last century. The states which still possess a legally based status of permanent neutrality are Switzerland and Austria.[14] The permanent neutrality of Switzerland is based on mutual unilateral declarations made by Switzerland and by the most important

---

[12] See above commentary to Section 1101.   [13] Schindler, in Delissen/Tanja (Eds.), 372.
[14] Bindschedler, *EPIL* 4 (1982), 133.

European powers, in connection with the Vienna Congress in 1815. The international legal basis of the permanent neutrality of Austria is also a unilateral act, namely the Austrian notification of the Federal Constitution Act of 26 October 1955. Whether, and to what extent, both states are under an international legal duty to maintain this status of permanent neutrality is not clear.

A permanently neutral state may not, in time of peace, accept any obligation which would render it impossible to fulfil, in times of armed conflict, its duties of neutrality. Therefore, a permanently neutral state may not become a member of a military alliance. In relation to Austria, there was a lively discussion as to whether the economic obligations involved in Austrian membership of the EC would be incompatible with its status of permanent neutrality. Whether this was true in the context of the division of Europe into two blocs is a question which no longer needs an answer. The political changes in Europe have led to closer co-operation between Eastern European states and the European Union. This being so, the question of the significance of economic ties for the status of permanent neutrality has become irrelevant in the European context.

In a more general way, permanent neutrality means a renunciation of the right of collective self-defence, i.e. the right to grant assistance, but not a renunciation of the right to accept help from others if the permanently neutral state is itself attacked.

In most other cases where states declared themselves as permanently neutral, the declarations were not of a legal, but of a political nature. Legal acts establishing permanent neutrality of the kind adopted by Switzerland and Austria are lacking in the case of states which during the past years have followed a policy of neutrality (Sweden, Finland, Ireland). In these cases, there may be some legal underpinning of neutrality in the principle of estoppel, namely where political declarations create a situation of confidence in which other states may rely on the state making such a declaration to remain neutral and where, due to that reliance, they have abstained from making defence preparations in relation to that state.

1106   **Except for those rules which, in a legally based permanent neutrality, apply in times of peace, neutrality begins with the outbreak of an armed conflict of significant scope between two other states.**

The status of neutrality as defined by international law becomes effective with the outbreak of an armed conflict between two other states.[15] Thus, the question arises of what constitutes an armed conflict within the meaning of the law of neutrality; in other words, what is the threshold of application of the law of neutrality? The law of neutrality leads to considerable modifications in the relationships between the neutral and the belligerent states, for instance as to the admissibility of exports, the sojourn of warships of the parties to the conflict in neutral waters, and the control of neutral trade. These fundamental changes are not triggered by every armed incident, but require an armed conflict of a certain duration and intensity. Thus, the

---

[15] Bothe, in Dekker/Post (Eds.) 205 ff.

Bothe

threshold of application of the law of neutrality is probably higher than that for the
rules of the law of war relating to the conduct of hostilities and the treatment of
prisoners, which are applicable also in conflicts of less intensity.

There is a traditional thesis, still defended in literature and by state organs, to the
effect that the application of the law of neutrality requires the existence of 'a war in
the legal sense'.[16] Whether and to what extent this thesis is a correct statement of
the current state of customary law depends on the definition of 'war in the legal
sense' under current international law. There is still a widespread opinion that, in
addition to the objective existence of armed hostilities, there must be a subjective
element: the intent to conduct a war (*animus belligerendi*). If this were correct a
state could, simply by declaring that it did not intend to conduct a war, evade all the
restraints imposed upon a party to the conflict by the law of neutrality. For states
not party to the conflict this construction would provide an excuse not to respect
the prohibition of supporting a belligerent. It is exactly in this sense that the construction has been used time and time again. However, the threshold of the application of the law of neutrality must be prevented from becoming in this way a
question for the subjective discretion of the states involved. Therefore, the threshold must be determined according to the object and purpose of the law of neutrality. This means that the law of neutrality must be applied in any conflict which has
reached a scope which renders its legal limitation by the application of the law of
neutrality meaningful and necessary. It is, however, impossible to establish this
threshold in a general way. One can only say that there must be a conflict of a certain duration and intensity.

On closer analysis, all those defending a 'subjective' notion of war come to a similar result if and to the extent that they tie the intent to conduct a war to a series of
objective criteria relevant for the character of the relationships between the parties
to a conflict as well as between these parties and neutral states. For them, the decisive question is whether and to what extent states use legal instruments typical of
the existence of a state of war; for instance the severance of diplomatic relations, the
treatment of nationals of the other party as enemy aliens, the exercise of control
over the commerce of third states, and similar measures.

It is apparent from the above that the determination of whether a particular conflict has reached the threshold of application of the law of neutrality is a matter of
complex legal construction both for the parties to the conflict and for third states.
In the interest of legal clarity, it is therefore desirable that states expressly clarify
their position in this respect. This legal construction is a matter to be decided by
governments, not by military command. Therefore, declarations and notifications
of a state's construction of the status of the conflict are relevant, but by no means
constitutive for the characterization of the conflict. The law of neutrality is applicable without a specific declaration on the part of the state not party to the conflict
being necessary. The difficulties described, however, have frequently led to situations in which different states evaluated the legal status of the same conflict in a different way (e.g. the Gulf War between Iran and Iraq), a fact which has led to
considerable legal insecurity.

[16] Castrén, 34 ff.; Greenwood, in Dekker/Post (Eds.), 212 ff.; Schindler, in Delissen/Tanja (Eds.), 375 ff.

Bothe

States not parties to a conflict which has not reached the threshold of application of the law of neutrality are not neutral in the legal sense, i.e. they are not bound by the particular duties of the law of neutrality. In those fields where the rules of international humanitarian law have a lower threshold of application than the law of neutrality, the use of the term 'other state not party to a conflict' is the logical consequence of this situation.[17]

The application of the law of neutrality requires the existence of an international conflict. There is no neutrality in relation to non-international conflicts. On the other hand, third states are subject to certain legal restrictions in relation to internal armed conflicts. According to a traditional rule of international law, support given to insurgents constitutes unlawful interference in the internal affairs of another state. If it reaches a certain intensity, this support is considered equivalent to an unlawful armed attack. Support given to an established government, in whatever form, was in former times generally considered as legal, each state being free to request the assistance of other states for the purpose of maintaining its internal order. This, however, is no longer uncontroversial, in particular because there have been a number of cases where the legitimacy of the government requesting the assistance was subject to doubt (e.g. Afghanistan, Vietnam). There is thus a growing tendency to consider the assistance given to parties to a civil war, even in the form of an 'intervention by invitation', as being generally inadmissible.[18] A prohibition of interference of this kind must not be confused with the duty of non-participation under the law of neutrality. Foreign intervention, whether lawful or not, can change the status of an internal conflict and render it an international one. In this case, the law of neutrality is indeed applicable.

1107 **Neutral status ceases with the end of an armed conflict or by the neutral state becoming a party to the conflict. However, neither limited actions of armed defence of neutrality nor breaches of single duties of neutrality by the state alone necessarily result in that state becoming a party to the conflict.**

The status of neutrality (except, of course, those rules of permanent neutrality which apply in times of peace) ends with the armed conflict. This obvious rule raises a number of practical problems similar to those concerning the beginning of neutral status. Under today's conditions, the end of a conflict can not always be clearly determined. The actual cessation of hostilities does not always lead to a modification in the relations between the parties to the conflict which would render the law of neutrality inapplicable. On the contrary, the resumption of arms exports, for instance, during an armistice, might even prompt the resurgence of the armed conflict and thus render futile a positive effect of the law of neutrality. On the other hand, an armistice may lead to the pacification of the situation which, after several years, can no longer be distinguished from normal peacetime relations. For this question, too, there are no sufficiently clear criteria of general validity. Within the meaning of the law of neutrality, a conflict must be considered as terminated

---

[17] See commentary to Section 1101.   [18] Akehurst, 'Civil War', *EPIL* 3, 88.

where, after the cessation of active hostilities, there is a certain degree of normalization of the relations between the parties to a conflict. There are specific rules for certain norms of the law of neutrality (e.g. Art. 111 GC III).

In the course of the conflict, a neutral state may become a party to the conflict. Whether and under what circumstances this occurs is not always easy to determine. Different cases must be distinguished.

The first possibility is that either a party to the conflict or the neutral state by unequivocal acts or declarations change the existing status, e.g. Germany and Italy during the Second World War by their declaration of war against the United States (which was neutral, but not behaving according to the law of neutrality) or Germany by its invasion of Norway. The question of whether this triggering of an armed conflict is or is not a violation of international law is irrelevant for the other question of whether the neutral status is ended. As long as states do not legally characterize their acts by declarations, the mere fact that hostilities are present between a neutral state and a party to the conflict must be evaluated in a differentiated way. Thus, the massive support given by the United States to the states at war with Germany did not render the United States a party to the conflict until the declaration of war just mentioned. Only where a hitherto neutral state participates to a significant extent in hostilities is there a change of status.

This becomes obvious if the duty of the neutral state to defend its neutrality, if necessary by the use of arms, is also considered. Where a party to a conflict tries to occupy parts of the neutral territory for use as a base for hostilities, the neutral state is bound to take military countermeasures. If it complies with this obligation, it cannot be considered as losing all the advantages of neutral status. It remains neutral despite the hostilities it wages with one of the parties of conflict.

The question of whether a change of a neutral status is effected by drawing the hitherto neutral state into the conflict must be distinguished from the different question of whether or not this change of status is brought about lawfully. In this respect, the change of status effected by a party to the conflict and by the neutral state itself must be distinguished. In addition, two levels of legal evaluation must be differentiated, namely the evaluation under the law of neutrality and that under the law relating to the international prohibition of the use of force.[19] Where a hitherto neutral state violates the law of neutrality by supporting a party to the conflict or in any other way, the affected party to the conflict is entitled to take reprisals, which are then subject to the general rules concerning reprisals, in particular the principle of proportionality.[20] According to traditional international law, reprisals could have involved the use of military force against the state violating the law. In this respect, the Charter of the United Nations requires a differentiated view. Armed reprisals are generally unlawful.[21] As a consequence, a reprisal involving the use of force against another state is now permissible only where the violation of the law triggering the reprisal itself constitutes an illegal armed attack. If this rule is applied in the context of an existing armed conflict, the question arises of whether the

---

[19] Concerning the problem of the parallel application of different levels of legal regulation see Schindler, in Delissen/Tanja (Eds.), 374 ff.

[20] Partsch, in *EPIL* 9, 330.   [21] Ibid., 332; Schindler, in Delissen/Tanja (Eds.), 381 ff.

Bothe

violation of neutrality is to the advantage of the aggressor or the victim. Support of the aggressor is illegal not only under the law of neutrality, but also under the law prohibiting the use of force. Illegal support for an aggressor, however, is not necessarily equivalent to an armed attack. Therefore, the victim of aggression reacting to a non-neutral service in favour of the aggressor is still subject to the prohibition of the use of force. In this case, it is therefore not necessarily legal to attack a state violating the law of neutrality and to make it, by that attack, a party to the conflict.

On the other hand, if a neutral state renders its support to the victim of aggression, this is counter to the law of neutrality, but not a breach of the prohibition of the use of force. The neutral state could claim the right of collective self-defence and thus become a party to the conflict without violating the international prohibition of the use of force. The question then arises of whether the right of collective self-defence serves as a justification also for the purposes of the law of neutrality, thus excluding the lawfulness of a countermeasure otherwise lawful under the law of neutrality. Such a conclusion would be contrary to a general principle of the law of war, namely the principle of equality of the parties regardless of the justification of the conflict.[22] Like international humanitarian law, the law of neutrality can effectively fulfil its function of restraining conflicts only if the question of which party is the aggressor and which the victim remains irrelevant for the evaluation of certain acts in the light of the law of neutrality. Therefore, reprisals taken against the state supporting the victim of aggression are admissible under the law of neutrality. Whether or not this support is legal under the rules relating to the prohibition of the use of force is reserved to a different level of analysis, for example where the question of the duty of the aggressor to pay damages is raised after the conflict.

II. THE RIGHTS AND DUTIES OF NEUTRAL STATES

1. General provisions

1108 **The territory of a neutral state is inviolable. It is prohibited to commit any act of hostility whatsoever on such territory (Art. 1 HC V).**

This rule formulates the fundamental right of the neutral state to remain outside the armed conflict and not to be adversely affected by it. Above all, this means that the armed forces of the parties to the conflict may not enter neutral territory. They may not in any way use this territory for their military operations, or for transit or similar purposes. It must again be stressed that this rule applies regardless of whether a party to the conflict is the aggressor or the victim of aggression. The right of self-defence does not legitimize the use of any means contrary to the laws of war.

---

[22] See Section 101. Therefore, Schindler's theory of optional neutrality (in Delissen/Tanja (Eds.), 373 et seq.) is problematic. Any attempt to mix in this way the law relating to the prevention of war and that relating to its conduct (and the law of neutrality is part of the latter) would negatively affect the functioning of the principle of reciprocity which is also the basis of the law of neutrality.

Nor does it legitimize military measures against states which have not themselves committed aggression, even if the use of their territory were useful or necessary for the exercise of the right of self-defence to be militarily effective. The right of self-defence does not constitute a comprehensive right of self-help against innocent third states. The inviolability of neutral territory applies not only to neutral land but also to neutral waters (internal waters, territorial sea, see Section 1117) and airspace (see Section 1149). As far as sea areas are concerned, this right is subject to a right of innocent passage. As far as the right of flight over sea areas is concerned, a distinction must be made between the territorial sea generally (no right of overflight) and international straits and shipping lanes through archipelagic waters, for both of which there is a right of overflight.

The inviolability of neutral territory also means that the neutral states must not be affected by collateral effects of hostilities. The parties to the conflict have no right to cause damage to neutral territory through hostilities themselves. Therefore, there is no rule of admissible collateral damage to the detriment of the neutral state (for collateral damage generally, see Section 455). If the effects of attacks directed against targets on the territory of a party to the conflict are felt on neutral territory, they are unlawful. Recognizing this rule, Allied governments paid compensation for damage occurring during the Second World War in Switzerland caused by attacks on targets in Germany which had an impact in Switzerland. Also in this respect, the principle that the relations between the neutral states and the parties to the conflict are generally governed by the law of peacetime applies.[23] An exception to this rule applies only where, as for example in maritime warfare, customary law recognizes a certain impact of hostilities on a neutral interest, in particular on neutral navigation, as being lawful. As to land warfare, there is no similar rule of customary law which would lower the normal standard of peacetime protection against transboundary impact. The fact that the use of weapons yielding high explosive power, in particular nuclear weapons, would thus be rendered illegal under the law of neutrality may render respect for this rule difficult in the case of an armed conflict. However, this fact has so far clearly not resulted in a change of practice and legal opinion which would have modified the traditional rule of the inviolability of the neutral territory.

The neutral state is bound to repel any violation of its neutrality, if necessary by force (Art. 5 HC V; Arts. 2, 9, 24 HC XIII). This obligation, however, is limited by the international legal prohibition of the use of force. The use of military force to defend neutrality is permissible only if it is legitimate self-defence against an armed attack.   1109

The duty of the neutral state to prevent its territory from being used by one of the parties to the conflict as a base for military operations is the corollary of the neutral's right not to be adversely affected by the conflict. Therefore it must prevent any attempt by a party to the conflict to use its territory for military operations, through

---

[23] Bothe, *GYIL* 34 (1991), 54, 59 ff.

invasion or in transit, by all means at its disposal. This duty, however, is limited to the defence feasible for the neutral state under the circumstances. A neutral state is certainly not obliged to destroy itself (see in particular the commentary to Section 1115).

In connection with this duty to defend neutrality, it has been debated whether and to what extent neutrality obliges the neutral state to undertake military efforts. The Austrian and Swiss concept is that of armed neutrality,[24] based on the idea that neutral states are indeed obliged to undertake military efforts in order to repel a violation of neutrality by the use of armed force. The neutrality policy of Costa Rica, on the other hand, is based on unarmed neutrality. This is certainly unobjectionable as long as no party to the conflict attempts to use the territory of the unarmed neutral state. In the absence of any effort by the neutral state to react to a violation of its territory, however, that state risks no longer being considered neutral by the party to the conflict adversely affected.

If the neutral state defends its neutrality it must respect the limits which international law imposes on military violence. There is no specific need for international legal justification of military measures which the state takes on its own territory, for instance if it drives troops out of its own territory. If military measures are employed outside the neutral state's own territory, they are admissible only to the extent that the violation constitutes an armed attack within the meaning of Art. 51 of the Charter and if the countermeasure taken constitutes a necessary and proportional reaction to that attack. Art. 51 of the Charter, thus, always marks the upper level of counter-force the neutral state may legally use[25]. In other words: the Charter of the United Nations grants a right to use counter-force; the law of neutrality may, under certain circumstances, impose an obligation to exercise this right.

1110   **A neutral state must not assist a party to the conflict. It is especially prohibited to supply warships, ammunition, or other war materials (Art. 6 HC XIII). Humanitarian assistance for victims of the conflict does not constitute a violation of neutrality even where it is for the benefit of only one party to the conflict (Art. 14 HC V).**

This rule formulates in a general way the principle of non-participation. The neutral state must abstain from any act which may have an impact on the outcome of the conflict. The second sentence names only a few examples of such forbidden assistance. Massive financial support for a party to the conflict also constitutes non-neutral service. This was the case with a number of Arab states during the conflict between Iran and Iraq who gave substantial financial support to the war effort of Iraq. The arms supplies by Western states to Iraq, too, were objectionable under the law of neutrality. The prohibition is absolute, and applies also where assistance is given to both parties. Section 1110 constitutes a concretization not of the duty of impartiality, but of the duty of non-participation. Therefore, it is unlawful for a

---

[24] Wildhaber, in Haller/Kölz/Müller/Thürer (Eds.), 423, esp. 434 ff.
[25] Greenwood, in Dinstein/Tabory (Eds.), 275 ff.; Lagoni, in *Festschrift Zeidler*, 1833, 1847 ff.

Bothe

neutral state to compensate an uneven relation of strength between the parties to the conflict by supplying arms or similar support.

The supply of any war material is forbidden (as to the definition, see comment to Section 1112, also Art. 44 HRLW). This rule, however, is among those which lend themselves to be modified where the Security Council adopts measures for the maintenance of peace.

As far as the humanitarian protection of the victims of the conflict is concerned, the only criterion for such assistance is need, and not equal benefit for the parties to the conflict. This idea was for the first time clearly formulated in Art. 70 AP I which states that humanitarian assistance may not be considered as an interference in the conflict. Humanitarian assistance, however, is subject to its own requirements of neutrality. Any assistance whose purpose is not to mitigate the need of victims, but to provide a military advantage to one party is not humanitarian. On the other hand, inequalities of assistance based on a difference in need and requirements do not violate the principle of humanitarian impartiality.

A neutral state may in no circumstances participate in acts of war by a party to the conflict.   1111

This rule names a further example of assistance forbidden according to Section 1110. It may be questionable what is considered to be forbidden participation in a particular case. If the neutral state takes part by engaging its own military forces, this is a clear example. Another example might be the supply of military advisors to the armed forces of a party to the conflict.

State practice has modified the former convention rule that a neutral state is not bound to prohibit export and transit of war material by private persons for the benefit of one of the parties to the conflict (Art. 7 HC V). To the extent that arms export is subject to control by the state, the permission of such export is to be considered as a non-neutral service.   1112

The traditional law of neutrality distinguished between unlawful assistance by the neutral state and assistance by private persons or private enterprises belonging to a neutral state. The latter was not attributed to the neutral state and there was no obligation on this state to prevent it. This rule has resulted in the private arms industry of neutral states supplying armaments in a relatively unimpeded way to a party to the conflict, and frequently to both sides.

The separation of the state and the private armaments industry is nowadays artificial and does not correspond with political reality. Arms production and arms trade are in many ways managed, promoted, and controlled by the state. Therefore it would simply be unrealistic if one did not attribute to the state the exports of that state's 'official' arms industry. Modern state practice accords with the rule of non-separation. Where states took the view that the law of neutrality applied, they did not permit arms exports by private enterprise, nor did they rely on the artificial separation between state and private enterprise. According to the current state of

Bothe

customary law, the correct view is that a state's permission to supply war material constitutes a non-neutral service.[26]

In addition to the question of the scope of application of the law of neutrality discussed above, this raises two additional questions. First, what kind of effort must a state make to prevent the export of war material, and secondly, what kinds of material constitute war material within the meaning of the rule. As to the first question, one has to assume that besides arms exports controlled by the state, there is a black market which evades state controls. The more stringent the controls, the greater the incentive to undertake transfers to circumvent them. Discussions about the supply of equipment for the production of chemical weapons in Libya and Iraq is an example. As to this question, there is no sufficient practice to produce an *opinio iuris*. In the field of chemical weapons, the new convention on their prohibition will entail specific duties of export control. In the area of nuclear weapons, the Non-Proliferation Treaty has a similar function for the non-nuclear weapon-owning states.

As to the definition of war materials which may not be supplied to the parties to the conflict, the problem must be distinguished from that of the definition of contraband. There is apparently no state practice to the effect that the prohibition of supply covers more than weapons *stricto sensu*, i.e. material which is capable of being used for killing enemy soldiers or destroying enemy goods. It is desirable that future treaties in the field of arms control should contain more far-reaching duties of control.

Another open question is whether the permission to grant licences or the non-prevention of re-exports are equivalent to the permission of exports.

Arms exports may have the effect of instigating a conflict. The Constitution of the Federal Republic of Germany, in Art. 26 of the Basic Law, has drawn lessons from this fact and has established a constitutional duty to restrict the export of weapons. This duty was implemented by the War Weapons Control Act. In addition, the export of materials relevant for armament may be restricted under the Foreign Economic Transactions Act. Both acts empower the Federal Government to prevent exports which are prohibited under the law of neutrality.[27]

1113   **Citizens of neutral states may, at their own risk, enter into the service of one of the parties to the conflict (Art. 6 HC V). In such a case, they must be treated as nationals of the respective party to the conflict (Art. 17 HC V). The prohibition against recruiting, using, financing, or training mercenaries must be respected (Art. 47 AP I; Mercenary Convention; see Section 303).**

1114   **It is prohibited to recruit and raise troops on neutral territory to assist one of the parties to the conflict (Art. 4 HC V).**

---

[26] Oeter, *Neutralität und Waffenhandel*, esp. 216 ff.

[27] Act implementing Art. 26, para. 2 of the Basic Law (*Gesetz über die Kontrolle von Kriegswaffen*) of 20 Apr. 1961, as promulgated 22 Nov. 1990, BGBl I 2506; Foreign Economic Transaction Regulation of 18 Dec. 1986, BGBl I 2671.

Bothe

While the troops of a neutral state may not take part in any war operations (see Section 1111), it cannot and is not required to prevent its nationals from entering the service of a party to the conflict on their own initiative and responsibility. This distinction between private and governmental assistance may, however, be misused. If the state tolerates the establishment of so-called volunteer corps, a not uncommon practice, this amounts to a non-neutral service. The same applies where (Section 1114) the neutral state tolerates publicity for the establishment of troops by the parties to the conflict. All acts and omissions of the neutral state are prohibited which further the military effort of a party to the conflict.

Further duties of prevention result from the Convention against recruitment, use, financing and training of mercenaries, opened for signature and ratification by the General Assembly of the United Nations on 4 December 1989. The parties to this Convention are bound to punish the recruitment of mercenaries. It must be taken into account, however, that the members of regular armed forces of a party to the conflict are not mercenaries within the meaning of the Convention. Recruitment for activities within the regular armed forces of another state thus does not constitute an activity which must be punished according to the Mercenaries Convention.

Still greater duties of prevention may apply when the Security Council imposes an obligation to abstain from any assistance to an aggressor. This may imply an obligation to prevent private assistance which does not exist under the general law of neutrality nor under the Mercenaries Convention. In the Federal Republic of Germany, recruitment for foreign military service and aiding such recruitment generally constitute criminal acts (s. 109h Penal Code).

2. War on Land

Troop or supply movements must not be carried out on neutral territory (Art. 2   **1115** **HC V). The neutral state may allow the transit of wounded persons and relief goods (Art. 14 HC V).**

This provision is a consequence of the prohibition of non-neutral services set out in Sections 1110 and 1112, and also of the prohibition against using neutral territory for the military purposes of a party to the conflict. Prohibited transport across neutral territory includes cases where a party to the conflict is granted landing rights for supply flights, a case which has some practical importance.

During the Second World War the prohibition of transit was in some cases not respected by neutral states under the pressure of circumstances. Neutral states have granted transit rights to belligerents in different ways. In most cases, this was the first step towards a neutral state being drawn into the conflict. On the other hand, states refusing transit rights were attacked.

The exact definition of forbidden supply movement presents difficulties. Transport of weapons belongs to this category. On the other hand, the movement of medical supplies or of raw materials for the war industry would be considered as permitted.

Bothe

The second sentence establishes an exception to the rule for the transport of wounded persons and relief supplies. There is a general principle of the law of war behind this rule (also expressed in Section 1110, second sentence) namely that humanitarian assistance to the victims of conflict, as a rule, does not constitute a non-neutral service.

1116   **It is not considered a non-neutral service for a neutral state to permit the use by a party to the conflict of generally accessible means of communications on its territory. The neutral state must not, however, install or permit on its territory special means of communication for a party to the conflict (Art. 3 HC V).**

In view of the great importance of telecommunications for modern high technology warfare, the rules of the law of neutrality relating to neutral telecommunciation installations are of particular significance. The relevant rules of Hague Convention V do not address modern problems of telecommunication with the necessary clarity, but they contain principles which remain valid and applicable today. Another element of the delimitation between permissible and impermissible use of neutral telecommunication installations is the idea of *courant normal*, which is of general importance for neutral commercial relations. The outbreak of an armed conflict does not result in an obligation for the neutral state to prevent the use of its telecommunication installations by a party to the conflict which used them or which had access to them before. Existing non-military telecommunication infrastructure, in particular that owned by a public telecommunications enterprise or administration of the neutral state, may be used by the parties to the conflict.

Thus, the parties may rent fixed lines for voice and data communication of a military nature and may be granted access from such lines to satellite communications. On the other hand, it is a non-neutral service for a neutral state to place at the disposal of a party to the conflict telecommunication installations not available to it under normal conditions (for instance its own military telecommunication infrastructure) or if it creates, or acquiesces in the creation of, new telecommunication infrastructure for the particular purposes of a party to the conflict.

1117   **Neutral states must intern forces of the parties to the conflict trespassing on neutral territory (Arts. 11 and 12 HC V). Escaped prisoners of war who are allowed to remain in the territory of the neutral state may be assigned a specific place of residence (Art 13 HC V).**

The treatment of military personnel and war material of the parties to the conflict which are found on neutral territory is unclear in many respects.

If whole units of the armed forces of a party to the conflict arrive on neutral territory, it would be a violation of the duty of non-participation if the neutral state permitted them to take part again in hostilities. Therefore, those troops must be interned (Art. 11 HC V). War material, too, has to be withheld until the end of the conflict (e.g. the military aircraft brought into Iran during the Gulf War, if the law of neutrality is applicable in that case).

Bothe

A logical consequence of this rule would be that the neutral state had to prevent escaped prisoners arriving on its territory from taking further part in the hostilities. Art. 13 HC V expressly states that such escaped prisoners must remain free. Certain authors conclude from this that they must be permitted to go back to their home country.[28] However, this is by no means clear. The provisions of the Third Geneva Convention provide for repatriation of prisoners of war on neutral territory only in certain cases and do not regulate the question comprehensively (see Arts. 110 and 111 GC III). This question should, whenever possible, be regulated by a specific agreement between the states concerned.

3. Naval warfare

a) General

The internal waters, archipelagic waters, and territorial sea of neutral states must be respected (Art. 1 HC XIII). It is prohibited to commit any act of war in such waters (Art. 2 HC XIII).   1118

The parties to the conflict are forbidden to use neutral ports or territorial waters as a base for naval operations (Art. 5 HC XIII).   1119

Acts of war are prohibited in neutral waters to the same extent as on neutral terri-tory (Art. 2 HC XIII). The acts of war which are forbidden include the exercise of the law of prize such as stop, visit, and search, orders to follow a specific course, and capture of merchant ships (Art. 2 HC XIII).   1120

Sections 1118–20 constitute the maritime aspect of the general principle (formu-lated in Section 1108) that the territory of a neutral state is inviolable and may not be used for the purpose of conducting hostilities. This rule, however, is somewhat modified for neutral territorial sea, as compared to the rule in land warfare, in that there is a right of innocent passage (Section 1126). The jurisdictional waters to be respected consist of the territorial sea and the internal waters belonging to the sea, i.e. sea areas on the landward side of the base line from which the territorial sea is measured (see Art. 8, United Nations Convention on the Law of the Sea). The exclu-sive economic zone and the sea area above the continental shelf do not constitute neutral waters within the meaning of Sections 1118–20. In those areas, acts of war are as a matter of principle permitted; they constitute a kind of freedom of the use of such waters, like navigation. The parties to the conflict must, however, in con-ducting hostilities take into account the economic interests of the neutral coastal state in whose exclusive economic zone hostilities are taking place.

The prohibited acts of war are not defined with any precision. Mere passage is not a forbidden act of war. Acts of war include shooting at enemy ships, take-off by military aircraft from aircraft carriers, laying mines, and also transmission of

---

[28] Castrén, 468.

Bothe

intelligence. Section 1120 clarifies that the exercise of the right of prize is also a prohibited act of war.

1121 **When a ship has been captured by a party to the conflict in the waters of a neutral state, the latter must, as long as the prize is still within its waters, use all means at its disposal to obtain the release of the prize and its crew. The prize crew must be interned (Art. 3, para. 1 HC XIII).**

Section 1121 reflects the duty to defend neutrality. If the right of prize is exercised in neutral waters contrary to the laws of neutrality, the neutral state must make an effort to undo this violation by freeing the prize captured in its waters. This liberation of the prize is not inconsistent with the prohibition of the use of force, since it constitutes an exercise of sovereign rights in the state's own jurisdictional area where the justification of self-defence is not required.

1122 **A neutral state may demand the release of a ship captured within its waters even if the ship has already left those neutral waters (Art. 3, para. 2 HC XIII).**

This rule clarifies the rights of the neutral state in case of an illegal taking of a prize in its waters. It is a secondary obligation derived from the primary rule in Section 1120: the situation must be re-established as if the violation of neutral waters had not occurred. Thus, the respective party to the conflict must render the prize illegally taken.

1123 **If a ship of a neutral state takes wounded, sick, or shipwrecked persons on board, it must, to the extent required by international law, ensure that these persons take no further part in hostilities (Art. 15 GC II).**

Section 1123 is the maritime aspect of Section 1117. As a matter of principle, combatants who fall into the power of a neutral state must be prevented from taking further part in hostilities. The reference in Art. 15 GC II to general international law is, however, somewhat problematic.

In land warfare, the transit of wounded and sick persons through neutral territory is permitted (Art. 14, para. 1 HC V). If one were to equate the situation of taking such persons aboard with their transit, it would be lawful to permit them to return to their own party. As a matter of principle, however, one would compare the situation rather with that of reception on neutral territory. Then, the general rule applies that any further participation of military personnel in hostilities must be prevented (Art. 14, para. 2 HC V). Only those seriously sick or heavily wounded whose complete recovery is unlikely may be repatriated. These rules for disabled prisoners of war (Art. 110 GC III) may be applied by analogy.

1124 **As regards the laying of sea mines, neutral states are subject to the same safety regulations as the parties to the conflict (Art. 4, para. 1 HC VIII). They must notify the location of minefields to the government of maritime states without delay (Art. 4, para. 2 HC VIII).**

Bothe

The neutral state which is bound to defend its neutrality may, as a matter of principle, do so by using the same means of warfare which the parties to the conflict can use. Defensive laying of sea mines therefore constitutes a lawful protective measure. However, the neutral state must then take the same precautionary measures in the interest of third parties which the parties to the conflict are required to take.

A neutral state is bound to use all means at its disposal to prevent the fitting out or   1125
arming of any vessel within its jurisdiction which it has reason to believe is
intended to be engaged in acts of war against the foreign power. It is also bound to
prevent the departure of any vessel that has been adapted entirely or partly within
its jurisdiction for use in war (Art. 8 HC XIII).

Section 1125 is the maritime version of the general prohibition of assisting parties to the conflict in their military effort. It has to be noted that in the field of naval warfare, the distinction between assistance by the state and by private persons or entities, which originally limited the prohibition as far as land warfare is concerned, has never been made. To that extent, the broader prohibition in the field of naval warfare corresponds to modern trends concerning the general regulation of arms exports.

b) Innocent passage through territorial sea and archipelagic waters; transit passage

Passage through the territorial sea and archipelagic waters of a neutral state by   1126
warships belonging to and prizes taken by a party to the conflict does not consti-
tute a violation of neutrality (Art. 10 HC XIII). While transit passage through inter-
national straits and archipelagic shipping lane passage include the right of
overflight (Arts. 38 and 53 United Nations Convention on the Law of the Sea) and
the right of submarine navigation, there are no such rights of innocent passage
outside those waterways. The right of innocent passage is subject to the following
provisions.

The principle of innocent passage constitutes an exception to the general rule of land warfare that a neutral state may not acquiesce in the presence of armed forces of a party to the conflict in areas subject to its jurisdiction. On the other hand, it confirms the rule that the relation between the neutral state and the parties to the conflict is as a matter of principle subject to the law of peacetime relations which also provides for such rights of passage.

This principle entails greater rights of innocent passage than those expressly provided for in Hague Convention XIII. The parties to the conflict also enjoy rights of transit passage through international straits and archipelagic shipping lanes passage granted to their warships in times of peace (see Arts. 37 and 53 United Nations Convention on the Law of the Sea).

This right of transit or innocent passage is, however, subject to a number of specific limitations designed to prevent the exercise of those rights from developing

Bothe

into the use of neutral jurisdictional areas for the purpose of conducting war contrary to the law of neutrality.

1127   **Warships of the parties to the conflict are, as a matter of principle, not permitted to remain in neutral ports, roadsteads or territorial sea for more than twenty-four hours. The neutral state may prolong this period, but may also altogether prohibit such vessels from remaining in its waters (Art. 12 HC XIII). Warships of the parties to the conflict may not extend their stay beyond the permissible time except on account of damage or bad weather. They must depart as soon as the cause of the delay has ceased to exist (Art. 14 HC XIII).**

The 'twenty-four hour-rule' is the most important exception to the rule that the rights of passage or transit existing in peacetime apply equally in times of armed conflict. The rationale is to prevent a party to the conflict from using neutral waters as a refuge from enemy ships. According to the text of the Hague Convention, the twenty-four hour rule applies to the 'stay'. Taking into account the object and purpose of this provision, however, any passage is also covered. This became controversial during the Second World War in the *Altmark* case, where a German auxiliary warship had spent two days passing through the coastal waters of Norway, which at the time was still neutral, in order to avoid being captured by the British fleet. At that time, Norway claimed that the twenty-four hour rule did not apply to mere passage. That view has not prevailed[29].

An exception to the twenty-four hour-rule applies where the passage through neutral waters is not possible within twenty-four hours. This will be the case particularly for archipelagic shipping lane passage. In that case, the rule is modified to the effect that the time required for the shortest possible passage is permitted.

1128   **In neutral ports and roadsteads, warships of the parties to the conflict may only carry out such repairs as are absolutely necessary to restore their seaworthiness. Restoring the combat readiness of these ships is no cause for extending the permissible duration of their stay. Activities to increase their fighting capability are also prohibited (Art. 17 HC XIII).**

1129   **Warships of the parties to the conflict may neither complete their crews nor replenish or increase their armament or their military supplies in neutral waters (Art. 18 HC XIII).**

1130   **Warships of the parties to the conflict may only revictual in neutral ports and roadsteads to bring up their supplies to a normal peacetime level (Art. 19 HC XIII).**

1131   **In neutral ports and roadsteads, warships of the parties to the conflict may only ship sufficient fuel to enable them to reach the nearest port in their own country (Art. 19 HC XIII). These ships may not again replenish their fuel supplies in a port of the same neutral state before three months have passed (Art. 20 HC XIII).**

[29] Schütz, *EPIL* 3, 14.

Bothe

Sections 1128–31 clarify the assistance permissible during a stay of ships of a party to the conflict in neutral waters. They constitute a compromise between the prohibition of assisting armed forces of the belligerents and the requirements of seafaring solidarity. Seafaring solidarity requires granting such help to a ship which is necessary, taking into account the seaworthiness of the ship, navigational difficulty caused by weather, and provision of food and fuel. Assistance must be strictly limited to those essential seafaring requirements.

If a warship of a party to the conflict stays in a neutral port without being entitled   1132
to do so and does not leave this port notwithstanding notification, the neutral
state may detain the ship and prevent it from departing for the duration of the
armed conflict (Art. 24 HC XIII). The crew of the detained ship may also be
detained. Its members may be left on the ship or brought either to another vessel
or ashore. In any case, a number of men sufficient to look after the vessel must be
left on board.

A warship of the party to the conflict which stays longer than the time permissible according to the rules stated above (i.e. over 24 hours or over the time required in view of the condition of either the ship or the sea) violates the laws of neutrality. The duty to defend neutrality then applies. The neutral state must detain the ship and ensure that it can take no further part in any hostilities.

A prize may only be brought into a neutral port if it is absolutely necessary on   1133
account of unseaworthiness of the prize, bad weather, or want of fuel or provi-
sions. It must leave as soon as the circumstances which justified its entry are at an
end (Art. 21 HC XIII).

If, after the cause for a stay has ceased to exist, a prize does not leave even after it   1134
has been ordered to do so by the neutral authorities, the neutral state must seek to
release the prize and its crew. The prize crew must be interned (Art. 21 HC XIII).
The same rule applies when a prize has entered a neutral port without authoriza-
tion (Art. 22 HC XIII).

Sections 1133 and 1135 clarify the preceding rules concerning the stay of prizes in neutral waters. As a general rule, the right of passage also applies to prizes, subject to the twenty-four hour rule. Prizes may not, however, be brought into neutral ports except for reasons of navigational stress. A violation of this rule (as in the cases discussed before) gives rise to the duty of the neutral state to defend its neutrality and to free the prize.

When warships of several parties to the conflict are present simultaneously in a   1135
neutral port or roadstead, a period of not less than twenty-four hours must elapse
between the departure of the ships belonging to one party and the departure of
the ships belonging to the other party (Art. 16 HC XIII).

Bothe

This rule is a variation of the requirement that no assistance must be given which affects the outcome of the conflict, and also reflects the principle of impartiality. The requirement of a fixed period between the departure of warships belonging to different parties prevents confrontations between them immediately after they leave neutral waters. Otherwise the order of departure may influence the outcome of the conflict.

1136 **A neutral state may allow warships of a party to the conflict to employ its pilots (Art. 11 HC XIII). It is bound to prevent, within the means at its disposal, any violation of the rules of neutrality within its waters and to exercise such surveillance as is required for this purpose (Art. 25 HC XIII).**

This rule further clarifies the limits of the prohibition of non-neutral service. In this case, the prohibition is modified in the interests of navigational safety.

1137 **A neutral state must apply impartially to all parties to the conflict any conditions, restrictions, or prohibitions which it imposes on admission into its ports, roadsteads, or waters of warships or prizes belonging to the parties to the conflict (Art. 9 HC XIII). A neutral state may forbid a warship which has failed to comply with its directions or which has violated its neutrality to enter its ports or roadsteads (Art. 9 HC XIII).**

Again, this rule clarifies the neutral duty of impartiality. Even in times of peace, but especially in times of armed conflict, the neutral state may regulate passage through its waters and any stay therein by imposing its own rules. In particular, it may limit passage rights. To the extent that it makes such rules, it is bound by the duty of equal treatment, and may not create more advantageous conditions for one party than for another. Nevertheless, in specific geographic circumstances, one party to the conflict may benefit from such rules more than another.

c) Control by the parties to the conflict

1138 **Warships of a party to the conflict are entitled to stop, visit, and search merchant ships flying the flag of a neutral state on the high seas and control the contents and destination of their cargo.**

The control of neutral commercial shipping by the parties to the conflict was traditionally a very important question until the recent past. The state of international customary law is controversial in many details concerning the extent of this control. The London Declaration of 1909 which codified these rights of control was never ratified, but is considered at least largely to constitute an expression of customary law.

In more recent conflicts, too, such rights of control were exercised without objection, although certain specific measures and the status of some conflicts were controversial.[30]

---

[30] Ronzitti, in Ronzitti (Ed.), *The Law of Naval Warfare*, 1, 7 et seq.; Gioia/Ronzitti, in Dekker/Post (Eds.),

Bothe

The control by the parties to the conflict of neutral shipping constitutes an essential exception to the principle that the neutral state may not be adversely affected by the existence of an armed conflict. These rights of control, however, are limited, although during the Second World War a tendency to expand those rights was evident.

The purpose of such control is to impede the provision of goods important for the war effort to the other party to the conflict. A key position is taken by the right of visit and search, i.e. the right of warships of a party to the conflict to stop neutral commercial ships and to search them in order to find out whether they have goods aboard which could assist the war effort of another party to the conflict.

Warships of a party to the conflict may use only such force as is necessary against   1139
neutral merchant ships to exercise such control. In particular, neutral merchant
ships which, although subject to control by a party to the conflict, resist inspec-
tion may be damaged or destroyed if it is not possible to prevent them from con-
tinuing their voyage by other means. The captain of the neutral ship shall
previously be warned in an appropriate manner. Rescue of shipwrecked persons
must be ensured.

As a last resort, the right of control described in Section 1137 may be exercised by using force. However, this is limited by a strict principle of necessity. Only such force is permissible which is indispensable to enforce the right of control, in particular to prevent a merchant ship from evading such control. The destruction of the neutral merchant ship is permissible only in exceptional circumstances, because a warship will generally have other means at its disposal to enforce its right of control.

To simplify such inspection, a party to the conflict may, subject to the approval of
the neutral state concerned, issue an inspection document (navicert) to the neu-   1140
tral vessel in the port of loading. A navicert issued by one party to the conflict is not
binding on the other party. The fact that the ship carries a navicert of another
party to the conflict does not justify any more far-reaching measures of control.

This rule describes the 'navicert system' which has often been used in practice.[31] The navicert makes it possible for the neutral ship to prove, in the case of control by a warship of a party to the conflict, by a document issued at the port of loading by that party to the conflict (usually by its diplomatic representative) that it is not carrying contraband. A navicert is only accepted by the party which issued it.

During the Second World War it was argued that carrying a navicert, which places a neutral merchant ship under the partial control of one belligerent, constitutes a non-neutral act because it favours the belligerent exercising this control. If this were so, neutral commerce would be unreasonably endangered because it could not protect itself against conflicting control claims of the parties.[32] In the end, how-

221, 231 ff.; Dinstein, *EPIL*, 19, 24 et seq.; Donner, *Die neutrale Handelsschiffahrt im begrenzten militärischen Konflikt*, 261 et seq.

[31] Meng, *EPIL* 3, 122.

ever, that argument did not prevail, as clearly stated in the last sentence of Section 1140.

1141   **The right of control shall not apply to merchant ships flying neutral flags and escorted by a neutral warship (convoy). In this case, however, a warship of a party to the conflict may request the commander of the neutral warship to specify the type and destination of the cargo.**

The right of convoy was long controversial.[33] The effect of the rule is that warships of the parties to the conflict may control neutral merchant ships but not neutral warships. The question then arises of whether the fact that certain neutral merchant ships are placed under the protection of neutral warships limits the right of control of the belligerents. In the Gulf conflict between Iran and Iraq, convoys of merchant ships flying neutral flags were indeed placed under the protection of warships of neutral states. In that case, the neutral states did not accept the rights of control of the parties to the conflict, essentially of Iran, which they otherwise tolerated. This practice seems to be a last step in the development which has led to the recognition of the right of neutral convoy.[34] In a lawful convoy, control is exercised by requiring the commander of the neutral warship to provide information concerning the type and destination of the cargo to the warship of the party to the conflict.

Whether a neutral state may place only neutral ships flying its own flag under the protection of its warships or whether it may grant such protection to the ships of other neutral states is less clear. The latter is probably the case. This practice may not, however, be used in order to disguise non-neutral service. Thus, it is problematic if a neutral state allows ships of another state, which has rendered non-neutral service to a party to the conflict, to fly its own flag and places reflagged merchant ships under the protection of its own warships.

1142   **If the cargo contains goods essential for war which are destined for the port of an adversary, such goods may be captured by the warship of the party to the conflict ('absolute contraband'). The parties to the conflict may notify to the neutral states lists of the goods which they deem to be essential for war. Any goods destined for the administration or the armed forces of the opposing party to the conflict will likewise be deemed contraband ('conditional contraband').**

As stated above, the rules concerning the control of neutral shipping are intended to prevent essential war goods from reaching the adversary. If control reveals essential war goods destined for the enemy aboard the ship, their further transportation may be prevented, subject to certain procedural rules. The first question arising in this connection is: what kinds of essential war goods are subject to this power to prevent further transportation ('contraband').[35] A distinction must be made

---

[32] Stödter, *EPIL* 193, 195.   [33] Stödter, *EPIL* 3, 128.

[34] Ronzitti, in Ronzitti (Ed.), *The Law of Naval Warfare*, 9; Bothe, in Delissen/Tanja (Eds.), 387, 394.

[35] Meng, *EPIL* 3, 122; Ronzitti, in Ronzitti (Ed.), *The Law of Naval Warfare*, 7 et seq.

Bothe

between absolute and conditional contraband. Absolute contraband comprises all essential war goods. Parties to the conflict have some discretion as to the determination of what is to be considered as essential for war. That distinction must always take into account the specific circumstances of the conflict. If the parties to the conflict set out their construction of goods essential for war in lists notified to the adversary, legal clarity is achieved. On the other hand, such lists have tended to be unacceptably wide. Absolute contraband is goods which must by their very nature be considered as essential for war, and must be distinguished from conditional contraband which comprises those goods destined for the administration and armed forces of the adversary, whether or not they otherwise serve essential purposes of war. Thus, equipment which would otherwise not be considered as war essential belongs to this category. Art. 24 of the London Declaration of 1909 refers also to food and clothing as conditional contraband. To the extent that such items are shipped for the purpose of humanitarian relief actions (Arts. 23, 59 GC IV; Art. 70 AP I), they may, of course, not be considered as contraband. Contraband may be captured by the controlling warship.

A ship carrying contraband is also subject to capture. 1143

As well as the cargo, the ship carrying such contraband is also subject to capture. Whether and to what extent this applies where only part of the cargo constitutes contraband is somewhat controversial.

A captured ship (prize) must be brought as safely as possible to a port of a party to 1144
the conflict or of a state allied with that party. In that port the permissibility of the
capture of ship and cargo are to be reviewed by a prize court. Ship and cargo may
be confiscated by the order of a prize court.

Capture is a provisional measure only. The legality of the capture must be reviewed in a judicial procedure as soon as possible. The principle '*toute prise doit être jugée*' applies. Only if the prize court finds that the ship was indeed carrying contraband a final determination concerning the ship and cargo is permissible. Cargo may be confiscated only after a prize court judgment. The same is true of the ship carrying that cargo and only if the contraband constituted more than half of the cargo, whether by value, weight, volume, or freight (Arts. 39 and 40 of the London Declaration of 1909). Bringing the prize to the port of a territory occupied by a party to the conflict is also permissible. The prize court may be established anywhere on the territory of the party to the conflict, in a territory occupied by it, or on the territory of an ally of that party.

If suspicion that a ship is carrying contraband, which led to control measures, 1145
proves unfounded, and if the neutral ship has not contributed to that suspicion,
the party to the conflict is obliged to compensate for any damage caused by the
delay.

Bothe

If the capture is not upheld by the prize court, and the cargo not confiscated, the control measure was unjustified. Delay of the shipping may have caused a considerable financial damage. Such expense must be paid by the party which exercised the control.

1146 **The parties to the conflict may not hold prize courts on neutral territory or on a vessel in neutral waters (Art. 4 HC XIII).**

This rule adds further precision to the principle that neutral territory may not be used for any act which causes damage to the enemy. The establishment of a prize court belongs to this category of activities.

d) Protection of neutral merchant shipping

1147 **Warships of neutral states may escort merchant ships flying the flag of the same or another neutral state.**

Freedom of neutral shipping, limited only by the rights of control just described, is by no means unchallenged. Recent experiences in the conflict between Iran and Iraq proved this. From a political point of view, impeding neutral shipping, especially oil tankers, has obvious benefits because the adversary will benefit from this shipping, although according to the rules just described those ships were not subject to capture and confiscation. Fuel constitutes contraband only if it is destined for a party to the conflict, not if it comes from a party to the conflict which uses revenue from sales of fuel to finance its war effort.[36] Nevertheless, in such a situation the temptation for the disadvantaged party to the conflict to impede navigation is great. In this or similar situations, the question arises of how neutral shipping can be protected.

The formation of convoys has proved an efficient means of protection. The advantage of convoys in relation to the rights of control concerning cargo and destination have already been described. The formation of convoys also means that those convoys, in a manner of speaking, represent the state, so that attacks against them constitute attacks against a neutral state which trigger its right of self-defence.[37]

It is understood that convoys operate within the applicable law of the sea and, in particular, must respect the rules concerning innocent passage and transit passage. The fact that the formation of a convoy also demonstrates military power does not mean that it constitutes a violation of the prohibition of the use of force. This was confirmed by the judgment of the ICJ in the *Corfu Channel* case.[38]

The formation of convoys may constitute a non-neutral service if merchant ships of a party to the conflict are placed under the protection of a neutral warship.

It is also doubtful whether it is possible to place merchant ships of a neutral state under the protection of a neutral warship if the flag state of the merchant ship

---

[36] Bothe, in Dekker/Post (Eds.), 211.   [37] Donner, *Die neutrale Handelsschiffahrt*, 285 ff.
[38] ICJ Reports 1949, 4, 28.

renders non-neutral services to a party to the conflict. This was the case with the passage of Kuwaiti tankers through the Gulf. Kuwait was certainly guilty of non-neutral services in favour of Iraq. This would have justified the taking of reprisals by Iran against Kuwaiti navigation. The United States placed Kuwaiti tankers under their protection, but only after reflagging the tankers with the American flag. Whether such reflagging could shield ships which would otherwise be a permissible object of reprisals is open to doubt.[39]

On international shipping routes and on the high seas, warships of neutral states   **1148**
may sweep mines to the extent necessary to protect and maintain neutral ship-
ping. Such minesweeping operations do not constitute a non-neutral service for
the benefit of the adversary of the minelaying party.

Sweeping mines on the high seas and in sea areas subject to transit rights is a means for neutral states to protect themselves, which attained considerable practical significance during the conflict between Iran and Iraq. For the purpose of legal evaluation, minesweeping in the jurisdictional waters of a party to the conflict and similar activities on the high seas must be distinguished. On the high seas, the first aspect to be considered is the law of the sea. Conducting hostilities is a lawful use of the high seas, although this is not explicitly stated in the Law of the Sea Convention. Minesweeping therefore constitutes a kind of self-help against a lawful activity. On the other hand, the high seas should be free for shipping, and this right has a great weight. The conduct of hostilities also limits the freedom of navigation of other states. Minesweeping therefore involves balancing two freedoms, similar to the conflicting interests involved in the conduct of hostilities on the high seas. Minesweeping undertaken to protect a state's freedom of shipping does not constitute an unacceptable limitation of the freedom of the parties to the conflict to conduct hostilities at sea.

From the point of view of the law of neutrality, minesweeping by neutral states constitutes an activity which benefits the adversary of the party which laid the mines. However, from the point of view of social significance, it is not the support for one of the parties which is the essential point, but the protection of the neutral state. Therefore, a minesweeping operation intended only to protect neutral shipping does not constitute a non-neutral service.

Unilateral minesweeping operations in the waters of a party of the conflict constitute a violation of the prohibition of the use of force. As a rule, they are illegal. However, there is no violation where a party to a conflict has laid mines in shipping lanes through which transit rights exist and which the minesweeping state is bound to keep open. This was confirmed by state practice during the conflict between Iran and Iraq.[40]

---

[39] Ronzitti, in Ronzitti (Ed.), *The Law of Naval Warfare*, 9; Bos, in Dekker/Post (Eds.), 219 et seq.
[40] Ronzitti, in Ronzitti (Ed.), *The Law of Naval Warfare*, 5.

Bothe

4. Aerial warfare

1149   **The airspace of a neutral state is inviolable (Art. 40 HRAW).**

Section 1149 formulates the application to airspace of the general rule of inviolability of neutral territory. This rule is of particular importance because, in the era of modern air warfare and missile technology, violations of airspace are easily committed.

The territorial jurisdiction of a neutral state extends to the limits of the atmosphere. Outer space above neutral territory is not subject to the neutral state's jurisdiction. Overflights by satellites and missiles moving in outer space therefore do not constitute a violation of neutrality.

The delimitation between airspace and outer space is still controversial. In both practice and theory, there are two main trends which, however, possess a number of variations. Functional theories focus on the kind of activity for which the delimitation is relevant. According to this view, satellites in orbit are typical space objects. Crossing a specific territory or stationing a satellite on a fixed point over the territory of a state does not constitute a violation of the territorial sovereignty of the respective states. Missiles only constitute typical space vehicles where they are at least partially brought into orbit around the earth where the centrifugal force and the attraction of the earth balance each other. Theories based on spacial concepts try to draw the line between airspace and outer space at a particular altitude, of roughly 100 kilometres.[41]

1150   **Parties to a conflict are forbidden to send military aircraft, rockets, or other missiles into neutral airspace (Art. 40 HRAW).**

As a consequence of the inviolability of neutral airspace, the parties to the conflict are not allowed to penetrate by aircraft or other flight objects the airspace of neutral states. For aircraft attacking targets over large distances this may involve significant detours.

Overflight by civilian aircraft does not constitute a violation of neutrality. The neutral state must, however, exercise all necessary controls in order to prevent civilian overflight from being used for military purposes. Under air traffic rules, this is rendered possible by the so-called 'war clause' of the Chicago Convention.

1151   **A neutral state is bound to prevent violations of its airspace. Aircraft which enter such space must be forced to leave or to put down. The crews of military aircraft of a party to the conflict who have been brought down must be interned (Art. 42 HRAW).**

The dangers for neutral airspace described in the commentary to Section 1149 lead to the question: what must a neutral state do in order to prevent such violations of

---

[41] Matte, *EPIL* 11, 303, 307.

Bothe

its airspace? It is undisputed that it must endeavour to prevent such violations. It is difficult, however, to determine the effort required for this purpose.[42] A neutral state must take economically feasible measures in order to create an aerial defence capacity. This includes at least simple radar observation of its airspace. On the other hand, it may not be required that each state possess the latest missile technology in order to protect its neutrality.

The defence must be feasible for the neutral state. In this respect, defence against missiles possessing nuclear warheads, which may after interception fall on neutral territory and cause damage therein, cannot be required.

Interception of aircraft by the airforce of a neutral state is undoubtedly among the measures which the neutral state is required to take. Aircraft entering its airspace must be forced to turn back or land. The obligation to intern their crews derives from the general principle described above.

Medical aircraft may be allowed to overfly the territory of a neutral state and to   1152
land therein (Art. 37 GC I; Art. 40 GC II; Art. 31 AP I; Art. 17 HRAW).

A neutral state may allow medical aircraft of a party to a conflict to overfly its territory or to land therein; this does not constitute non-neutral service. On the contrary, it is a form of humanitarian assistance, subject to rules similar to those concerning land warfare.

Overflight and stopover require permission. A neutral state may place conditions   1153
and restrictions on overflight (Art. 37, para. 2 GC I; Art. 40, para. 2 GC II; Art. 31
AP I).

Section 1153 regulates the procedure to be respected in overflights authorized in accordance with Section 1152. Even medical aircraft are not permitted to penetrate into neutral airspace without authorization. On the contrary, they require specific authorization, the granting of which is in the discretion of the neutral state.

If a neutral state grants such permission it may be subject to conditions, especially as to routes which must be followed and necessary stopovers. At a stopover an aircraft may be inspected to verify that it is medical transport (Art. 31, para. 3 AP I). If the neutral state grants authorization to and imposes conditions on medical flights, the duty of impartiality applies. Both sides must be treated equally. In this case also identical treatment is not required. Often, geographic factors will result in one party using such transit flights, and the other not. The fact that the possibility of transit favours one party more than the other does not constitute a violation of the requirement of impartiality.

The neutral state is not bound to tolerate flights which are not authorized or which violate conditions lawfully imposed. It may attack a medical aircraft flying illegally if there is no other means to prevent it from continuing the flight, or subject it to scrutiny. Given the risk of abuse of medical flights, it may even be

---

[42] Madders, *EPIL* 4, 14 ff.; Millet, *Annales de droit international médical* 35 (1991), 63, 69; Torelli, *Annales de droit international médical* 35 (1991), 25, 44.

concluded that the neutral state has a duty not to tolerate unauthorized medical flights over its territory, and to take appropriate countermeasures.

1154 **The right of neutral aircraft to overfly the territory of the parties to the conflict is regulated by the general rules of international law on the protection of national airspace and the rules of international air traffic.**

Under general international law applicable in times of peace, there is no general right for foreign aircraft, whether private or state-owned, to overfly the territory of another state or to land therein. For private non-scheduled air services, the Chicago Convention provides certain rights of overflight and landing. However, these rights do not apply in armed conflicts. According to the 'war clause' of the Chicago Convention (Art. 89), the provisions of the Convention do not affect the freedom of action of the contracting parties in a war, be they belligerent or neutral. Traffic rights for scheduled air services are, as a rule, derived from bilateral agreements. Whether and to what extent these rights are affected by the fact that one of the contracting parties is a party to a conflict with a third state is a question to be regulated by the relevant agreement. Generally speaking, the legal situation is that a state which is party to a conflict is relatively free to grant or not to grant rights of overflight to aircraft flying neutral flags, subject, in particular, to the provisions of bilateral air transport agreements.

Special rules apply to airspace above specific types of jurisdictional waters. As stated above, the right of innocent passage over territorial sea does not comprise overflight. As far as overflight is concerned, territorial sea is treated in the same way as the land areas around it. An exception to this rule applies to international straits and archipelagic waters. In this case, the right of transit or passage (Arts. 38 and 53 United Nations Convention on the Law of the Sea) includes a right of overflight (see commentary to Section 1108). It is submitted that these rules are now customary law.

1155 **The relevant rules of naval warfare apply to the control, capture, and confiscation of neutral aircraft above sea areas and to the treatment of their passengers and crew (Art. 35 HRAW). An aircraft which does not carry clearly visible neutral national emblems may be treated as enemy aircraft.**

The increase in air traffic raised the question (originally rather theoretical) of the control of neutral air commerce. The analogy to neutral shipping offered itself. When the Hague Rules of Air Warfare were elaborated, the rules concerning the control of neutral shipping were imported comprehensively. There is, however, relatively little state practice in this matter. As it can only be applied by analogy, not every detail of the rules concerning the control of neutral shipping applies. The special character of air traffic must be taken into account. As far as air traffic over the high seas is concerned, account must be taken of the fact that aircraft constitute a considerable threat to warships of the parties to the conflict. Thus, those ships will be inclined to react to a perceived threat where the identity of an aircraft is not beyond doubt. The shooting down of an Iranian civilian airbus by a US warship during the conflict between Iran and Iraq shows the kind of tragic errors which may result. The principle must be maintained that both belligerent and neutral warships, as in the case just mentioned, must endeavour to ascertain the nationality and category of an aircraft before it is attacked. This is only possible where neutral aircraft and civilian aircraft of the parties to the conflict do everything feasible to facilitate their identification. An aircraft which is not identifiable and does not carry any exterior emblem of nationality must be considered as an enemy military aircraft and may therefore be attacked.

12

Enforcement of International Humanitarian Law

Introductory Remarks

1. *Enforcement in general.* One of the peculiarities of international law is that its legal rules are not enforced through a central body. In this respect it differs fundamentally from domestic law, and herein lies its weakness which is so deplored in literature.[1]

A solitary exception exists in respect of the maintenance of international peace and security; Chapter VII of the UN Charter grants the United Nations Security Council competence to employ coercive measures against a threat to or breach of the peace or against an act of aggression. Particularly in the Security Council's latest practice, this coercive competence has been broadened. Serious and continuous human rights violations, acts of terrorism, and overthrowing democratic institutions have been considered to constitute threats to peace. Thus the Security Council, invoking its responsibility for world peace, condemned Iraqi repression of the Kurdish people and, in Resolution 688 (1991) of 5 April 1991, compelled Iraq to permit international humanitarian organizations access to persons in need of help. Recently it has been possible through Security Council efforts to alleviate the distress and persecution of the Kurdish people. Furthermore, in the Yugoslav conflict and the civil war in Somalia, serious human rights violations perpetrated against sections of the population and difficulties in distribution of essential aid supplies have caused the Security Council to intervene or tighten its sanctions. In the Yugoslav conflict the Security Council has prohibited military flights in Bosnian airspace, tightened inspections, and authorized enforcement of control and aid measures by armed force to ensure the protection of humanitarian aid convoys. These actions were based upon Chapter VII of the UN Charter.[2] Finally the Security Council has appointed an impartial commission of experts to investigate reports of violations of international human rights provisions in the Yugoslav conflict.[3]

The Commission on Human Rights has also initiated an assessment and

---

[1] Cf. Dahm/Delbrück/Wolfrum, 89 for further supporting evidence.

[2] SC Res. 770 (1992) of 13 Aug. 1992, 781 (1992) of 9 Oct. 1992, 816 (1993) of 31 Mar. 1993, 819 (1993) of 16 Apr. 1993, 859 (1993) of 24 Aug. 1993, and in particular 1003 (1995) of 5 July 1995.

[3] SC Res. 780 (1992) of 6 Oct. 1992, Doc. S/25274 of 10 Feb. 1993 (Report of the Commission).

documentation of human rights violations committed during fighting in the former Yugoslavia (mass shootings, torture, rape, ethnically motivated expulsions) and authorized criminal prosecution for these actions in its special session in August 1992. Resolution 1992/S–1/1 of 14 August 1992 (para. 9) states that persons who commit or order violations of the four Geneva Conventions or its two additional Protocols are to be held individually criminally responsible. The report of the Special Rapporteur T. Mazowiecki[4] speaks of the continuation of intense and widespread human rights violations. In order to secure distribution of humanitarian aid supplies, the Security Council eventually authorized military intervention in Somalia following the example of the military action against Iraq.[5]

This practice confirms that serious and continuing human rights violations by a country are no longer considered its internal affair, and that the community of states can intervene through its co-operative organs. However, sufficient political will on the part of the world community is necessary for effective use of available instruments. Apart from this, enforcement of international law often lies with individual members of the international community which have recourse to different enforcement methods. Retaliation, reprisal, and self-defence are regarded as classic forms of national enforcement of international law obligations. Under this heading belong also demands for compensation (state responsibility), punishment of individuals, or as exercised *vis-à-vis* the military leaders of Haiti, sanctions directed against the property or assets of individuals.[6] The punishment of individuals under the heading 'punishment of war criminals' takes on special meaning in regard to the enforcement of international humanitarian law.[7] Geneva law has most recently developed specific instruments[8] to secure both interstate and domestic enforcement. Among these are the institutions of fact finding Commission (Art. 90 AP I) and the protecting power. Within each individual country, every effort is being made to publicize the content of international humanitarian law.

2. *Historic development.* International law norms for the punishment of war crimes have evolved along with the development of international law rules on warfare. They are understood primarily as a means for enforcement of international humanitarian law. However, the development of international treaty law on the punishment of war criminals has limped along behind the developmental pace of rules on warfare.[9] The punishment of war criminals through the injured state was thus based primarily upon customary international law, disregarding the amnesty clauses of peace treaties pre-dating World War I[10] concerning the punishment of

---

[4] UN Doc. A/47/635 of 6 Nov. 1992.   [5] SC Res. 794 of 3 Dec. 1992 (Operation Restore Hope).
[6] SC Res. 841 of 16 June 1993.   [7] Appleman, 53.   [8] Kwakwa, 159 ff.
[9] Regarding prosecution of war crimes in the Middle Ages cf. Keen; Sunga, 18. Punishment was already discussed for Napoleon following his return from Elba. In a statement made on 13 Mar. 1815 in Vienna by the powers which had defeated Napoleon, the countries alleged that Napoleon had placed himself above the law, exposing himself to public retribution as an enemy of world peace. After his defeat, however, no criminal proceedings were initiated against him. Instead, by agreement of the Great Powers, he was treated as both a prisoner of war and a security risk and accordingly interned on St Helena.
[10] Jeschek, *EPIL* 4, 294 (295); Lachs, *War Crimes*, correctly emphasizes the Preamble of Hague Convention IV: until a more complete code of war can be developed, the High Contracting Parties think it

war crimes. The Hague Conventions of 1899 and 1907 contained no express regulation of individual responsibility for offences against the laws and practices of war. However, they also did not limit individual responsibility or the possibility of prosecution by the injured state. Specific indications of the possibility of criminal prosecution for war crimes are to be found, however, in Arts. 41 and 56, para. 2 HagueReg. Art. 41 HagueReg addresses the violation of cease-fire terms by private individuals and provides that compensation from and punishment of the accused parties can be demanded. Pursuant to Art. 56, para. 2 HagueReg, all seizure, destruction, or wilful damage to common and institutional property, historic monuments, or works of art and science is prohibited and punishable. A comparable rule is found in Art. 28 of the Geneva Convention of 1906, pursuant to which the states parties agreed 'to repress, in time of war, individual acts of robbery and ill-treatment of the sick and wounded of the armies, as well as to punish, as ursurpations of military insigna, the wrongful use of the flag and brassard of the Red Cross'. These provisions assume the liability to punishment of individuals, but fail to incorporate detailed regulations for prosecution. Under these provisions, punishment could be carried out by a state which had taken its opponent's personnel prisoner.[11] Thus, although a series of treaties governing the rules of warfare already existed before World War I, a treaty securing an enforcement mechanism for punishment of war criminals was lacking and recourse to customary international law was necessary.

At the end of World War I the punishment of those who had violated customary or treaty-made rules of warfare was considered at the preparatory meeting for the Paris Peace Conferences. This meeting established a Commission whose task was to investigate responsibility for the war's outbreak. More specifically, the Commission was responsible for determining offences against the rules of warfare committed by Germany and its allies, and was mandated to establish a criminal court for the prosecution of responsible individuals. The Commission listed thirty-two war crimes.[12] The Treaty of Versailles planned for punishment of individuals

suitable to stipulate that, in instances which are not covered by the provisions of the order accepted by them, the population and the belligerent parties remain under the protection and control of international law, as these follow from the established usages of civilized peoples, the laws of humanity and the demands of public conscience.

[11] Draper, in *IYHR* 6 (1976), 9–48 (15).

[12] United Nations War Crimes Commission, *History of the United Nations War Crimes Commission and the Development of the Laws of War*, London 1948, 34–5: (1) Murders and massacres; systematic terrorism. (2) Putting hostages to death. (3) Torture of civilians. (4) Deliberate starvation of civilians. (5) Rape. (6) Kidnapping of girls and women for the purpose of enforced prostitution. (7) Deportation of civilians. (8) Internment of civilians. (9) Forced labour of civilians in connection with the military operations of the enemy. (10) Usurpation of sovereignty during military occupation. (11) Compulsory enlistment of soldiers among the inhabitants of occupied territory. (12) Attempts to denationalize the inhabitants of occupied territory. (13) Pillage. (14) Confiscation of property. (15) Exactions of illegitimate contributions and requisitions. (16) Debasement of currency and issue of spurious currency. (17) Imposition of collective penalties. (18) Wanton devastation and destruction of property. (19) Deliberate bombardment of undefended places. (20) Wanton destruction of religious, charitable, educational, and historic buildings and monuments. (21) Destruction of merchant ships and passenger vessels without warning and without provision for the safety of passengers and crew. (22) Destruction of fishing boats and of relief ships. (23) Deliberate bombing of hospitals. (24) Attack on and destruction of hospital ships. (25) Breach of other rules relating to the Red Cross. (26) Use of deleterious and asphyxiating gases. (27) Use of explosive or expanding bullets, and other

who had violated rules of warfare through the military tribunals of the Allied and Associated Powers (Arts. 228–30), whereby offenders were to be handed over by the German Reich. This form of prosecution broke down when the German government[13] refused to surrender individuals accused of having commited war crimes. Instead, punishment of war criminals was undertaken by the Supreme Court of the German Reich (*Reichsgericht*) on the basis of a law passed on 18 December 1919.[14]

After the establishment of the League of Nations, the Commission entrusted with the preparation of a statute for the Permanent International Court of Justice made an attempt to develop a code on international criminal law. The proposals submitted in 1920 proposed punishment of violations of international law through an international court. However, the recommendation was not pursued further in the League of Nations. Proposals for punishment of war crimes are found in the Geneva Conventions of 1929.[15]

Despite these first steps, at the outbreak of World War II no general international law codification existed concerning the prosecution of war crimes. The various attempts and proposals for regulation of this problem made clear, however, that there were three possible types of tribunal for punishment of war crimes: an international criminal court, the courts of the injured state, or the courts of the war criminal's home state. If punishment is to be pursued by the home state, the prosecution of war criminals can only be regarded as an effective means of enforcement of the law of war if the latter is under an obligation to prosecute (i.e. Art. 56, para. 2 HagueReg).

Already during World War II the intention was voiced to punish German and Japanese war criminals. In 1942, stepping into the place of older institutions, a United Nations War Crimes Commission was set up and entrusted with preparation[16] to that end. At the end of 1943 a programme for prosecution of war criminals was agreed upon at the Moscow Conference between the major powers (the United States, the United Kingdom, and the former USSR).[17]

inhumane appliances. (28) Directions to give no quarter. (29) Ill-treatment of the wounded and prisoners of war. (30) Employment of prisoners of war on unauthorized works. (31) Misuse of flags of truce. (32) Poisoning of wells. (Reprinted also in *AJIL* 14 (1920), 114, 115); Wells, 96–7.

[13] Art. 227 of the Treaty of Versailles considered the establishment of an international tribunal against Kaiser Wilhelm II; charges were to be brought against him for violation of international moral law and of sanctity of the contracts. The provision stipulated that the court 'should decide [pursuant to the] applied principles of international policy'. The trial's execution, however, foundered on the Netherlands' refusal to extradite. Art. 230 of the Treaty of Sèvres provided for the sentencing of those responsible for the crimes against the Armenians. This treaty was not ratified, however, and stipulations of this sort were absent from the later Treaty of Lausanne.

[14] Of the 901 persons against whom proceedings were initiated, only thirteen were convicted. As these penalties were deemed to be too light, comprehensive execution of them did not ensue. The fact that the punishment of war criminals following World War I was considered unsatisfactory led to the establishment of the International Military Tribunal after World War II.

[15] Art. 30: 'On the request of a belligerent, an enquiry shall be instituted, in a manner to be decided between the interested parties, concerning any alleged violation of the Convention; when such violation has been established the belligerents shall put an end to and repress it as promptly as possible.' Cf. Pictet, *Humanitarian Law and the Protection of War Victims*, 68.

[16] Cf. *History of the UN War Crimes Commission and the Development of the Laws of War*, 1948; Schwelb, *BYIL* 23 (1946), 363–76; Bierzanek, *War Crimes*, 573.

[17] The Moscow Declaration reads: 'Those German officers and men and members of the Nazi party who have been responsible for, or have taken a consenting part in the above atrocities, massacres, and executions, will be sent back to the countries in which their abominable deeds were done in order that they may

On 8 August 1945 the United States, the United Kingdom, France, and the former USSR signed the Agreement for the Prosecution and Punishment of the Major War Criminals of the European Axis Powers, which nineteen other states ratified before the conclusion of the Nuremberg Trials. An integral part of this Agreement is the Charter of the International Military Tribunal, in an addendum.[18] The Tribunal's trials against the principal war criminals began in Nuremberg on 20 November 1945.

According to Art. 6 lit. a of its Statute, the Tribunal was competent to try crimes against the peace, war crimes, and crimes against humanity, which constitute three different offences.[19] Art. 6 of the Statute defines the concept of war crimes as: 'violations of the laws or customs of war. Such violation shall include, but not be limited to, murder, ill-treatment or deportation to slave labour or for any other purpose of civilian population of or in occupied territory, murder or ill-treatment of prisoners of war or persons on the seas, killing of hostages, plunder of public or private property, wanton destruction of cities, towns or villages, or devastation not justified by military necessity.'

To prove the legitimacy of punishment based upon this agreement the Tribunal stated that these acts had long been recognized as war crimes, either as customary or treaty law. Reference was made in this respect to Arts. 46, 50, 52, and 56 HagueReg and to Arts. 2, 3, 4, 46, and 51 of the 1929 Geneva Convention Relative to the Treatment of Prisoners of War.[20]

In addition to the Germans, Japan's political and military decision makers were also subjected to criminal prosecutions after World War II. The Allies had expressed an intent to do so in the Potsdam Declaration of 26 July 1945. The relevant conditions set down in the Declaration of Surrender were explicitly accepted by Japan. Through a proclamation by the chief commanding officers of the Allied armed forces on 19 January 1946, an International Military Tribunal for the Far East was established and the Statute of the Tribunal was appended to it. Japan accepted the judgments passed by the International Military Tribunal in the San Francisco Peace Treaty.[21]

The International Military Tribunals of Nuremberg and Tokyo conducted trials and imposed penalties against a number of German and Japanese personalities. Further trials against groups of German persons were carried out by American military courts on the basis of Control Council Law No. 10, which followed the

be judged and punished according to the laws of these liberated countries and of the free governments which will be created therein. . . . The above declaration is without prejudice to the case of the major criminals, whose offences have no particular geographical location and who will be punished by the joint decision of the Governments of the Allies.'

[18] Text: *AJIL* 39 (1945), Suppl. 258.

[19] These three different offences had already been provided for in the proposals of the Commission on the Responsibility of the Authors of War and on Enforcement of Penalties appointed by the Preliminary Peace Conference of 1919; *AJIL* 14 (1920), 95. According to Greenspan, 419, on the other hand, the term war crimes is to be understood generically as including conventional war crimes, crimes against humanity, and crimes against peace, as well as genocide.

[20] For the trials before the International Military Tribunal cf. Appleman, 70 ff. Ipsen, *Völkerrecht*, 536 ff.

[21] For the Tokyo Processes see: Schwarzenberger, in *Current Legal Problems* 3 (1950), 289; Röling/Rüter (Eds.).

provisions of the Nuremberg Statutes with modifications. Similar war crimes trials took place against Japanese military personnel before courts in the United States, the United Kingdom, Australia, Canada, and the Netherlands.[22]

Intensive efforts were made in the United Nations to create a comprehensive international criminal law modelled on the London Agreement of 8 August 1945. These endeavours have to date remained unsuccessful. The International Law Commission in particular has increased its efforts (UN Doc. A/CN.4/457 of 15 Feb. 1994, 6 et seq.) to create a Code of Crimes Against the Peace and Security of Mankind. These efforts were influenced by violations of the prohibition on war and of international humanitarian law committed in the most recent international and civil wars.[23]

The law applied by the International Military Tribunals following World War II has had no significant precedential effect so far. This is even true in respect of the prosecution of war crimes. Thus in the 1971 military process against Lieutenant Calley and Captain Medina, both prosecuted for the massacre in My Lai of over 100 Vietnamese civilians, including children, the 'Uniform Code of Military Justice' alone was considered. No reference to the international law elements of war crimes was made.[24] Had the principles of the decision against General Yamashita[25] been considered, the superiors of both officers would also have been held responsible.[26] Although Bangladesh announced in April 1973 that it would prosecute 195 Pakistanis for genocide, war crimes, crimes against humanity, and serious violations of the Geneva Conventions in the face of intense political pressure, it refrained from this action, instead transferring the accused parties to Pakistan.[27]

Despite a lack of practice it has to be assumed in the meantime that a broad *opinio juris* exists that individuals who commit war crimes, crimes against peace, or crimes against humanity can be held responsible for those acts under national or international criminal law.[28] This proposition has recently been supported by a decision of the Security Council to prosecute those who have committed war crimes in the former Yugoslavia. A substantial number of these crimes are covered by the Four Geneva Conventions of 1949 and the two Additional Protocols.

Although the Red Cross has not succeeded in developing its own 'Model Law' for punishing war criminals which would serve as a model for the legislation,[29] the Four Geneva Conventions of 12 August 1949 do contain rules governing the prosecution of grave breaches of the Conventions (Arts. 49 & 50 GC I; Arts. 50 & 51 GC II; Arts. 129 & 130 GC III; Arts. 146 & 147 GC IV). These rules offer national legislatures sufficient grounds for prosecution. Art. 50 GC I (Art. 51 GC II; Art. 130 GC III; Art. 147 GC IV) contains a definition of the term 'grave breaches'. Specific abuses defined in the individual Conventions fall into this category, to the extent that they are com-

---

[22] For full details see Piccigallo, 44 ff.   [23] Cf. Sunga, 133 ff.

[24] Friedmann, L. (Ed.), Vol. II, 1708.   [25] Cf. Lael.

[26] Friedmann (Ed.), Vol. II, 1599; Ipsen, 540; Lyon, in Baird, (Ed.), *From Nuremberg to My Lai* (1972), 139–49.

[27] Cf. Paust/Blaustein, *Vanderbilt Journal of Transnational Law* 11 (1978), 1–38.

[28] Sunga, 35; Brownlie, *Principles of Public International Law*, 562; Dinstein, *Israel Law Review* 20 (1985), 206–42; Dahm/Delbrück/Wolfrum, I/2 (forthcoming).

[29] Cf. Pictet, *Humanitarian Law and the Protection of War Victims*, 70.

mitted against persons or goods protected by the Convention. A number of breaches named in the Conventions had already previously been recognized as war crimes by customary international law. The contents of GC II address in principle the same issues as GC I. The second Convention, however, contains in its paragraph on naval warfare a number of special provisions resulting from the problems posed by naval warfare.[30] The same holds true for GC III, which rewrites individual standards of conduct in an effort to protect prisoners of war, and makes violations of these provisions a grave breach of the Convention.[31] Lastly, GC IV also expands the scope of obligations, thus expanding the meaning of 'grave breach'.

The indicated provisions circumscribe the necessary elements of a criminal offence, yet without the precision of a national penal code; concrete statements about the range of punishments are nowhere to be found. An exception is made regarding prosecution of criminal offences against prisoners of war (Arts. 82 ff. GC III). However, the indicated provisions are not directly applicable without more. The parties to the treaty are only obliged to enact 'all legislation necessary to provide effective penal sanctions'. With this provision the Geneva Conventions decided on the third of the named prosecution methods, namely prosecution of war criminals by the state to which the transgressor belongs. Corresponding obligations to investigate and prosecute exist in Art. 49, para. 2 GC I; Art. 50, para. 2 GC II; Art. 129, para. 2 GC III; Art. 146, para. 2 GC IV). This duty of the home state does not, however, create any monopoly on investigation and prosecution on its side. The ability to investigate and prosecute is left fully open to other states. In this respect, other contracting states interested in prosecuting war crimes are as much empowered to do so as the custodial state (for prisoners of war or internees).

In accordance with Art. 49, para. 2 GC I, the country of the offender, instead of conducting a prosecution itself, can hand such a person over for trial to another contracting state interested in the prosecution, provided that sufficient incriminatory evidence is produced. The principle *aut dedere aut punire* is thus valid. To the extent that such extradition is possible it is regulated by the domestic law of the home state. According to German constitutional law, any attempted extradition of German nationals would be contrary to Art. 16 GG. Normally the state interested in prosecution will most likely be either the injured state or the native country of the accused. However, extradition is not limited to these states. A request for extradition can be made by all High Contracting Parties, even states neutral in the conflict, as long as they demonstrate an abstract interest in the prosecution of the grave breaches committed and produce corresponding incriminating evidence. With this, Geneva Law secures the prosecution of war criminals by all contracting states.[32]

The punishment of prisoners of war in the custodial state for grave breaches can occur under the terms of either the custodial state's domestic law or international (and thus also Geneva) law.[33] The above-mentioned lack of precision in Geneva Law is balanced by the fact that Section VI, Chap. III (Arts. 84–108) of GC III contains a list of guarantees for the criminal proceedings as well as limits to sentences.

---

[30] Arts. 22, 24, 25, and 27 GC II.   [31] Art. 13 GC III.   [32] Jescheck, *EPIL* 4, 297.

[33] See Art. 99, para. 1 GC III.

Equally the statute of the International Tribunal for the Prosecution of Persons Responsible for Serious Violations of International Humanitarian Law Committed in the Territory of the Former Yugoslavia is based on the prosecution of war criminals in accordance with international law.[34]

No explicit regulation is to be found in Geneva Law governing the prosecution of war criminals in instances where the accused individual acted under orders. Art. 49 para. 2 GC I makes it clear, however, that both the person who acts and that person's commander may have committed a grave breach. The practice of the trials against war criminals immediately following World War II is consistent with this language. The Geneva Law of 1949 denies a war criminal's claim that he acted as an organ of state and that his behaviour is therefore attributable to the state and not to him personally.[35] The Geneva Conventions, however, give no indication of the extent to which following orders can exonerate a subordinate. The Conventions do not provide that grave breaches can also be committed through acts of omission, although the International Military Tribunals recognized these as violations immediately following World War II.

The First Additional Protocol of 1977 (AP I) lists further grave breaches. Art. 11, para. 4 and Art. 85, para. 3 are examples. The Geneva Conventions of 1949 are also expanded by AP I in that both acts and omissions can produce grave breaches. The Second Additional Protocol (AP II) does not mention grave breaches. Art. 6 nevertheless regulates prosecution and punishment of criminal offences connected with armed conflict. The AP II presumes application of domestic criminal law, whereby the domestic power of sentence is subordinate to the demands of the Protocol.

I. GENERAL

1201   **Violations of international humanitarian law have been committed by parties to nearly every armed conflict. Both published reports and internal findings show, however, that the protective provisions of international humanitarian law prevented or reduced great suffering in many cases.**

International law faces the same problems concerning violations as every other legal system, although this is not to be understood as an excuse for violations. Legal systems formulate what their citizens should do, the realization of which being fully dependent on the effectiveness of law enforcement. It is imperative for the effective implementation of humanitarian law that its contents be known by persons involved in a conflict, that those persons be aware that violations carry disciplinary or penal consequences, and that persistent breach may lead to an escalation of the conflict. In this regard, compliance with humanitarian law is in the interest of every individual party to the conflict. The developments in former Yugoslavia, in particular, indicate that public opinion, particularly the mass media, are in the position to

[34] UN Doc. S/25704 3 May 1993.   [35] Cf. Matthei, *RDMilG* (1980), 259 ff.

keep conflicts under strict surveillance and to document breaches of international humanitarian law. Furthermore, there is a growing tendency to use the spectre of public documentation as a weapon to deter abuses as well as to lay the foundations for later prosecutions. The inquiries of the Security Council and the Commission on Human Rights in the case of former Yugoslavia are to be seen in this light. Apart from this, military leaders or responsible political organs are themselves under an obligation to investigate possible breaches of humanitarian law, to suppress them, and to document corresponding investigations and measures taken.

The following factors can induce the parties to a conflict to counteract disobedi-   1202
ence of the law applicable in armed conflicts and thus to enforce observance of
international humanitarian law:

— **consideration for public opinion;**

— **reciprocal interests of the parties to the conflict;**

— **maintenance of discipline;**

— **fear of reprisals;**

— **penal and disciplinary measures;**

— **fear of payment of compensation;**

— **activities of protecting powers;**

— **international fact finding;**

— **the activities of the International Committee of the Red Cross (ICRC);**

— **diplomatic activities;**

— **national implementing measures;**

— **dissemination of humanitarian law; and**

— **personal conviction and responsibility of the individual.**

1. The obligation to observe international humanitarian law addresses itself both to states parties to the conflict and to individuals. Incentives to comply with the law are diverse.

2. In these days of mass media, the role which public opinion plays in humanitarian law enforcement is growing both within states parties to a conflict and in other countries. There are numerous examples of this. One is the US entry into World War II after breaches committed in territories of, and occupied by, the German Reich. The course of the Vietnam conflict was clearly influenced by public opinion both from within the United States and from outside. Pictures broadcast from Iraq, former Yugoslavia, and Somalia contributed substantially to the willingness of the community of states to attempt to contain these conflicts.

3. An important element in guaranteeing respect for humanitarian law results from the idea of reciprocity.[36] No party to a conflict can expect its opponent to observe

---

[36] Simma, *EPIL* 7, 400–4 for further supporting evidence.

Wolfrum

rules of warfare which it does not itself respect. The expectation of mutual advantages is one of the guarantees for the implementation of international law in general[37] as well as international humanitarian law specifically.

4. A breach of international humanitarian law can be countered by the opponent through an act normally contrary to international law (reprisal). This responding violation of international law finds its justification in the principle of reciprocity.[38] Here in particular exists a real danger of further escalation. The Geneva Law, particularly AP I, limits the permissibility of reprisals.[39]

5. Fear of criminal or disciplinary punishment—i.e. in addition to the deterrent effect of past convictions—is another means by which adherence to humanitarian law can be guaranteed. These measures alone are not sufficient, however. Rather it is the duty of superiors to make their troops aware that the conduct of war is subject to limitation and that adherence to the rules of warfare is in the interest of every single combatant. A precondition for this is that international humanitarian law has been implemented in national law and made generally known to the troops.

6. International law recognizes the possibility of allowing a state to claim compensation for breaches of international law. This instrument is not fully standardized, but is another means of guaranteeing application of international law.[40] The claims for compensation made against Iraq are an example.[41]

7. One institution provided in Geneva Law to secure its enforcement is that of protecting powers.[42] The International Committee of the Red Cross also has the task of ensuring observation of the rights of protected persons (prisoners of war, injured and shipwrecked persons, civilians, etc.).

8. Finally the possibility exists that states not party to the original conflict may intervene against grave breaches of international humanitarian law. The protection of individuals, according to modern international law, is no longer the internal affair of a state, and the possibility exists for intervention by international organizations (United Nations) or regional organizations or arrangements (CSCE in the Yugoslavian conflict).[43]

---

[37] Verdross/Simma, 49.

[38] Kimminich, *Einführung in das Völkerrecht*, 480.

[39] See *supra* Sections 477 ff. and *infra* 1206.

[40] Cf. Dahm/Delbrück/Wolfrum, I/1, 90.

[41] Cf. *Criteria of the Administrative Council of the United Nations Compensation Commission* S/AC.26/1991/1 and 2 of 2 Aug. 1991; S/AC.26/1991/3, 4, and 5 of 23 Oct. 1991; S/AC.26/1991/Rev. 1 of 17 Mar. 1992; S/AC.26/1992/8 of 27 Jan. 1992, and S/AC.26/1992/9 of Mar. 1992; Report of 1 Sep. 1992 on the activities of the United Nations Compensation Commission S/24589 of 28 Sep. 1992.

[42] See *infra* Sections 1215–17.

[43] See Introductory Remarks, above.

Wolfrum

II. PUBLIC OPINION

The publishing of a violation of international law may render an essential contribution to enforcing behaviour is in compliance with international law. To this end, considering the global information network, the media (press, broadcasting, television) and their aids (radio, satellites) can be employed today in an incomparably better and thus more efficient manner than has been the case in previous armed conflicts. When offences against international law become known, each party to the conflict must expect that truthful enemy reports on its violations of international law will impair the fighting morale of its forces and the consent of its own population.

1203

Reference has already been made to the increasing significance of public opinion for enforcement of international humanitarian law.

III. RECIPROCAL INTERESTS OF THE PARTIES TO THE CONFLICT

Only those who themselves comply with the provisions of international humanitarian law can expect the adversary to observe the dictates of humanity in an armed conflict. No one shall be guided by the suspicion that soldiers of the other party to the conflict might not observe these rules. Soldiers must treat their opponents in the same manner that they themselves wish to be treated.

1204

The significance of reciprocity has already been discussed.

IV. MAINTENANCE OF DISCIPLINE

Ordering or tolerating violations of international law leads to subordinates' doubts as to the justification of their own side's activities. It can also undermine the authority of the military leader giving such an order and can jeopardize the discipline of the forces.

1205

Violations of the law of warfare have a negative influence on subordinates in many regards. These violations can lead to relaxation of discipline, as a propensity develops among subordinates themselves to disregard international humanitarian law. Above all, however, a superior who acts contrary to international law endangers his own authority. He cannot expect that his orders will be followed unquestioningly in the future.

Wolfrum

V. REPRISALS

1206   **The use of reprisals can cause an adversary who is contravening international law to cease that violation. Reprisals are permissible only in exceptional cases and for the purpose of enforcing compliance with international law. They require a decision at the highest political level (see Sections 476–9).**

1. Reprisals are a means of enforcement of international humanitarian law. Because of humanitarian considerations, the Geneva Law provides in particular for restrictions of reprisals. Therefore Art. 20 AP I prohibits reprisals against the wounded, sick, and shipwrecked. The same is true in regard to civilians (Art. 51(6) AP I) and civilian objects (Art. 52(1) AP I), cultural property (Art. 53 AP I), indispensable objects (Art. 54(3) AP I), and the natural environment (Art. 55(2) AP I) as well as facilities and installations which contain dangerous forces (Art. 56(4) AP I). Restrictions on reprisals arise from Art. 46 GC I (prohibition of reprisals against the wounded, sick, personnel, buildings, or material protected by the Convention), Art. 47 GC II (prohibition of reprisals against the wounded, sick, shipwrecked, personnel, buildings, or material protected by the Convention), Art. 13 GC III (Prohibition of reprisals against prisoners of war), and Art. 33 GC IV (Prohibition of reprisals against protected persons and their possessions).

2. In any case, the decision to take retaliatory measures lies at the political level. A military leader does not have the right to decide to answer an unlawful act of his opponent with an unlawful act of his own. Such measures constitute violations or grave breaches of humanitarian law and may result in disciplinary or criminal proceedings.

VI. PENAL AND DISCIPLINARY MEASURES

1207   **Each member of the armed forces who has violated the rules of international humanitarian law must be aware of the fact that he can be prosecuted according to penal or disciplinary provisions.**

1. This regulation refers to every violation, both grave breaches[44] and others. The consequences of a grave breach are always of a penal nature; other violations may be punished through disciplinary procedures.

2. In accordance with Art. 49, para. 2 GC I (likewise Art. 50, para. 2 GC II; Art. 129, para. 2 GC III; Art. 146, para. 2 GC IV) every state party is under an obligation to investigate persons accused of the commission or ordering of a grave breach. The provisions of the Geneva Convention explicitly state that the commission of a grave

---

[44] See Sections 1208 and 1209.

breach and an order which leads to one are equally serious. The commander and the subordinate who acts on the command are equally responsible. No possibility exists for the subordinate to escape penal responsibility through reference to his orders. Geneva Law is not explicit, but the same conclusion can be inferred from the objective and purpose of the indicated provisions. In this respect, older agreements can also be invoked. The 1922 Washington Treaty Relating to the Use of Submarines and Noxious Gases in Warfare already eliminated the defence of following orders for violations committed under higher command.[45] A similar regulation is found in the Statute of the International Military Tribunal of 8 August 1945.[46] Whether a subordinate has the right to refuse an order in such cases has not yet been dealt with in international treaties. Attempts to enshrine the right to refuse an order violating international humanitarian law in AP I failed.[47]

3. In accordance with Art. 86(2) AP I, superiors whose subordinates violate the Convention will not be relieved of criminal or disciplinary responsibility if they were aware, or under the circumstances should have been aware, that the subordinate was committing or was going to commit such a violation. The superior will be liable if he has failed to take all possible measures to foreclose or repress such violation, and if the person committing such violation was under his command.[48] Art. 86(2) AP I is to be read in connection with Art. 87 AP I (Duties of Military Leaders). Section 1207 does not state this principle clearly enough. The principle, however, corresponds to German penal law, under which a failure to act is as culpable as an action, if both a duty and possibility to act exist.

4. Art. 86, para. 2 AP I is based largely on the decision in the war crime proceedings against General Yamashita. He was judged by the United States Military Commission in Manila for war crimes his troops had committed in the Philippines. The Commission decided in this matter that: '. . . the gist of the charge is an unlawful breach of duty by the petitioner as an army commander to control the operations of the members of his command by "permitting them to commit" the extensive and widespread atrocities specified. The question then is whether the law of war imposes on an army commander a duty to take such appropriate measures as are within his power to control the troops under his command for the prevention of the specified acts which are violations of the law of war and which are likely to attend the occupation of hostile territory by an uncontrolled soldiery, and whether he may be charged with personal responsibility for his failure to take such measures when violations result . . . [t]he purpose of the law of war . . . to protect civilian populations and prisoners of war from brutality would largely be defeated if the

---

[45] See Art. 3: 'the Signatory Powers . . . further declare, that any person in the service . . . who shall violate any of those rules, whether or not such a person is under orders of a government superior, shall be deemed to have violated the laws of war and shall be liable to trial and punishment as if for an act of piracy', *AJIL* 16 (1922), Suppl. 58.

[46] 'The fact that the Defendant acted pursuant to order of his government or of a superior shall not free him from responsibility, but may be considered in mitigation of punishment if the Tribunal determines that justice so requires'.

[47] Cf. Matthei, *RDMilG* (1980), 266 ff.   [48] Cf. ICRC *Commentary*, Art. 86, para. 3543.

Wolfrum

commander of an invading army could with impunity neglect to take reasonable measures for their protection. Hence the law of war presupposes that its violation is to be avoided through the control of the operations of war by commanders who are to some extent responsible for their subordinates.'[49]

5. The superior's responsibility for actions is a logical consequence of Art. 1 HagueReg, according to which militia and volunteer corps fall under this treaty only if they are commanded 'by a person responsible for his subordinates'.[50] The same notion is to be found in Art. 39 GC III, according to which each prisoner of war camp is placed under the immediate authority of a responsible commissioned officer. From that responsibility of the superior results his specific accountability for violations by his subordinates.

6. Art. 49, para. 2 GC I[51] obliges states to take action if they receive knowledge of grave breaches having been committed. Such obligation does not only come into existence if states are exhorted by other states to initiate investigations. Investigations must be made in any case. Further, it is of no consequence who has committed a breach. Investigations and eventual prosecutions must be initiated against nationals and citizens of allies, as well as citizens of opponent states.

7. Even if the home country does not itself undertake the investigation and ensuing prosecution, it is obliged under Art. 49, para. 1 GC I to extradite alleged violators to another interested state party for trial, as long as such state party can produce a *prima facie* case against the suspects. In this regard, the general principle of international law is clearly reflected, in which the state having custody over the accused person is itself under an obligation either to prosecute or to extradite the suspect. Art. 49, para. 2 GC I does not contain a further specification of the potential states which may ask for extradition if they are interested in prosecuting.[52] The only restrictions provided by Geneva Convention Law in this respect are the reference to the domestic law of the extraditing state and the requirement of sufficient incriminating evidence. The extradition of German nationals is generally ruled out by Art. 16 of the German Basic Law.

1208   **The four Geneva Conventions and Additional Protocol I oblige the contracting parties to make grave breaches of the protective provisions liable to punishment and to take all suitable measures to ensure compliance with the Conventions (Arts. 49, 50 GC I; Arts. 50, 51 GC II; Arts. 129, 130 GC III; Arts. 146, 147 GC IV; Art. 85 AP I).**

1. These provisions impose a twofold obligation on the contracting states. They must shape their domestic law, in particular their criminal and military codes of

---

[49] Decision of 7 Dec. 1945, in Friedmann (Ed.), Vol. 2, 1596.   [50] Also Art. 4A 2 GC III; Art. 43.
[51] Also Art. 50 GC I.
[52] Critical of this is Levie, *The Code of International Armed Conflict*, Vol. 2, 892.

discipline, so that the punishment of grave breaches[53] of international humanitarian law is ensured. This assumes that both the elements constituting the offence and the range of punishment are established for each offence. Such obligation already exists in times of peace. In addition, the contracting parties must employ further measures to ensure that the additional protective provisions of the Convention are observed and that offences which do not constitute grave breaches are prosecuted according to domestic law. This follows primarily from Art. 49, para. 3 GC I.

2. Art. 85, para. 1 AP I ensures that the provisions of the four Geneva Conventions for punishment of violations and grave breaches are applied to the punishment of corresponding breaches of the First Additional Protocol. Apart from that, Art. 85, paras. 2 and 4 AP I elaborate and expand the Regulations of the four Geneva Conventions concerning protected persons and objects.[54]

3. In accordance with Art. 49, para. 4 GC I, the contracting states are not entirely free in organizing the legal procedure. Minimum standards of international law, as reflected in Arts. 105 ff. GC III, have to be respected.

Each state shall make the following grave breaches of international humanitarian law liable to punishment and prosecution (Art. 49 GC I; Art. 50 GC II; Art. 129 GC III; Art. 146 GC IV; Art. 85 AP I):   1209

—Indictable offences against protected persons (wounded, sick, medical personnel, chaplains, prisoners of war, inhabitants of occupied territory, other civilians), such as wilful killing, mutilation, torture, or inhumane treatment, including biological experiments, wilfully causing great suffering, serious injury to body or health, taking of hostages (Arts. 3, 49–51 GC I; Arts. 3, 50, 51 GC II; Arts. 3, 129, 130 GC III; Arts. 3, 146, 147 GC IV; Arts. 11, para. 2, 85, para. 3 lit. a AP I).

1. The indicated provisions list the grave breaches. They are there tailored to the objectives of the individual Geneva Conventions and are supplemented through Art. 85, paras. 2–4 AP I.

2. Protected persons include the injured and sick (Art. 13 GC I[55]) at sea as well as shipwrecked[56] (Art. 13 GC II), prisoners of war (Art. 4 GC III), and civilians (Art. 4 GC

---

[53] See Section 1209.   [54] For the term 'grave breach' see Section 1209.
[55] Also belonging to this category are persons accompanying the armed forces without being members, such as civilian crew members of military aircraft, war correspondents, army contractors, members of work units, or services responsible for the care of military personnel; cf. Levie, *The Code of International Armed Conflict*, Vol. I, 6 ff.
[56] It is irrelevant whether the shipwrecked persons have fallen into the hands of the detaining state or not. For example, Admiral Dönitz was accused before the Nürnberg Military Tribunal of having given the command that shipwrecked persons of hostile nations were not to be rescued. He was not convicted, since a similar command on the side of the Allies had been given to the commanding officers of British and American submarines. A British military tribunal condemned the crew members of a German submarine that had opened fire on the crew of a sinking Greek ship after they had climbed into lifeboats. Pursuant to

IV). This category of persons is supplemented (Art. 85, paras. 2–4 AP I) by persons who have participated in military operations and fallen into enemy hands (Arts. 44, 45 AP I);[57] injured, sick, and shipwrecked of the opposing party (Art. 8 AP I);[58] medical and religious personnel (Art. 8 AP I); and persons *hors de combat* (Art. 85, para. 3 lit. e AP I).

3. The term 'wilful killing' covers all cases in which a protected person is killed. 'Wilful killing' includes active deeds as well as omission if the omission was committed with intent to cause the death of a protected person. The reduction of rations for prisoners of war resulting in their starvation falls into the category of wilful killing.

4. 'Mutilation' comprises any serious invasion of physical integrity that causes residual damage. The scope of this grave breach of international humanitarian law overlaps with that of serious injury of physical body or health.[59]

5. 'Torture' or 'inhumane treatment' refers to cases in which suffering is inflicted upon persons, e.g. in order to extract confessions or information from them or from other persons. For a more accurate interpretation of this provision, the Convention against Torture and other Cruel, Inhumane or Degrading Treatment or Punishment of 10 December 1984[60] can be applied. This provides that torture comprises any treatment by which great physical or spiritual pain or suffering is inflicted.

6. The prohibition of 'inhumane treatment' refers to Art. 12 GC II, pursuant to which protected persons are to be treated humanely. The prohibition of inhumane treatment refers to all offences against this principle. According to Art. 27 GC IV, all protected persons must be treated humanely. The obligation of humane treatment is practically a guiding theme for the four Geneva Conventions.[61] The principle originates from the Hague and was also contained in both Geneva Conventions of 1929. The word 'treatment' must be understood in the broadest possible sense. It prohibits principally any use of force or intimidation which cannot be justified by military necessity or a legitimate desire for security. On this basis, the term is not limited to the physical condition of the concerned person. On the contrary, any treatment which substantially injures human dignity constitutes a violation. Complete isolation from the external world or from family members will fall under this category.

7. The prohibition of 'biological experiments' refers to experiments on the human body or health. This means that the use of prisoners of war or protected persons for

the London Protocol of 1936 the commanding officer of a submarine is not allowed to sink a civilian merchant vessel if he is not in a position to save the crew.

[57] See Sections 301–30; 601; this term is broader than the notion of prisoners of war in GC III.

[58] More far-reaching than GC I; see Sections 603, 605, as well as Levie, *The Code of International Armed Conflict*, Vol. 1, 7 ff.

[59] See Sections 606 ff.   [60] BGBE 1990 I 246.

[61] In accordance with Art. 13 GC III prisoners must be treated humanely.

scientific experiments is strictly prohibited.[62] Medical care is not forbidden, even when it entails new medical procedures. It is then at all times essential that the sole purpose of such treatment is to improve the state of health of the person concerned. In practice, the differentiation between medical care and medical experimentation may cause difficulties. In consequence special significance is attached to the free consent to the medical treatment by the person in question.[63] Lastly, only medical treatment given to the civilian population of the host state may be employed on protected persons under its custody.

8. The prohibition of the wilful imposition of 'great suffering' corresponds in essence with the prohibition of torture and inhumane treatment, including biological experimentation. This includes both infliction of suffering as punishment or revenge and that brought about by other motives, for example through unmitigated cruelty, torture, or biological experiments. Pursuant to the wording of the four Conventions, this prohibition does not refer exclusively to physical suffering, but applies equally to psychological suffering. Thus, solitary confinement and penal measures may also fall within the notion of 'inhumane treatment'.

9. The prohibition of causing 'serious detriment to physical integrity or health' covers the physical side of this rule.

10. A wilful attack directed, in violation of the Protocol, against the civilian population or individual civilians which results in death or grave detriment to body or health constitutes a grave breach according to Art. 85, para. 3 lit. a AP I. A prohibition of attacks upon the civilian population or individual civilians is contained in Art. 51, para. 2 AP I.[64] In this context, the terms 'civilian population', 'civilians' and 'attack', are defined in Article 50 AP I. The terms 'civilian population' and 'civilians' are defined negatively. Civilians are all those persons who are not members of the armed forces in accordance with Art. 43 AP I or members of the regular or irregular forces according to Arts. 13 Nos. 1–3, 6 GC I (apart from the regular forces in the same sense, the organized militias and volunteer corps belonging to a state party to the conflict, the organized militias and volunteer corps belonging to organized resistance movements, and inhabitants of an unoccupied territory who, on the approach of the enemy, spontaneously take up arms to resist). In any case of doubt a person is presumed to be civilian. The civilian population is the sum of all civilians (Art. 50, para. 2 AP I), but this body does not lose its civilian status if individuals who are not civilians are found among its numbers.

11. The term 'attacks' includes both offensive and defensive use of force against the opponent, whether by land, air, or sea, in the opponent's state territory or in the

---

[62] In this respect Geneva Convention Law refers to the decisions in the trials of war criminals following World War II. Cf. e.g. proceedings before the US military tribunal against Field Marshall Milch, who was cleared of this charge, Law Reports of Trials of War Criminals, Vols. VII–IX (1948), Case No. 39.
[63] On this point see Section 608.
[64] Cf. Levie, *The Code of International Armed Conflict*, Vol. I, 67 ff.

territory of a party to the conflict controlled by the opponent. A grave breach of AP I is committed if an attack is directed against the civilian population or individual civilians of such areas.[65] Attacks which harm the civilian population incidentally do not fall under the prohibition of Art. 85, para. 3 lit. a.

12. The prerequisite for a grave breach is intent; the attack must be intentionally directed at the civilian population or individual civilians and the intent must embrace physical consequences. If this is not the case, there is no grave breach, but rather a violation of the Protocol which gives rise to disciplinary proceedings.

13. In accordance with Art. 51, para. 1 AP I, even a threat made with the primary goal of spreading fear through the civilian population is forbidden. Such offences are breaches, but not grave breaches, of the Protocol.

— **Compelling prisoners of war and civilians to serve in the forces of the adversary (Arts. 129–131 GC III).**

14. This prohibition derives from Art. 130 GC III, which forbids the pressing of prisoners of war into such service, and the compulsion of a prisoner of war to serve in the fighting forces of the detaining power. In accordance with Art. 23 HagueReg it is forbidden for the belligerent country to enlist nationals of the opposing party to participate in the conduct of war against their own country. This is also true in case where they were enlisted before the outbreak of war. It is likewise prohibited to impose an obligation on the civilian population of an occupied area to serve in the occupier's forces or to work for military purposes.[66] The rationale, according to Art. 52 of Hague IV, is that the population should not be obliged to participate in the conduct of war against their homeland. In the war crime trials after World War II, several judgments condemned offences against this principle.[67]

— **Deportation, illegal transfer, or confinement of protected civilians (Arts. 146–148 GC IV; Arts. 50, 51, 57, 85, para. 4 lit. a AP I).**

15. The prohibition of deportation and illegal transfer of civilians[68] results from Art. 147 GC IV. It embraces breaches of Arts. 45 and 49 GC IV. A transfer of the population is allowed only if it serves the security of the population involved. Deportation for the deployment of labour is forbidden, whether of not such labour is of military or civilian significance. The Hague Law does not contain a particular prohibition of this sort, but in the aftermath of World War I the deportation of sections of the Belgian civilian population to Germany for compulsory work was already seen as unlawful, even by the German *Reichstag*.[69] Today, Art. 49 GC IV

---

[65] Cf. Partsch, in Bothe/Partsch/Solf, 516; Solf, ibid. 300 ff.   [66] Greenspan, 177.

[67] Cf. the proceedings against Milch, *loc. cit.*, 39.

[68] For reference to the term 'Civilians' see Sections 541–6.

[69] A number of war criminals were convicted of violations against this principle after World War II; cf. the process against IG-Farben, in US Military Tribunal *Law Reports of Trials of War Criminals*, vol. X, 1949, 1 (53); Krupp *et al.*, ibid. 69 (142); Milch *loc. cit.*, 39.

contains the necessary clarification. Individual or mass deportations, as well as displacement of protected persons from occupied areas to territories of the occupying power or elsewhere, is forbidden, whatever the reasons underlying such displacement. Art. 45 GC IV also forbids the delivery of protected persons to another power.

16. A special ruling for children is contained in Art. 78 AP I. This provides that evacuation of children who are not nationals of the evacuating power is acceptable only for medical treatment and with the written consent of the parents or those primarily responsible for the care of children. Evacuation of children from an occupied area is permitted for reasons of safety. A violation of Art. 78 AP I constitutes a breach of the prohibition of 'illegal transfer'.

17. The prohibition of illegal confinement of civilians creates practical problems. The occupying power has the right to take prisoners under certain conditions, for its security or for criminal prosecution. However, confinement or internment is forbidden without legitimate reason.

— **Starvation of civilians by destroying, removing, or rendering useless objects indispensable to the survival of the civilian population (e.g. foodstuffs, means for the production of foodstuffs, drinking water installations and supplies, irrigation works) (Art. 54 AP I; Art. 14 AP II).**

18. In accordance with Art. 51 AP I and Art. 13 AP II, the civilian population and individual civilians enjoy general protection from dangers arising from military action. This principle is enforced by Art. 54, paras. 1 and 2 AP I and Art. 14 AP II, which prohibit the starvation of the civilian population as a means of conducting war. The objective is to preserve facilities, institutions, and objects indispensable for the survival of the civilian population.

19. Even though these codifications were introduced into international humanitarian law by the Additional Protocols, their groundwork was laid in Arts. 23 and 53 GC IV. Pursuant to these provisions, passage is to be guaranteed for shipments of medicines and medical supplies, objects necessary for religious services, and essential foodstuffs, clothing, and medicines for those in special need of protection. Art. 53 GC IV prohibits unnecessary destruction of movable and immovable property.[70]

20. The catalogue of grave breaches contained in Art. 85 AP I does not expressly mention the violation of Art. 54 AP I. Starvation of a population through destruction of facilities, institutions, and objects necessary for survival, however, always constitutes an attack on the civilian population (Art. 85, para. 3 lit. a AP I).

---

[70] Art. 13 AP II acquires greater significance since the rules of Protocol II governing non-international armed conflict lack a clause regarding general protection of objects such as that found in Art. 52 AP I. See Sections 451–63.

— **Destruction or appropriation of goods, carried out unlawfully and wantonly without any military necessity (Art. 50 GC I; Art. 147 GC IV).**

21. This prohibition summarizes a number of grave breaches of the Geneva Law. In accordance with Art. 50 GC I, the destruction and appropriation of protected goods constitutes a grave breach if it is not justified by military necessity, and if protected goods are taken on a large scale, unlawfully, and arbitrarily. The term 'protected goods' is defined in Arts. 33–6 GC I. Medical institutions, whether fixed or mobile, come within the ambit of this provision. Other goods protected under GC II include mobile medical units, coastal rescue craft, hospital ships, transport ships for the wounded, and air ambulances (Arts. 22, 23, 24, 25, 27, 28, 38, and 39). Finally, GC IV prohibits the destruction of property within the occupied territory by an occupying power (Art. 53), unless destruction is clearly necessary to fulfil military objectives. Not included in this prohibition is the destruction of property at the battle-front.

22. The expropriation of protected objects is also forbidden unless the special requirements of the Geneva Conventions for such types of appropriations are met.

— **Launching an indiscriminate attack in the knowledge that it will have adverse effects on civilian life and civilian objects (Art. 85, para. 3 lit. b AP I).**

23. The prohibition, and punishment as a grave breach, of an 'indiscriminate attack in the knowledge that such attack will have adverse effects on civilian life and civilian objects' (collateral damage) corresponds with Art. 85, para. 3 lit. b and Art. 51, para. 4 AP I. This prohibition is a concretization of the obligations enshrined in Arts. 48 and 52 AP I.[71] The regulation of Art. 85, para. 3 lit. b AP I serves to reinforce the general principle that military actions against combatants must be aimed at military objects (Arts. 48 and 52 AP I), and Art. 52 AP I defines the term 'civilian objects'.

24. The regulation of Art. 85, para. 3 lit. b AP I contains two qualifications: the indiscriminate attack must be intentional and it must be known in advance that this attack will lead to a disproportionately high loss of life, wounding of civilians, or damage to civilian property.

25. Specification of which collateral damage is considered 'disproportionate' can be found in Art. 57, para. 2 lit. a(iii) AP I.[72] This provides that a balance is required between concrete, direct military advantage and the requirement that the civilian population be protected. However, Art. 57, para. 2 lit.a AP I is broader in regard to the situations covered than the penal standard in Art. 85, para. 3 AP I. Art. 57, para. 2 lit. a(i) and (ii) AP I require particular precautionary measures when planning and carrying out attacks. An attack, however, will only be considered illegal when the prerequisites of Art. 57, para. 2(iii) AP I are fulfilled, i.e. when the precautionary

---

[71] See Sections 451–63.   [72] Ibid.

measures were manifestly insufficient. A serious breach of AP I is committed however, when knowledge of the disproportionality of collateral damage exists.[73]

26. An attack on civilians with the 'primary goal' of spreading terror throughout the
civilian population constitutes a grave breach (Art. 85, para. 2 lit. a AP I). Pursuant
to Art. 51, para. 2 (second sentence) AP I this is strictly forbidden, although in practice these types of terror attacks are frequently committed. Two of the most prominent examples since World War II are the Iraqi attacks on Israeli cities during the
Gulf War (1991) and the bombardment by the Yugoslav army and Serbian militia
during the Yugoslav conflict (1991/92).[74]

— **Launching an attack against works or installations containing dangerous
   forces (dams, dykes, and nuclear electricity generating stations), expecting
   that such an attack will cause excessive loss of life, injury to civilians, or damage to civilian objects (Art. 85, para. 3 lit. c AP I; Art. 15 AP II).**

27. This regulation is based on Art. 85, para. 3 lit. c AP I. Reference is made to Art.
56 AP I, by which some institutions enjoy absolute protection. Institutions of this
sort must also not be attacked if they are of military significance to the extent that
the attack can lead to the release of dangerous forces (overflow, radioactivity) which
would lead to grievous injury of the civilian population. This holds equally true
whether the attack on such facilities is deliberate or the incidental result of strikes
on other military objects.

28. A comparable rule is found in Art. 15 AP II. AP II, however, does not recognize
the concept of grave breaches, and prosecution of breaches is by domestic criminal
law.

— **Launching an attack against an undefended locality, demilitarized zone, or
   neutralized zone (Art. 85, para. 3 lit. d AP I; Art. 15 AP II).**

29. Undefended localities are described in Art. 59 AP I.[75] Localities of this sort may
not be attacked by the parties to the conflict for any reason. The same is true for
demilitarized zones, according to Art. 60 AP I.[76] A grave breach of international
humanitarian law is committed if an undefended locality or demilitarized zone is
intentionally made the object of attack which results in death or serious harm to the
physical integrity or health of persons in the area.

— **Launching an attack against defenceless persons (Art. 85, para. 3 lit. e AP I).**

30. The category of defenceless persons is defined by Art. 41 AP I. This notion covers persons who find themselves under the control of a hostile party, who unmistakably announce their intention to surrender, or who are unconscious or

---

[73] Partsch, in Bothe/Partsch/Solf, 516. ICRC *Commentary*, Art. 85, para. 3479.
[74] See Section 451.   [75] See Sections 458–61.   [76] See Sections 461–3.

Wolfrum

otherwise unable to defend themselves due to injury or sickness, as long as they refrain from hostile actions and do not attempt to escape. A grave breach is committed if the attacker knows that the person is incapable of fighting. It is not enough, however, to say that the attacker was obliged to infer this from the circumstances.[77]

— Unjustifiable delay in the repatriation of prisoners of war and civilians (Art. 85, para. 4 lit. b AP I).

31. In accordance with Art. 109 GC III, seriously wounded or seriously ill prisoners of war must be repatriated to their own countries even during a military conflict. In addition, after termination of the hostilities an obligation exists to release and repatriate prisoners of war immediately. Unjustifiable delay in repatriation constitutes a grave breach. A delay is unjustifiable when there are no objective reasons for it and the delay furthers no corresponding reasons which the custodian state has invoked.

32. The situation concerning the civilian population differs from that of prisoners of war. In accordance with Art. 35 GC IV all protected persons who wish to leave the conflict area during the course of the conflict have the right to do so, as long as their departure does not conflict with national interests. In other words, a grave breach is committed if civilians are denied departure without sufficient reason.[78]

33. A grave breach is also committed according to Art. 85, para. 4 lit. b AP I if a civilian population lawfully displaced in accordance with Art. 49 GC IV is not allowed to return promptly. This should be differentiated from the rule contained in Art. 85, para. 4 lit. a AP I, which provides that a grave breach is committed if the occupying power either uses a portion of its own civilian population to colonize an occupied territory (in violation of Art. 49 GC IV) or expatriates segments of the civilian population native to an occupied territory (in violation of Art. 49 GC IV). Art. 49 GC IV sets strict limits on the resettlement of civilian populations native to occupied territories. Violations of these constitute grave breaches under Art. 147 GC IV. In this respect Art. 85, para. 4 lit. a AP I has a merely repetitive character.

34. On the other hand, the classification of colonization of an occupied territory by the occupying power's civilian population as a grave breach is new to humanitarian law. The reasons underlying this reclassification (Art. 49, para. 6 GC IV) as a grave breach are recent experiences in the Middle East, as well as the desire to protect established populations from foreign infiltration and control. In addition, this provision is intended to prevent the creeping annexion of occupied territories. It has gained greatly in significance in the light of the Yugoslav conflict.

---

[77] Partsch, in: Bothe/Partsch/Solf, 517; ICRC *Commentary*, Art. 85, para. 3493.
[78] ICRC *Commentary*, Art. 85, para. 3509.   ·

— The practice of apartheid and other inhumane and degrading practices based on racial discrimination (Art. 85, para. 4 lit. c AP I).

35. Examples of such serious breaches include segregation on the basis of race within prisoner of war camps, or bad treatment (or worse) handling of specific ethnic groups. Most of the practices condemned here fall under the category of 'inhumane practices'. The notion of 'apartheid' is defined by the International Convention on the Suppression and Punishment of the Crime of Apartheid.[79] The term 'racial discrimination' is from Art. 1 of the International Convention on the Elimination of all Forms of Racial Discrimination, GA Res. 2106 A (XX) of 21 December 1965.

— Extensive destruction of cultural property and places of worship (Art. 85, para. 4 lit. d AP I; Art. 16 AP II).

36. Arts. 53 AP I and 16 AP II, without prejudice to the Protection of Cultural Property in the Event of Armed Conflict,[80] forbid all acts of hostility directed against historical monuments, works of art, or places of worship which constitute the cultural or intellectual heritage of peoples and which have been given special protection based upon specific conventions, for example within the framework of a competent international organization.[81] More specifically, it is forbidden to use such articles to attain military objectives.[82]

37. According to Art. 85, para. 4 lit. d AP I, a breach of the duty to protect cultural property constitutes a grave breach of the Protocol if the attack was directed at such a protected object, if the object was plainly protected, and if it suffered extensive damage. No violation occurs if the object attacked was being used primarily to support military objectives (Art. 53, lit. b AP I) or was located in the immediate vicinity of a military facility. The violation can be attributed to any military leader, even one in charge of a small unit, as long as that leader was competent to decide upon the target of the attack concerned.

— Prevention of a fair and regular trial (Art. 3, para. 3 lit. d GC I; Art. 3, para. 1 lit. d GC III; Art. 85, para. 4 lit. e AP I).

38. GC Art. 3, para. 1 lit. d prohibits the passing of sentences and carrying out of executions without previous judgment pronounced by a regularly constituted court, affording all the judicial guarantees which are recognized as indispensable by civilized people. Art. 50 GC I does not classify this violation as a grave breach of the Convention. The situation in GC III and GC IV is different.

39. Arts. 99–108 GC III and Arts. 71–5 and 126 GC IV contain corresponding procedural guarantees, as does Art. 75 AP I.[83]

[79] G Res. 3068 (XXVIII) of 30 Nov. 1973.   [80] See above.
[81] See Section 901.   [82] See Section 903.
[83] See Sections 714–26.

40. According to Art. 130 GC III and Art. 147 GC IV, the wilful deprivation of a prisoner of war's right to a fair and impartial trial, as described in GC III and IV, is a grave breach. This principle is also found in Art. 85, para. 4 lit. e of AP I where it is expanded to encompass all protected peoples.

— **Perfidious (Art. 37 AP I) use of recognized protective signs (Art. 53, para. 1 GC I; Art. 45 GC II; Art. 185, para. 3 lit. f AP I; Art. 12 AP II).**

41. The improper use of the Red Cross or Red Crescent emblem or any other emblems, signs, or signals which create such illusion was originally forbidden by Art. 53, para. 1 GC I. Art. 45 GC II prohibits the misuse of emblems designated for hospital ships. Art. 38 AP I expands this prohibition to include improper use of the Red Cross and misuse of all other symbols, markings, or signals adopted by the Geneva Conventions and Protocols.[84] The abuse of any other international symbols, markings, or signals, such as the flag of truce, is also prohibited.

42. According to Art. 85, para. 3 lit. f AP I, perfidious use of the distinctive emblems of the Red Cross in violation of Art. 37 AP I is a grave breach, if it is wilfully committed and leads to death or serious injury. The word 'perfidious', as used in Art. 85, para. 3 lit. f, makes clear that the action must be intended to deceive the opponent. Unintentional use of these symbols does not constitute a grave breach.

— **Use of prohibited weapons.**

43. This prohibitive norm is based upon Art. 23 HagueReg and specific international treaties. Forbidden weapons include particularly those which cause superfluous injury and unnecessary suffering.[85]

44. Neither the Geneva nor the Hague Law sees the infringement of this provision as a grave breach. Its characterization as such in national regulations is nonetheless allowed. This supports the special significance placed upon these prohibitions for humanitarian purposes.[86]

1210   Serious violations of international humanitarian law are covered by the general subject matters identified in the German national penal code (*Strafgesetzbuch*, or StGB), which particularly include offences against:

— life (ss. 211 ff.);

— body and health (ss. 223 ff.);

— personal liberty (ss. 234 ff.);

---

[84] Counted among these are the individual indications and identifying features in accordance with Art. 38 GC I; GC IV, Annex I, Art. 6; Art. 66 AP I and Annex I; see Section 473.

[85] Art. 35, para. 1 AP I; cf. also the Biological Weapons Convention as well as the St Petersburg Declaration of 1868 and the Declaration of 1899 on the prohibition of dum-dum bullets; see Section 402.

[86] Also Greenspan, 317.

— personal property (ss. 242 ff.);

— offences constituting a public danger (ss. 306 ff.); and

— offences committed in execution of official duties (ss. 331 ff.).

1. The regulations concerning all the grave breaches listed in Section 1209 have been incorporated into German criminal law statutes. The injury and killing of civilians as well as the seizure or destruction of property during armed conflicts breach numerous penal provisions. The actions may be justified if committed within the framework of a military conflict. However, there is no justification for violations of international humanitarian law.

2. Sections 211 ff. of the German Penal Code cover all crimes involving death, i.e. offences of which the collective shame lies in the killing of one or more individuals. Included in these provisions are offences causing the death of protected persons, for example by starving persons to death, through indiscriminate attacks, assaults on facilities containing dangerous forces, aggression against undefended localities, perfidious and unauthorized use of recognized protective symbols, or the use of forbidden weapons.

3. If the above-mentioned actions lead to non-fatal personal injury, then the violations will be termed offences against the bodily integrity of others (s. 223 StGB). These provisions protect the bodily integrity and health of all persons, while the effects of violations can be either physical or psychological in nature.[87]

4. Compelling prisoners of war and civilians to serve in the armed forces of the adversary falls under the statutory crime of s. 240 StGB. Deportation, illegal transfer, or confinement of protected civilians is also punishable under s. 240 StGB, and may also fall under the rubric of persecution under s. 239 StGB (false imprisonment). The same is true of unjustifiable delay in the repatriation of prisoners of war and civilians. For the case of hostage-taking, which is forbidden by international humanitarian law, s. 239b StGB. The minimum sentence for such actions is five years' imprisonment.

5. The destruction of public and private property and its unjust expropriation, neither of which is permissible under the law of war, is made punishable by s.303 StGB (destruction of property), ss. 242 ff. StGB (theft) or ss. 249 ff. StGB (robbery). In the case of destruction of private or public property, ss. 306 ff. StGB (offences dangerous to the public) will generally apply.

6. In addition, in specific cases of grave breaches of international humanitarian law, the elements necessary for criminal offences by officials in the course of duty (s. 331 StGB) may be present.

---

[87] Schönke/Schröder, *Strafgesetzbuch, Kommentar* (1991 edn.), 24. s. 223, No. 1.

1211   According to s. 125 of the Administrative Offences Act (*Ordnungswidrig-keitengesetz*), the misuse of the emblem of the Red Cross or of the heraldic emblem of Switzerland constitutes an administrative offence, liable to a fine (see Section 638).

Section 1211 expands upon Section 1209. According to Section 1211, a misuse of a recognized protective emblem is a grave breach, if wilfully committed and causing death or serious injury. An administrative offence is committed whenever the Red Cross or Red Crescent are used without authorization, even if the conditions required in Section 1209 have not occurred.

1212   The abuse of distinctive emblems and names which, according to the rules of international law, are equal in status to the Red Cross may also be prosecuted (s. 125, para. 4, Administrative Offences Act).

See Section 1211.

1213   When a disciplinary superior learns about incidents substantiating suspicion that international law has been violated, he shall clarify the facts and consider whether disciplinary measures are to be taken. If the disciplinary offence constitutes a criminal offence, he shall refer the case to the appropriate criminal prosecution authority when criminal prosecution seems to be indicated (Sections 28, para. 1, 29, paras. 2 and 3 Military Disciplinary Code, in connection with Art. 87, para. 3 AP I).

1. Section 1213 expands upon Section 1207. Not only can criminal responsibility attach to superiors for a grave breach by their subordinates , but the officers themselves are generally under an obligation to prevent such injuries, and if necessary to report such violations,[88] and further to impose disciplinary or criminal punishment.[89]

2. The question of whether disciplinary punishment is sufficient or whether the case should be referred to criminal prosecutors is decided in Germany by martial law. According to Section 29, para. 3 of the German Military Disciplinary Code, a case must be referred to federal prosecutors when any suspicion exists that a criminal offence has occurred. The possibility of military disciplinary punishment remains even after a case has been handed over to the prosecutor.

VII. COMPENSATION

1214   A party to a conflict which does not comply with the provisions of international humanitarian law shall be liable to pay compensation. It shall be responsible for

---

[88] Art. 87, para. 1 AP I.   [89] Art. 87, para. 3 AP I.

all acts committed by persons forming part of its armed forces (Art. 91 AP I; Art. 3 HC IV).

1. The obligation to compensate can be traced to Art. 91 AP I, which copies Art. 3 HC IV verbatim. At the time that this norm was written, it was believed that this article would provide an effective method for enforcement of the Hague Regulations. It corresponds with the principle, as developed both in state practice and in international decisions, that a breach of international law caused by an individual state will serve as grounds for its responsibility.[90]

2. In practice, however, this basic principle of the law of war has never been enforced. More often, the victor demands compensatory payment from the defeated (reparation) without extracting compensation for each individual violation. This tendency attempts to counter Art. 51 GC I (Art. 52 GC II, Art. 131 GC III, and Art. 148 GC IV), as the contracting states strive to free themselves or another state from responsibility for breaches committed.

3. The obligation to provide compensation for violations of international humanitarian law applies equally to each party to the conflict, whether aggressor or defender.

4. The service regulations speak only of the violation of the humanitarian law of war. A compensatory obligation for breach of the law concerning the conduct of war does not fall within its scope.

5. Pursuant to Art. 91 AP I compensation must be paid only if violation of international humanitarian law causes compensatable damages (personal injuries, material and property damage, etc). An obligation to compensate for simple violation of law has not yet been accepted under international law.

6. The second sentence of Section 1214 evolved from the system of international law of state responsibility. Pursuant to this, a state is accountable only for the acts of persons acting in an official capacity. The sentence is clear on the point that every act of a member of the armed forces, whether or not committed under orders, and whether or not they fall within the realm of duties, is attributable to the relevant state. Thus liability is strict.

VIII. PROTECTING POWERS AND THEIR SUBSTITUTES

It is the duty of the parties to a conflict from the beginning of that conflict to   1215
appoint protecting powers to safeguard the interests of these parties (Art. 5, para.

---

[90] Ipsen, *Völkerrecht*, 490 for further supporting evidence.

1 AP I). For this purpose, each party to the conflict shall designate a protecting power (Art. 8, para. 1 GC I; Art. 8, para. 1 GC II; Art. 8, para. 1 GC III; Art. 9, para. 1 GC IV). The party involved shall, without delay and for the same purpose, permit the activities of a protecting power which has been acknowledged by it as such after designation by the adverse party. The International Committee of the Red Cross may assist in the designation of protecting powers (Art. 5, para. 3 AP I).

1. The institution of the protecting power is of ancient nature. Its incorporation into an international agreement, however, occurred for the first time in Art. 86 of the Geneva Convention of 1929 relative to the Treatment of Prisoners of War. The four Geneva Conventions of 1949 all contain provisions regarding protecting powers (Arts. 8–10 GC I; Arts. 8–10 GC II; Arts. 8–10 GC III; and Art. 9–11 GC IV). They regulate the procedure of appointment and the functions of the protecting powers, although rather imperfectly. Further particulars of the procedure of the designation of a protecting power appear in Art. 5, para. 1 AP I; this relies on the proceedings developed by international customary law.

2. There are four possibilities for the appointment of a protecting power. Art. 5, para. 2 AP I provides first for appointment through a trilateral agreement between the determining party, the opposing party, and the protecting power. Following this, a belligerent appoints a state not party to the conflict to safeguard its interests in view of the other parties engaged in the conflict. The prospective protecting power, as well as the state with which the party is actively engaged in armed conflict must agree to this selection. The second and more likely possibility is that the appointment of protecting powers will be accomplished through the mediation efforts of the International Committee of the Red Cross (ICRC) after the trilateral method fails. The reasons why states could not agree in the appointment of protecting powers are irrelevant for the involvement of the ICRC. In order to achieve the appointment of protecting powers the ICRC can summon a party—here the third procedure comes into play—to present it with a list of at least five states that it judges to be acceptable to act as a protecting power against the hostile party. Each opposing party can be called concurrently to submit a list of at least five states which they would recognize as protecting powers. The ICRC compares both lists and requests the consent of a state specified on both lists to act as a protecting power. If no appointment of a protecting power is reached through this method, the possibility exists that the parties will designate the ICRC or another international organization as a substitute protecting power in accordance with Art. 5, para. 4 AP I.[91]

3. The duties of the protecting powers are enshrined in Art. 5, para. 1 AP I. According to that provision they must safeguard the interests of the parties to the conflict. The functions of the protecting powers are not completely defined. As follows from the four Geneva Conventions, it is the duty of the protecting powers to ensure compliance with international humanitarian law.[92]

[91] See Section 1216.   [92] See Section 1217.

If there is no protecting power, the parties to the conflict are obliged to accept an   1216
offer of the International Committee of the Red Cross or of any other impartial
and efficient organization to act as a substitute (Art. 5, para. 4 AP I).

The final possibility is that the parties to the conflict recognize the ICRC or another
impartial organization as a substitute protecting power. Despite unclear wording it
seems that a corresponding obligation to accept exists. Only this interpretation of
the obligation contained in Art. 5, para. 1 AP I allows the contracting states to avail
themselves of the system of protecting powers.

Protecting powers and their substitutes shall have a duty to safeguard the inter-   1217
ests of the party to the conflict which has designated them and to encourage compliance with international humanitarian law in an impartial manner (Art. 5 AP I).

The protecting power's duties are described generally in Art. 5, para. 1 AP I, which
gives protecting powers the duty to safeguard the interests of the parties to the conflict. The particulars of their functions as protecting powers follow from the rights
of the countries they represent pursuant to Geneva Law. According to Art. 126,
paras. 1–3 GC III the representatives or delegates of the protecting powers have a
free right of access to the places of internment of prisoners of war.[93] According to
Art. 143, paras. 1–4 GC IV they have the right to enter all places where protected persons may be.This is particularly true for places of internment, confinement, or
work. In accordance with Art. 30 GC IV protected persons can appeal to the protecting powers of the ICRC and of any other aid organization. According to Art. 105,
para. 5 GC III the representatives of protecting powers have the right to attend trials of war criminals. The same holds true for trials of civilians in occupied territories
(Art. 74, para. 1 GC IV). Finally, in accordance with Art. 55, para. 3 GC IV, it can be
determined by protecting powers whether sufficient foodstuffs and medical supplies are available in the occupied territories. In addition, according to Art. 5 of the
Regulations for the Execution of the Convention for the Protection of Cultural
Property in the Event of Armed Conflict, protecting powers can also verify violations of that Convention.

IX. INTERNATIONAL FACT FINDING

The International Fact Finding Commission (Art. 90 AP I) was established on 25   1218
June 1991. It is comprised of fifteen independent members and shall investigate
any incident alleged to be a grave breach or a serious violation of the rules of international humanitarian law within states which have recognized the competence
of the Commission.

---

[93] See Sections 714–26.

Wolfrum

1. Art. 52 GC I, Art. 53 GC II, Art. 132 GC III, and Art. 149 GC IV had previously provided for the creation of a fact-finding commission upon the request of a party to a conflict. Although the ICRC *Commentary* has always seen this provision as binding,[94] such an investigation has never yet been conducted. The probability for this is also slight, as the accused party can escape simply by refusing to permit an international investigation of the incident. Art. 90 AP I attempts to improve the procedure. A thorough revision of the procedure has not been achieved, however, since Art. 90 AP I finally provided for a consensual institution of such a fact-finding commission. However, a party can declare in advance by signing or ratifying AP I that it recognizes the competence of such a fact-finding commission *vis-à-vis* every other contracting party which accepts the same obligation. Such declarations have been submitted by 42 states (as of July 1995).[95] The functions of the Commission are: the investigation of all activities alleged to constitute a grave breach or other serious violation of the Geneva Conventions or AP I; good offices contributing to adherence to the Geneva Conventions and AP I; other investigations at the request of one party to a conflict and with the agreement of the other.

2. In accordance with Art. 90, para. 5 lit. c AP I the Commission does not publicly communicate the results of its fact-finding, unless all parties to the conflict so request.

1219   In the case of serious violations, the contracting parties are further bound to act, jointly or individually, in co-operation with the United Nations and in conformity with the United Nations Charter (Art. 89 AP I).

1. Art. 89 AP I is only understandable in the light of the history of its creation. It is the result of a long debate over whether to prohibit all reprisals or to allow them only under strictly limited conditions.[96]

2. Art. 89 AP I explains which actions the contracting states of AP I or the United Nations respectively can take to ensure observance of international humanitarian law. The most likely measures arise from Chapter VII of the UN Charter, i.e. economic and military measures through the Security Council. The Security Council has taken this path in the cases of Iraq, Somalia, and the former Yugoslavia.

3. With Security Council Resolution 688 of 5 April 1991, serious violations of human rights are classified as a threat to the peace and security of the region, thus clearing the way for Security Council activities based on Chapter VII of the Charter.

[94] Pictet (Ed.), *Commentary*, Vol. III, 632.

[95] Algeria, Australia, Austria, Belarus, Belgium, Bolivia, Bosnia and Herzegovina, Brazil, Bulgaria, Canada, Cape Verde, Czech Republic, Chile, Croatia, Denmark, Finland, Germany, Holy See, Hungary, Iceland, Italy, Liechtenstein, Luxembourg, Madagascar, Malta, The Netherlands, New Zealand, Norway, Poland, Portugal, Qatar, Roumania, Russian Federation, Seychelles, Slovakia, Slovenia, Spain, Sweden, Switzerland, Togo, Ukraine, United Arab Emirates, and Uruguay. For a history of negotiations see Kussbach 'Commission internationale d'établissement des faits', *RDMilG* 20 (1981) 78; Partsch, in Bothe/Partsch/Solf, 537 ff.

[96] See Section 1206.

Wolfrum

Until that time, no Security Council Resolution had taken so serious a step. The Security Council had addressed serious human rights violations in South Rhodesia in Resolutions 217 of 20 November 1965 and 221 of 19 April 1966, but its measures were justified by the danger of military conflict between South Rhodesia and neighbouring states.

3. The line adopted in Resolution 688 was pursued by the Security Council also in the case of Somalia. Resolution 794 of 3 December 1992 focuses exclusively on serious human rights violations which justify measures pursuant to Chapter VII. The Security Council entered the case of the former Yugoslavia as a result of violations of international humanitarian law. Resolutions 764 of 13 July 1992 and 780 of 6 October 1992 emphasized the obligation of parties to the conflict to obey international humanitarian law and initiated steps towards the prosecution of war criminals. Even if the measures enforced pursuant to Chapter VII relied mainly on the violation of Bosnia-Herzegovina's territorial integrity, the serious violations of international humanitarian law also legitimized the measures.

X. THE INTERNATIONAL COMMITTEE OF THE RED CROSS

The International Committee of the Red Cross (ICRC) is an independent human-   1220
itarian organization based in Geneva. Its principal purpose is to provide protection and assistance to the victims of armed conflict. The members of the ICRC and delegates acting in its name are Swiss citizens. The Geneva Conventions and their Additional Protocols recognize the special status of the ICRC and assign specific tasks to it, including visiting prisoners of war and civilian internees, providing relief to the population of occupied territories, selecting and transmitting information concerning missing persons, (Central Tracing Agency), and offering its good offices to facilitate the establishment of hospital and safety zones. The ICRC is entirely dedicated to promoting the faithful application of the Geneva Conventions and their Additional Protocols. It endeavours to ensure the protection of military and civilian victims of armed conflict, and to serve as a neutral intermediary between belligerents. According to the Geneva Conventions the ICRC has a general right of initiative in humanitarian matters. Owing to its humanitarian activity, which is guided by the principles of humanity, impartiality, neutrality, independence, voluntary service, unity, and universality, the ICRC enjoys high respect and deserves support.

1. The ICRC is, in practice, the organ which monitors observance of the four Geneva Conventions and both Additional Protocols. It is assured through the nature of its organization that the ICRC performs its duties independently of government influence (including the Swiss government). The ICRC has continuous or temporary delegations in foreign countries which represent its interests to the host state's authorities.

Wolfrum

2. According to its own Statutes and Art. 6 of the Statutes of the Red Cross, the duties of the Committee are *inter alia*: to secure observation of the basic principles of the Red Cross; to work for the strengthening of international humanitarian law; to enforce humanitarian measures in civil wars and domestic conflicts; and to serve as protection and aid for military and civilian victims in such conflicts and as a mediator in humanitarian questions between parties to the conflict. In addition, the ICRC performs duties assigned to it by the Geneva Conventions and Additional Protocols. Of importance among these are the visiting of prisoners of war and interned civilians as well as the maintenance of the International Tracing Service. In addition, it is generally recognized that the ICRC monitors observance of Geneva Convention law, even though it has no express supervisory authority in this respect. It can only notify one party of violations complained of by another party and in this way initiate dialogue between the two conflicting parties.[97]

XI. DIPLOMATIC ACTIVITIES

1221   Compliance with international law may be ensured by using protest, good offices, mediation, investigation, and diplomatic intervention, whether by neutral states or by international bodies and religious or humanitarian organizations, as well as by sanctions decided upon by the United Nations Security Council.

1. Violations of international humanitarian law can trigger reactions from other states, when violations reach a certain gravity. Apart from measures taken by the United Nations,[98] it is quite possible that individual states or humanitarian organizations will engage in diplomatic intervention. With this intervention, in addition to the influence of bad publicity, diplomatic pressure can be brought to bear on the state to adhere to humanitarian provisions. Examples can be found in the recent history of international law, in which states have countered massive breaches of international law with sanctions, although they themselves were not directly involved in the conflict. The most appropriate example to date involves sanctions imposed by the community of states in response to the taking of hostages at the American Embassy in Teheran. On 22 April 1980, the European Community Foreign Ministers resolved, in the framework of European political cooperation, to carry out measures necessary for the imposition of sanctions against Iran.[99] The International Court upheld this concerted action in its later decision[100] on the hostage-taking in Teheran. It determined that international law violations concern the entire international law community and called upon that community to assist in this effort. A further example is the economic sanctions against Poland in reaction to the imposition of martial law on 13 November 1981.

---

[97] For organization and functions of the ICRC, cf.: Bindschedler Robert, *EPIL* 5, 248–54; Durand, *Histoire du Comité international de la Croix-Rouge*. Schlögel, in: Wolfrum (ed.), *United Nations: Law, Policies and Practice* (1995), 814 et seq.

[98] See Section 1219.   [99] *EC Bulletin* 1980, No. 4, 26 ff.   [100] ICJ Reports 1980, 3, 43 ff.

2. Such reactions can only be triggered through serious breaches of public international law, including that of humanitarian law.

XII. NATIONAL IMPLEMENTING MEASURES

According to Art. 59, para. 2 of the Basic Law of the Federal Republic of Germany   1222
international treaties become part of German law by the passing of a Federal Act.
Art. 25 of the Basic Law states that general rules of international law are part of the
national law, being directly applicable and taking precedence over all acts. This
applies also to the basic principles of humanitarian law. The relative weakness of
international measures to secure the performance of obligations under humanitarian law calls for national implementing efforts among which military manuals
are of particular importance.

The laws of international humanitarian law are an integral part of the German law
system, binding upon individuals as directly applicable law. Military regulations in
this context gain significance by importing humanitarian rules into the military
sphere and by making the humanitarian provisions known.

XIII. DISSEMINATION OF HUMANITARIAN LAW

Effective implementation is dependent upon dissemination of humanitarian law.   1223
Providing information about it is the necessary basis from which to educate and
to further the attitude of peoples towards a greater acceptance of these principles
as an achievement of the social and cultural development of mankind.

It has already been pointed out[101] that the observance of international humanitarian law can only be expected if all authorities, armed forces, and peoples are made
familiar with its contents.

XIV. PERSONAL RESPONSIBILITY OF THE INDIVIDUAL

Each individual shall be responsible for realizing the ideals of international   1224
humanitarian law and observing its provisions. Military leaders shall highlight
this by their own behaviour. They shall make clear that everyone is required by his
or her conscience to stand up for the preservation of the law.

---

[101] See Section 1201.

International humanitarian law is also binding on every individual. In addition, a powerful moral obligation flows from the realization that the objective of international law is to reduce, as far as possible, the human suffering caused by military conflicts.

Appendix 1: List of International Instruments

16 April 1856	Declaration respecting Maritime Law (Paris Declaration—ParisDecl 1856)
22 August 1864	Convention for the Amelioration of the Condition of the Wounded in Armies in the Field (now replaced by the First Geneva Convention of 1949)
29 Nov.11 Dec. 1868	Declaration Renouncing the use, in Time of War, of Explosive Projectiles under 400 Grammes Weight (St. Petersburg Declaration—PetersburgDecl 1868)
29 July 1899	Hague Declaration concerning Expanding Bullets (DumDum Bullets—HagueDecl 1899)
21 December 1904	Convention for the Exemption of Hospital Ships, in Time of War, from the Payment of all Dues and Taxes Imposed for the Benefit of the State
18 October 1907	Hague Convention (I) for the Pacific Settlement of International Disputes
18 October 1907	Hague Convention (II) respecting the Limitation of the Employment of Force for the Recovery of Contract Debts
18 October 1907	Hague Convention (III) relative to the Opening of Hostilities (HC III)
18 October 1907	Hague Convention (IV) respecting the Laws and Customs of War on Land (HC IV)
18 October 1907	Hague Convention (V) respecting the Rights and Duties of Neutral Powers and Persons in Case of War on Land (HC V)
18 October 1907	Hague Convention (VI) relating to the Status of Merchant Ships at the Outbreak of Hostilities (HC VI)
18 October 1907	Hague Convention (VII) relating to the Conversion of Merchant Ships into War-Ships (HC VII)
18 October 1907	Hague Convention (VIII) relative to the Laying of Automatic Submarine Contact Mines (HC VIII)
18 October 1907	Hague Convention (IX) concerning Bombardment by Naval Forces in Time of War (HC IX)
18 October 1907	Hague Convention (X) for the Adaptation to Naval War of the Principles of the Geneva Convention (now replaced by the Second Geneva Convention of 1949)
18 October 1907	Hague Convention (XI) relative to Certain Restrictions with regard to the Exercise of the Right of Capture in Naval War (HC XI)
18 October 1907	Hague Convention (XII) relative to the Creation of an International Prize Court (not entered into force)
18 October 1907	Hague Convention (XIII) concerning the Rights and Duties of Neutral Powers in Naval War (HC XIII)
18 October 1907	Hague Declaration (XIV) Prohibiting the Discharge of Projectiles and Explosives from Balloons (not entered into force)
26 February 1909	Declaration Concerning the Laws of Naval War (London Declaration—LondonDecl 1909)
19 February 1923	Hague Rules of Air Warfare, drafted by a Commission of Jurists (HRAW 1923)

17 June 1925	Protocol for the Prohibition of the Use of Asphyxiating, Poisonous or Other Gases, and of Bacteriological Methods of Warfare (Geneva Gas Protocol—GasProt)
27 July 1929	Convention for the Amelioration of the Condition of the Wounded and Sick in Armies in the Field (replaced by the First Geneva Convention of 1949)
27 July 1929	Convention relative to the Treatment of Prisoners of War (replaced by the Third Geneva Convention of 1949)
15 April 1935	Treaty on the Protection of Artistic and Scientific Institutions and Historic Monuments (Roerich Pact)
6 November 1936	*Procès-Verbal* relating to the Rules of Submarine Warfare set forth in Part IV of the Treaty of London of 22 April 1930 (London Protocol—LondonProt 1936)
9 December 1948	Convention on the Prevention and Punishment of the Crime of Genocide (Genocide Convention—GenocidConv)
12 August 1949	Geneva Convention (I) for the Amelioration of the Condition of Wounded and Sick in Armed Forces in the Field (GC I)
12 August 1949	Geneva Convention (II) for the Amelioration of the Wounded, Sick and Shipwrecked Members of Armed Forces at Sea (GC II)
12 August 1949	Geneva Convention (III) relative to the Treatment of Prisoners of War (GC III)
12 August 1949	Geneva Convention (IV) relative to the Protection of Civilian Persons in Time of War (GC IV)
14 May 1954	Convention for the Protection of Cultural Property in the Event of Armed Conflict (Cultural Property Convention—CultPropConv)
10 April 1972	Convention on the Prohibition of the Development, Production and Stockpiling of Bacteriological (Biological) and Toxin Weapons and on their Destruction (Biological Weapons Convention—BWC)
18 May 1977	Convention on the Prohibition of Military or any Other Hostile Use of Environmental Modification Techniques (ENMOD)
8 June 1977	Protocol Additional to the Geneva Conventions of 12 August 1949, and Relating to the Protection of Victims of International Armed Conflicts (Protocol I—AP I)
8 June 1977	Protocol Additional to the Geneva Conventions of 12 August 1949, and Relating to the Protection of Victims of Non-International Armed Conflicts (Protocol II—AP II)
10 October 1980	`Convention on Prohibitions or Restrictions on the Use of Certain Conventional Weapons Which May be Deemed to be Excessively Injurious or to Have Indiscriminate Effects (Inhumane Weapons Convention—WeaponsConv)
4 December 1989	International Convention Against the Recruitment, Use, Financing and Training of Mercenaries (Mercenary Convention—MercenaryConv)
9 December 1994	Convention on the Safety of United Nations and Associated Personnel

Appendix 2: Distinctive emblems

1.	or	**1** 38 **2** 41 **5** 18		**Red Cross / Red Crescent** Military and civil medical services : medical and military religious personnel, medical units and transports as well as civilian religious personnel employed in medical units and in civilian services
2.		**1** 44		International Red Cross Organization
3.		**4** Appendix 1, **para 6**		Hospital and Safety Zones
4.	PG or PW	**3** 23 **para 4**		Prisoner of War Camp
5.	IC	**4** 83		Internment Camp
6.		**5** 66 **para 4, 6**		**Distinctive Sign of Civil Defence** Civil Defence : Personnel, buildings and material of civil defence organizations

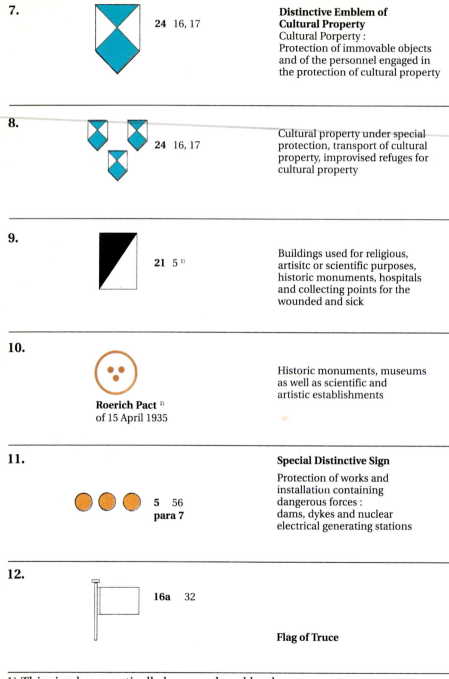

7. 24 16, 17

Distinctive Emblem of Cultural Property
Cultural Porperty :
Protection of immovable objects and of the personnel engaged in the protection of cultural property

8. 24 16, 17

Cultural property under special protection, transport of cultural property, improvised refuges for cultural property

9. 21 5 [1]

Buildings used for religious, artisitc or scientific purposes, historic monuments, hospitals and collecting points for the wounded and sick

10.

Roerich Pact [2]
of 15 April 1935

Historic monuments, museums as well as scientific and artistic establishments

11. 5 56
para 7

Special Distinctive Sign

Protection of works and installation containing dangerous forces :
dams, dykes and nuclear electrical generating stations

12. **16a** 32

Flag of Truce

1) This sign has practically been replaced by the distinctive emblem of cultural property (24 16, 17)
2) Applies only to North and South American countries

Appendix 3: Military and Red Cross Manuals on International Humanitarian Law

Partie III: *Précis d'instruction pour breveté d'Etat-Major et breveté d'administration militaire*

(6) *Ordre Général* -J/797- **Le conseiller en droit de la guerre** (CDG), 22 Feb. 91

(7) *Directive Provisoire sur* **l'enseignement de droit de la guerre** *au sein des forces armées*, Dec. 1990

BULGARIA

Jordan Puntschew, *Osnovnite poloshenijana meshdunarodnogo humanitarno pravo, Vojenno Izdatelstvo* 1991, 29 p

CANADA

(1) **Manual on the Geneva Conventions** of 12 August 1949, Canadian Forces Publication (CFP) 122

(2) **Unit Guide** to the Geneva Conventions, CFP 318 (4)

(3) Canadian Forces Office of the Judge Advocate General, **You and the Law of War**, 25 Articles
(*Vous et le droit de la guerre*)

(4) Canadian Forces Office of the Judge Advocate General, **Basic Law of Armed Conflict.** Course 9001
(*Cours de base—Droit de la guerre*)

(5) General Military Training—Volume 4—**Unit to the Geneva Conventions.**
(*Guide Régimentaire des conventions de Genève*)

(6) **Canadian Forces Law of Armed Conflict Manual** (Second Draft) 1984

CHINA

(1) Teaching Programme on the Law of War in People's Liberation Army of China (P.L.A.), 1991

(2) The Dissemination and Education of Armed Conflicts Law in the P.L.A., 1991

CZECH REPUBLIC

Frédéric de Mulinen, **Prírucka mezinárodního humanitárního práva pro ozbrojené síly,** Prague 1991, *Übersetzung aus dem Englischen* (see below, International Committee of the Red Cross, No. 7)

Haagské úmluvy v systému mezinárodního humanitárního práva, I. *díl* 1992, II. *díl* 1993

Zenevské úmluvy o ochrané obétí ozbrojenych konfkliktu z 12. *srpna* 1949, *Dodatkové pro-tokoly z 8. cervna* 1977

DENMARK

(1) *Dansk Rode Kors,* **Menneskerettigheder under vaebnede konflikter**

(2) *Dansk Rode Kors, Humanitaer Folkeret.* **Tekstsamling om humanitaer folkeret** *under veabnede konflikter*

FINLAND

(1) Gunnar Rosén, **Folkrätt i Krig, Handbok,** *Finlands Röda Kors* 1989, 187 p

(2) **Kausainväliset sopimukset** [International Agreements]

FRANCE

(1) **Le droit des gens et les conventions internationales,** *Bulletin officiel du Ministère de la guerre,* no. 110–0, 1955

(2) *Décret N 75–675 portant* **règlement de discipline générale dans les armées,** *28 juillet* 1975, *Journal officiel, Lois et décrets,* 1975, pages 7732–38; *modifié par décret* no. 78–1024 *du 11 octobre 1978* (BOC. 1979, p. 1712), décret no. 82–598 *du 12 juillet* 1982 (BOC. p. 3037), décret no. 85–914 *du 21 août 1985* (BOC. p. 5643), *décret* no. 87–233 *du 2 avril 1987* (BOC. p. 1560): articles 7, 8 para. 3, 9b, 10

GERMANY

(1) *ZDv* 15/1 *Humanitäres Völkerrecht in bewaffneten Konflikten—***Grundsätze***—*(in preparation)

(2) *ZDv* 15/2 *Humanitäres Völkerrecht in bewaffneten Konflikten—***Handbuch***—*1992 Humanitarian Law in Armed Conflicts—**Manual**—1992

(3) *ZDv* 15/3 *Humanitäres Völkerrecht in bewaffneten Konflikten—***Textsammlung***—*1991

(4) *ZDv* 15/4 *Humanitäres Völkerrecht in bewaffneten Konflikten—***Sammlung von Fällen mit Lösungen***—*(in preparation)

(5) **Die Genfer Rotkreuz-Abkommen** 12.August 1949 also *das Abkommen betreffend die Gesetze und Gebräuche des Landkrieges vom 18. Oktober 1907 und Anlage (Haager Landkriegsordnung), mit einer Einführung von Dr. Anton Schlögel,* 8. Aufl. 1988, XII

(6) **Handbuch des Deutschen Roten Kreuzes** *zum IV. Genfer Rotkreuz-Abkommen und zu den Zusatzprotokollen*:
Band 1: *Das* **IV. Genfer Abkommen** vom 12. August 1949 zum Schutze von Zivilpersonen in Kriegszeiten, **Textband,** *Bearbeiter*: Wolfgang Voit and Elmar Rauch, 1980 (Text of the Fourth Geneva Convention in German, English, French, and Russian),
Band 2: Zusatzprotokolle *zu den Genfer Abkommen vom 12. August 1949 über den Schutz der Opfer bewaffneter Konflikte,* **Textband,** *Bearbeiter*: Wolfgang Voit and Elmar Rauch, 1981 (Texts of the Additional Protocols in German, English, French, and Russian),
Heft 3: *Der Schutz der* **Zivilkrankenhäuser** *und ihres Personals, Bearbeiter*: Hans Giani, 1980,
Heft 4: Zivilschutz, *Bearbeiter*: Georg Bock, 1981
Heft 5: *Der Schutz im Bereich der* **öffentlichen Verwaltung,** *Bearbeiter*: Walter Hofmann, 1982
Heft 6: Polizei (*Vollzugspolizei der Länder, Bundesgrenz-schutz*), *Bearbeiter*: Ernst Rasch and H. Joppich, 1983
Heft 7: Heft für Juristen, *Bearbeiter*: Wolfgang Voit and Michael Bothe, 1984

(7) *Es begann in Solferino, Die Genfer Rotkreuz-Abkommen, Problemfälle—Beispiele—*

Sachverhalte, Lösung der beschriebenen Fälle, Handbuch für Lehrkräfte, Juristen und Konventionsbeauftragte, Deutsches Rotes Kreuz, Verfasser: Horst Seibt

(8) *Deutsches Rotes Kreuz,* **Das Amtliche Auskunftsbüro** (AAB) *der Bundesrepublik Deutschland nach den Genfer Abkommen, Handbuch mit Dienstanweisungen,* Bonn, 3. *Auflage, Stand* 1.8.1988

HUNGARY

Ferenc Almási, **A hadijogról** [Law of War] Zrínyi Kiadó, 1990

ISRAEL

(1) Brigadier General Ben-Zion Farhy, Military Advocate General, Israel Defense Forces, Current Legal Trends In The Areas Administered By Israel, May 1986

(2) Brigadier General Dov Shevi, Military Advocate General, Israel Defence Forces, The Status of the Legal Adviser to the Armed Forces: His Functions and Powers, *RDMilG* 1983, 259–76

(3) Representation of accused persons under the Israeli Military Justice System, *RDMilG* 1981, 359–85

ITALY

(1) *Stato Maggiore dell'Esercito, III Reparto, Ufficio Addestramento,* N. 1000/A/2: **Manuale del Combattente,** *Capo XVIII: Comportamento des Militare in Guerra* (106–11)

(2) *Stato Maggiore dell'Esercito,* **Raccolta delle convenzioni internazionali che riguardano la guerra terrestre**

(3) *Stato Maggiore dell'Esercito,* **Istruzioni concernenti I prigionieri die guerra memici**

(4) *Stato Maggiore dell'Esercito,* **Raccolta delle leggi nazionali relative ai conflitti armati ed alla neutralita'che riguardano la guerra terrestre**

(5) *Stato Maggiore dell'Esercito,* **Diritto umanitario e sua introduzione nelle regolamentazione dell'esertico italiano,** *volume primo: Leggi ed usi di guerra, 1991; volume secondo allegati: La protezione delle vittime della guerra*

(6) *Stato Maggiore della difesa,* **Manuale di diritto umanitario,** *volume I: Usi e convenzioni di guerra; volume II: Istruzioni concernenti i prigioneri di guerra nemeci; Volume III: Raccolta delle convenzioni internazionali relative ai conflitti armati; Volume IV: Raccolta delle leggi nazionali relative ai conflitti armati ed alle neutralita; Volume V: Indice analitico alfabetico ralativo al diritto umanitario dei conflitti armati vigenti in Italia*

(7) David Brunelli, *Reati contro le leggi e gli usi di guerra*

(8) Alessandro Marazzi, *Nozioni die diritto bellico*

(9) Pietro Verri, *Appunti die diritto bellico*

(10) Pietro Verri, *Dizionario die diritto internazionale dei conflitti armati*

(11) Pietro Verri, *Diritto per la pace e diritto nella guerra*

(12) *Rassegna della Giustizia Militare, Estratto del* n. 4–5 anno 1978, **I Protocolli Aggiuntivi alle Convenzioni di Ginevra** *del 12 Agosto 1949, traduzione e introduzione del Generale C.A.*(a) Pietro Verri

(13) Arturo Marcheggiano, *Diritti e doveri del cappellano militare in tempo die guerra*

JAPAN

(1) Sumio Adachi, *Gendai senso hohki ron* (The Modern Laws of War)

(2) Yuko Kurihara, *Defence of Japan*.

NETHERLANDS

(1) *Koninklijke Landmacht*, VS 27–412/1, Deel 1: **Toepassing Humanitar Oorlogsrecht** (*7 oktober 1993*)

(2) *Koninklijke Landmacht*, VS 27–412/2, Deel 2: **Verdragen Humanitair Orlogsrecht**

(3) **Handboek for de soldaat**, 1991

(4) MP 11–20/A, B, C, *Ministerie van Defensie*, **Humanitair Oorlogsrecht**

(5) *Ministerie van Buitenlandse Zaken*, Notification of 23 June 1989 concerning implementation measures relative to the Geneva Conventions and the Additional Protocols

NEW ZEALAND

New Zealand Defence Force, DM 112, *Interim Law of Armed Conflict Manual* (26 November 1992)

NIGERIA

Operational Code of Conduct for Nigerian Forces. Directive to all Officers and Men of the Armed Forces of the Federal Republic of Nigeria on Conduct of Military Operations, 1967

NORWAY

(1) *Overnskomster*, **Vedrorende Krigens Rett** *Som Norge Star Tilsluttet, Utgitt Av Det Kgl. Utenriksdepartement*, 1961, Grondahl & Sons *Boktrykkeri*

(2) Norges Rode Kors, **Menneskeretter i Krig**. *Genevekonvensjonene og andre folkerettsregler for vaepnet kamp*

(3) Norges Rode Kors, **Menneskerettigheter i Vaepnede Konflikter**

(4) Norges Rode Kors, **Prinsipper for opptreden i waepnede konflikter**

(5) Terje Lund, **Krigens Folkerett**, 5. Utgave 1992

(6) Terje Lund, *Undervisningsveiledning i Krigens Folkerett for Forsvarets Skoler*, 1990

POLAND

(1) **Miedzynarodowe Prawo Konfliktów Zbrojnych**, *Zbiór dokumentów, Wyboru dokonal oraz opatrzyl wstepem i przypisami* Marian Flemming, *Agencja Artekon, Warszawa*, 1991

(2) Marian Flemming, *Umowy Miedzynarodowe o ochronie ofiar wojny, Opracowal i wstepem opatrzyl, Polksi Czerwony Krzyz, Osrodek upowszechniania miedzynarodowego prawa humanitarnego, Panstwowy Zaklad Wydawnictw Lekarskich*, 1987

(3) Remigiusz Bierzanek, *Woina a prawo miedzynarodowe*, 1982

(4) A. Górbiel, *Problemy miedzynarodowego prawa wojennego, Wydawnictwo Ministerstwa Obrony Narodowej*, 1966

(5) Teofil Lésko, *Miedzynarodowe prawo konfliktów zbrojnych*, 1982

ROUMANIA

(1) Ionel Closca/Ion Suceava, *Dreptul International Umanitar*, 1992

(2) *Asociatia Romana de Drept Umanitar, Dreptul International Umanitar al Conflictelor Armate. Documente*, 1993

(3) *Asociatia Romana de Drept Umanitar, Protocoalele Aditionale la Conventiile de la Geneva din 12 August 1949 cu Privire la Protectia Victimelor de Razboi*, 1992

(4) Ionel Closca, *Razboiul naval si legile lui*, 1991

(5) Carmen Grigore/Ionel Closca/Gheorghe Badescu, *La protection des biens culturels en Roumanie*, 1994

RUSSIA

(1) *Prikas Ministra Oboronyi* SSSR No. 75, *16 Fevralja 1990 g ob objavlenii schenevskich konventsii o zaschtschitje schertv voinyi ot 12 Avgusta 1949 goda u dopolnitelnych protokolow k knim*, 1990

(2) I.N.Artsibasov/S.A.Jegorov, **Voorushenny Konflikt**: *Pravo, Politika, diplomatsija*, Mocow 1989

(3) **Voennoe Pravo**, *Utchebnik dlja voennyx akademii, pod redaktsiei* General-polkovnika justitsii A. G. Gornogo, 1984; *Glava 17: Osnovnye poloshenija meshdunarodnogo prava (voennye aspekti)*, 282–313

(4) **Voennomorskoj meshdunarodno-pravovoj spravocnik**, 1966

SPAIN

(1) *Estado Mayor del Ejercito*, **El Derrecho de los Confictos Armados, Manual**, 1995

(2) *Cruz Roja Española, I curso para mandos militares de las fuerzas armadas*

(3) *Temario Curso para Mandos Militares*. I–XVII

SWEDEN

(1) **Krigets Lagar**. *Folkrättsliga Konventioner Gällande under Krig, Neutralitet och Ockupation. Konventionssammling utgiven av Folkrättskommittén*, 1979

(2) **Folkrätten i Krig**, *Rättsregler under Väpnade Konflikter—tolkning, tillämpning och undervisning. Betänkande av folkrättskommittén*, 1984

International Humanitarian Law in Armed Conflict with reference to the Swedish Total Defence System, Stockholm 1991

(3) Torgil Wulff/ Ove Bring, **Handbok i Militärfolkrätt**, *Regler om Gränsskydd, Krigföring och Humanitet*, 1987

(4) *Totalförsvarets folkrättsförordning, svensk författningssamling* 1990:12

(5) *Överbefälhavens föreskrifter: Folkrättsliga rodgirare inom försvarsmakten*, 1988–07–07, *Utbildning i folkrätts inom försvarsmakten*, 1990–02–16,

SWITZERLAND

(1) **Gefallene, verstorbene, schwerverwundete, schwerkranke und vermisste Militärpersonen im Krieg,** (*Gefallenen- und Vermisstendienst/GVD*) **Militaires tombés, décédés, grands blessés et grands malades portés disparus en temps de guerre**

(2) **Gesetze und Gebräuche des Krieges,** 1984 **Lois et coutumes de la guerre Leggi e usi de la guerra**

(3) *Gesetze und Gebräuche des Krieges,* **Lehrschrift,** 1984

(4) *Gesetze und Gebräuche des Krieges,* (**Auszug und Kommentar**) *Règlement* 51.7/II d, 1987

(5) **Staatsverträge über bewaffnete Konflikte und Neutralität,** *Nachdruck* 1982 **Conventions internationales concernant des conflits armés et la neutralité**

(6) **Schweizerisches Inventar der Kulturgüter** *von nationaler und regionaler Bedeutung* **Inventaire suisse des biens culturels d'importance nationale et regionale**

(7) **Karte der Kulturgüter Carte des biens culturels Carta dei beni culturali**

(8) **Kriegsvölkerrechtliche Grundsätze für den Kommandanten,** 1991

UGANDA

Code of Conduct for the Army, Legal Notice No. 6 of 1986

UNITED KINGDOM

(1) JSP 381, *Aide-Mémoire* on the Law of Armed Conflict, 1 S.

(2) The War Office, WO Code No. 12333, **The Law Of War On Land**; Part III of the *Manual Of Military Law*, 1958

(3) Ministry of Defence, D/DAT/13/35/66 Army Code 71130, **The Law of Armed Conflict**, 1981

(4) *Manual of Air Force Law*, Fifth edn., Vol. II, Part VI: The Law of Armed Conflict. **International Conventions and Agreements**, 1982

USA

(1) Department of the Army Pamphlet No. 27–161–1, **International Law, Volume I**, 1964

561

(2) Department of the Army Pamphlet No. 27–161–2, **International Law Volume II**, 1962

(3) Department of the Army Pamphlet No. 27–1, **Treaties Governing Land Warfare**, 1956

(4) Department of the Army Pamphlet No. 27–1–1, **Protocols to the Geneva Conventions** of 12 August 1949, 1979

(5) Department of the Army Field Manual No. 27–2, **Your Conduct in Combat under the law of war**, 1984

(6) Department of the Army Field Manual No. 27–10, **The Law of Land Warfare**, 1956, 236 S.; Change No. 1, 1976

(7) Department of the Army Staff Officers Field Manual FM 101–31–1, **Nuclear Weapons Employment Doctrine And Procedures**, 1977

(8) Headquarters United States Army, Europe, and Seventh Army (USAREUR), Pamphlet No. 350–27, **Combat Code of the USAREUR Soldier**, 1984

(9) Department of the Army Field Manual FM 100–20, **Low Intensity Conflict**, 1981

(10) The Judge Advocate General's School, United States Army, Charlottesville, Virginia, **Operational Law Handbook** *for the Deploying Judge Advocate*, 1984

(11) The Judge Advocate General's School, United States Army, Charlottesville, Virginia, *Law of War Training Material*, 1986

(12) The Judge Advocate General's School, United States Army, Charlottesville, Virginia, *Operational Law* (OpLaw): *Judge Advocate Exercise Participation*, 1988

(13) The Judge Advocate General's School, United States Army, Charlottesville, Virginia, *Operational Law* (OpLaw): *Deployment Checklist*, 1988

(14) The Judge Advocate General's School, United States Army, Charlottesville, Virginia, ADI–14, *The Geneva Conventions and the Soldier, Instructor's guide for use with lesson plan for TF* 21–4228

(15) Department of the Air Force, AFP 110–31, *International Law*—**The Conduct of Armed Conflict and Air Operations**, 1976

(16) Department of the Air Force, AFP 110–34, *Commander's Handbook on the Law of Armed Conflict*, 1980

(17) Department of the Air Force, AFP 200–17, **Targeting and International Law**, 1978

(18) Department of the Navy, NWP 9 A/FMFM 1–10, **The Commander's Handbook on the Law of Naval Operations**, 1989 and **Annotated Supplement** to the *Commanders Handbook* on the Law of Naval Operations (Rev. A)/FMFM 1–10, 1989

(19) Department of Defense (DoD) Directive No. 5100.77, DoD *Law of War Program*, 10 July 1979

(20) DoD Directive No 1300.7, *Training and Education Measures Necessary to Support the Code of Conduct*, Department of Defense, 19 December 1984

(21) The Joint Chiefs of Staff, MJCS 59–83, *Implementation of the DoD Law of War Program*, 1 June 1983

(22) Department of the Navy, SECNAVINST 3300.1A JAG 10, *Law of Armed Conflict (Law of War) program to insure compliance by the naval establishment*, 2 May 1980

3M SelfCheck™ System

Customer name: Bhatt, Debolina

Title: The handbook of humanitarian law in armed conflicts / edited by Dieter Fleck ... [et al.]
ID: 30114012408319
Due: 22-11-16

Total items: 1
15/11/2016 14:38
Overdue: 0

Thank you for using the
3M SelfCheck™ System.

(23) The Atlantic Command Headquarters of the Commander in Chief, CINCLANTINST 3300.3A (JL1), *DoD Law of War Instruction*, DoD 9 June 1981

(24) Commander in Chief US Pacific Fleet, CINCPACFLTINST 3300.9 (03J), *Implementation of DoD LAW of War Program*, 20 Dec. 1984

(25) Department of the Navy, SECNAVINST 1000.9 Op–09BL, *Code of Conduct for Members of the Armed Forces of the United States*, 1979

(26) Department of the Navy, OPNAVINST 3300.52 JAG:133, *Law of Armed Conflict (Law of War) Program to ensure compliance by the US Navy and Naval Reserve*, 18 March 1983

(27) DoD Directive No 5100.69, *DoD Program for Prisoners of War and Other Detainees*, 27 Dec. 1972

(28) Department of the Navy, JAGINST 3300.2A JAG:103, *Law of Armed Conflict Resource Materials*, 1990

(29) White House, *Amending the Code of Conduct for Members of the Armed Forces of the United States*, 28 March 1988

YUGOSLAVIA (SERBIA AND MONTENEGRO)

Propisi o primeni pravila medjunarodnog ratnog prava *u Oruzanim snagama SFRJ [Richtlinie zur Anwendung des Kriegsvölkerrechts in den Streitkräften der Sozialistischen Bundesrepublik Jugoslawien, hrsg vom Bundesminister für Nationale Verteidigung]*, 1988

INTERNATIONAL COMMITTEE OF THE RED CROSS

(1) **The Geneva Conventions** of 12 August 1949, reprint 1986

(2) **Protocols Additional to the Geneva Conventions** of 12 August 1949, 1977, X

(3) *International Law Concerning the conduct of Hostilities.* **Collection of Hague Conventions and some other Treaties**, 1989

(4) Waldemar A. Solf/ J. Ashley Roach, **Index of International Humanitarian Law**, 1987, XXVI

(5) **Rules for behaviour in combat**, 1985

(6) **Summary of the Geneva Conventions** of 12 August 1949 **and their Additional Protocols**, 1984

(7) Fréderic de Mulinen, **Handbook on the Law of War** *for Armed Forces*, 1987, XXIV *Law of War Summary for Commanders, Law of War Rules for Behaviour in Action, Law of War Training Programme*

(8) Francoise Bory, **Origin and Development of International Humanitarian Law**, 1982

(9) Alma Baccino-Astrada, **Handbook on the Rights and duties of Medical Personnel in Armed Conflicts**, Geneva 1989

(10) **Manual for the Use of Technical Means of Identification** *by Hospital Ships, Coastal Rescue Craft, Other Protected Craft and Medical Aircraft*, 1990

(11) **Guidelines for Tracing in Disasters**, 1989

SELECTIVE BIBLIOGRAPHY

Abi-Saab, G., 'Wars of National Liberation in the Geneva Conventions and Protocols', *Receuil des Cours* 165 (1979–IV), 353.

Abi-Saab, R., *Droit international et conflits internes* (1987).

——*The General Principles of Humanitarian Law according to the International Court of Justice*, *IRRC* 29 (1987), 367.

Adachi, S., 'La conception asiatique', *UNESCO/Institut Henri Dunant* (Eds.), *Les dimensions internationales du droit humanitaire* (1986), 31–8.

Akehurst, M. B., 'Civil War', in Bernhardt (Ed.) *EPIL*, 81.

Aldrich, G. H., 'Progressive Development of the Laws of War: A Reply to Criticisms of the 1977 Geneva Protocol I', VaJIntL 26 (1986), 693–720 .

——'Prospects for the United States Ratification of Acdditional Protocol I to the 1949 Geneva Conventions', *AJIL* 85 (1991), 1–20.

——'New Life for the Laws of War', *AJIL* 75 (1981), 764–83.

Alexander, L. M., 'International Straits', in Robertson (Ed.), *International Law Studies* Vol. 64. *The Law of Naval Operations*, Newport, Rhode Island (1991), 91–108 [L. M. Alexander, *Straits*].

American Law Institute, *Restatement of Foreign Relations Law*, Third (1987).

Anderson, W. S., 'Submarines and Disarmament Conferences', *USNIP* Vol. 53 (January 1927), 50–69.

Antoine, P., 'Droit international humanitaire et protection de l'environnement en cas de conflit armé', *RIC* 74 (1992), 537–58 .

Appleman, J. A., *Military Tribunals and International Crimes* (1954).

Arrassen, M., *Conduite des hostilités, droit des conflits armés et désarmement* (1986).

Attard, D. J., *The Exclusive Economic Zone in International Law*, Oxford (1987).

Aubert, M., 'Le Comité international de la Croix-Rouge et le problème des armes causant des maux superflus ou frappant sans discrimination', *RIC* 72 (1990), 521–41.

Baccino-Astrada, A., *Handbook on the Rights and Duties of Medical Personnel in Armed Conflicts* (1989).

Bailey, S., 'Cease-fires, Truces and Armistices in the Practice of the UN Security Council', *AJIL* 71 (1977), 461.

Baker, B., 'Legal Protections for the Environment in Times of Armed Conflict', VaJIntL 33 (1993), 351–83.

Balladore Pallieri, G., *Diritto bellico*,2nd Edn. (1954).

Bar-Yaacov, N., 'The Applicability of the Laws of War to Judea and Samaria (the West Bank) and to the Gaza Strip', Israel Law Review 24 (1990), 485.

Baxter, R. R.,' Comportement des combattants et conduite des hostilités (Droit de la Haye)', UNESCO/Institut Henry Dunant (Eds.), *Les dimensions internationales du droit humanitaire*, (1986), 117–62 .

——'Armistices and other forms of Suspension of Hostilities', *Receuil des Cours* 149 (1976), 353.

——'The Privy Council on the Qualifications of Belligerents', *AJIL* 63 (1969), 290.

——'Multilateral Treaties as Evidence of Customary International Law', *BYIL* 41 (1965–6), 286.

——'Passage of Ships Through International Waterways in Time of War', *BYIL* (1954), 187–216.

Bello, E., *African Customary Humanitarian Law* (1980).

Berber, F.; *Lehrbuch des Völkerrechts*. Vol. 2: *Kriegsrecht*, 2nd Edn., München (1969).

Bernauer, T., *The Chemistry of Regime Formation: Explaining International Cooperation for a Comprehensive Ban on Chemical Weapons* (1993).

——*The Projected Chemical Weapons Convention: A Guide to the Negotiations in the Conference on Disarmament* (1990) (UN Doc. UNIDIR/90/7).

Bernhardt, R. (Ed.), *Encyclopedia of Public International Law*, Instalments 1–12, Amsterdam/New York/Oxford/Tokyo (1981–90) [*EPIL*].

Best, G., *Humanity in Warfare: The Modern History of the International Law of Armed Conflicts* (1980).

Bierzanek, R., 'Reprisals as a Means of Enforcing the Laws of Warfare: The Old and the New Law', in Cassese (Ed.), *The New Humanitarian Law of Armed Conflict* (1979), 232–57.

——'War Crimes: History and Definition', in Bassiouni/Nanda (Eds.), *A Treatise on International Criminal Law* (1973), 559–80.

Bindschedler, R., 'Neutrality; Concept and General Rules', *EPIL* 4, 9.

——'Permanent Neutrality of States', *EPIL*, 4, 82, .

Bindschedler-Robert, D., 'Red Cross', *EPIL* 5, 248–54.

Blake, B. (Ed.), *Jane's Underwater Warfare Systems 1990–91*, 2nd Edn., Coulsdon (1990) [*Jane's Underwater Warfare Systems*].

Blix, H., 'Moyens et méthodes de combat', in UNESCO/Institut Henry Dunant (Eds.), *Les dimensions internationales du droit humanitaire*, (1986), 163–81.

——'Area Bombardment: Rules and Reasons', *BYIL* 49 (1978) 31–69.

Bluntschli, J. C., *Das moderne Völkerrecht der civilisierten Staaten* (1872).

Bock, I., *Die Entwicklung des Minenrechts von 1900–1960*, Hamburg (1963).

Boissier, P., *From Solferino to Tsushima* (1978).

Born, W.-R., *Die offene Stadt, Schutzzonen und Guerrillakämpfer. Regelungen zum Schutz der Zivilbevölkerung in Kriegszeiten* (1978).

Boss, A., 'Neutrality at Sea, Comments', in Dekker/Post (Eds.), *The Gulf War of 1980–1988*, (1992), 217–19.

Bothe, M. 'Rechtsfragen der Rüstungskontrolle im Vertragsvölkerrecht der Gegenwart', *Berichte der Deutschen Gesellschaft für Völkerrecht Heft* 30 (1990), 31–93.

——'Chemical Warfare', *EPIL* 3, 83–5.

——'Land Warfare', *EPIL* 3, 239–42.

——'War Graves', *EPIL* 4, 315–16.

——'The Protection of the Environmnet in Times of Armed Conflict', *GYIL* 34 (1991), 54–62.

——'Commentary on the 1977 Geneva Protocol I', in N. Ronzitti (Ed.), *The Law of Naval Warfare*, 760–7 [M. Bothe, Commentary].

——'Neutrality at Sea', in Dekker/Post (Eds.), *The Gulf War of 1980–1988* (1992), 205–11.

——'Neutrality in Naval Warfare: What is Left of traditional international law?', in Delissen/Tanja (Eds.), *Humanitarian Law of Armed Conflict—Challenges Ahead, Essaysin Honour of Frits Kalshoven* (1991), 387–405.

——*Das völkerrechtliche Verbot des Einsatzes chemischer und bakteriologischer Waffen* (1973).

Bothe M./Ipsen, K./Partsch, K. J., 'Die Konferenz über humanitäres Völkerrecht—Verlauf und Ergebnisse', *ZaöRV* 38 (1978), 1–85.

Bothe M./Macalister-Smith, P./Kurzidem, T. (Eds.), *National Implementation of Humanitarian Law*. Proceedings of an Internatio-nal Colloquium held at Bad Homburg, June 17–19, 1988 (1990).

Bothe, M./Partsch, K. J./Solf, W. A., *New Rules for Victims of Armed Conflicts*, The Hague/Boston/London (1982) [Bothe/Partsch/Solf].

566

Bouchez, L. J., 'Bays and Gulfs', *EPIL* 11, 45–8.

Bouvier, A., 'La protection de l'environnement naturel en période de conflit armé', *RIC* 73 (1991), 599–611.

——'Travaux récents relatifs à la protection de l'environnement en période de conflit armé', *RIC* 74 (1992), 578–91.

Bowett, D. W., 'Reprisals involving Recourse to Armed Force', *AJIL* 66 (1972), 1.

——*Self-Defence in International Law* (1958).

——*UN Forces* (1964).

Böhmert, V., 'Londoner Seerechtskonferenz 1908/09', *WVR II*, 428–31.

Bretton, P., 'Le problème des "méthodes et moyens de guerre ou de combat" dans les Protocoles Additionnels aux Conventions de Genève du 12 août 1949', *Revue Générale de Droit International Public* 82 (1978), 32–81.

——'Principes humanitaires et impératifs militaires dans le domaine des armes classiques à travers le droit international actuel', in *Soçiété Française pour le Droit International, Colloque de Montpellier—le droit international et les armes* (1983), 35–50.

Breucker, J. de, 'Pour les vingt ans de la Convention de la Haye du 14 Mai 1954 pour la protection des biens culturels', *RevBelgDI* 11 (1975), 525 ff.

Bring, O.E./Reimann, H.B., 'Redressing a Wrong Question: The 1977 Protocols Additional to the 1949 Geneva Conventions and the Issue of Nuclear Weapons', *Netherlands International Law Review* 33 (1986), 99–105.

Brownlie, I., *Principles of Public International Law*, 4th Edn., (1990).

——'Some Legal Aspects of the Use of Nuclear Weapons', *ICLQ* 14 (1965), 437–51.

——*International Law and the Use of Force by States* (1963).

Bruha, T., 'Bombardment', *EPIL* 3, 53–6.

Bugnion, F., *L'emblème de la Croix Rouge* (1977).

Buß, R., Der *Kombattantenstatus—die kriegsrechtliche Entstehung eines Rechtsbegriffs und seine Ausgestaltung in Verträgen des 19. und 20. Jahrhunderts, Bochumer Schriften zur Friedenssicherung und zum humanitären Völkerrecht, Bd. 12*, Bochum (1992).

Carnahan, B. M., 'The Law of Land Mine Warfare: Protocol II to the United Nations Convention on Certain Conventional Weapons', *Military Law Review* 105 (1984), 73–95.

——'"Linebacker II" and Protocol I: The Convergence of Law and Professionalism', *American University Law Review* 31 (1982), 861–70.

——'The Law of Air Bombardment in its Historical Context', *Air Force Law Review* 17 (1975), 39–60.

Cassese, A., 'A Tentative Appraisal of the Old and the New Humanitarian Law of Armed Conflict', in Cassese (Ed.), *The New Humanitarian Law of Armed Conflict* (1979), 461–501.

——'The Geneva Protocols of 1977 on the Humanitarian Law of Armed Conflict and Customary International Law', *UCLA Pacific Basin Law Journal* 3 (1984) 55–118.

——'The Prohibition of Indiscriminate Means of Warfare', *Declarations on Principles, Festschrift für B.V.A. Röling* (1977), 171–94.

——(Ed.), *The Current Legal Regulation of the Use of Force* (1987).

——(Ed.), *The New Humanitarian Law of Armed Conflict* (1979).

Castrén, E. 'The Illegality of Nuclear Weapons', *University of Toledo Law Review* 3 (1971), 89–98.

——*The Present Law of War and Neutrality* (1954).

Cauderay, G. C., 'Les mines antipersonnel', *RIC* 75 (1993), 293–309.

Chayes, A., *The Cuban Missile Crisis* (1974).

Clingan, Th. A. Jr., 'Submarine Mines in International Law', *International Law Studies* 64. *The Law of Naval Operations*, Edited by H. B. Robertson, Newport, Rhode Island (1991), 351–61 [Th. A. Clingan Jr., Mines].

Coll, A.R./Arend, A.C., *The Falklands War: Lessons for Strategy, Diplomacy and International Law* (1985).

Colombos, C. J., *Internationales Seerecht*, German translation of the 5th English Edn. 1962, München/Berlin (1963).

——'The Actual Value of the Declaration of London of 1909', *Revue Héllenique de Droit International* 12 (1959), 10–20.

Condorelli, L./Boisson de Chazournes, L., 'Quelques remarques à propos de l'obligation des etats de "respecter et faire respecter" le droit international humanitaire "en toutes circonstances", in Swinarski (Ed.) *Etudes et essais sur le droit international humanitaire et sur les principes de la croix-rouge en l'honneur de (Jean Pictet)* (1984), 17.

Dahm, G./Delbrück, J./Wolfrum, R., *Völkerrecht* I/1, 2nd Edn., 1989; I/2, 2nd Edn. (1993).

Danzinger, R., 'The Persian Gulf Tanker War', *USNIP* 111 (May 1985), 160–7.

David, E., 'A propos de certaines justifications théoriques à l'emploi de l'arme nucléaire', in Swinarski (Ed.), 325–42.

Dekker, I./Post, H. (Eds.), *The Gulf War of 1980–88* (1991).

Delbrück, J., 'Proportionality,' *EPIL* 7, 396–400.

——'War, Effect on Treaties', *EPIL* 4, 310.

——(Ed.), *Friedensdokumente aus fünf Jahrhunderten. Abrüstung—Kriegsverhütung—Rüstungskontrolle* (1984 ff.).

Delissen, A. J. M./Tanja, G. J. (Eds.), *Humanitarian Law of Armed Conflict—Challenges Ahead. Essays in Honour of Frits Kalshoven*, (1991).

Denny, M., 'The Impact of Article 82 of Protocol I on the Organization of a Division SJA Office', *Army Lawyer* 14 (1980).

DeSaussure, H., 'Belligerent Air Operations and the 1977 Geneva Protocol I', *Annals of Air and Space Law* 4 (1979), 459–82.

Detter De Lupis, I., *The Law of War* (1987).

Dinstein, Y., 'Siege Warfare and the Starvation of Civilians', in Delissen/Tanja (Eds.), *Humanitarian Law of Armed Conflict: Challenges Ahead. Essays in Honour of F. Kalshoven* (1991) 145–52.

——*War, Aggression and Self-Defence* (1988).

——'Military Necessity', *EPIL* 3, 274–6.

——'Neutrality in Sea Warfare', *EPIL*, 4, 82,.

——'Prisoners of War', *EPIL* 4, 146–52.

——'Warfare, Methods and Means', *EPIL* 4, 338–43.

——'International Criminal Law', *Israel Law Review* 20 (1985), 206–42.

——*The Defence of Obedience to Superior Orders in International Law* (1965).

——'The Laws of War at Sea', *IYHR* (1980), 38–69.

——'The Release of Prisoners of War', in Swinarski (Ed.), 38–45.

Dinstein, Y./Tabory, M., (Eds.) *International Law at a Time of Perplexity, Essays in Honour of Shabtai Rosenne* (1989), 273.

Dischler, L., 'Fryatt-Fall', *WVR* I, 606–8.

Djurovic G., *L'Agence centrale de recherches du Comité international de la Croix-Rouge* (1981).

Domke, M., 'Feindbegriff', *WVR* I, 509–11.

Donner, M., *Die neutrale Handelsschiffahrt im begrenzten militärischen Konflikt* (1994,.

Doswald-Beck, L., 'The Value of the Geneva Protocols for the Protection of Civilians', in Meyer (Ed.), *Armed Conflict and the New Law: Aspects of the 1977 Geneva Protocols and the 1981 Weapons Convention* (1989), 137–72.

Doswald-Beck, L./Cauderay, G. C., 'Le développement des nouvelles armes antipersonnels', *RIC* 72 (1990), 620–35.

Downey, W. G. Jr., 'Captured Enemy Property, Booty of War and Seized Enemy Property', *AJIL* (1950) 488–504.

Draper, G. I. A. D., 'Le développement du droit international humanitaire', in UNESCO/ Institut Henri Dunant (Eds.), *Les dimensions internationales du droit humanitaire* (1986), 89–114.

——'Indiscriminate Attack', *EPIL* 3, 219–21.

——'Implementation and Enforcement of the Geneva Conventions and of the two Additional Protocols', *Recueil des Cours* 164 III (1979), 1–54.

——'Wars of National Liberation and War Criminality', in Howard (Ed.) *Restraints in War* (1979), 135.

——'Role of legal advisers in armed forces', *IRRC* (1978) 6–17.

——'The Modern Pattern of War Criminality', *IYHR* 6 (1976), 9–48.

——'Military Necessity and Humanitarian Imperatives', *RDPMDG* (1973), 129–51.

——'The Interaction of Christianity and Chivalry in the Historical Development of Law of War', *IRRC* 7 (1965), 3.

Durand, A., *From Sarajevo to Hiroshima* (1984).

——*Histoire du Comité international de la Croix-Rouge*, 2 Bde (1978).

Eberlin, P., 'Underwater acoustic identification of hospital ships', *IRRC* 267 (Nov.–Dec. 1988), 505–28.

Eichen, K.-D./Walz, D., '*Neuere Entwicklungen auf dem Gebiet des humanitären Völkerrechts. Ausgewählte Rechtsfragen des I. Zusatzprotokolls zu den Genfer Abkommen*', *NZWehrr* 30 (1988), 146–56, 195–213.

Epping, V., 'Die Novellierungen im Bereich des Rüstungsexportkontrollrechts', *Recht der internationalen Wirtschaft* (1991), 461–70.

Ermacora, F., 'Der Afghanistankonflikt im Lichte des humanitären Völkerrechts', in Haller/Kölz/Müller/Thürer (Eds.), *Im Dienst an der Gemeinschaft, Festschrift für Dietrich Schindler* (1989), 201–14.

Falk, R., *The Vietnam War and International Law*, (1966–75), 4 vols.

——'International Law Aspects of Repatriation of Prisoners of War During Hostilities', *AJIL* 67 (1973), 465–78.

Falk, R./Meyrowitz, L./Sanderson, J., 'Nuclear Weapons and International Law', in *Indian Journal of International Law* 20 (1980), 541–95.

Feist, R., 'Manual for the Use of Technical Means of Identification', *HUV-I* (1990), 211–12.

Fenrick, W. J., 'Military Objectives in the Law of Naval Warfare', in Heintschel v. Heinegg (Ed.), *The Military Objective and the Principle of Distinction in the Law of Naval Warfare, Bochumer Schriften zur Friedenssicherung und zum humanitären Völkerrecht, Bd. 7*, Bochum (1991), 1–44.

——'La Convention sur les armes classiques: un traité modeste mais utile', *RIC* 72 (1990), 542–55.

——'The Exclusion Zone Device in the Law of Naval Warfare', *CYIL* Vol. XXIV (1986), 91–126.

——'The Rule of Proportionality and Protocol I in Conventional Warfare', *Military Law Review* 98 (1982), 91–127.

——'New Development in the Law Concerning the Use of Conventional Weapons in Armed Conflict', *CYIL* 19 (1981), 229–56.

Fischer, H., 'Neue Studien über "Der geplante Tod" von James Bacque', *HUV-I*, (3/1991), 117–18.

——'Die Rückführung von marrokanischen Kriegsgefangenen in der Hand der Polisario', *HUV-I* (1/1990), 14–16.

——'Limitation and Prohibition of the Use of Certain Weapons in Non-international Armed Conflicts', *Yearbook of the International Institute of Humanitarian Law* (1989–90), 117–80.

Fischer, H., 'Internationales öffentliches Luft- und Weltraumrecht', in K. Ipsen, *Völkerrecht*, 51, 52 [Fischer, in Ipsen, *Völkerrecht*].

——*Der Einsatz von Nuklearwaffen nach Art.51 des I. Zusatzprotokolls zu den Genfer Konventionen von 1949* (1985).

Fischer H./Wallenfels M., 'Bildberichterstattung und der Schutz der Kriegsgefangenen im Zeitalter des Satellitenfernsehens', in Institut für Friedenssicherungsrecht und Humanitäres Völkerrecht (Ed.), *Beiträge zum humanitären Völkerrecht, zur völkerrechtlichen Friedenssicherung und zum völkerrechtlichen Individualschutz, Festgabe für Georg Bock* (1993), 17–47.

Fleck, D., '*Military Manuals on International Humanitarian Law Applicable in Armed Conflicts. Consultations of Government Experts in Koblenz (Germany), 7–11 October 1991*', *HUV-I* (4/1991), 213–15 .

——'The Protocols Additional to the Geneva Conventions and Customary International Law', *RDMilG* 29 (1990), 495–517; *Law and State*, Vol 43, 119–25.

——'Topical Approaches Towards Developing the Laws of Armed Conflicts at Sea', in Delissen/Tanja (Eds.), *Essays in Honour of Frits Kalshoven*, The Hague 1990, 407–23 [Fleck, *Topical Approaches*].

——'Die Zusatzprotokolle zu den Genfer Abkommen und das Völkergewohnheitsrecht', *NZWehrr* 1990, 1.

——'NATO-Strategie und Völkerrecht', *NZWehrr* 29 (1987), 221–9.

——'Suspension of Hostilities', *EPIL* 4, 239.

——'Ruses of War and Prohibition of Perfidy', *RDMilG* (1974), 269–314.

——(Ed.), *The Gladisch Committee on the Law of Naval Warfare, Bochumer Schriften zur Friedenssicherung und zum Humanitären Völkerrecht Band 5*, Bochum 1990 [Fleck (Ed.), *The Gladisch Committee*].

——(Ed.), *Beiträge zur Weiterentwicklung des humanitären Völkerrechts für bewaffnete Konflikte*, Hamburg (1973) [Fleck, *Beiträge*].

——*Der Rotkreuz-"Entwurf von Regeln zur Einschränkung der Gefahren, denen die Zivilbevölkerung in Kriegszeiten ausgesetzt ist" (Neu-Delhi 1957) als Beitrag zur Schaffung einer rechtlichen Ordnung bestimmter Kriegshandlungen des Luftkriegs* (1964).

Forch, S./Harndt, R., 'Neue Regeln für den Einsatz von Kernwaffen?', *Juristische Rundschau* (1986), 45–50.

Forsythe, D. P., 'The Legal Management of Internal War', *AJIL* 72 (1978), 272.

Frailé, R., *La guerre biologique et chimique: le sort d'une interdiction* (1982).

Francioni, 'The Gulf of Sidra Incident (*United States* v. *Libya*) and International Law', *Ital YIL* 5 (1980/81), 85–109.

——'The Status of the Gulf of Sirte in International Law', *Syracuse Journal of International Law & Commerce* 11 (1984), 311–26.

Frey, H., *Die disziplinarische und gerichtliche Bestrafung von Kriegsgefangenen* (1948).

Friedmann, L. (Ed.), *The law of war: A documentary history* (1972), 2 vols.

Friedman, N., 'The Vincennes Incident', *USNIP* 115 (May 1989), 74–8.

Fujita, H., 'Commentary on the 1856 Paris Declaration', in Ronzitti (Ed.), *The Law of Naval Warfare*, 66–75.

Furet, M. F./Martinez, J. E./Dorandeu, H., *La Guerre et le droit*, 1979.

Furrer, H.-P., *Perfidie in der Geschichte und im heutigen Kriegsvölkerrecht* (1988).

Gardam, J. G., *Non-Combatant Immunity as a Norm of International Humanitarian Law* (1993).

Garner, J. W., *International Law and the World War*, Vol. 1, London (1920) [Garner, Vol. 1].

——'War Zones and Submarine Warfare', *AJIL* (1915), 594–626.

Gasser, H.-P., 'Die Aktivitäten des Internationalen Komitees vom Roten Kreuz im Golfkrieg', in Voit (Ed.), *Das humanitäre Völkerrecht im Golfkrieg und andere Rotkreuz-Fragen, Bochumer Schriften zur Friedenssicherung und zum Humanitären Völkerrecht* (1992), 5–28.

——'Das humanitäre Völkerrecht', in Haug, H., *Menschlichkeit für alle, Die Weltbewegung des Roten Kreuzes und des Roten Halbmonds* (1991), Kapitel IV, 499–599.

——'Humanitäres Völkerrecht in Aktion: Einige erste Folgerungen aus der Operation "Desert Storm"', *HUV-I* (4/1991), 30–3.

——'Some Legal Issues Concerning Ratification of the 1977 Geneva Protocols', in Meyer, M. A. (Ed.), *Armed Conflict and the New Law: Aspects of the 1977 Geneva Protocols and the 1981 Weapons Convention* (1989), 81–104.

——'Armed Conflict within a State, Some Reflections on the State of the Law Relative to the Conduct of Military Operations in Non-International Armed Conflicts', in Haller/Kölz/Müller/Thürer (Eds.), 225–40.

——'An Appeal for Ratification by the United States', in 'AGORA: The US Decision not to Ratify Protocol I to the Geneva Conventions on the Protection of War Victims', *AJIL* 81 (1987), 912–25.

——'Genfer Abkommen und Terrorismusverbot', in *Völkerrecht im Dienste des Menschen, Festschrift für Hans Haug* (1986), 69–80.

——'Scrutiny', *Australian Yearbook of International Law* 9 (1985), 345–58.

——'The Protection of Journalists in Dangerous Missions', *IRRC* (1983), 3–18.

Geck, W. K., 'Warships', *EPIL* 4, 346–52.

——'Allbeteiligungsklausel', *WVR* II, 28–9.

Gilchrist, S. F., 'The Cordon Sanitaire: Is It Useful? Is It Practical?', *Naval War College Review* 35 (1982), 60–72.

Gilliland, J., 'Submarines and Targets: Suggestions for New Codified Rules of Submarine Warfare', *Georgetown Law Journal* (1985), 975–1005.

Gimmerthal, M., *Kriegslist und Perfidieverbot im Zusatzprotokoll vom 10. Juni 1977 zu den vier Genfer Rotkreuz-Abkommen von 1949 (Zusatzprotokoll I), Bochumer Schriften zur Friedenssicherung und zum Humanitären Völkerrecht Band 4*, Bochum (1990).

Gioia, A./Ronzitti, N., 'The law of neutrality; third states' commercial rights and duties', in Dekker/Post (Eds.), *The Gulf War of 1980–1988* (1992), 221–42.

Gloria, Ch., 'Internationales öffentliches Seerecht', in Ipsen, K. *Völkerrecht*, 47–50 [Gloria, Ch. in Ipsen, K.].

Goldblat, J. 'Legal Protection of the Environment Against the Effects of Military Activities', È 22 (1991), 399–406.

Goldie, L. F. E., 'Commentary on the 1937 Nyon Agreements', in Ronzitti, N. (Ed.), *The Law of Naval Warfare*, 489–502 [Goldie, *Commentary*].

——'Maritime War Zones & Exclusion Zones', *International Law Studies* Vol. 64. *The Law of Naval Operations*. Edited by H.B. Robertson, Newport, Rhode Island (1991), 156–204 [Goldie, *Maritime War Zones*].

Goldman, R. K., 'International Humanitarian Law: Americas Watch's Experience in Monitoring Internal Armed Conflicts', *American University Journal of International Law and Policy* 9 (1993), 49–94.

Granat, M. G., 'Modern Small-Arms Ammunition in International Law', *Netherlands International Law Review* 40 (1993), 149–68.

Gray, C., 'The British Position in regard to the Gulf Conflict', *ICLQ* (1998), 420–28.

Green, L. C., *The Contemporary Law of Armed Conflicts*, (1993).

——'The Environment and the Law of Conventional Warfare', *CYIL* 24 (1991), 222–37.

Green, L. C., 'Nuclear Weapons and the Law of Armed Conflict', in *Denver Journal of International Law and Policy* 17 (1988), 1–27.

Green, L. C., *Essays on the Modern Law of War* (1985).

——*Superior Orders in National and International Law* (1976).

Greenspan, M., *The Modern Law of Land Warfare* (1959).

Greenwood, C., 'Neutrality at Sea: Comments', in Dekker/Post (Eds.), *The Gulf War of 1980–1988*, (1992), 212–16.

——'New World Order or Old?', *Modern Law Review* 55 (1992), 153.

——'Customary Law Status of the 1977 Geneva Protocols', in Delissen/Tanja (Eds.) *Humanitarian Law of Armed Conflict: Challenges Ahead. Essays in Honour of F. Kalshoven* (1991), 93–114.

——'Iraq's Invasion in Kuwait', *NZWehrr* (1991), 45–56.

——'Self-Defence and the Conduct of International Armed Conflict', in Dinstein/Tabory (Eds.) *International Law at a Time of Perplexity* (1989), 273.

——'Terrorism and Humanitarian Law', *IYHR* 19 (1989), 187.

——'The Twilight of the Law of Belligerent Reprisals', *NYIL* 20 (1989), 35–69.

——'The Concept of War in Modern International Law', *ICLQ* 36 (1987), 283 .

——'The relationship between *ius ad bellum* and *ius in bello*', *Review of International Studies* 9 (1983), 221.

Greig, D. W., 'Self-defence and the Security Council', *ICLQ* 40 (1991), 366.

Grewe, W. G., *Epochen der Völkerrechtsgeschichte* (1984).

Grob, F., *The Relativity of War and Peace* (1947).

Guichard, L., *The Naval Blockade 1914–1918*, New York 1930 .

Guttry, A. de 'Commentary on the 1907 Hague Convention VI', in Ronzitti, N. (Ed.), *The Law of Naval Warfare*, 84–91.

Hackel, E., *Das militärische Objekt* (1980).

Hailbronner, K., 'Die Notsituation im Luftkriegsrecht', in Fleck (Ed.), *Beiträge zur Weiterentwicklung des humanitären Völkerrechts für bewaffnete Konflikte* (1973).

Hall, J. A., *The Law of Naval Warfare*, 2nd edn., London 1921.

Haller, W./Kölz, A./Müller, G./Thürer, D. (Eds.), *Im Dienst an der Gemeinschaft, Festschrift für Dietrich Schindler* (1989) .

Hallerbach, R., 'Die "kontrollierte Mine" gehorcht der Stimme ihres Herrn', *Europäische Wehrkunde* (10/85), 572–5.

Hampson, F. J., 'Mercenaries: Diagnosis before Proscription': *NYIL* 32 (1991), 3 .

Hampson, F., 'The Geneva Conventions and the Detention of Civilians and Alleged Prisoners of War', *Public Law* (1991), 507–22.

Hampson, F. J., 'Belligerent Reprisals and the 1977 Protocols to the Geneva Conventions 1949', *ICLQ* 37 (1988), 818–43.

Hanke, H. M., 'Les Règles de La Haye de 1923 conçernant la guerre aérienne', *RIC* 75 (1993), 13–49.

Harvey, A. H., 'The Maintenance of Control over Prisoners of War', *RDMilG* (1963), 127–51.

Haug, H. (Ed.), *Menschlichkeit für Alle, Die Weltbewegung des Roten Kreuzes und des Roten Halbmondes* (1991).

Hegelsom, G. J. F. van, 'Methods and Means of Combat in Naval Warfare', in W. Heintschel v. Heinegg (Ed.), *Methods and Means of Combat in Naval Warfare, Bochumer Schriften zur Friedenssicherung und zum humanitären Völkerrecht, Bd. 8*, Bochum (1992), 1–59.

Heintschel v. Heinegg, W., 'Exclusion Zones, Mines, Abuse of Neutral Flags and Insignia, Booty in Naval Warfare', in Fleck (Ed.), *The Gladisch Committee on the Law of Naval Warfare*, 39–59.

572

——'Visit, Search, Diversion and Capture: Conditions of Applicability', Part I, *CYIL* Vol. XXIX (1991), 283–329.

——'Das "militärische Ziel" im Sinne von Art. 52 Abs. 2 des I. Zusatzprotokolls', *HUV-I* (1989), (Heft 3), 51.

——*Der Ägäis-Konflikt. Die Abgrenzung des Festlandsockels zwischen Griechenland und der Türkei und das Problem der Inseln im Seevölkerrecht*, Berlin 1989 [W. Heintschel von Heinegg, *Ägäis-Konflikt*].

Heintschel v. Heinegg/Donner, M., 'New Developments in the Protection of the Natural Environment in Naval Armed Conflicts', *GYIL* 37 (1994), to be published in 1995.

Heintschel von Heinegg, W. (Ed.), *Methods and Means of Combat in Naval Warfare. Report & Commentaries of the Round-Table of Experts on International Humanitarian Law Applicable to Armed Conflicts at Sea, Institut Méditerranéen d'Études Stratégiques, Université de Toulon et du Var, 19–23 October 1990, Bochumer Schriften zur Friedenssicherung und zum Humanitären Völkerrecht Band 8*, Bochum (1992) [Heintschel von Heinegg (Ed.), *Methods and Means*].

——(Ed.), *The Military Objective and the Principle of Distinction in the Law of Naval Warfare. Report, Commentaries and Proceedings of the Round Table of Experts on International Humanitarian Law Applicable to Armed Conflicts at Sea, Ruhr-Universität Bochum, 10–14 November 1989, Bochumer Schriften zur Friedenssicherung und zum Humanitären Völkerrecht Band 7*, Bochum 1991 [Heintschel von Heinegg (Ed.), *Military Objective*].

Helm, H. G., 'Die rechtliche Stellung der Troßschiffe einer Kriegsmarine', *Marine Rundschau* 54 (1957), 152–6.

Heydte, F. A. Frhr. v. d., 'Air Warfare', *EPIL* 3, 6–10.

——'Military Objectives', *EPIL* 3, 276–9.

——'Atomare Kriegführung und Völkerrecht', *AVR* 9 (1961), 162–82.

Higgins, A. P., 'Ships of War as Prize', *BYIL* 1925, 103–10.

——'Enemy Ships in Port at the Outbreak of War', *BYIL* (1922/3), 55–78.

Higgins, R., *The Development of International Law by the Political Organs of the United Nations* (1963).

Hill, N. D., 'The Origin of the Law of Unneutral Service', *AJIL* 23 (1929), 56–67.

Hingorani, R., *Prisoners of War* (1982) .

Hinz, J., *Das Kriegsgefangenenrecht: Unter besonderer Berücksichtigung seiner Entwicklung durch das Genfer Abkommen vom 12. August 1949* (1955).

Hoffmann, R. F., 'Offensive Mine Warfare: A Forgotten Strategy', *USNIP* 103 (May 1977), 142–55.

Hofs, H., *Sind Kampfhandlungen in der ausschließlichen Wirtschaftszone eines neutralen Staates völkerrechtlich mit der Neutralität des Staates vereinbar? Wie haben sich deutsche Kriegsschiffe in der schwedischen Wirtschaftszone zu verhalten?, Führungsakademie der Bundeswehr*, Hamburg (1987).

Holland, T. E., *Studies in International Law* (1898).

Hoog, G., 'Mines', *EPIL* 3, 284–85.

Howard, M. (Ed.), *Restraints in War* (1979).

Hönes, E. R., 'Zur Kennzeichnung des Kulturguts nach der Haager Konvention vom 14. Mai 1954', in *Die Öffentliche Verwaltung* (1988), 538–47.

ICRC *Commentary*, see Sandoz/Swinarski/Zimmermann (Eds.).

Ide, W., 'Der Minenkampf in Nordsee und Ostsee', *Europäische Wehrkunde* (7/1989), 447–54.

International Committee of the Red Cross, *Report on its Activities during the Second World War*, Vol. I, (1948).

International Institute of Humanitarian Law, *San Remo Manual on International Law Applicable to Armed Conflicts at Sea, Prepared by a Group of International Lawyers and Naval Experts*, (1994).

International Institute of Humanitarian Law, 'Declaration on the Rules of International Humanitarian Law Governing the Conduct of Hostilities in Non-International Armed Conflicts', *IRRC* (September-October 1990), 404–8.

Ipsen, K., 'Auswirkungen des Golfkriegs auf das humanitäre Völkerrecht', in Voit (Ed.), *Das humanitäre Völkerrecht im Golfkrieg und andere Rotkreuzfragen, Bochumer Schriften zur Friedenssicherung und zum Humanitären Völkerrecht* (1992), 29–48.

——'Kombattanten und Kriegsgefangene', in Schöttler/Hoffmann (Eds.), *Die Genfer Zusatzprotokolle*, 139 ff.

——*Völkerrecht*, 3rd edn. (1990).

——'Kommentierung zu Art. 87a', in Dolzer (Ed.), *Kommentar zum Bonner Grundgesetz, Loseblattsammlung*, Heidelberg [BK].

——'Perfidy', *EPIL* 4, 130–3.

——'War, Ruses', *EPIL* 4, 330–1.

——'Die "offene Stadt" und die Schutzzonen des Genfer Rechts', in Fleck (Ed.), *Beiträge zur Weiterentwicklung des humanitären Völkerrechts für bewaffnete Konflikte* (1973), 149–210.

——*Rechtsgrundlagen und Institutionalisierung der atlantisch-westeuropäischen Verteidigung* (1967).

Istituto Internazionale di Diritto Umanitario, *La Protezione Internazionale dei Beni Culturali/ The International Protection of Cultural Property*, Rome (1986).

Jacobs, F./Roberts (Eds.), *The Effect of Treaties in Domestic Law* (1987).

Jacobson, J. L., 'The Law of Submarine Warfare Today', in Robertson, H. B., *The Law of Naval Operations, International Law Studies* Vol. 64. 1991, 205–40, [Jacobson, *Submarine Warfare*].

Jakovljevic, B., 'Armed Conflict in Jugoslavia, Agreements in the Field of International Humanitarian Law and Practice', *HUV-I* (3/1992), 108–11.

Jennings, R. Y., 'The Caroline Case', *AJIL* 32 (1938), 82.

Jescheck, H. H., 'War Crimes', *EPIL* 4, 294–8.

Johnson, D. H. N., 'Prize Law', *EPIL* 4, 154–9.

Jopp, H. D., *Marine 2000. Neue wehrtechnische Entwicklungen und ihr Einfluß auf die Seekriegführung* (1989).

Junod, S., *Protection of the Victims of Armed Conflict—Falklands/Malvinas Conflict* (1985).

Juschka, K. O., 'Kriegsvölkerrecht und Bundeswehrverwaltung', in *Bundeswehrverwaltung* (1972).

Kalshoven, F., 'Les principes juridiques qui sous-tendent la Convention sur les armes classiques', *RIC* 72 (1990), 556–67.

——'Belligerent Reprisals Revisited', *NYIL* 21 (1990), 43–80.

——'Arms, Armaments and International Law', *Recueil des Cours* 191 (1985 II) 183–341.

——'Applicability of Customary International Law in Non-International Armed Conflicts', in Cassese (Ed.), *Current Problems of International Law* (1975) 267–85.

——'Commentary on the 1909 London Declaration', in Ronzitti (Ed.), *The Law of Naval Warfare*, 257–75 [F. Kalshoven, *Commentary*].

——'Conventional Weaponry: The Law From St. Petersburg to Lucerne and Beyond', in Meyer (Ed.), *Armed Conflict and the New Law: Aspects of the 1977 Geneva Protocols and the 1981 Weapons Convention* (1989) 251–70.

——*Constraints on the Waging of War* (1987).

——*The Law of Warfare* (1973).

——*Belligerent Reprisals* (1971).

——(Ed.), *Assisting the Victims of Armed Conflict and Other Disasters* (1989).

Kassapis, G., *C-Waffen: der völkerrechtliche Hintergrund der Genfer Verhandlungen über ihre Eliminierung* (1986).

Keen, M. H., *The Laws of War in the Late Middle Ages* (1965).

Keenan, T.P., 'Die Operation "Wüstensturm" aus der Sicht des aktiven Rechtsberaters', *HUV-I* (4/1991), 34–7.

Keeva, M., 'Lawyers in the War Room', *American Bar Association Journal*, (December 1991), 52.

Khadduri, M., 'The Law of War and Peace', in *Islam* (1955).

Kimminich, O., *Einführung in das Völkerrecht*, 4th Edn. (1990).

——'Der Einfluß des humanitären Völkerrechts auf die Kernwaffenfrage', in *Staatsrecht, Völkerrecht, Europarecht, Festschrift für Hans-Jürgen Schlochauer* (1981), 407–23.

——*Schutz der Menschen in bewaffneten Konflikten* (1979).

Kischlat, W.-D., *Das Übereinkommen über das Verbot der Entwicklung, Herstellung und Lagerung bakteriologischer (biologischer) Waffen und von Toxin-Waffen sowie über die Vernichtung solcher Waffen* (1976).

Kiss, A., 'Les Protocoles additionnels aux Conventions de Genève de 1977 et la protection de biens de l'environnement', in Swinarski (Ed.), 181–92.

Knackstedt, H., 'Kriegspropaganda', *WVR* II, 353–4.

——'Das bewaffnete Handelsschiff im Seekrieg', *Marine Rundschau* 56 (1959), 69–77.

Kowark, H./Taylor, S. M., 'Die Räumung des Suezkanals', *Marine Rundschau* 71 (1974), 724–36.

Kotzsch, L., 'The Concept of War', *Contemporary History and International Law* (1956).

Köpfer, J., *Die Neutralität im Wandel der Erscheinungsformen militärischer Auseinandersetzung* (1975).

Krüger-Sprengel, F., 'Kriegslist und Perfidieverbot', *NZWehrr* 13 (1971), 161–70.

Kunz, J.L., 'Kriegsrecht im Allgemeinen', *WVR* II, 354–9.

——'The Laws of War', *AJIL* (1956), 313–37.

——'Die koreanische Kriegsgefangenenfrage', *Archiv des Völkerrechts* 4 (1954), 408–23.

——'Ending the War with Germany', *AJIL* 46 (1952), 114 .

——'The Chaotic Status of the Laws of War and the Urgent Necessity for their Revision', *AJIL* 45 (1951), 37–61.

——*Kriegsrecht und Neutralitätsrecht* (1935).

Kussbach, E., 'La neutralité permanente et les Nation Unies; nouvelles perspectives après les changements fondamentaux en Europe de l'Est', *Annales de droit international médical* 35 (1991), 82–95.

——'Le développement du statut des combattants et le droit international humanitaire', *RDMilG* XXII (1983), 377–418.

——'Neutral Trading', *EPIL* 4, 7–9.

Kühner, R., *Vorbehalte zu multilateralen völkerrechtlichen Verträgen* (1986).

Kwakwa, E., *The International Law of Armed Conflict: Personal and Material Fields of Application* (1992).

Lachs, M., *War Crimes* (1945).

Lael, J., *The Yamashita Precedent* (1982).

Lagoni, R., 'The Work of the Gladisch Committee in Today's Persepctive', in Fleck (Ed.), *The Gladisch Committee*, 63–76 [R. Lagoni, *Gladisch*].

——'Gewaltverbot, Seekriegsrecht und Schiffahrtsfreiheit im Golfkrieg', in *Festschrift für Wolfgang Zeidler* (1987), 1833 ff.

——'Cables, Submarine', *EPIL* 11, 48–51.

——'Merchant Ships', *EPIL* 11, 228–33.

Lamar, S., 'The Treatment of Prisoners of War: The Role of the International Committee of the Red Cross in the War Between Iran and Iraq', *Emory International Law Review* 5 (1991), 243–83.

Landolt, S., *Die rechtliche Stellung des Generalkommissars für Kulturgut*, Dissertation, Zürich (1973).

Lautenschläger, K., 'The Submarine in Naval Warfare, 1901–2001', *International Security* Vol. 11 (1986–7), 94–140.

Lauterpacht, E./Greenwood, C./Weller, M., and Bethlehem, D., *The Kuwait Crisis, Basic Documents* (1991), Vol. I.

Lauterpacht, E., 'The Legal "Irrelevance" of the State of War', *Proceedings of the American Society of International Law* 62 (1968), 58.

Lauterpacht, E. (Ed.), *The Kuwait Crisis*.

Lauterpacht, H., 'The Limits of Operation of the Laws of War', *BYIL* 30 (1953), 206.

Leckow, R., 'The Iran–Iraq Conflict in the Gulf: The Law of War Zones', *ICLQ* 1988, 629–44.

Leibler, A., 'Deliberate Wartime Environmental Damage: New Challenges for International Law', *California Western International Law Journal* 23 (1992), 67–137.

Lentföhr, Ch., 'Schwedischer Vorschlag zur Neuregelung des Einsatzes von Minen im Seekrieg', *HUV-I* (3/1989), 38–41.

Levie, H. S., 'Commentary on the 1907 Hague Convention VIII', in Ronzitti (Ed.), *The Law of Naval Warfare* (1988), 140–8 [Levie, *Commentary*].

——*Mine Warfare at Sea*, Dordrecht/Boston/London (1992) [H. S. Levie, *Mine Warfare at Sea*].

——'Means and Methods of Combat at Sea', *Syracuse Journal of International Law & Commerce* 14 (1988), 727–39.

——*The Code of International Armed Conflict*, Vol. 2 (1985).

——'Documents on Prisoners of War', *US Naval War College, International Law Studies* 60 (1979).

——'Prisoners of War', *US Naval War College International Law Studies* 59 (1978).

——'Procedures for the Protection of Prisoners of War in Vietnam: A four-way problem', *Proceedings of the Amercian Society of International Law* (1971), 209–14.

——'The Maltreatment of Prisoners of War in Vietnam', in Falk (Ed.), *The Vietnam War and International Law*, Vol. 2 (1969), 361–97.

——'The Nature and Scope of the Armistice Agreement', *AJIL* 50 (1956), 880.

Lijnzaad, L./Tanja, G. J., 'Protection of the Environment in Times of Armed Conflict: The Iraq–Kuwait War', *Netherlands International Law Review* 40 (1993), 169–99.

Lombardi, A. V., *Bürgerkrieg und Völkerrecht, Die Anwendbarkeit völkerrechtlicher Normen in nicht-zwischenstaatlichen bewaffneten Konflikten* (1976).

Lyon, 'The Case of General Yamashita', in Baird (Ed.), *From Nuremberg to My Lai* (1972), 139–49.

Maaß, R., *Der Söldner und seine kriegsvölkerrechtliche Rechtsstellung als Kombattant und Kriegsgefangener, Bochumer Schriften zur Friedenssicherung und zum Humanitären Völkerrecht, Bd. 2* (1990).

Macalister-Smith, P., 'Protection de la population civile et interdiction d'utiliser la famine comme méthode de guerre', *RIC* 73 (1991), 464–84.

——'Emblems, Internationally Protected', *EPIL* 9, 113–19.

Madders, K. J., 'Internment', *EPIL*, 3, 224–33.

——'Neutrality in Air Warfare', *EPIL* 4, 14–16.

——'War, Use of Propaganda in', *EPIL* 4, 334–6.

Majid, A. A., 'Treaty Amendment Inspired by Korean Plane Tragedy: Custom Clarified or Confused?', *GYIL* 29 (1986) 190–226.

Makagiansar, M., 'The thirteenth anniversary of the Convention for the Protection of Cultural Property in the Event of Armed Conflict: Results and Prospects', in Istituto Internazionale di Diritto Umanitario, *La Protezione Internazionale dei Beni Culturali/ The International Protection of Cultural Property*, Rome (1986), 27–40.

Mallison, W. T., 'Studies in the Law of Naval Warfare: Submarines in General and Limited Wars', *International Law Studies* Vol. LVIII, Washington (1968).

Marauhn, T., 'Die Vorschriften über Rüstungsbeschränkung im "Vertrag über die abschließende Regelung in bezug auf Deutschland"', in *HUV-I* (4/1991), 62–9.

Martens, F. von, *Völkerrecht, 2 Band* (1886).

Matte, N. M., 'Space Law' *EPIL* 11, 303–9.

Matthei, D., 'Befehlsverweigerung aus humanitären Gründen', *RDMilG* (1980), 257–83.

McCoubrey, H., *International Humanitarian Law: The Regulation of Armed Conflicts* (1990).

McDougal, M. S./Feliciano, J. P., 'International Coercion and World Public Order: The General Principles of the Law of War', *Yale Law Journal* 67 (1958), 771–845.

McNair, A., *The Effect of War upon Treaties* (1943).

McNair, A., 'The Legal Meaning of War', *Transactions of the Grotius Society* 11 (1925), 45.

McNair, A./Watts, A. D., *The Legal Effects of War* (1966), 4th edn.

Meng, W., 'Contraband', *EPIL* 3, 122.

——'War', *EPIL* 4, 282.

Meron, T., 'Prisoners of War, Civilians and Diplomats in the Gulf Crisis', *American Journal of International Law* 85 (1991), 104–16.

——*Human Rights and Humanitarian Norms as Customary International Law* (1989).

——'Neutrality, The Right of Shipping and the Use of Force in the Persian Gulf—Remarks', in *Proceedings of the American Society of International Law* 82 (1988), 164–9.

Meyer, M. A. (Ed.), *Armed Conflict and the New Law: Aspects of the 1977 Geneva Protocols and the 1981 Weapons Convention* (1989).

Meyrowitz, H., 'Quel droit de la guerre pour l'OTAN?', *Etudes Internationales* 17 (1986), 549–69.

——'Le Protocole Additionnel I aux Conventions de Genève de 1949 et le droit de la guerre maritime', *Revue Générale de Droit International Public* 89 (1985), 243–98.

——'Buts de guerre et objectifs militaires', *RDMilG* 22 (1983), 93–115.

——'Le statut des armes nucléaires en droit international', *GYIL* 25 (1982), 219–51 and *GYIL* 26 (1983), 161–97.

——'Le Protocole Additionnel I et le droit général de la guerre', *RDMilG* 21 (1982), 119–34.

——'Le bombardement stratégique d'après le Protocole additionnel I aux Conventions de Genève', *ZaöRV* 41 (1981), 1–68.

——'La stratégie nucléaire et le Protocole additionnel I aux Concentions de Genève de 1949', *Revue Générale de Droit International Public* 83 (1979), 904–61.

——'The Law of War in the Vietnamese Conflict', in Falk (Ed.), *The Vietnam War and International Law*, Vol. 2 (1969), 516–71.

——'Réflexions à propos du centenaire de la Déclaration de Saint-Pétersbourg', in *RIC* 50 (1968), 541–55.

Michel, P.-F (Ed.), *The Gulf Conflict 1990–91* (1991).

Miller, R. I., *The Law of War* (1975).

Millet, A. S., *La neutralité aérienne, Annales de droit international médical* 35 (1991), 63–81.

Mirimanoff-Chilikine, J., 'Protection de la population et des personnes civiles contre les dangers résultant des opérations militaires', *Revue Belge de Droit International* 7 (1971), 619–70 and 8 (1972), 101–42.

Miyazaki, S., 'The Martens Clause and International Humanitarian Law', in Swinarski (Ed.), 433–44.

Momtaz, D., 'Les règles relatives à la protection de l'environnement au cours des conflits armés à l'épreuve du conflit entre l'Iraq et le Koweit', *Annuaire Francais de Droit International* 37 (1991), 203–19.

Moritz, G., 'Völkerrechtlicher Status des Zivilpersonals der Streitkräfte im Falle eines bewaffneten Konflikts internationalen Charakters', in *Bundeswehrverwaltung* (1965).

Mossop, J. C. M., 'Hospital Ships in the Second World War', *BYIL* XXIV (1947), 160–215, 398–406.

Mulinen, F. de, 'A propos de la conférence de Lucerne et Lugano sur l'emploi de certaines armes conventionnelles', *Annales d'Etudes Internationales* 8 (1977) 111–32.

Murray, C., 'The 1977 Protocols and the Conflict in Southern Africa', *ICLQ* 33 (1984), 462.

Münch, F., 'War, Laws of History', *EPIL* 4, 326.

——'Die Martens'sche Klausel und die Grundlagen des Völkerrechts', *ZaöRV* 36 (1976), 347–73.

Nahlik, S. E., 'From Reprisals to Individual Penal Responsibility', in Delissen/Tanja (Eds.), 165–76.

——'International Law and Nuclear Weapons', in *Im Dienst an der Gemeinschaft. Festschrift für Dietrich Schindler* (1989), 283–99.

——'On some deficiencies of the Hague Convention of 1954 on the protection of cultural property in the event of armed conflict', *Annuaire de l'Association des Anciens de l'Academie (La Haye)*, 27 (1976) 5, 100–8 [Nahlik, *Deficiencies*].

——'La protection internationale des biens culturels en cas de conflit armé', *Recueil des Cours* 120 (1967 I), 64–163.

Ney, M. C., *Der Einsatz von Atomwaffen im Lichte des Völkerrechts* (1985).

Noeske, R., 'Moderne Seeminen für die Deutsche Marine', *Marineforum* 10 (1988), 348–52.

Nordquist, M. H./Wachenfeld, M. G., 'Legal Aspects of Reflagging Kuwaiti Tankers and Laying of Mines in the Persian Gulf', *GYIL* 31 (1988), 138–64.

Norton, P. M., 'Between the Ideology and the Reality: the Shadow of the Law of Neutrality', *Harvard Journal of International Law* 17 (1976), 249.

Nwogugu, E. I., 'Commentary on Submarine Warfare', in Ronzitti (Ed.), *The Law of Naval Warfare*, 353–65.

O'Brien, W. V., *The Conduct of Just and Limited War* (1981).

O'Connell, D.P., *The International Law of the Sea* (Ed. I.A. Shearer), Vol. II, Oxford (1984) [O'Connell, Vol. II].

——'Limited War at Sea' in Howard (Ed.), *Restraints on War* (1979), 123.

——'International Law and Contemporary Naval Operations', *BYIL* 1970, 18–85.

——*The Influence of Law on Sea Power*, Manchester (1975) [O'Connell, *Influence*].

——'The Legality of Naval Cruise Missiles', *AJIL* 1972, 785–94.

Oeter, S., *Neutralität und Waffenhandel* (1992).

——'Bürgerkrieg in Jugoslawien—Konflikt um Kroatien—Serbisch–Kroatischer Krieg? Völkerrechtliche Überlegungen zum militärischen Konflikt um das Erbe Jugoslawiens', *HUV-I* (5/1992), 4–10.

Oppenheim, L./Lauterpacht, H., *International Law*, Vol.II: *Disputes, War and Neutrality*, 7th edn. (1952).

Ottmüller, R., *Die Anwendung von Seekriegsrecht in militärischen Konflikten seit 1945* (1978).

Parks, W. H., 'Air War and the Law of War', *The Air Force Law Review* 32 (1990), 1–225.

——'Le protocole sur les armes incendiaires', *RIC* 72 (1990), 584–604.

——'Submarine-Launched Cruise Missile and International Law: A Response', *USNIP* 103 (September 1977), 120–3.

Partsch, K. J., 'Armed Conflict', *EPIL* 3, 25.

——'Armed Conflict, Fundamental Rules', *EPIL* 3, 28.

——'Humanitarian Law and Armed Conflict', *EPIL* 3, 215.

——'Reprisals', *EPIL* 9, 330–5.

——'Die Bestrafung der Rassendiskriminierung nach den internationalen Abkommen und die Verwirklichung der Verpflichtungen in nationalen Strafrechtordnungen', *GYIL* 20 (1977), 119–38.

Patrnogic, J./Jakovlevic, B., *International Humanitarian Law in the Contemporary World*, San Remo (1991).

Paust J./Blaustein A. P., 'War Crimes and Due Process: The Bangladesh Experience', *Vanderbilt Journal of Transnational Law* 11 (1978), 1–38.

Peace, D. L., 'Major Maritime Events in the Persian Gulf War', *Proceedings of the American Society of International Law* 82 (1988), 146–54.

Pechstein, M., 'Die Ratifizierung der Zusatzprotokolle zu den Genfer Konventionen durch die Bundesrepublik Deutschland', AVR 30 (1992), 281–97.

Penna, L.R., 'Customary International Law and Protocol I: An Analysis of Some Provisions', in Swinarski (Ed.), 201–25.

Petersen, Ch. H., 'Die Operationen der sowjetischen Marine für die Wiedereröffnung der Häfen in Bangladesh. März 1972–Juni 1974', *Marine Rundschau* 72 (1975), 665–76.

Phillips, C. G., 'Capture at Sea in Perspective', *USNIP* 91 (April 1965), 60–7.

Piccigallo, Ph., *The Japanese on Trial: Allied War Crimes* (1979).

Pictet, J. S., *Development and Principles of International Humanitarian Law*, Geneva (1985).

——*Die Grundsätze des Roten Kreuzes, Kommentar, Genf und Bonn* (1990).

——*Development and Principles of International Humanitarian Law* (1985).

——*Humanitarian Law and the Protection of War Victims* (1975).

——(Ed.), *Conventions de Genève, Commentaire* (1952 ff.).

——(Ed.), *The Geneva Conventions of 12 August 1949, Commentary*, Vol I (Geneva 1952), Vol. II (Geneva 1960), Vol. III (Geneva 1960), Vol. IV (Geneva 1958).

Pilloud, C., 'Protection des victimes des conflits armés: II. Prisonniers de guerre', in Institut Henry Dunant/UNESCO (Eds.), *Les dimensions internationales du droit humanitaire*, Paris/Genève (1986), 199–218.

——'Les Conventions de Genève de 1949 pour la protection des victimes de la guerre, les Protocoles additionnels de 1977 et les armes nucléaires', *GYIL* 21 (1978) 1.

Plant, G. (Ed.), *Environmental Protection and the Law of War: A 'Fifth Geneva' Convention on the Protection of the Environment in Time of Armed Conflict* (1992).

Plattner, D., 'La Convention de 1980 sur les armes classiques et l'applicabilité de règles relatives aux moyens de combat dans un conflit armé non international', *RIC* 72 (1990), 605–19.

Platzöder, R., 'Überlegungen zur völkerrechtskonformen Verwendung von C-Waffen', *NZWehrr* 29 (1987), 177–94.

Playfair, E. (Ed.), *International Law and the Administration of Occupied Territories, Two Decades of Israeli Occupation of the West Bank and Gaza Strip* (1992).

Pogany, I., (Ed.), *Nuclear Weapons and International Law* (1987).

Politakis, G. P., 'Stratagems and the Prohibition of Perfidy with a Special Reference to the Law of War at Sea', *Austrian Journal of Public International Law* 45 (1993), 253–308.

——'Waging War at Sea: The Legality of War Zones', *Netherlands International Law Review* XXXVIII (1991/92), 125–72.

Preux, J. de, *Geneva Convention Relative to the Treatment of Prisoners of War* (1960).

Prugh, G. S., 'American Issues and Friendly Reservations Regarding Protocol I, Additional to the Geneva Conventions', *RDMilG* 31 (1992), 223–85.

Quigley, J., 'Iran and Iraq and the Obligations to Release and Repatriate Prisoners of War After the Close of Hostilities', *American Journal of International Law and Policy* 5 (1989), 73–86.

Rabus, W., 'Booty in Sea Warfare', *EPIL* 3, 68–71.

Rajan, H. P., 'The Legal Regime of Archipelagos', *GYIL* 29 (1986), 137–53.

Randelzhofer, A., 'Civilian Objects', *EPIL* 3, 93–6.

——'Flächenbombardement und Völkerrecht', in *Um Recht und Freiheit. Festschrift für F.A. von der Heydte* (1977), Vol.I, 471–93.

Rauch, E., *The Protocol Additional to the Geneva Conventions for the Protection of Victims of International Armed Conflicts and the United Nations Convention on the Law of the Sea: Repercussions on the Law of Naval Warfare*, Berlin (1984) [E. Rauch, *The Protocol Additional*].

——'Biological Warfare', *EPIL* 3, 45–7.

——'The Protection of the Civilian Population in International Armed Conflicts and the Use of Landmines', *GYIL* 24 (1981), 262–87.

——'L'emploi d'armes nucléaires et la réaffirmation et le développement du droit international humanitaire applicables dans les conflits armés', *Revue Hellénique du droit international* 33 (1980), 1–60.

——'Le concept de nécessité militaire dans le droit de la guerre', *RDMilG* 19 (1980), 205–37.

Rauschning, D., 'Nuclear Warfare and Nuclear Weapons', *EPIL* 4, 44–50.

Reimann, H.B., 'Das internationale Regime der ABC-Waffen und dessen Gemeinsamkeiten mit Grundsätzen des humanitären Kriegsvölkerrechtes', in Haller, W./Kölz, A./Müller, G./Thürer, D. (Eds.), *Im Dienst an der Gemeinschaft, Festschrift für Dietrich Schindler* (1989), 301–10 .

Rice, D./Gavshon, A., *The Sinking of the Belgrano* (1984).

Roach, J. A., 'Certain Conventional Weapons Convention : Arms Control or Humanitarian Law', *Military Law Review* 105 (1984), 3–72.

Roberts, A., 'La destruction de l'environnement pendant la guerre du Golfe de 1991', *RIC* 72 (1990), 559–77.

——'Prolonged Military Occupation: The Israeli-Occupied Territories Since 1967', *AJIL* 84 (1990) 44 ff.

Roberts, A./Guelff, R., *Documents on the Laws of War* (1989) 2nd edn.

Roberts, G. B., 'The New Rules for Waging War: The Case against Ratification of Additional Protocol I', *VaJIntL* 26 (1985), 109–70.

Robertson, H. B., 'Modern Technology and the Law of Armed Conflict at Sea', *International Law Studies* 64. The Law of Naval Operations. Edited by H. B. Robertson, Newport, Rhode Island (1991), 362–83 [Robertson, *Technology*].

Robinson, N. A., 'International Law and the Destruction of Nature in the Gulf War', *Environmental Policy & Law* 21 (1991), 216–20.

Rodriguez Iglesias, G. C., 'State Ships', *EPIL* 11, 320–23.

Rogers, A. P. V., 'Mines, pièges et autres dispositifs similaires', *RIC* 72 (1990), 568–83.

——'Conduct of Combat and Risks Run by the Civilian Population', *RDMilG* 21 (1982), 293–322.

Rojahn, O., 'Ships, Visit and Search', *EPIL* 4, 224–6.

Ronzitti, N., 'La guerre du Golfe, le déminage et la circulation des navires', *Annuaire Francais de Droit International* XXXIII (1987), 647–62.

——'Introductory: The Crises of the Traditonal Law Regulating International Armed Conflict at Sea and the Need for its Revision', in Ronzitti, (Ed.), *The Law of Naval Warfare* (1988), 1–58.

——*Rescuing Nationals Abroad* (1985).

Ronzitti, N. (Ed.), *The Law of Naval Warfare. A Collection of Agreements and Documents with Commentaries*, Dordrecht/Boston/London (1988).

Rosas, A., *The Legal Status of Prisoners of War*, Helsinki (1976).

Rosenblad, E., *International Humanitarian Law of Armed Conflict. Some Aspects of the Principle of Distinction and Related Problems* (1979).

——'Area Bombing and International Law', *RDMilG* 15 (1976) 53–111.

Rosenne, S., *Israel's Armistice Agreements with the Arab States* (1951).

Rostow, E., 'Until What? Enforcement Action or Collective Self-Defense?' *AJIL* 85 (1991), 506.

Rousseau, C., *Le droit des Conflits Armés* (1983).

Rovine, A., (Ed.), *Digest of United States Practice in International Law*.

Rowe, P. J., *The Gulf War 1990–91 in International and English Law*, London (1993).

——*Defence. The Legal Implications. Military Law and the Laws of War* (1987).

Röling, B., 'Crimes against Peace', *EPIL* 3, 132–6.

Röling, B./Rüter, C. F. (Eds.), *The Tokyo Judgment*, Vol. 3 (1977).

Rudolf, W., 'Über den internationalen Schutz von Kulturgütern', in *Festschrift Döring* (1989), 853.

Ruegger, P., 'L'organisation de la Croix-Rouge Internationale sous ses aspects juridiques', *Recueil des Cours* 82 (1953 I), Leyde (1954), 381 ff.

Runciman, S., *The Fall of Constantinople* (1969).

Russell, F. H., *The Just War in the Middle Ages* (1975).

Sandoz, Y., 'Nouveau développement du droit international: interdiction ou restriction d'utiliser certaines armes classiques', *Revue Internationale de la Croix-Rouge* 63 (1981), 3–19.

——'Le droit d'initiative du Comité international de la Croix-Rouge', *Jahrbuch für Internationales Recht* 22 (1979), 352–73.

——'The Application of Humanitarian Law by the Armed Forces of the United Nations Organization', *IRRC* 20 (1978), 274.

——*Des armes interdites en droit de la guerre* (1975).

Sandoz, Y./Swinarski, C./Zimmermann, B. (Eds.), *Commentary on the Additional Protocols of 8 June 1977 to the Geneva Conventions of 12 August 1949, Geneva 1987* [ICRC *Commentary*].

San Remo Manual, see: International Institute of Humanitarian Law, *San Remo Manual on International Law Applicable to Armed Conflicts at Sea, Prepared by a Group of International Lawyers and Naval Experts* (June 1994).

Sassòli, M., *Bedeutung einer Kodifikation für das allgemeine Völkerrecht mit besonderer Betrachtung der Regeln zum Schutze der Zivilbevölkerung vor den Auswirkungen von Feindseligkeiten*, Basel/Frankfurt a. M. (1990).

——'The National Information Bureau in aid of the victims of armed conflicts', *IRRC* 1987, 6–24.

——'The Status, Treatment and Repatriation of Deserters under International Humanitarian Law', in *International Institute of Humanitarian Law* (Ed.), *Yearbook 1985* (1986), 9–36.

Sánchez Rodríguez, L. I., 'Commentary on the 1977 Environmental Modification Convention', in Ronzitti (Ed.), *The Law of Naval Warfare*, 661–72 [Sánchez Rodríguez, *Commentary*].

Schachter, O., 'United Nations Law in the Gulf Conflict', *AJIL* 85 (1991) 452.

Scheidl, F. J., *Die Kriegsgefangenenschaft von den ältesten Zeiten bis zur Gegenwart* (1943).

Scheuner, U., 'Beuterecht im Seekrieg', *WVR* I, 199–201.

——'Kursanweisung', *WVR* II, 385.

——'Prisenrecht', *WVR* II, 794–802.

Schindler, D., 'Tranformations in the Law of Neutrality since 1945', in Delissen/Tanja (Eds.), 367–86.

——'Probleme des Humanitären Völkerrechts und der Neutralität im Golfkonflikt, 1990–1991', *Schweizerische Zeitschrift für internationales und europäisches Recht*, 1, 1991, 3–23.

Schindler, D., 'L'évolution du droit de la guerre des Conventions de la Haye aux Protocoles Additionnels aux Conventions de Genève', *RDMilG* 21 (1982) 23–33.

——'State of War, Belligerency, Armed Conflict', in Cassese (Ed.), *The New Humanitarian Law of Armed Conflict* (1979), 3.

Schindler, D., 'The Different Types of Armed Conflict', *Receuil des Cours* 163 (1979-II), 117–63.
——'United Nations Forces and International Humanitarian Law', in Swiniarski (Ed.), 521–30.
Schindler, D./Toman, J., *The Laws of Armed Conflicts. A Collection of Conventions, Resolutions and Other Documents*, 3rd edn., Geneva (1988).
Schlögel, A., 'Völkerrechtliche Aspekte des Einsatzes des Hospitalschiffes "Helgoland"', *Jahrbuch für Internationales Recht* (1973), 92–112.
—— 'IRC-International Red Cross' in Wolfrum (Ed.), *United Nations: Law, Policies and Practice* (1995), 814 et seq.
Schneider, H., 'Zur Auslegung des Art. 118 Abs. 1 der Genfer Konvention über die Behandlung von Kriegsgefangenen von 1949', *HUV-I* (2/1989), 13–21 .
Schönborn, W., 'Der Widerstand feindlicher Handelsschiffe gegen Visitationen und Aufbringung', *Archiv für öffentliches Recht* (1918), 161–74.
Schöttler, H./Hoffmann, B. (Eds.), *Die Genfer Zusatzprotokolle*, (1993).
Schramm, G., 'Die Umwandlung von Kauffahrteischiffen in Kriegsschiffe auf hoher See während eines Krieges', *Marine Rundschau* 22 (1911), 1255–66, 1539–54.
Schütz, H.-J., 'The Altmark', *EPIL* 3, 14, 1992.
Schwarzenberger, G., *International Law as Applied by International Courts and Tribunals/ Vol.II: The Law of Armed Conflict* (1968).
——'The Law of Armed Conflict: A Civilized Interlude?', *Yearbook of World Affairs* 28 (1974), 293–309.
——*The Legality of Nuclear Weapons* (1958).
——'The Problem of an International Criminal Law', *Current Legal Problems* 3 (1950), 263–97.
Schwelb, E., 'The United Nations War Crimes Commission', *BYIL* 23 (1946), 363–76.
Seidl-Hohenveldern, I., 'La neutralité permante: l'expérience autrichienne, *Annales de droit international médical* 35 (1991), 96–103.
——'Der Begriff der Neutralität in den bewaffneten Konflikten der Gegenwart', in *Zum Recht und Freiheit, Festschrift für Friedrich August Freiherr von der Heydte* (1977), Vol. 1, 593–613.
Seyersted, F., *United Nations Forces in the Law of Peace and War* (1966).
Shamgar, M., 'The observance of international law in the administered territories', 1 IYHR (1971), 262 ff.
Sharma, S. P., *The Indo-Pakistan Maritime Conflict 1965* (1979).
Shearer, I. A., 'Commentary on the 1907 Hague Convention XI', in Ronzitti (Ed.), *The Law of Naval Warfare*, 183–91 [Shearer, *Commentary*].
Shields-Delessert, C. *Release and repatriation of prisoners of war at the end of active hostilities: a study of Article 118, paragraph I, of the Third Geneva Convention relative to the treatment of prisoners of war* (1977) .
Simma, B., 'Reciprocity', *EPIL* 7, 400–4.
Singh, N., 'Armed Conflicts and Humanitarian Laws of Ancient India', Swinarski (Ed.), 531.
Singh, N./McWhinney, E., Nuclear Weapons and Contemporary International Law, 2nd edn. (1989).
Sofaer, A., 'The United States Decision not to Ratify Protocol I', *AJIL* 82 (1988), 784–7.
Sohler, H., 'U-Bootkrieg und Völkerrecht', *Marine Rundschau* (1956), Beiheft 1 .
Solf, W. A., 'Cultural Property, Protection in Armed Conflict', *EPIL* 9, 64–8.
'Protection of Civilians against the Effects of Hostilities under Customary International Law and under Protocol I', *The American University Journal of International Law and Policy* 1 (1986), 107–35.
——'Siege', *EPIL* 4, 226–7.
Sommaruga, C., 'Respect for international humanitarian law: ICRC review of five years of activity (1987–1991)', *IRRC* 286 (January-February 1992), 74–93.

Spaight, J.M., *Air Power and War Rights* 3rd edn. (1947).

Spetzler, E., *Luftkrieg und Menschlichkeit* (1956).

Spieker, H., 'Haager Regeln des Luftkriegs von 1923', in *HUV-I* (3/1990), 134–8.

Spinnler, P. *Das Kriegsgefangenenrecht im Koreankonflikt: Eine Untersuchung über die Konfrontation des traditionellen Kriegsgefangenenrechts mit Erscheinungsformen moderner bewaffneter Konflikte* (1976) .

Stein, E., 'Impacts of New Weapons Technology on International Law', *Recueil des Cours* 133 (1971 II), 223–388.

Steinicke, D., *Das Navicertsystem: Eine völkerechtliche Unter-suchung von Maßnahmen der britischen Seehandelskontrolle im 1. und 2. Weltkrieg, Vol. 2* (1966).

Sticher, C., 'Noriega als Kriegsgefangener in den USA vor Gericht', *HUV-I* (2/1990), 64–71.

Stock, T., 'Die zukünftige Konvention zum Verbot der Chemiewaffen—Ein Schritt zur Vernichtung einer vom humanitären Völkerrecht geächteten Waffenart', *HUV-I* 5 (1992), 50–60.

Stone, J., *Legal Controls of International Conflict* (1954).

Stödter, R., 'Convoy', *EPIL* 3, 128–30.

——'Safe-Conduct and Safe Passage', *EPIL* 1, (1992), 825–6.

Strebel, H., 'Martens' Clause', *EPIL* 3, 252–3.

——'Die Haager Konvention zum Schutze der Kulturgüter im Falle eines bewaffneten Konfliktes', *ZAöRV* 16 (1955), 35–75.

Strupp, K./Schlochauer, H.-J. (Eds.), *Wörterbuch des Völkerrechts, 3 Bände und Register*, 2nd Edn., (1960–1962) [*WVR*].

Sultan, H., 'La conception islamique', in UNESCO/Institut Henri Dunant (Eds.), *Les dimensions internationales du droit humanitaire*, 47–60 .

Sunga, L. S., *Individual Responsibility in International Law for Serious Human Rights Violations* (1992).

Swinarski, Chr. (Ed.), *Etudes et essais sur le droit international humanitaire et sur les principes de la Croix-Rouge an l'honneur de Jean Pictet*, Genève, La Haye (1984).

Tavernier, P., 'Combatants and Non-Combatants', in Dekker/Post (Eds.), *The Gulf War of 1980–1988*, (1992), 129–46.

Taylor, T., 'The Chemical Weapons Convention and Prospects for Implementation', *ICLQ* 42 (1993), 912–19.

Terfloth, K., *Das Seebeuterecht an gesunkenen Schiffen*, Bonn (1955).

Thorpe, A. G. Y., 'Mine Warfare at Sea—Some Legal Aspects of the Future', *Ocean Development and International Law* 18 (1987), 255–78.

Toman, J., 'La Protection des biens culturels en cas de conflit armé non international', in *Festschrift D. Schindler* (1989), 311–39.

Torelli, M., 'La neutralité', *Annales de droit international médical* 35 (1991), 25–59 .

Truver, S. C., 'The Legal Status of Submarine Launched Cruise Missiles', *USNIP* 103 (August 1977), 82–4.

Tucker, R., *The Law of War and Neutrality at Sea* (1957).

UNESCO/Institut Henry Dunant (Eds.), *Les dimensions internationales du droit humanitaire* (1986).

United States Department of Defense, *Final Report to Congress: Conduct of the Persian Gulf War* (1992).

United States Department of the Navy, *The United States Navy in Desert Shield and Desert Storm* (1991).

Venturini, G., 'Commentary on the 1907 Hague Convention VII', in Ronzitti (Ed.), *The Law of Naval Warfare*, 120–8 [G. Venturini, *Commentary*].

Venturini, G., *Necessità e proporzionalità nell'uso della forza militare in diritto internazionale* (1988).

Verdross, A./Simma, B., *Universelles Völkerrecht*, 3rd edn., Berlin 1984.

Verosta, S., 'Neutralization', *EPIL* 4, 31.

Verzijl, J. H. W., 'International Law in Historical Perspective, Vol.IX-A: *The Laws of War* (1978).

Vignes, D., 'Commentary on the 1936 Montreux Convention', in Ronzitti (Ed.), *The Law of Naval Warfare*, 468–82 [D. Vignes, *Commentary*].

Villar, R., *Merchant Ships at War: The Falklands Experience*, London 1984.

Vitzthum, W. Graf, 'Rechtsfragen der Rüstungskontrolle im Vertragsvölkerrecht der Gegenwart', *Berichte der Deutschen Gesellschaft für Völkerrecht Heft 30* (1990), 95–149.

Waldock, H., 'The Regulation of the Use of Force by Individual States in International Law', *Recueils des Cours* 81 (1952), 51.

Wallaw, I. F., *Die völkerrechtliche Zulässigkeit der Ausfuhr kriegswichtiger Güter aus neutralen Staaten* (1970), (Diss. Hamburg).

Weller, M., 'The Use of Force in Collective Security', in Dekker/Post (Eds.), 77.

Wells, *War Crimes and Laws of War* 2nd edn. (1991).

White, N. D./McCoubrey, H., 'International Law and the Use of Force in the Gulf', *International Relations* 10 (1991), 347–73.

Whiteman, M. M., *Digest of International Law*, Vol. 10, Washington (1968) [Whiteman, Vol. X].

Willemin, G./Heacock, R., *The International Committee of the Red Cross*, Boston/The Hague (1984).

Wildhaber, L., 'Muss die dauernde Neutralität bewaffnet sein?', in Haller/Kölz/Müller/Thürer (Eds.), *Im Dienst an der Gemeinschaft, Festschrift für Dietrich Schindler* (1989), 429–41.

Wilson, H. A., *International Law and the Use of Force by National Liberation Movements* (1988).

Witteler, S., 'Der Krieg im Golf und seine Auswirkungen auf die natürliche Umwelt: Notwendige Überlegungen zu den umweltschützenden Vorschriften des humanitären Völkerrechts', *HUV-I* (4/1991), 48–58.

Wolf, J., 'Ships, Diverting and Ordering into Port', *EPIL* 4, 223–4.

Wolfrum, R., 'The Emerging Customary Law of Marine Zones: State Practice and the Convention on the Law of the Sea', *NYIL* 1987, 121–44.

Würkner-Theis, G., *Fernverlegte Minen und humanitäres Völkerrecht* (1990).

York, C., 'International Law and the Collateral Effects of War on the Environment: The Persian Gulf', *South African Journal on Human Rights* 7 (1991), 269–90.

'International Law and the Collateral Effects of War on the Environment: The Persian Gulf', *South African Journal on Human Rights* 7 (1991), 269–90.

Zayas, A. M. de, 'Civilian Population, Protection', *EPIL* 3, 96–101.

——'London Naval Conference of 1908/1909', *EPIL* 3, 249–51.

——' Open Towns', *EPIL* 4, 69–71.

——*The Wehrmacht War Crimes Bureau 1939–1945*, Nebraska (1989).

Zemanek, K., 'Merchant Ships, Armed', *EPIL* 3, 258–60.

——'The Athenia', *EPIL* 3, 41.

——*Neutrality in Land Warfare*, EPIL 4 (1982), 16–19.

Zuppi, A. L., *Die bewaffnete Auseinandersetzung zwischen dem Vereinigten Königreich und Argentinien im Südatlantik aus völkerrechtlicher Sicht*, Köln/Berlin/Bonn/München (1990).

INDEX

Figures refer to Sections